Data Wrangling on AWS

Clean and organize complex data for analysis

Navnit Shukla

Sankar M

Sam Palani

BIRMINGHAM—MUMBAI

Data Wrangling on AWS

Publishing Product Manager: Heramb Bhavsar
Book Project Manager: Kirti Pisat
Content Development Editor: Joseph Sunil
Technical Editor: Sweety Pagaria
Copy Editor: Safis Editing
Proofreader: Safis Editing
Indexer: Sejal Dsilva
Production Designer: Shyam Sundar Korumilli
DevRel Marketing Coordinator: Nivedita Singh

First published: July 2023

Production reference: 1280723

Published by Packt Publishing Ltd.
Grosvenor House
11 St Paul's Square
Birmingham
B3 1RB, UK.

ISBN 978-1-80181-090-6

www.packtpub.com

I am grateful to my grandmother, Radhika Shukla, my mother, Asha Shukla, my grandfather, I.D. Shukla, and my father, N.K. Shukla, for their unwavering support and the sacrifices they have made. They have been a constant source of inspiration and have shown me the true power of determination. I would also like to express my heartfelt gratitude to my loving wife, Anchal Dubey, and my son, Anav Shukla, for being my steadfast companions on our shared life journey. Their love and encouragement have fueled my ambitions and brought immense joy to my life.

- Navnit Shukla

I am thankful to my wife, Krithiha Kumar, for her unwavering support and motivation in all my endeavors. I would thank my son and daughter for their love, curiosity, creativity, and boundless energy, which has inspired me every day to explore further and dream big.

- Sankar Sundaram

Contributors

About the authors

Navnit Shukla is a passionate individual with a love for technology. He pursued engineering studies in electronics and communication at Dr. A.P.J. Abdul Kalam Technical University in Lucknow (formerly U.P.T.U), setting the stage for his future endeavors. At the age of 25, he ventured across the oceans to the United States, where he now resides in the beautiful Orange County, California, alongside his loving wife and son. Immersed in the world of IT since 2009, he has gained extensive experience and knowledge within the industry. For the past four years, he has worked with **Amazon Web Services (AWS)** as a specialist solution architect – analytics. In this role, he is entrusted with the responsibility of assisting organizations of all sizes in architecting, building, and seamlessly operating solutions on the dynamic AWS Cloud platform. Beyond his professional pursuits, he finds immense joy in spending quality time with his family and friends, exploring new places, creating precious memories, and embarking on exciting adventures.

I am deeply grateful to those who have been by my side, offering unwavering support throughout my journey. I extend a heartfelt thank you to my beloved wife, Anchal Dubey, and my devoted parents, whose encouragement and belief in me have been invaluable.

Sankar M has been working in the IT industry since 2007, specializing in databases, data warehouses, and the analytics space for many years. As a specialized data architect, he helps customers build and modernize data architectures and helps them build secure, scalable, and performant data lake, database, and data warehouse solutions. Prior to joining AWS, he worked with multiple customers in implementing complex data architectures.

Sam Palani has over 18+ years as a developer, data engineer, data scientist, startup co-founder, and IT leader. He holds a master's in Business Administration with a dual specialization in Information Technology. His professional career spans 5 countries across financial services, management consulting, and the technology industries. He is currently Sr Leader for Machine Learning and AI at Amazon Web Services, where he is responsible for multiple lines of the business, product strategy, and thought leadership. Sam is also a practicing data scientist, a writer with multiple publications, a speaker at key industry conferences, and an active open-source contributor. Outside work, he loves hiking, photography, experimenting with food, and reading.

About the reviewer

Naresh Rohra is an accomplished data modeler and lead analyst with a passion for harnessing the potential of cutting-edge technologies to unlock valuable insights from complex datasets. With over a decade of experience in the field of data modeling, he has successfully navigated the dynamic landscape of data wrangling and analysis, earning him a reputation as a leading expert. He has expertly designed various data models related to OLTP and OLAP systems. He has worked with renowned organizations like TCS, Cognizant, and Tech Mahindra.

I extend heartfelt thanks to my colleagues and family for their constant encouragement throughout my book review journey. To my beloved daughter, Ginisha, you are the luminescent star that adorns my night sky.

Roja Boina is an engineering senior advisor. She provides data-driven solutions to enterprises. She takes pride in her get-it-done attitude. She enjoys defining requirements, designing, developing, testing, and delivering backend applications, and communicating data through visualizations. She is very passionate about being a **Women in Tech** (**WIT**) advocate and being a part of WIT communities. Outside of her 9-5 job, she loves to volunteer for non-profits and mentor fellow women in STEM. She believes in having a growth mindset.

Table of Contents

3

Introducing AWS SDK for pandas 75

4

Introduction to SageMaker Data Wrangler 131

Part 3: AWS Data Management and Analysis

5

Working with Amazon S3 151

6

Working with AWS Glue 175

7

Working with Athena 203

8

Working with QuickSight 245

Part 4: Advanced Data Manipulation and ML Data Optimization

9

Building an End-to-End Data-Wrangling Pipeline with AWS SDK for Pandas 273

10

Data Processing for Machine Learning with SageMaker Data Wrangler 329

Part 5: Ensuring Data Lake Security and Monitoring

11

Data Lake Security and Monitoring 369

Preface

Welcome to the world of *Data Wrangling on AWS*! In this comprehensive book, we will explore the exciting field of data wrangling and uncover the immense potential of leveraging **Amazon Web Services** (**AWS**) for efficient and effective data manipulation and preparation. Whether you are a data professional, a data scientist, or someone interested in harnessing the power of data, this book will provide you with the knowledge and tools to excel in the realm of data wrangling on the AWS platform.

Data wrangling, also known as data preparation or data munging, is a critical step in the data analysis process. It involves transforming raw data into a clean, structured format that is ready for analysis. With the exponential growth of data and the increasing need for data-driven decision-making, mastering the art of data wrangling has become essential for extracting valuable insights from vast and complex datasets.

In this book, we will guide you through a series of chapters, each focusing on a specific aspect of data wrangling on AWS. We will explore various AWS services and tools that empower you to efficiently manipulate, transform, and prepare your data for analysis. From AWS Glue and Athena to SageMaker Data Wrangler and QuickSight, we will delve into the powerful capabilities of these services and uncover their potential for unlocking valuable insights from your data.

Throughout the chapters, you will learn how to leverage AWS's cloud infrastructure and robust data processing capabilities to streamline your data-wrangling workflows. You will discover practical techniques, best practices, and hands-on examples that will equip you with the skills to tackle real-world data challenges and extract meaningful information from your datasets.

So, whether you are just starting your journey in data wrangling or looking to expand your knowledge in the AWS ecosystem, this book is your comprehensive guide to mastering data wrangling on AWS. Get ready to unlock the power of data and unleash its full potential with the help of AWS's cutting-edge technologies and tools.

Let's dive in and embark on an exciting journey into the world of data wrangling on AWS!

Who this book is for

Data Wrangling on AWS is designed for a wide range of individuals who are interested in mastering the art of data wrangling and leveraging the power of AWS for efficient and effective data manipulation and preparation. The book caters to the following audience:

- **Data Professionals**: Data engineers, data analysts, and data scientists who work with large and complex datasets and want to enhance their data-wrangling skills on the AWS platform
- **AWS Users**: Individuals who are already familiar with AWS and want to explore the specific services and tools available for data wrangling

- **Business Analysts**: Professionals involved in data-driven decision-making and analysis who need to acquire data-wrangling skills to derive valuable insights from their data
- **IT Professionals**: Technology enthusiasts and IT practitioners who want to expand their knowledge of data wrangling on the AWS platform

While prior experience with data wrangling or AWS is beneficial, the book provides a solid foundation for beginners and gradually progresses to more advanced topics. Familiarity with basic programming concepts and SQL would be advantageous but is not mandatory. The book combines theoretical explanations with practical examples and hands-on exercises, making it accessible to individuals with different backgrounds and skill levels.

What this book covers

Chapter 1, Getting Started with Data Wrangling: In the opening chapter, you will embark on a journey into the world of data wrangling and discover the power of leveraging AWS for efficient and effective data manipulation and preparation. This chapter serves as a solid foundation, providing you with an overview of the key concepts and tools you'll encounter throughout the book.

Chapter 2, Introduction to AWS Glue DataBrew: In this chapter, you will discover the powerful capabilities of AWS Glue DataBrew for data wrangling and data preparation tasks. This chapter will guide you through the process of leveraging AWS Glue DataBrew to cleanse, transform, and enrich your data, ensuring its quality and usability for further analysis.

Chapter 3, Introducing AWS SDK for pandas: In this chapter, you will be introduced to the versatile capabilities of AWS Data Wrangler for data wrangling tasks on the AWS platform. This chapter will provide you with a comprehensive understanding of AWS Data Wrangler and how it can empower you to efficiently manipulate and prepare your data for analysis.

Chapter 4, Introduction to SageMaker Data Wrangler: In this chapter, you will discover the capabilities of Amazon SageMaker Data Wrangler for data wrangling tasks within the Amazon SageMaker ecosystem. This chapter will equip you with the knowledge and skills to leverage Amazon SageMaker Data Wrangler's powerful features to efficiently preprocess and prepare your data for machine learning projects.

Chapter 5, Working with Amazon S3: In this chapter, you will delve into the world of **Amazon Simple Storage Service** (**S3**) and explore its vast potential for storing, organizing, and accessing your data. This chapter will provide you with a comprehensive understanding of Amazon S3 and how it can be leveraged for effective data management and manipulation.

Chapter 6, Working with AWS Glue: In this chapter, you will dive into the powerful capabilities of AWS Glue, a fully managed **extract, transform, and load** (**ETL**) service provided by AWS. This chapter will guide you through the process of leveraging AWS Glue to automate and streamline your data preparation and transformation workflows.

Chapter 7, Working with Athena: In this chapter, you will explore the powerful capabilities of Amazon Athena, a serverless query service that enables you to analyze data directly in Amazon S3 using standard SQL queries. This chapter will guide you through the process of leveraging Amazon Athena to unlock valuable insights from your data, without the need for complex data processing infrastructure.

Chapter 8, Working with QuickSight: In this chapter, you will discover the power of Amazon QuickSight, a fast, cloud-powered **business intelligence** (**BI**) service provided by AWS. This chapter will guide you through the process of leveraging QuickSight to create interactive dashboards and visualizations, enabling you to gain valuable insights from your data.

Chapter 9, Building an End-to-End Data-Wrangling Pipeline with AWS SDK for Pandas: In this chapter, you will explore the powerful combination of AWS Data Wrangler and pandas, a popular Python library for data manipulation and analysis. This chapter will guide you through the process of leveraging pandas operations within AWS Data Wrangler to perform advanced data transformations and analysis on your datasets.

Chapter 10, Data Processing for Machine Learning with SageMaker Data Wrangler: In this chapter, you will delve into the world of **machine learning** (**ML**) data optimization using the powerful capabilities of AWS SageMaker Data Wrangler. This chapter will guide you through the process of leveraging SageMaker Data Wrangler to preprocess and prepare your data for ML projects, maximizing the performance and accuracy of your ML models.

Chapter 11, Data Lake Security and Monitoring: In this chapter, you will be introduced to **Identity and Access Management** (**IAM**) on AWS and how closely Data Wrangler integrates with AWS' security features. We will show how you can interact directly with Amazon Cloudwatch logs, query against logs, and return the logs as a data frame.

To get the most out of this book

To get the most out of this book, it is helpful to have a basic understanding of data concepts and familiarity with data manipulation techniques. Some prior exposure to programming languages, such as Python or SQL, will also be beneficial, as we will be utilizing these languages for data-wrangling tasks. Additionally, a foundational understanding of cloud computing and AWS will aid in grasping the concepts and tools discussed throughout the book. While not essential, having hands-on experience with AWS services such as Amazon S3 and AWS Glue will further enhance your learning experience. By having these prerequisites in place, you will be able to fully engage with the content and successfully apply the techniques and practices covered in *Data Wrangling on AWS*.

Software/hardware covered in the book	Operating system requirements
AWS	Windows, macOS, or Linux

If you are using the digital version of this book, we advise you to type the code yourself or access the code from the book's GitHub repository (a link is available in the next section). Doing so will help you avoid any potential errors related to the copying and pasting of code.

Download the example code files

You can download the example code files for this book from GitHub at `https://github.com/PacktPublishing/Data-Wrangling-on-AWS`. If there's an update to the code, it will be updated in the GitHub repository.

We also have other code bundles from our rich catalog of books and videos available at `https://github.com/PacktPublishing/`. Check them out!

Conventions used

There are a number of text conventions used throughout this book.

`Code in text`: Indicates code words in text, database table names, folder names, filenames, file extensions, pathnames, dummy URLs, user input, and Twitter handles. Here is an example: "Mount the downloaded `WebStorm-10*.dmg` disk image file as another disk in your system."

A block of code is set as follows:

```
import sys
import awswrangler as wr
print(wr.__version__)
```

When we wish to draw your attention to a particular part of a code block, the relevant lines or items are set in bold:

```
ROW FORMAT SERDE 'org.apache.hadoop.hive.serde2.RegexSerDe' WITH
SERDEPROPERTIES (
    "input.regex" = "^([\\w\\s.+-]{11})\\s([\\w\\s.+-]{8})\\s([\\
    w\\s.+-]{9})\\s([\\w]{4})\\s([\\d]{4})\\s([\\d]{4})")
LOCATION 's3://<<location your file/'
```

Any command-line input or output is written as follows:

```
git clone https://github.com/aws-samples/aws-database-
migrationsamples.git
cd aws-database-migration-samples/mysql/sampledb/v1/
```

Bold: Indicates a new term, an important word, or words that you see onscreen. For instance, words in menus or dialog boxes appear in **bold**. Here is an example: "Click on the **Upload** button."

> **Tips or important notes**
> Appear like this.

Get in touch

Feedback from our readers is always welcome.

General feedback: If you have questions about any aspect of this book, email us at `customercare@packtpub.com` and mention the book title in the subject of your message.

Errata: Although we have taken every care to ensure the accuracy of our content, mistakes do happen. If you have found a mistake in this book, we would be grateful if you would report this to us. Please visit `www.packtpub.com/support/errata` and fill in the form.

Piracy: If you come across any illegal copies of our works in any form on the internet, we would be grateful if you would provide us with the location address or website name. Please contact us at `copyright@packt.com` with a link to the material.

If you are interested in becoming an author: If there is a topic that you have expertise in and you are interested in either writing or contributing to a book, please visit `authors.packtpub.com`.

Share Your Thoughts

Once you've read *Data Wrangling on AWS*, we'd love to hear your thoughts! Scan the QR code below to go straight to the Amazon review page for this book and share your feedback.

`https://packt.link/r/1-801-81090-7`

Your review is important to us and the tech community and will help us make sure we're delivering excellent quality content.

Download a free PDF copy of this book

Thanks for purchasing this book!

Do you like to read on the go but are unable to carry your print books everywhere? Is your eBook purchase not compatible with the device of your choice?

Don't worry, now with every Packt book you get a DRM-free PDF version of that book at no cost.

Read anywhere, any place, on any device. Search, copy, and paste code from your favorite technical books directly into your application.

The perks don't stop there, you can get exclusive access to discounts, newsletters, and great free content in your inbox daily

Follow these simple steps to get the benefits:

1. Scan the QR code or visit the link below

`https://packt.link/free-ebook/9781801810906`

2. Submit your proof of purchase
3. That's it! We'll send your free PDF and other benefits to your email directly

Part 1: Unleashing Data Wrangling with AWS

This section marks the beginning of an exciting journey, where we explore the realm of data wrangling and unveil the remarkable capabilities of AWS for data manipulation and preparation. This section lays a solid foundation that provides you with insights into key concepts and essential tools that will pave the way for your data-wrangling endeavors throughout the book.

This part has the following chapter:

1

Getting Started with Data Wrangling

In the introductory section of this book, we listed use cases regarding how organizations use data to bring value to customers. Apart from that, organizations collect a lot of other data so that they can understand the finances of customers, which helps them share it with stakeholders, including log data for security, system health checks, and customer data, which is required for working on use cases such as Customer 360s.

We talked about all these use cases and how collecting data from different data sources is required to solve them. However, from collecting data to solving these business use cases, one very important step is to clean the data. That is where data wrangling comes into the picture.

In this chapter, we are going to learn the basics of data wrangling and cover the following topics:

- Introducing data wrangling
- The steps involved in data wrangling
- Best practices for data wrangling
- Options available within **Amazon Web Services** (**AWS**) to perform data wrangling

Introducing data wrangling

For organizations to become data-driven to provide value to customers or make more informed business decisions, they need to collect a lot of data from different data sources such as clickstreams, log data, transactional systems, and flat files and store them in different data stores such as data lakes, databases, and data warehouses as **raw data**. Once this data is stored in different data stores, it needs to be cleansed, transformed, organized, and joined from different data sources to provide more meaningful information to downstream applications such as machine learning models to provide product recommendations or look for traffic conditions. Alternatively, it can be used by business or data analytics to extract meaningful business information:

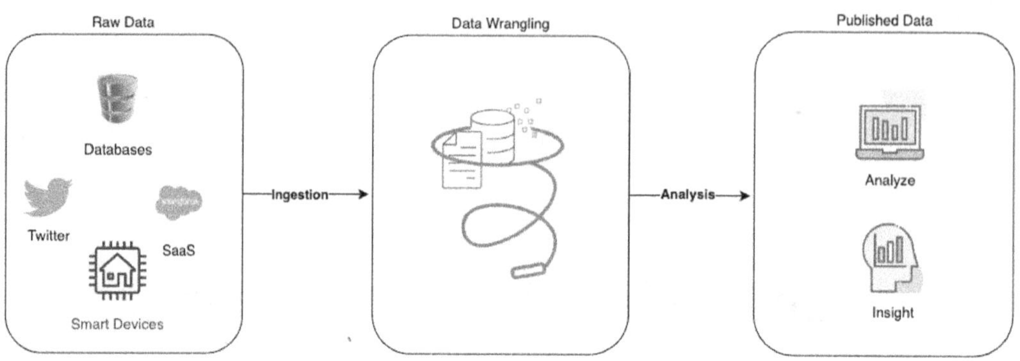

Figure 1.1: Data pipeline

The 80-20 rule of data analysis

When organizations collect data from different data sources, it is not of much use initially. It is estimated that data scientists spend about 80% of their time cleaning data. This means that only 20% of their time will be spent analyzing and creating insights from the data science process:

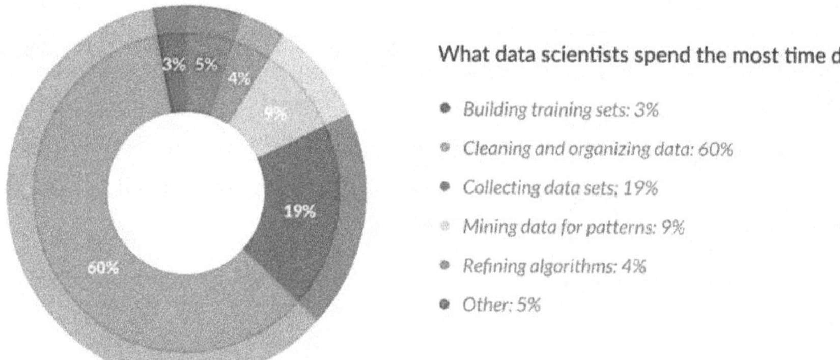

Figure 1.2: Work distribution of a data scientist

Now that we understand the basic concept of data wrangling, we'll learn why it is essential, and the various benefits we get from it.

Advantages of data wrangling

If we go back to the analogy of oil, when we first extract it, it is in the form of crude oil, which is not of much use. To make it useful, it has to go through a refinery, where the crude oil is put in a distillation unit. In this distillation process, the liquids and vapors are separated into petroleum components called fractions according to their boiling points. Heavy fractions are on the bottom while light fractions are on the top, as seen here:

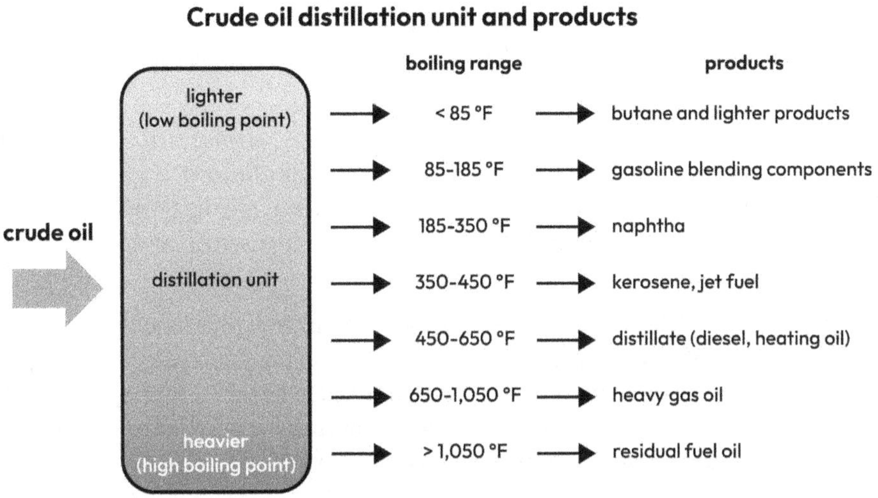

Crude oil distillation unit and products

crude oil

distillation unit

	boiling range	products
lighter (low boiling point)	< 85 °F	butane and lighter products
	85-185 °F	gasoline blending components
	185-350 °F	naphtha
	350-450 °F	kerosene, jet fuel
	450-650 °F	distillate (diesel, heating oil)
	650-1,050 °F	heavy gas oil
heavier (high boiling point)	> 1,050 °F	residual fuel oil

Figure 1.3: Crude oil processing

The following figure showcases how oil processing correlates to the data wrangling process:

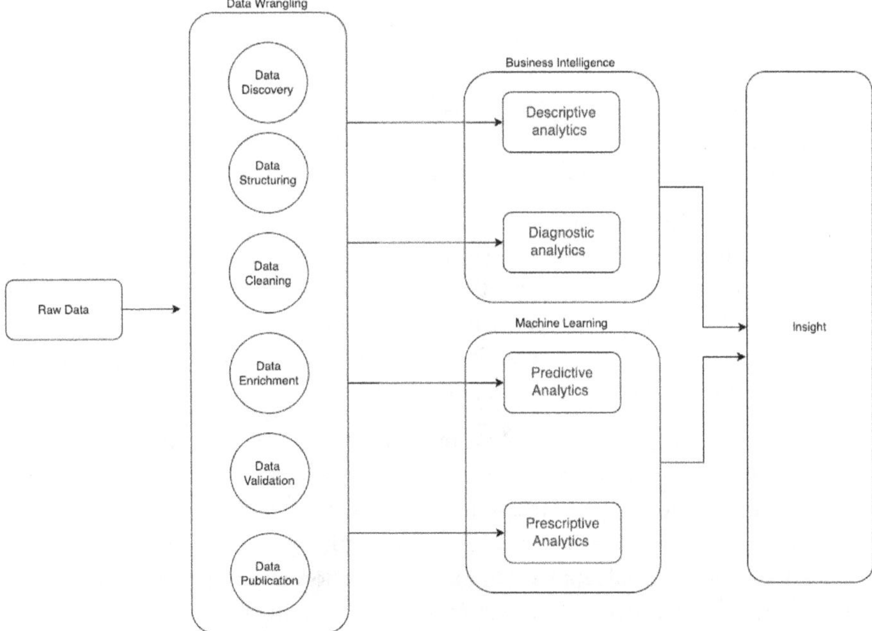

Figure 1.4: The data wrangling process

Data wrangling brings many advantages:

- **Enhanced data quality**: Data wrangling helps improve the overall quality of the data. It involves identifying and handling missing values, outliers, inconsistencies, and errors. By addressing these issues, data wrangling ensures that the data used for analysis is accurate and reliable, leading to more robust and trustworthy results.
- **Improved data consistency**: Raw data often comes from various sources or in different formats, resulting in inconsistencies in naming conventions, units of measurement, or data structure. Data wrangling allows you to standardize and harmonize the data, ensuring consistency across the dataset. Consistent data enables easier integration and comparison of information, facilitating effective analysis and interpretation.
- **Increased data completeness**: Incomplete data can pose challenges during analysis and modeling. Data wrangling methods allow you to handle missing data by applying techniques such as imputation, where missing values are estimated or filled in based on existing information. By dealing with missing data appropriately, data wrangling helps ensure a more complete dataset, reducing potential biases and improving the accuracy of analyses.
- **Facilitates data integration**: Organizations often have data spread across multiple systems and sources, making integration a complex task. Data wrangling helps in merging and integrating data from various sources, allowing analysts to work with a unified dataset. This integration facilitates a holistic view of the data, enabling comprehensive analyses and insights that might not be possible when working with fragmented data.
- **Streamlined data transformation**: Data wrangling provides the tools and techniques to transform raw data into a format suitable for analysis. This transformation includes tasks such as data normalization, aggregation, filtering, and reformatting. By streamlining these processes, data wrangling simplifies the data preparation stage, saving time and effort for analysts and enabling them to focus more on the actual analysis and interpret the results.
- **Enables effective feature engineering**: Feature engineering involves creating new derived variables or transforming existing variables to improve the performance of machine learning models. Data wrangling provides a foundation for feature engineering by preparing the data in a way that allows for meaningful transformations. By performing tasks such as scaling, encoding categorical variables, or creating interaction terms, data wrangling helps derive informative features that enhance the predictive power of models.
- **Supports data exploration and visualization**: Data wrangling often involves **exploratory data analysis** (**EDA**), where analysts gain insights and understand patterns in the data before formal modeling. By cleaning and preparing the data, data wrangling enables effective data exploration, helping analysts uncover relationships, identify trends, and visualize the data using charts, graphs, or other visual representations. These exploratory steps are crucial for forming hypotheses, making data-driven decisions, and communicating insights effectively.

Now that we have learned about the advantages of data wrangling, let's understand the steps involved in the data wrangling process.

The steps involved in data wrangling

Similar to crude oil, raw data has to go through multiple data wrangling steps to become meaningful. In this section, we are going to learn the six-step process involved in data wrangling:

1. Data discovery
2. Data structuring
3. Data cleaning
4. Data enrichment
5. Data validation
6. Data publishing

Before we begin, it's important to understand these activities may or may not need to be followed sequentially, or in some cases, you may skip any of these steps.

Also, keep in mind that these steps are iterative and differ for different personas, such as data analysts, data scientists, and data engineers.

As an example, data discovery for data engineers may vary from what data discovery means for a data analyst or data scientist:

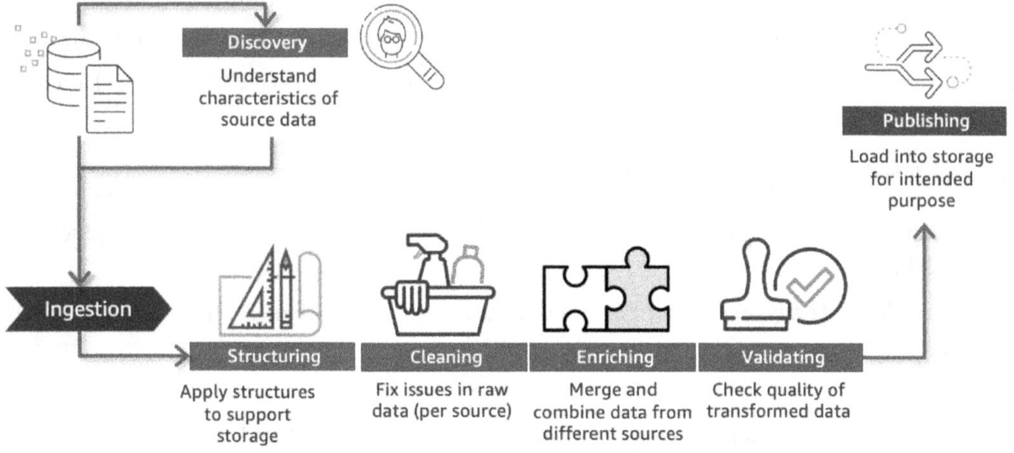

Figure 1.5: The steps of the data-wrangling process

Let's start learning about these steps in detail.

Data discovery

The first step of the data wrangling process is data discovery. This is one of the most important steps of data wrangling. In data discovery, we familiarize ourselves with the kind of data we have as raw data, what use case we are looking to solve with that data, what kind of relationships exist between the raw data, what the data format will look like, such as CSV or Parquet, what kind of tools are available for storing, transforming, and querying this data, and how we wish to organize this data, such as by folder structure, file size, partitions, and so on to make it easy to access.

Let's understand this by looking at an example.

In this example, we will try to understand how data discovery varies based on the persona. Let's assume we have two colleagues, James and Jean. James is a data engineer while Jean is a data analyst, and they both work for a car-selling company.

Jean is new to the organization and she is required to analyze car sales numbers for Southern California. She has reached out to James and asked him for data from the sales table from the production system.

Here is the data discovery process for Jane (a data analyst):

1. Jane has to identify the data she needs to generate the sales report (for example, sales transaction data, vehicle details data, customer data, and so on).
2. Jane has to find where the sales data resides (a database, file share, CRM, and so on).
3. Jane has to identify how much data she needs (from the last 12 months, the last month, and so on).
4. Jane has to identify what kind of tool she is going to use (Amazon QuickSight, Power BI, and so on).
5. Jane has to identify the format she needs the data to be in so that it works with the tools she has.
6. Jane has to identify where she is looking to store this data – in a data lake (Amazon S3), on her desktop, a file share, and sandbox environment, and so on.

Here is the data discovery process for James (a data engineer):

1. Which system has requested data? For example, Amazon RDS, Salesforce CRM, Production SFTP location, and so on.
2. How will the data be extracted? For example, using services such as Amazon DMS or AWS Glue or writing a script.
3. What will the schedule look like? Daily, weekly, or monthly?
4. What will the file format look like? For example, CSV, Parquet, orc, and so on.
5. How will the data be stored in the provided store?

Data structuring

To support existing and future business use cases to serve its customers better, the organization must collect unprecedented amounts of data from different data sources and in different varieties. In modern data architecture, most of the time, the data is stored in data lakes since a data lake allows you to store all kinds of data files, whether it is structured data, unstructured data, images, audio, video, or something else, and it will be of different shapes and sizes in its raw form. When data is in its raw form, it lacks a definitive structure, which is required for it to be stored in databases or data warehouses or used to build analytics or machine learning models. At this point, it is not optimized for cost and performance.

In addition, when you work with streaming data such as clickstreams and log analytics, not all the data fields (columns) are used in analytics.

At this stage of data wrangling, we try to optimize the raw dataset for cost and performance benefits by performing partitioning and converting file types (for example, CSV into Parquet).

Once again, let's consider our friends James and Jean to understand this.

For Jean, the data analyst, data structuring means that she is looking to do direct queries or store data in a memory store of a BI tool, in the case of Amazon QuickSight called the SPICE layer, which provides faster access to data.

For James, the data engineer, when he is extracting data from a production system and looking to store it in a data lake such as Amazon S3, he must consider what the file format will look like. He can partition it by geographical regions, such as county, state, or region, or by date – for example, year=YYYY, month=MM, and day=DD.

Data cleaning

The next step of the data wrangling process is data cleaning. The previous two steps give us an idea of how the data looks and how it is stored. In the data cleaning step, we start working with raw data to make it meaningful so that we can define future use cases.

In the data cleaning step, we try to make data meaningful by doing the following:

- Removing unwanted columns, duplicate values, and filling null value columns to improve the data's readiness
- Performing data validation such as identifying missing values for mandatory columns such as First Name, Last Name, SSN, Phone No., and so on
- Validating or fixing data type for better optimization of storage and performance
- Identifying and fixing outliers
- Removing garbage data or unwanted values, such as special characters

Both James and Jane can perform similar data cleaning tasks; however, their scale might vary. For James, these tasks must be done for the entire dataset. For Jane, they may only have to perform them on the data from Southern California, and granularity might vary as well. For James, maybe it is only limited to regions such as Southern California, Northern California, and so on, while for Jean, it might be city level or even ZIP code.

Data enrichment

Up until the data cleaning step, we were primarily working on single data sources and making them meaningful for future use. However, in the real world, most of the time, data is fragmented and stored in multiple disparate data stores, and to support use cases such as building personalization or recommendation solutions or building Customer 360s or log forensics, we need to join the data from different data stores.

For example, to build a Customer 360 solution, you need data from the **Customer Relationship Manager** (**CRM**) systems, clickstream logs, relational databases, and so on.

So, in the data enrichment step, we build the process that will enhance the raw data with relevant data obtained from different sources.

Data validation

There is a very interesting term in computer science called **garbage in, garbage out** (**GIGO**). GIGO is the concept that flawed or defective (garbage) input data produces defective output.

In other words, the quality of the output is determined by the quality of the input. So, if we provide bad data as input, we will get inaccurate results.

In the data validation step, we address this issue by performing various data quality checks:

- Business validation of data accuracy
- Validate data security
- Validate result consistency across the entire dataset
- Validate data quality by validating data quality checks such as the following:
    - Number of records
    - Duplicate values
    - Missing values
    - Outliers
    - Distinct values
    - Unique values
    - Correlation

There is a lot of overlap between data cleaning and data validation and yes, there are a lot of similarities between these two processes. However, data validation is done on the resulting dataset, while data cleaning is primarily done on the raw dataset.

Data publishing

After completing all the data wrangling steps, the data is ready to be used for analytics so that it can solve business problems.

So, the final step is to publish the data to the end user with the required access and permission.

In this step, we primarily concentrate on how the data is being exposed to the end user and where the final data gets stored – that is, in a relational database, a data warehouse, curated or user zones in a data lake, or through the **Secure File Transfer Protocol** (**SFTP**).

The choice of data storage depends on the tool through which the end user is looking to access the data. For example, if the end user is looking to access data through BI tools such as Amazon QuickSight, Power BI, Informatica, and so on, a relational data store will be an ideal choice. If it is accessed by a data scientist, ideally, it should be stored in an object store.

We will learn about the different kinds of data stores we can use to store raw and wrangled data later in this book.

In this section, we learned about the various steps of the data wrangling process through our friends James and Jean and how these steps may or may not vary based on personas. Now, let's understand the best practices for data wrangling.

Best practices for data wrangling

There are many ways and tools available to perform data wrangling, depending on how data wrangling is performed and by whom. For example, if you are working on real-time use cases such as providing product recommendations or fraud detection, your choice of tool and process for performing data wrangling will be a lot different compared to when you are looking to build a **business intelligence** (**BI**) dashboard to show sales numbers.

Regardless of the kind of use cases you are looking to solve, some standard best practices can be applied in each case that will help make your job easier as a data wrangler.

Identifying the business use case

It's recommended that you decide which service or tool you are looking to use for data wrangling before you write a single line of code. It is super important to identify the business use case as this will set the stage for data wrangling processes and make the job of identifying the services you are looking to use easier. For example, if you have a business use case such as analyzing HR data for small organizations where you just need to concatenate a few columns, remove a few columns, remove duplicates, remove NULL values, and so on from a small dataset that contains 10,000 records, and only a few users will be looking to access the wrangled data, then you don't need to invest a ton of money to find a fancy data wrangling tool available on the market – you can simply use Excel sheets for your work.

However, when you have a business use case, such as processing claims data you receive from different partners where you need to work with semi-structured files such as JSON, or non-structured datasets such as XML files to extract only a few files' data such as their claim ID and customer information, and you are looking to perform complex data wrangling processes such as joins, finding patterns using regex, and so on, then you should look to write scripts or subscribe to any enterprise-grade tool for your work.

Identifying the data source and bringing the right data

After identifying the business use case, it is important to identify which data sources are required to solve it. Identifying this source will help you choose what kind of services are required to bring the data, frequency, and end storage. For example, if you are looking to build a credit card fraud detection solution, you need to bring in credit card transaction data in real time; even cleaning and processing the data should be done in real time. Machine learning inference also needs to be run on real-time data.

Similarly, if you are building a sales dashboard, you may need to bring in data from a CRM system such as Salesforce or a transactional datastore such as Oracle, Microsoft SQL Server, and so on.

After identifying the right data sources, it is important to bring in the right data from these data sources as it will help you solve the business use cases and make the data wrangling process easy.

Identifying your audience

When you perform data wrangling, one important aspect is to identify your audience. Knowing your audience will help you identify what kind of data they are looking to consume. For example, marketing teams may have different data wrangling requirements compared to data science teams or business executives.

This will also give you an idea of where you are looking to present the data – for example, a data scientist team may need data in an object store such as Amazon S3, business analysts may need data in flat files such as CSV, BI developers may need data in a transactional data store, and business users may need data in applications.

With that, we have covered the best practices of data wrangling. Next, we will explore the different options that are available within AWS to perform data wrangling.

Options available for data wrangling on AWS

Depending on customer needs, data sources, and team expertise, AWS provides multiple options for data wrangling. In this section, we will cover the most common options that are available with AWS.

AWS Glue DataBrew

Released in 2020, AWS Glue DataBrew is a visual data preparation tool that makes it easy for you to clean and normalize data so that you can prepare it for analytics and machine learning. The visual UI provided by this service allows data analysts with no coding or scripting experience to accomplish all aspects of data wrangling. It comes with a rich set of common pre-built data transformation actions that can simplify these data wrangling activities. Similar to any **Software as a service (SaaS)** (`https://en.wikipedia.org/wiki/Software_as_a_service`), customers can start using the web UI without the need to provision any servers and only need to pay for the resources they use.

SageMaker Data Wrangler

Similar to AWS Glue DataBrew, AWS also provides SageMaker Data Wrangler, a web UI-based data wrangling service catered more toward data scientists. If the primary use case is around building a machine learning pipeline, SageMaker Data Wrangler should be the preference. It integrates directly with SageMaker Studio, where data that's been prepared using SageMaker Data Wrangler can be fed into a data pipeline to build, train, and deploy machine learning models. It comes with pre-configured data transformations to impute missing data with means or medians, one-hot encoding, and time series-specific transformers that are required for preparing data for machine learning.

AWS SDK for pandas

For customers with a strong data integration team with coding and scripting experience, AWS SDK for pandas (`https://github.com/aws/aws-sdk-pandas`) is a great option. Built on top of other open source projects, it offers abstracted functions for executing typical data wrangling tasks such as loading/unloading data from various databases, data warehouses, and object data stores such as Amazon S3. AWS SDK for pandas simplifies integration with common AWS services such as Athena, Glue, Redshift, Timestream, OpenSearch, Neptune, DynamoDB, and S3. It also supports common databases such as MySQL and SQL Server.

Summary

In this chapter, we learned about the basics of data wrangling, why it is important, the steps and best practices of data wrangling, and how the data wrangling steps vary based on persona. We also talked about the different data wrangling options available in AWS.

In the upcoming chapters, we will dive deep into each of these options and learn how to use these services to perform data wrangling.

Part 2: Data Wrangling with AWS Tools

In this section, we will explore three powerful AWS tools designed to streamline data-wrangling and preparation tasks. First, we'll delve into AWS Glue DataBrew, learning how to cleanse, transform, and enrich data to ensure high-quality and usable datasets. After that, we'll uncover the versatility of the AWS SDK for pandas, gaining a comprehensive understanding of efficient data manipulation and preparation on the AWS platform. Finally, we'll explore Amazon SageMaker Data Wrangler, equipping you with the skills to seamlessly preprocess and prepare data for impactful machine learning projects.

This part has the following chapters:

- *Chapter 2, Introduction to AWS Glue DataBrew*
- *Chapter 3, Introducing AWS SDK for pandas*
- *Chapter 4, Introduction to SageMaker Data Wrangler*

2

Introduction to AWS Glue DataBrew

The previous chapter discussed how organizations are transitioning toward modern data architecture. A crucial aspect of modern data architecture is enabling access to data for every individual in the organization. This promotes data-driven decision-making, leading to empowered users, increased productivity, and, ultimately, higher profits and greater customer and employee satisfaction.

This chapter focuses on **Amazon Web Services** (**AWS**) Glue DataBrew and its application in data wrangling. The following topics will be covered:

- The benefits of using AWS Glue DataBrew
- Starting to use AWS Glue DataBrew
- Working with AWS Glue DataBrew

Why AWS Glue DataBrew?

Having the right tools is a crucial factor in enabling organizations to become data-driven, and AWS Glue DataBrew is one such tool. It is part of the AWS Glue family, which was introduced at re:Invent 2020.

Initially, when AWS Glue was launched in August 2017, it was targeted at developers and data engineers who were writing Apache Spark code. The goal was to provide them with a platform that offered both compute and storage resources to run their Spark code. This allowed them to take advantage of the speed and ease of use of Apache Spark, which is 100 times faster than Hadoop for large-scale data processing, while also leveraging the benefits of the cloud, such as elasticity, performance, and cost-effectiveness.

As the adoption of the public cloud increased and became more mainstream over time, AWS Glue evolved to meet the changing needs of enterprises. Initially, it was primarily used as an ETL tool, but it has since expanded to become a more comprehensive data governance tool. This expansion includes the addition of features such as a Python engine, Glue Data Catalog, Glue crawlers, and AWS Glue Studio. Additionally, the persona of users has evolved beyond just developers to now include business personnel such as data analysts, business analysts, product managers, and data scientists.

Despite the addition of new features, including a UI experience to author Glue ETL jobs and the introduction of Glue Studio in 2021, there has been a common request for greater ease of use. While these features cater primarily to performing ETL using Apache Spark, they still require some level of coding or scripting knowledge.

Business users require a tool that eliminates the delay between data producers and data consumers, between developers and business users. They seek an easy-to-use tool, such as Microsoft Excel, without the need to learn programming or scripting languages such as Scala, PySpark, Python, or SQL. Typically, in enterprises, business users rely heavily on BI developers to build dashboards based on different KPIs that enable them to make critical business decisions and identify any anomalies. However, making minor changes to KPIs, data sources, or even data can take a week or more.

Apart from ease of use, customers also need a solution that scales. While Microsoft Excel is one of the best data-wrangling tools, it lacks scalability. Although it is ideal for small datasets with thousands of records, it struggles when the data grows to tens of thousands or millions of records.

Based on interactions with organizations of all sizes, ranging from small start-ups to large enterprises looking to establish a data-driven culture or enable **data as a service** (**DaaS**), the biggest challenge is how to provide secure and high-quality data access. Customers want a tool that enables them to perform data wrangling without downloading data to their local machines, which poses significant data security risks and can cause data quality issues, particularly in verticals such as life sciences or government and financial institutions. Although AWS Glue enables the building of ETL pipelines, performing data analysis requires downloading data from data lakes (Amazon S3) or data warehouses such as Amazon Redshift or Snowflake to a local desktop, leading to data security and quality risks, or the use of third-party tools, which pose data security risks as data has to move from the AWS cloud to third-party tools via the internet, adding to the cost.

For example, many data privacy laws, such as the EU **General Data Protection Regulation** (**GDPR**), the **California Consumer Privacy Act** (**CCPA**), and the **Health Insurance Portability and Accountability Act** (**HIPAA**) of 1996, now restrict companies' use of customer data, where to store it, and which tools they can use. For instance, traveling with a laptop with data that should not go beyond national boundaries or using non-HIPAA-compliant tools may pose legal and financial challenges for organizations.

One of the challenges in working with big data is maintaining data quality. For instance, tools such as Excel may not provide the same level of precision as Spark, especially when working with large datasets in the cloud. Moreover, few tools on the market offer an easy-to-use UI built on open source technologies such as Apache Spark.

This is where AWS Glue DataBrew comes in. It is a no-code/low-code, serverless visual data preparation tool from AWS that enables data professionals, such as data analysts, business analysts, BI developers, and data scientists, to perform data wrangling without writing any code. It provides over 300 ready-to-use transformations to automate the data-wrangling process, including data discovery, structuring, quality checks, cleaning, validation, anomaly detection, and **personally identifiable information** (**PII**) identification. This reduces the time it takes to prepare data for analytics and machine learning by up to 80%.

One key feature of AWS Glue DataBrew is its serverless nature, which provides agility by eliminating the need to manage infrastructure tasks such as resource provisioning, scaling, high availability, and server maintenance. AWS Glue DataBrew is built on the open source Apache Spark, providing the scale and speed of Spark without licensing costs. It is particularly well suited for big data projects where data is stored in a data lake such as Amazon S3.

In addition to being serverless, AWS Glue DataBrew offers advanced data profiling, visual data lineage, integration with data pipelines, and the ability to prepare data for advanced machine learning use cases.

The following figure illustrates how DataBrew works at a high level.

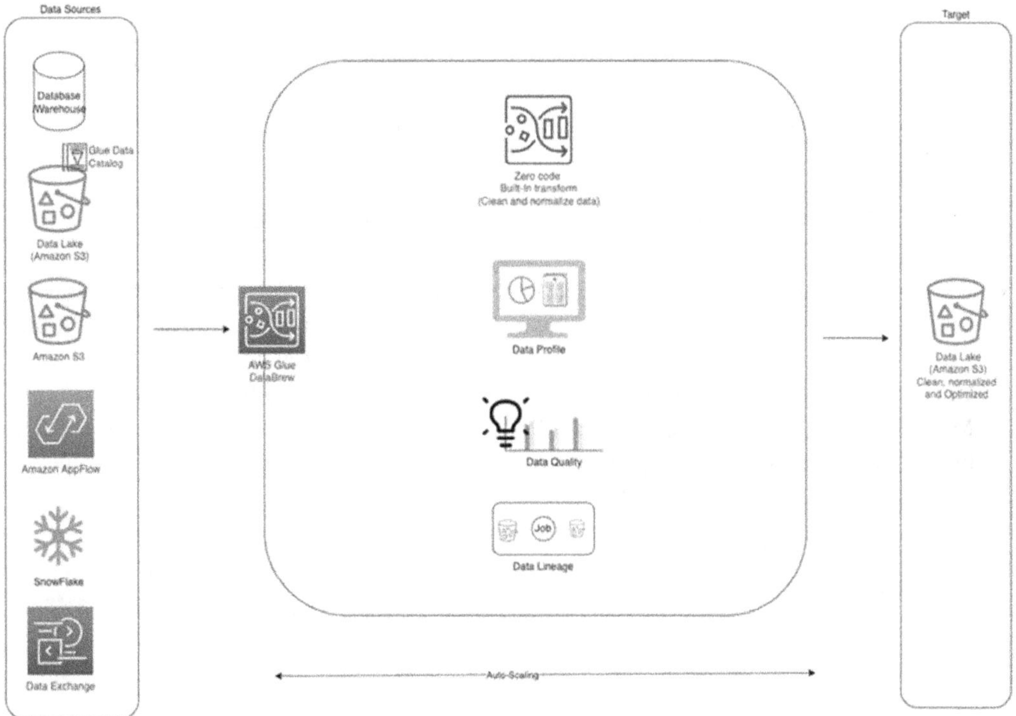

Figure 2.1: How DataBrew works at a high level

To lay the groundwork for building data-wrangling solutions on AWS Glue DataBrew, let us first delve into its basic building blocks.

AWS Glue DataBrew's basic building blocks

Here are the core building blocks of DataBrew:

- **Projects**: In DataBrew, a project encompasses all the necessary components for you to explore, comprehend, merge, clean, and standardize your data visually. Creating a project establishes a workspace that stores information about your data, the transformations applied to it, and the scheduled jobs that transform it.

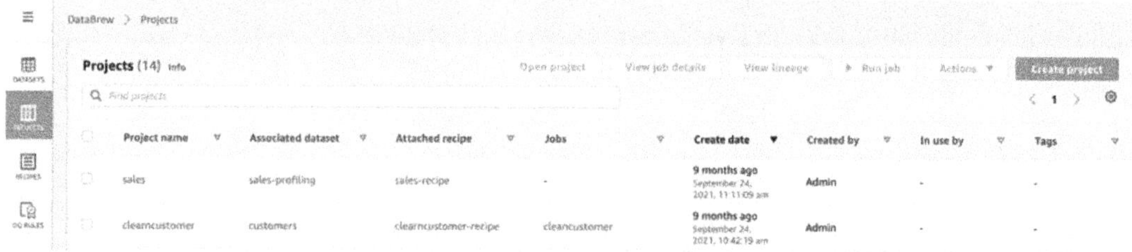

Figure 2.2: Projects list in the AWS Glue DataBrew console

- **DataBrew datasets**: With DataBrew datasets, you can create new datasets from various data sources. These sources include files uploaded from your local machine, data stored in the Amazon S3 data lake, metadata available in the AWS Glue Data Catalog crawled by the AWS Glue crawler, and data from different SaaS data sources, such as Datadog, Salesforce, and Marketo, through Amazon AppFlow. Additionally, AWS Data Exchange provides access to a broad range of third-party data products and makes them available to be used in DataBrew.

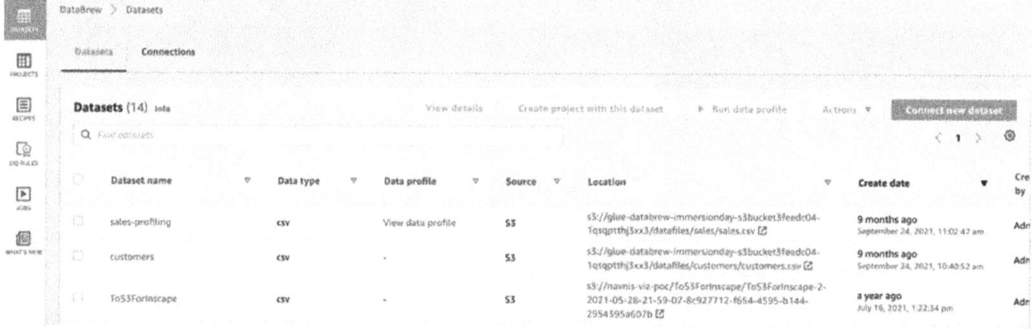

Figure 2.3: Datasets list in the AWS Glue DataBrew console

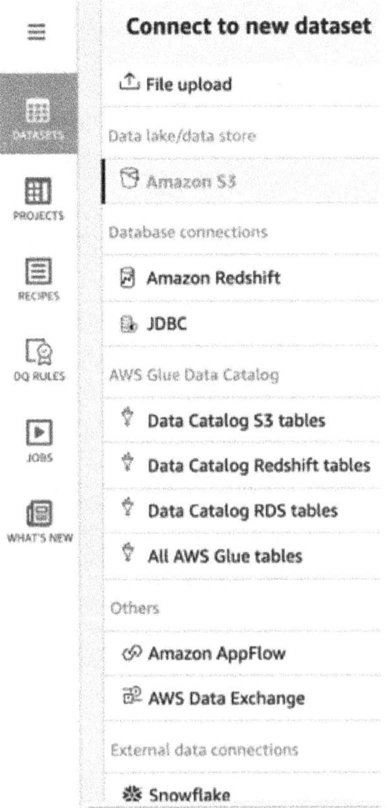

Figure 2.4: Data source list in the AWS Glue DataBrew console

- **Recipe**: In AWS Glue DataBrew, a recipe is a set of transformation steps that you create or modify while working on a project. You can publish a recipe as a stand-alone entity. A published recipe consists only of the transformation steps, without any reference to the original data. You can share the published recipe by downloading it in YAML or JSON format. Recipes can have multiple published versions, which you publish from a project. You can also have multiple working copies of the same recipe, as you progress through multiple drafts.

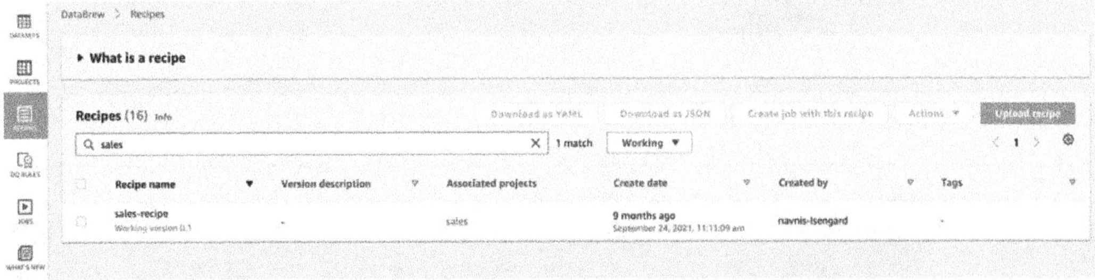

Figure 2.5: Recipe lists in the AWS Glue DataBrew console

- **Job**: In AWS Glue DataBrew, a job is a set of instructions that can be performed on a dataset or project. There are two types of jobs available:
    - **Recipe jobs**: A recipe job runs all the transformations in a recipe against the dataset or project and produces an output in a different file format, which can be saved to an Amazon S3 bucket in the same or an external AWS account
    - **Profile jobs**: A profile job examines the dataset to provide information about correlation, value distribution, column statistics, and more

  For recipe jobs, you can define job output settings such as the file type and Amazon S3 path to the output object. You can also compress the output. Additionally, you can associate a schedule with a job and choose how often and when you want the job to run. AWS Glue DataBrew offers a variety of scheduling options, including `cron` settings.

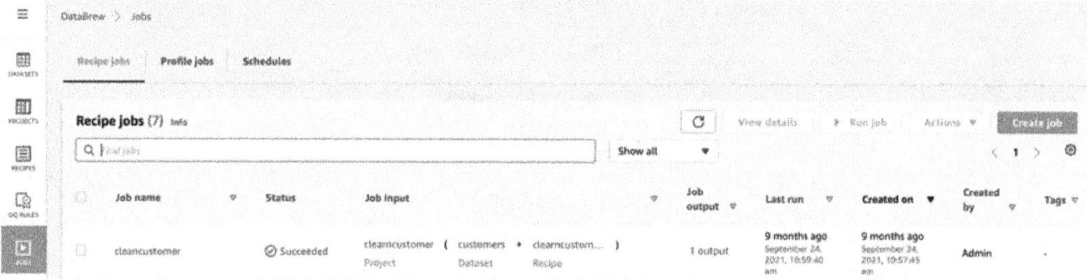

Figure 2.6: Job lists in the AWS Glue DataBrew console

- **DataBrew data lineage**: Data lineage allows you to easily track and visualize the origin, events, and target of your datasets, providing a clear understanding of the path your data has taken.

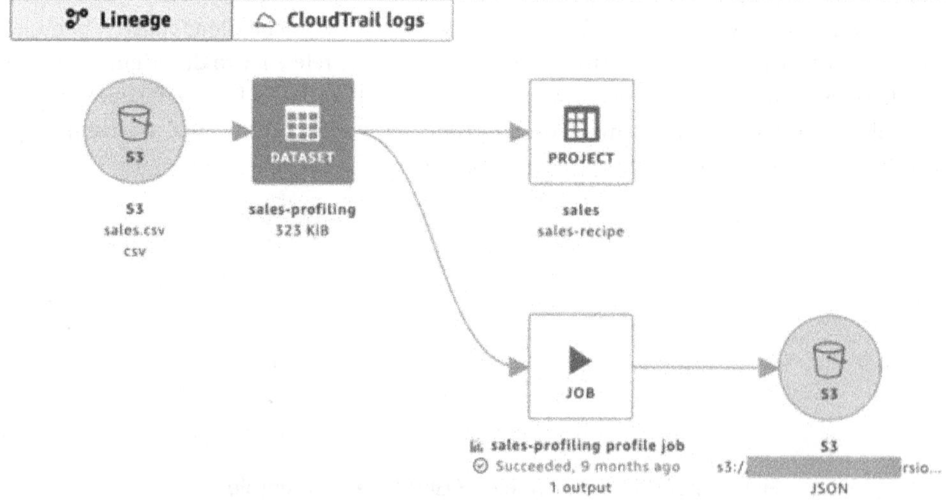

Figure 2.7: Data linage visual in the AWS Glue DataBrew console

- **Data profiling**: Data profiling is one of the most important features available as part of Glue DataBrew. At its core, AWS Glue DataBrew enables users to create comprehensive data profiles for their datasets effortlessly. By running a data profile job through AWS Glue DataBrew, users can obtain valuable information about the current shape of their data. This includes a deep understanding of the context of the content, the underlying structure of the data, and the intricate relationships between various data elements.

  Through advanced algorithms and intelligent analysis, AWS Glue DataBrew profiles meticulously examine each data point, providing descriptive statistics, data distribution insights, and data quality assessments. They help data professionals identify potential anomalies, missing values, and inconsistencies, enabling them to make informed decisions and take necessary actions to improve data quality.

  AWS Glue DataBrew profiles also offer visualizations and intuitive dashboards, presenting the data profile in an easily understandable format. This enables users to grasp complex patterns, spot trends, and extract meaningful insights from their datasets more efficiently.

  With its user-friendly interface and powerful capabilities, AWS Glue DataBrew profiles empower data professionals to unlock the hidden potential of their datasets. By harnessing the insights derived from the data profile, they can make informed decisions, enhance the data quality, and drive impactful outcomes for their organizations.

  According to a Harvard Business Review report, only 3% of companies' data meets basic quality standards, and on average, 47% of newly created data records have at least one critical error (i.e., those that impact their work).

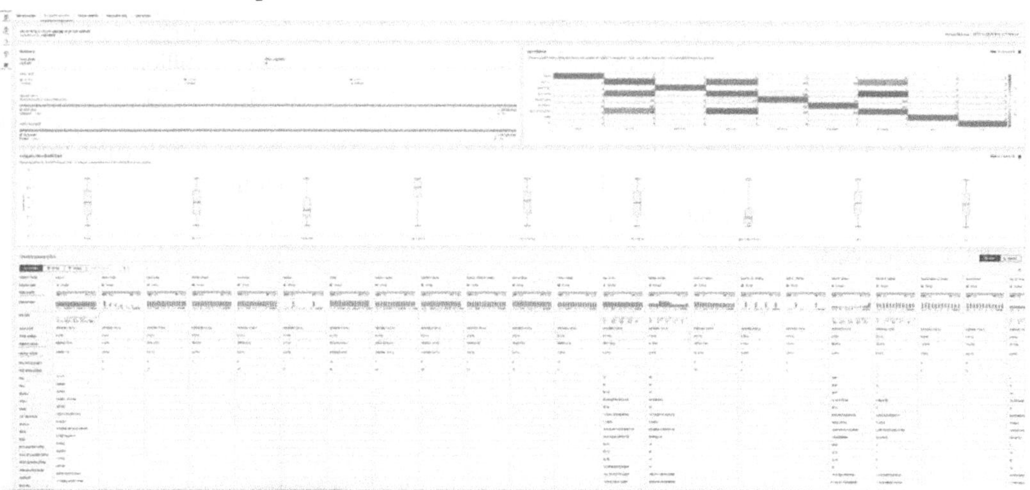

Figure 2.8: Data profile visual in the AWS Glue DataBrew console

Now that we have checked out the basics of AWS Glue DataBrew, let's get started with using it for various tasks.

Getting started with AWS Glue DataBrew

One of the most effective ways to learn about any service or tool is through hands-on experience or by learning from examples. We will follow the same approach. In this guide and subsequent tutorials, we will be using the AWS console to learn about AWS Glue DataBrew as a data-wrangling tool. The first requirement for working with AWS Glue DataBrew is data. We previously discussed how data is the new oil, but when it is in raw form, it has little to no value. Before we proceed, it is crucial to understand the pricing model of any service.

Understanding the pricing of AWS Glue DataBrew

It is important to note that the pricing for AWS services varies between regions and is subject to change. In this section, we will be discussing pricing in the us-east-1 region. AWS Glue DataBrew has various components, such as projects, datasets, jobs, and recipes.

Let's start with datasets. A dataset is created when you bring data from different data stores, including S3, AWS Glue Data Catalog, Redshift, Snowflake, Amazon AppFlow, and AWS Data Exchange. Customers are not charged for using AWS Glue DataBrew connectors such as JDBC drivers (a JDBC driver is a software component that allows Java applications to connect and interact with a specific type of database). However, customers are responsible for the cost of the Glue Data Catalog, which is very minimal. For example, you can store up to a million objects for free. If you store more than a million objects, you will be charged $1.00 per 100,000 objects over a million, per month. An object in the AWS Glue Data Catalog is a table, table version, partition, or database.

The first million access requests to the AWS Glue Data Catalog per month are free. If you exceed a million requests in a month, you will be charged $1.00 per million requests over the first million. Common requests include `CreateTable`, `CreatePartition`, `GetTable`, and `GetPartitions`.

Moving on to projects, this is where things get interesting. Glue DataBrew charges mostly come from DataBrew interactive sessions. A DataBrew interactive session is initiated after the data in a DataBrew project is loaded. Customers are billed for the total number of sessions used, which are calculated in 30-minute increments.

When you interact with a Glue DataBrew project, such as adding a recipe or filtering data through either the UI or the DataBrew API/CLI/SKD, you will be initiating a session. The session will remain active even if you are not doing anything, but it will automatically close at the end of the current 30-minute period. It is important to close the session if you are going for a break or you are not working on it. The cost of a session is $1.00.

For example, say you initiate an interactive session at 09:00 A.M. and work until 09:20 A.M., go for a break, and then initiate another session at 09:30 A.M., and work hard for the next hour, complete all your work, and go for another break. When you look at your AWS bill the next day, you will see $3.00 added to your bill even though the first session was only 20 minutes long.

In a different scenario, say you open a project for 2 minutes and close it, and then open the same project after 5 minutes and work for 10 minutes, close it, and repeat the same activity five times in a period of 30 minutes; it would only cost you $1. This is because every time you open a session, AWS Glue DataBrew assigns resources to provide quicker access and reduce the latency to assign resources to each project.

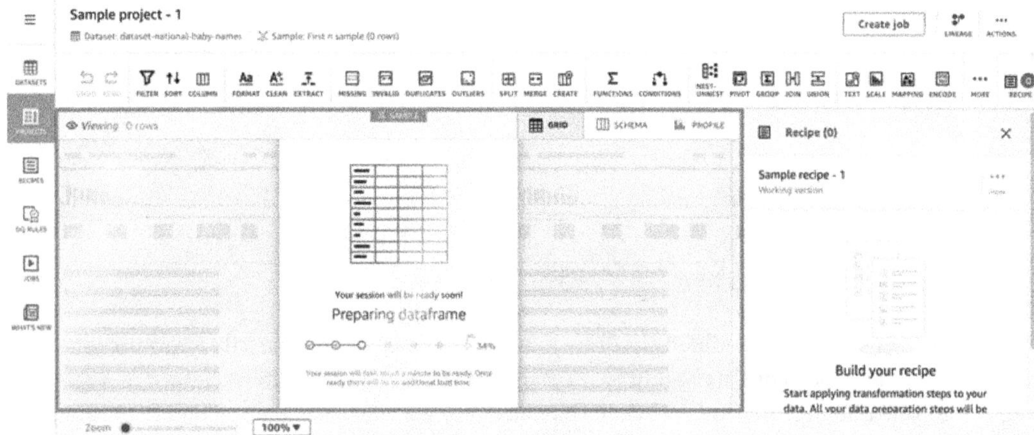

Figure 2.9: Glue DataBrew interactive session getting initiated

AWS Glue DataBrew jobs also play a role in determining the pricing. When you create a dataset, you won't have a data profile overview available for review. To generate the data profile overview, you need to run a data profile that creates an AWS Glue DataBrew job for you. In the upcoming sections, we'll learn about the various options available for configuring our job before running it. However, for pricing purposes, one important configuration option to be aware of is how many nodes you assign to your job. This option can be found under **Advanced job settings - optional**. Note that this option is called *optional* because AWS Glue DataBrew has a default configuration of five nodes.

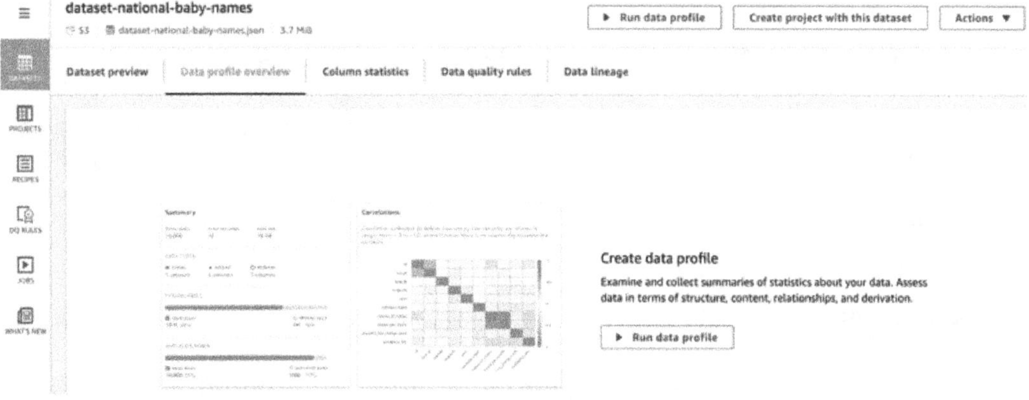

Figure 2.10: Data profile overview section when a dataset is created

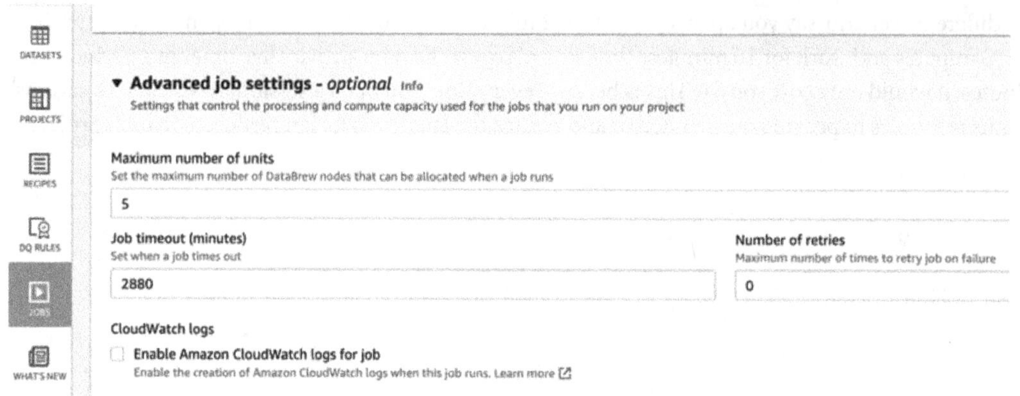

Figure 2.11: Advanced job settings with default configurations

To determine the cost of AWS Glue DataBrew jobs, the number of nodes used to run the job is a crucial factor. Each node consists of four vCPUs and 16 GB of memory and is charged at a rate of $0.48 per node per hour. However, AWS Glue DataBrew jobs are billed for a minimum of one minute. To illustrate, let's consider an example where a job was run for 20 minutes with 10 nodes. The cost would be calculated as follows:

1 node/hour = $0.48

10 nodes/hour = $0.48 x 10 = $4.80/hour

Since AWS Glue DataBrew jobs are billed for a minimum of 1 minute, we can convert 20 minutes into a third of an hour. Thus, the final cost would be $4.80 x 1/3 = $1.60. When you have finished building a recipe for your project against a sample dataset and are ready to apply the same recipe to the entire dataset, you can create a job with the recipe. Now that we have covered the pricing aspect of AWS Glue DataBrew, let's move on to performing some data-wrangling tasks using Glue DataBrew.

Using AWS Glue DataBrew for data wrangling

In this section, we will explore how AWS Glue DataBrew can be utilized for various data-wrangling tasks, including the following:

- Data discovery
- Data structuring
- Data cleaning
- Data enrichment
- Data validation
- Data publication

Before we begin, the first step is to identify the data source, acquire the dataset, and make it available for data wrangling.

Identifying the dataset

To demonstrate the data-wrangling steps and tasks, we will be using human resources data generated using the Random HR Data Generator Excel macro available on the internet. We will be using a sample size of 5 million records with the following attributes:

`Emp ID, Name Prefix, First Name, Middle Initial, Last Name, Gender, E Mail, Father's Name, Mother's Name, Mother's Maiden Name, Date of Birth, Time of Birth, Age in Yrs., Weight in Kgs., Date of Joining, Quarter of Joining, Half of Joining, Year of Joining, Month of Joining, Month Name of Joining, Short Month, Day of Joining, DOW of Joining, Short DOW, Age in Company (Years), Salary, Last % Hike, SSN, Phone No., Place Name, County, City, State, Zip, Region, User Name, Password.`

After identifying the dataset, the next step is to download it from the internet.

Currently, AWS Glue DataBrew supports CSV, TSV, JSON, JSONL, ORC, Parquet, and XLSX formats.

Downloading the sample dataset

We will be using the Syntactic Human Resource dataset available on the internet, which can be downloaded from `https://eforexcel.com/wp/downloads-16-sample-csv-files-data-sets-for-testing/`.

However, in a real-world production environment, data is typically extracted from various sources, such as the web, SFTP, databases, and IoT sensors, and ingested into a data lake (S3) or other data stores, such as file shares, databases, and data warehouses, using services such as AWS Glue (which we will cover in an upcoming chapter).

For example, the following architecture demonstrates how AWS Glue with a Python engine can be used to bring data from an FTP location and store it in Amazon S3.

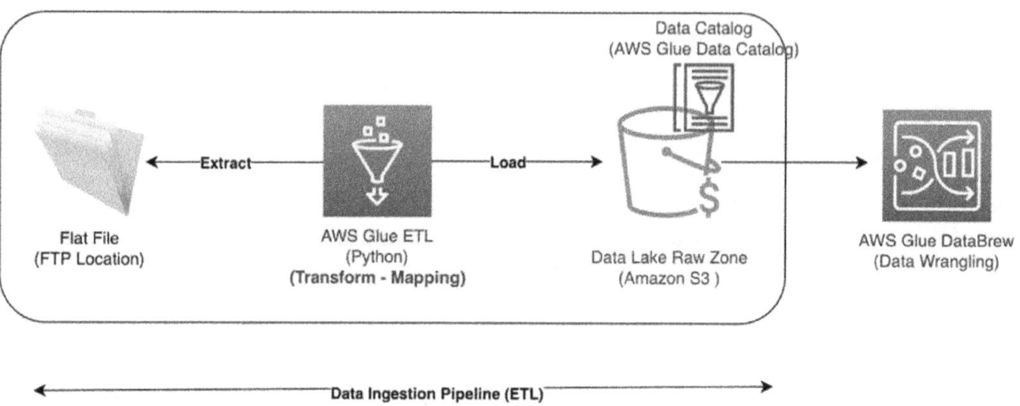

Figure 2.12: Data pipeline to bring data from the FTP location

After downloading the data, the next step is to upload the dataset to Amazon S3. To accomplish this, follow these steps:

1. Go to the AWS console.
2. If you already have an S3 bucket, search for it in the bucket list. Otherwise, create a new bucket.
3. Click on the **Upload** button.
4. Click on **Add Files**, or simply drag and drop the file from your local machine.
5. Click **Upload**.

You may have noticed that my Amazon S3 bucket name has a `raw-` prefix. This prefix is used to differentiate between different stages of data processing in a data lake. In the raw layer, data is stored as is, in its raw form. This allows us to have a single source of truth and use the data for future use cases. I will cover more details about data lakes and their best practices in upcoming chapters.

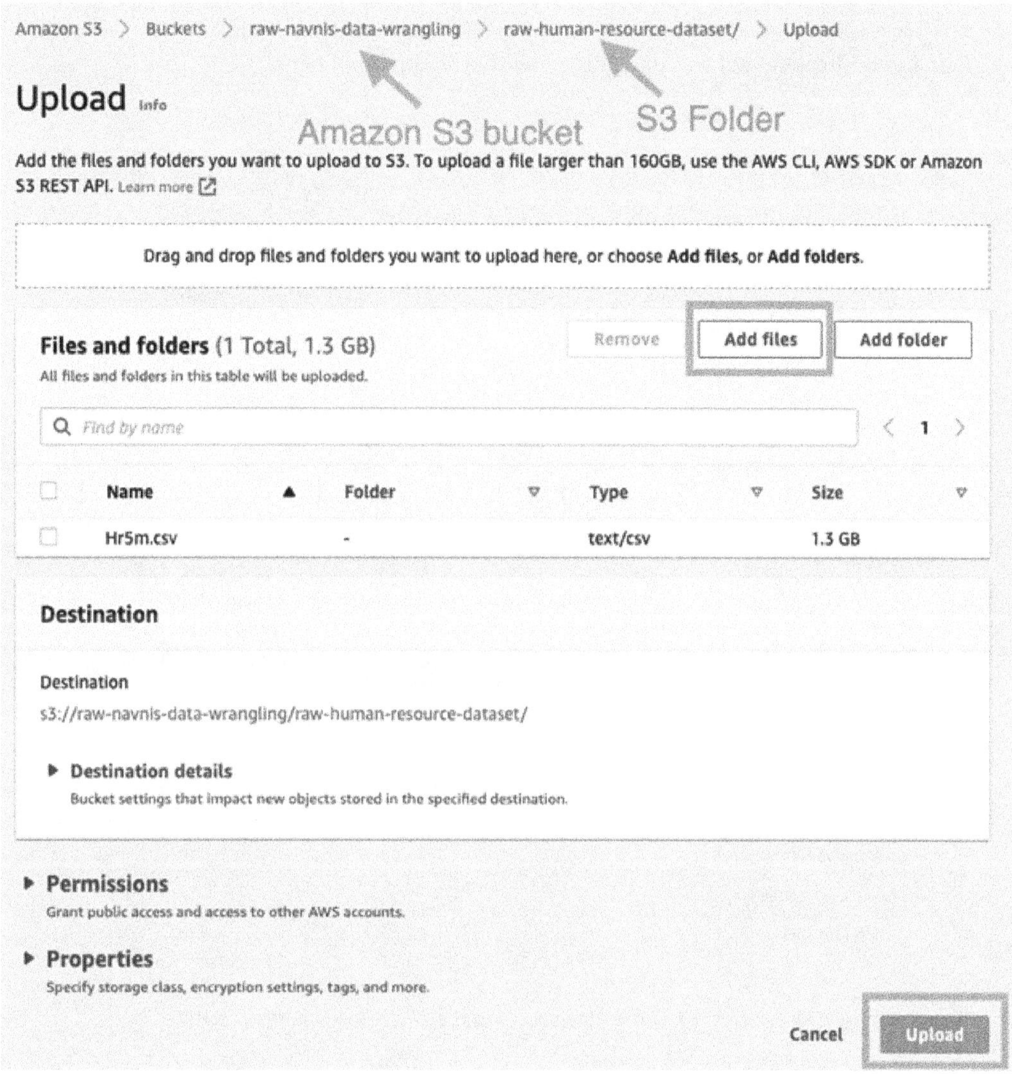

Amazon S3 > Buckets > raw-navnis-data-wrangling > raw-human-resource-dataset/ > Upload

Upload Info

Amazon S3 bucket

S3 Folder

Add the files and folders you want to upload to S3. To upload a file larger than 160GB, use the AWS CLI, AWS SDK or Amazon S3 REST API. Learn more

Drag and drop files and folders you want to upload here, or choose **Add files**, or **Add folders**.

Files and folders (1 Total, 1.3 GB)

All files and folders in this table will be uploaded.

Remove | Add files | Add folder

Find by name

Name	Folder	Type	Size
Hr5m.csv	-	text/csv	1.3 GB

Destination

Destination

s3://raw-navnis-data-wrangling/raw-human-resource-dataset/

Destination details

Bucket settings that impact new objects stored in the specified destination.

Permissions

Grant public access and access to other AWS accounts.

Properties

Specify storage class, encryption settings, tags, and more.

Cancel | Upload

Figure 2.13: Amazon S3 data lake folder structure

After the data has been made available on the raw layer of an Amazon S3 bucket, the next step is to create an AWS Glue dataset. In DataBrew, a dataset is comprised of metadata collected about the data. Data can be connected directly or exported to files and loaded from Amazon S3 or a local drive:

To create a DataBrew dataset, follow these steps:

1. Go to AWS Glue DataBrew.
2. On the left-hand side, click on **Datasets** and then click on **Connect new dataset**.

3. Provide a dataset name (e.g., `raw-human-resource`) and select the S3 bucket where the human resources dataset was uploaded, as shown in the figure here:

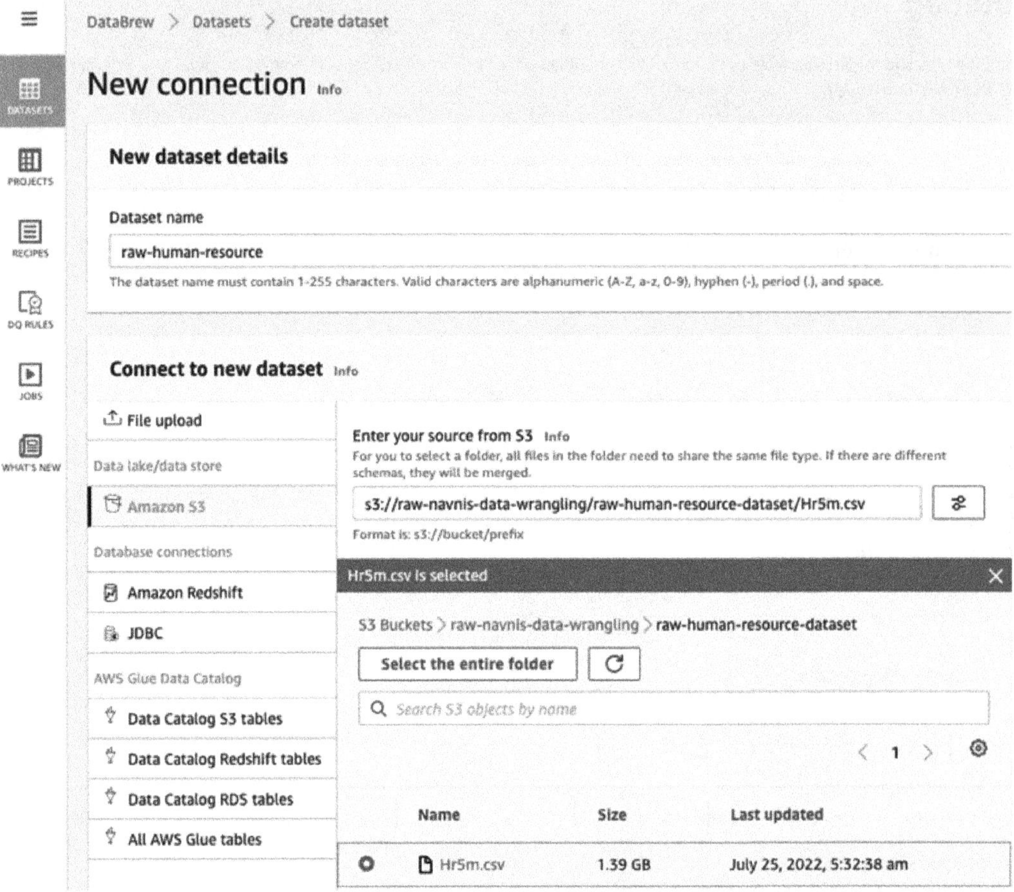

Figure 2.14: Amazon S3 as the data source in the AWS Glue DataBrew console

- Under **Additional configurations**, select **CSV** as the file format, select **Comma (,)** as the delimiter (since this is the default for CSV files), and keep **Treat first row as header** checked under **Column header values**.

DataBrew has an interesting feature where data can be previewed before creating the dataset, which can help in data discovery. Click on **Preview data** to perform some data discovery.

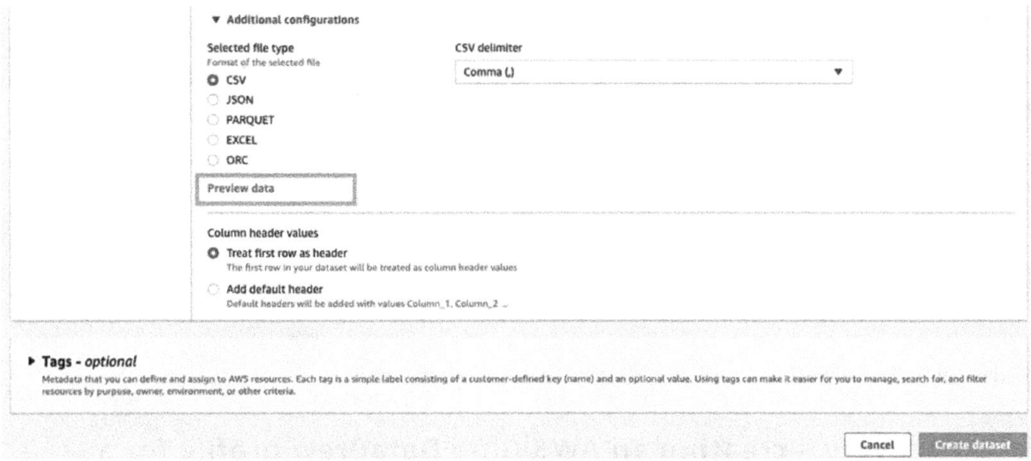

▼ Additional configurations

Selected file type

CSV

JSON

PARQUET

EXCEL

ORC

Preview data

CSV delimiter

Comma (,)

Column header values

Treat first row as header

Add default header

▸ Tags - *optional*

Cancel

Create dataset

Figure 2.15: Preview data option in the AWS Glue DataBrew console

The **Preview data** section allows users to see what the data and data structure look like.

Figure 2.16: Dataset preview in the AWS Glue DataBrew console

Once the dataset has been reviewed, click on **Create dataset**.

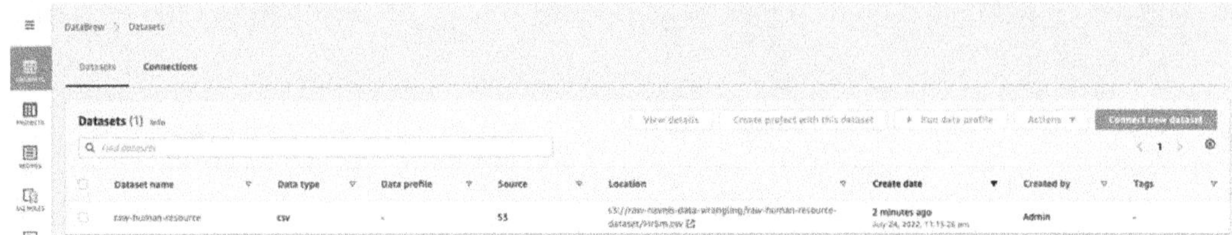

Figure 2.17: Dataset in the AWS Glue DataBrew console

The dataset will now be ready, and data discovery can be performed.

Data discovery – creating an AWS Glue DataBrew profile for a dataset

To create an AWS Glue DataBrew data profile for a dataset, follow these steps:

1. Choose a job name, for example, `raw-human-resource-profile-job`.
2. Select **Full Dataset** for the job run sample.
3. Choose the S3 location where you want to store the profile output in JSON format, which can be used for automating tasks such as data quality checks and PII identification.
4. Keep the rest of the options as the defaults.
5. Under **Permissions**, choose **Create new IAM role** and provide a name for the role, such as `human-resource`.
6. Click on **Create and run job.**
7. Wait for the data profile to be generated.

After the data profile is created, you can review it in the summary section, which provides useful information about the dataset, including the following:

- The size of the dataset, which serves as a good data quality check to ensure no data loss has occurred during ingestion
- The data type of the dataset, including the number of integer, double, and string columns
- Any duplicate rows or missing cells, which can help identify data quality issues

In the example provided, the dataset has 5 million rows and no missing cells or duplicate rows, indicating high data quality. Reviewing the data profile can provide a point of reference for comparing data in the source system to what is in the target system.

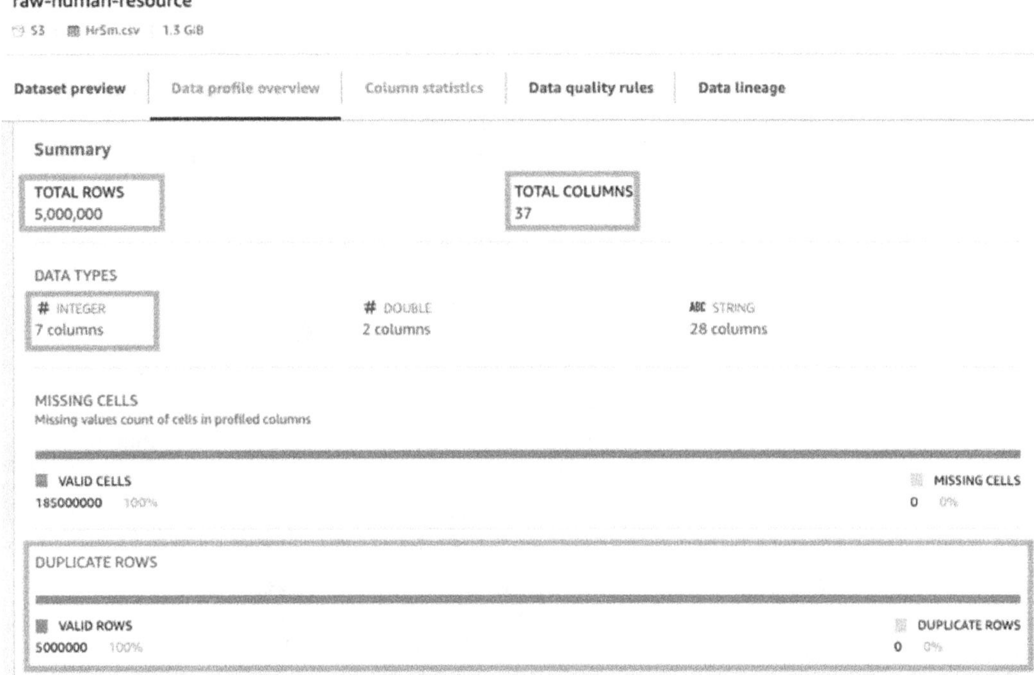

Figure 2.18: Data profile overview in the AWS Glue console

Correlations

The correlation coefficient (r) measures the degree of association between two variables, ranging from -1.0 to +1.0, with 0 indicating no relationship between the variables. The following interpretation can be made based on the value of r:

- Exactly -1: A perfect negative (downward-sloping) linear relationship
- -0.70: A strong negative (downward-sloping) linear relationship
- -0.50: A moderate negative (downhill-sloping) relationship
- -0.30: A weak negative (downhill-sloping) linear relationship
- 0: No linear relationship

- +0.30: A weak positive (upward-sloping) linear relationship
- +0.50: A moderate positive (upward-sloping) linear relationship
- +0.70: A strong positive (upward-sloping) linear relationship
- Exactly +1: A perfect positive (upward-sloping) linear relationship

In the given correlation coefficient diagram, the `Year of Joining` and `Age in Company` variables have a strong relationship, but in the opposite direction. This means that if one variable increases (e.g., `Year of Joining` moves from 2018 to 2016 with reference to the year 2022), the other variable decreases (i.e., `Age in Company` also decreases by two years).

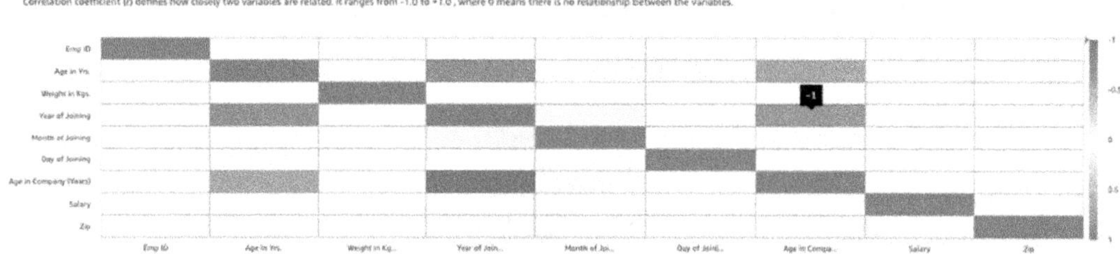

Figure 2.19: Correlation coefficient

The correlation coefficient between `Age in Company` (in years) and `Age in Yrs.` is +65, indicating that there is a positive correlation between these two variables. This means that if someone is older in age, they are likely to have spent more time in the company, and therefore, they are a more tenured employee. However, it is important to note that this correlation coefficient does not always hold true in all cases, and other factors may also influence an employee's tenure in a company.

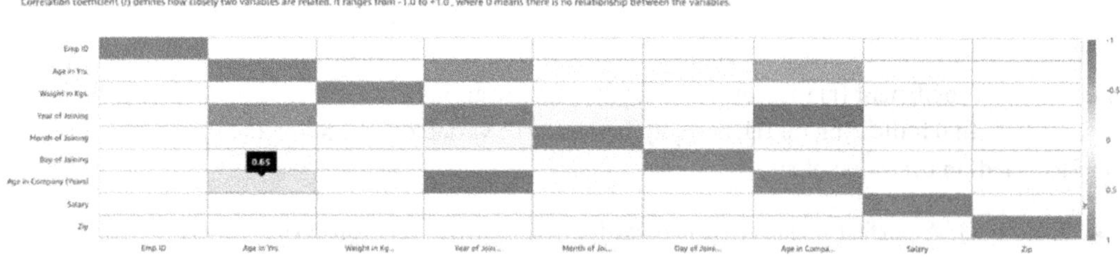

Figure 2.20: Correlation coefficient

Value distribution

The value distribution of a dataset indicates how well the data is spread out, and it serves as a good indicator of data skew. For instance, if we consider the `Salary` column, it appears to be equally distributed, which is a positive indicator of a well-distributed dataset.

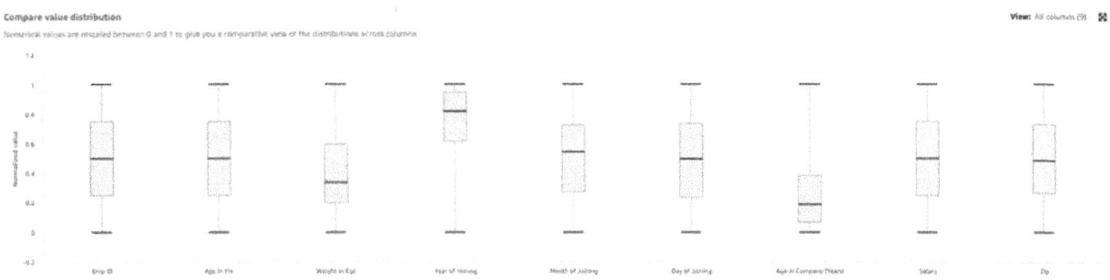

Figure 2.21: Value distribution

Columns summary

The summary section of a column in a profile provides valuable information about its characteristics, including its distribution, missing values, unique values, distinct values, median, minimum, mode, outliers, and skewness. Understanding these data values can aid in feature engineering. For example, skewness is a way to see whether data is lopsided or not. It tells us how much the data differs from being perfectly balanced. If the skewness is positive, it means there is more data on the right side, making the tail on that side longer or fatter. If the skewness is negative, it means there is more data on the left side, making the tail on that side longer or fatter. If the skewness is 0, it means the data is perfectly balanced.

For instance, examining the summary of the `Ages in Yrs.` column can give you a good idea of the ages of employees in a company. The minimum age for employees is around 21 years, the maximum age is 60 years, and the mean age is 40.50 years.

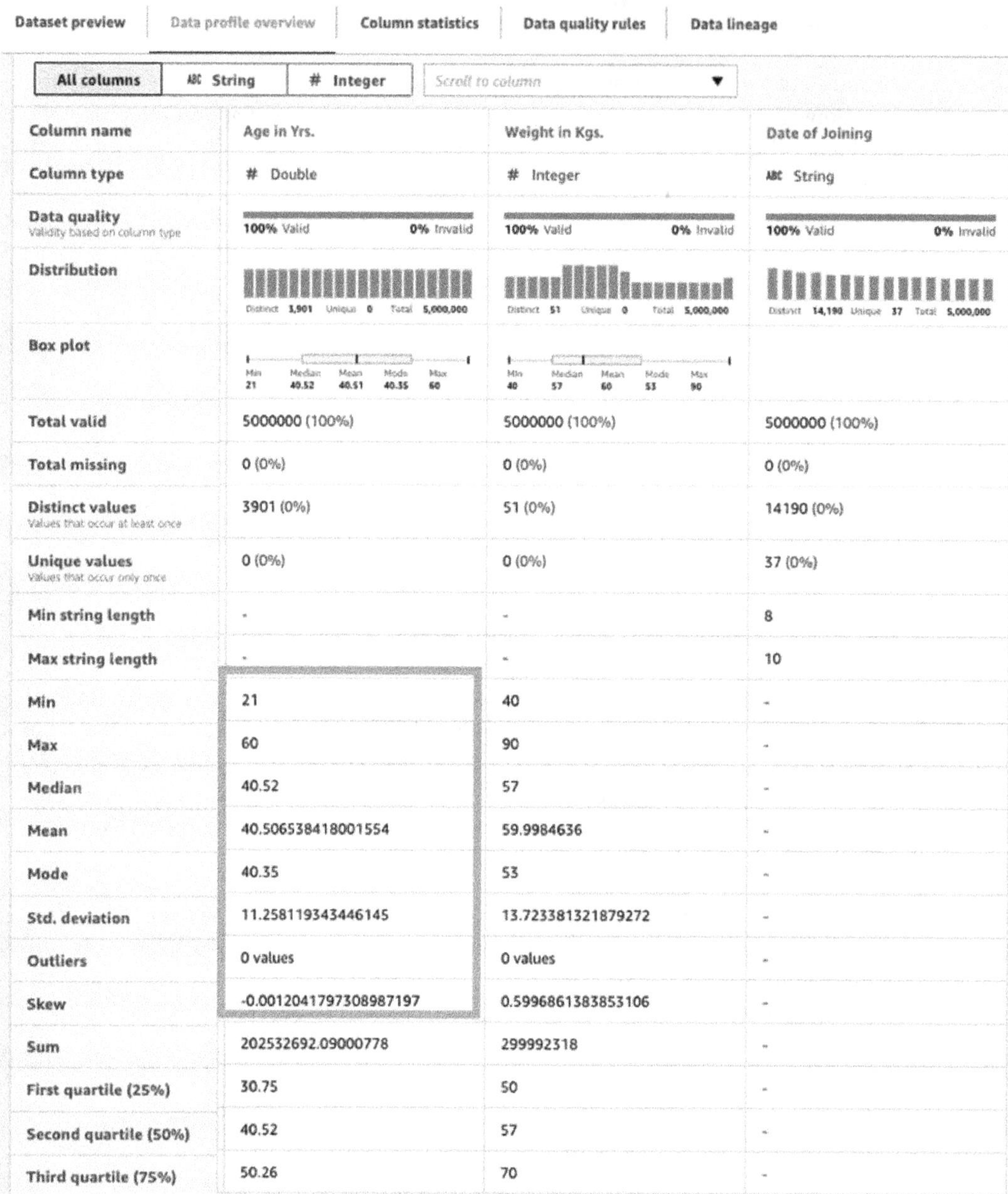

Dataset preview | Data profile overview | Column statistics | Data quality rules | Data lineage

All columns | ABC String | # Integer | Scroll to column

Column name	Age in Yrs.	Weight in Kgs.	Date of Joining
Column type	# Double	# Integer	ABC String
Data quality Validity based on column type	100% Valid 0% Invalid	100% Valid 0% Invalid	100% Valid 0% Invalid
Distribution	Distinct 3,901 Unique 0 Total 5,000,000	Distinct 51 Unique 0 Total 5,000,000	Distinct 14,190 Unique 37 Total 5,000,000
Box plot	Min 21 Median 40.52 Mean 40.51 Mode 40.35 Max 60	Min 40 Median 57 Mean 60 Mode 53 Max 90	
Total valid	5000000 (100%)	5000000 (100%)	5000000 (100%)
Total missing	0 (0%)	0 (0%)	0 (0%)
Distinct values Values that occur at least once	3901 (0%)	51 (0%)	14190 (0%)
Unique values Values that occur only once	0 (0%)	0 (0%)	37 (0%)
Min string length	-	-	8
Max string length	-	-	10
Min	21	40	-
Max	60	90	-
Median	40.52	57	-
Mean	40.506538418001554	59.9984636	-
Mode	40.35	53	-
Std. deviation	11.258119343446145	13.723381321879272	-
Outliers	0 values	0 values	-
Skew	-0.0012041797308987197	0.5996861383853106	-
Sum	202532692.09000778	299992318	-
First quartile (25%)	30.75	50	-
Second quartile (50%)	40.52	57	-
Third quartile (75%)	50.26	70	-

Figure 2.22: Data profile overview in the AWS Glue DataBrew console

Data cleaning and enrichment – AWS Glue DataBrew transforms

To create a project in DataBrew, which is a collection of data exploration, cleaning, and normalization information, please follow these steps:

1. Go to the DataBrew console and select **Projects**.
2. Click **Create project**.
3. Enter a name for the project, such as `basic-transform-human-resource-project`.
4. Keep the default recipe name.
5. Select **My datasets** and choose the `raw-human-resource` dataset created in the previous section.
6. Keep the default sampling size of **500**.
7. Under **Permissions**, select the IAM role created under the data profile section for the role name.
8. Click **Create project**.

To build a recipe for your project, open the project in the AWS Glue DataBrew interactive session and follow the instructions to create a set of data-wrangling steps, or actions.

One of the common data-wrangling tasks is merging multiple columns into one, such as merging name or date columns. To perform this task in AWS Glue DataBrew, use the **MERGE** transform, which allows you to merge multiple columns and create a single column.

Figure 2.23: Merge columns

To perform the task, follow these steps:

1. Open the **basic-transform-human-resource-project** project created in the previous step.
2. Click on **MERGE** in the top menu.

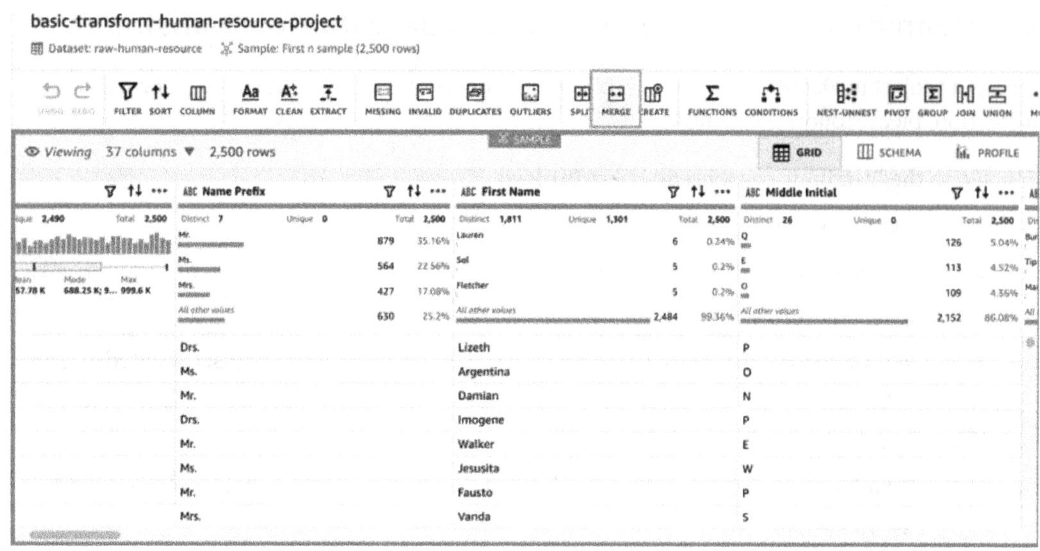

Figure 2.24: MERGE option

3. Select **Name Prefix**, **First Name**, **Middle Initial**, and **Last Name** as the source columns.
4. Add a space as the separator.
5. Provide a new column name, such as `Employee_Full_Name`.

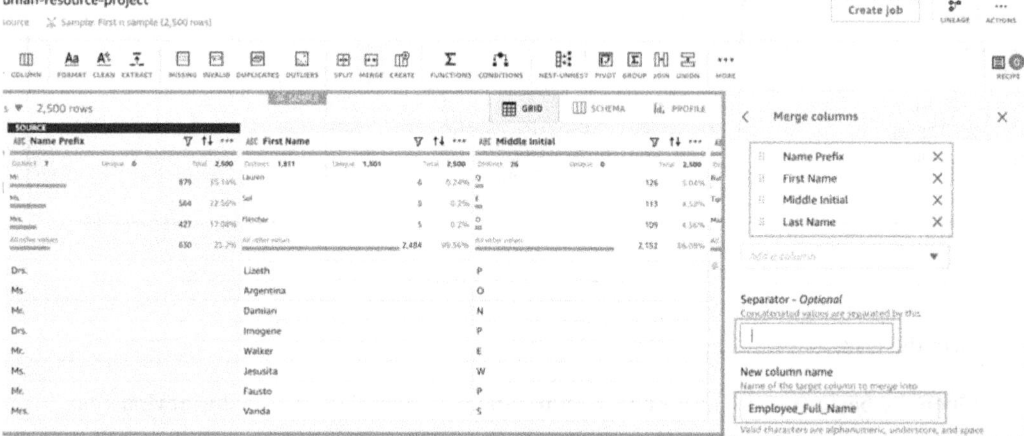

Figure 2.25: Merge columns list

6. Click on **Apply**.

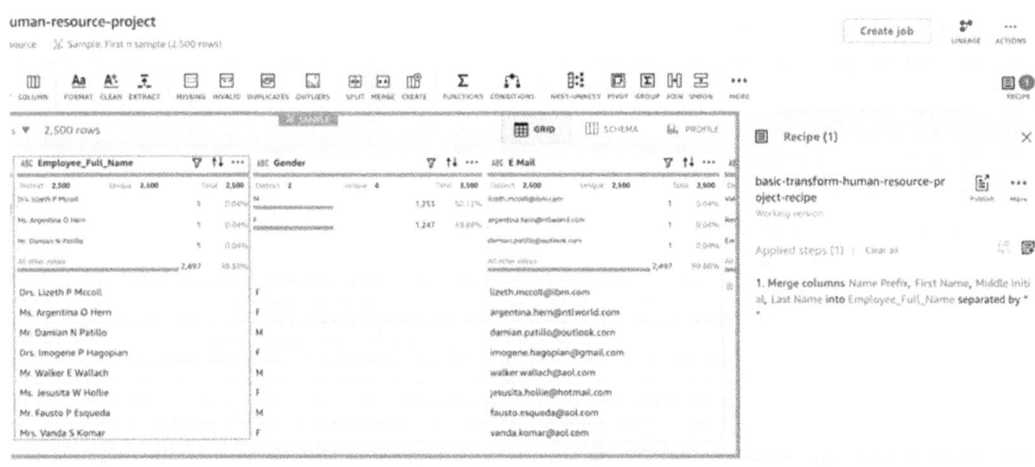

Figure 2.26: Merge column output

7. Delete unwanted columns.

   To delete columns, go to the **COLUMNS** icon and click on **Delete**. Select the column you want to delete from the drop-down menu and click on **Apply**. Delete columns such as **Short Month**, **DOW of Joining**, and **Short DOW**.

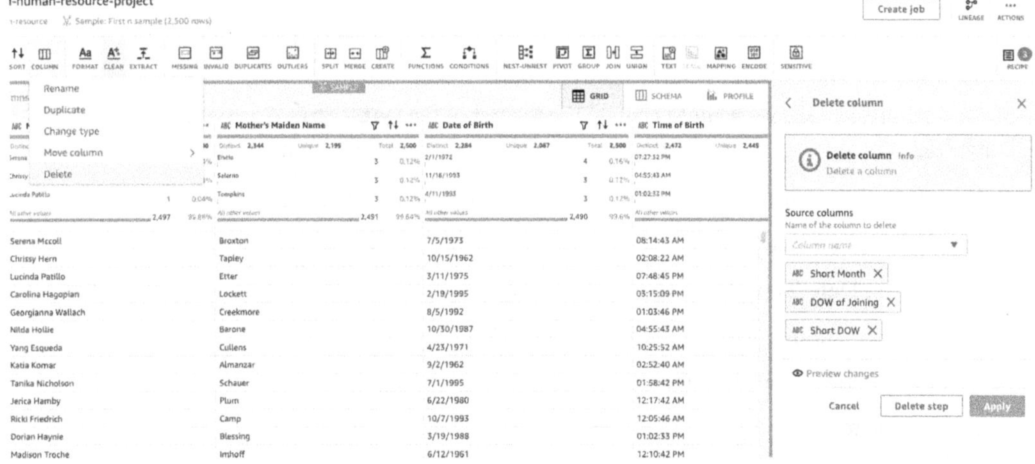

Figure 2.27: Delete column option in the AWS Glue DataBrew console

8. Format the date columns.

AWS Glue DataBrew offers various data format options based on the type of data, including the following:

- String formatting:
    - Convert to uppercase
    - Convert to lowercase
    - Convert to capital case
    - Convert to sentence case
- Numeric formatting:
    - Decimal precision
    - Thousands separator
    - Abbreviate numbers
- Date-time formats:
    - ISO
    - US
    - UK
- Phone number

To illustrate, let's say we want to change the format of the `Date of Joining` column from `mm/dd/yyyy` to `month*dd,*yyyy` to make it more readable. To do this, follow these steps:

I. Select the ellipsis (dot dot dot) above the `Data of Joining` column.

II. Choose **Format**.

III. Select **Date-Time Formats**.

IV. Choose **month*dd,*yyyy** from the menu that appears.

V. Click on **Preview** to review the new column.

VI. If you're satisfied with the changes, click on **Apply**.

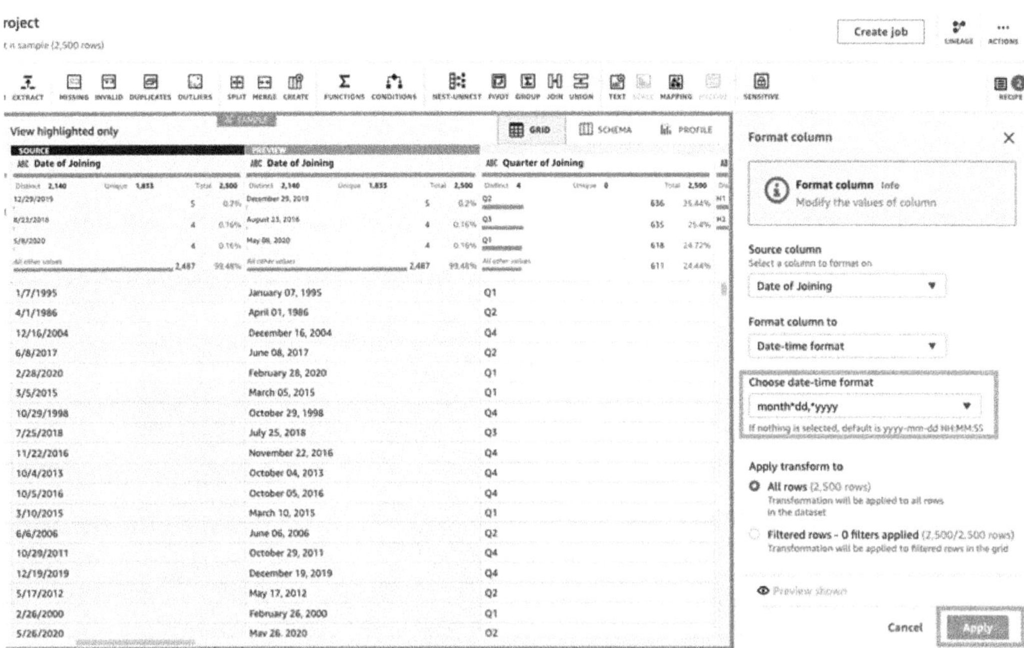

Figure 2.28: Data formatting in the AWS Glue DataBrew console

9. Rename the column.

   During dataset analysis, it was discovered that some column names, such as **Phone No.**, end with a dot. To resolve this issue, the column should be renamed. To change a column name, select the column and click on the three dots, then choose the **Rename** option.

   To update the column name, choose a new name. For example, **Phone No.** can be changed to **Phone**. Once the new name has been chosen, click on **Apply**.

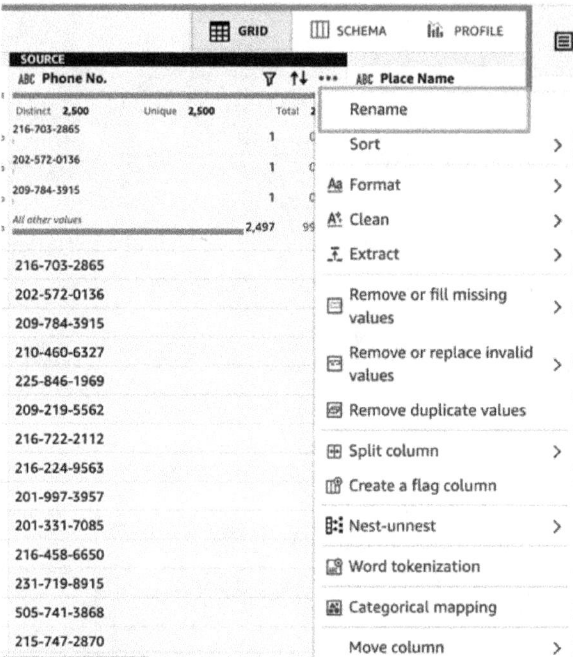

Figure 2.29: Rename columns in the the AWS Glue DataBrew console

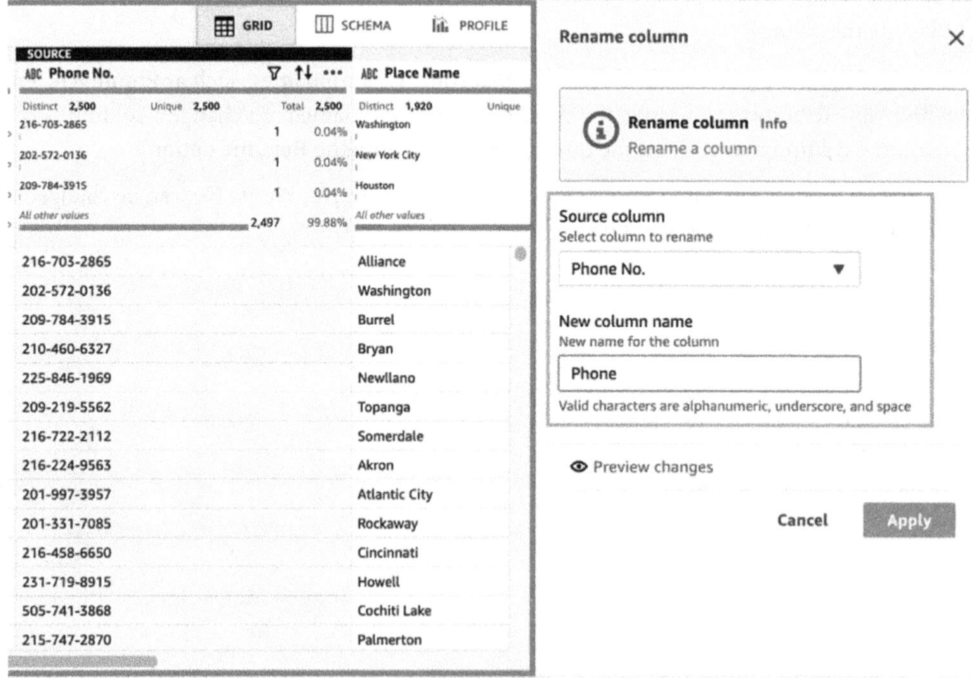

Figure 2.30: Rename column option in the AWS Glue DataBrew console

10. Redact sensitive columns.

    AWS Glue DataBrew offers a highly useful feature that involves redacting sensitive columns. This feature is particularly helpful when building solutions such as DaaS, enabling self-service, or sharing data internally or externally. Redacting sensitive data is a critical requirement in all such cases:

    I. To redact sensitive columns, start by reviewing the dataset and identifying columns that contain sensitive information, such as Social Security Numbers, phone numbers, usernames, and passwords. Once identified, you can use the **SENSITIVE** icon in AWS Glue DataBrew to select and redact values from these columns.

    II. To perform data redaction, select the **SENSITIVE** icon and choose the **Redact values** option. Then, select the source columns and keep the rest of the options as the defaults (i.e., use the redact symbol, #) before clicking on **Apply**.

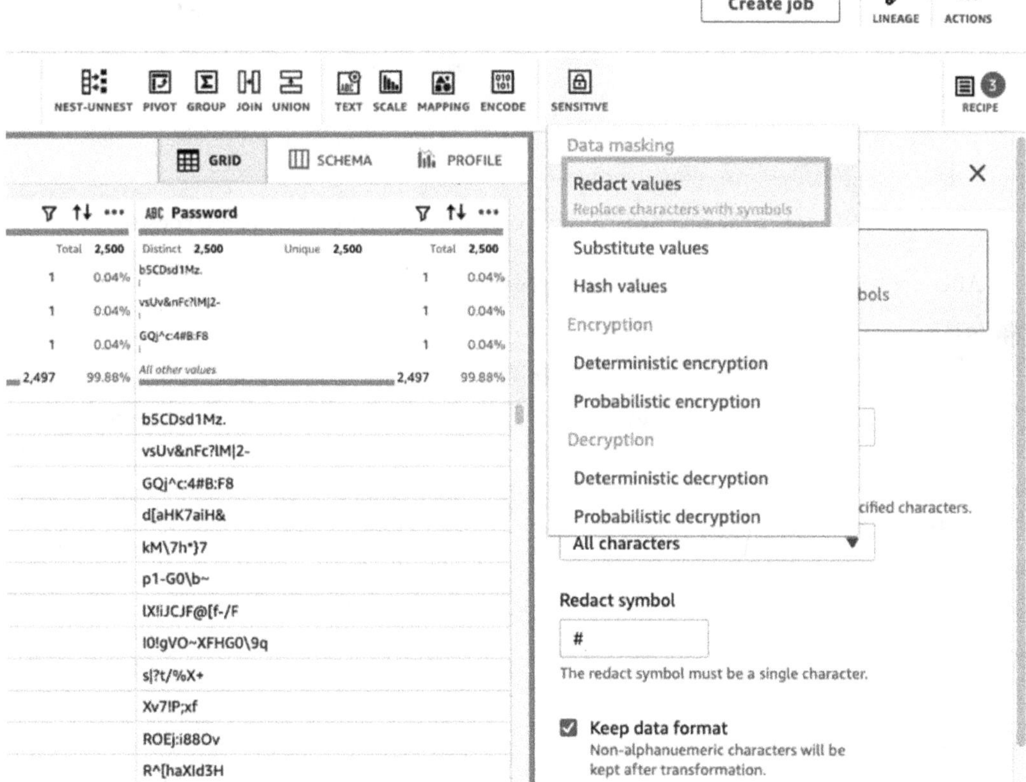

Figure 2.31: Sensitive columns Redact values option in the AWS Glue DataBrew console

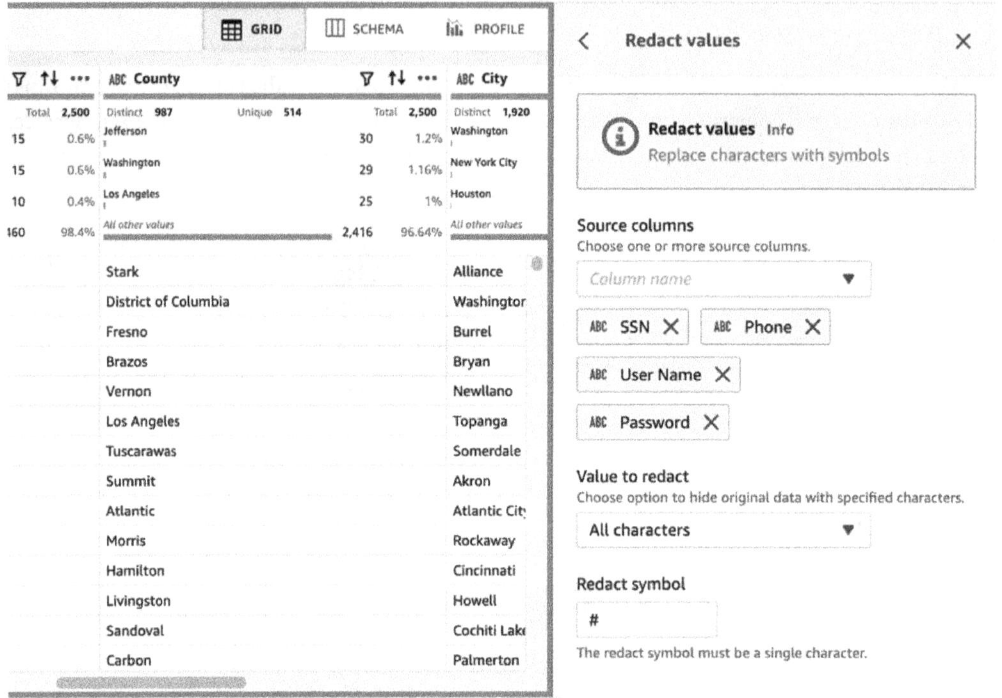

Figure 2.32: Sensitive columns Redact values option in the AWS Glue DataBrew console

After applying the recipe, you'll be able to see the hashed column.

ABC SSN	ABC Phone No.
Distinct 1 Unique 0 Total 2,500	Distinct 1 Unique 0 Total 2,
###-##-#### 2,500 100%	###-###-#### 2,500 1
###-##-####	###-###-####
###-##-####	###-###-####
###-##-####	###-###-####
###-##-####	###-###-####
###-##-####	###-###-####
###-##-####	###-###-####
###-##-####	###-###-####
###-##-####	###-###-####
###-##-####	###-###-####

Figure 2.33: Sensitive columns redaction in the AWS Glue DataBrew

11. Perform deterministic encryption.

    To perform deterministic encryption, follow these steps:

    I. Click on the **SENSITIVE** icon and navigate to the **Encryption** section.

    II. Select **Deterministic encryption**.

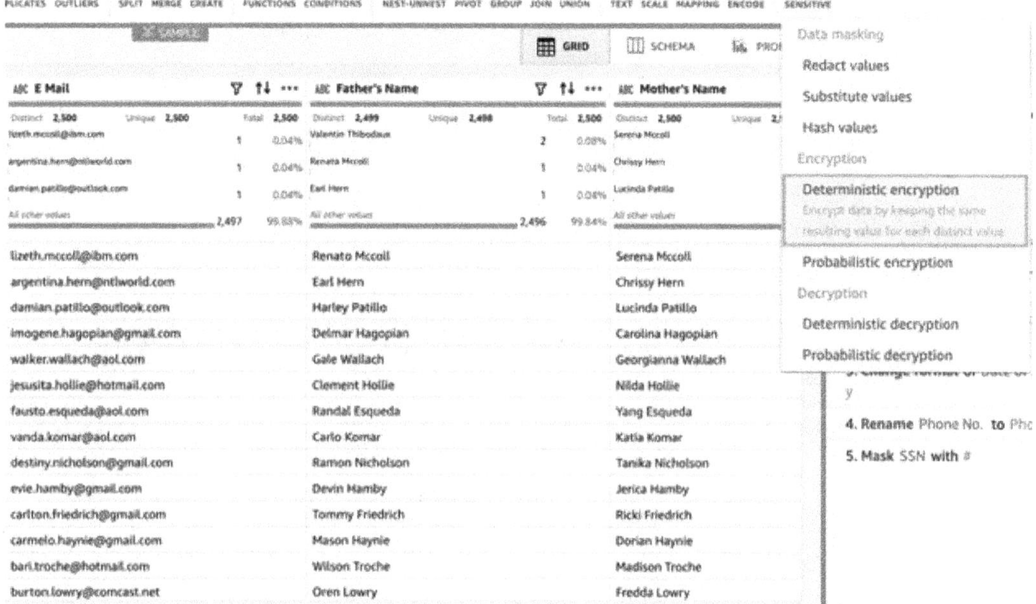

Figure 2.34: Sensitive columns Deterministic encryption option in the AWS Glue DataBrew console

    III. Choose the columns you want to encrypt, such as `Employee_Full_Name`, `E Mail`, and `Date of Birth`.

    IV. Select the **secret** option and choose the default DataBrew secret key.

    V. Click on **Apply** and you will be able to see the encrypted data.

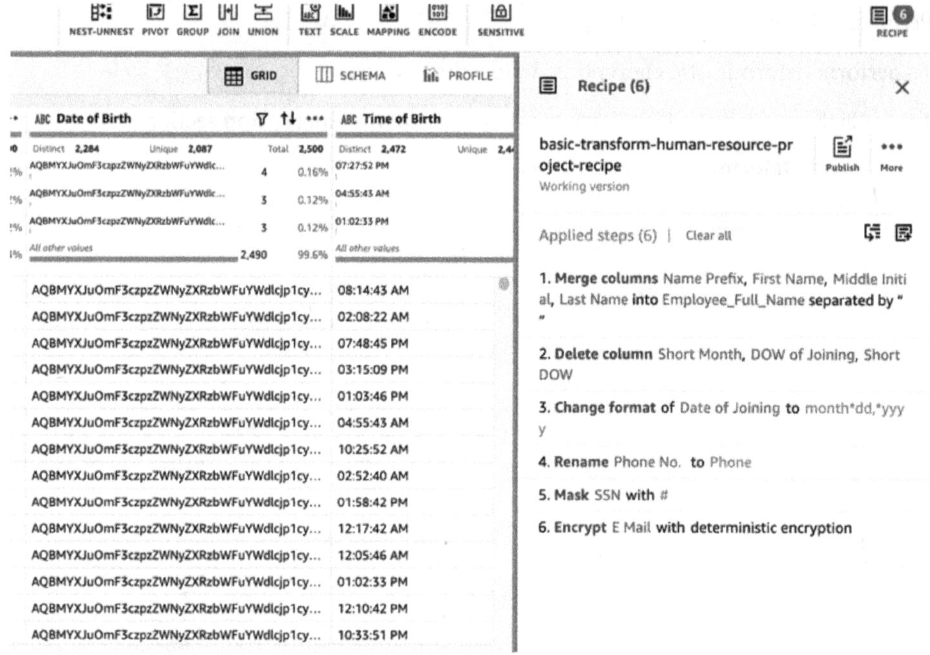

Figure 2.35: Sensitive columns deterministic encryption output in the AWS Glue DataBrew console

12. Group based on gender.

    First, group the data based on gender. Then, we can analyze how the salary is distributed between males and females.

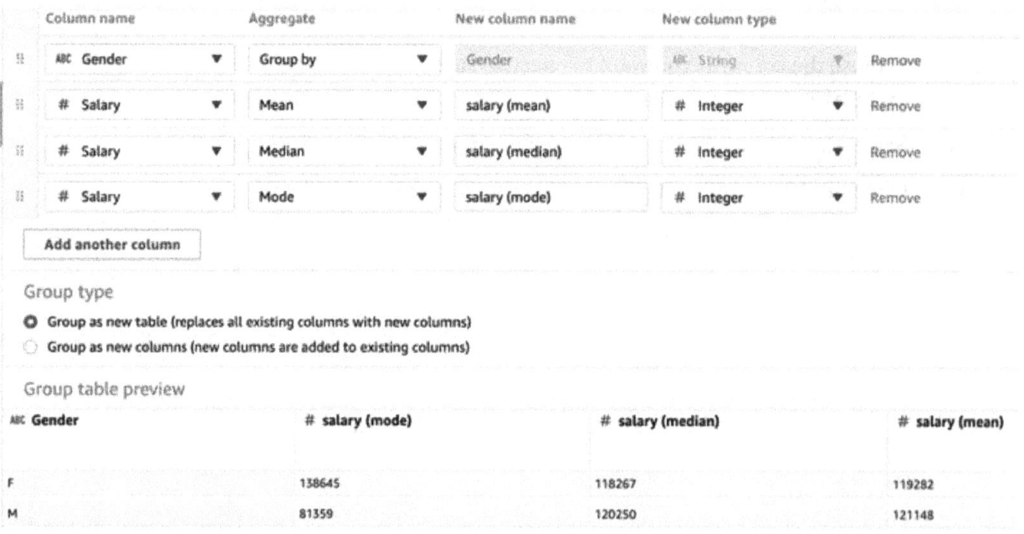

Figure 2.36: Group by output in the AWS Glue DataBrew console

13. Join the dataset.

    Joining datasets involves combining two or more tables based on a common key. It is a crucial step in the data-wrangling process, allowing for data enrichment.

    AWS Glue DataBrew supports several types of joins, including the following:

    - **Inner join**: This is the default join type in Glue DataBrew. It returns records that have matching values in both tables based on the join key.

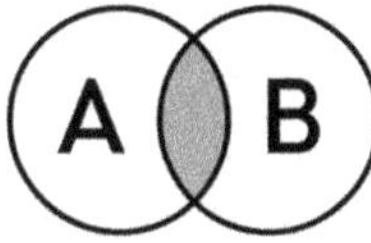

Figure 2.37: Inner join Venn diagram

    - **Left join**: This returns all records from the left table and the matched records from the right table based on the join key.

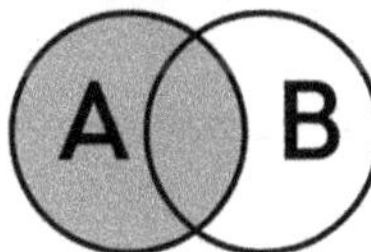

Figure 2.38: Left join Venn diagram

    - **Right join**: This returns all records from the right table and the matched records from the left table based on the join key.

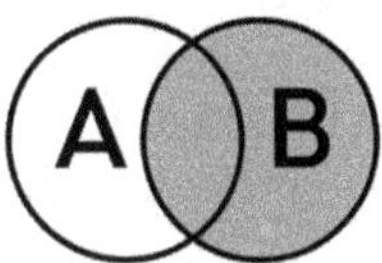

Figure 2.39: Right join Venn diagram

    - **Outer join**: This returns all rows from Table A and Table B, regardless of the join condition.

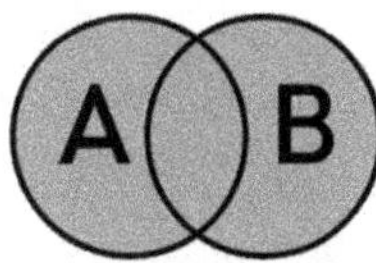

Figure 2.40: Outer join Venn diagram

- **Left excluding join**: This returns all rows from Table A, excluding the rows that meet the join condition.

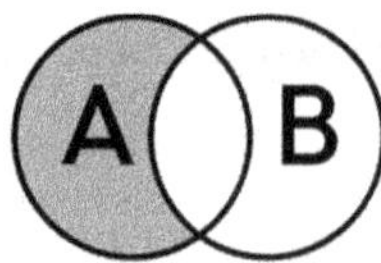

Figure 2.41: Left excluding join Venn diagram

- **Right excluding join**: This returns all rows from Table B, excluding the rows that meet the join condition.

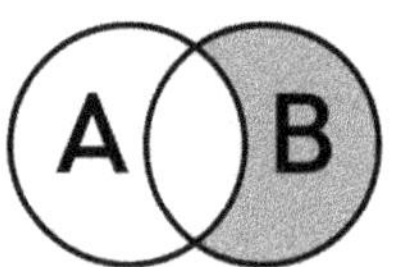

Figure 2.42: Right excluding join Venn diagram

- **Outer excluding join**: This returns all rows from Table A and Table B, excluding the rows that meet the join condition.

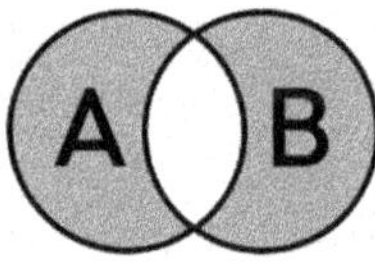

Figure 2.43: Outer excluding join Venn diagram

Each join type has a different effect on the resulting dataset. It is important to understand these differences in order to choose the appropriate join for your data analysis needs.

To perform a join in AWS Glue DataBrew, follow these steps:

I. Open your project and click on the **JOIN** icon to access the join option.

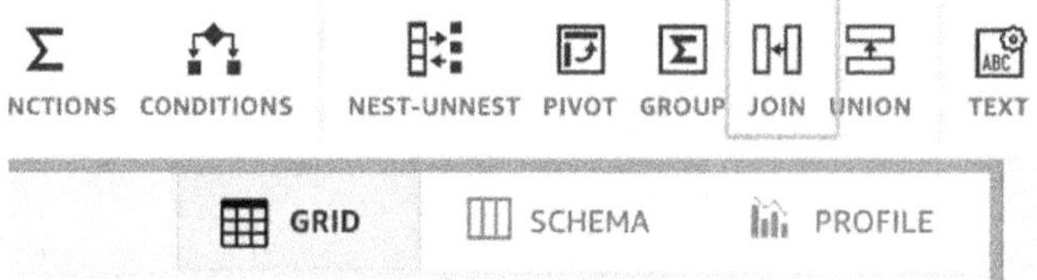

Figure 2.44: JOIN option in AWS Glue DataBrew

II. Choose the dataset you want to join. If you only have one dataset, you can perform a self-join (or self-inner join) by joining the dataset with itself.

III. Select the join type and column you want to join on, then click **Finish**. Your project will now have a joined dataset.

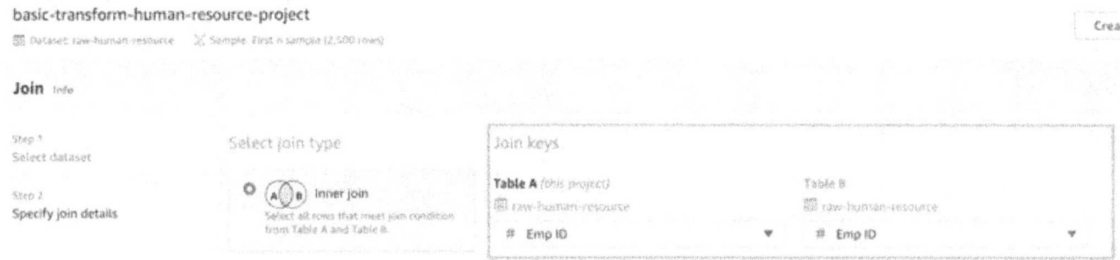

Figure 2.45: Join option in AWS Glue DataBrew

Now that you know how to perform data transformation using AWS Glue DataBrew, you can try out other transformations on your own. The next step is to learn how to perform data quality checks using AWS Glue DataBrew.

Data validation – performing data quality checks using AWS Glue DataBrew

This section will focus on using AWS Glue DataBrew to perform data validation and quality checks with real-world examples.

In this first example, we will learn how to use AWS Glue DataBrew to identify and correct data quality issues. But first, let's briefly discuss data quality issues and why it's important to address them. As we discussed in the previous chapter, organizations are striving to become data-driven, and for such organizations, it's crucial to address any data quality challenges they face or have the necessary tools and processes in place to deal with data quality issues.

According to a report by KPMG, 77% of CEOs are concerned about whether their organization is keeping up with new technologies, and data and analytics will be a top area of investment over the next three years. Additionally, 84% of CEOs are worried about the quality of the data they're basing their critical business decisions on. Poor data quality is not just a technology issue, as it can have a significant impact on businesses. According to a research paper by Gartner in 2018, organizations believe that poor data quality costs an average of $15 million per year in losses.

A popular consumer tool, Zestimate, powered by artificial intelligence to estimate the value of homes, by Zillow is a prime example of data quality issues. Zillow employed distinctive algorithms that regularly updated its database of property values multiple times per week. These algorithms took into account information derived from both publicly available data and data submitted by users. Zillow claimed that its Zestimate, which was the estimated property value provided for both on-market and off-market homes, had a median error rate of 1.9% for on-market homes nationwide, while off-market homes had a median error rate of 6.9%. However, it is important to note that the accuracy of Zestimates relied heavily on the accuracy of the underlying data. If crucial details such as the number of bedrooms or bathrooms, square footage, or lot size of a home were inaccurately recorded on Zillow, it would result in a significant deviation in the Zestimate provided. This issue eventually led to Zillow buying many houses at much higher prices than they sold because of Zestimate's failure. Consequently, Zillow decided to shut down its home-buying business, which resulted in thousands of layoffs and millions of dollars in losses.

In another example, data quality issues caused the real-time e-commerce site of a prominent credit history provider to crash. Upon investigation, they found that the website was expecting alphabetic characters in the comment field, which unfortunately had an unreadable TAB character in it that caused a cascading system failure.

As we briefly discussed in the previous chapter, the computer science concept of **garbage in, garbage out (GIGO)** determines the quality of data. The quality of the output of data is determined by the quality of its input. In layman's terms, if we provide bad data as input, we will get bad data as output. Data quality issues relate to completeness, consistency, validity, accuracy, uniqueness, integrity, and timeliness.

Now that we understand the impact of data quality on technology and business, let's move forward with our example of building data quality rules on AWS Glue DataBrew to identify and fix issues.

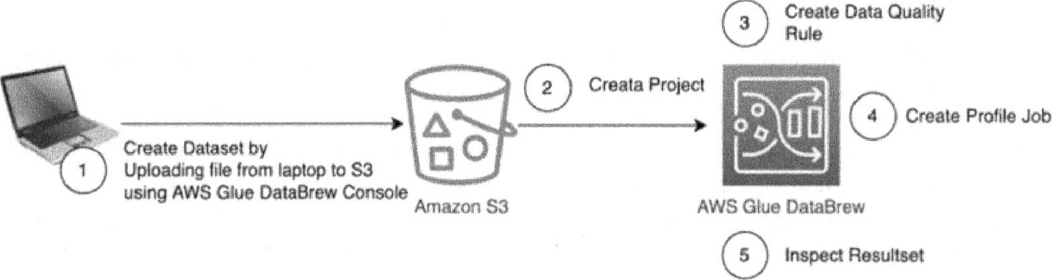

Figure 2.46: Data quality check architecture in AWS Glue DataBrew

If you wish to follow along, I will be providing step-by-step instructions for creating data quality rules.

To create data quality rules, please follow the steps mentioned here:

1. Click on the **DQ Rules** option.
2. Provide a name for your data quality ruleset. For instance, you may name it `data-quality-human-resource`.
3. In the **Choose dataset** section, select the dataset that you created in *step 2*. Once you have selected the dataset, the system will provide you with recommendations for data quality rules.

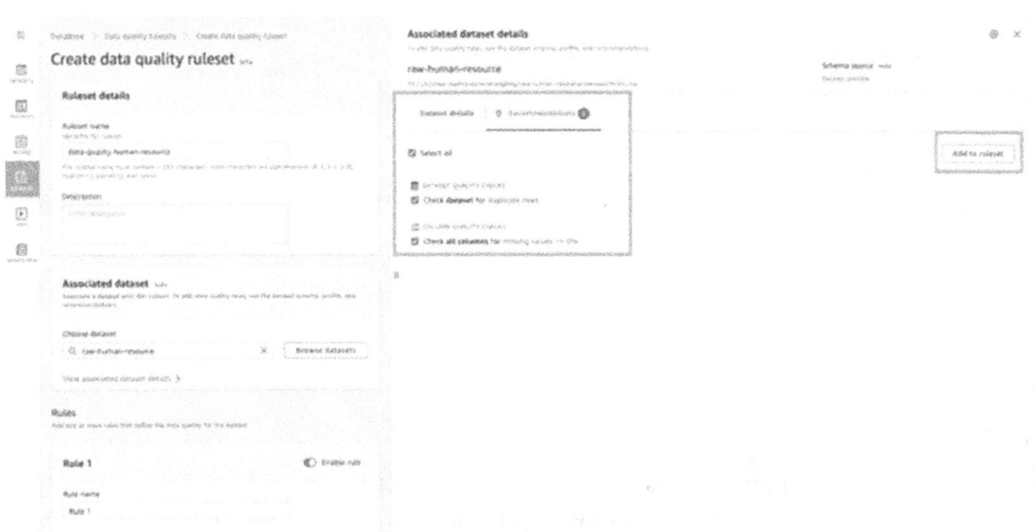

Figure 2.47: Data quality default recommendation before data quality check

For this dataset, the following recommendations are being displayed:

- Check for duplicate rows in the dataset
- Ensure that there are no missing values in any column

To create a data profile, follow these steps provided:

1. Provide a name for the job. For example, you may name it `raw-human-resource-profile-job`.
2. Select **Full Dataset** as the option for **Job Run Sample**.
3. Choose an S3 location where you would like to store your profile output in the **Job Output Settings** section.
4. Leave the remaining options as the defaults.
5. In the **Permissions** section, click on **Create new IAM role** and provide a new IAM role suffix.
6. Finally, click on **Create and run job** to create the data profile. It will take some time to generate the data profile.

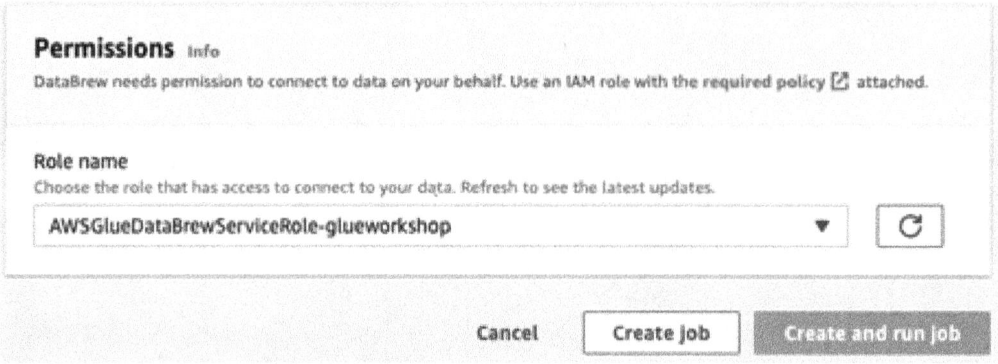

Permissions Info

DataBrew needs permission to connect to data on your behalf. Use an IAM role with the required policy attached.

Role name

Choose the role that has access to connect to your data. Refresh to see the latest updates.

AWSGlueDataBrewServiceRole-glueworkshop

Cancel | Create job | Create and run job

Figure 2.48: Creating the data profile job

After completing the data profile job and returning to the **Data quality rules** section, select the `raw-human-resource` dataset to view the 53 generated data quality recommendations in the AWS Glue DataBrew console. While not all recommendations may be useful, it's advisable to review all of them and add relevant ones to the ruleset.

From the recommendations list, the following data quality recommendations were selected and added to the ruleset:

1. Check for duplicate rows in the dataset.
2. Ensure that all columns have no missing values (0% missing values).
3. Verify that the `Age in Yrs.` column contains values between 21 and 60.
4. Ensure that the `Quarter of Joining` column only contains values from the list `["Q3","Q2","Q1","Q4"]`.
5. Verify that the `SSN` column has a length of 11 characters.
6. Ensure that the `Phone No.` column has a length of 12 characters.

These recommendations were provided as part of the data quality rule suggestions. To create custom data quality rules using the Glue DataBrew console, read on.

In order to create custom data quality rules using the Glue DataBrew console, we must first define what rules we want to build. Here are some rules we want to create:

1. **Validate the row count**: We have downloaded the dataset of 5 million records. Let's validate whether the count matches.
2. **The employee ID, email address, and SSN should be unique**: These values should always be unique.
3. **The employee ID and email address should not be null**: Usually, we don't want these values to be null.
4. **The employee ID and employee age in years shouldn't have negative values**: We want to validate that the values in these columns are positive.
5. **The SSN data format should be in the format (xxx-xx-xxxx).**

Let's start building the data quality rules:

1. Validate the row count.

   To check the total row count, let's perform the following steps:

   I. Create a new rule.

   II. Name the rule (e.g., `Row count == 5 million`).

   III. Choose **Individual check for each column** for the data quality check scope.

   IV. Select **All data quality checks are met (AND)** as the rule success criteria.

   V. Choose **Number of rows** as the data quality check.

   VI. Select **Is equals** as the condition.

   VII. Enter `5000000` as the value.

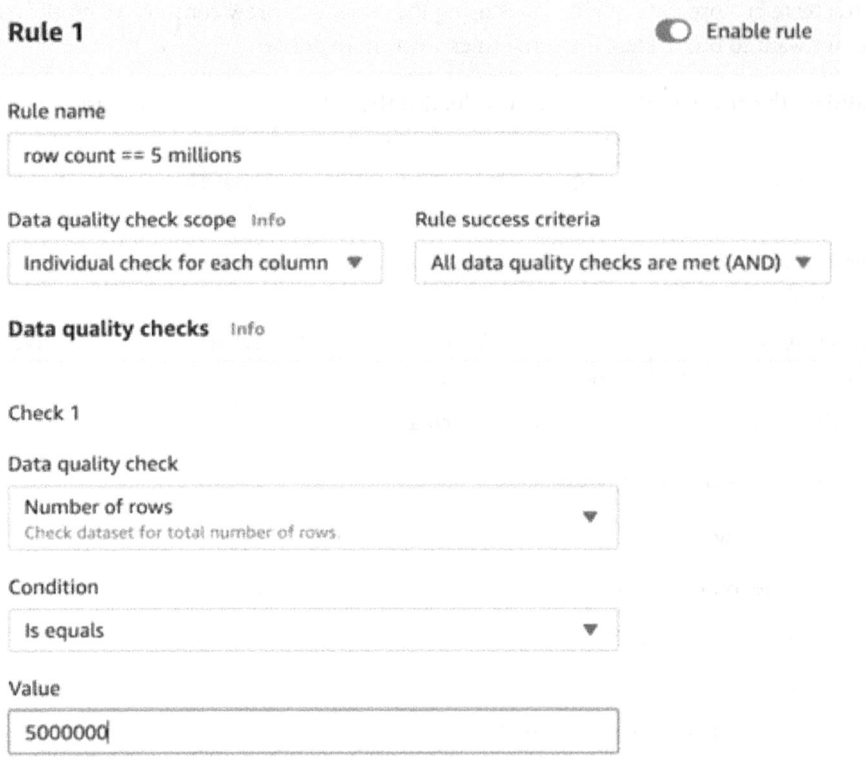

Figure 2.49: Data quality check

2. To verify that the specified columns contain only unique values, follow these instructions:

   I. Click on **Add rule**.

   II. Enter a name for the rule, for example, `Check Unique Values in Columns`.

   III. Select **Common checks for chosen columns** as the data quality check scope.

   IV. For **Rule success criteria**, select **All data quality checks are met (AND)**.

   V. Select the **Emp ID**, **E Mail**, and **SSN** columns under **Selected columns**.

   VI. Under **Check 1**, select **Unique values** under **Data quality check**.

   VII. Select **Is equals** under **Condition**.

VIII. Enter `100` for **Value**, and select **%(percent) rows** from the drop-down menu.

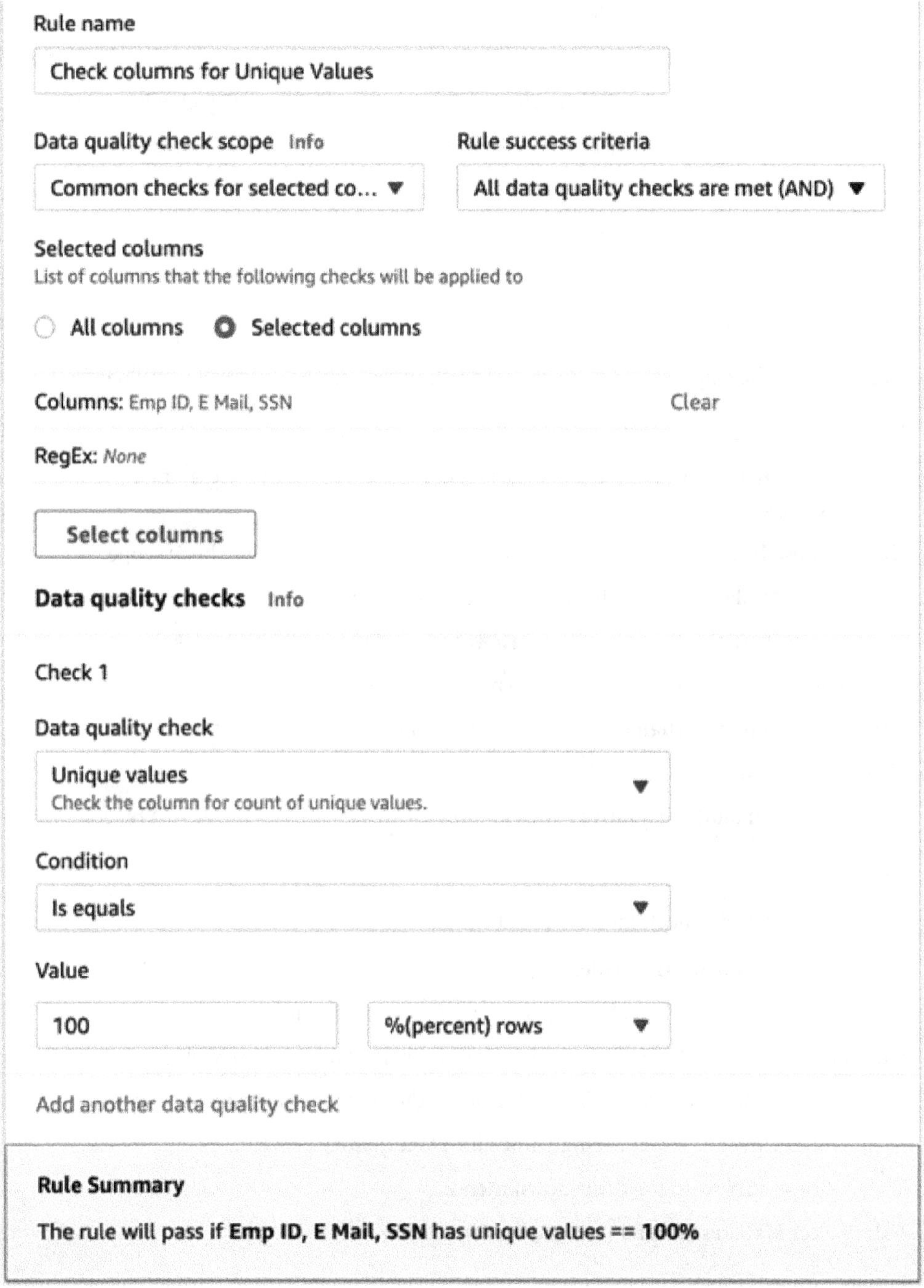

Rule name

Check columns for Unique Values

Data quality check scope Info

Common checks for selected co...

Rule success criteria

All data quality checks are met (AND)

Selected columns

List of columns that the following checks will be applied to

All columns Selected columns

Columns: Emp ID, E Mail, SSN Clear

RegEx: *None*

Select columns

Data quality checks Info

Check 1

Data quality check

Unique values

Check the column for count of unique values.

Condition

Is equals

Value

100 %(percent) rows

Add another data quality check

Rule Summary

The rule will pass if **Emp ID, E Mail, SSN** has unique values == **100%**

Figure 2.50: Data verification

3. To ensure that the employee ID and email address are not null, follow these steps:

   I. Choose **Add another rule**.

   II. Enter a name for the rule, such as `Check for Null Employee ID and Email`.

   III. Choose **Common checks for selected columns** for **Data quality check scope**.

   IV. Choose **All data quality checks are met (AND)** for **Rule success criteria**.

   V. Select **Emp ID** and **Email** under **Selected columns**.

   VI. For **Data quality check**, choose **Value is not missing**.

   VII. Choose **Greater than or equals** for **Condition**.

   VIII. Enter `100` as the threshold value and select **%(percent) rows** from the drop-down menu.

4. To ensure that the employee ID and age columns contain only positive values, follow these steps:

   I. Click **Add another rule**.

   II. Enter a name for the rule, such as `Check emp ID and age for positive values`.

   III. Choose **Individual check for each column** as the data quality check scope.

   IV. Select **All data quality checks are met (AND)** as the rule success criteria.

   V. For the first check, choose **Numeric values** as the data quality check.

   VI. Select **Emp ID** from the drop-down menu.

   VII. Choose **Greater than or equal to** for the condition.

   VIII. Select **Custom value** for the value and enter `0`.

   IX. Click **Add another quality check** and repeat steps 5-8 for the **Age in Yrs.** column.

5. Validate the SSN data format.

   Follow these steps to check the SSN data format:

   I. Click on **Add another rule**.

   II. Enter a name for the rule, such as `Verify SSN format`.

   III. Select **Individual check for each column** for the data quality check scope.

   IV. Choose **All data quality checks are met (AND)** for the rule success criteria.

   V. Under **Check 1**, select **String values** for **Data quality check**.

   VI. Choose **SSN** from the drop-down menu.

   VII. Select **Matches (RegEx pattern)** for **Condition**.

VIII. Enter the RegEx value `^\d{3}-\d{2}-\d{4}$` to verify the SSN format.

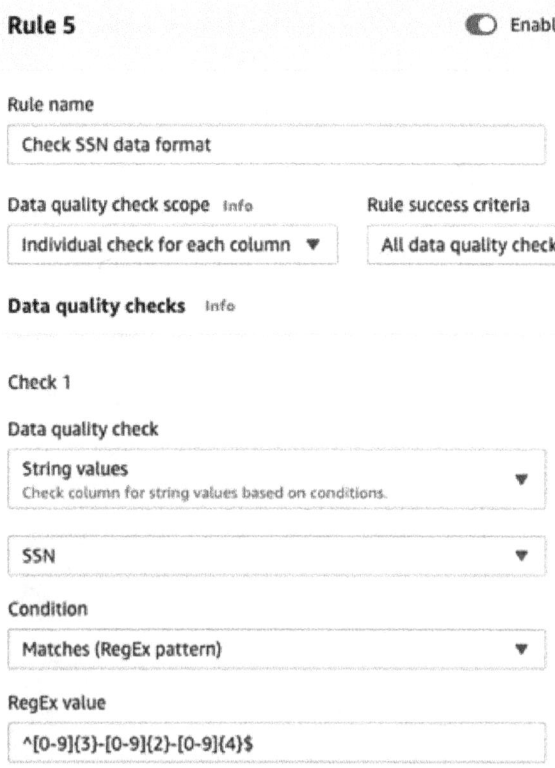

Figure 2.51: Validating the SSN format

The next step involves executing data quality checks by applying the ruleset to the profile job that was created earlier. To run the job with default options, ensure that the role name you created during data profile generation in the previous section is selected.

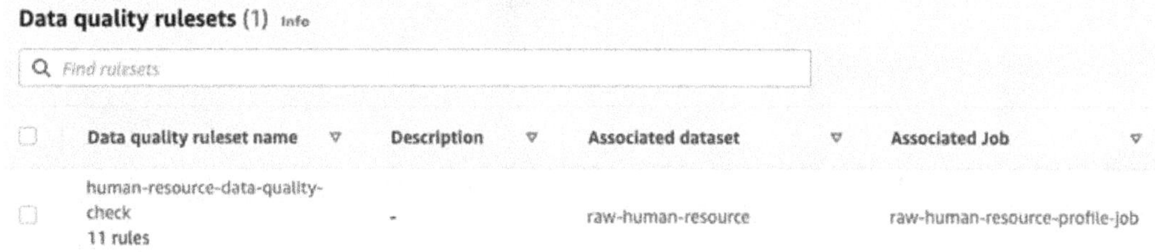

Figure 2.52: Checking the role names

Click on **Run job** and a new pop-up window will appear. It is important to decide whether to run the job against the full dataset or a customer sample, depending on the use case. If it is a mission-critical application, it is recommended to select the full dataset.

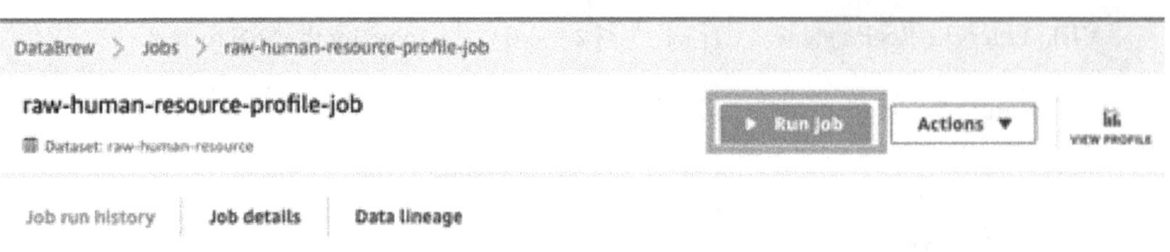

Figure 2.53: Run profile job

After running the job, wait for it to complete. It is important to note that keeping the default options is essential.

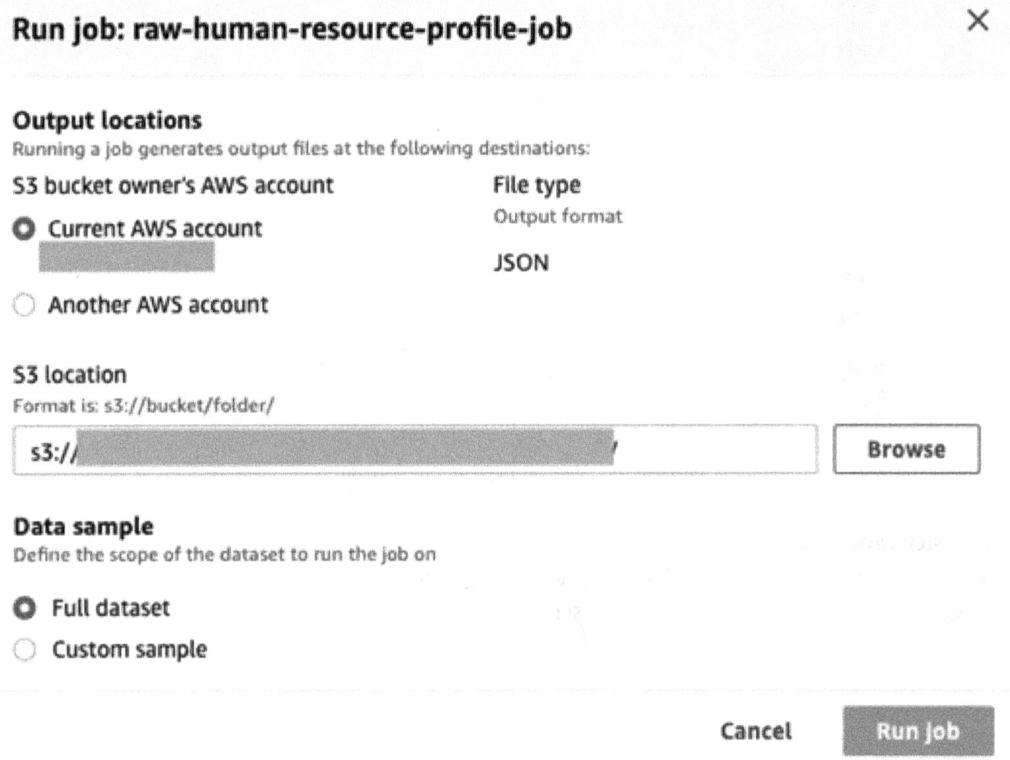

Figure 2.54: Inspect data quality rules validation results

After waiting for the job to complete, which typically takes about 17 minutes (but may vary), the next step involves inspecting the results of the data quality rules validation.

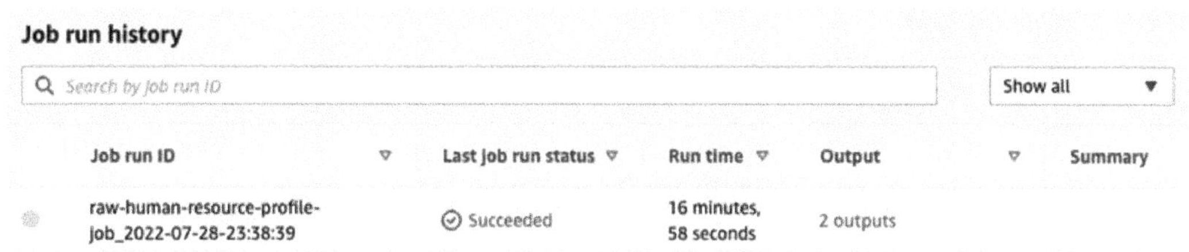

Figure 2.55: Job execution summary

To do this, follow these steps:

1. Go to the **Jobs** page on the DataBrew console and select the **Profile jobs** tab.
2. Wait for the profile job status to change to **Succeeded**.
3. Once the job is complete, select **View data profile**.

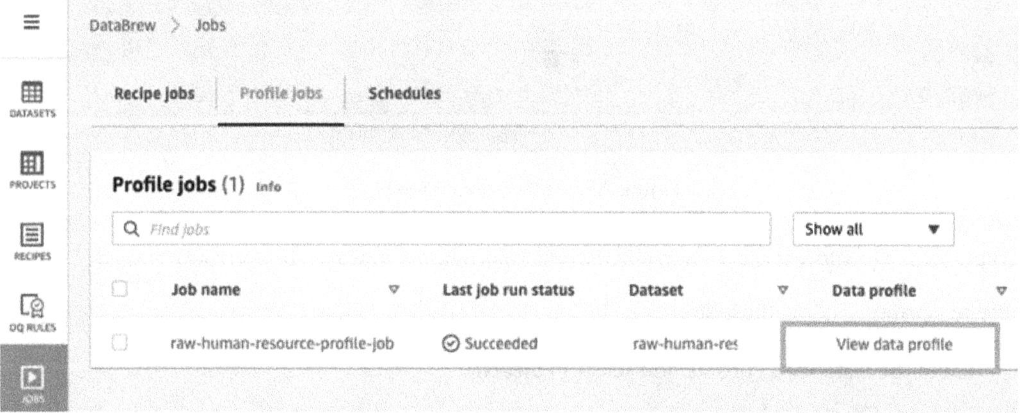

Figure 2.56: Viewing the data profile

4. Click on the **Data quality rules** tab to view the status of all data quality checks.

On this platform, you can view the status of all your data quality checks. Fortunately, in our case, only one data quality rule failed, and the rest were successful.

Based on the data quality check, we have discovered that there are duplicate values for `Emp ID`, `E Mail`, and `SSN`. To confirm this, navigate to the **Column Statistics** tab and select the `Emp ID` column.

Scroll down to the **Top Distinct Values** section. By simply looking at this table, we have identified that there is a significant number of duplicate values for `Emp ID`. Similarly, you will be able to identify duplicate values for `E Mail` and `SSN`.

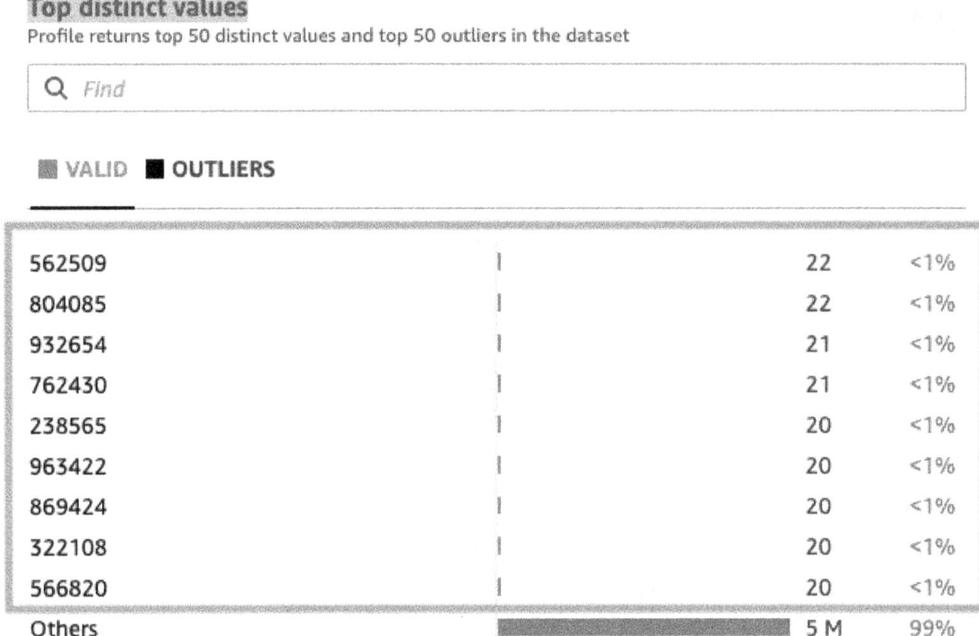

Figure 2.57: Top distinct values

The next step is to address the data quality issues. To do so, the first step is to create a project.

To create a project, follow these steps:

1. Go to the DataBrew console and select **Projects**.
2. Click on **Create project**.
3. Enter a name for the project (e.g., `human-resource-project-data-quality-check`) under **Project name**.
4. Under **Select a dataset**, choose **My datasets**.
5. Select the `raw-human-resource` dataset.
6. Keep the sampling size at its default value.
7. Under **Permissions**, select the IAM role that was previously created for our DataBrew profile job under **Role name**.
8. Click **Create project**.

Once the project has been created, the Glue DataBrew interactive session will be launched. Now, let's remove the duplicate values from the `Emp ID` column.

To do this, follow these steps:

1. Select the `Emp ID` column.
2. Click on the **More options** icon (three dots) to see all the available transforms for this column.
3. Choose **Remove duplicate values**.

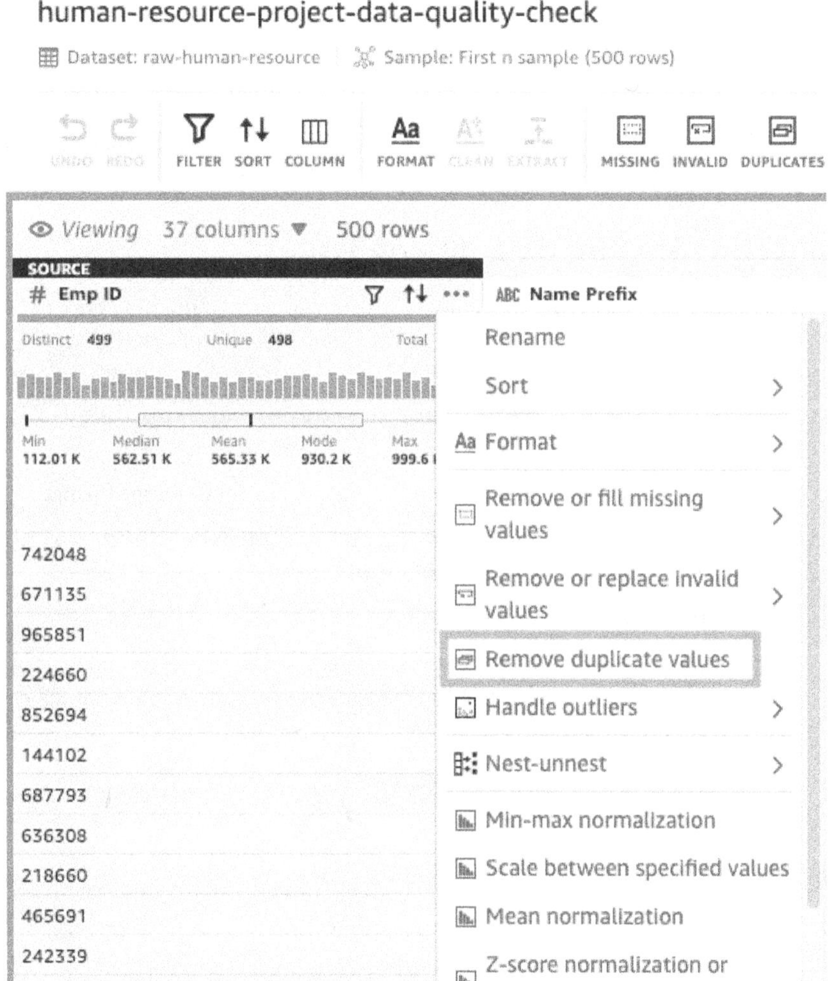

Figure 2.58: Remove duplicate values option

4. Perform similar steps for the `SSN` and `E Mail` columns.

You may have noticed that three new recipes were created for us. However, when a recipe is applied in the Glue DataBrew interactive session, it is only applied to the sample of data.

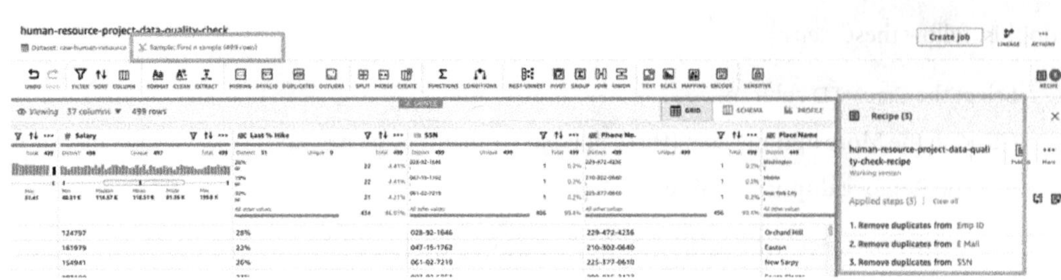

Figure 2.59: Glue DataBrew session sample

The next step is to create a job to apply these recipes to the entire dataset. To do so, we need to create a new job.

Data publication – fixing data quality issues

The next step is to create a DataBrew job to run these transforms against the full dataset:

1. On the project details page, select **Create job**.
2. Enter a name for the job (e.g., `human-resource-after-dataquality-fix`) under **Job name**.
3. Under **Job output settings**, select **CSV** as the file type for the final storage format.
4. Enter the S3 bucket location for the output (e.g., `s3://navnis-data-warngling-curated/human-resource/`) under **S3 location**.
5. Choose **None** as the compression type.

Wait for the job to complete:

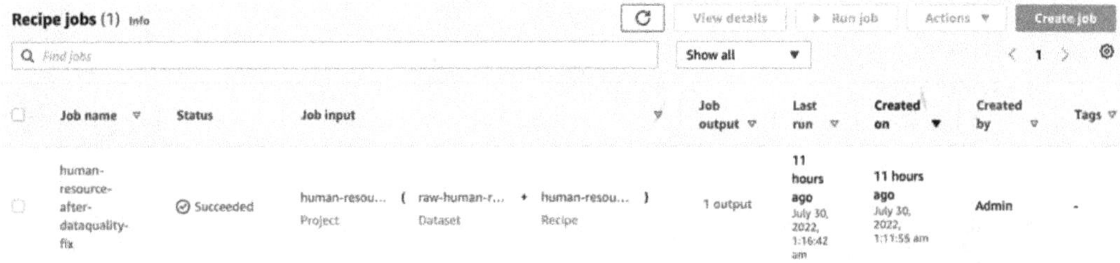

Figure 2.60: Job list in AWS Glue DataBrew console

Validation of data quality check with corrected dataset

Now, we need to validate the data quality check with the corrected dataset. Here are the steps to follow:

1. The first step is to create a dataset from the corrected dataset (you can follow the steps outlined earlier).

Figure 2.61: Dataset list in AWS Glue DataBrew console

2. Next, we need to run a data quality rule against the data quality check. Follow these steps:

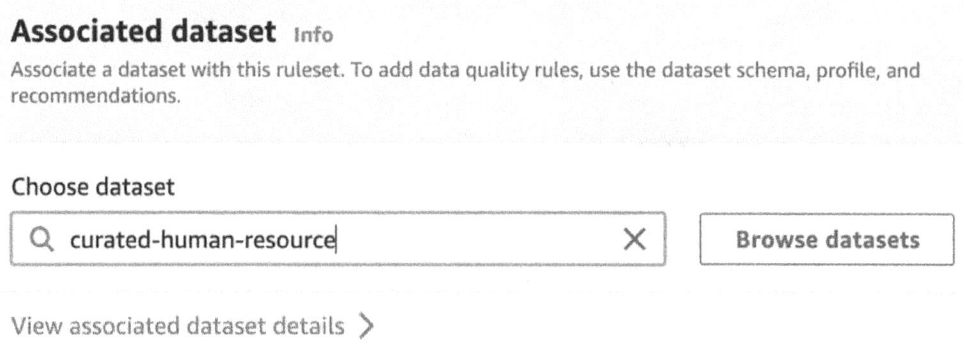

Associated dataset Info

Associate a dataset with this ruleset. To add data quality rules, use the dataset schema, profile, and recommendations.

Choose dataset

curated-human-resource

Browse datasets

View associated dataset details

Figure 2.62: Choosing the dataset

3. Choose **DQ Rules** and select the ruleset you created earlier.
4. Select **Duplicate** on the **Actions** menu.
5. Browse the newly created dataset on the associate dataset.
6. Click on **Create ruleset** at the end.

7. Select the newly created data quality ruleset and click on **Click profile job with ruleset**.
8. Follow the previously described steps to create a new profile job.

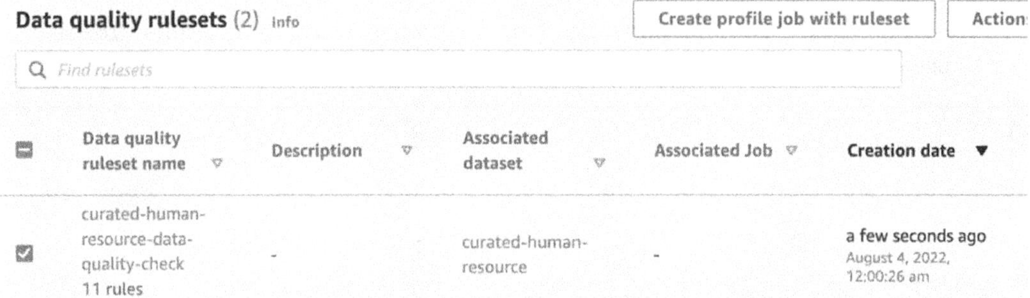

Figure 2.63: Data quality rulesets list in AWS Glue DataBrew console

Once it completes, you will be able to validate the data quality. You will see that all the rules have passed except **Check total record count** because you removed the duplicate values.

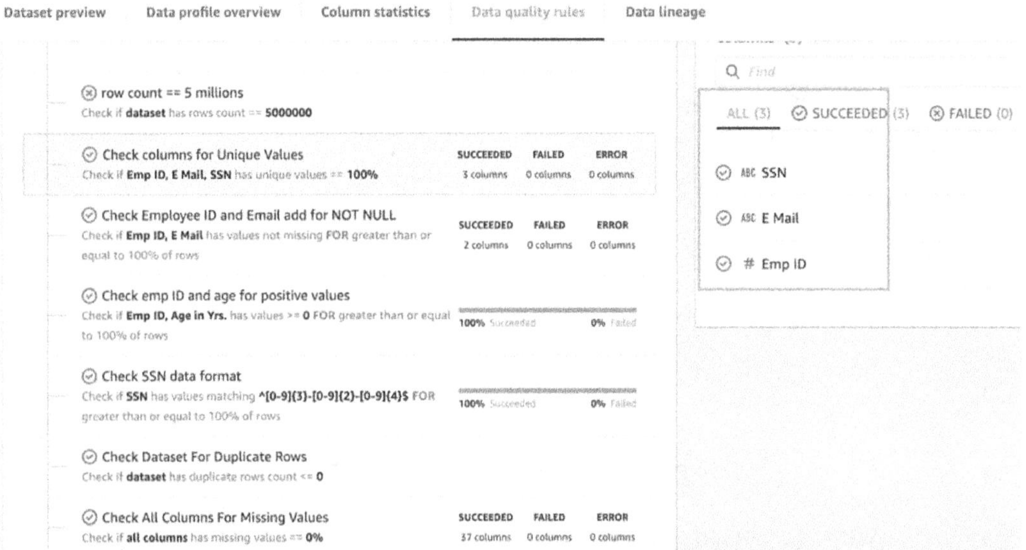

Figure 2.64: Applying the recipe on the dataset

On the **Column statistics** page, under **Top distinct values** for the **Emp ID** column, you can see the distinct values. Similarly, you can see the distinct values for the `SSN` and `E Mail` columns.

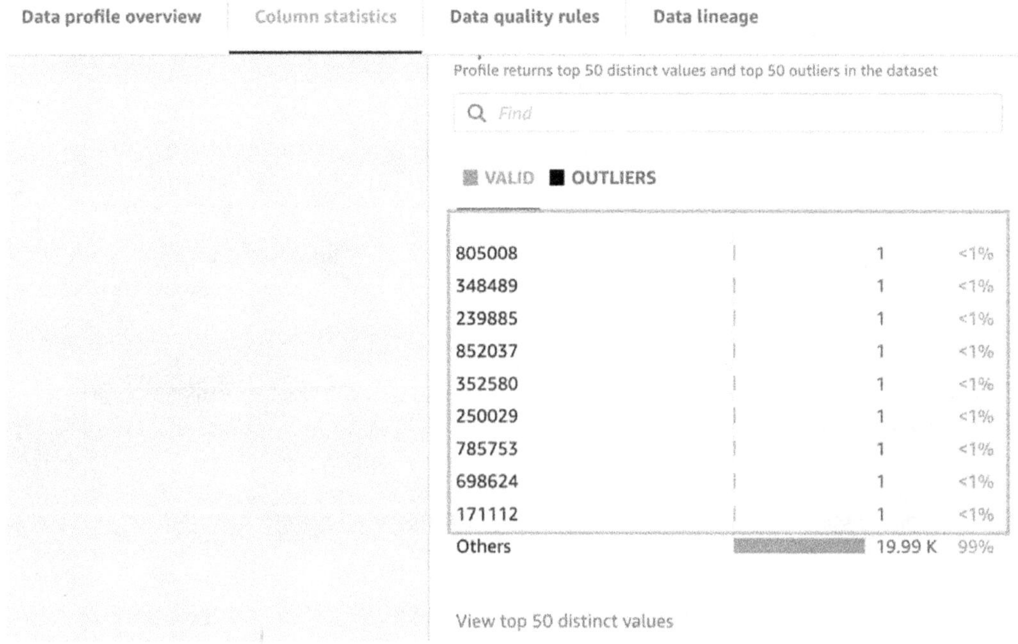

Figure 2.65: Distinct values for columns

Finally, you can see the data quality check information after fixing the issue in the AWS Glue DataBrew console.

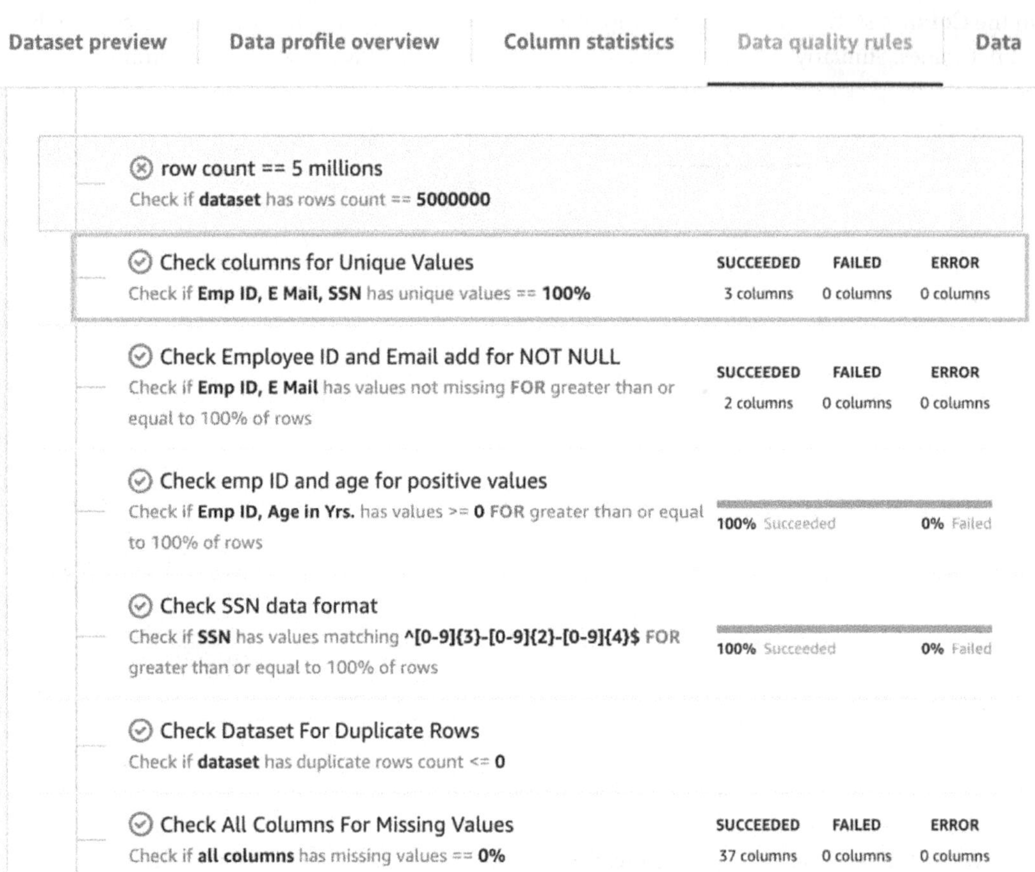

Figure 2.66: Data quality check information after fixing the issue

Throughout this section, we have gained an understanding of how Glue DataBrew can assist in recognizing and resolving data quality concerns. Although the techniques presented were manual, it's important to note that in practice, it's preferable to implement an event-driven data quality check. This approach involves automatically identifying any data quality issues as they arise, such as the absence of a valid Social Security Number or an employee ID, and taking appropriate measures, such as alerting the business or application owner, allowing them to validate the data and implement necessary fixes.

Event-driven data quality check using Glue DataBrew

In this architecture, every time a file is uploaded to Amazon S3, an EventBridge rule triggers a Step Functions state machine.

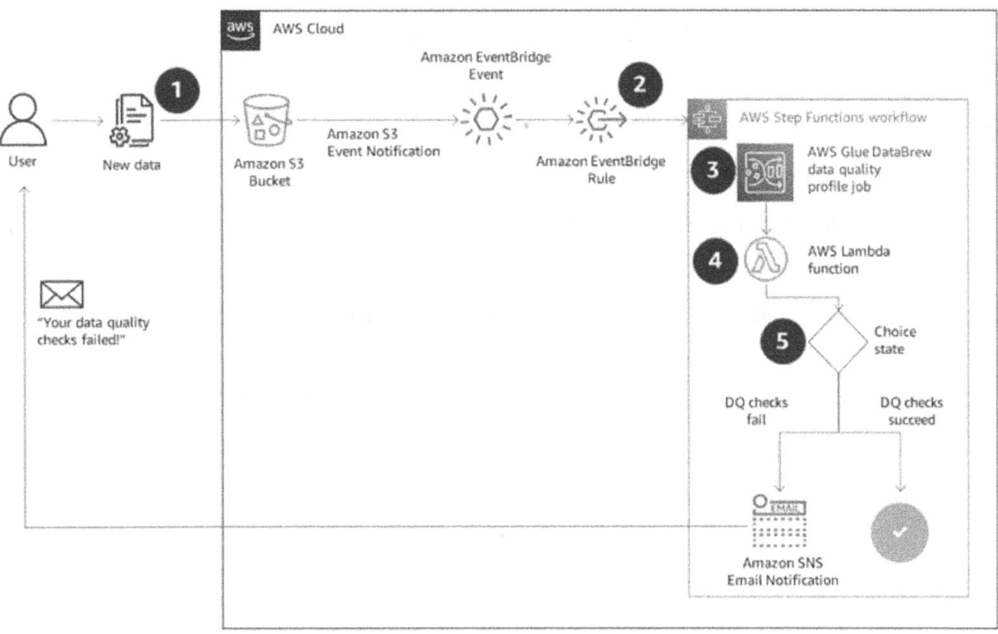

Figure 2.67: Event-driven data quality check

The state machine initiates a DataBrew profile job that is configured with a set of data quality rules and the resulting output is stored in Amazon S3. A Lambda function is used to read the data quality results from Amazon S3 and returns a Boolean response to the state machine. The function returns `false` if one or more rules in the ruleset fail and returns `true` if all rules succeed. If the Boolean response is `false`, the state machine sends an email notification to Amazon SNS and ends in a failed status. Conversely, if the Boolean response is `true`, the state machine ends in a successful status. The next step in this process is to learn how to identify PII data using AWS Glue DataBrew.

Data protection with AWS Glue DataBrew

Organizations face challenges beyond data quality, including identifying and securing personal information. News of data breaches is common, such as the LinkedIn data breach in 2021 where data associated with 700 million users was posted for sale on the Dark Web, impacting 92% of LinkedIn's user base. Similarly, Yahoo! reported in 2017 that 32 million accounts were accessed through a cookie-based attack. Regulatory and compliance requirements, such as FedRAMP, FINMA, HIPAA, and PCI, also necessitate secure data processing and storage. AWS Glue DataBrew offers features to help you secure and comply with these requirements.

Encryption at rest

Encryption at rest is a security measure that involves encrypting data when it is stored in a local storage device, such as a hard disk, to prevent unauthorized access to confidential information in case the device is accessed by attackers. AWS Glue DataBrew offers support for data encryption at rest for both DataBrew projects and jobs. With AWS **Key Management Service** (**KMS**), jobs can read and write encrypted data.

To enable encryption at rest in a job, follow these steps:

1. Go to **Job output settings**.
2. Select **Additional configuration – optional**.
3. Check **Enable encryption for job output file**.
4. Choose between using SSE-S3 (Amazon S3-managed encryption keys) or AWS KMS.

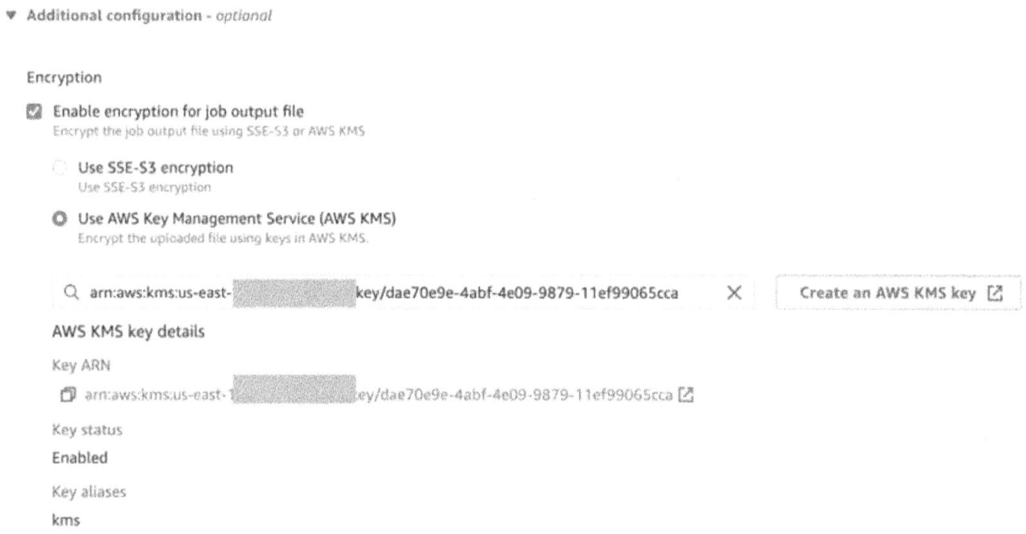

Figure 2.68: AWS KMS encryption in AWS Glue DataBrew job

Encryption in transit

Encryption in transit is the process of securing your data by encrypting it while it's being transmitted between services over the internet, such as when connecting databases using a JDBC connection.

To enable encryption in transit, AWS offers **Secure Sockets Layer** (**SSL**) encryption. AWS Glue DataBrew leverages SSL for JDBC, which is a built-in feature of AWS Glue since it uses the JDBC connector provided by AWS Glue.

Identifying and handling PII

A critical part of data security is the identification, redaction, replacement, encryption, and decryption of PII data, such as first name, last name, email address, SSN, and phone number. It gets even more complex when we talk about identifying and protecting sensitive data at scale. Even after identification, it is not easy to implement a solution around the redaction, masking, or encryption of sensitive data at scale.

You can use AWS Glue DataBrew to obfuscate PII data during the data preparation step. Based on your requirements, there are different PII data redaction mechanisms available. You have the option to obfuscate the PII data so that users can't revert it, or you can make the obfuscation reversible.

The following techniques can be employed to mask data:

- **Substitution**: This involves replacing PII data values, such as names, addresses, and Social Security Numbers, with other authentic-looking values, such as pseudonyms, dummy addresses, or randomly generated identifiers
- **Shuffling**: This technique shuffles the values from the same column across different rows
- **Deterministic encryption**: This involves applying deterministic encryption algorithms to the column values, which always produce the same ciphertext for a given value
- **Probabilistic encryption**: In this technique, probabilistic encryption algorithms are applied to the column values, producing different ciphertext each time it is used
- **Decryption**: This involves decrypting columns based on encryption keys
- **Nulling out or deletion**: A particular field can be replaced with a null value or the entire column can be deleted
- **Masking out**: This technique employs character scrambling or masks certain portions in the columns
- **Hashing**: Hash functions can be applied to the column values as a means of masking

Let's look at an example to understand this. In the data quality section, we learned how to create a dataset and profile it. Here are the steps:

1. Create a new dataset called `raw-human-resource-pii-dataset`, referring to the previous section.

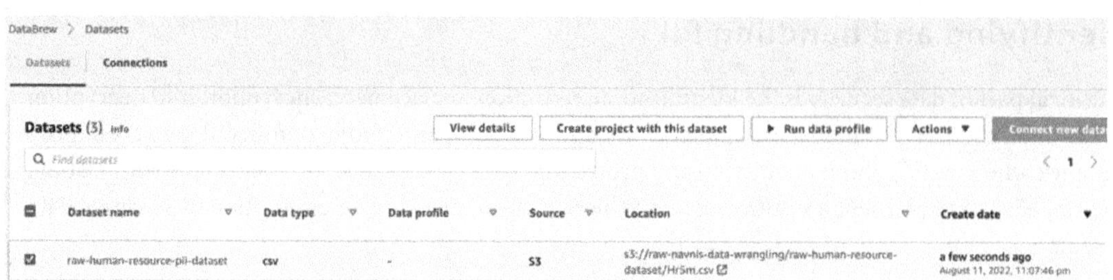

Figure 2.69: Datasets in AWS Glue DataBrew

2. Select the newly created dataset and click on **Run data profile**.
3. Create a profile job when prompted.
4. Keep the job name and job run sample as the defaults.
5. Specify the Amazon S3 path where you want to store your data profile information as JSON in the job output settings.
6. Enable **PII statistics** under **Dataset level configurations**, and select **All categories** under PII categories. Note that in production, you may want to choose what is relevant to your data.

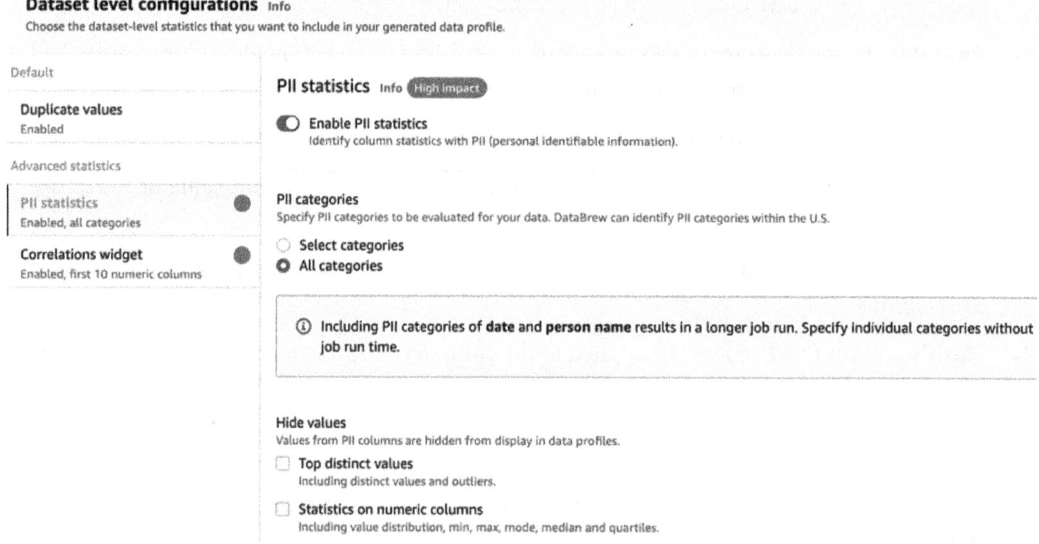

Figure 2.70: PII configuration in AWS Glue DataBrew

7. Keep the rest of the options as the defaults.
8. Select the role name that we created during the data quality rule.

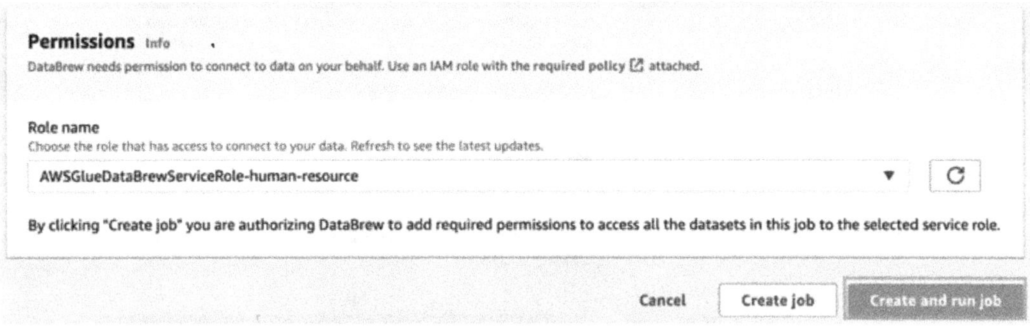

Permissions Info

DataBrew needs permission to connect to data on your behalf. Use an IAM role with the required policy attached.

Role name

Choose the role that has access to connect to your data. Refresh to see the latest updates.

AWSGlueDataBrewServiceRole-human-resource

By clicking "Create job" you are authorizing DataBrew to add required permissions to access all the datasets in this job to the selected service role.

Cancel | Create job | Create and run job

Figure 2.71: Added role in the Glue DataBrew job

9. Wait for the profile job to complete.

Once the job is complete, you will be able to see the stats in the Data Profile overview section in **Datasets**. For our dataset, it shows that 17 columns are PII.

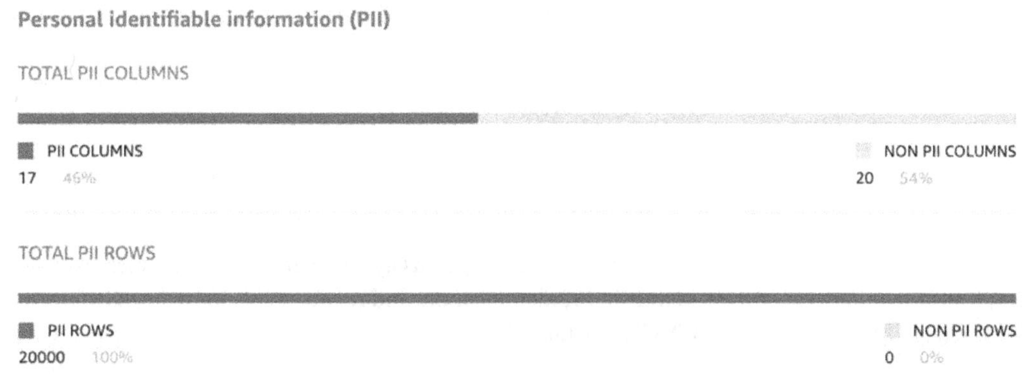

Personal identifiable information (PII)

TOTAL PII COLUMNS

PII COLUMNS 17 46% — NON PII COLUMNS 20 54%

TOTAL PII ROWS

PII ROWS 20000 100% — NON PII ROWS 0 0%

Figure 2.72: PII summary for dataset

When you scroll down, you will find columns, such as E Mail, Date of birth, Date of joining, SSN, and Phone, that have 100% PII rows.

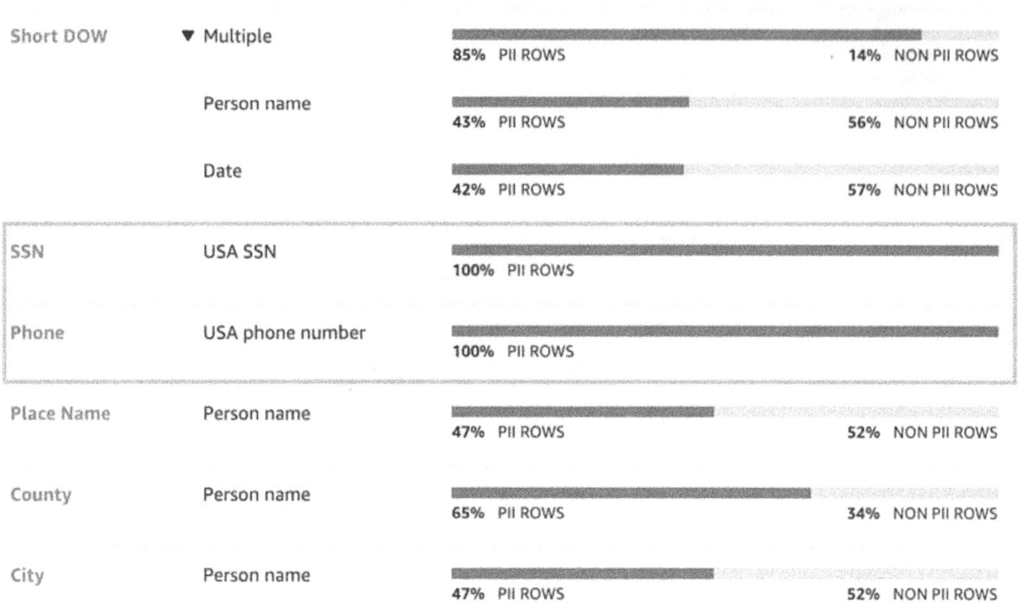

Figure 2.73: PII stats for columns

Now that we have identified the PII columns, the next step is to redact and encrypt the **PII** column. You can perform this task using the steps described in the AWS Glue DataBrew transform section.

With a fair understanding of the various data security options available in AWS Glue, such as data encryption at rest, data encryption in transit, PII identification, and redaction, the next step is to learn about the data lineage feature of AWS Glue DataBrew.

Take the following examples:

- **Testing and development environments**: When creating testing and development environments, it is often necessary to use representative data that mimics real-world scenarios. However, exposing sensitive PII data in these environments can pose a security risk. By obfuscating the PII data using AWS Glue DataBrew, you can ensure data privacy while still maintaining the realism needed for effective testing and development.
- **Data analytics and reporting**: In situations where data needs to be shared with analysts or third-party vendors for data analytics or reporting purposes, obfuscating PII data becomes crucial to comply with privacy regulations and maintain confidentiality. AWS Glue DataBrew can help anonymize or replace sensitive information with authentic-looking values, allowing analysts to work with the data while protecting individual privacy.

- **Data sharing and collaboration**: Collaborative projects often involve sharing datasets across teams or organizations. In these cases, sensitive information must be safeguarded. By utilizing AWS Glue DataBrew to obfuscate PII data, you can share datasets securely while still maintaining the integrity and utility of the data for collaborative analysis and decision-making.
- **Machine learning training**: Machine learning models often require large datasets for training. When working with sensitive PII data, obfuscating this information is vital to protect individuals' privacy. AWS Glue DataBrew can help replace or transform PII data to ensure that the training data remains anonymous and compliant with data protection regulations.
- **Compliance with data privacy regulations**: Organizations operating in industries such as healthcare, finance, or e-commerce must adhere to stringent data privacy regulations such as GDPR or HIPAA. Obfuscating PII data using AWS Glue DataBrew helps ensure compliance with these regulations by minimizing the risk of unauthorized access to sensitive information.

Data lineage and data publication

Data lineage and data publication are critical aspects of data management. Data lineage is the process of tracking data as it moves from its origin to its consumption, and AWS Glue offers a data lineage feature, though it is still in the early stages of development. Compared to enterprise tools such as Talend and Collibra, AWS Glue's data lineage feature has limited integration with external services and provides limited information about datasets and recipes at each stage. Despite its limitations, the data lineage feature in AWS Glue DataBrew is a valuable addition, and it is hoped that it will incorporate more features in the future.

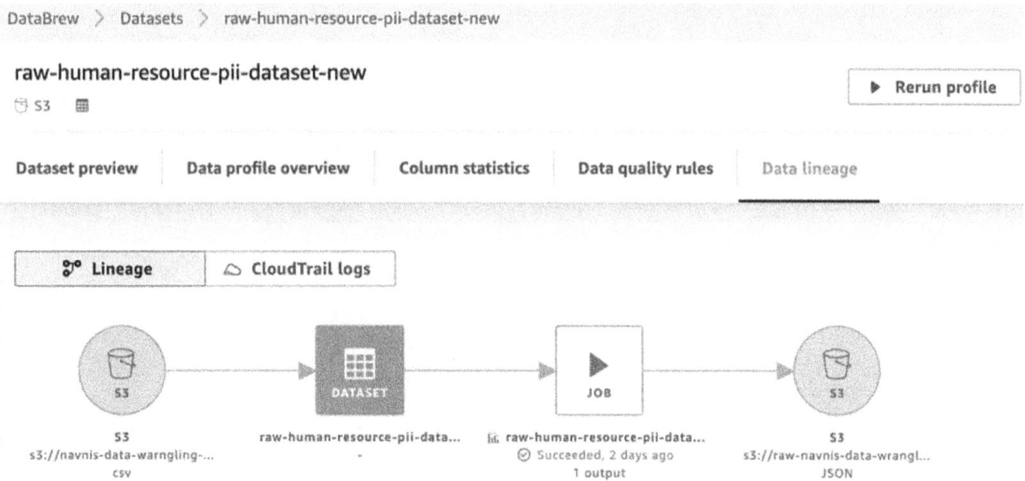

Figure 2.74: Data lineage in AWS Glue DataBrew

Summary

In this chapter, we explored the capabilities of AWS Glue DataBrew, a no-code data-wrangling service provided by AWS. We learned how to perform various data-wrangling tasks, including data discovery, data enrichment, identifying and redacting PII, and performing data quality checks. We also learned about data profiling and its usefulness. In the next chapter, we will delve into AWS Glue Data Wrangler, an open source data-wrangling option built on Python.

3
Introducing AWS SDK for pandas

In this chapter, we will explore the AWS SDK for pandas package and understand its building blocks. We will explore in detail different modes of installing the AWS SDK for pandas package for various use cases and will also show you how to customize the package further to suit your specific project needs. We will also learn the integrations of this package with AWS services and how it helps to perform common data-wrangling activities in an efficient manner. So, by the end of this chapter, you can expect to understand AWS SDK for pandas and its building blocks, the standard and custom installation options for different use cases, and integration with AWS services such as Amazon S3, Amazon RDS, Amazon Redshift, and Amazon Athena.

This chapter covers the following topics:

- AWS SDK for pandas
- Building blocks for AWS SDK for pandas
- Customizing, building, and installing AWS SDK for pandas
- Configuration options for AWS SDK for pandas
- The features of AWS SDK for pandas with different AWS services

AWS SDK for pandas

AWS SDK for pandas (previously known as AWS Data Wrangler) is a Python library that enhances the AWS **Software Development Kit** (**SDK**) with additional functionalities and also provides an interface with a pandas DataFrame. This is an open source initiative by the AWS Professional Services team that offers easy integration with an array of AWS services. In addition to the existing functionalities of the AWS SDK, integration with the pandas library provides a rich set of features to perform data wrangling and data integration activities.

AWS SDK for pandas was initially known as the `awswrangler` package and was created around July 2019 by the AWS Professional Services team. AWS SDK for pandas is an open source initiative published under the Apache 2.0 license. The framework has gone through a rebranding exercise to change its name to AWS SDK for pandas as of August 2022. However, everything with respect to the library remains the same, and the name was changed to better align with the AWS ecosystem. From here on in, we will use the term `awswrangler` in the book to refer to the AWS SDK for pandas library.

Customers who use the AWS ecosystem can access services and perform tasks through programmatic means with the language of their choice using the AWS SDK. As of October 2022, the AWS SDK supports 12 programming languages, including C++, Go, Python, Rust, JavaScript, Kotlin, Java, Node.JS, PHP, Ruby, Swift, and .NET. The features available in each SDK are well documented in the AWS documentation (`https://aws.amazon.com/developer/tools/`). For customers who use the Python programming language, AWS SDK for Python (also called Boto3) provides a mechanism to interact with AWS services.

AWS SDK for pandas was created to work on top of Boto3 and also to provide integration with pandas DataFrames and AWS services. The code base is actively maintained by a group of volunteers from within and outside AWS. There were around 95 releases until October 2022, which is more than two releases per month on average and provides an indication of the features that are added constantly to make the library more helpful. The following graph shows the commits that have been made to the repository in the past year, which shows how the code base is actively managed by the team.

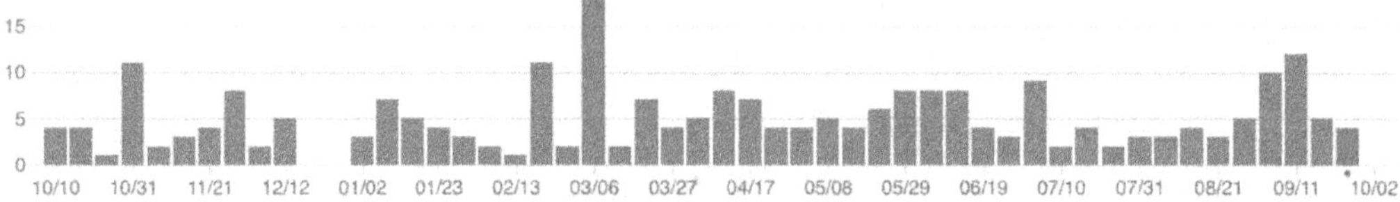

Figure 3.1: The AWS SDK for pandas repository code commits

For all practical purposes, if you use pandas for data wrangling or data integration activities, AWS SDK for pandas will provide you with functions that can effectively *load or read* data *to or from* AWS services such as S3, RDS, NoSQL databases, and Redshift in an easier and more performant manner, using libraries such as `pyarrow`. Once data is available in the pandas DataFrame, users utilize the rich ecosystem of the pandas library to perform data-wrangling activities on the dataset. Now that we have learned what AWS SDK for pandas is all about, let us check out the building blocks that make up the SDK.

Building blocks of AWS SDK for pandas

In this section, we will explore the building blocks for the AWS SDK for pandas library, such as Apache Arrow, pandas, and Boto3.

Arrow

Apache Arrow (`https://arrow.apache.org/`) is an in-memory, column-oriented (similar to the DataFrame format) data format used in many systems and programming languages for efficient in-memory analytical operations on modern hardware. Users might be already aware of the Parquet file format, which helps to store data in columnar format on disc, but when the data is loaded into memory, it's mapped differently by different runtimes (Spark loads data into DataFrames after Parquet files are read from disk). So, when data needs to be exchanged across systems, it needs serialization/deserialization to convert it from one format to another. One advantage of using Arrow is the ability to store data in the columnar format in memory, supporting analytical operations and efficiently transferring data between different runtime environments without the need to serialize and deserialize data. Many different projects and teams utilize the Arrow library, such as pandas and Spark. This is beneficial to Python developers who work with pandas and NumPy data.

For example, in PySpark programming, we would serialize/deserialize data between a Python UDF and a **Java Virtual Machine** (**JVM**) environment. Because a PySpark program is written in Python, it will eventually get executed in a JVM. This process involves converting data into pickle format for serialization and deserialization activities, which are time-consuming. With Arrow-based serialization, data can be moved efficiently and much faster between JVM and Python processes.

According to Wes McKinney, "*Apache Arrow defines a binary "serialization" protocol for arranging a collection of Arrow columnar arrays (called a "record batch") that can be used for messaging and interprocess communication. You can put the protocol anywhere, including on disk, which can later be memory-mapped or read into memory and sent elsewhere. Arrow protocol is designed so that you can "map" a blob of Arrow data without doing any deserialization, so performing analytics on Arrow protocol data on disk can use memory-mapping and pay effectively zero cost*" (`https://stackoverflow.com/questions/56472727/difference-between-apache-parquet-and-arrow`).

pandas

At its heart, the `awswrangler` library brings the pandas DataFrame much closer to the AWS ecosystem. In addition to that, `awswrangler` has methods that simplify common activities (listing S3 objects created after a specific time) using prebuilt modules on top of Boto3 capabilities. pandas is an open source library written for the Python programming language that provides a fast and performant data structure for most data analysis workloads. The Python programming language has a wide variety of libraries for machine learning, and pandas helps people to use Python to perform data analysis activities as well. The pandas library (`https://pandas.pydata.org/`) can help users to transform their data into different formats based on projects needs, and it also has wider integration with multiple tools.

Boto3

AWS SDK for Python (Boto3) (`https://boto3.amazonaws.com/v1/documentation/api/latest/index.html`) provides capabilities for users to programmatically access AWS services and perform various actions through Python code. This helps to automate common tasks and also helps to deploy production-grade applications in the cloud. Boto3 uses AWS credentials to authenticate the API calls being made to AWS services, and the access is restricted based on AWS credentials provided through an **Identity and Access Management** (**IAM**) service.

Boto3 provides both a high-level object-oriented API (resource) and a low-level API (client) to access AWS services:

- Clients provide a low-level interface to AWS services whose methods map one to one with service APIs. All service operations are supported by clients. Responses are returned as Python dictionaries. It is up to users to traverse and process the response for the attributes they need.
- Resources provide a higher-level abstraction than the raw, low-level calls made by service clients. To use resources, you invoke the resource method of a session and pass in an AWS service name. They might not have all the functionalities of the services such as the low-level API, but they are simpler and powerful to use once you understand the concepts.
- Sessions manage the state of a particular configuration and typically store information such as user credentials, AWS Regions, and other configurations related to a user profile. This lets users customize their code by connecting to different AWS accounts and Regions using different credentials.

> **Fun tip**
>
> Boto is a Portuguese name given to a type of freshwater dolphin, native to the Amazon river. The name was chosen by the author of the original Boto library, Mitch Garnaat, as a reference to the company.

Now we have learned about the building blocks of the `awswrangler` package, let us explore various options to customize and install `awswrangler` in various AWS services and environments.

Customizing, building, and installing AWS SDK for pandas for different use cases

AWS SDK for pandas can be installed in different programming environments to perform data-wrangling activities. Let us consider the following examples, which will help us understand the usage of `awswrangler` across different environments:

- A business user from Project A wants to install AWS SDK for pandas on a local machine and perform a proof of concept for a new project. The user also wants to do the same in an Amazon EC2 instance to test the solution with data from an AWS environment.

- An IT person from Project A wants to use AWS SDK for pandas on a Lambda function to perform data-wrangling activities on low-volume data.
- An IT person from Project B wants to use AWS SDK for pandas on a Glue Python shell to perform data-wrangling activities on data extracted from a source database. The team expects the transformations will take more than 15 minutes (the Lambda execution time limit). The team also has another data project that consumes and transforms larger data volumes, and they want to utilize the Glue Spark shell for data transformation and use Glue bookmarks for incremental data processing.
- A data analyst from Project B wants to perform data-wrangling activities before passing the data to a custom ML model. They want to utilize AWS SDK for pandas on SageMaker notebooks to perform exploratory analysis of the data.
- A project manager from a strategic initiative wants his team to implement a "big data pipeline" and also use AWS SDK for pandas for data preparatory activities. The team would like to utilize AWS SDK for pandas in EMR jobs for data-wrangling activities.

Standard and custom installation on your local machine or Amazon EC2

A business user from Project A can install AWS SDK for pandas from PyPI or Conda on their local machine or EC2 instance. Python users can install packages from two popular packaging systems, PIP and Conda. Most distributions of Python come with `pip` preinstalled. pip comes preinstalled from Python 2.7 upward, and pip3 is preinstalled from Python 3.4 and above by default.

The advantage of using PIP is that it can be used on the command line, and it installs all the required dependencies along with the package. The syntax to install `awswrangler` through pip is given here:

Python 2.x:

```
pip install awswrangler
```

Python 3.x:

```
pip3 install awswrangler
```

When you execute this command, the following additional packages are installed as well, which are used inside `awswrangler` as dependencies. However, as a user, we need to execute only the preceding command, and the rest is taken care of by the pip package installer:

```
Installing collected packages: numpy, pytz, six, python-dateutil, pandas, pyarrow, python-utils, progressbar2, pyparsing
, packaging, soupsieve, beautifulsoup4, urllib3, jmespath, botocore, certifi, charset-normalizer, idna, requests, asn1cr
ypto, scramp, lxml, s3transfer, boto3, redshift-connector, decorator, ply, jsonpath-ng, opensearch-py, pymysql, requests
-aws4auth, nest-asyncio, aenum, typing-extensions, frozenlist, multidict, asynctest, aiosignal, yarl, attrs, async-timeo
ut, aiohttp, isodate, gremlinpython, zipp, importlib-metadata, pg8000, backoff, et-xmlfile, openpyxl, awswrangler
Successfully installed aenum-3.1.11 aiohttp-3.8.1 aiosignal-1.2.0 asn1crypto-1.5.1 async-timeout-4.0.2 asynctest-0.13.0
attrs-22.1.0 awswrangler-2.16.1 backoff-2.1.2 beautifulsoup4-4.11.1 boto3-1.24.62 botocore-1.27.62 certifi-2022.6.15 cha
rset-normalizer-2.0.12 decorator-5.1.1 et-xmlfile-1.1.0 frozenlist-1.3.1 gremlinpython-3.6.1 idna-3.3 importlib-metadata
-4.12.0 isodate-0.6.1 jmespath-1.0.1 jsonpath-ng-1.5.3 lxml-4.9.1 multidict-6.0.2 nest-asyncio-1.5.5 numpy-1.21.6 openpy
xl-3.0.10 opensearch-py-1.1.0 packaging-21.3 pandas-1.3.5 pg8000-1.29.1 ply-3.11 progressbar2-4.0.0 pyarrow-7.0.0 pymysq
l-1.0.2 pyparsing-3.0.9 python-dateutil-2.8.2 python-utils-3.3.3 pytz-2022.2.1 redshift-connector-2.0.908 requests-2.28.
0 requests-aws4auth-1.1.2 s3transfer-0.6.0 scramp-1.4.1 six-1.16.0 soupsieve-2.3.2.post1 typing-extensions-4.3.0 urllib3
-1.26.12 yarl-1.8.1 zipp-3.8.1
WARNING: You are using pip version 20.1.1; however, version 22.2.2 is available.
You should consider upgrading via the '/home/ec2-user/awssdk4pandas/bin/python3 -m pip install --upgrade pip' command.
(awssdk4pandas) [ec2-user@ip-10-20-1-201 ~]$
```

Figure 3.2: Additional packages installed with awswrangler

The preceding screenshot shows the additional packages that get installed along with AWS SDK for pandas.

Once installed, you can successfully verify the installation by printing the `awswrangler` version in the Python shell as follows. At this stage, we have successfully installed `awswrangler` and can start using it in Python programs for various data-wrangling activities:

```
(dms_blog) [ec2-user@ip-10-20-1-28 ~]$ python3
Python 3.7.10 (default, Jun  3 2021, 00:02:01)
[GCC 7.3.1 20180712 (Red Hat 7.3.1-13)] on linux
Type "help", "copyright", "credits" or "license" for more information.
>>> import awswrangler as wr
>>> print(wr.__version__)
2.16.1
>>>
```

Figure 3.3: The installed version of awswrangler

> **Fun tip**
>
> **PIP** is a recursive acronym that stands for **PIP Installs Python.** It was first introduced as `pyinstall` in 2008 by Ian Bicking (the creator of the `virtualenv` package) as an alternative to `easy_install`.

Installing awswrangler in a virtual environment

Users can create a virtual environment where they can install the `awswrangler` libraries without impacting the existing projects on that machine. Consider a situation where you already have pandas version 1.3.6 being used for another project, and the project code won't work with pandas version 1.3.5. Now, if you install `awswrangler` using the `pip` command, it will install pandas version 1.3.5, and now you have two conflicting versions of the same library on your machine, which can cause programs to crash. So, it is a best practice to create Python virtual environments to work on separate projects with conflicting dependencies. From here on in, we will use this virtual environment to install and modify the `awswrangler` package.

You can use the `activate` and `deactivate` commands to get into a Python virtual environment. This allows you to move across different projects and work on them without impacting each other. The following screenshot shows the packages installed on the new virtual environment and the `python3` environment. Using the `pip3 list` command after the `deactivate` command will show the libraries from the `python3` default installation.

```
$python3 --version
Python 3.9.12
$python3 -m venv awspandas
$ls
awspandas
$source awspandas/bin/activate
(awspandas) $pip3 list  --disable-pip-version-check
Package    Version
---------- -------
pip        22.0.4
setuptools 58.1.0
(awspandas) $deactivate
$pip3 list
Package                      Version
---------------------------- -----------
aenum                        3.1.11
aiohttp                      3.8.1
aiosignal                    1.2.0
asn1crypto                   1.5.1
async-timeout                4.0.2
attrs                        22.1.0
awscli                       1.25.50
```

Figure 3.4: The Python virtual environment

Custom installation

One major advantage of open source libraries is the capability to customize and add additional code segments to suit your project needs as necessary. You can apply the following steps to perform a custom installation of AWS SDK for pandas, adding modules specific to your project needs.

As a prerequisite, activate the virtual environment and install `python3` and `git` on your laptop/EC2 machine:

- To install `git` on a Mac, you can use the `brew` command
- To install `git` on an EC2 instance, you can use `sudo yum install git`:

1. Download or copy the code base to your local machine or EC2 instance:

   I. Copy the git repository URL from the `aws-sdk-pandas` repository (`https://github.com/aws/aws-sdk-pandas`).

II. Using the link, clone the entire git repository to your local machine/EC2 for further development:

```
(awspandas) $git --version
git version 2.37.3
(awspandas) $git clone https://github.com/aws/aws-sdk-pandas
Cloning into 'aws-sdk-pandas'...
remote: Enumerating objects: 13000, done.
remote: Counting objects: 100% (565/565), done.
remote: Compressing objects: 100% (264/264), done.
remote: Total 13000 (delta 388), reused 431 (delta 299), pack-reused 12435
Receiving objects: 100% (13000/13000), 8.00 MiB | 7.91 MiB/s, done.
Resolving deltas: 100% (9773/9773), done.
(awspandas) $
```

Figure 3.5: The awswrangler git copy

2. Go to the code base and explore the code. You can make changes to the existing code and add additional modules for your project needs:

   I. Navigate inside the installation path for `awswrangler` and explore the different folders. You should see the code under the folder named `awswrangler` and there are individual folders for different services.

   II. For the purpose of this learning, let us modify the `__init__.py` file, which will be executed when we import `awswrangler` inside our Python code. Explore the modules that are imported for various AWS services/`awswrangler` functionalities. You can see an `import` statement that gets variables from the `__metadata__.py` file. Append a new variable to the `import` statement with a new variable, `__message__`, as shown here, and save the file.

```
from awswrangler.__metadata__ import __description__, __license__, __title__, __version__,__message_
_ # noqa
from awswrangler._config import config  # noqa
```

Figure 3.6: The awswrangler init.py file

   III. Open the `__metadata__.py` file and change the `__description__` fields, as shown here. Also, add another variable, `__message__`, which was imported into the `__init__.py` module in the previous step, and save the file.

```
__title__: str = "awswrangler"
__description__: str = "Pandas on AWS.Updated for custom intallation."
__version__: str = "2.17.0"
__license__: str = "Apache License 2.0"
__message__: str = "This was changed as a part of Learning exercise."
~
```

Figure 3.7: The awswrangler metadata.py file

3. Install `awswrangler` from the custom code that was modified on your local machine or EC2 instance:

   I. Navigate to the top-level folder where the `awswrangler` code is available.

   II. Execute the `pip3 install .` command, as shown here. This will install `awswrangler` on your machine with the local code base that has your custom changes.

```
(awspandas) $cd aws-sdk-pandas
(awspandas) $ls
CODE_OF_CONDUCT.md                awswrangler                    test_infra
CONTRIBUTING.md                   building                       tests
CONTRIBUTING_COMMON_ERRORS.md     docs                           tox.ini
LICENSE.txt                       fix.sh                         tutorials
NOTICE.txt                        poetry.lock                    validate.sh
README.md                         pyproject.toml
THIRD_PARTY.txt                   test.sh
(awspandas) $pip3 install .
Processing /Users/ssmsun/Documents/Initiatives/DataWranglerbook/code/aws-sdk-pandas
  Installing build dependencies ... done
  Getting requirements to build wheel ... done
  Preparing metadata (pyproject.toml) ... done
Collecting botocore<2.0.0,>=1.27.11
  Downloading botocore-1.27.82-py3-none-any.whl (9.2 MB)
     ---------------------------------------- 9.2/9.2 MB 25.5 MB/s eta 0:00:00
```

Figure 3.8: awswrangler installation on your local machine

4. Verify and start using the `awswrangler` custom installation:

   I. Open a Python shell and import `awswrangler`.

   II. Print the `__message__` and `__description__` variables to see whether we have installed the `awswrangler` package from our local machine/EC2 instance with the changes that were made in the earlier steps.

```
(awspandas) $python3
Python 3.9.12 (main, Apr  5 2022, 01:53:17)
[Clang 12.0.0 ] :: Anaconda, Inc. on darwin
Type "help", "copyright", "credits" or "license" for more information.
>>> import awswrangler as wr
>>> print(wr.__description__)
Pandas on AWS.Updated for custom intallation.
>>> print(wr.__message__)
This was changed as a part of Learning exercise.
>>>
```

Figure 3.9: Verifying the awswrangler local installation with custom changes

5. As a final step, you can validate that the changes we made are only restricted to our virtual environment by moving out of the virtual environment and installing the `awswrangler` package using the `pip3 install awswrangler` command (which will install the package from the `pypi` remote repository without our custom code changes):

```
(awspandas) $deactivate
$pip3 install awswrangler
Requirement already satisfied: awswrangler in /Users/ssmsun/miniconda3/lib/python3.9/site-packages (
2.16.1)

$python3
Python 3.9.12 (main, Apr  5 2022, 01:53:17)
[Clang 12.0.0 ] :: Anaconda, Inc. on darwin
Type "help", "copyright", "credits" or "license" for more information.
>>> import awswrangler as wr
>>> print(wr.__description__)
Pandas on AWS.
>>> print(wr.__message__)
Traceback (most recent call last):
  File "<stdin>", line 1, in <module>
AttributeError: module 'awswrangler' has no attribute '__message__'
>>>
```

Figure 3.10: Multiple versions of awswrangler with a Python virtual environment

We saw how to install the `awswrangler` package on a local machine/EC2 instance by simply using the `pip` command. We also downloaded the code from the `awswrangler` git repository, made the changes that are needed for our project, and installed the changed version of `awswrangler`. We also learned how to install packages inside virtual environments so that the changes made for one project do not conflict with other projects.

Congratulations on completing this step! You can play around with the package for some time here to understand more. Once you are done exploring, let us move to the next section, where we have to help an IT person install `awswrangler` with a Lambda function.

Standard and custom installation with Lambda functions

For most use cases, including a situation such as the IT person from Project A processing small volume data, we will want to deploy and execute data integration code in a serverless environment. AWS Lambda is a serverless, event-driven compute service that lets you run code for virtually any type of application or backend service without provisioning or managing servers. Lambda comes preloaded with a wide variety of important libraries, but the user has to package the libraries that are not available in the default environment along with the code when it is deployed to a Lambda function.

For smaller libraries, users can package dependencies along with the code and upload it to a Lambda function. We will see how to create a ZIP archive containing the dependent libraries for a Lambda function (`https://docs.aws.amazon.com/Lambda/latest/dg/python-package.html#python-package-create-package-with-dependency`). To do this, create a new Python virtual environment and install the new packages in the virtual environment. This will install the dependent packages under a `pip install` path on your machine. You can then move those packages to the deployment folder of your Lambda function and archive them as a ZIP file to be uploaded into the Lambda function.

Lambda functions can also have layers, which are saved in a ZIP file with the additional code/libraries. It can also contain a custom runtime, data, or configuration file. Using layers in a Lambda function will reduce the size of the deployment package, and the same Lambda layer can be shared across multiple Lambda functions, promoting reusable code components. Also, this helps to separate the responsibility of managing code segments among different teams. In addition, when you deploy code and dependencies in a single ZIP file, the Lambda function is not editable in the console, adding more difficulty in code maintenance. Currently, Lambda layers can be created with `.zip` file archives.

With all the preceding content, where would we use Lambda layers? Consider a situation where there is a central data warehouse, and different project teams access data from it using Lambda functions as microservices, and use it for different purposes. There are requirements to provide access only to certain user groups within the organization and also to perform data masking when accessing data. The database administrators are also worried about too many concurrent users accessing the database and leaving idle open connections that could strain the database. The individual project teams are also concerned about using and maintaining database drivers to connect to the warehouse, and they don't have experience in managing database connection state, configurations, and so on. The ideal solution is to create a Lambda layer to access the warehouse that meets all preceding requirements, which will be maintained by the database administration team, and individual teams can utilize that Lambda layer to develop their code in Lambda functions. This promotes code reuse, separation of responsibilities, and quicker development cycles.

In the same context, users can use AWS SDK for pandas from Lambda layers. There are two options for using AWS SDK for pandas in your Lambda code.

Standard installation – a Lambda managed layer

Create a Python Lambda function in the AWS Console with a Python 3.9 runtime. Scroll down the Lambda function overview screen until you reach the bottom of the page, where you can find the **Layers** section:

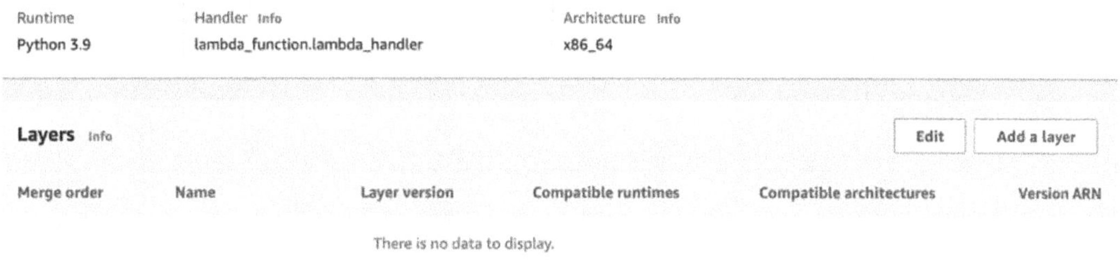

Runtime	Handler Info	Architecture Info
Python 3.9	lambda_function.lambda_handler	x86_64

Layers Info — Edit — Add a layer

Merge order	Name	Layer version	Compatible runtimes	Compatible architectures	Version ARN

There is no data to display.

Figure 3.11: awswrangler Lambda installation

You can then choose to add a layer; choose the **AWSSDKPandas-Python39** layer, as shown in the following screenshot. The version number might change in the future as new releases are added by the AWS team. This is a layer that the AWS team has curated for your usage, removing and optimizing the components, thereby reducing the package size.

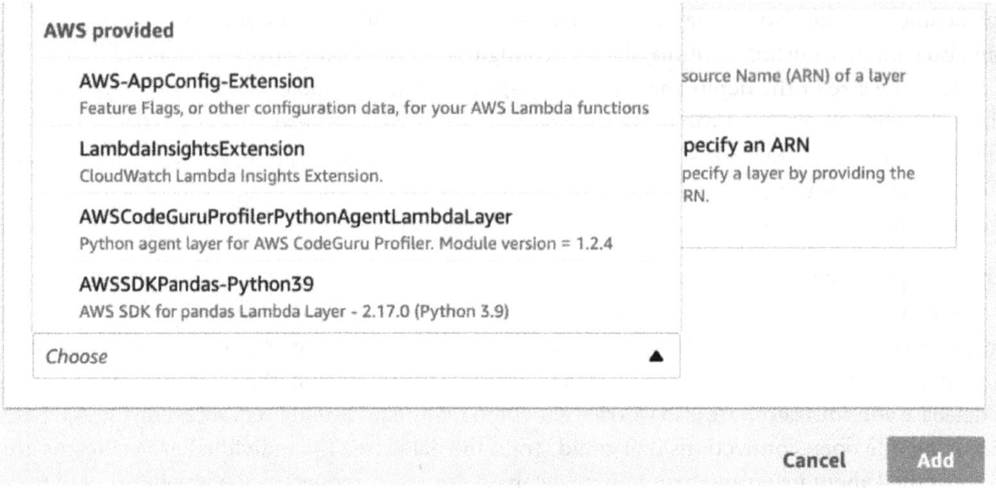

AWS provided

AWS-AppConfig-Extension
Feature Flags, or other configuration data, for your AWS Lambda functions

LambdaInsightsExtension
CloudWatch Lambda Insights Extension.

AWSCodeGuruProfilerPythonAgentLambdaLayer
Python agent layer for AWS CodeGuru Profiler. Module version = 1.2.4

AWSSDKPandas-Python39
AWS SDK for pandas Lambda Layer - 2.17.0 (Python 3.9)

Choose

source Name (ARN) of a layer

pecify an ARN
pecify a layer by providing the RN.

Cancel
Add

Figure 3.12: awswrangler Lambda installation – the managed layer options for Python 3.9

The usage of AWS SDK for pandas from an AWS managed layer is the simplest and easiest option if you want to use a package without any custom modifications of your own. Also, note that there might be a delay of up to one week or more before the new features are released or made available in the AWS managed layer. Now, you can also create the Lambda function with different Python versions and different architecture and still utilize `awswrangler` for that version. The following screenshot shows the `awswrangler` layer available in the Lambda function created with Python 3.8 and ARM architecture.

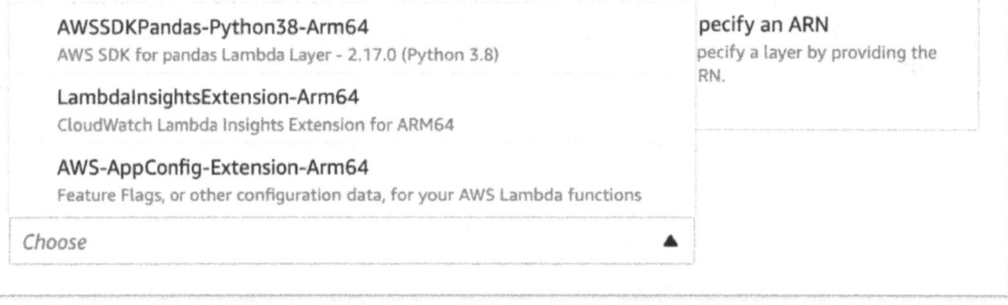

Figure 3.13: awswrangler Lambda installation – the managed layer options for Python 3.8

Custom installation – creating a custom managed layer

There is also a situation where you will want to use AWS SDK for pandas with some modifications and custom code added to suit your needs. We will upload the `.zip` archive file into a custom layer and then use it in the Lambda function. There is a Lambda service limit (`https://docs.aws.`

amazon.com/Lambda/latest/dg/gettingstarted-limits.html#function-configuration-deployment-and-execution) – the entire Lambda deployment package size should be less than 250 MB unzipped (50 MB zipped).

As shown in the following screenshots, if we archive the contents of the awswrangler library, it is around 86 MB zipped without including the actual Lambda code. This exceeds the limit of the Lambda deployment package size:

```
(awspandas) $ls
aws-sdk-pandas  awspandas
(awspandas) $cd awspandas/lib/python3.9/site-packages
(awspandas) $zip -r ../../../../awswrangler.zip .
  adding: pandas-1.5.0.dist-info/ (stored 0%)
  adding: pandas-1.5.0.dist-info/RECORD (deflated 69%)
```

Figure 3.14: awswrangler Lambda installation – creating a custom Lambda package

```
(awspandas) $ls -lh
total 197032
drwxr-xr-x  29 ssmsun  staff   928B Sep 28 14:30 aws-sdk-pandas
drwxr-xr-x   8 ssmsun  staff   256B Sep 28 14:48 awspandas
-rw-r--r--   1 ssmsun  staff    86M Sep 28 16:23 awswrangler.zip
```

Figure 3.15: awswrangler Lambda installation – verify the created Lambda package

So, we must build the Lambda package in an optimal manner to upload it into a Lambda function. Luckily, we have a script that can help us perform exactly that activity. Follow the following steps to get a ZIP file that is less than 50 MB to upload to the Lambda function.

Here are the prerequisites:

- We will utilize the awswrangler local repository that we utilized for the local machine/EC2 instance setup. Remember the changes that we made in the __init__.py for message and description variables? We will print them out in the Lambda function to verify our installation.
- A Docker daemon needs to run on your machine, which we will use to build the Lambda layer. Also, note that Docker should have enough memory allocated to build code to avoid any out-of-memory errors during the process. Note that the following screenshot allocates 8 GB of memory for Docker to utilize, so regardless of your physical machine capacity, Docker needs to have enough memory and compute to complete the build successfully.

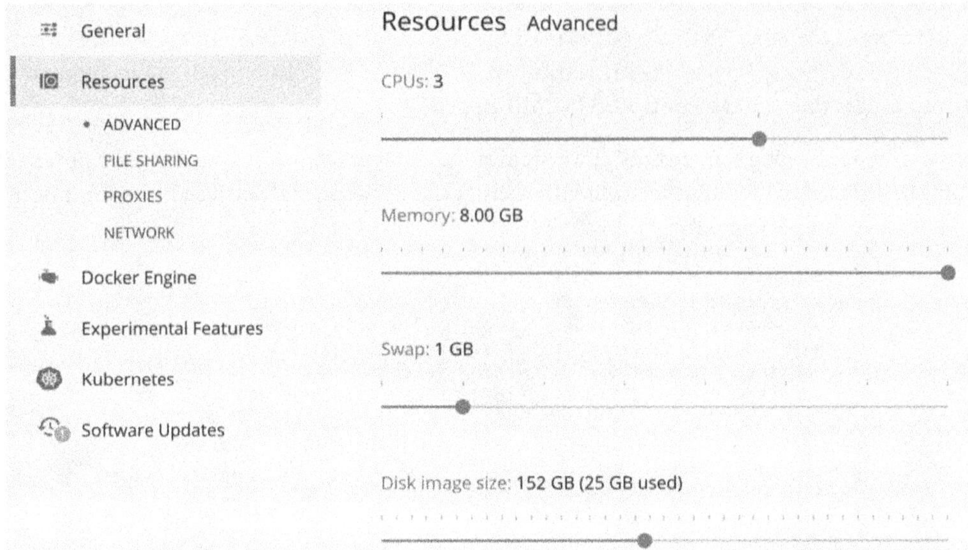

Figure 3.16: awswrangler custom Lambda installation – container memory configuration

We will now get started, as follows:

1. Go to the source code path and execute the command to build Lambda layers that can be added to AWS Lambda functions. Now, execute the `sh build-Lambda-layers.sh` command to kickstart the `awswrangler` custom build.

```
(awspandas) $ls
build-docs.sh              build-wheel.sh              publish.sh
build-lambda-layers.sh  lambda
(awspandas) $sh build-lambda-layers.sh
++ python -c 'import awswrangler as wr; print(wr.__version__)'
+ VERSION=2.17.0
```

Figure 3.17: awswrangler custom Lambda installation – building the Lambda layer

> **Note**
>
> This step will take a lot of time to get completed. This code will build Lambda layers for the Python 3.7, Python 3.8, and Python 3.9 distributions.

Open the code for `build-Lambda-layers.sh`, and comment out the Python 3.7 and Python 3.8 lines in the build process if you plan to deploy this library with the Python 3.9 environment only.

```
#  # Python 3.7
#  docker run \
#    --volume "$DIR_NAME":/aws-data-wrangler/ \
#    --workdir /aws-data-wrangler/building/lambda \
#    --rm \
#    awswrangler-build-py37 \
#    build-lambda-layer.sh "${VERSION}-py3.7" "ninja-build"
#fi

# Python 3.8
#docker run \
#  --volume "$DIR_NAME":/aws-data-wrangler/ \
#  --workdir /aws-data-wrangler/building/lambda \
#  --rm \
#  awswrangler-build-py38 \
#  build-lambda-layer.sh "${VERSION}-py3.8${ARCH_SUFFIX}" "ninja-build"

# Python 3.9
docker run \
  --volume "$DIR_NAME":/aws-data-wrangler/ \
  --workdir /aws-data-wrangler/building/lambda \
  --rm \
  awswrangler-build-py39 \
  build-lambda-layer.sh "${VERSION}-py3.9${ARCH_SUFFIX}" "ninja-build"
```

Figure 3.18: awswrangler custom Lambda installation – Python 3.9

The preceding screenshot shows the commented code segments for Python 3.7 and Python 3.8 highlighted.

2. Once the build is complete, you should see zipped files created for three Python versions, 3.7, 3.8, and 3.9. Remember to change the build function to the specific Python version or versions that your Lambda applications use. You can see that the zipped files are now around ~44–46 MB in size.

```
(awspandas) $ls -lh ../dist
total 279048
-rw-r--r--  1 ssmsun  staff   246K Sep 28 22:17 awswrangler-2.17.1-py3-none-any.whl
-rw-r--r--  1 ssmsun  staff    44M Sep 30 11:41 awswrangler-layer-2.17.0-py3.7.zip
-rw-r--r--  1 ssmsun  staff    46M Sep 30 13:33 awswrangler-layer-2.17.0-py3.8.zip
-rw-r--r--@ 1 ssmsun  staff    46M Sep 30 16:06 awswrangler-layer-2.17.0-py3.9.zip
```

Figure 3.19: awswrangler custom Lambda installation – verifying the created Lambda layers

3. Create a Lambda function with Lambda version 3.9, and then create a custom layer in the Lambda console.

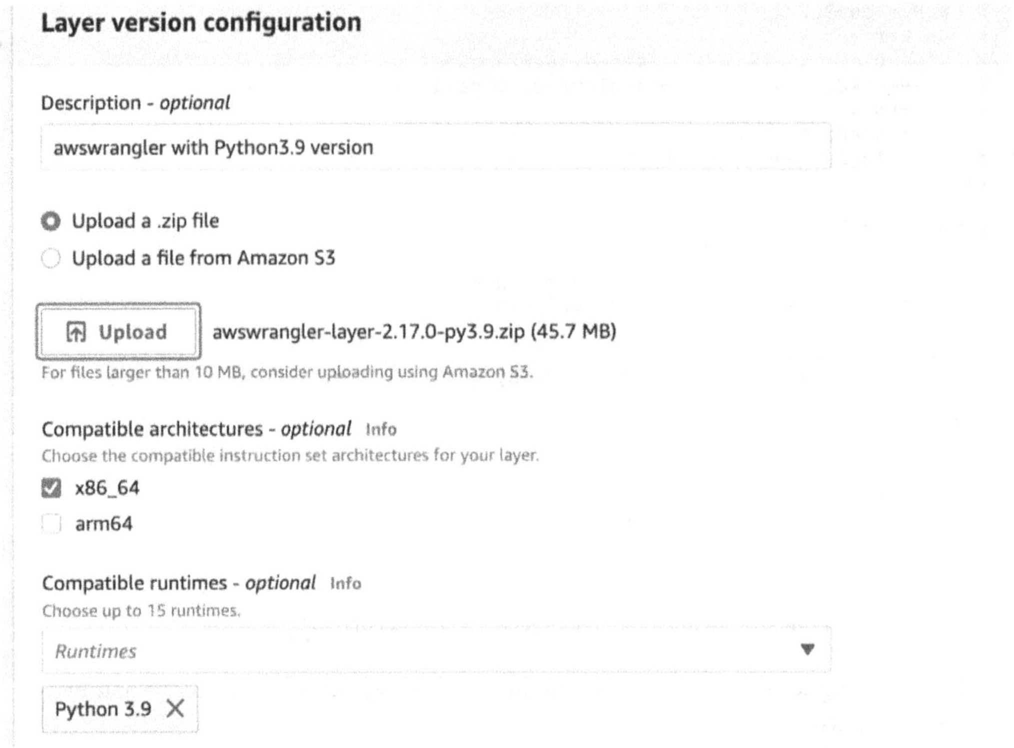

Layer version configuration

Description - *optional*

awswrangler with Python3.9 version

Upload a .zip file

Upload a file from Amazon S3

Upload awswrangler-layer-2.17.0-py3.9.zip (45.7 MB)

For files larger than 10 MB, consider uploading using Amazon S3.

Compatible architectures - *optional* Info

Choose the compatible instruction set architectures for your layer.

x86_64

arm64

Compatible runtimes - *optional* Info

Choose up to 15 runtimes.

Runtimes

Python 3.9 X

Figure 3.20: awswrangler custom Lambda installation – uploading the custom Lambda layers

4. Create a Lambda function with the Python 3.9 runtime and paste the following code into it:

```
import json
import awswrangler as wr

def Lambda_handler(event, context):
    # TODO implement
    print(wr.__version__)
    print(wr.__description__)
    print(wr.__message__)
    return {
        'statusCode': 200,
        'body': json.dumps('Hello from Lambda!')
    }
```

5. Attach the custom Lambda layer created in *step 3* to the Lambda function.

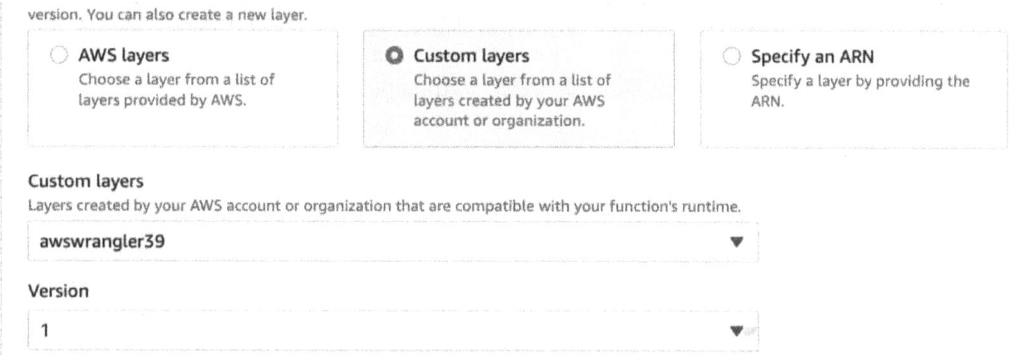

version. You can also create a new layer.

AWS layers
Choose a layer from a list of layers provided by AWS.

Custom layers
Choose a layer from a list of layers created by your AWS account or organization.

Specify an ARN
Specify a layer by providing the ARN.

Custom layers
Layers created by your AWS account or organization that are compatible with your function's runtime.

awswrangler39

Version

1

Figure 3.21: awswrangler custom Lambda installation – attaching the custom layer to the Lambda function

6. Execute the Lambda function and look at the **Execution results** tab. You should be able to see a message that confirms the `awswrangler` package is built from our custom code base.

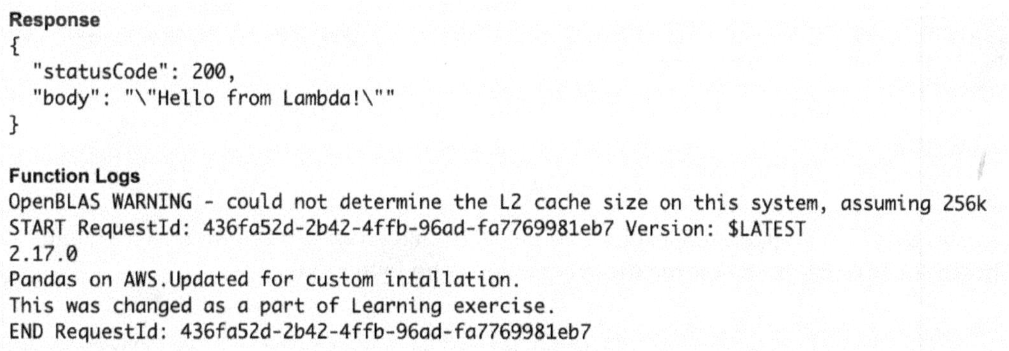

Response
```
{
  "statusCode": 200,
  "body": "\"Hello from Lambda!\""
}
```

Function Logs
```
OpenBLAS WARNING - could not determine the L2 cache size on this system, assuming 256k
START RequestId: 436fa52d-2b42-4ffb-96ad-fa7769981eb7 Version: $LATEST
2.17.0
Pandas on AWS.Updated for custom intallation.
This was changed as a part of Learning exercise.
END RequestId: 436fa52d-2b42-4ffb-96ad-fa7769981eb7
```

Figure 3.22: awswrangler custom Lambda installation – verifying the Lambda output

Standard and custom installation for AWS Glue jobs

We will look at the scenario where the IT person from Project B wants to use AWS SDK for pandas on a Glue Python shell to perform data-wrangling activities on data from a source database. Glue jobs have three modes of execution – Python shell, Spark ETL, and Spark Streaming ETL. Python shell job mode is used to process small-scale file processing that doesn't require an Apache Spark environment. For larger data volumes and distributed processing, you can use Spark job mode, and for streaming pipelines, you can choose Spark Streaming job mode. We will see how to install `awswrangler` for Python shell and Spark jobs.

Standard installation of awswrangler for a Python shell job

The Python shell job environment comes in two different Python versions, 3.6 and 3.9 (the default is Python 3.6). We can attach external libraries to a Glue Python shell job using wheel files. Wheel files are part of the Python ecosystem and help in the Python package installation process, making it faster and more stable:

- The AWS Glue Python 3.6 environment doesn't come preinstalled with `awswrangler`. Refer to the already installed libraries (`https://docs.aws.amazon.com/glue/latest/dg/add-job-python.html#python-shell-supported-library`) in the Python Glue job environment before adding additional libraries. We have to attach the `wheel` file for the `awswrangler` version that we want to use in our Glue job and attach to it, as documented in the following steps:

    I. For Python 3.6 jobs, you can download the wheel files from the public artifacts bucket using the following syntax: `s3://aws-data-wrangler-public-artifacts/releases/<version>/ awswrangler-<version>-py3-none-any.whl`.

```
(awspandas) $aws s3 cp s3://aws-data-wrangler-public-artifacts/releases/2.14.0/awswrangler-2.14.0-py3-none-any.whl .
download: s3://aws-data-wrangler-public-artifacts/releases/2.14.0/awswrangler-2.14.0-py3-none-any.whl to ./awswrangler-2.14.0-py3-none-any.whl
```

Figure 3.23: awswrangler glue installation – downloading the wheel file

> **Note**
>
> `awswrangler` dropped support for Python 3.6 from `awswrangler` version 2.15, and hence, it will throw an error if you use later versions with Python 3.6.

    II. Upload the wheel file into an S3 bucket and copy the S3 URL. Create a Glue job with Python version 3.6 and provide the wheel file in the Python library path section under **Advanced properties** on the job details page.

Libraries Info
Python library path
s3://athenaresults-sankar/awswrangler/awswrangler-2.14.0-py3-none-any.whl

Figure 3.24: awswrangler glue installation – uploading the wheel file

    III. Paste the following code into the script window and save the job:

```
import sys
```

```
import awswrangler as wr
print(wr.__version__)
```

IV. Execute the code and verify the output in CloudWatch Logs, checking whether `awswrangler` was successfully loaded into the Glue Python shell job.

```
Successfully installed asn1crypto-1.5.1 awswrangler-2.14.0 beautifulsoup4-4.11.1 boto3-1.23.10 botocore-1.26.10 certifi-2022.9.24
normalizer-2.0.12 decorator-5.1.1 et-xmlfile-1.1.0 idna-3.4 jmespath-0.10.0 jsonpath-ng-1.5.3 lxml-4.9.1 numpy-1.18.5 openpyxl-3.0
py-1.1.0 packaging-21.3 pandas-1.1.5 pg8000-1.22.1 ply-3.11 progressbar2-3.55.0 pyarrow-6.0.1 pymysql-1.0.2 pyparsing-3.0.9 python
python-utils-3.3.3 pytz-2022.2.1 redshift-connector-2.0.909 requests-2.27.1 requests-aws4auth-1.1.2 s3transfer-0.5.2 scramp-1.4.1
59.6.0 six-1.16.0 soupsieve-2.3.2.post1 urllib3-1.26.12 xlrd-2.0.1 xlwt-1.3.0

2.14.0
```

Figure 3.25: awswrangler glue installation – checking that awswrangler has been loaded in the Lambda environment

- Python 3.9 comes with `awswrangler` version 2.15.1 preinstalled. When creating a job, enable the **Load common analytics libraries (recommended)** checkbox. For situations where you want to use a different version of `awswrangler`, you have to attach the wheel file similar to the way we did in the Python 3.6 environment. However, if you want to use the 2.15.1 version of `awswrangler`, which is preinstalled, follow these steps:

  I. Create a job with Python version 3.9 and select the **Load common analytics libraries (recommended)** checkbox.

Type

The type of ETL job. This is set automatically based on the types of data sources you have selected.

Python Shell

Python version

Python 3.9 ▼

☑ Load common analytics libraries (recommended)

Include common Python libraries from pypi.org such as pandas, numpy and s3fs. Uncheck if you are loading your own libraries, and wish to avoid version conflicts.

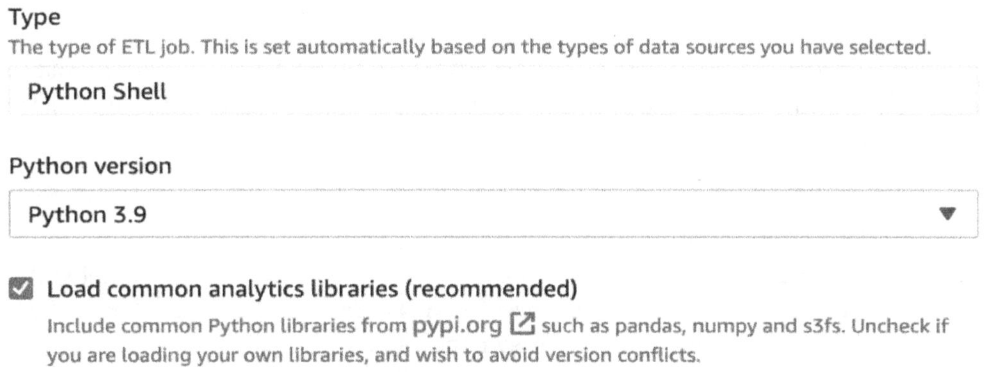

Figure 3.26: awswrangler glue installation – createing a Python 3.9 shell job

  II. Paste the sample code used in the Python 3.6 job to print the `awswrangler` version. Save and execute the job. The output will show the version of `awswrangler` used in the Python shell job. You can see this by clicking on the output logs link in the Glue Python shell job.

```
Setup complete. Starting script execution:
----
2.15.1
No newer events at this moment. Auto retry paused. Resume
```

Figure 3.27: awswrangler glue installation – verifying the awswrangler version

In order to use newer versions of `awswrangler`, follow the steps similar to the Python 3.6 shell to add a new wheel file. The following screenshot shows the output of uploading `awswrangler` version 2.17 to the Glue Python shell, which is a more recent version compared to `awswrangler` 2.15.1.

```
pyparsing-3.0.9 python-dateutil-2.8.2 python-utils-3.3.3 pytz-2022.2.1 redshift-connector-2.0.909 requests-2.28
s3transfer-0.6.0 scramp-1.4.1 setuptools-65.4.0 six-1.16.0 soupsieve-2.3.2.post1 urllib3-1.26.12 yarl-1.8.1

[notice] A new release of pip available: 22.1.2 -> 22.2.2
[notice] To update, run: pip install --upgrade pip

Setup complete. Starting script execution:
----
2.17.0
```

Figure 3.28: awswrangler glue installation – verifying the awswrangler version (a custom version installation)

Custom installation of awswrangler for Python shell jobs

We will utilize the `poetry` library to create a custom wheel file from the `awswrangler` repository where we made our changes. We will utilize the `awswrangler` local repository that we utilized for our local machine/EC2 instance setup:

1. You can install Poetry using the `pip3 install poetry` command in your Python virtual environment.
2. Execute the `build_wheel.sh` script from the local repository to build the wheel file, as shown in the following figure, and the wheel file will be created using the `poetry.lock` configurations, provided along with the `awswrangler` repository.

```
(awspandas) $poetry --version
Poetry (version 1.2.1)
(awspandas) $cd aws-sdk-pandas/building
(awspandas) $sh build-wheel.sh
+ pushd ..
~/Documents/Initiatives/DataWranglerbook/code/aws-sdk-pandas ~/Documents/Initiatives/DataWranglerboo
k/code/aws-sdk-pandas/building
+ rm -rf 'dist/*.whl'
+ poetry build -f wheel
Creating virtualenv awswrangler-Muv3bMem-py3.9 in /Users/ssmsun/Library/Caches/pypoetry/virtualenvs
Building awswrangler (2.17.0)
(awspandas) $ls ../dist
awswrangler-2.17.0-py3-none-any.whl
(awspandas) $
```

Figure 3.29: awswrangler glue custom installation – the prerequisites

3. Upload the wheel file into an S3 bucket, create a Glue Python shell job (Python version 3.9), and provide the wheel file S3 location.
4. Paste the following code to verify that we are using the custom version of `awswrangler`:

```
import sys
import awswrangler as wr
print(wr.__version__)
print(wr.__description__)
print(wr.__message__)
```

5. Execute the job and verify the output in CloudWatch Logs.

```
pymysql-1.0.2 pyparsing-3.0.9 python-dateutil-2.8.2 python-utils-3.3.3 pytz-2022.2.1 redshift-connector-2.0.909 requests-2.28
aws4auth-1.1.2 s3transfer-0.6.0 scramp-1.4.1 setuptools-65.4.0 six-1.16.0 soupsieve-2.3.2.post1 urllib3-1.26.12 yarl-1.8.1

[notice] A new release of pip available: 22.1.2 -> 22.2.2
[notice] To update, run: pip install --upgrade pip

Setup complete. Starting script execution:
----

2.17.0
Pandas on AWS.Updated for custom intallation.
This was changed as a part of Learning exercise.
```

Figure 3.30: awswrangler glue custom installation – verifying the awswrangler installation

Now that you have explored different options for installing `awswrangler` in a Python shell, you can use it effectively for all activities related to Python.

Standard installation of awswrangler on a Glue Spark job

A Glue spark job can be created with the Glue 0.90 (Spark 2.2), Glue 1.0 (Spark 2,4), Glue 2.0 (Spark 2.4), and Glue3.0 (Spark3.1) versions. `awswrangler` has support only from Glue version 2.0 and before, as it has compiled dependencies (C/C++). The default is Glue 3.0, which is the latest version, and you should have the latest Glue 3.0 version for all new jobs and, wherever possible, upgrade to it. This has the latest features from Spark and the AWS Glue service, providing a better, more secure, and more performant environment to run your jobs. We will install `awswrangler` using the following steps:

1. Create a Glue 3.0 job and provide the job parameters as follows:

```
- key: --additional-python-modules    values:
pyarrow==2,awswrangler==<<version>
```

Job parameters Info

Key | Value - *optional*

--additional-python- | awswrangler==2.17. | Remove

Figure 3.31: awswrangler glue standard installation – job parameter configuration

2. Paste the following code in the script window, save the job, and click to run it:

```
import sys
from awsglue.transforms import *
from awsglue.utils import getResolvedOptions
from pyspark.context import SparkContext
from awsglue.context import GlueContext
from awsglue.job import Job
import awswrangler as wr
## @params: [JOB_NAME]
args = getResolvedOptions(sys.argv, ['JOB_NAME'])

sc = SparkContext()
glueContext = GlueContext(sc)
spark = glueContext.spark_session
job = Job(glueContext)
job.init(args['JOB_NAME'], args)
print(wr.__version__)
job.commit()
```

3. Check CloudWatch Logs once the job completes execution. You should see the version of `awswrangler` being printed there successfully:

```
2022-09-30 16:06:07,219 main INFO Log4j appears to be running in a Servlet environment, but there's no log4j-web module available. If you
support, please add the log4j-web JAR to your web archive or server lib directory.

2.17.0
```

Figure 3.32: awswrangler glue standard installation – verifying the output

Custom installation of awswrangler on a Glue Spark job

For custom installation of `awswrangler`, users can follow the following steps to install a custom `awswrangler` build from a wheel file, in a similar way to the Python shell job:

1. The steps are similar to those in the Python shell job. Perform *steps 1–3* in the Python shell job custom installation to create the wheel file. Upload your wheel file to an S3 location.
2. Attach the wheel file to the Glue spark job by providing the wheel file location as a part of the job parameters, as shown in the following screenshot.

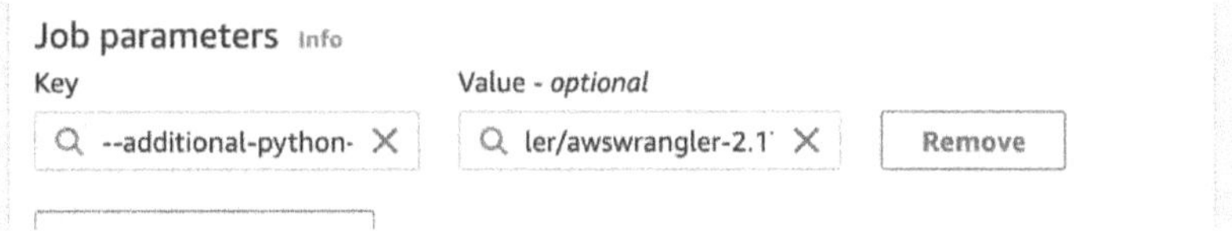

Figure 3.33: awswrangler Glue Spark custom installation – attaching the wheel file to a job

3. Copy and paste the code from the earlier Spark program and execute the Spark job. Verify the output logs to see whether the custom library has been installed in the Glue spark job.

```
2022-10-02 11:59:56,721 main INFO Log4j appears to be running in a Servlet environment, but there's no log4j-web module available.
better web container support, please add the log4j-web JAR to your web archive or server lib directory.

2.17.0
Pandas on AWS.Updated for custom intallation.
This was changed as a part of Learning exercise.
```

Figure 3.34: awswrangler glue spark custom installation – verifying the output

Additionally, you can click on the error logs and verify the log content, showing the installation of `awswrangler` from the wheel file.

```
INFO    2022-10-02 11:59:54,819 26668   com.amazonaws.services.glue.PythonModuleInstaller       [main]  Processing ./awswrangler-2.17.1-py3-none-
any.whlCollecting boto3<2.0.0,>=1.24.11  Downloading boto3-1.24.84-py3-none-any.whl (132 kB)     ━━━━━━━━━━━━━━━━━━━━━━━━━━━━━━━━━━━━
132.5/132.5 kB 4.6 MB/s eta 0:00:00Collecting progressbar2<5.0.0,>=4.0.0  Downloading progressbar2-4.0.0-py2.py3-none-any.whl (26 kB)Collecting
backoff<3.0.0,>=1.11.1  Downloading backoff-2.1.2-py3-none-any.whl (14 kB)Requirement already satisfied: pymysql<2.0.0,>=1.0.0 in /home/spark
/.local/lib/python3.7/site-packages (from awswrangler==2.17.1) (1.0.2)Collecting requests-aws4auth<2.0.0,>=1.1.1  Downloading requests_aws4auth-
1.1.2-py2.py3-none-any.whl (24 kB)Collecting redshift-connector<2.1.0,>=2.0.889  Downloading redshift_connector-2.0.909-py3-none-any.whl (112 kB)
━━━━━━━━━━━━━━━━━━━━━━━━━━━━━━━━━━━━ 112.1/112.1 kB 3.0 MB/s eta 0:00:00Collecting opensearch-py<3,>=1  Downloading opensearch_py-2.0.0-
py2.py3-none-any.whl (204 kB)    ━━━━━━━━━━━━━━━━━━━━━━━━━━━━━━━━━━━━ 204.6/204.6 kB 5.7 MB/s eta 0:00:00Requirement already satisfied:
pandas<2.0.0,>=1.2.0 in /home/spark/.local/lib/python3.7/site-packages (from awswrangler==2.17.1) (1.3.2)Collecting numpy<2.0.0,>=1.21.0
```

Figure 3.35: awswrangler glue spark custom installation – verifying the output in the error logs

Standard and custom installation on Amazon SageMaker notebooks

Amazon SageMaker notebooks can be used to develop code interactively for Python and PySpark applications.

For a SageMaker python3 notebook, `awswrangler` can be installed by running a command, as shown here. Users can utilize both the Conda and pip package management systems to install external libraries (`https://docs.aws.amazon.com/SageMaker/latest/dg/nbi-add-external.html`) in Notebook instances:

```
!pip install awswrangler==<version>
```

```
[3]: import awswrangler as wr

[4]: print(wr.__version__)

     2.17.0

[2]: !pip install awswrangler==2.17.0

     Looking in indexes: https://pypi.org/simple, https://pip.repos.neuron.amazonaws.com
     Collecting awswrangler==2.17.0
       Downloading awswrangler-2.17.0-py3-none-any.whl (251 kB)
          ---------------------------------------- 251.6/251.6 KB 2.2 MB/s eta 0:00:0000:0100:01
     Requirement already satisfied: pymysql<2.0.0,>=1.0.0 in /home/ec2-user/anaconda3/envs/python3/lib/python3.8/site
```

Figure 3.36: awswrangler SageMaker standard installation

Also, note that the installation is persisted only during the session, and if the EC2 instance that supports the SageMaker notebook is restarted, you have to run the installation step again. Users can leverage SageMaker life cycle policies to install the required libraries (`https://docs.aws.amazon.com/SageMaker/latest/dg/nbi-lifecycle-config-install.html`) on SageMaker during the instance startup phase. When the development happens through SageMaker instances, we can set up SageMaker notebook life cycle policies to install `awswrangler` on all compatible kernels. We can add the `pip install` statement as a part of the life cycle policies so that `awswrangler` can be attached to kernels when the instance is created, and users need not worry about installing the required packages.

Custom installation

To use the custom `awswrangler` package, upload the ZIP file that we generated for the Lambda function earlier, and upload the package in the same folder as the script for simplicity. If the custom library is uploaded in a different path, we need to include the path where the `awswrangler` source code is available to `sys.path`.

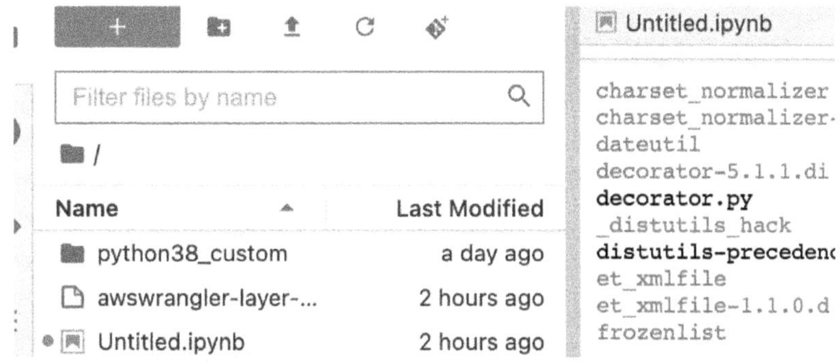

Figure 3.37: awswrangler SageMaker custom installation – uploading the custom library

Import `awswrangler` from the custom path, rather than installing it through the `pip` command, and you can now verify that the changes are available for use within the notebook.

```
from platform import python_version
print(python_version())
```

```
3.8.12
```

```
from python38_custom import awswrangler as wr1
```

```
print(wr1.__version__)
print(wr1.__description__)
print(wr1.__message__)
```

```
2.17.0
Pandas on AWS.Updated for custom intallation.
This was changed as a part of Learning exercise
```

Figure 3.38: awswrangler SageMaker custom installation – checking the installation status

Installing AWS SDK for pandas for EMR usage

We can install `awswrangler` on a new EMR cluster by configuring the bootstrap scripts. Create a bootstrap script with the following commands and upload it into an S3 bucket:

```
#!/usr/bin/env bash
set -ex
sudo pip3 install pyarrow==2 awswrangler==2.17.0
```

Create an EMR cluster with the needed software for your project, and also enable JupyterHub and Livy if you want to develop scripts interactively using Jupyter notebooks. We will launch a Jupyter notebook that is associated with this cluster. You can verify `awswrangler` by printing the version name and description, as we did earlier.

```
import awswrangler as wr
print(wr.__version__)
print(wr.__description__)
Last executed at 2022-10-02 21:16:49 in 71ms


2.17.0
Pandas on AWS.
```

Figure 3.39: awswrangler EMR installation – checking the installation status

You could also verify the awswrangler installation with the sc.list_packages() command to list the packages from the sparkContext object.

```
[2]: sc.list_packages()
     Last executed at 2022-10-02 21:14:26 in 1.31s


     aenum (3.1.11)
     aiohttp (3.8.1)
     aiosignal (1.2.0)
     asn1crypto (1.5.1)
     async-timeout (4.0.2)
     asynctest (0.13.0)
     attrs (22.1.0)
     aws-cfn-bootstrap (2.0)
     awswrangler (2.17.0)
     backoff (2.1.2)
     beautifulsoup4 (4.9.3)
```

Figure 3.40: awswrangler EMR installation – checking the installed packages

You could upload the custom awswrangler package on an EMR cluster and install it for usage in an EMR cluster. Refer to the EMR documentation (https://docs.aws.amazon.com/emr/latest/ReleaseGuide/emr-jupyterhub-install-kernels-libs.html) to install additional packages and kernels.

We have spent a considerable amount of time installing awswrangler in different environments to enable different personas across your organization to utilize the awswrangler library. Also, we showed how to make changes to awswrangler and deploy it across all environments to suit your organization's needs more appropriately. The AWS SDK for pandas library already provides a lot of capabilities, and most customers can use the official library in their projects, so we provided approaches to using it for different personas. If your project requires the customization of the awswrangler library for your needs, we also showed different ways to achieve that. Now, we will explore how to set the configuration options to make awswrangler more customized for your project's specific needs.

Configuration options for AWS SDK for pandas

There are options to configure global variables in `awswrangler`, which will help us to make the `awswrangler` library more customized for our specific use cases. We will look in depth at how to set up configurations to customize the working of `awswrangler`.

Setting up global variables

Global configuration variables can be set up through two different mechanisms in `awswrangler`:

- **Environment variables**: Create environment variables in the operating system/kernel environment where the `awswrangler` package will be executed. For example, in a Jupyter notebook, use the `%env` command to set values for environment variables. This is loaded when the `awswrangler` object is instantiated.
- **Wrangler config variables**: You can also set up values for environment variables using the `wrangler` object directly. Use the `awswrangler.config.<<variable name>>` syntax to assign a value for that configuration.

How does a config get applied?

Python has an interesting feature called decorators to add functionality to existing code. This is also called metaprogramming because a part of the program tries to modify another part of the program at compile time. The decorator ensures that configurations are applied before the function is called, using the `@decorator_func` syntax within the `awswrangler` source code for different services.

Refer to the following screenshot, where the decorator function is applied before the Athena `read_sql_query` function, which will set the global variables relevant to Athena in the code. The `apply_configs` function is defined in the `config.py` script, which you can read if needed to understand it in greater depth.

```
@apply_configs
def read_sql_query(
    sql: str,
    database: str,
    ctas_approach: bool = True,
    unload_approach: bool = False,
    unload_parameters: Optional[Dict[str, Any]] = None,
    categories: Optional[List[str]] = None,
    chunksize: Optional[Union[int, bool]] = None,
    s3_output: Optional[str] = None,
    workgroup: Optional[str] = None,
```

Figure 3.41: awswrangler – a config.py code snippet

The following categories of variables are available in the `awswrangler` package. However, users can add configuration variables to the code based on specific project needs:

- **Endpoint URL**: Provide an endpoint URL for various services that will be used by `awswrangler` to connect with an AWS environment. To connect programmatically to an AWS service, you use an endpoint, which is the entry point for an AWS web service. The AWS SDKs and the AWS **Command Line Interface** (**CLI**) automatically use the default endpoint for each service in an AWS Region, but you can specify an alternative endpoint for your API requests using this variable. One example would be to connect to a particular Region or use an FIPS endpoint for enhanced security using TLS connections.
- **botocore configuration variables**: These are configuration parameters for the boto environment. For more details on the parameters that can be passed to a botocore configuration, refer to the boto3 documentation. Some examples of the parameters in a boto3 configuration are the Region name, output format, connection timeout, and retries. Refer to the botocore documentation (`https://botocore.amazonaws.com/v1/documentation/api/latest/reference/config.html`) for more details on variables that can be configured.
- **General configuration variables**: These are general configurations that are used in various services to affect the way they behave – for example, we can configure a block size parameter to read data from S3.

Parameters related to Athena cache behavior

`awswrangler` can retrieve the results from Athena queries that have already been executed within a specific time period. We can configure this behavior using configuration variables to return the pre-executed data within *X* seconds, or *X* queries, so that a user can get valid data more quickly. The following variables help to configure Athena cache behavior:

- `MAX_CACHE_SECONDS`: `awswrangler` can check in Athena's history whether this query has been run before. If so, and its completion time is less than `max_cache_seconds` from the current query, `awswrangler` skips the query execution and just returns the same results as last time.
- `MAX_CACHE_QUERY_INSPECTIONS`: This is the maximum number of queries that will be inspected from the history to try to find some result to reuse. It only takes effect if `max_cache_seconds` > 0.
- `MAX_REMOTE_CACHE_ENTRIES`: This is the maximum number of queries that will be retrieved from AWS for cache inspection. It only takes effect if `max_cache_seconds` > 0 and the default value is `50`.
- `MAX_LOCAL_CACHE_ENTRIES`: This is the maximum number of queries for which metadata will be cached locally. This will reduce latency and also enables keeping more than `max_remote_cache_entries` available for the cache. This value should not be smaller than `max_remote_cache_entries`. It only takes effect if `max_cache_seconds` > 0 and the default value is `100`.

Parameters used across different services

The following parameters are used when interacting with Amazon S3 using the `awswrangler` package. They will help to improve the performance of read/write operations:

- `CONCURRENT_PARTIONING`: If `True`, this will increase the parallelism (using threads) level when writing to partitions. It will decrease the writing time and increase memory usage.
- `S3_BLOCK_SIZE`: This configuration is used to read files from S3, either in specified block sizes or completely in one shot if the value is set as `-1` for this variable.

Common use cases for configuring

We can configure `awswrangler` so that the same settings are repeated across multiple commands, meaning that we don't need to type them every time. Also, when we execute programs across multiple environments, global configurations help us to set default values that will customize an `awswrangler` execution specific to that environment.

Consider a situation where we need to execute Athena queries against a test database and a production database. The region, account, and cache factors are different between test and production queries. Rather than configuring them individually in each API call, we can customize them using global configurations once.

The other advantage here is that you can customize the configuration variables to add your own variables, as well as to further customize the behavior of `awswrangler` for your project.

We have learned various ways to install and configure an `awswrangler` package for your specific use cases so far. Now, we will explore the integration of various AWS services with `awswrangler` and how to use it efficiently with those services.

The features of AWS SDK for pandas with different AWS services

We will now explore the integration of the `awswrangler` package with AWS services. `awswrangler` works with more AWS services, and we explained its integration with some commonly used services such as Amazon S3, RDS databases, Amazon Redshift, and Amazon Athena.

Amazon S3

Amazon's **Simple Storage Service** (**S3**) is the largest and most performant object storage service for structured, semi-structured, and unstructured data and the storage service of choice to build a data lake. Amazon S3 allows you to migrate, store, manage, and secure all structured and unstructured data at an unlimited scale. With an S3 data lake, you can break down data silos, analyze diverse datasets, manage data access in one centralized place, and accelerate machine learning. Amazon S3 is secure by design, scalable on demand, and durable against the failure of an entire AWS Availability Zone. You can use AWS native services and integrate with third-party service providers to run applications on your data lake.

The following are the major functionalities that are available in `awswrangler` with Amazon S3:

- **Reading/downloading data from S3**: We have functions to read data from an S3 path for the JSON, CSV, Excel, Parquet, and fixed width file formats into a pandas DataFrame. These functions help to load data from an S3 location into a DataFrame to process it with pandas functions. They also provide additional capabilities for partition push-down, load objects that are modified/loaded after a certain time (for incremental data loads), load data in configurable chunks for bigger files, and provide multiple formatting options on data (pandas or PyArrow arguments).

  To get data from an S3 location to a local path/on-premise server, users can utilize the download function and perform further processing on the data on the local machine. Similarly, if the users want to query the data from S3 objects to debug and understand metadata for catalog updates, both S3 Select and the `read_parquet_metadata` functions will help.

- **Writing/uploading data to S3**: The data can be written to S3 in various file formats such as JSON, CSV, Parquet, and Excel using the `awswrangler` library. Users can choose to store datasets in various formats in S3. These functions also provide options to create partitions and update the Glue catalog so that data can be queried through the Athena and Redshift Spectrum. The data can be saved in various modes, such as append (adding new files), overwrite (replacing all files under a target path), and overwrite partition (overwriting files only in that partition). Users can configure the S3 functions to support schema evolution (allow missing or new columns) and also allow partition projection for Athena.

If you want to export data to S3 from a local/on-premise location, the `upload` function can be leveraged. The `download` and `upload` functions read and write data using filesystem functions and use multithreading logic for efficiency.

What is different in Parquet file handling?

To read and write other file formats, `awswrangler` uses pandas functions to read and write the files. However, for Parquet file loading/writing, `awswrangler` will utilize the Arrow library for faster data loading and map them in memory. Read the benefits of using the Arrow library in the introduction section for additional details.

Amazon S3 practical examples with awswrangler

Let's use some practical examples to further understand the concept of `awswrangler` reading/writing to S3.

We will load CSV data from a recent weather dataset and store it in JSON and Parquet format. Then, we will load the data in each format and validate its loading time in each format:

1. Install the `memory_profiler` library in the notebook to track memory usage, as well as the time taken to load and unload data:

```
1]: !pip install memory_profiler

    Looking in indexes: https://pypi.org/simple, https://pip.repos.neuron.amazonaws.com
    Collecting memory_profiler
      Downloading memory_profiler-0.60.0.tar.gz (38 kB)
      Preparing metadata (setup.py) ... done
    Requirement already satisfied: psutil in /home/ec2-user/anaconda3/envs/amazonei pytorch latest p37/lib/python3
```

Figure 3.42: S3 integration – installing the memory profiler

2. We will load ~4 GB data into a pandas DataFrame, which, by the way, is a big dataset to perform our data load benchmarking.

```
(base) ssmsun@38f9d355c9cf aws-data-wrangler % aws s3 ls s3://noaa-ghcn-pds/csv/by_year/202 --hum
an-readable --summarize
2022-10-05 13:59:29    1.5 GiB 2020.csv
2022-10-05 13:57:46    1.5 GiB 2021.csv
2022-10-05 13:57:37    1.1 GiB 2022.csv

Total Objects: 3
   Total Size: 4.1 GiB
```

Figure 3.43: S3 integration – the CSV file listing to understand the size of the files

The following screenshot shows the storage size of similar data volumes from parquet files (Snappy-compressed), and it is way less. This shows the value of storing datasets in Parquet format, as it stores datasets efficiently and also highly performant when running analytical queries.

```
2ebfc_0.snappy.parquet
2022-10-05 13:57:36    4.6 KiB parquet/by_year/YEAR=2022/ELEMENT=WT10/aba894e511414a32b2b4fed17f2
2ebfc_0.snappy.parquet
2022-10-05 13:57:36   15.0 KiB parquet/by_year/YEAR=2022/ELEMENT=WT11/aba894e511414a32b2b4fed17f2
2ebfc_0.snappy.parquet

Total Objects: 383
   Total Size: 286.6 MiB
```

Figure 3.44: S3 integration – the Parquet file listing to understand the size of the files

3. Verify the time taken to load data in the CSV and parquet file formats.

The Parquet file loading metrics are shown here:

```
%%time
%%memit
#Load compressed parquet file of size 286MB
weather_data=wr.s3.read_parquet("s3://noaa-ghcn-pds/parquet/by_year/YEAR=202")

peak memory: 26221.25 MiB, increment: 26067.42 MiB
CPU times: user 2min 19s, sys: 28.6 s, total: 2min 48s
Wall time: 2min 26s

weather_data.info()

<class 'pandas.core.frame.DataFrame'>
RangeIndex: 98619752 entries, 0 to 98619751
Data columns (total 7 columns):
 #   Column      Dtype
---  ------      -----
 0   ID          string
 1   DATE        string
 2   DATA_VALUE  Int64
 3   M_FLAG      string
 4   Q_FLAG      string
 5   S_FLAG      string
 6   OBS_TIME    string
dtypes: Int64(1), string(6)
memory usage: 5.2 GB
```

Figure 3.45: S3 integration – the Parquet file load metrics

The preceding metrics for the Parquet file was taken from a `t3.xlarge` instance. A similar instance failed to load the CSV file into memory, threw an error, and got stuck. Since loading a CSV file is a memory-intensive operation, we changed the notebook instance from `t3.xlarge` to `r5.2xlarge`. With that change, CSV files are able to load much faster, as shown in the following screenshot.

```
%%time
%%memit
#Load CSV file with 4.1GB of data
weather_data=wr.s3.read_csv("s3://noaa-ghcn-pds/csv/by_year/202")

peak memory: 28901.76 MiB, increment: 28747.74 MiB
CPU times: user 1min 15s, sys: 32.1 s, total: 1min 47s
Wall time: 1min 13s

weather_data.info()

<class 'pandas.core.frame.DataFrame'>
RangeIndex: 98707563 entries, 0 to 98707562
Data columns (total 9 columns):
 #   Column       Dtype
---  ------       -----
 0   Unnamed: 0   int64
 1   ID           object
 2   DATE         int64
 3   ELEMENT      object
 4   DATA_VALUE   int64
 5   M_FLAG       object
 6   Q_FLAG       object
 7   S_FLAG       object
 8   OBS_TIME     float64
dtypes: float64(1), int64(3), object(5)
memory usage: 6.6+ GB
```

Figure 3.46: S3 integration – the CSV file load metrics

This essentially demonstrates the advantage of using the right compute capacity for specific use cases to get better performance.

The preceding exercise also shows how easy it is to read data in different formats and highlights the benefits of storing data in the Parquet file format for analytical use cases.

Other awswrangler S3 functions

The following are some of the additional functions that `awswrangler` can perform:

- **Copy objects**: We use the `S3.copy` function from boto3 to copy one object at a time. Typically, users iterate over a function to copy multiple objects. `awswrangler` makes it easy to simply copy multiple files from one S3 prefix/folder to another S3 location. The `copy` function appends the source files to the new location. The merge objects function can either overwrite the files in the target location or append files to the target location based on configuration parameters.
- **List objects**: This function takes suffix and prefix arguments to filter files from the `s3` path. It takes the wildcard character format for file listing. This is achieved through a filename match library (`https://docs.python.org/3/library/fnmatch.html`). It can also filter files by timestamp after listing the files, which is very advantageous when listing files from a path for incremental data processing.

  The following screenshot shows the list of files that are created after a specific timestamp from an S3 location. You can see that the location already has a CSV file, but the list object doesn't list any files when we restrict the list to show only the files that were changed/uploaded in the last minute.

```
#This filter is done after listing of files from S3 path
path="s3://athenaresults-sankar/awswrangler/data/"
wr.s3.list_objects(path)
```

```
['s3://athenaresults-sankar/awswrangler/data/9f41c2b191014610a9bf2791635f23a6.csv']
```

```
#List files created in the last 1 minute
from datetime import datetime,timezone,timedelta
wr.s3.list_objects(path,last_modified_begin=datetime.now(timezone.utc)- timedelta(minutes = 1))
```

```
[]
```

Figure 3.47: S3 integration – listing only the incremental files

  Create a CSV file in the same location and list objects that were created in the last minute. Now, you can see that the new file is listed in the S3 path and does not list the older files. This can help you to identify new files that were created after a specific time period.

```
import pandas as pd
df = pd.DataFrame({
    "id": [1, 2],
    "value": ["ABC", "DEF"]})

wr.s3.to_csv(df=df,path=path,index=False,dataset=True,mode="overwrite")

{'paths': ['s3://athenaresults-sankar/awswrangler/data/c8d458b1139347f880387223f96b48e4.csv'],
 'partitions_values': {}}

wr.s3.list_objects(path,last_modified_begin=datetime.now(timezone.utc)- timedelta(minutes = 1))

['s3://athenaresults-sankar/awswrangler/data/c8d458b1139347f880387223f96b48e4.csv']
```

Figure 3.48: S3 integration – listing only the incremental files (continued)

Challenge exercise

You can use this function in your custom code to create incremental data processing logic. Every time you execute the read function, only newer files that were created after the last successful run should be processed.

Hint

You can use DynamoDB to store the timestamp from the ETL job once it is successfully completed as part of the last step of the job. The next execution of the job should retrieve the latest timestamp for every new execution, and it should only list files between the timestamp from the last successfully completed job run and the timestamp of the start of the current job run. Add a lock mechanism as a part of the initialization step of the job (or before reading the files) to avoid two jobs running in parallel reading the data at the same time. The DynamoDB table should store state information with a primary key and a sort key as a combination of a job identifier and an S3 path, and store start timestamp and stop timestamp information for each job and S3 path combination.

- **Describe objects**: Users can execute a boto3 `head_object` command for a single file or for a prefix (which can be done in parallel threads for improved performance). The advantage of using this function is that it doesn't download the object; instead, it gets only the metadata of the S3 object.

Usage

You can use the describe object command with filters (time or job identifier prefix) to identify the list of new files and their sizes. This can help to identify the scope to optimize your output file size once the job is completed.

- **Delete objects**: Using this function, we can delete a huge number of files concurrently using threads, similar to other objects. It also captures errors and tries to delete the files for a specific number of times (five attempts) to avoid intermittent errors.

> **Warning**
>
> With great power comes great responsibility. Use this function with caution and couple this with S3 versioning and other features to avoid accidental deletions in production situations.

- **A wait object**: A waiter function is called every five seconds until a successful state (e.g., the availability of an S3 object) is reached. An error is returned after 20 failed checks. We can use the waiter config to mention the wait time and maximum retries before an error is thrown. The advantage of using `awswrangler` is to have concurrent execution on multiple waiting objects. One use case of this is to wait for a trigger file to be available in a path before starting the job execution.
- **Data retrieval using S3 select queries**: Users can utilize the S3 select functionality to read specific S3 files and apply filters on the data within a single S3 object. This method currently supports CSV, JSON, Parquet, and some files with custom delimiters. The advantage of this approach is that it enables your applications to retrieve only the subset of data that is needed for processing. With this approach, we push the data filtering part to S3, which is much faster (up to 400% faster; in some cases, it could be slower) and cheaper (up to 80% cheaper) for certain workloads. Consider an example of a huge compressed ZIP file that has a million records, and an application needs to process only 100 records from a filter condition. With the traditional approach, the entire file is downloaded to the client side and then filtered to get the data, but with S3 Select, we can un-compress data, filter it, and then download it on the client side.

  S3 Select works on objects stored in the CSV, JSON, or Apache Parquet formats. S3 Select also supports compression of CSV and JSON objects with GZIP or BZIP2, and server-side encrypted objects. S3 Select can be executed only against a single file and can't be run against multiple files (for which AWS services such as Athena and Redshift will help).

  S3 Select when used in the AWS console only supports 40 MB of data. One use case is to explore a file for errors quickly without running through custom processing. We can use an S3 Select query to identify records with null values in a column before starting the ETL process.

The following screenshot shows an example of using S3 Select on a CSV file:

```
%%time
%%memit
weather_data=wr.s3.select_query(
    sql='SELECT * FROM s3object s where s.DATA_VALUE<>\'0\'',
    path='s3://noaa-ghcn-pds/csv/by_year/2022.csv',
    input_serialization = 'CSV',
    input_serialization_params={
        'FileHeaderInfo': 'Use'
    },
    use_threads=True,
)

peak memory: 39506.35 MiB, increment: 19722.42 MiB
CPU times: user 4min 17s, sys: 55.2 s, total: 5min 12s
Wall time: 4min 7s
```

```
weather_data.head(5)
```

		ID	DATE	ELEMENT	DATA_VALUE	M_FLAG	Q_FLAG	S_FLAG	OBS_TIME
0	0	AE000041196	20220101	TAVG	204	H		S	
1	1	AEM00041194	20220101	TAVG	211	H		S	

Figure 3.49: S3 integration – S3 Select queries

It takes four minutes to get the results back from the query, which reads 1 GB of data in the CSV format, as the data is stored in an uncompressed format and it needs to read all the data, but less data will be transferred between systems. The benefits will be more pronounced when transferring high-volume data in a low-bandwidth network. Also, note that this test was done on a high-memory and high-bandwidth machine, which can load the entire file much faster and filter the data quickly in memory. So, if your only need is better performance, you also need to consider the data storage format and compute and memory resources available to your machine before using S3 Select or filtering data after reading the entire object into your compute layer.

- **Merging datasets on an S3 data lake**: The merge upsert table function will help to perform `upsert` operations on existing files. This function takes a primary key and performs an `upsert` operation. The underlying logic is to drop the records from the existing table, which has the same primary key from the DataFrame that has the new records to be loaded into the table. This will create a final table with the new records inserted, and the existing records will be updated with the most recent value.

Note

This is not a performant solution for larger tables, as loading an entire table in memory is not an efficient operation. Users should think of using transactional data lake formats such as Hudi, Iceberg, Delta, or Lake Formation governed tables if they deal with huge data volumes and use Apache Spark to process the data.

Amazon Athena

`awswrangler` has good integration with Amazon Athena. It helps to load results from an Athena query into a pandas DataFrame for further wrangling activities, in order to ensure that `awswrangler` utilizes the following logic to evaluate whether a query has to be executed or retrieve results from the previous execution in a faster manner.

The following screenshot shows some simple steps involved in creating a Glue table using `awswrangler` and querying the table using it. We can set configuration variables once during program execution, and the queries are executed quickly without a lot of parameters and additional coding.

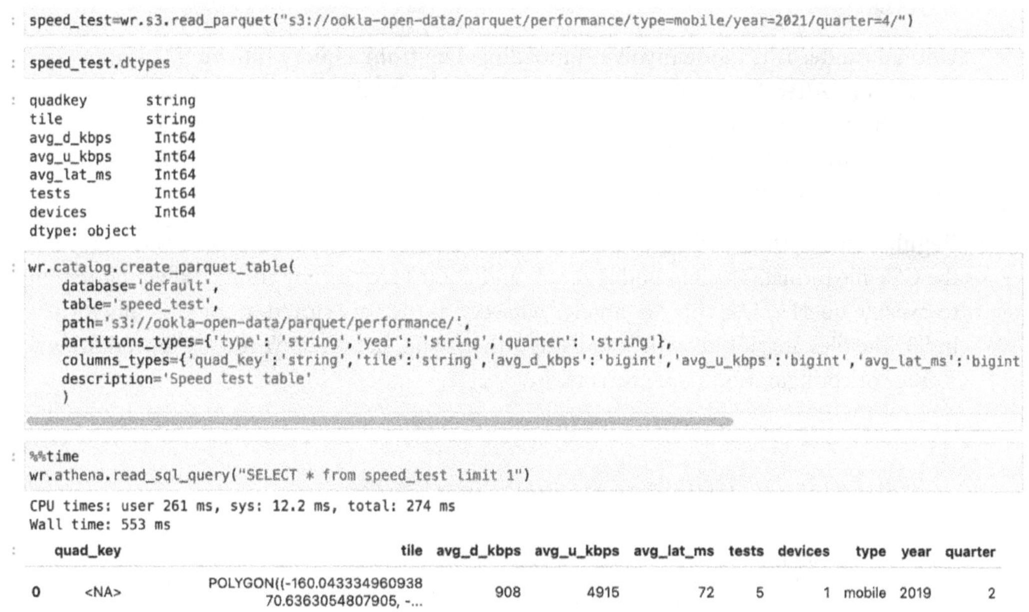

Figure 3.50: Athena integration – creating a table in the AWS Glue catalog

The following are the steps involved in fetching data from an `awswrangler` query/table API call:

1. When you submit a read SQL table API call internally, the table name gets appended with a select statement and gets executed through a read SQL query API call.
2. There are a lot of arguments to configure the working of query submission. We can use the `params` argument to format the query.
3. Evaluate whether the query is available in the local cache (which gets updated with every new query execution and stores 100 queries by default). This step also looks for queries from the remote cache (the Athena service query history) based on configuration parameters, including past *X* queries or past *X* seconds.

4. If there is no hit in the cache step, the query is submitted for execution by `awswrangler` in either **Create Table as Statement** (**CTAS**), UNLOAD, or regular mode:

   - **CTAS mode**: This is the **default mode**, and it involves wrapping a query within a `create table as` statement, with data stored in an S3 location in the Parquet format. This method also creates a table with the output of the query in a CTAS database, which is provided as an input argument. The Parquet file is then loaded into a DataFrame using the `awswrangler` S3 read parquet file API. Also, the temporary tables will be deleted at the end of the query execution to avoid cluttering the tables from each query. Use this for bigger datasets where performance is necessary and it also needs permissions to create and drop temporary CTAS tables.
   - **Unload mode**: This mode involves unloading data from a query into an S3 location as a Parquet file. After that, similar to CTAS, we will load the dataset into a pandas DataFrame using the `awswrangler` S3 read parquet file API. Use this for bigger datasets and data that is exported to S3 in the Parquet format. Note that this method doesn't create Glue tables before loading in a DataFrame.
   - **Regular mode**: This mode uses the Athena output location where the results are saved in the CSV file format. This method is simple and doesn't require any additional configuration to execute queries. Use this for smaller datasets, as they are stored in the CSV file format in S3. The files are stored by default using Athena and, hence, don't require any additional storage or configuration requirements.

The following diagram summarizes the `awswrangler` Athena query execution flow:

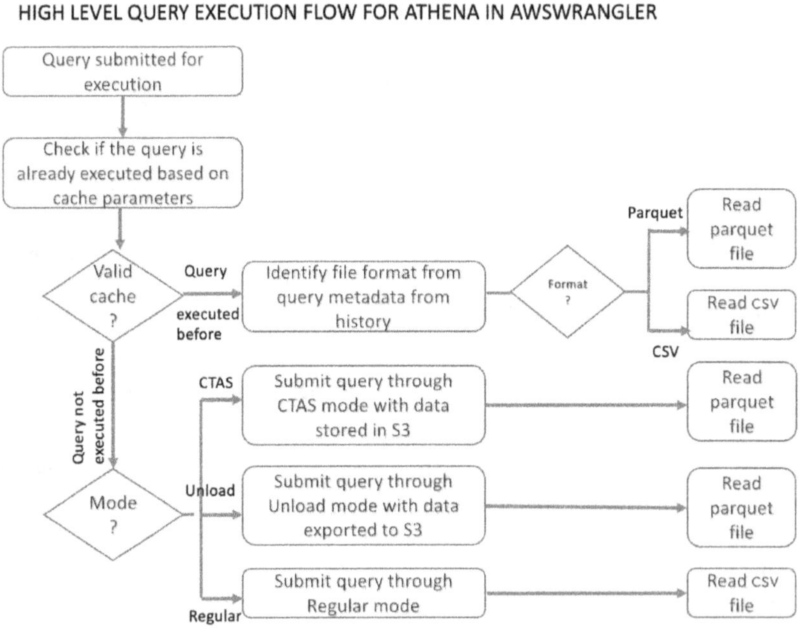

Figure 3.51: Athena integration – the query execution workflow

How to utilize query metadata for performance

The pandas DataFrame also has a `query_metadata` dictionary, which is similar to the output of the `GetQueryExecution` command from Athena that retrieves each query metadata. In the following screenshot, you can see information such as when the query started and finished, where the results are stored, the format of the file, and so on.

```
result_type

results.query_metadata

{'QueryExecutionId': 'a551b95f-c7e6-4423-b3ef-a2994f05e7f6',
 'Query': 'CREATE TABLE "default"."temp_table_1712a308609b46218042dcbb4286ab3d"\nWITH(\n    external_location = \'s3://
aws-athena-query-results-473373155991-us-east-2/temp_table_1712a308609b46218042dcbb4286ab3d\',\n    format = \'PARQUE
T\')\nAS SELECT date,time,bytes,method,uri,result_type from cloudfront_logs limit 1',
 'StatementType': 'DDL',
 'ResultConfiguration': {'OutputLocation': 's3://aws-athena-query-results-473373155991-us-east-2/tables/a551b95f-c7e6-4
423-b3ef-a2994f05e7f6'},
 'QueryExecutionContext': {'Database': 'default'},
 'Status': {'State': 'SUCCEEDED',
  'SubmissionDateTime': datetime.datetime(2022, 10, 4, 1, 29, 33, 922000, tzinfo=tzlocal()),
  'CompletionDateTime': datetime.datetime(2022, 10, 4, 1, 29, 35, 338000, tzinfo=tzlocal())},
 'Statistics': {'EngineExecutionTimeInMillis': 1289,
  'DataScannedInBytes': 1495,
  'DataManifestLocation': 's3://aws-athena-query-results-473373155991-us-east-2/tables/a551b95f-c7e6-4423-b3ef-a2994f05
e7f6-manifest.csv',
  'TotalExecutionTimeInMillis': 1416,
  'QueryQueueTimeInMillis': 106,
  'QueryPlanningTimeInMillis': 156,
  'ServiceProcessingTimeInMillis': 21},
 'WorkGroup': 'primary',
 'EngineVersion': {'SelectedEngineVersion': 'AUTO',
  'EffectiveEngineVersion': 'Athena engine version 2'}}
```

Figure 3.52: Athena integration – getting query metadata from Athena

However, we also have a bunch of important attributes under the "Statistics" segment. They provide information on the query wait time, the planning time, the execution time, and also the data scanned. Note that Athena queries are charged based on the data scanned:

```
TotalExecutionTime =  EngineExecutionTime(includes QueryPlanningTime)
+ QueryQueueTime + ServiceProcessingTime
```

Here is an example from the preceding case – 1,416 ms = 1,289 ms + 106 ms + 21 ms.

The `EngineExecution` time was 1,289 ms, out of which `Queryplanningtime` was 156 ms. So, the actual execution time for the query in the Athena engine was 1,133ms.

Let's understand the terms used in the preceding query here:

- `TotalExecutionTime`: The number of ms that Athena took to run a DDL or DML query.
- `EngineExecutionTime`: The number of ms that the Athena engine took to run the query. The more complex the query and the larger the data volume, the longer this phase takes.
- `QueryPlanningTime`: The number of ms that Athena took to plan the query processing flow.

- `QueryQueueTime`: The number of ms that the query was in the query queue waiting for resources. This is a variable time and depends on the availability of resources at the specific Region and time.
- `ServiceProcessingTime`: The number of ms that Athena took to process the query results after the query engine finished running the query. If a query spends too much time in this phase, we write a big dataset to S3 and try to reduce the size of the resulting set.

You can use these metrics to look at where each query spends time and then optimize them. However, note that these metrics don't include any network latencies and delays outside of the Athena query engine.

How does Athena cache work?

We can enable cache logic by setting the `MAX_CACHE_SECONDS` variable to be greater than zero. This will help decrease the query execution time (by skipping the execution entirely and reusing the past execution results if they are still available).

The following steps are evaluated while performing cache validation:

1. Check whether the `MAX_CACHE_SECONDS` variable is greater than zero; if it's set to zero or less, return immediately and the queries are executed every time they are called. This is needed for use cases where data is updated more frequently and you require recent data rather than lower query execution times.
2. Retrieve queries based on `MAX_REMOTE_CACHE_ENTRIES` from the Athena history log using pagination. Check whether the query details are available in the local cache; if not, append the query details to the local cache object. The local cache stores the data about the most recent 100 queries so that the data can be retrieved much faster than the remote cache. In this `awswrangler` Athena context, the cache can be understood as the storage for query metadata details, such as the query execution ID and query completion time.
3. Sort the list of queries from the local cache and the remote cache based on the condition that the elapsed seconds query completion time is not greater than `MAX_CACHE_SECONDS`.
4. Parse the query so that a successful match can be made with older queries. Currently, the query is stripped of white space and trailing semicolons and leading and trailing brackets are removed so that the queries can be matched to a reasonable degree of confidence.
5. If the older query is CTAS (executed with `awswrangler` CTAS mode), then parse and take the inner query before it can be compared with a new query. Compare both queries, and if there is a match, return the cache match as a success.

For example, let us execute a simple query that extracts data from an example table, crawled on CloudFront logs and stored in an S3 bucket. You could use any table for this demonstration of Athena cache functionality.

```
%%time
wr.athena.read_sql_query("SELECT date,time,bytes,method,uri,referrer,result_type from cloudfront_logs limit 1")

CPU times: user 298 ms, sys: 12.7 ms, total: 311 ms
Wall time: 3.42 s
```

	date	time	bytes	method	uri	referrer	result_type
0	2022-02-18	16:12:03	481	GET	/	-	Error

```
%%time
wr.athena.read_sql_query("SELECT date,time,bytes,method,uri,referrer,result_type from          cloudfront_logs limit 1;

CPU times: user 87.3 ms, sys: 2.99 ms, total: 90.2 ms
Wall time: 333 ms
```

	date	time	bytes	method	uri	referrer	result_type
0	2022-02-18	16:12:03	481	GET	/	-	Error

Figure 3.53: Athena integration – Athena cache functionality

You can see that the first run of the query took 3.42 seconds, and the second query ran in ~300 ms. This translates into 11x time reduction from our initial run. However, based on the complexity of the initial query, we can save a lot of time by simply reusing the existing results and not executing it again. Also, note the query has some extra spaces before the table name and a trailing semicolon, which are removed before comparing queries.

However, as mentioned before, the benefits are realized only when a similar query is executed. Refer to the following example, where we only selected a subset of columns from the query. We found that the **referrer** column doesn't have any data in our specific dataset, and we wanted to remove the column from our result set. As you can see, the query without the referrer column takes 2.63 seconds to retrieve data.

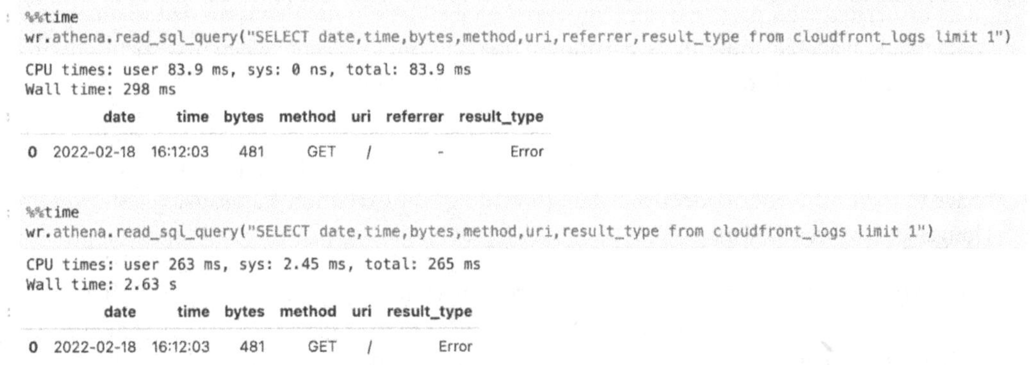
%%time
wr.athena.read_sql_query("SELECT date,time,bytes,method,uri,referrer,result_type from cloudfront_logs limit 1")
CPU times: user 83.9 ms, sys: 0 ns, total: 83.9 ms
Wall time: 298 ms
date time bytes method uri referrer result_type
0 2022-02-18 16:12:03 481 GET / - Error
%%time
wr.athena.read_sql_query("SELECT date,time,bytes,method,uri,result_type from cloudfront_logs limit 1")
CPU times: user 263 ms, sys: 2.45 ms, total: 265 ms
Wall time: 2.63 s
date time bytes method uri result_type
0 2022-02-18 16:12:03 481 GET / Error

Figure 3.54: Athena integration – Athena cache functionality limitation when SQL is changed

Challenge

You can expand the query architecture to match queries that had a wider dataset earlier and then apply filters to get a smaller dataset. Expand on the high-level process listed in the following list.

1. Identify the older query and split the `where` clause and `from` clause in the queries before comparison.
2. Parse the new query in a similar format and compare it with the older query. If the new query has more filters than the old query or/and fewer columns than the old query, we can use the data from the old query and apply the filters in the pandas DataFrame and return the results, such as the following:

```
Query 1:  select * from hr. employee where city='NY'
Query 2:  select * from hr. employee where city='NY' and join_
date>'2020-10-01'
```

Here, we can see that `Query 2` is a subset of `Query 1`, and we can use the already executed data and apply further filters on the columns in the pandas DataFrame.

Also, there is tremendous scope for improving the query matching logic to improve the cache hit, and the updates you make can be contributed back to the AWS SDK for pandas repository. Happy coding!!!

Also, It provides many helpful modules, a couple of which are listed here:

- **Repair table**: This runs the `MSCK REPAIR` command to update the table metadata with the most recent data from the storage layer. This function executes Hive's metastore consistency check – `MSCK REPAIR TABLE <tablename>`. The command recovers partitions and data associated with partitions and updates the table definition. This is needed to query the data that is available under those partitions. This is useful to execute when new partitions are created from an ETL job that doesn't update the Glue catalog.
- **Wait query**: This iterates through the query status every 250 ms until the query moves to either FAILED, SUCCEEDED, or CANCELLED status (the final status for a query execution). You have to customize your code if you want to verify query execution status, using a shorter or longer polling mechanism.

The `awswrangler` package takes care of data type conversion internally. The Parquet files from the resulting folder are read using S3 read functions (which in turn uses `pyarrow` to read the S3 object). The data type conversion of the Parquet files – arrow – `athena` are handled internally within the `awswrangler` package. The following snippet from the `data_types.py` module shows the conversion of the `pyarrow` and `athena` data types.

```
def pyarrow2athena(  # pylint: disable=too-many-branches,too-many-return-statements
    dtype: pa.DataType, ignore_null: bool = False
) -> str:
    """Pyarrow to Athena data types conversion."""
    if pa.types.is_int8(dtype):
        return "tinyint"
    if pa.types.is_int16(dtype) or pa.types.is_uint8(dtype):
        return "smallint"
    if pa.types.is_int32(dtype) or pa.types.is_uint16(dtype):
        return "int"
    if pa.types.is_int64(dtype) or pa.types.is_uint32(dtype):
        return "bigint"
    if pa.types.is_uint64(dtype):
        raise exceptions.UnsupportedType("There is no support for uint64, please conside
    if pa.types.is_float32(dtype):
        return "float"
    if pa.types.is_float64(dtype):
```

Figure 3.55: Athena integration – pyarrow data type conversions

RDS databases

There is a good amount of integration functionalities available within `awswrangler` to connect with relational databases, such as Postgres, Oracle, SQL Server, and MySQL. In addition to this, `awswrangler` supports DataAPI-based access to Redshift and Aurora Serverless databases.

`awswrangler` uses additional libraries to connect with the databases, which need to be installed as well. The following diagram shows the additional libraries needed to connect with different database engines.

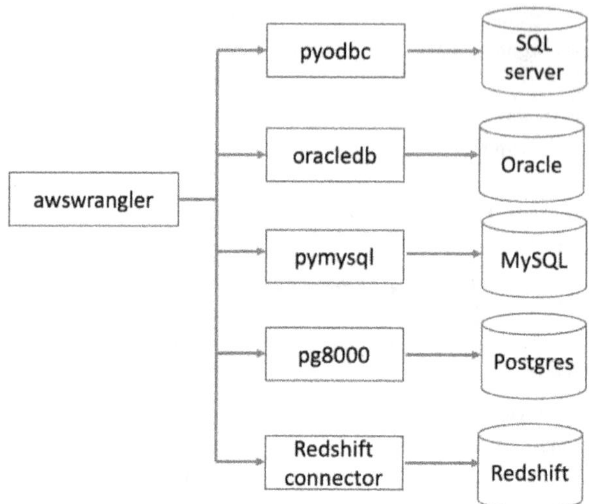

Figure 3.56: RDS integration – database engines and recommended drivers

We have to ensure that the extra Python libraries are installed when we try to connect to those database engines. To connect with Redshift and Aurora Serverless as well IAM authentication, we can use DataAPI, which also helps to manage database connections more effectively.

The following common modules/functionalities are available for all database engines:

- **Connect to database**: This checks whether an extra Python library is available for the database engine and provides an error if the Python library needed to make a database connection is missing. The connect module requires an existing Glue connection or secret identifier to provide database login details. For example, a secret should have the following fields to make a database connection:

```
{
        "host":"hostname.region.rds.amazonaws.com",
        "username":"testuser",
        "password":"testpassword", "engine":"mysql", "port":"3306"
}
```

  `awswrangler` will internally format the connection string from the secrets manager or Glue connection and use the **Create a connection** object (`pymysql` in the case of MySQL, `pyodbc` in the case of `sqlserver`, etc.) and return to the calling code. This connection object can be used from that point onward to read and write to the database.

- **Reading from database**: There are a couple of options to read from database engines – Read from SQL and Read from table. Read from table will create a select query on the table and again call the Read from SQL module.

The query is formatted and submitted through the connection object, which is passed as an argument to the **Read from SQL** module. The code will execute the query using cursors from the connection object.

Once the data is retrieved from the execution, it's loaded into a `pyarrow` array to enable faster loading of data from the record object in the cursor execution. We can then quickly convert it to a pandas DataFrame and return to the calling function to further process the data.

The following screenshot shows a quick example of loading the Ookla speed test data from S3 (4.1 million records) in three minutes, with the lowest instance size for the notebook and database. The intent of this exercise is to show the ease with which data can be loaded and queried with `awswrangler`.

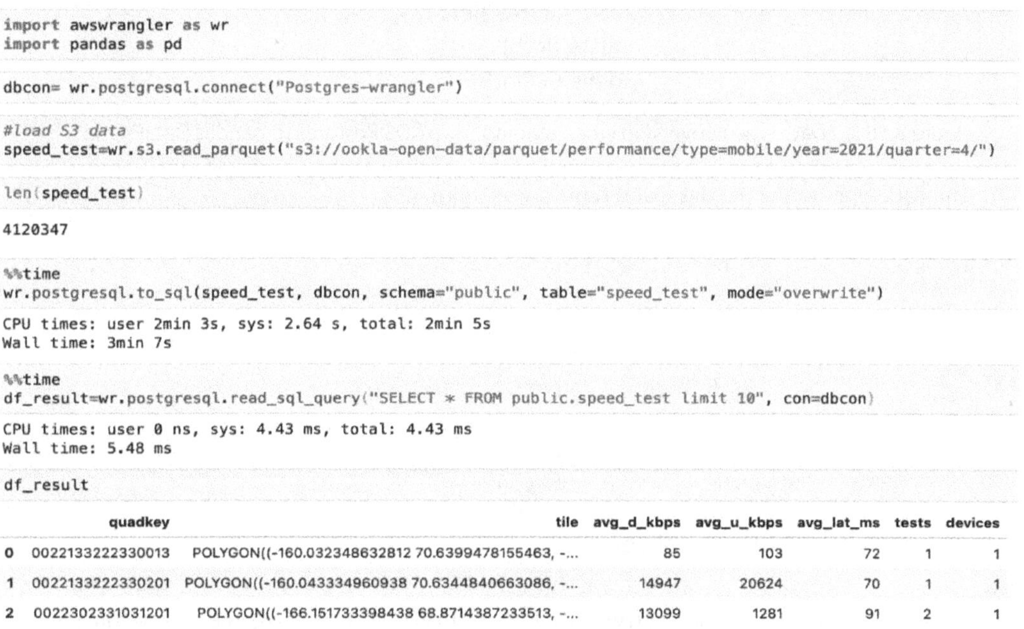

```
import awswrangler as wr
import pandas as pd

dbcon= wr.postgresql.connect("Postgres-wrangler")

#load S3 data
speed_test=wr.s3.read_parquet("s3://ookla-open-data/parquet/performance/type=mobile/year=2021/quarter=4/")

len(speed_test)

4120347

%%time
wr.postgresql.to_sql(speed_test, dbcon, schema="public", table="speed_test", mode="overwrite")

CPU times: user 2min 3s, sys: 2.64 s, total: 2min 5s
Wall time: 3min 7s

%%time
df_result=wr.postgresql.read_sql_query("SELECT * FROM public.speed_test limit 10", con=dbcon)

CPU times: user 0 ns, sys: 4.43 ms, total: 4.43 ms
Wall time: 5.48 ms

df_result
```

	quadkey	tile	avg_d_kbps	avg_u_kbps	avg_lat_ms	tests	devices
0	0022133222330013	POLYGON((-160.032348632812 70.6399478155463, -...	85	103	72	1	1
1	0022133222330201	POLYGON((-160.043334960938 70.6344840663086, -...	14947	20624	70	1	1
2	0022302331031201	POLYGON((-166.151733398438 68.8714387233513, -...	13099	1281	91	2	1

Figure 3.57: RDS integration – loading sample data from RDS

You can also see that the data types are changed based on Arrow and the pandas DataFrame.

The data types in the Postgres instance are as follows:

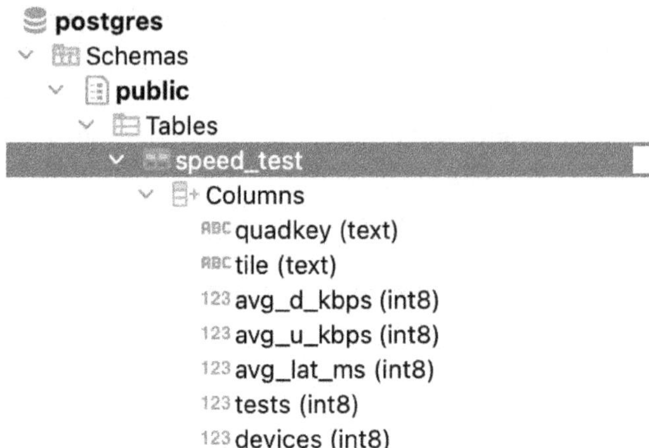

Figure 3.58 (a): Data type conversion when loading from RDS Postgres to pandas DataFrame

The data types in the pandas DataFrame are as follows:

```
df_result.dtypes
```

```
quadkey        string
tile           string
avg_d_kbps      Int64
avg_u_kbps      Int64
avg_lat_ms      Int64
tests           Int64
devices         Int64
dtype: object
```

Figure 3.58 (b): Data type conversion when loading from RDS Postgres to a pandas DataFrame

- **Writing to database**: We can use the `to_sql` function from each database engine module to write a pandas DataFrame into a table. This validates the connection object and then creates the tables if they're not there already (drops and recreates tables if the mode is set to overwrite). Based on the different modes, the data gets updated differently:

- **Upsert**: This updates the specific set of columns when there is a match to a list of matching columns (mostly to identify unique records). This is for cases where there is an existing table with Column1, Column2, and Column3 as primary key columns. When we `upsert`, we check whether the new record matches with existing records on Column1, Column2, and Column3, and if there is a match, we will update the rest of the columns (or a subset of the rest of the columns). If there is no match with Column1, Column2, and Column3, the new record will be inserted into the table.
- **Append**: This inserts new records into the table. We can check whether the record matches an existing record by matching it with a specific set of columns and then choose to ignore it if there is a match. If there is no match, the record can be inserted into the table.

We will emulate a data update + insert (upsert) situation for a Postgres database using the following steps:

1. Extract a couple of records using quad key values from the table:

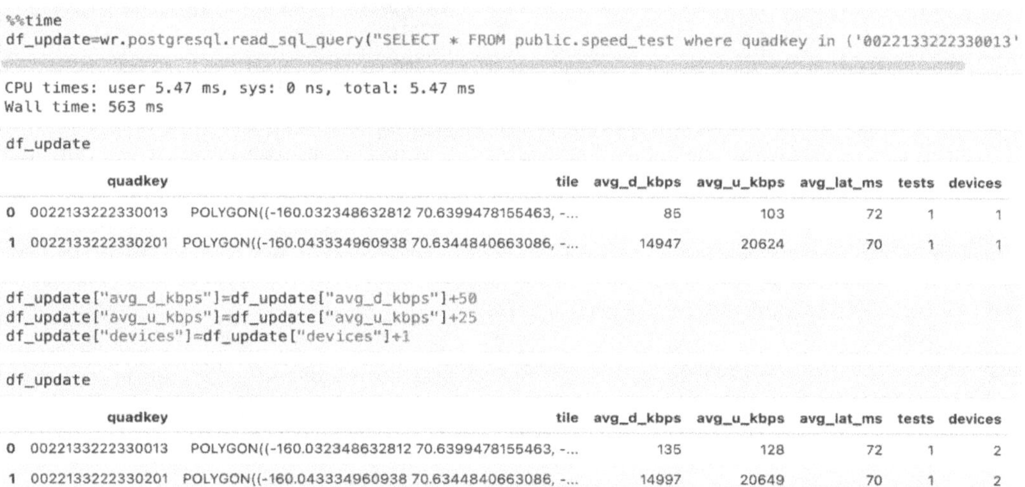

```
%%time
df_update=wr.postgresql.read_sql_query("SELECT * FROM public.speed_test where quadkey in ('0022133222330013'
```

```
CPU times: user 5.47 ms, sys: 0 ns, total: 5.47 ms
Wall time: 563 ms
```

```
df_update
```

	quadkey	tile	avg_d_kbps	avg_u_kbps	avg_lat_ms	tests	devices
0	0022133222330013	POLYGON((-160.032348632812 70.6399478155463, -...	85	103	72	1	1
1	0022133222330201	POLYGON((-160.043334960938 70.6344840663086, -...	14947	20624	70	1	1

```
df_update["avg_d_kbps"]=df_update["avg_d_kbps"]+50
df_update["avg_u_kbps"]=df_update["avg_u_kbps"]+25
df_update["devices"]=df_update["devices"]+1
```

```
df_update
```

	quadkey	tile	avg_d_kbps	avg_u_kbps	avg_lat_ms	tests	devices
0	0022133222330013	POLYGON((-160.032348632812 70.6399478155463, -...	135	128	72	1	2
1	0022133222330201	POLYGON((-160.043334960938 70.6344840663086, -...	14997	20649	70	1	2

Figure 3.59: RDS integration – emulate the upsert logic to extract data from the existing table

2. Update the DataFrame to change the values of those records. These two records are used to test the update situation in upsert.

```
%%time
df_update=wr.postgresql.read_sql_query("SELECT * FROM public.speed_test where quadkey in ('0022133222330013'
```

```
CPU times: user 5.47 ms, sys: 0 ns, total: 5.47 ms
Wall time: 563 ms
```

```
df_update
```

	quadkey	tile	avg_d_kbps	avg_u_kbps	avg_lat_ms	tests	devices
0	0022133222330013	POLYGON((-160.032348632812 70.6399478155463, -...	85	103	72	1	1
1	0022133222330201	POLYGON((-160.043334960938 70.6344840663086, -...	14947	20624	70	1	1

```
df_update["avg_d_kbps"]=df_update["avg_d_kbps"]+50
df_update["avg_u_kbps"]=df_update["avg_u_kbps"]+25
df_update["devices"]=df_update["devices"]+1
```

```
df_update
```

	quadkey	tile	avg_d_kbps	avg_u_kbps	avg_lat_ms	tests	devices
0	0022133222330013	POLYGON((-160.032348632812 70.6399478155463, -...	135	128	72	1	2
1	0022133222330201	POLYGON((-160.043334960938 70.6344840663086, -...	14997	20649	70	1	2

Figure 3.60: RDS integration – emulating upsert logic to update extracted records

3. Insert a new record into the pandas DataFrame to test it. This record will be used to validate the insert situation in upsert.

```
new_record={"quadkey":"0000000000000000","tile":"POLYGON","avg_d_kbps":50,"avg_u_kbps":25,"avg_lat_ms":5,"tests":1,"device
df_update.append(new_record, ignore_index=True)
```

	quadkey	tile	avg_d_kbps	avg_u_kbps	avg_lat_ms	tests	devices
0	0022133222330013	POLYGON((-160.032348632812 70.6399478155463, -...	135	128	72	1	2
1	0022133222330201	POLYGON((-160.043334960938 70.6344840663086, -...	14997	20649	70	1	2
2	0000000000000000	POLYGON	50	25	5	1	1

Figure 3.61: RDS integration – emulating upsert logic to generate a new record to insert into the table

4. Change the table to create a unique index so that upsert situations will work in Postgres:

```
ALTER TABLE postgres.public.speed_test
ADD CONSTRAINT UI_quadkey_index UNIQUE (quadkey);
```

5. Test the upsert situation by executing the command with the `upsert` option:

```
%%time
wr.postgresql.to_sql(df_update, dbcon, schema="public", table="speed_test", mode="upsert",
                    upsert_conflict_columns=['quadkey'],)

CPU times: user 4.25 ms, sys: 191 µs, total: 4.44 ms
Wall time: 7.69 ms

%%time
df_update1=wr.postgresql.read_sql_query("SELECT * FROM public.speed_test where quadkey in ('0022133222330013','00221332223

CPU times: user 4.94 ms, sys: 17 µs, total: 4.96 ms
Wall time: 4.46 ms

df_update1
```

	quadkey	tile	avg_d_kbps	avg_u_kbps	avg_lat_ms	tests	devices
0	0000000000000000	POLYGON	50	25	5	1	1
1	0022133222330013	POLYGON((-160.032348632812 70.6399478155463, -...	135	128	72	1	2
2	0022133222330201	POLYGON((-160.043334960938 70.6344840663086, -...	14997	20649	70	1	2

Figure 3.62: RDS integration – validating the upsert logic

This will help us to create data pipelines to update and insert data in existing Postgres tables in a simple and effective manner. You can also customize this code further to suit your project needs.

In the SageMaker notebook environment we used earlier, the `pg8000` library was preinstalled, so we were able to execute commands successfully after installing the `awswrangler` package:

```
!pip list | grep pg8000
pg8000                                   1.29.1
```

Figure 3.63: RDS integration – SageMaker database library availability verification

If `pg8000` or another Python library for your database engine is not available in the environment, then you need to install it before proceeding further. If it's a Lambda function, you add it through Lambda layers.

Redshift

The `awswrangler` module has additional functionalities available to connect with Redshift; the aforementioned common functions are present in Redshift as well. However, we have additional functionalities that are specific to the Redshift warehouse, as listed here:

- **Connecting to the data warehouse**: We can connect with a username/password similar to other RDS databases, or we can connect using temporary login credentials for a database username provided you have IAM permissions to get credentials on the Redshift cluster (`https://docs.aws.amazon.com/cli/latest/reference/redshift/get-cluster-credentials.html`).

- **Writing/loading data to a data warehouse**:
  - **Loading from a pandas DataFrame**: There are a couple of options to load data from a DataFrame into a Redshift table. The `to_sql` function, which was used earlier similar to RDS, can be used. Another option is to use the `copy` method, which uses a Parquet file in S3 as a staging area and utilizes the Redshift `COPY` command to load data. This method has more overhead in configuration, but it is more effective when there are a higher number of records, as Redshift loads data in parallel threads.
  - **Loading directly from an S3 file**: This method is more efficient if you want to load data from S3 directly into Redshift without loading data into a pandas DataFrame. This method uses the `COPY` command to move data into Redshift.

The following steps are performed to write data into the Redshift data warehouse using the `copy` command.

Copy the speed test data and load it into an S3 bucket within the same region as your Redshift cluster. In the following example, we will downside the data to 100,000 records (still a reasonable volume) to illustrate the Redshift load process:

```
speed_test=wr.s3.read_parquet("s3://ookla-open-data/parquet/performance/type=mobile/year=2021/quarter=4/")

df1=speed_test.head(100000)

wr.s3.to_parquet(df1,"s3://                    /awswrangler/data/redshift_load_speed_test.parquet")

{'paths': ['s3://                    /awswrangler/data/redshift_load_speed_test.parquet'],
 'partitions_values': {}}
```

Figure 3.64: Redshift integration – preparing data to be loaded into Redshift

Use case 1: Migrate data from S3 to Redshift without any modification. Load the data into the Redshift data warehouse as follows:

```
%%time
#Method1 - Load S3 files directly into Redshift
wr.redshift.copy_from_files(path="s3://                    /awswrangler/data/",
                            con=con,schema="public", table="speed_test",mode="overwrite"
                            ,iam_role="arn:aws:iam::473373155991:role/RedshiftImmersionRole"
                            ,path_ignore_suffix=".txt")

CPU times: user 107 ms, sys: 11.1 ms, total: 118 ms
Wall time: 2.86 s
```

Figure 3.65: Redshift integration – loading data into Redshift

Query the data from Redshift and verify whether the table has been loaded as expected:

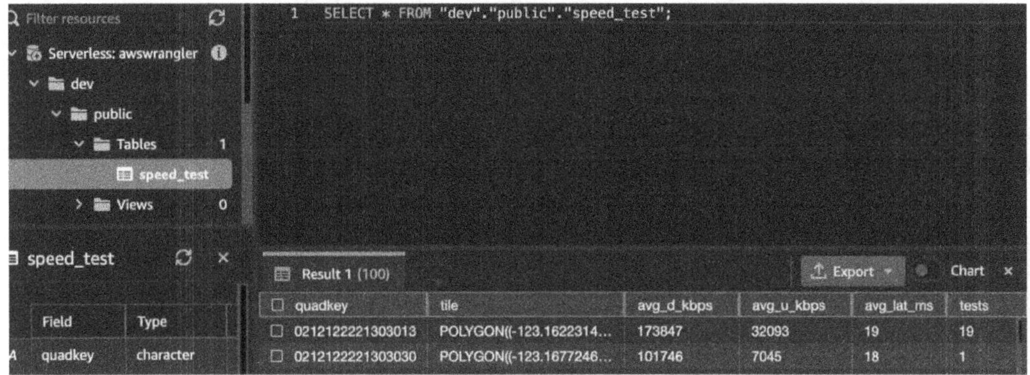

Figure 3.66: Redshift integration – querying data from Redshift

Use case 2: Migrate the data from S3 after some modifications through an ETL process. Load the data from an S3 file into a pandas DataFrame and perform ETL modifications on the data as necessary, using pandas transformations.

```
#Usecase2 - Load S3 files into Pandas, make some changes and load it to Redshift using S3 copy command
speed_test=wr.s3.read_parquet("s3://ookla-open-data/parquet/performance/type=mobile/year=2021/quarter=4/")
```

```
#Usecase2 - Perform ETL transformations
speed_test_load=speed_test.drop('tile',axis=1)
speed_test_load['newdevices']=speed_test_load['devices']+1
speed_test_load['avg_usedbandwidth']=speed_test_load['avg_d_kbps']+speed_test_load['avg_u_kbps']
```

```
speed_test_load.head(2)
```

	quadkey	avg_d_kbps	avg_u_kbps	avg_lat_ms	tests	devices	newdevices	avg_usedbandwidth
0	0022133222330013	85	103	72	1	1	2	188
1	0022133222330201	14947	20624	70	1	1	2	35571

Figure 3.67: Redshift integration – transforming data before loading it into Redshift

After the transformations are complete, load the data into a Redshift table. The record set has 100,000 records, and we will use the `copy` function and validate the total time for loading to complete.

```
%%time
#Path variable here is the S3 staging path for loading to Redshift
wr.redshift.copy(df=speed_test_load, path="s3://                    /awswrangler/data-staging/",
                 con=con,schema="public", table="speed_test_uc2",mode="overwrite",
                 iam_role="arn:aws:iam::473373155991:role/RedshiftImmersionRole")
```

```
CPU times: user 3.31 s, sys: 318 ms, total: 3.63 s
Wall time: 8.48 s
```

Figure 3.68: Redshift integration – loading data into Redshift from S3 using the COPY command

We can verify the staging file getting created in the S3 path provided in the aforementioned `copy` command. To be clear, we ran this statement twice, and it took 15 seconds during the first run and 8 seconds during the second run. So, the load time depends on multiple factors, including bandwidth and the capacity available at that time.

Users can query the data from Redshift and validate the new table to ensure that the changes made are loaded into it.

avg_lat_ms	tests	devices	newdevices	avg_usedbandwidth
22	1	1	2	400783
29	5	3	4	69938
31	2	1	2	5879

Figure 3.69: Redshift integration – the query loaded data from Redshift

As a part of this use case, we will also explore the `to_sql` function to write data into Redshift, but this will use `INSERT` statements to load the data and is not as performant as the `copy` command. However, this method won't have the overhead of storing data in the S3 staging path.

```
6]: %%time
#Use case - Load S3 files into Pandas, make some changes and load it to Redshift using insert command directly
speed_test=wr.redshift.to_sql(df=speed_test_load,con=con,schema="public",table="speed_test_uc3")

CPU times: user 1min 28s, sys: 3.19 s, total: 1min 32s
Wall time: 18min 34s
```

Figure 3.70: Redshift integration – loading data into Redshift using the to_sql function

You can see that this takes 18 minutes, which is much higher than the first two methodologies. Of course, this time depends on multiple factors, but this use case gives you an idea of what happens when the data is smaller, such as reference table loading.

We can further reduce the loading time by using the `chunksize` parameter. By default, `chunksize` is configured for 200 records, so records get loaded in batches of 200. This factor can be increased based on the capacity of the machine on which it's run. The following screenshot shows the execution time with the `chunksize` parameter set to 2000. Still, this option takes more time compared to the `copy` function.

```
%%time
#Use case - Load S3 files into Pandas, make some changes and load it to Redshift using insert command directly
speed_test=wr.redshift.to_sql(df=speed_test_load,con=con,schema="public",table="speed_test_uc3",chunksize=2000)

CPU times: user 1min 4s, sys: 1.63 s, total: 1min 6s
Wall time: 12min 29s
```

Figure 3.71: Redshift integration – loading data into Redshift using the to_sql function and the chunksize parameter

- Reading/exporting data from the data warehouse:
  - **Unloading data into a pandas DataFrame**: There are a couple of options to export data from Redshift. The `unload` method will export data from Redshift to an S3 staging path and then load it into a pandas DataFrame; this is supposed to be a high throughput option with additional IAM permissions to unload data, but it can help with performance on large datasets. For smaller datasets, users can directly load data into a pandas DataFrame using `read_from_sql`.
  - **Unloading files directly to S3**: This method is more efficient if you want to export data from Redshift directly into S3/a data lake without loading data into a pandas DataFrame. This method uses the UNLOAD command to move data from Redshift to S3 quickly.

We will look at a couple of use cases similar to the Redshift data loading scenario to understand this better.

Use case 1: The data from Redshift needs to be exported to an S3 data lake from where it will be shared with external users, with a pre-signed URL that expires in a week:

```
%%time
#select query helps you remove certain columns or make changes as necessary
wr.redshift.unload_to_files(sql="select * from public.speed_test",
                            path="s3://                    /awswrangler/data-staging/rsexport/",
                            con=con,
                            iam_role="arn:aws:iam::473373155991:role/RedshiftImmersionRole")

CPU times: user 11.4 ms, sys: 255 µs, total: 11.7 ms
Wall time: 4.73 s
```

Figure 3.72: Redshift integration – exporting data from Redshift using the unload function

The data will be loaded in the configured S3 path, and you can use the S3 Select functionality in the AWS console to verify that the data has populated as expected. Also, you can see there are multiple Parquet files available in the S3 path because the UNLOAD command exports data from Redshift in a parallel manner, thus completing the export in a faster time.


```
{
  "quadkey": "0022133222330013",
  "tile": "POLYGON((-160.032348632812 70.6399478155463, -160.02685546875 70.6399478155463, -160.02685546875 70.6381267305321, -1
  "avg_d_kbps": 85,
  "avg_u_kbps": 103,
  "avg_lat_ms": 72,
  "tests": 1,
  "devices": 1
}
```


Figure 3.73: Redshift integration – Redshift data exported in S3 and queried using S3 Select in the AWS console

Use case 2: The data from Redshift is exported to S3 and then transformed before being shared with a specific customer team.

We can use the `unload` command to export files to an S3 staging location and load them into a pandas DataFrame. You can also see the results from the DataFrame printed as follows:

```
%%time
#select query helps you remove certain columns or make changes as necessary
wr.redshift.unload(sql="select * from public.speed_test",
                   path="s3://                /awswrangler/data-staging/rsexport_stg/",
                   con=con,
                   iam_role="arn:aws:iam::473373155991:role/RedshiftImmersionRole")

CPU times: user 13.8 s, sys: 2.01 s, total: 15.8 s
Wall time: 16.3 s
```

	quadkey	tile	avg_d_kbps	avg_u_kbps	avg_lat_ms	tests	devices
0	0022133222330013	POLYGON((-160.032348632812 70.6399478155463, -...	85	103	72	1	1
1	0022133222330201	POLYGON((-160.043334960938 70.6344840663086, -...	14947	20624	70	1	1

Figure 3.74: Redshift integration – exporting data from a pandas DataFrame and an S3 staging location

We can use the `read_from_sql` function to directly load data into a pandas DataFrame. We can see in the following figure that the data was loaded much faster with a direct SQL load function. However, this test was done on a `t3.2xlarge` machine, and your response time might vary based on machine capacity and other factors. You can run this test for your specific workloads and use either `unload` or a direct SQL export as necessary:

```
%%time
#select query helps you remove certain columns or make changes as necessary
wr.redshift.read_sql_query(sql="select * from public.speed_test", con=con)

CPU times: user 1.2 s, sys: 37.9 ms, total: 1.24 s
Wall time: 5.27 s
```

	quadkey	tile	avg_d_kbps	avg_u_kbps	avg_lat_ms	tests	devices
0	0212320201112030	POLYGON((-123.123779296875 44.0481157308235, -...	17609	5433	51	8	4
1	0212320201112032	POLYGON((-123.123779296875 44.0441673535722, -...	20644	10528	47	8	3
2	0212320201112033	POLYGON((-123.118286132812 44.0441673535722, -...	89217	16508	38	7	4
3	0212320201112100	POLYGON((-123.11279296875 44.0560116957853, -1...	309396	28648	26	14	8

Figure 3.75: Redshift integration – exporting data from the pandas DataFrame directly

The takeaway here is that writing to S3 is a parallel activity, but it creates an additional step before loading data into a pandas DataFrame. You should evaluate the different export options based on the use case, compute/storage capacity, and the size of the exported data.

The following table will give you a high-level idea of using different functions to load and unload data from Redshift using `redshift-connector`:

	Load from pandas DataFrame	Load from S3 storage	Export to pandas DataFrame	Export to S3 storage
Redshift data < 1K records	`to_sql` function	`copy_from_files`	`read_from_sql`	`unload_to_files`
Redshift data > 1K records	`copy` function	`copy_from_files`	`unload` or `read_from_sql`	`unload_to_files`

Table 3.1: Functions for RedShift

In addition to using the preceding `redshift-connector` method, we can also use the Redshift DataAPI to connect with Redshift and execute our queries through `awswrangler`.

Challenge

You can use Redshift Upsert mode to update existing records and insert new records, similar to how we did it in RDS. This will help you to use `awswrangler` in your data pipeline to load data into Redshift on a scheduled frequency.

Summary

In this chapter, we learned how to use AWS SDK for pandas (aka `awswrangler`). We explored various components available in the `awswrangler` library and how it brings pandas DataFrames closer to the AWS ecosystem. We learned how to customize and install the library for different use cases and development environments. We also looked at `awswrangler` integration with AWS services, such as Amazon S3, Amazon RDS, Amazon Redshift, and Amazon Athena, and the different features available within `awswrangler`.

In the next chapter, we will learn about SageMaker Data Wrangler, which helps us perform data-wrangling activities as a part of ML pipelines.

4

Introduction to SageMaker Data Wrangler

Data processing is an integral part of **machine learning** (**ML**). In fact, it is not a stretch to say that ML models are only as good as the data that is used to train them. According to a *Forbes* survey from 2016, 80% of the time spent on an ML engineering project is data preparation. That is an astonishingly high percentage of time. Why is that the case? Due to the inherent characteristics of data in the real world, data preparation is both tedious and resource intensive. This real-world data is often referred to as dirty, unclean, noisy, or raw data in ML. In almost all cases, this is the type of data you begin your ML process with. Even in rare scenarios where you think you have good data, you still need to ensure that it is in the right format and scale it to be useful. Applying ML algorithms on this raw data would not give quality results as they would fail to identify patterns, detect anomalies correctly, or generalize well enough outside their development and training environment.

In today's connected and digital world, data is generated more rapidly than it can be consumed and processed. This enormous quantity of data that is being generated can be a real advantage for building ML models for applications that were previously unexplored or thought impossible. However, this also presents a few challenges. Let's look at some of them next.

One of the main challenges is the data quantity. Due to the sheer volume of data that is generated, we need frameworks and tools that can ingest, process, and store the relevant attributes. We need tools that are robust and can scale automatically to meet data ingestion needs. The next challenge is the quality of data. In the real world, data is hardly ever perfect; you have to deal with challenges such as inaccuracies, inconsistencies, missing data, and multiple data formats, to name a few. Here, we need tools that can prepare and clean this data so that it can be used as input to our ML pipelines. Since a lot of this data cleaning is repeatable and time-consuming, these tools should natively support reusability so that data processing practitioners can operate with this effectively with the least amount of friction possible. Data practitioners seldom work in silos. They are usually part of a larger team within the organization and will often need to collaborate with other cross-functional teams. It is also important that the tools they use for data processing support this collaboration and integrate with the organization's existing tools and repositories.

In recent years, we have made a deliberate effort to build responsible ML models—models that are fair and free from biases. This is a hard problem to solve. One primary reason why this is hard with real-world data is the inherent bias that can be present in such data. These biases can be in the form of imbalance or underrepresentation of a certain class. Bias can also creep in due to the selection of specific data sources. In addition, there may be historical biases in certain datasets that make their way into your ML data. Detecting bias is also hard because it is not always visible with standard data visualization and profiling tools. You often need to calculate additional metrics to dig out these hidden biases. This, again, can be both tedious and time-consuming if done manually. Even if scripted or programmed, they can be error-prone. If these biases are left undetected and not corrected, they can directly be transferred to the ML models that are trained on this data, thereby resulting in real-world ML models that are biased. While it is important to understand that in data science there exist scenarios where biases are indeed needed for our ML models to be able to generalize well in the real world, it is beyond the scope of this book to cover that. For now, we will assume bias in data is something that we need to detect and correct as part of data preparation. As such, our data preparation and processing tools for ML must be able to detect and fix these biases in raw data natively. Data preparation for ML involves multiple steps such as data transformation, feature engineering, and data visualization and validation. Data preparation for ML encompasses everything that is needed to get the data in a format that can be used for training ML models. More specifically, data preparation includes data preprocessing and feature engineering. While standalone data preparation tools have grown in adoption, data preparation remains tedious, time-consuming, and complex. Most of these tools often lack an integrated framework, which is essential for building ML pipelines. The ability to have data preparation integrated with ML pipelines ensures that these are repeatable, reusable, and deployable. This further enables ML engineers to build an **ML operations** (**MLOps**) pipeline.

As you saw in earlier chapters, **Amazon Web Services** (**AWS**) offers various purpose-built tools for data processing such as Glue and **Elastic MapReduce** (**EMR**). While all the tools we have covered so far can be used for ML, in this chapter, we will cover an introduction to SageMaker Data Wrangler, which is a purpose-built tool for ML. SageMaker Data Wrangler is a data processing tool that enables data scientists to import, transform, and analyze data specifically for ML. SageMaker Data Wrangler has over 300 built-in transformations that are commonly used for processing data for ML. With SageMaker Data Wrangler, data scientists can create automated data orchestration workflows and generate insights into data quality. Using Data Wrangler, you can easily take your experiment code into production. Without manually sifting through and translating hundreds of lines of data preparation and ingestion code, you can export your prepared data directly import data from multiple data sources, such as **Amazon Simple Storage Service** (**Amazon S3**), Amazon Athena, Amazon Redshift, Snowflake, and Databricks, and process your data with over 300 built-in data transformations and a library of code snippets so that you can quickly normalize, transform, and combine features without writing any code. You can also bring your custom transformations in PySpark, **Structured Query Language** (**SQL**), or pandas. In fact, you do not need to import your dataset at all to begin exploring Data Wrangler. A recently released feature for Data Wrangler enables you to start experimenting with Data Wrangler even faster by using a sample dataset and following suggested actions to easily navigate the product for the first time. Once you have processed the raw data, you can export it directly to S3 or directly to a feature store such as SageMaker Feature Store.

Data Wrangler supports additional integrations, allowing you to integrate with other data stores such as Snowflake, thereby enabling data scientists to accomplish data preparation, cleaning, and feature engineering tasks with less effort and time. In addition to directly exporting processed data, you can also export all your data preparation workflow directly to a notebook with a single click to easily bring it into production. This ability to export your entire data processing flow as code is extremely useful when integrating data processing with multiple workflow automation and orchestration tools such as Apache Airflow, SageMaker Pipelines, and AWS Step Functions, among others. In other words, SageMaker Data Wrangler can reduce the time it takes to aggregate and prepare data for ML and directly empower data scientists to spend more time creating ML models. Overall, Data Wrangler not only gives you a powerful set of data visualizations and data transformations, but it also gives you the capability to productionize your workflows very quickly. As the name suggests, Amazon SageMaker Data Wrangler is a feature within Amazon SageMaker Studio. For the sake of clarity, there used to exist an open source version of Data Wrangler outside SageMaker Studio, which has now been renamed AWS SDK for pandas. Amazon SageMaker Studio is a web-based **integrated development environment (IDE)** for ML. SageMaker Studio provides all the tools needed for a data scientist to build, train, and deploy ML models. SageMaker Studio has a number of features to do bias detection, data processing, **automated ML (AutoML)**, ML training, model deployments, and MLOps. As such, to use SageMaker Data Wrangler from SageMaker Studio, you must first ensure that you have set up Amazon SageMaker Studio. While a detailed overview of all the features offered with SageMaker Studio is out of the scope of this book, we have included a *SageMaker Studio setup prerequisites* section at the end of this chapter to enable you to set up and get started with SageMaker Data Wrangler quickly. As of the writing of this book, SageMaker Data Wrangler works with tabular and time series data. In summary, Amazon SageMaker Data Wrangler is a feature of Amazon SageMaker that makes it faster for data scientists and engineers to prepare data for ML applications via a visual interface. Data Wrangler reduces the time it takes to aggregate and prepare data for ML from weeks to minutes. SageMaker Data Wrangler's core functionalities include correcting data issues such as data imbalances and missing data, as well as transforming the data specifically for ML. In the following section, we will cover some of the core capabilities of SageMaker Data Wrangler.

Data import

Before you start to process your data using SageMaker Data Wrangler, you first need to import data into Data Wrangler. Using Data Wrangler, you can connect and import data from a variety of data stores. When you start Data Wrangler for the first time, the first screen you get asks whether you want to import data or use a sample dataset:

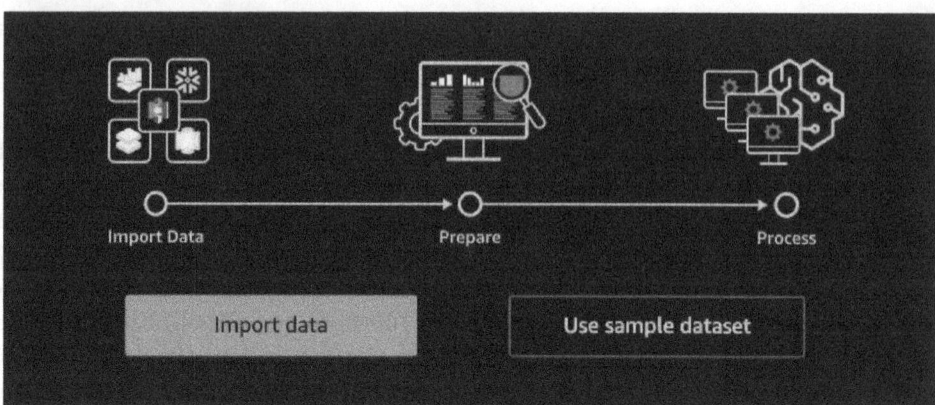

Figure 4.1 – Data Wrangler import

Amazon S3 is an object-based data store that has quickly become the de facto storage of the internet. Due to its low cost per GB and high levels of reliability, you can store and retrieve any amount of data, at any time, from anywhere on the web using Amazon S3. You can upload and access data both using the console or programmatically using APIs, which is also the most common way to work with data in Amazon S3. Amazon S3 implements bucket and object architecture. You can think of a bucket as a folder and objects as files that are logically stored inside the bucket. SageMaker Data Wrangler supports a native connection to Amazon S3. When you connect Data Wrangler to your data in Amazon S3, it uses S3 Select to query and preview your data before actually importing it. This enables data science practitioners to get a profile of the data including its features to make sure everything looks okay to proceed with data processing. S3 Select is also very fast; in fact, it is designed to increase query performance by up to 400% and reduce querying costs by as much as 80%. It works by retrieving a subset of an object's data (using simple SQL expressions) instead of the entire object, which can be up to 5 TB in size. When importing data from Amazon S3, you can either choose to import a single file or multiple files from the same bucket. You can also choose to import the entire file or a portion as a sample. However, when working with multiple files, you need to ensure that the files must be in the same folder within your S3 bucket *AND* must share the same header or have no header. Supported file formats include **JavaScript Object Notation** (**JSON**), **comma-separated values** (**CSV**), Parquet, and **Optimized Row Columnar** (**ORC**). In addition to Amazon S3, Data Wrangler also supports a native connection to **Amazon Athena** for importing data. Amazon Athena is a serverless interactive query service that makes it easy to analyze data directly in Amazon S3 using standard SQL. In Athena, tables and databases are containers for the metadata definitions that define a schema for underlying source data. For each dataset, a table needs to exist in Athena. Databases are a logical grouping of tables and also hold only metadata and schema information for a dataset. Using Data Wrangler, you can query Athena databases and import the results in Data Wrangler. Similar to Amazon S3, when importing data from Athena, you can import either the entire dataset or a portion of the dataset as a sample. Large enterprises will often have a data warehouse setup. Data Wrangler supports native integrations to data warehouse services such as **Amazon Redshift** and **Snowflake**. Amazon Redshift is a fully managed, PB-scale data warehouse service in the cloud. You can connect to and query one or more Amazon Redshift clusters in Data Wrangler. Additionally, Data Wrangler offers seamless integration with Snowflake, allowing you to effortlessly prepare data stored in Snowflake for ML tasks. With a simple and intuitive interface, you can establish a direct connection to Snowflake without the need for any coding. Moreover, Data Wrangler facilitates data integration by enabling you to combine your Snowflake data with information residing in Amazon S3, as well as data extracted through Amazon Athena and Amazon Redshift. If you prefer to utilize Databricks as your data source, Data Wrangler supports connection to this data processing service as well. By leveraging the **Java Database Connectivity** (**JDBC**) import functionality, you can import datasets from your Databricks database. Once connected, you can specify a SQL query to extract the required data and seamlessly import it into Data Wrangler for further processing.

Data orchestration

Data orchestration can be defined as the process of combining data from various sources, including the steps to import, transform, and load it to the destination data source, with the fundamental principle being the ability to automate all the steps involved in the data preparation steps in a repeatable and reusable form, which can then be integrated with the overall ML pipelines. While data orchestration can be used in a wider context that can also include resource provisioning, scaling, and monitoring, the core of data orchestration is creating and automation data workflows, and this is where we will focus for the remainder of the book. The other heavy-lifting tasks of provisioning, scaling, and monitoring are taken care of by AWS. SageMaker Data Wrangler uses a data flow to connect the datasets and perform transformation and analysis steps. This data flow can be used to define your data pipeline and consists of all the steps that are involved in data preparation. When you create a data flow in Data Wrangler, it automatically provisions the resources needed to run your analysis and transformations that you will define inside your flow. While there is a default option, you also have the flexibility of choosing a supported instance type based on your specific data preparation needs. Data flow creation in SageMaker Data Wrangler is GUI based. When you first import your data (or use a sample dataset), Data Wrangler automatically infers the data types of the columns in your data source and creates a new data frame. Both the data source and the data frame appear in the data flow UI of Data Wrangler. Data Wrangler allows you to easily add additional steps to your data pipeline using the data flow UI. Data Wrangler steps can be categorized as transform, analysis, join, and concatenate. A transform step—as the name indicates—consists of applying transformations to your data. A join step includes a join operation with another dataset. A concatenate step, on the other hand, includes a concatenate operation with another dataset. You can use the analysis step to add ad hoc analysis that may be helpful with your data preparation. Spending time on data preparation early in the ML life cycle can significantly improve the model performance and also significantly reduce training time and cost. In most real-life scenarios, data preparation is iterative and includes multiple passes; as such, you will end up doing multiple transformations on the same dataset, and these will appear stacked in the data flow UI. All the steps in your data flow can be updated or deleted directly from the data flow UI (shown in *Figure 4.2*) or the table UI:

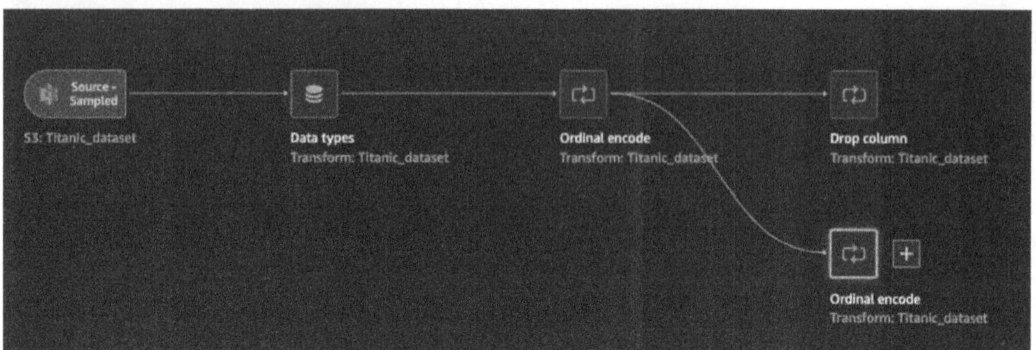

Figure 4.2 – Data Wrangler data flow UI

We will go through the details of a data flow in the next chapter, where we will cover a step-by-step example of creating a data flow. All the steps in your data flow can be saved and exported as a file with the `.flow` extension. This enables the process to be repeatable, version controlled, and integrated with the overall ML pipeline. Additionally, you can also use AWS services such as Amazon EventBridge and AWS Lambda to schedule automatic runs of these data flows. Finally, since this orchestration is logically separated from compute and storage, you can optimize resource utilization by turning off instances when not in use and still retain all the steps in the flow that can be executed as needed.

Data transformation

Data processing for ML primarily includes data transformation. At its core, SageMaker Data Wrangler includes over 300 built-in transformations that are commonly used for cleaning, transforming, and featurizing your data specifically for data science and ML. Using these built-in transformations, you can transform columns within your dataset without having to write any code. In addition to these built-in transformations, you can add custom transformations using PySpark, Python, pandas, and PySpark SQL. Some of these transformations operate in place, while others create a new output column in your dataset. Whenever you incorporate a transform into your data flow, it introduces a new step in the process. Each added transform modifies your dataset and generates a fresh data frame as a result. Subsequently, any subsequent transforms you apply will be performed on this updated data frame. In the real world, datasets are often imbalanced. This imbalance can be in the form of an underrepresented class or sometimes even a complete absence due to sampling errors. Needless to say, this is one of the starting issues that must be tackled in data processing and can also be time-consuming to detect and fix. SageMaker Data Wrangler includes a balance data operation that enables data practitioners to quickly balance imported datasets. The balance operation within Data Wrangler enables standard data balance operations. These include the following:

- **Random oversampling**: This operation randomly duplicates instances from the minority class
- **Random undersampling**: Similar to random oversampling, this operation randomly removes samples from the overrepresented class
- **Synthetic Minority Oversampling Technique** (**SMOTE**): SMOTE utilizes samples from the underrepresented category to interpolate new synthetic minority samples

In addition to the built-in one-click transforms, Data Wrangler also supports custom transforms. Custom transforms enable data scientists to work with packages and frameworks that they are already familiar with to write custom transform operations. These include the use of defined functions via Python, PySpark, PySpark (SQL), or pandas. Data Wrangler also allows you to use popular libraries by importing them in the custom code block of the custom transform operation. There are, however, some restrictions using custom transform operations, which we will cover in depth in the next chapter. You can also implement custom formulas via PySpark SQL to generate new columns or features for your dataset. As we briefly looked at in the *Data orchestration* section, SageMaker Data Wrangler data transformations also support standard join and concatenation operations. SageMaker Data Wrangler also works with non-numeric data. It includes built-in transforms for one-hot encoding, categorial encoding, and similarity encoding, among others. In addition, depending on the type of data science or ML problem at hand, it might be useful to featurize text. Data Wrangler transforms include capabilities to vectorize text data—that is, create meaningful numeric embeddings from text data in the form of vectors, which can then be used to perform numeric operations. Another commonly seen data type in ML is time series data. This is data that is indexed to a specific time. SageMaker Data Wrangler transforms include a number of options to work with time series data. This includes commonly used operations such as grouping time series data, handling missing values within time series data, extracting features from time series data, and using rolling windows within time series data. The following screenshot shows the built-in transformations available in Data Wrangler:

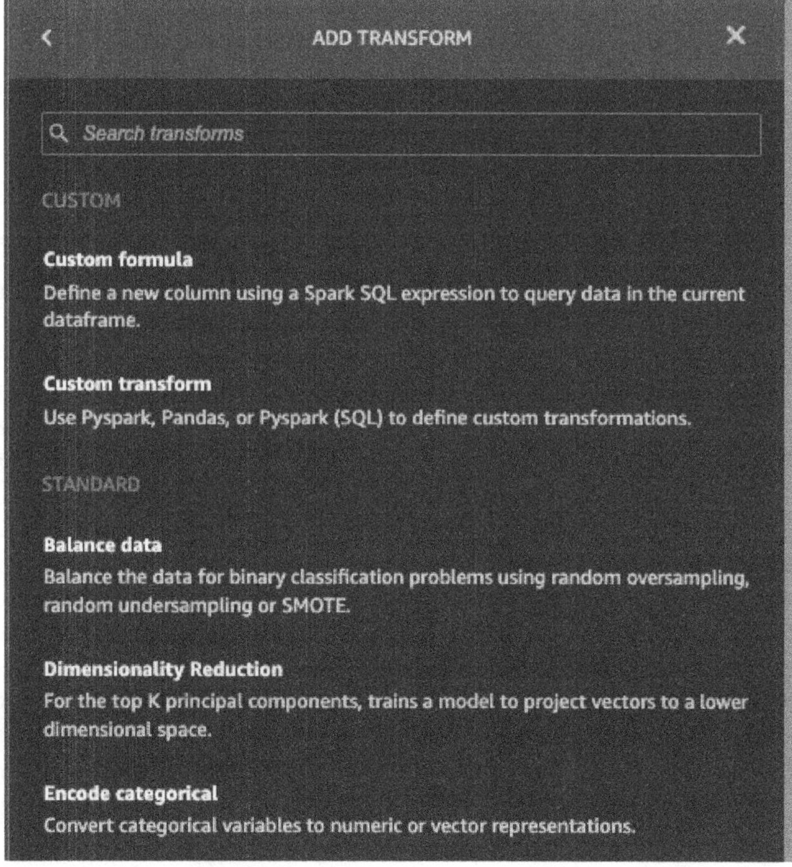

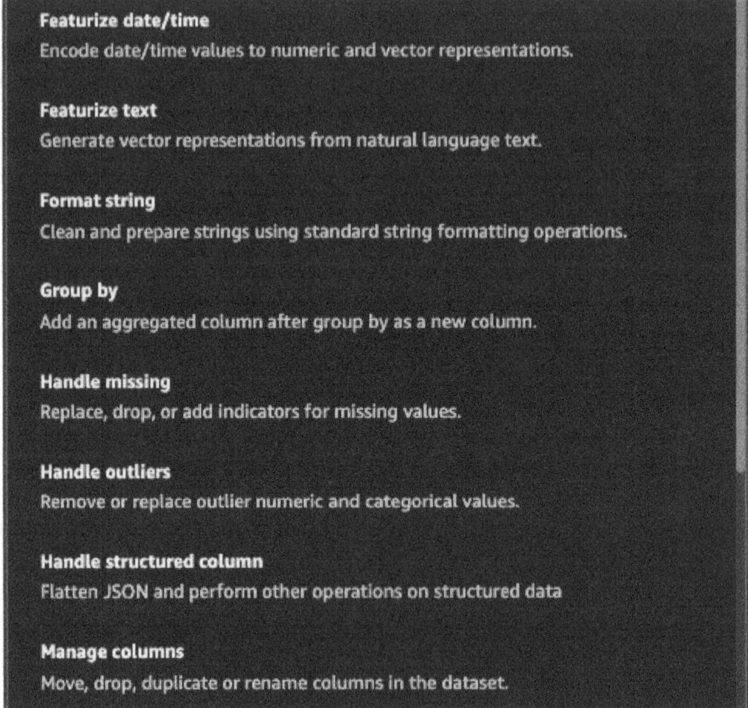

Figure 4.3 – Data Wrangler built-in transformations

Insights and data quality

Generating insight reports on data and quality is part of data profiling. Data profiling is a broader term that includes all the processes involved in reviewing the data source, understanding the structure and composition of data, generating useful summaries and statistics from the data, and studying any inherent relationships that exist between various features in the dataset. Before you even begin to take steps to process your data, you must first understand the state of your data. As such, data profiling is most often one of the first steps done after the data is imported into Data Wrangler. Data Wrangler provides a built-in feature to generate an insight report on data and quality. This report works either on the entire dataset that you import into Data Wrangler or on the sample if you sampled the data after importing data into Data Wrangler. The report gives you a quick insight into common data issues such as imbalances in the data, target leakage, and so on. You can also find out additional information about your data, such as missing values, outliers, and other descriptive statistics. In addition to the report being available for viewing online, the generated report can be downloaded for offline viewing and sharing. The summary section of the report provides a concise overview of the data, encompassing various aspects such as missing values, invalid values, feature types, outlier counts, and more. Additionally, it may highlight high-severity warnings that indicate potential issues within the dataset. While generating the report, you can optionally choose a target column. Once a target column is selected in Data Wrangler, it automatically generates a corresponding target column analysis. Additionally, Data Wrangler arranges the features in descending order based on their predictive strength. When choosing a target column, it is necessary to specify whether you are addressing a regression or a classification problem. Data Wrangler also provides additional insights on your samples, such as if they contain duplicates or anomalous records. While some duplicate data might be valid, it is often a result of errors in data collection or sampling. You can manage duplicate data using the **Drop duplicates** option. Anomalous records are identified by Data Wrangler using an isolation forest algorithm. This associates an anomaly score with each record of the dataset. One of the most interesting and often useful features of the insight report is **Quick Model**. Data Wrangler creates a quick model on a sample of your data, which provides an estimate of the expected predicted quality of a model that you train on your data. For the quick model, Data Wrangler trains an XGBoost model on the sample of your data with the default hyperparameters. It automatically splits the sample into training and test sets before training the quick model. It does minimal automatic data preprocessing, and an early stopping is applied on the training for efficiency. A summary of the model performance is generated with metrics such as accuracy, F1, R2, **Root Mean Squared Error** (**RMSE**), and so on, depending on whether you choose a regression or a classification problem. For example, if you choose a classification problem, a confusion matrix is generated along with the summary, as shown here:

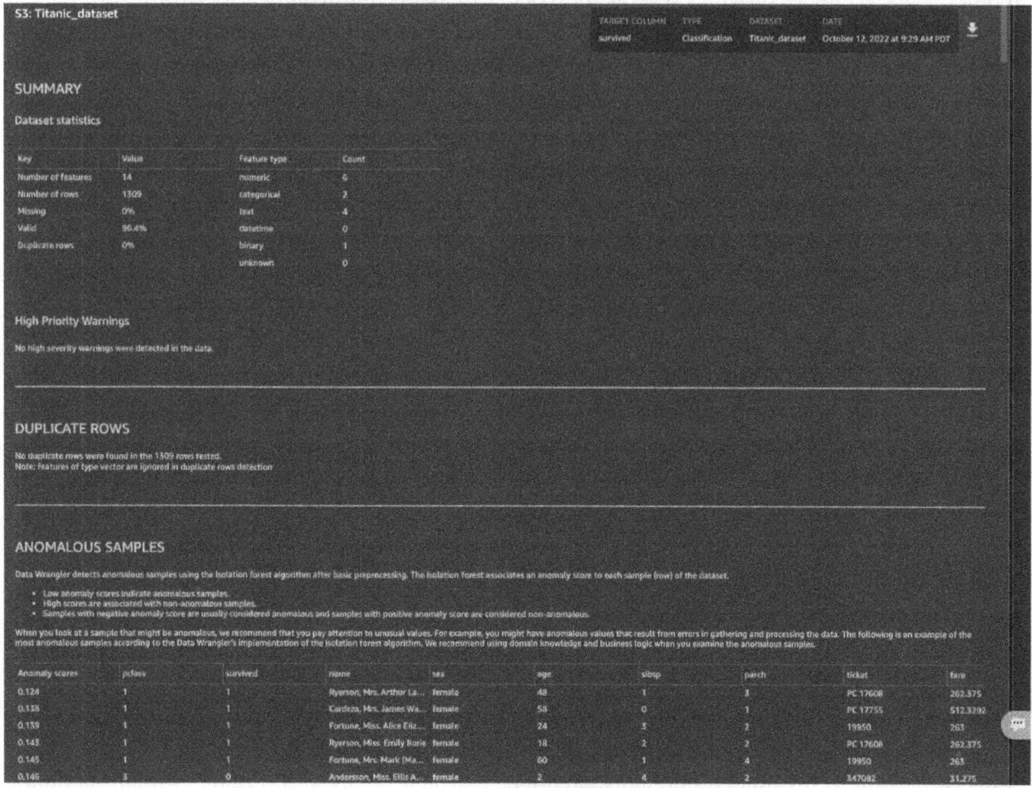

Figure 4.4 – Data insight report

Data analysis

Closely related to generating insights on data and quality is the ability to quickly analyze the imported data. Data analysis is part of the data profiling phase and lets you get a better understanding of the data before you can move to processing your data for ML. SageMaker Data Wrangler includes built-in analyses that help you generate visualizations and data analyses in a few clicks. In addition, you can also create your own custom analysis using custom code. Using data visualizations, you can get a quick overview of your entire dataset. It provides an accessible way to see and understand trends, outliers, and patterns in data. Data Wrangler provides out-of-the-box analysis tools, including histograms and scatter plots. You can create these visualizations with a few clicks and customize them with your own code. In addition to the visualizations, under analysis, you can also create table summaries. Table summaries enable data practitioners to quickly summarize your data and can contain important characteristics of the data, such as the number of records, and descriptive statistics such as mean and standard deviation. Data Wrangler also includes analysis specifically for data science and ML. One of them is for detecting multicollinearity in data. Multicollinearity refers to a situation where there is a correlation between two or more predictor variables. These predictor variables represent the features within your dataset that are utilized to predict a target variable. In the presence of multicollinearity, the predictor variables exhibit not only predictiveness toward the target variable but also toward each other. Data Wrangler provides several approaches to assess multicollinearity within your data, including the **Variance Inflation Factor** (**VIF**), **Principal Component Analysis** (**PCA**), and **Lasso feature selection**. The VIF quantifies how much the variance of the estimated regression coefficients is inflated if your predictors are correlated. A high VIF indicates that the associated predictor has a strong correlation with other predictors, which can compromise the reliability of the regression model. PCA is commonly used for dimensionality reduction in ML, allowing for easier data visualization and noise reduction, thereby resulting in the avoidance of correlated features. Similarly, Lasso feature selection can reduce the coefficient of less important features to zero, effectively eliminating them from the model. This helps in reducing model complexity and preventing overfitting. These measures assist in identifying and quantifying the degree of multicollinearity present in your dataset. We will look at these techniques in more detail in the next chapter. Detecting anomalies in time series data is another analysis provided by Data Wrangler that is commonly used when working with such data. Time series data can include trends and seasonality. A trend is a long-term change (increase or decrease) in the data. This can be linear or exponential and sometimes can also change in direction. Seasonality, on the other hand, is a repeating cycle in the series with fixed frequencies. Data Wrangler employs a decomposition technique to analyze time series data, separating it into a predicted term and an error term. The predicted term captures the seasonality and trend of the time series, while the residuals represent the error term. Within the error term, you have the flexibility to define a threshold, indicating the number of standard deviations the residual can deviate from the mean to be identified as an anomaly. Additionally, Data Wrangler offers the capability to decompose the seasonal trend within time series data. By utilizing the Seasonal-Trend decomposition visualization, you can determine the presence of seasonality in your time series data. The decomposition process employed by Data Wrangler leverages the **Seasonal-Trend decomposition using LOESS** (**STL**) method to separate the time series into its distinct components—namely, seasonal, trend, and residual. Providing data scientists and data practitioners the ability to generate these quickly without the need of having to write any code significantly improves the data processing workflow and makes it more efficient. The following screenshot shows the feature correlation report for our dataset:

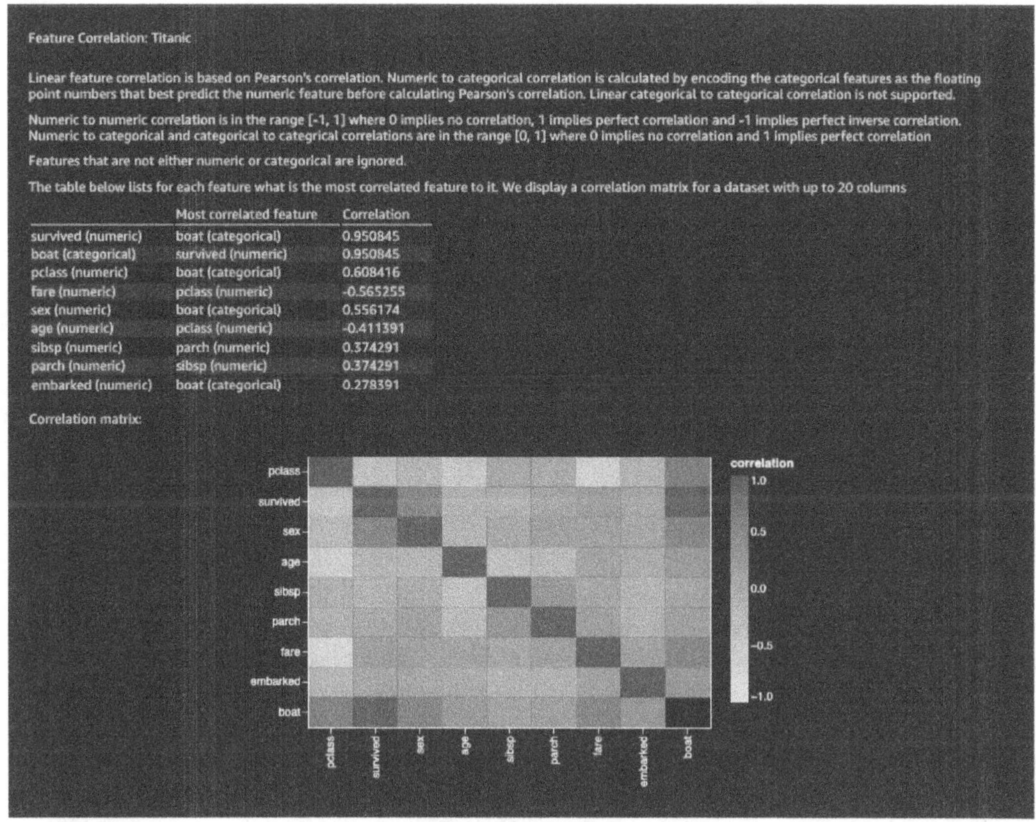

Figure 4.5 – Data analysis report: feature correlation

Data export

So far, we've looked at Data Wrangler capabilities that enable you to import data into Data Wrangler and perform analysis and transformations. SageMaker Data Wrangler enables you to export all or part of these transformations as a data flow. In most cases, data processing consists of a series of transformations. Each of these transformations can be referred to as a step in Data Wrangler. A Data Wrangler flow is made up of a series of nodes that represent the import of your data and the transformations that you've performed. As we covered earlier, one of the first steps in Data Wrangler is to import data from a supported data source. As such, the data source is the first node in your data flow. Following the previous step, the next node in the data flow is the Data Types node. This node signifies that Data Wrangler has executed a transformation to convert the dataset into a format that is suitable for further analysis and processing. Each transformation that is added to the data flow is represented as a new node, enabling a visual representation of the sequence of operations performed on the dataset. Think of this data flow as a code file that includes all the code and sequences of your data transformations. Data Wrangler supports exporting these transformations to multiple supported destinations and formats that include Amazon S3, SageMaker Pipelines, SageMaker Feature Store, and as standard Python code. In the case of S3, Data Wrangler allows you to export your processed data to a bucket location in S3. You can specify this S3 location as a destination node or use the **Export** option to export the processed data or transformation results to S3. In addition to the exported data, the flow itself is saved to the S3 bucket location. When you choose S3 as the destination, you do that by adding a destination node, which is the S3 bucket location. Data Wrangler allows you to add multiple destination nodes. The export happens using a Data Wrangler job, which behind the scenes is a SageMaker processing job. When you create a Data Wrangler export job, you can specify the number of instances and a supported instance type. Data Wrangler also allows you to export to SageMaker Pipelines, which is a SageMaker feature for building end-to-end ML workflows that take advantage of direct SageMaker integration. You can export your entire flow or some of the steps from your data flow to SageMaker Pipelines. Data Wrangler will create a Jupyter notebook that you can use to define, instantiate, run, and manage a pipeline. Feature stores have gained prominence in ML. Features are specific columns in your dataset. A feature store contains processed data along with some associated metadata and acts as a central repository for all the processed data or features that can be used by various data science teams within their ML workflows. Data Wrangler enables you to export features you've created to Amazon SageMaker Feature Store, which is another SageMaker service to store and discover features. Using Data Wrangler, you can either update existing feature groups or create completely new feature groups in SageMaker Feature Store. You can use either a Jupyter notebook or a destination node to update your feature group with the observations in the dataset or create a feature group in Feature Store. Finally, you can also export all the transformations in your data flow as Python code that you can integrate with any data processing workflow. Since the exported code will have references to SageMaker and AWS resources, you will need to make sure that the environment or workflow with which you integrate has access to the AWS resources referenced.

SageMaker Studio setup prerequisites

SageMaker Data Wrangler is available as a service within Amazon SageMaker Studio. While you can still use some of the SageMaker Data Wrangler features via APIs, for the purposes of this book, we will be using Data Wrangler from within SageMaker Studio. In this section, we will cover a brief overview of SageMaker Studio and how to set up a SageMaker Studio domain and users in your AWS account.

Prerequisites

Before we can start setting up SageMaker Studio, there are a few prerequisites, as follows:

- An AWS account.

- An **Identity and Access Management** (**IAM**) role with the appropriate policy and permissions attached. There is an `AmazonSageMakerFullAccess` AWS managed policy that you can use as is or as a starting point to create your custom policy.

Studio domain

You will start by creating and onboarding a SageMaker domain using the AWS console. A SageMaker domain includes an **Amazon Elastic File System** (**Amazon EFS**) volume, a list of authorized studio users, and a variety of security, application, policy, and **Amazon Virtual Private Cloud** (**Amazon VPC**) configurations. When you are creating a domain, you can choose how you want to onboard users on the domain. You have two options: use AWS IAM Identity Center (successor to **AWS Single Sign-On**, or **AWS SSO**) or AWS IAM for authentication methods. Choose the IAM Identity Center option if you are integrating SageMaker Studio with an existing SSO or creating a new SSO setup; else, choose the IAM authentication option. It is important to remember that you cannot change this after the domain has been created unless you delete and recreate the domain. When you use IAM authentication, you can choose either the **Quick setup** or the **Standard setup** option for onboarding a domain. For the scope of this book, we will consider IAM authentication with **Quick setup**.

Studio onboarding steps

Let's look at the steps for studio onboarding:

1. Log in to your AWS account and navigate to the SageMaker console.
2. From the **Control panel** option on the left, choose **Studio**, as illustrated here:

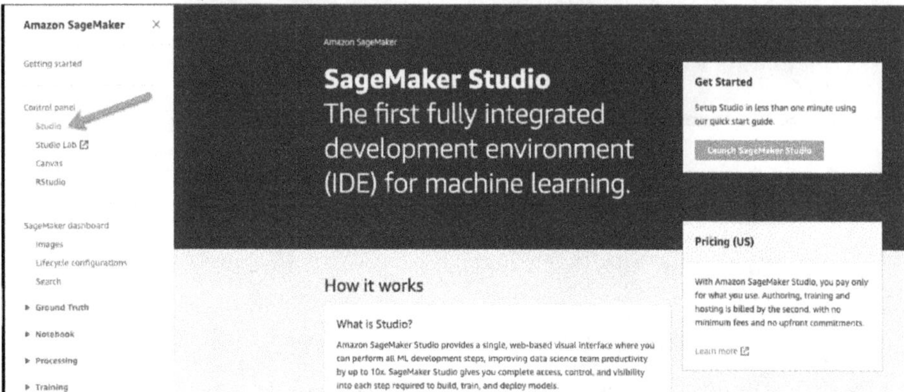

Figure 4.6 – SageMaker console

3. Click on the **Launch SageMaker Studio** button. If this is your first time, you will be taken to the **Setup SageMaker Domain** page with options for **Quick setup** and **Standard setup**:

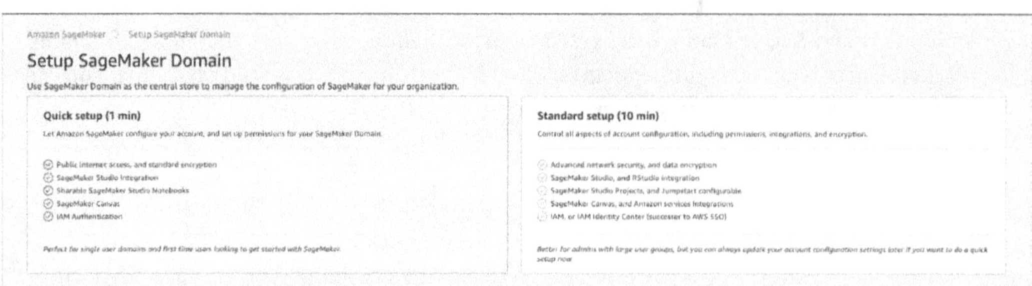

Figure 4.7 – Domain setup options

Quick setup is selected by default. Keep that unchanged.

4. Next, you need to provide a username for the default admin user and choose a default execution role for your domain, as illustrated in the following screenshot. If you do not already have a SageMaker execution role in your account, you can create one using the built-in policy mentioned in the *Prerequisites* section:

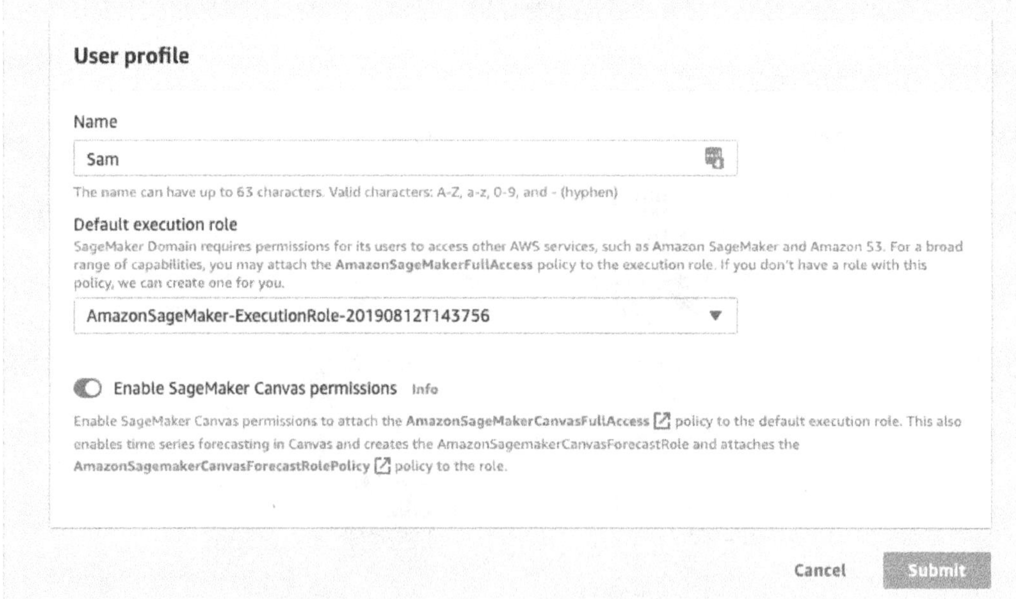

Figure 4.8 – SageMaker Studio execution role

SageMaker Canvas is not in scope for this book. You can either leave the option enabled or disable it here before you proceed.

5. Once you click on **Submit**, the domain creation process is started. Behind the scenes, SageMaker will create a Studio domain for you, provision the AWS services required (such as EFS), and create a default user for the domain. This will take a few minutes, and the domain status will show as **Pending** till it completes:

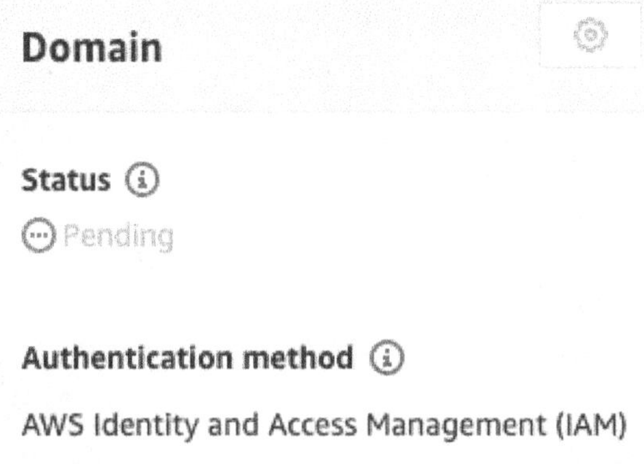

Figure 4.9 – Checking domain creation status

6. After domain creation is complete, the status will change to **Ready**, and you can log in to SageMaker Studio using the default user. To log in, choose **Studio** from the **Launch app** button in the console, as illustrated here:

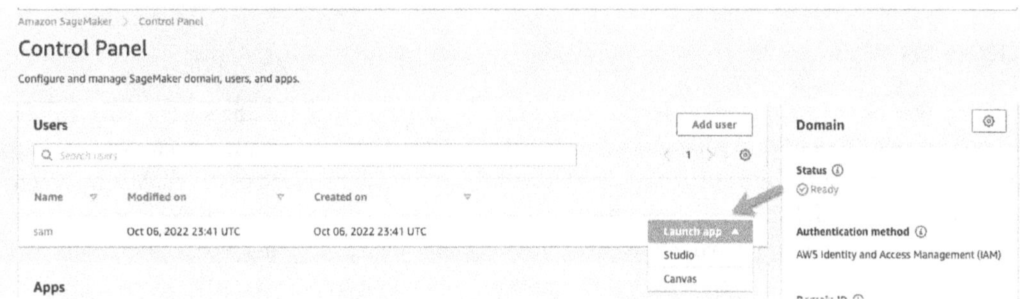

Figure 4.10 – Launching SageMaker Studio

7. The first time logging in to SageMaker Studio takes a few minutes as it needs to provision a default application. Subsequent logins are quicker. Once the application creation is complete and the login is successful, the SageMaker Studio IDE landing page should open:

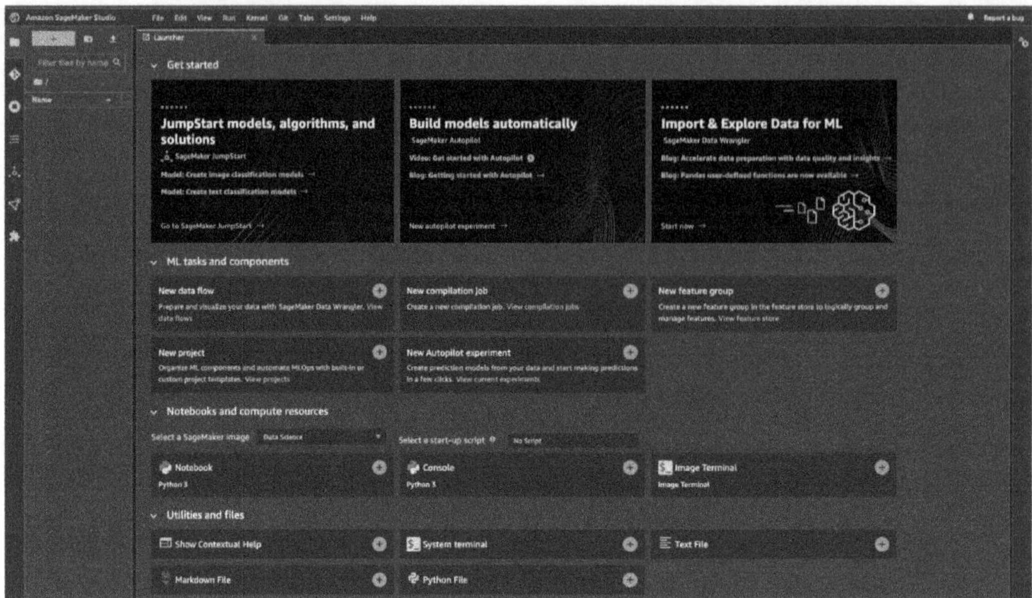

Figure 4.11 – SageMaker Studio IDE

That's it—from here on, you are ready to follow along with all the Data Wrangler examples in the book.

Summary

In this chapter, we covered an introduction to data processing on AWS, specifically focusing on ML and data science. We looked at how data processing for ML is unique and why it is such a critical and significant component of the overall ML workflow. We went through some of the challenges when dealing with large and distributed datasets and data sources and how to work with these at scale. We discussed the importance of having a reliable and repeatable data processing workflow for ML. We then covered some of the key capabilities that are needed in tooling and the frameworks used for data processing for ML, which include the ability to detect bias present in real-world data, the ability to detect and fix data imbalances, the ability to perform quick and error-free transformations and run preprocessing reports and visualizations at scale, as well as the ability to ingest data at scale.

As enterprises move from experimentation and research to production, the focus switches to operations. Here, we covered data processing for ML in the context of operations and, specifically, MLOps. We discussed why it is important for the tools and frameworks to integrate seamlessly with pipelines at the enterprise. Next, we had an introduction to SageMaker Data Wrangler, a SageMaker service that is purpose-built for data processing for ML. We did a detailed walkthrough of the key capabilities of SageMaker Data Wrangler and how they help solve some of the specific data processing challenges that we covered earlier. A data processing tool is only as important as the data source it can support, and we looked at the supported data sources for Data Wrangler, as well as the integration points with other AWS and third-party services. Once the data processing tasks and transformations are done, we discussed how the processed data can be exported. We looked at the various formats in which data can be exported, as well as the various export destinations supported by Data Wrangler. In addition to the processed data, we also need the processing steps and transformations to be consistent and repeatable; here, we looked at how the transformations can be exported in the form of data flows.

SageMaker Data Wrangler is a component of SageMaker Studio. One of the prerequisites for using Data Wrangler is to set up SageMaker Studio. We wrapped up the chapter by going over how to set up a SageMaker Studio domain in your AWS account and how to onboard users and accounts. Data processing is one of the most challenging and time-consuming areas of ML. If done correctly, it can lead to a direct performance gain for your ML models. SageMaker Data Wrangler provides capabilities that enable data scientists and ML practitioners to perform data processing at scale while integrating with the organization's overall ML workflow. The **Quick setup** option uses default settings and allows internet access and shareable notebooks.

Part 3: AWS Data Management and Analysis

In this section, we'll explore essential AWS services for effective data management and analysis. *Chapter 5* introduces Amazon S3, revealing its potential as a robust storage and organization solution for your data. *Chapter 6* dives into AWS Glue, demonstrating how this powerful ETL service automates data preparation and transformation workflows. *Chapter 7* unveils Amazon Athena, a serverless query service enabling valuable insights through SQL queries directly on Amazon S3 data. Finally, *Chapter 8* explores Amazon QuickSight, a fast BI service for creating interactive dashboards and visualizations to gain valuable insights from your data.

This part has the following chapters:

- *Chapter 5, Working with Amazon S3*
- *Chapter 6, Working with AWS Glue*
- *Chapter 7, Working with Athena*
- *Chapter 8, Working with QuickSight*

5
Working with Amazon S3

In previous chapters, we repeatedly discussed the concepts of big data and data lakes and how organizations are using them to store and extract valuable insights from their data through various data wrangling processes, as outlined in *Chapter 1*, using **Amazon Web Services** (**AWS**) services such as AWS Glue DataBrew, the AWS SDK for Pandas, and SageMaker Data Wrangler. This chapter will delve deeper into the specifics of big data and data lakes.

Specifically, we will be covering the following topics:

- The definition and concept of big data
- The characteristics of big data
- The concept and definition of a data lake
- Best practices for building a data lake on **Amazon Simple Storage Service** (**Amazon S3**)
- The layout and organization of data on Amazon S3

We will begin by exploring the definition and characteristics of big data.

What is big data?

Big data refers to extremely large datasets that are too complex and diverse to be processed and analyzed using traditional data management and analytics tools. Big data often comes from multiple sources, such as sensors, social media, and e-commerce platforms, and it may include structured, semi-structured, and unstructured data.

The volume, velocity, and variety of big data present significant challenges for data management and analysis. Traditional data storage and processing systems are not designed to handle such large and complex datasets, and they may not be able to provide the performance, scalability, and flexibility required for big data applications.

To overcome these challenges, organizations have turned to big data technologies, such as Apache Hadoop, Apache Spark, and Apache Flink. These technologies are designed to support the storage, processing, and analysis of big data at scale, and they provide a distributed and parallel architecture that can handle large volumes of data.

Big data technologies have enabled organizations to extract valuable insights and knowledge from their data, and they have become key enablers of data-driven decision-making and innovation processes. For example, big data technologies are used in a wide range of applications, such as fraud detection, recommendation systems, and predictive maintenance.

Despite the many benefits of big data technologies, there are also challenges and limitations to consider. For example, big data systems can be complex and difficult to manage, and they may require specialized skills and expertise. In addition, big data systems may raise privacy and security concerns, and they may require careful management to ensure the integrity and quality of the data.

As we have learned, the term "*big data*" refers to a vast amount of structured, semi-structured, and unstructured data that is typically complex and requires significant computing power to process. However, the definition of big data can be relative and depends on the storage and compute options available.

For example, 1 GB of data may be considered big data for someone who is using Excel to process it, but it may not be for someone using the Apache Spark framework on a laptop with 32 GB of RAM. Similarly, when data grows to 1 TB, it may require external databases and **extract, transform, and load** (**ETL**) tools for processing. But when the data expands to tens of TBs, it may necessitate the use of distributed processing options either on-premises or in the cloud, using storage systems such as **Hadoop Distributed File System** (**HDFS**) and processing frameworks such as Hadoop, or object stores such as Amazon S3 and processing using AWS services such as AWS Glue. However, even with these options, when the data expands to hundreds of TBs, it may be considered big data even for AWS Glue, and it may be expensive to process, reducing its business value and requiring options such as **Amazon Elastic MapReduce** (**Amazon EMR**).

Customers' perspectives of what constitutes big data can also vary; some may consider a few terabytes of data to be big data, while others may consider petabytes or even exabytes of data to be big data. This perspective is also relative in comparison to how large technology companies such as Amazon, Facebook, Google, and Apple store and process data, which can reach multiple petabytes or even exabytes.

According to *Statista*, the world will be creating, capturing, copying, and consuming 181 zettabytes (1 zettabyte = 1,024 exabytes) (`https://www.statista.com/statistics/871513/worldwide-data-created/`) by the year 2025.

Overall, big data is a critical aspect of modern data management and analysis, and it presents both opportunities and challenges for organizations. By leveraging the right tools and technologies, organizations can unlock the value of their data and drive business growth and innovation.

Now we have a fair understanding of big data, let's understand its key characteristics.

5 Vs of big data

The 5 Vs of big data are five key characteristics that define the concept of big data. These characteristics help to understand the nature of big data and how it can be effectively analyzed and used. Let's look at these in more detail, as follows:

- **Volume**: Big data refers to extremely large datasets that are too large to be processed using traditional methods. These datasets can range from a few terabytes to several petabytes in size.

  For example, Twitter alone generates over 500 million tweets per day, which amounts to a large volume of data that must be stored, processed, and analyzed. Another example of big data would be data generated by large e-commerce companies such as Amazon. This data may include customer purchase history, website clickstream data, and customer service interactions. This data can be collected from various sources such as online transactions, mobile apps, social media, emails, and customer service interactions. All of this data can add up to terabytes or even petabytes of data that must be stored, processed, and analyzed in order to gain insights that can be used to improve the customer experience and increase revenue.

- **Variety**: Big data often comes in a variety of formats, including structured, semi-structured, and unstructured data. Structured data is organized in a predictable way, such as in a spreadsheet, while unstructured data is more free-form, such as social media posts or emails. An example of variety in big data would be an e-commerce company such as Amazon collecting data from a variety of sources, such as the following:
  - Structured data from transactional systems such as **point-of-sale** (**POS**) systems, inventory management systems, and **customer relationship management** (**CRM**) systems
  - Semi-structured data such as log files and XML files
  - Unstructured data such as customer reviews, social media posts, and images and videos

- **Velocity**: Big data is generated at an incredibly fast rate, with millions or even billions of data points being generated every second. This high velocity means that traditional methods of data processing and analysis may not be able to keep up with the volume and variety of data being generated.

  For example, a manufacturing company may have hundreds or thousands of sensors on their production line, generating data on machine performance, temperature, vibration, and other parameters. This data must be collected, processed, and analyzed in real time to detect and respond to issues before they cause downtime or quality problems.

- **Veracity**: The quality and accuracy of big data can vary widely. It is important to carefully assess the veracity of big data before using it for decision-making or analysis.

An example of veracity in big data would be a healthcare organization collecting data from **electronic health records** (**EHRs**) and wearable devices. This data may come from different sources and may be incomplete, inconsistent, or biased. For example, patient self-reported data from wearables may not be as accurate as data from clinical measurements. Additionally, EHRs may contain errors or inconsistencies due to manual data entry or different formatting standards. To make sense of this data and use it for decision-making and diagnosis, the organization would need to apply data cleaning, normalization, and validation techniques to ensure the veracity of the data.

Another example of veracity in big data could be a social media platform that is collecting data on users' posts, comments, and likes. The veracity of the data would be questionable, as the users' posts and comments may not be an accurate representation of their thoughts and feelings; they may contain typos, sarcasm, and other forms of figurative language that could be misinterpreted. Additionally, some users may post fake information or false statements, which would make it difficult to trust the data. To address these issues, the platform would need to apply **natural language processing** (**NLP**) and **machine learning** (**ML**) techniques to understand the context of the data and filter out unreliable or fake information.

- **Value**: The value of big data lies in its ability to provide insights and inform decision-making. By analyzing and interpreting large volumes of data, organizations can gain valuable insights that can help drive business strategy and improve operational efficiency.

  An example of value in big data would be a financial services company using data analytics to detect fraudulent activities in real time. The company would collect a large volume of data from various sources such as transactions, customer behavior, and social media. By analyzing this data, the company could identify patterns and anomalies that might indicate fraudulent activities and take action to prevent losses. In this example, the value of the data comes from its ability to detect fraud and protect the company's assets and reputation, which would create overall value for the company and its customers.

In conclusion, the 5 Vs of big data (volume, variety, velocity, veracity, and value) describe the key characteristics of big data and how it can be effectively used to drive business strategy and decision-making.

In this section of the chapter, we learned how customers create data lakes to collect and extract valuable insights from their data. Now, we will delve deeper into understanding the concept of a data lake, the reasons for its necessity, the various layers of a data lake, and the best practices for building one on Amazon S3, but before that, let's understand what a data lake is.

What is a data lake?

A data lake is a centralized repository that allows organizations to store all of their structured and unstructured data at any scale. This approach to data storage and management provides organizations with a single, unified platform for storing and managing data from a variety of different sources, including social media, sensors, and transactional systems.

Data lakes are designed to support the storage of large amounts of data in its raw format, allowing it to be processed and analyzed at a later stage by various teams within the organization. This approach to data storage and management provides organizations with the flexibility to collect and store data from a wide range of sources, without the need to preprocess or structure the data in any specific way.

One of the key benefits of using a data lake is that it allows organizations to store and manage data from a variety of different sources, including both structured and unstructured data. This means that organizations can collect and store data from sources such as social media feeds, sensor data, and transactional systems, and then use this data to gain insights and make data-driven decisions.

Another key benefit of data lakes is that they provide organizations with the flexibility to process and analyze data in a variety of different ways. This is because data in a data lake is stored in its raw format, allowing it to be accessed and analyzed by various teams within the organization, such as data scientists, business analysts, and data engineers.

Let's explore these benefits in detail, as follows:

- **Cost-effective storage**: Data lakes can store large volumes of data at a lower cost than traditional data warehouses. This is because data lakes use commodity hardware and open source technologies, which are generally less expensive than proprietary solutions.
- **Flexibility—schema on read**: Data lakes allow you to store data in its raw, original format, without the need to transform or structure it upfront. This allows you to defer the decision on how to use the data until it is needed, giving you more flexibility in your data management strategy.
- **Scalability—decoupling of storage and compute**: Data lakes are designed to scale horizontally, meaning that you can easily add more storage and processing power as needed. This makes them well suited for handling large volumes of data and sudden spikes in data volume.
- **Integration**: Data lakes can integrate with a wide range of data sources and analytics tools, allowing you to bring together data from multiple sources and perform a variety of analyses on it.
- **Collaboration**: Data lakes allow multiple users and teams to access and analyze data, fostering collaboration and supporting data-driven decision-making.

Overall, data lakes provide organizations with a powerful tool for managing and analyzing large amounts of data from a variety of different sources. By allowing organizations to collect, store, and manage data in its raw format, data lakes provide the flexibility and scalability needed to support a wide range of data-driven applications and use cases.

Building a data lake on Amazon S3

Amazon S3 is a cloud-based storage service that provides scalable, durable, and secure storage for data and media. Amazon S3 is a popular choice for storing and managing data as it offers high performance, reliability, and flexibility.

In this chapter, we will discuss the process of building a data lake on Amazon S3. A data lake is a centralized repository that allows organizations to store all of their structured and unstructured data at any scale. One of the most popular platforms for building a data lake is Amazon S3. Amazon S3 is a highly durable and scalable storage service that makes it easy to store and analyze large amounts of data.

Let's look at the steps involved when building a data lake on Amazon S3:

1. The first step in building a data lake on Amazon S3 is to design the data architecture. This involves identifying the types and sources of data that will be stored in the data lake, as well as the data ingestion, processing, and analysis pipelines that will be used. It is important to consider the performance, scalability, and security requirements of the data lake and to choose the right storage, computing, and networking resources.
2. The next step in building a data lake on Amazon S3 is to prepare and organize the data. This involves cleaning, transforming, and enriching the data to make it suitable for analysis and visualization. It is important to ensure the quality, consistency, and completeness of the data and to apply appropriate metadata, tagging, and cataloging to facilitate data discovery and access.
3. Once the data is prepared and organized, it can be loaded into the data lake on Amazon S3. This can be done using a variety of tools and techniques, such as batch processing, real-time streaming, and bulk import. It is important to choose the right file format and compression method for the data and to apply the right partitioning and indexing strategies to support efficient data storage and querying.
4. After the data is loaded into the data lake on Amazon S3, it can be accessed and queried using a variety of tools and frameworks. This could include **Structured Query Language** (**SQL**)-based query engines such as Amazon Redshift and Amazon Athena, as well as big data frameworks such as Apache Spark and Apache Flink. It is important to choose the right tools and technologies that can support the performance, scalability, and flexibility requirements of the data lake.
5. Finally, the data in the data lake on Amazon S3 can be used for a variety of purposes, such as reporting, analytics, ML, and data visualization. This can be done using a variety of tools and platforms, such as dashboarding and visualization tools, data science notebooks, and analytics and ML platforms. It is important to choose the right tools and technologies that can support the data lake and the intended use cases.

In summary, building a data lake on Amazon S3 requires careful planning, design, and execution. By leveraging the right tools and technologies, organizations can create a scalable, secure, and cost-effective platform for storing, processing, and analyzing large datasets.

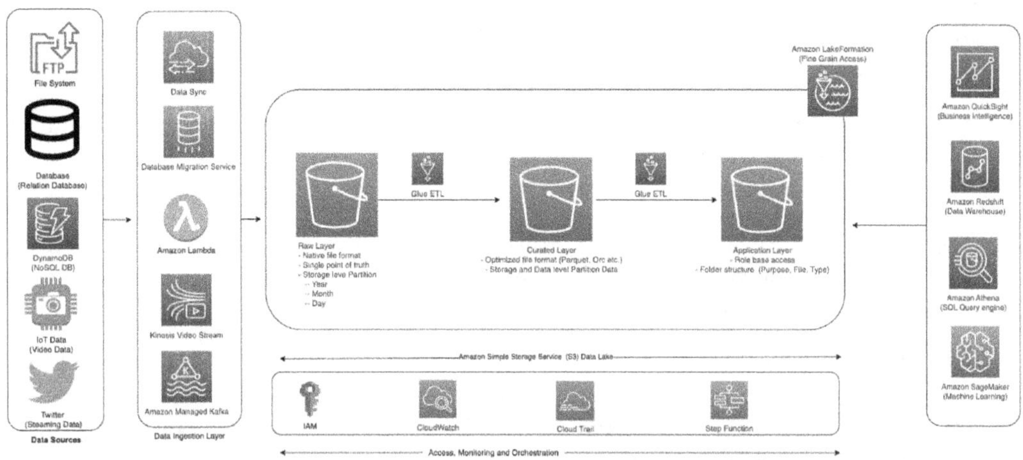

Figure 5.1 – High-level data lake architecture in AWS

Advantages of building a data lake on Amazon S3

In the previous section, you learned how you can build a data lake on Amazon S3, but you must be wondering why you should build a data lake on Amazon S3—that's what we will try to explore in this section.

Here are some key advantages of building a data lake on Amazon S3:

- **Scalability**: Amazon S3 is highly scalable and can handle large amounts of data, making it an ideal option for building a data lake. An example of scalability in Amazon S3 would be a company that starts with a small amount of data and, over time, the volume of data it collects and stores in its data lake increases significantly. With Amazon S3, the company can easily scale its data storage to accommodate this growth in data volume without needing to worry about running out of storage space. For instance, an organization starts with 50 GB of data, and over time, the data volume increases to 100 TB. It can easily scale its data storage in Amazon S3 to handle this increase in data volume, without needing to worry about running out of storage space or having to migrate data to a new storage system.
- **Cost-effective**: Amazon S3 is a cost-effective solution for data storage and allows you to only pay for the storage you use. For example, a company wants to store 1 PB of data in a data lake. If it were to store the data on-premises, it would have to purchase and maintain expensive storage infrastructure, which could be costly. With Amazon S3, the company can store the same amount of data at a lower cost because it only pays for the storage it uses, and it doesn't have to worry about the additional costs associated with maintaining and upgrading storage infrastructure. Additionally, Amazon S3 also offers cost-effective data retrieval options, such as Amazon S3 Select and Amazon S3 Glacier, which allow you to retrieve only the data you need, reducing data retrieval costs.

- **Data security**: Amazon S3 provides robust security features such as encryption, access controls, and compliance with various regulations. Here are some examples:
    - **At-rest encryption**: An organization uses Amazon S3's **Server-Side Encryption** (**SSE**) feature to encrypt all patient data stored in its data lake. This ensures that the data is protected even if the data lake is compromised.
    - **Access control**: An organization uses Amazon S3's access control features, such as bucket policies and **access control lists** (**ACLs**), to restrict access to patient data to only authorized individuals and systems.
    - **Compliance**: An organization uses Amazon S3's compliance features, such as support for the **Health Insurance Portability and Accountability Act** (**HIPAA**) and the **Payment Card Industry Data Security Standard** (**PCI DSS**), to ensure that the data lake meets the regulatory requirements for storing sensitive patient data.
    - **Audit**: An organization uses AWS CloudTrail and AWS Config to log and monitor access to patient data in the data lake. This allows the organization to detect and respond to any unauthorized access to patient data.
- **Flexibility**: Amazon S3 supports multiple data types and formats, allowing you to store structured, semi-structured, and unstructured data in the same data lake. For example, a company collects structured data (such as customer transactions) in a **comma-separated values** (**CSV**) format, semi-structured data (such as social media comments) in **JavaScript Object Notation** (**JSON**) format, and unstructured data (such as website logs) in text format. With Amazon S3, the company can easily store all these types of data in the same data lake without worrying about compatibility issues.
- **Integration with other AWS services**: Amazon S3 can be easily integrated with other AWS services such as Glue, Kinesis, and Redshift for data processing, analysis, and visualization.
- **Data management and governance**: Amazon S3 provides features for data cataloging, metadata management, data lineage, and data governance, which makes it easy to manage and organize large amounts of data.
- **Durability and availability**: Durability and availability are two important concepts in Amazon S3. Durability refers to the ability of Amazon S3 to sustain the loss of data due to hardware failures, while availability refers to the ability of Amazon S3 to provide the stored data to the users when they request it. Durability is measured in terms of the **annual failure rate** (**AFR**)—the percentage of objects that are expected to be lost in a given year. Amazon S3 provides durability of 11 9s, which means that the AFR is 0.000000001, or one in a billion. This high level of durability means that data stored in Amazon S3 is highly unlikely to be lost.

  Availability is measured in terms of the percentage of time that objects are successfully retrievable, and Amazon S3 provides availability of 4 9s, which means that objects are expected to be retrievable 99.99% of the time. This high level of availability means that users can expect to be able to access their data stored in Amazon S3 almost all the time.

- **Easy to access and share**: Amazon S3 allows easy access and sharing of data with different teams and users, which facilitates collaboration and self-service analytics.

Design principles to design a data lake on Amazon S3

Several design principles can be followed when creating a data lake on Amazon S3, as follows:

- **Use a flat file structure**: In a data lake, it is generally recommended to use a flat file structure rather than a hierarchical one. This means that all data is stored at the same level of the filesystem, rather than being organized into subfolders or nested directories. A flat file structure allows for easier and more flexible data access, as data can be easily queried without the need to navigate through a complex directory structure.
- **Use partitioning**: Partitioning is the process of dividing your data into logical sections based on attributes such as date, location, or product. This can help improve the performance and efficiency of your data lake by allowing you to easily access and query specific subsets of data.
- **Use object tagging**: Object tagging allows you to attach metadata to your data in the form of key-value pairs. This metadata can be used to describe the data, classify it, or provide additional context. Object tagging can be useful for organizing and managing large volumes of data in your data lake.
- **Use data governance**: It is important to have proper data governance in place when creating a data lake. This includes defining roles and responsibilities, establishing data policies and standards, and implementing security and compliance controls.
- **Use data management tools**: Data management tools, such as AWS Glue or Amazon EMR, can be useful for organizing, cleansing, and transforming data in your data lake. These tools can also help automate data pipelines and improve the efficiency of data processing.

In conclusion, following these design principles can help you create a well-organized and efficient data lake on Amazon S3. A flat file structure, partitioning, object tagging, data governance, and the use of data management tools can all contribute to a successful data lake design.

Data lake layouts

A data lake layout refers to the way that data is organized and structured within a data lake. This can include the physical location of the data within the data lake, as well as the logical organization of the data into different categories, such as structured and unstructured data.

In general, data lake layouts are designed to support the efficient storage and management of large amounts of data from a variety of different sources. This can include organizing data by source, by type, or by some other criterion that is relevant to the organization's data management needs.

Some common elements of data lake layouts include the following:

- **Physical location**: The physical location of the data within the data lake, such as on-premises storage or cloud-based storage
- **Logical organization**: The logical organization of the data into different categories, such as structured and unstructured data
- **Data lineage**: The history of the data, including where it came from, how it was processed, and how it has been used
- **Metadata**: Information about the data, such as its format, quality, and relevance to the organization
- **Security and access control**: Policies and mechanisms for controlling who can access the data, and for ensuring the confidentiality, integrity, and availability of the data

Overall, the goal of a data lake layout is to provide a flexible and scalable framework for storing and managing large amounts of data in a way that supports the organization's data management needs.

Organizing and structuring data within an Amazon S3 data lake

There are several different ways that data can be organized and structured within a data lake, depending on the specific needs and requirements of the organization. Some common data layout patterns in data lakes include the following:

- **Structured versus unstructured data**: Data in a data lake can be organized into different categories based on whether it is structured or unstructured. Structured data is data that is organized into a fixed format, such as rows and columns in a database table. Unstructured data, on the other hand, is data that does not have a fixed format, such as text documents, images, or audio and video files.
- **Data by source**: Data in a data lake can be organized by the source from which it was collected, such as social media feeds, sensor data, or transactional systems. This can help organizations to manage and analyze data from different sources in a consistent and coordinated way.
- **Data by type**: Data in a data lake can also be organized by type, such as customer data, product data, or sales data. This can help organizations quickly and easily access data that is relevant to their specific needs and use cases.
- **Data by time**: Data in a data lake can also be organized by time, such as data from a specific time period or data that was updated or modified within a specific time frame. This can help organizations to analyze trends and patterns over time and to perform time-series analysis.

Overall, the specific data layout pattern that is used in a data lake will depend on the specific needs and requirements of the organization. The key is to choose a data layout pattern that supports the efficient and effective storage, management, and analysis of the organization's data.

Process of building a data lake on Amazon S3

Now, let's understand how to build a data lake on Amazon S3.

To begin, you will need to create an AWS account if you don't already have one. Once you have an AWS account, you can create an S3 bucket to store your data. An S3 bucket is a logical unit of storage that is used to store objects, which are the individual pieces of data that make up your data lake.

Once you have created your S3 bucket, you can begin uploading data to it. There are several ways to do this, including using the AWS Management Console, the AWS **Command Line Interface** (**CLI**), and programmatic APIs. For example, you can use the AWS CLI to upload data to your S3 bucket with the following command:

```
aws s3 cp <local_file_path> s3://<your_bucket_name>/<object_key>
```

After you have uploaded your data to your S3 bucket, you can organize it by creating folders and subfolders within the bucket. This will make it easier to manage and access your data. You can also apply tags to your data to help you identify and categorize it.

Once your data is organized and tagged, you can start querying it using Amazon Athena, which is a serverless interactive query service that makes it easy to analyze data in Amazon S3 using SQL. Athena is integrated with S3, so you can easily query data in your S3 bucket using SQL.

You can also use other tools and services to access and analyze your data in your data lake on S3. For example, you can use Amazon EMR to process and analyze large datasets using a managed Hadoop framework. You can also use Amazon Redshift to perform fast, complex queries on your data using a managed data warehouse.

In summary, building a data lake on Amazon S3 is a simple and cost-effective way to store and analyze large amounts of data. By using S3 to store your data, you can take advantage of its durability and scalability, and you can use tools such as Athena and EMR to easily access and analyze your data.

Selecting the right file format for a data lake

Selecting the right file format for a data lake on Amazon S3 is an important decision that can impact the performance and efficiency of the data lake. There are several factors to consider when choosing a file format, including the type and structure of the data, the intended use of the data, and compatibility with other systems and tools.

One of the most popular file formats for a data lake in Amazon S3 is the Apache Parquet format. This columnar file format is optimized for big data analytics and supports complex data types, such as nested data structures and arrays. It is also highly efficient as it allows for compression and supports efficient data skipping, which can improve query performance.

Another popular file format for a data lake in Amazon S3 is the Apache **Optimized Row Columnar** (**ORC**) format. This format is similar to Parquet but offers additional features, such as support for complex data types, indexing, and predicate pushdown. ORC files are also highly efficient and support fast data ingestion and query processing.

In addition to Parquet and ORC, other file formats may be suitable for a data lake in Amazon S3, depending on the specific needs of the data and the use case. For example, the Apache Avro format is a popular choice for data serialization and supports a wide range of data types. The Apache JSON format is another option for storing data in a data lake, as it is human-readable and easy to integrate with other systems.

Ultimately, the right file format for a data lake in Amazon S3 will depend on the specific needs and requirements of the data and the intended use of the data lake. It is important to carefully evaluate the available options and choose a file format that will support efficient data storage, processing, and analysis.

Apart from columnar and row-based file formats, which we discussed earlier, one other important characteristic of a file format is being splittable in nature. In data lakes, splittable file formats are preferred as they allow for efficient and parallel processing of large datasets. Let's understand the difference between splittable and unsplittable file formats.

A splittable file format is a file format that can be divided into smaller chunks and processed independently, and the individual chunks of data can be recombined to form the original file. Examples of splittable file formats include Hadoop's HDFS and Apache Cassandra's **Sorted Strings Table (SSTable)**.

An unsplittable file format, on the other hand, is a file format that cannot be divided and processed independently. An example of an unsplittable file format is a PDF file. Since it's a binary file format and you might not be able to extract the content easily, it cannot be split into chunks of data and processed.

It is important to note that some files can be converted to a splittable format—for example, CSV from Excel, and JSON from PDF. So, it's always good to do a conversion of files to a splittable format before storing them in a data lake if needed.

	Splittable	Unsplittable
File format	Single-line delimited CSV	Multi-lined CSV
	Single-line delimited JSON	Multi-lined JSON
	Apache Parquet	
	Apache ORC	
	Apache Avro	
	Apache Parquet with row-level snappy compression	
	Apache ORC with row-level snappy compression	
	Apache Parquet with gzip compression	
	XML	
Compression type	bzip2	gzip
	zstd	LZO
		snappy

Table 5.1 – File formats and compression types

Now we have a fair understanding of columnar/splittable and row-based/unsplittable file formats, let's consolidate this with an example, where we will be comparing how performance and cost will be affected based on your file type.

In this example, we will be using the *Amazon Customer Reviews* dataset, which you can find here: `https://registry.opendata.aws/amazon-reviews/`.

This dataset contains 130 million records of customer reviews since 1995, in both **tab-separated values** (**TSV**) and Parquet file formats.

```
(base) navnis@38f9d36a27bd ~ % aws s3 ls s3://amazon-reviews-pds/
                              PRE parquet/
                              PRE tsv/
```

Figure 5.2 – Data in Amazon Customer Reviews open dataset

TSV is similar to **CSV**. It is a simple file format for storing data in a tabular format—for example, a database table or spreadsheet data—with each row of the table represented as a separate line in the file and each cell in the table separated by a tab character.

Parquet is a column-oriented file format for storing large amounts of data in a file. It is used for storing data in a distributed environment, such as in a Hadoop cluster. Parquet is optimized for efficient querying and storage of data and is designed to work with data processing frameworks such as Apache Spark and Impala.

To start with, we create two tables—table 1 (`amazon_reviews_tsv`), which is built on the TSV dataset, and table 2 (`amazon_reviews_parquet`), which is built on the Parquet dataset. The `amazon_reviews_parquet` table is not only using the Parquet file format but is also partitioned by `product_category`, as illustrated in the following screenshot:

```
(base)                          % aws s3 ls s3://amazon-reviews-pds/parquet/
                           PRE product_category=Apparel/
                           PRE product_category=Automotive/
                           PRE product_category=Baby/
                           PRE product_category=Beauty/
                           PRE product_category=Books/
                           PRE product_category=Camera/
                           PRE product_category=Digital_Ebook_Purchase/
                           PRE product_category=Digital_Music_Purchase/
                           PRE product_category=Digital_Software/
                           PRE product_category=Digital_Video_Download/
                           PRE product_category=Digital_Video_Games/
                           PRE product_category=Electronics/
                           PRE product_category=Furniture/
                           PRE product_category=Gift_Card/
                           PRE product_category=Grocery/
                           PRE product_category=Health_&_Personal_Care/
                           PRE product_category=Home/
                           PRE product_category=Home_Entertainment/
```

Figure 5.3 – Parquet dataset with partitions

This SQL code is for the `amazon_reviews_tsv` table definition:

```
CREATE EXTERNAL TABLE amazon_reviews_tsv(
  marketplace string,
  customer_id string,
  review_id string,
  product_id string,
  product_parent string,
  product_title string,
  product_category string,
  star_rating int,
  helpful_votes int,
  total_votes int,
  vine string,
  verified_purchase string,
  review_headline string,
  review_body string,
  review_date date)
ROW FORMAT DELIMITED
  FIELDS TERMINATED BY '\t'
  ESCAPED BY '\\'
  LINES TERMINATED BY '\n'
LOCATION
  's3://amazon-reviews-pds/tsv/'
TBLPROPERTIES ("skip.header.line.count"="1");
```

This SQL is for the `amazon_reviews_parquet` table definition partitioned by `product_category`:

```
CREATE EXTERNAL TABLE `amazon_reviews_parquet`(
  `marketplace` string,
  `customer_id``string,
  `review_id` string,
  `product_id` string,
  `product_parent` string,
  `product_title` string,
  `star_rating` int,
  `helpful_votes` int,
  `total_votes` int,
  `vine` string,
  `verified_purchase` string,
  `review_headline` string,
  `review_body` string,
  `review_date` bigint,
```

```
  `year` int)
PARTITIONED BY ( `product_category` string )
STORED AS PARQUET
LOCATION 's3://amazon-reviews-pds/parquet';
```

The following table compares the execution time, data scan, and cost between the TSV and Parquet tables:

Query	Execution time		Data scan (GB)		Cost ($5/TB scan)	
	TSV (`amazon_reviews_tsv`)	Parquet (`amazon_reviews_parquet`)	TSV	Parquet	TSV	Parquet
`SELECT count(*) FROM`	1 min 2.54 sec	704 ms	32.22 GB	0	$0.15	$0

`SELECT count(*) FROM "<table>"`
 	
`WHERE marketplace = 'US'`
	1 min 25.66 sec	1.298 sec	32.22 GB	5.28 MB	$0.15	$0.000025

`SELECT * FROM "<table>"`
 	
`WHERE marketplace = 'US'`
 	
`limit 1000;`
	1.08 sec	669 ms	1.88 MB	2.69 MB		

`select distinct product_category from "<table_name>"`	1 min 16 sec	1.38 sec	32.22 GB	0		0

SELECT product_id, product_title, count(*) as num_reviews, avg(star_rating) as avg_stars FROM <table_name> where product_category='Toys' GROUP BY 1, 2 ORDER BY 3 DESC limit 100;	1 min 17 sec	2.27 sec	32.22 GB	215 MB	$0.15	$0.00102

Table 5.2 – Table comparing execution time, data scan, and cost between TSV and Parquet files

If you review the table stats around execution time, data scan, and cost, you will get a fair idea of why you want to have data stored in an optimized columnar file format such as Parquet.

For example, when you have data stored in TSV without partition, in most of the queries, you need to scan either the entire dataset (for example, `running count(*)` or `distinct`) or a chunk of the dataset.

Similarly, when you have data stored in Parquet with partitions in cases such as `count(*)` and `distinct`, it doesn't require you to scan the dataset as it maintains the stats about the data. If you have to run a filter statement such as a `WHERE` clause in TSV, it has to scan the entire dataset, and if data is partitioned, it has only gone through a specific partition, which eventually makes your query faster as it scans a lot less data.

Selecting the right compression method for a data lake

Selecting the right compression method for a data lake in Amazon S3 is an important decision that can impact the performance and efficiency of the data lake. Compression can help reduce the storage space required for the data, as well as improve the speed of data transfer and query processing.

One of the most popular compression methods for a data lake in Amazon S3 is the Snappy compression algorithm. This algorithm is designed for high-speed data compression and decompression, and it can provide a good balance between compression ratio and performance. Snappy is supported by many popular big data frameworks, such as Apache Spark and Apache Flink, and it can be easily integrated into data pipelines and applications.

Another popular compression method for a data lake in Amazon S3 is the gzip compression algorithm. This algorithm is widely used for data compression and provides a higher compression ratio than Snappy. However, gzip can be slower than Snappy, and it may not be suitable for real-time or interactive data processing applications.

In addition to Snappy and gzip, other compression algorithms may be suitable for a data lake in Amazon S3, depending on the specific needs of the data and the use case. For example, the LZO algorithm is a popular choice for data compression, as it provides a high compression ratio and good performance. The LZ4 algorithm is another option, as it offers a high compression speed and low memory usage.

Ultimately, the right compression method for a data lake in Amazon S3 will depend on the specific needs and requirements of the data and the intended use of the data lake. It is important to carefully evaluate the available options and choose a compression algorithm that will support efficient data storage, processing, and analysis.

Choosing the right partitioning strategy for a data lake

Choosing the right partitioning strategy for a data lake is an important decision that can impact the performance and efficiency of the data lake. Partitioning is the process of dividing a large dataset into smaller, more manageable pieces, known as partitions. Each partition is stored and managed separately and can be queried and processed independently.

One of the most common partitioning strategies for a data lake is to partition the data by time. This can be useful for data that is generated at regular intervals, such as sensor data, log data, or financial data. Time-based partitioning allows for efficient querying and processing of data within a specific time range, and it can also support data archiving and data retention policies. You can see an example of partitioning by date here:

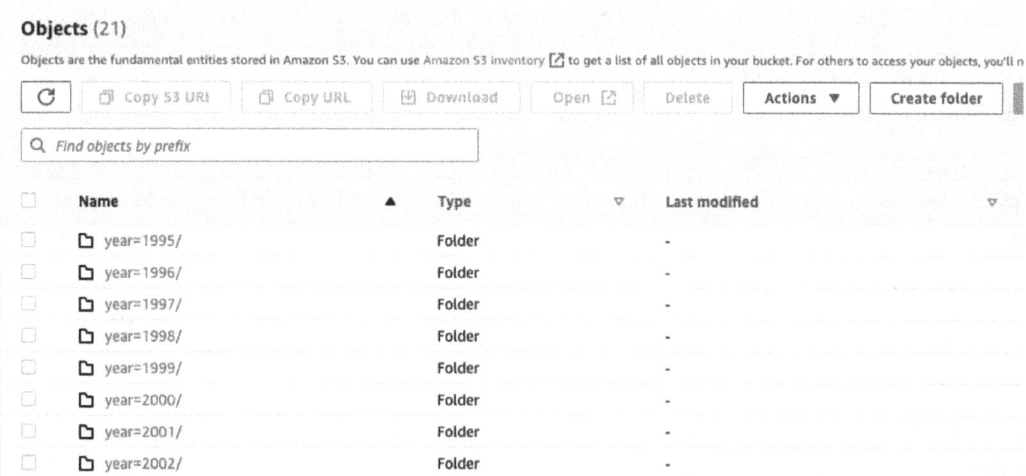

Figure 5.4 – Partitioning by date

Another popular partitioning strategy for a data lake is to partition the data by location. This can be useful for data that is related to a specific geographic area, such as weather data, traffic data, or retail data. Location-based partitioning allows for efficient querying and processing of data within a specific geographic area, and it can also support data privacy and data sovereignty requirements. Here's a screenshot example of how to partition by location:

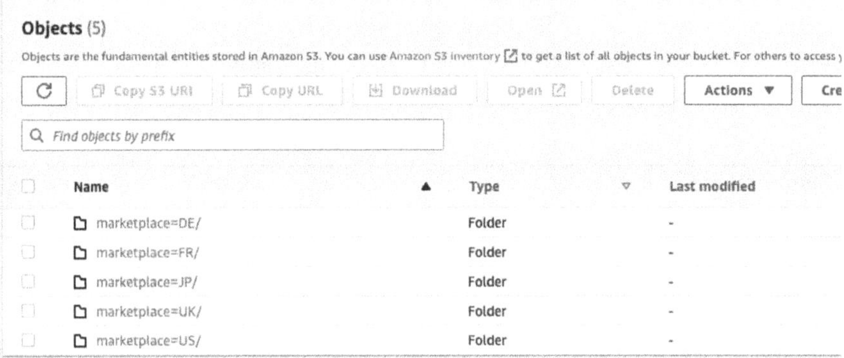

Figure 5.5 – Partitioning by location

In addition to time-based and location-based partitioning, other strategies may be suitable for a data lake, depending on the specific needs and requirements of the data. For example, data can be partitioned by customer, product, event type, or any other relevant attribute. It is important to carefully evaluate the available options and choose a partitioning strategy that will support efficient data storage, processing, and analysis.

Configuring Amazon S3 Lifecycle for a data lake

Configuring Amazon S3 Lifecycle for a data lake involves defining rules and policies for managing the data stored in the data lake. Amazon S3 Lifecycle allows for the automatic management of data based on the age and usage of the data. This can help reduce storage costs and improve the performance and efficiency of the data lake.

To configure Amazon S3 Lifecycle for a data lake, first, create a lifecycle policy in the Amazon S3 console. This can be done by selecting a data lake bucket and choosing **Lifecycle** from the **Management** tab, as illustrated in *Figure 5.6*. Then, create a new rule and specify conditions and actions for the rule.

The conditions for the lifecycle rule can be based on the age of the data, the storage class of the data, or the number of days since the data was last accessed. For example, a rule can be created to move data that has not been accessed in the last 90 days to the S3 Glacier storage class, which is a lower-cost storage option for infrequently accessed data.

The actions for the lifecycle rule can include transitioning the data to a different storage class, archiving the data to S3 Glacier Deep Archive, or deleting the data. For example, a rule can be created to delete data that has not been accessed in the last 365 days, to reduce the storage cost and free up space in the data lake:

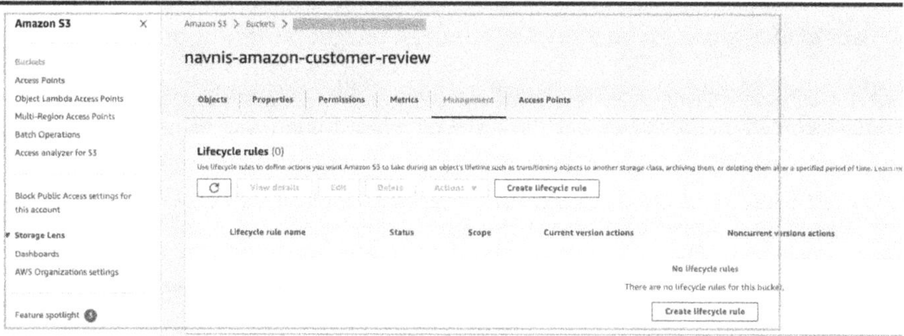

Figure 5.6 – Amazon S3 lifecycle rule

Click on **Create lifecycle rule** to create a data lifecycle for data that resides in that Amazon S3 bucket. You should then see a screen like this:

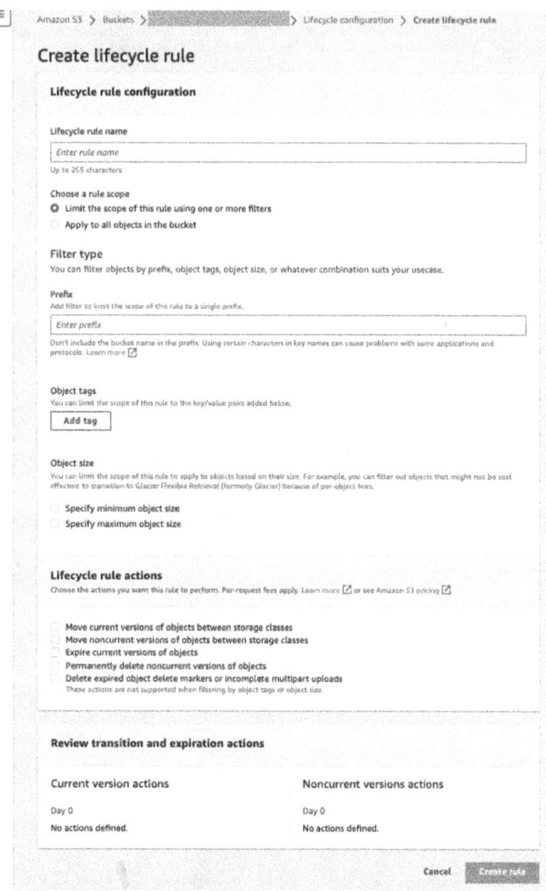

Figure 5.7 – Configuring an Amazon S3 lifecycle rule

Apart from Amazon S3 Lifecycle, Amazon S3 also offers Amazon S3 Intelligent-Tiering.

Amazon S3 Intelligent-Tiering is a storage class that automatically moves data to the most cost-effective storage tier, based on changing access patterns. The data is automatically transitioned between two access tiers: one for frequently accessed data and another for infrequently accessed data. This helps you optimize costs while ensuring that frequently accessed data is always available with low latency.

In summary, S3 Intelligent-Tiering can move data from a less frequently accessed tier to an S3 frequent tier based on the access pattern. But lifecycle policies only cause data to move toward further infrequent access tiers (not vice versa).

You can configure Amazon S3 Intelligent-Tiering by creating or selecting an existing bucket that you want to use for intelligent tiering. From the **Properties** tab for the bucket, select **Intelligent-Tiering** from the list of storage classes. Once you have selected the **Intelligent-Tiering** class, you can configure several settings for the bucket, such as object lock, versioning, and events. You can also set up lifecycle rules to move objects between the frequent and infrequent access tiers automatically based on certain conditions. *Figure 5.8* and *Figure 5.9* illustrate how to configure Intelligent-Tiering:

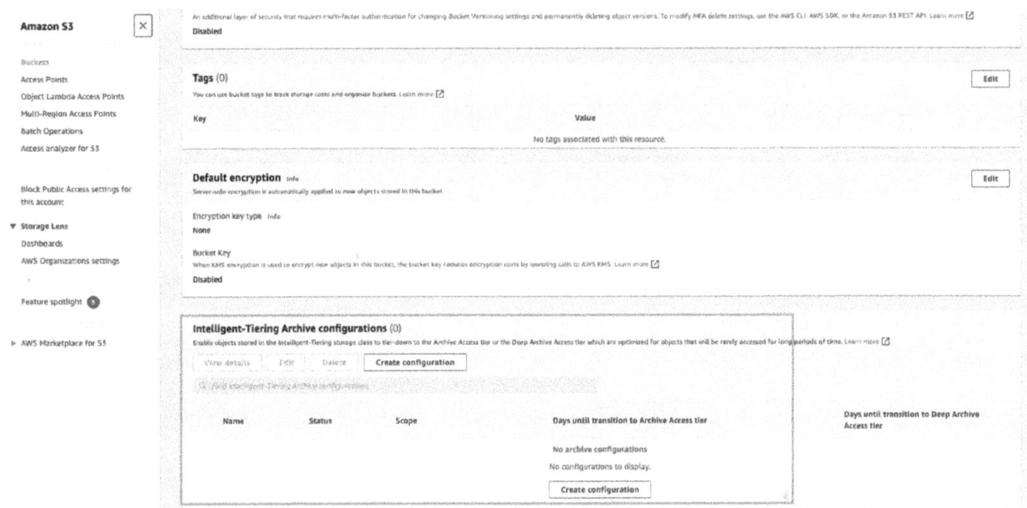

Figure 5.8 – Configuring Amazon S3 Intelligent-Tiering

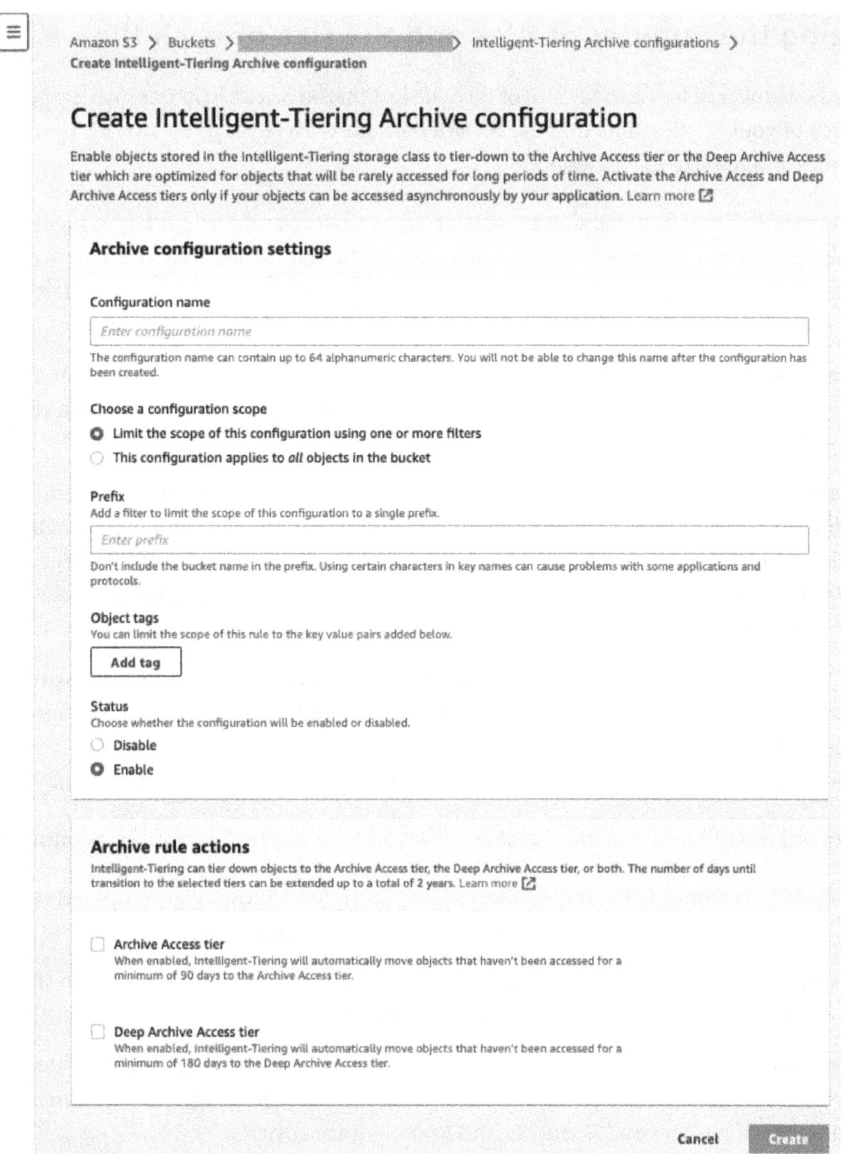

Figure 5.9 – Amazon S3 Intelligent-Tiering configuration

It is important to carefully evaluate the lifecycle rules and policies for a data lake and to choose the right options that will support the performance, scalability, and cost-efficiency of the data lake. It is also important to regularly review and update lifecycle rules and policies to ensure that they are still relevant and effective.

Optimizing the number of files and the size of each file

Optimizing the number of files and the size of each file in Amazon S3 can help improve the performance and efficiency of your applications that use S3 as a data store. Here are a few tips for optimizing the number of files and file size in Amazon S3:

- **Use large file sizes**: In general, it is more efficient to store and retrieve larger files rather than smaller ones. This is because S3 charges for data transfer and request fees, and these fees are based on the number of requests made rather than the amount of data transferred. Therefore, using larger file sizes can help reduce the number of requests and lower the overall cost of using S3.
- **Use a consistent file size**: Using a consistent file size can make it easier to manage and process your data. It can also improve the performance of your applications, as the data can be more easily split and processed in parallel.
- **Use a reasonable number of files**: While using larger file sizes can be more efficient, having too few files can lead to very large files that may be difficult to manage and process. On the other hand, having too many small files can also be inefficient as it may result in a large number of requests and increased costs. Finding a balance between file size and the number of files can help optimize performance and cost.
- **Use prefixes and partitioning**: Using prefixes and partitioning can help you organize and manage large numbers of files in S3. Prefixes allow you to group related files together, while partitioning allows you to divide your data into logical sections based on attributes such as date or location. This can make it easier to access and process specific subsets of data.

There are several ways to optimize the number of files and file size in Amazon S3, as outlined here:

- **Use multipart uploads for larger files**: Multipart upload allows you to upload large files in smaller chunks, which can be more efficient than uploading one large file.
- **Use smaller file sizes**: Instead of uploading one large file, try breaking it up into smaller files. This can reduce the time it takes to upload and download the files.
- **Use object lifecycle policies**: As discussed in an earlier section, setting up object lifecycle policies to automatically delete or archive older files that are no longer needed can help reduce the number of files in your S3 bucket and lower storage costs.
- Use AWS Glue or AWS EMR to run analytics on your data in S3, and then delete unnecessary data from your S3 bucket.
- As discussed in the previous section, using AWS S3 Intelligent-Tiering, S3 **Standard-Infrequent Access (Standard-IA)**, and S3 **One Zone-Infrequent Access (One Zone-IA)** for storing files that are not frequently accessed may help reduce the costs associated with storing these files.
- Enabling server-side compression for files in your S3 bucket can help reduce the amount of storage space required.

In conclusion, optimizing the number of files and file size in Amazon S3 involves finding a balance that helps improve performance and efficiency while minimizing cost. Using large file sizes, a consistent file size, and a reasonable number of files, and utilizing prefixes and partitioning can all help optimize the use of S3 for your data storage needs.

In this section, we learned how to optimize your data lake. In the next section, we will discuss the challenges and considerations one should be aware of when building a data lake.

Challenges and considerations when building a data lake on Amazon S3

When building a data lake on Amazon S3 or data lake in general, here are some challenges and considerations one should be aware of:

- **Data ingestion**: The process of bringing data into a data lake can be challenging, particularly when the data comes from multiple sources with varying formats and structures. This can lead to difficulties in ensuring data quality and consistency. Additionally, handling large volumes of data can be a challenge, particularly as the data grows. Another issue is keeping schema changes consistent throughout all downstream applications.
- **Data governance**: Maintaining data quality, security, and regulatory compliance can be difficult when dealing with a large volume of data in a data lake. Implementing policies and standards for data classification, quality, and retention, as well as managing access and permissions, including **role-based access control** (**RBAC**) and data encryption, can be challenging. Additionally, tracking data sources and usage through lineage and auditing, managing data retention and archiving, and protecting against data breaches and unauthorized access can be difficult.
- **Data management**: Organizing and managing the vast amounts of data stored in flat files and object storage can be a challenge. Additionally, incorporating data lineage and governance into data management processes, managing storage and retrieval costs, and integrating the data lake with other data management and analytics tools and services can be challenging. Ensuring data quality and consistency, providing data access and self-service to different users and teams, managing scalability and performance as data volume increases, and managing data backup and **disaster recovery** (**DR**) are also challenges in the management of data in a data lake.
- **Data processing**: Data processing within a data lake—including tasks such as data transformation, cleaning, and analysis—can be difficult and may require specialized tools and technologies such as AWS Glue, Kinesis, and so on. Challenges may include integrating with other AWS services and tools for data processing and analysis, managing the costs of data processing and compute resources, handling both real-time and batch processing, maintaining data quality and consistency, providing access and self-service to different users and teams, securing sensitive data, and meeting performance and availability requirements.

- **Data access**: Enabling easy and efficient access to the data within the data lake for different users and groups can be a complex task, especially if you are working in a multi-tenancy environment.
- **Cost**: The cost of storing and processing large amounts of data on Amazon S3 can be significant and needs to be carefully managed. That's why setting up an S3 bucket lifecycle is important.
- **Data security**: It's necessary to ensure sensitive data is protected and meets compliance requirements. We are going to explore data security challenges in the chapter on security and monitoring.
- **Performance**: Data lake performance should be optimized to ensure that data is easily accessible for analysis and reporting. That's why it is super important to ensure the best practices described in the *Organizing and structuring data within an Amazon S3 data lake* section are implemented.

Summary

In this chapter, we have discussed what big data is, the characteristics of big data, what a data lake is, why we need data lakes, and how a data lake can be built on Amazon S3 by providing an overview of the benefits of data lakes, the different layers of a data lake, and the best practices for building a data lake on Amazon S3. We also provided details on organizing and managing the data within a data lake on S3, including using features such as file formats, partitions, S3 lifecycle management, Amazon S3 Intelligent-Tiering, and so on. The chapter also discussed some challenges and considerations when building a data lake on Amazon S3, such as cost and performance.

In the next chapter, we are going to learn about AWS Glue. AWS Glue is a data integration service that lets you bring data from different data sources and allows you to perform ETL on top of it using frameworks such as Apache Spark and Python.

6
Working with AWS Glue

In the preceding chapter, we discussed various data storage types, including data warehouses, data lakes, data lakehouses, and data meshes, along with their key differences.

This chapter will explore the distinct components of AWS Glue, providing insight into how they can aid in data wrangling tasks.

After completing this chapter, you will be able to comprehend and define how AWS Glue can be utilized for data wrangling. You will also be capable of explaining the fundamental concepts associated with various AWS Glue features, such as AWS Glue Data Catalog, AWS Glue connections, AWS Glue crawlers, AWS Glue Schema Registry, AWS Glue jobs, AWS Glue development endpoints, AWS Glue interactive sessions, and AWS Glue triggers.

The following topics will be covered in this chapter:

- Spark basics
- AWS Glue features
- Data discovery using AWS Glue
- Data ingestion using AWS Glue

What is Apache Spark?

Apache Spark is a unified analytics engine for processing big data, developed as an open source project in 2009 at the University of California, Berkeley's AMPLab. Initially, it was created as a class project to address the limitations of the Hadoop framework in exchanging data between iterations through HDFS for machine learning use cases. The objective was to design a new framework for fast interactive processing, including machine learning and interactive data analysis, while retaining the implicit data parallelism and fault tolerance of MapReduce and HDFS from the Hadoop framework. It incorporates in-memory caching and is optimized for analytics workloads of any size.

Apache Spark was open sourced in 2010 under a BSD License, and in 2013, the project was contributed to the Apache Software Foundation. In 2014, Spark became a top-level Apache project. It has garnered over 1.7 thousand contributors and over 30K stargazers on GitHub.

According to the Spark documentation, the engine provides high-level APIs in Java, Scala, Python, and R, and supports general execution graphs through an optimized engine. Additionally, it offers a range of advanced tools that make it easier to work with different types of data and perform specific tasks. For example, Spark SQL allows you to process structured data and execute SQL queries. If you prefer using pandas for your data analysis, you can also use the pandas API on Spark to leverage its capabilities. For machine learning tasks, there's MLlib, which provides tools and algorithms to help you build and train models. If you're working with graph data, GraphX is available to assist with graph processing. Lastly, if you need to perform computations on data streams and handle incremental updates, you can use Structured Streaming, which enables stream processing with Spark.

Apache Spark architecture

At a high level, Apache Spark operates on a leader and worker node architecture, where there is a central coordinator and several distributed worker nodes. It comprises a driver, multiple executors, and a cluster manager. The driver program transforms the user's code into multiple tasks that can be distributed across worker nodes. The executor runs on the worker node and executes the task assigned to it. A cluster manager is required to mediate between the driver and worker node.

The collaboration of the driver and worker nodes is referred to as the Spark cluster, and the effective combination of the driver and workers is known as the Spark application.

A Spark application can be launched with the help of the cluster manager. There are many cluster manager types:

- **Standalone**: This is a straightforward cluster manager that comes bundled with Spark. It provides a simple way to set up and manage your cluster.
- **Apache Mesos**: Mesos is a versatile cluster manager that can handle various workloads, including running Hadoop MapReduce and service applications. However, it is worth noting that Mesos is now deprecated and may not be the preferred choice.
- **Hadoop YARN**: YARN is the resource manager that's used in both Hadoop 2 and Hadoop 3. It offers cluster management capabilities and can be used with Spark for running and allocating resources.
- **Kubernetes**: Kubernetes is an open source system designed for automating the process of deploying, scaling, and managing containerized applications. It can also be used to manage Spark clusters, providing flexibility and scalability:

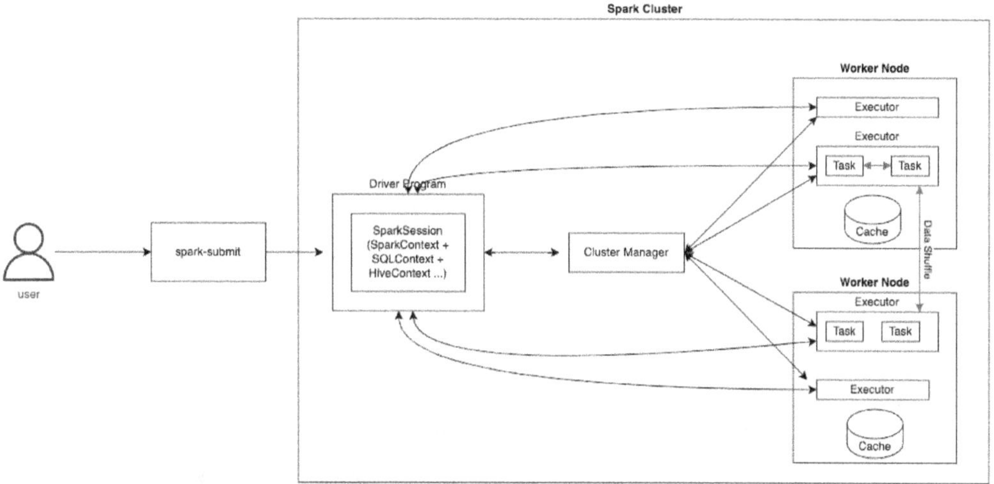

Figure 6.1 – Apache Spark architecture

Let's understand the responsibility of the driver:

- The driver is a Java process that is responsible for running the `main()` method of Scala, Python, and Java
- It executes user code and creates a SparkSession, which is responsible for creating **Resilient Distributed Datasets (RDD)**
- It creates lineage, both logical and physical plans
- The driver is responsible for scheduling the execution of the tasks by coordinating with the cluster manager
- It keeps track of data of metadata that has been cached in the executor's memory

Let's understand the responsibility of the executors:

- Executors consist of cores (slot), memory, and local storage
- Slots indicate the threads that are available to perform parallel work for Spark
- They also consist of two types of memory:
  - **Working memory**: This is utilized by Spark workloads
  - **Storage memory**: Half of the memory (storage) is used for persisted objects
- They also consist of disks, which are attached directly and provide space for shuffle partitions (Spark shuffle partitions are the intermediate divisions of data during the shuffling process to facilitate data exchange between stages) for the shuffle stages

- They are responsible for running individual tasks and returning them to the driver:

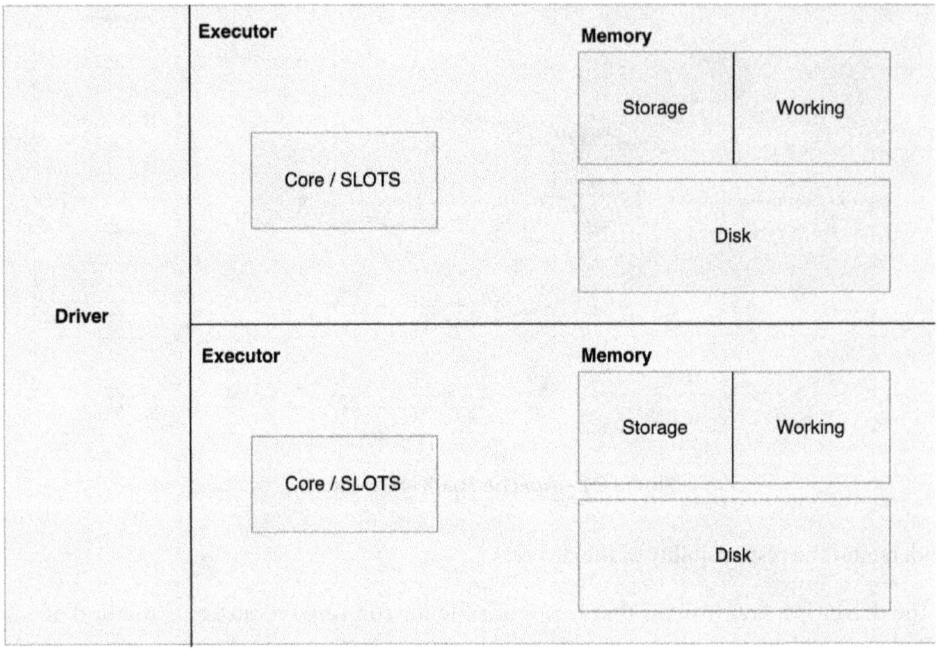

Figure 6.2 – Apache Spark executors

To start running applications on a Spark cluster, you can utilize the `spark-submit` script located in Spark's `bin` directory. This script serves as a unified interface that allows you to launch your applications without the need to configure them specifically for each cluster manager supported by Spark. This means you can seamlessly use different cluster managers without having to modify your application setup for each one individually.

Now that we have gained a reasonable understanding of the Apache Spark architecture, let's proceed to explore the Apache Spark framework.

Apache Spark framework

The Apache Spark framework is a unified analytics engine for large-scale data processing. It consists of four main components: Spark Core, Spark SQL, Spark Streaming, and GraphX.

Apache Spark Core is the foundation or fundamental unit of the Spark platform that provides in-memory computing capabilities. Spark Core facilitates parallel and distributed processing, task scheduling, dispatching, and basic I/O functionalities. Spark Core can be accessed through an **application programming interface** (**API**) developed for Scala, Python, Java, and R. The Spark API reduces the complexity of a distributed parallel processing engine. Spark utilizes a special type of data structure called RDD to handle data. RDD represents a logical collection of data that is spread across multiple machines in the cluster.

Here are some key modules in Spark and what they offer:

- **Spark SQL**: This module focuses on processing structured data. It introduces a programming abstraction called DataFrames, which provides a convenient way to work with structured data. Additionally, Spark SQL can be used as a distributed SQL query engine, allowing you to query and analyze data using SQL-like syntax.
- **Spark Streaming**: With Spark Streaming, you can build powerful applications that process both real-time streaming data and historical data. It inherits Spark's user-friendly nature and fault-tolerance capabilities, making it easier to develop interactive and analytical applications that can handle continuous streams of data.
- **GraphX**: GraphX is an engine built on top of Spark that specializes in graph computation. It empowers users to interactively create, transform, and reason about large-scale graph data. This is particularly useful for applications that involve analyzing and processing data with complex relationships, such as social networks or web graphs:

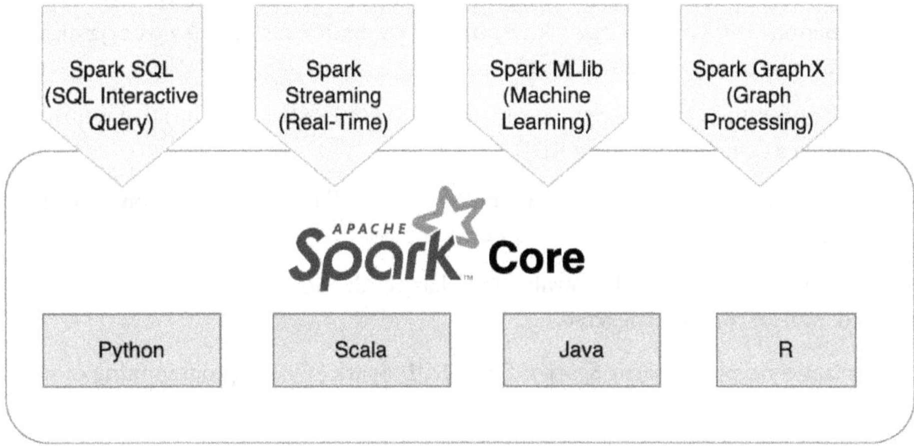

Figure 6.3 – The Apache Spark framework

Resilient Distributed Datasets

Spark introduces the concept of RDD. It is a logical collection of data partitioned across different machines. RDD is the fundamental data structure of Spark. It is an immutable, fault-tolerant, distributed collection of objects of any type that operate in parallel:

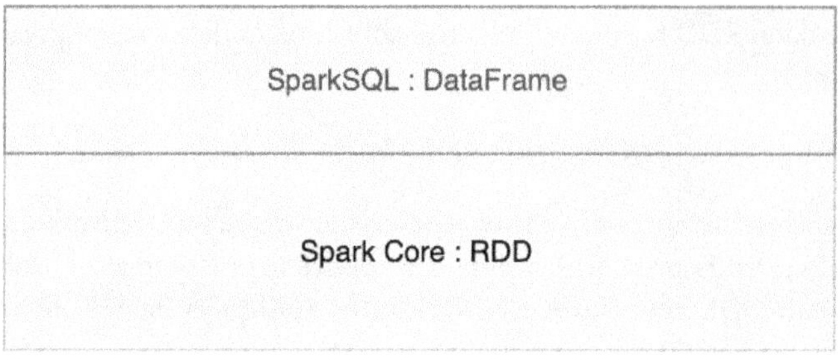

Figure 6.4 – Spark framework

RDDs are immutable but you can modify them with transformations. However, these transformations return a new RDD, while the original RDD remains the same.

RDDs support two types of operations:

- **Transformations** are operations (for example, `select`, `read`, `filter`, `groupBy`, `sort`, and so on) that are performed on an RDD and which yield a new RDD containing the result.

  The official Spark page provides a comprehensive list of all available transformations (`https://spark.apache.org/docs/1.2.1/programming-guide.html#transformations`).

- **Actions** are operations (for example, `reduce`, `count`, `first`, and so on) that return a value after running a computation on an RDD.

  The official Spark page provides a comprehensive list of all the available actions (`https://spark.apache.org/docs/1.2.1/programming-guide.html#actions`).

Transformations in Spark are called "lazy evaluation." Lazy evaluation means the transformation will not be executed until an action is triggered.

Another important concept in Apache Spark is Spark SQL. Spark SQL is a programming module for structured data processing.

Datasets and DataFrames

According to the Apache Spark documentation, DataFrames are a crucial aspect of any framework. DataFrames consist of named columns and can be thought of as tables in a relational database or a DataFrame in R/Python but with enhanced optimizations. They can be created from a variety of sources, including structured data files, tables in Hive, external databases, or existing RDDs. The DataFrame API is available in Scala, Java, Python, and R, with Scala and Java representing DataFrames as a dataset of rows; in the Java API, `Dataset<Row>` is used to represent a DataFrame. Now that we understand Apache Spark, we can start learning about AWS Glue and its building blocks.

AWS Glue building blocks

AWS Glue Crawler allows you to crawl data from various data sources, including S3, and databases such as Redshift, MySQL, MSSQL, Oracle, and MongoDB, among others. Once the crawling process is complete, AWS Glue Crawler automatically creates or updates tables in the AWS Glue Data Catalog. A list of supported data sources can be found at `https://docs.aws.amazon.com/glue/latest/dg/crawler-data-stores.html`:

- **AWS Glue Data Catalog**: The AWS Glue Data Catalog is a centralized catalog that stores metadata from various data stores. These can be used by other AWS services such as Amazon Athena, Amazon QuickSight, Amazon EMR, and Amazon Redshift.
- **AWS Glue Triggers**: AWS Glue Triggers enable you to create schedules that can manually or automatically start one or more AWS Glue Crawlers or AWS Glue ETL jobs. Triggers can be configured to fire on demand, based on a schedule, or based on a combination of events.
- **AWS Glue Workflows**: AWS Glue Workflows enable you to orchestrate the execution of Glue ETL and Glue Crawler using a Glue Trigger.
- **AWS Glue ETL**: AWS Glue ETL allows users to create **Extract, Transform, and Load** (ETL) pipelines using Python, PySpark, or Scala. With Glue ETL, you can process data from various data sources, perform transformations, and eventually write to different data sources (such as Amazon Redshift, Oracle, OpenSearch, and Amazon S3). You have the option to choose from different processing engines: for distributed processing, you can choose between PySpark and Scala, while for non-distributed processing, you can select Python:

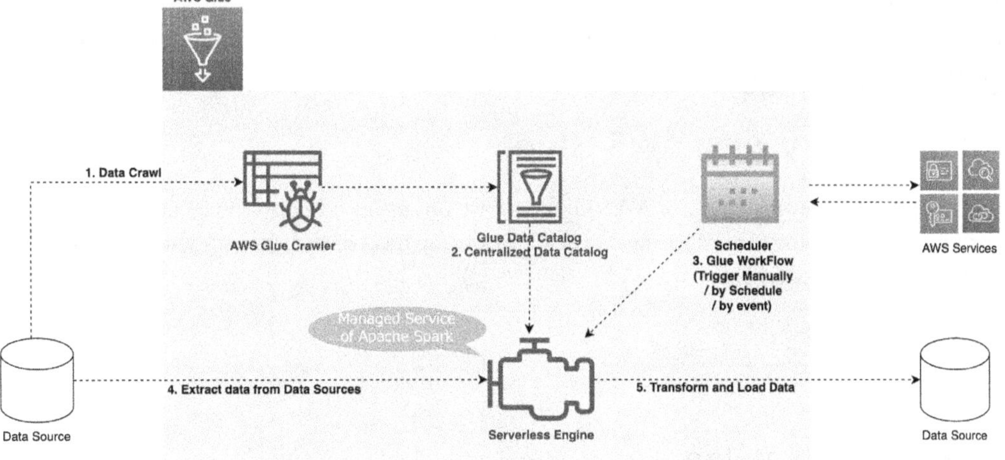

Figure 6.5 – Simple data pipeline using AWS Glue

- **AWS Glue interactive sessions**: AWS Glue interactive sessions provide a managed Jupyter notebook-based **integrated development environment** (**IDE**) for developing and testing AWS Glue ETL scripts.
- **AWS Glue Schema Registry**: AWS Glue Schema Registry is a tool that allows users to have centralized control over data stream schemas. It seamlessly works with popular data streaming platforms such as Apache Kafka, Amazon Kinesis, and AWS Lambda. With AWS Glue Schema Registry, you can easily manage and govern the schemas used in your data streams, ensuring consistency and compatibility across different components of your data processing pipeline.
- **AWS Glue Blueprint**: AWS Glue Blueprint allows users to scale similar ETL use cases by parameterizing a single workflow to handle them all – for example, crawling different S3 buckets. Blueprint examples can be found here: `https://github.com/awslabs/aws-glue-blueprint-libs/tree/master/samples`.
- **AWS Glue Connections**: AWS Glue Connections are catalog objects that provide a convenient way for users to create and store connection information for different data stores. These connections act as a bridge between AWS Glue and various data sources. With AWS Glue Connections, you can easily configure and manage the necessary connection details for your data stores.

  In addition to standard data stores, AWS Glue Connections also support Marketplace AWS Glue Connectors. These connectors enable integration with third-party data stores such as Apache Hudi, Google Big Query, and Elasticsearch. This means you can seamlessly connect and interact with these external data sources using AWS Glue, making it easier to access and process data from diverse systems in a unified manner.

We have now gained a fundamental understanding of Apache Spark and AWS Glue's building blocks. In the following discussion, we will delve into the various components of AWS Glue to comprehend how it can be employed in data wrangling.

Data discovery with AWS Glue

One of the unique features that sets AWS Glue apart from other ETL tools is its ability to create a centralized data catalog. This catalog is crucial for performing data discovery and relies on two important components of Glue:

- Glue Data Catalog
- Glue Data Crawler

AWS Glue Data Catalog

A data catalog is a centralized storage of metadata for data stored in different data stores, such as data lakes, data warehouses, relational databases, and non-relational databases. The metadata contains information about columns, data formats, locations, and serialization/deserialization mechanisms. Hive Metastore is one of the most popular metadata products used in the industry. However, it uses

relational database management systems (RDBMSs) such as MySQL and PostgreSQL. The problem with using an RDBMS for Hive metadata is managing and maintaining it, especially for production workloads where high availability, scaling, and redundancy must be taken into account. This increases the complexity and cost of the solution. AWS Glue Data Catalog solves this problem with its serverless nature, eliminating the need for additional administrative overhead in managing the infrastructure.

AWS Glue Data Catalog is comprised of the following:

- Databases
- Tables
- Partitions
- Partition indexes

Databases

In AWS Glue, a database is a grouping of metadata tables. Whenever a table is created in AWS Glue Data Catalog, it must be associated with a specific database. It's not possible to have the same table present in multiple databases:

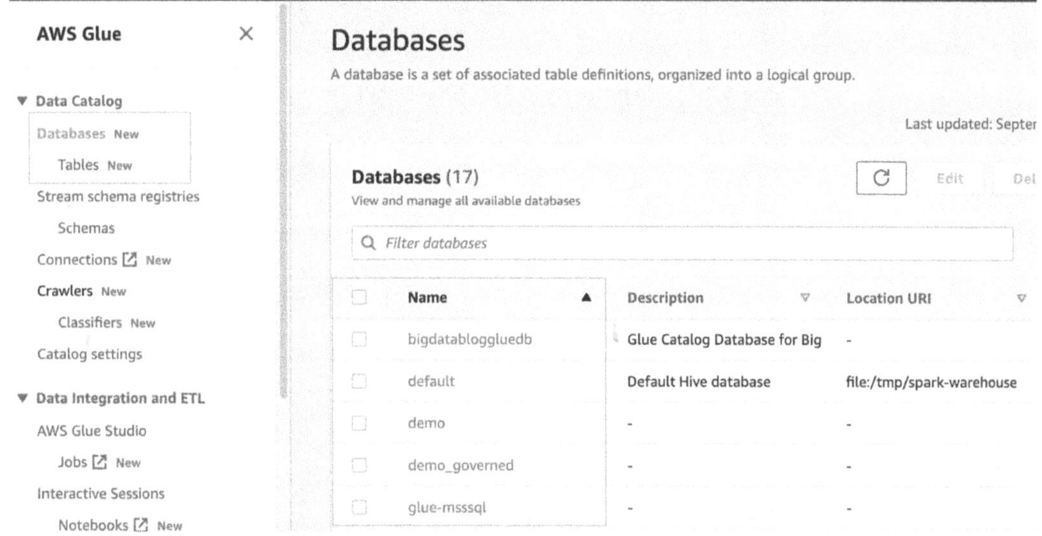

Figure 6.6 – Databases in AWS Glue Data Catalog

Tables

An AWS Glue Data Catalog table is a metadata representation of your data. It contains various information about your data, such as its name, description, location, input/output format, serialization libraries, schema, partitions, indexes, and more.

AWS Glue Data Catalog supports versioning of tables, which means that whenever a table is updated, a new version of the table is created by default. This is a crucial feature for identifying any schema changes in the source and preventing downstream application failures due to such changes. Check out this blog post, which explains how to detect any changes in the structures of your data source using AWS Glue: `https://aws.amazon.com/blogs/big-data/identify-source-schema-changes-using-aws-glue/`:

Figure 6.7 – Table property in AWS Glue Data Catalog

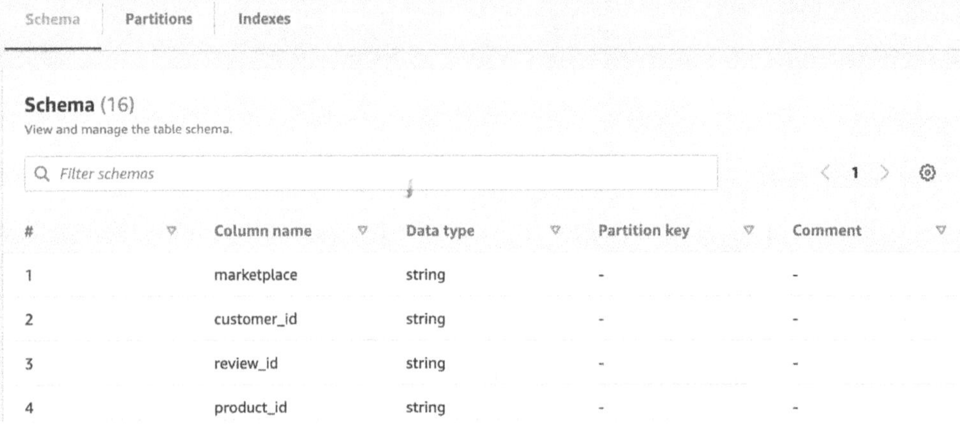

Figure 6.8 – Table property in AWS Glue Data Catalog

Partitions

Partitioning is a strategy that's used to optimize query performance by dividing a table based on the values of specific column(s). A table can have multiple partition keys that define a specific partition (also known as a partition specification). This technique improves query performance by reducing the amount of data that needs to be processed to answer a specific query:

Figure 6.9 – Partition in an AWS Glue Data Catalog table

Glue Connections

AWS Glue provides Glue Connections to allow you to connect to different data sources. Glue Connections store important information such as login credentials, connection strings (URIs), and VPC configuration details (VPC subnet and security group information), all of which are needed to establish a connection to a data source:

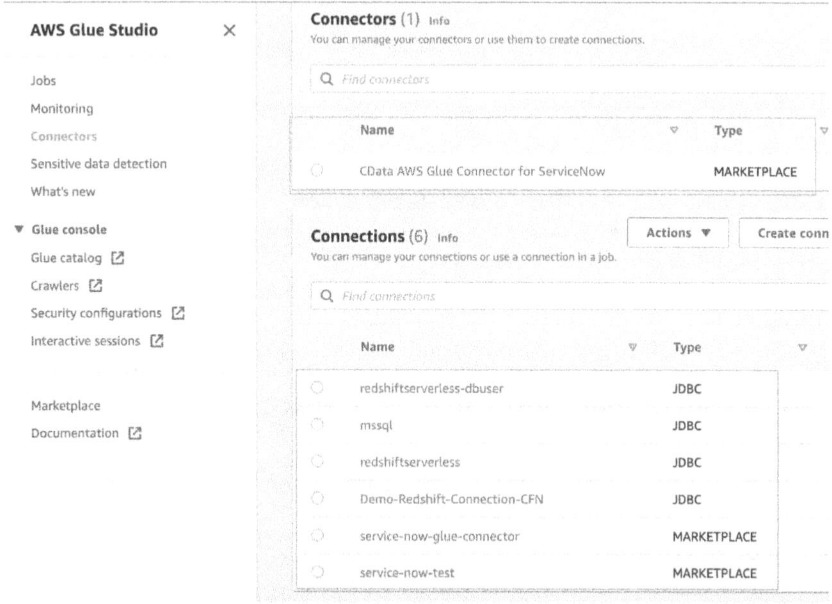

Figure 6.10 – AWS Glue Connections

Having covered the basics of AWS Glue Data Catalog, our next topic of discussion will be AWS Glue crawlers and classifiers, and their role in facilitating data discovery.

AWS Glue crawlers

A Glue crawler lets you crawl the data from different types of data stores, infer the schema, and populate AWS Glue Data Catalog with the metadata for the dataset that was crawled:

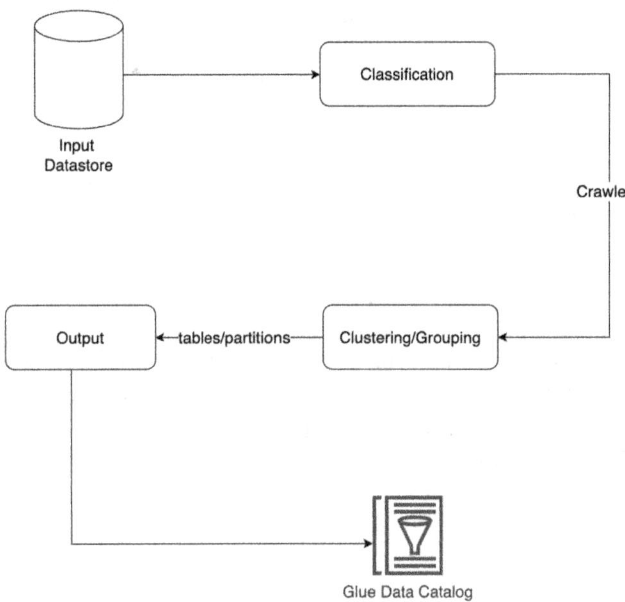

Figure 6.11 – Workflow of a Glue crawler

The Glue Crawler workflow consists of several stages:

1. **Classification**:

   In AWS Glue, a Classifier is responsible for examining the data in a data store and determining its format. Once the format is recognized, the Classifier generates the appropriate schema for the data.

   To perform this task, Glue provides both built-in and custom classifiers. When you create and run a Glue Crawler, it first applies the custom classifiers that you specify in the order defined within your crawler configuration. These custom classifiers are given priority during the schema recognition process.

The crawler also assigns a certainty number to indicate the level of confidence in the format recognition. A certainty value of 1.0 means that the crawler is 100% certain about creating the correct schema.

If none of the classifiers return a certainty value of 1.0, the crawler selects the classifier with the highest certainty value. However, if none of the classifiers return a certainty value greater than 0.0, AWS Glue returns a default classification string of **UNKNOWN**, indicating that the format could not be determined with confidence.

2. **Grouping/clustering**:

   The output from the classification stage is used by the crawler and the data is grouped based on crawler schema, classification, and other properties.

3. **Output**:

   In this stage, the Glue Data Catalog Glue API writes the table or partition objects that were created in the clustering stage. To avoid duplication of table(s), the crawler creates a table with a hash string suffix if the table(s) already exists from the previous run.

The inner workings of a crawler for Amazon S3

The Glue Crawler workflow is divided into multiple stages. The crawler is primarily used to crawl data from Amazon S3, and you may be wondering how it works. By default, the crawler reads all the data from the specified S3 path. It classifies each file available in S3 and maintains the metadata in the crawler's service-side storage, which is different from AWS Glue Data Catalog and not exposed to the customer. In subsequent runs, the crawler reuses the stored metadata and only crawls the newly added files. This reduces the crawler's execution time in subsequent runs. If a new version of the same file is uploaded, the crawler treats it as a new file and includes it in the new crawl.

The crawler samples the data based on its file size and reads the initial 1 to 10 MB of data. If the file size is larger than 10 MB, it ensures that at least one record is read.

For JDBC, Amazon DynamoDB, and Amazon DocumentDB, the crawler workflow is the same, but the logic tables are decided based on the database engine. For JDBC, Glue crawlers connect to the database server and extract the schema from the database that matches the included path value in the crawler settings.

Let's look at an example of performing data crawling and accessing the crawled data using Amazon Athena. In this example, we will do the following:

1. Explore the Covid-19 open source dataset.
2. Create a Glue Catalog database.
3. Create a Glue crawler to crawl the Covid-19 dataset.
4. Use Athena to query the dataset.

To illustrate this example, we will be utilizing the Covid-19 dataset, which can be found in Open Data on AWS:

1. Go to the **Registry of Open Data on AWS** (`https://registry.opendata.aws/`) page. In the **Search datasets** search box, put `COVID-19 Data Lake` as the search clause. You should see one dataset, **COVID-19 Data Lake**, as a result.
2. Click on the **Details** (`https://registry.opendata.aws/aws-covid19-lake/`) link on the page; you will see the AWS resource information about how to access the dataset
3. You can access data using the AWS CLI (`https://aws.amazon.com/cli/`) from the Amazon S3 location:

```
aws s3 ls --no-sign-request s3://covid19-lake/
```

4. For our example, we are looking to use a subset of the Covid-19 dataset:

```
aws s3 ls  s3://covid19-lake/rearc-covid-19-testing-data/
```

   To proceed with this example, the next step is to create a Glue Catalog database.

5. Go to the AWS Glue console (`https://console.aws.amazon.com/glue/`) and click **Databases** on the left.
6. Create a database called `chapter6_covid19` by clicking **Add Database**, then **Create**:

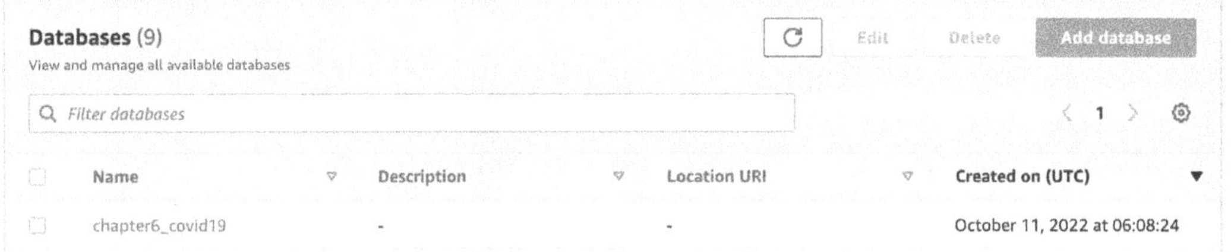

Figure 6.12 – AWS Glue – Databases

   To proceed with this example, the next step is to create a Glue crawler.

7. Click **Crawlers** on the left.
8. Click **Create Crawler**.
9. On the **Set crawler properties** page, provide a name for the new crawler, such as `chapter-gluecrawler`, and click **Next**.
10. On the **Choose data sources and classifiers** page, select **Not Yet** under **Data source configuration**
11. Click **Add a data store**, select **In a different account** under **Location of S3 data**, set `s3://covid19-lake/rearc-covid-19-testing-data/` under **S3 path**, and click **Add an S3 data source**. Then, click **Next** and keep the rest of the options at their defaults.

12. On the **Configure security settings** page, click **Create new IAM role** and provide `AWSGlueServiceRole-covid19`. Then, click **Create** and then **Next**.
13. On the **Set output and scheduling** page, under the **Output configuration** section, choose `chapter6_covid19` from the **Database** drop-down list. Enter `covid19_` as the prefix that's added to tables (optional) and under **Crawler schedule**, keep the frequency set to **on demand**.
14. Review all the configurations and click **Create crawler**:

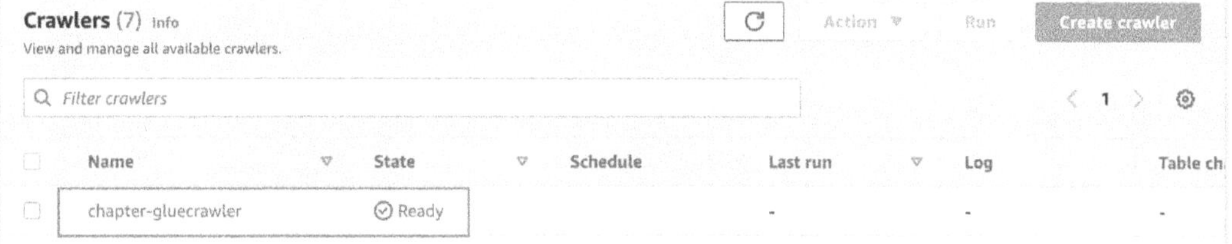

Figure 6.13 – AWS Glue – Crawlers

15. Now that we have created the crawler, click the checkbox next to it and choose to run the crawler by clicking the **Run** button at the top of the page. It will take a minute or two for the crawler to finish:

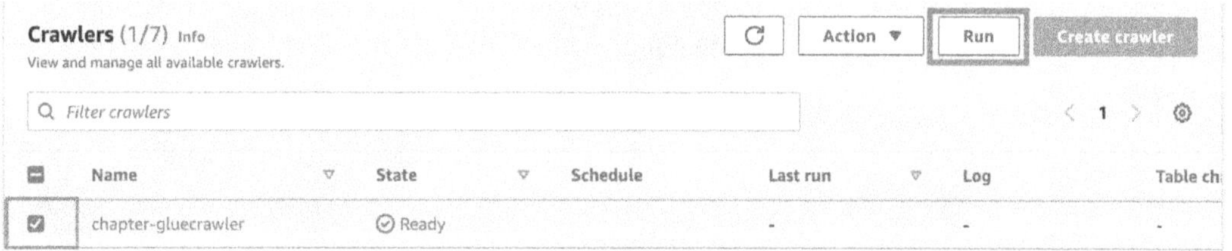

Figure 6.14 – AWS Glue – Run

Once the crawler has completed successfully, it will list four tables. Let's go to the database and explore the table definition:

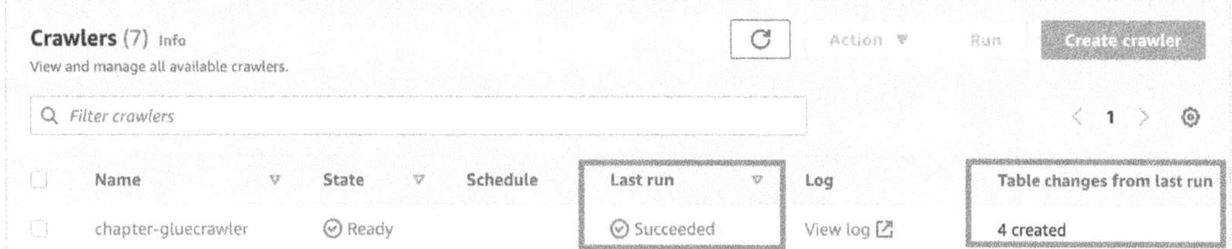

Figure 6.15 – AWS Glue – Crawlers status

Observing the table location and classification, we can see that it is pointing to the Covid-19 dataset and extracting the database definition for different file types – in this case, CSV and JSON. As you have learned, Glue Crawler allows you to crawl data from different AWS accounts, which is very useful when building a centralized data catalog where data is stored in different AWS accounts:

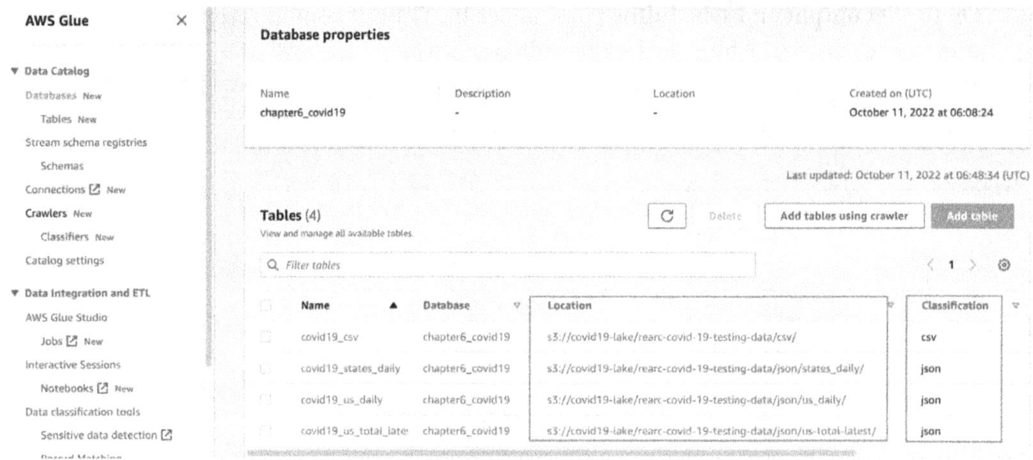

Figure 6.16 – AWS Glue Data Catalog tables

By clicking on the table's name – in this case, `'covid19_csv'` – you can explore the table definition. As we learned previously, this provides valuable information about the table, including statistics and metadata:

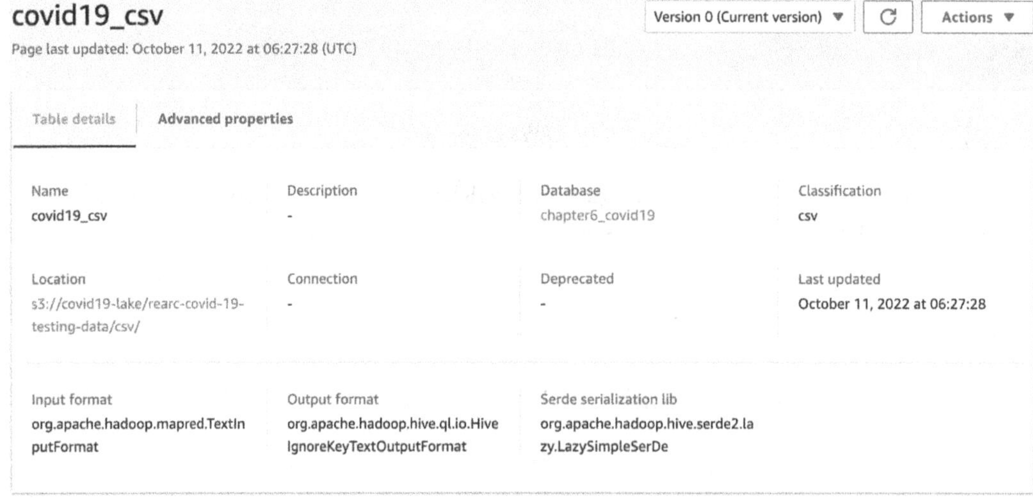

Figure 6.17 – AWS Glue Catalog table properties

Table stats

In AWS Glue, table stats refer to the statistical information about a table in Glue Data Catalog. These stats include the number of total and distinct values in each column, the minimum and maximum values, and the average length of the values. This information is important for query optimization and performance tuning:

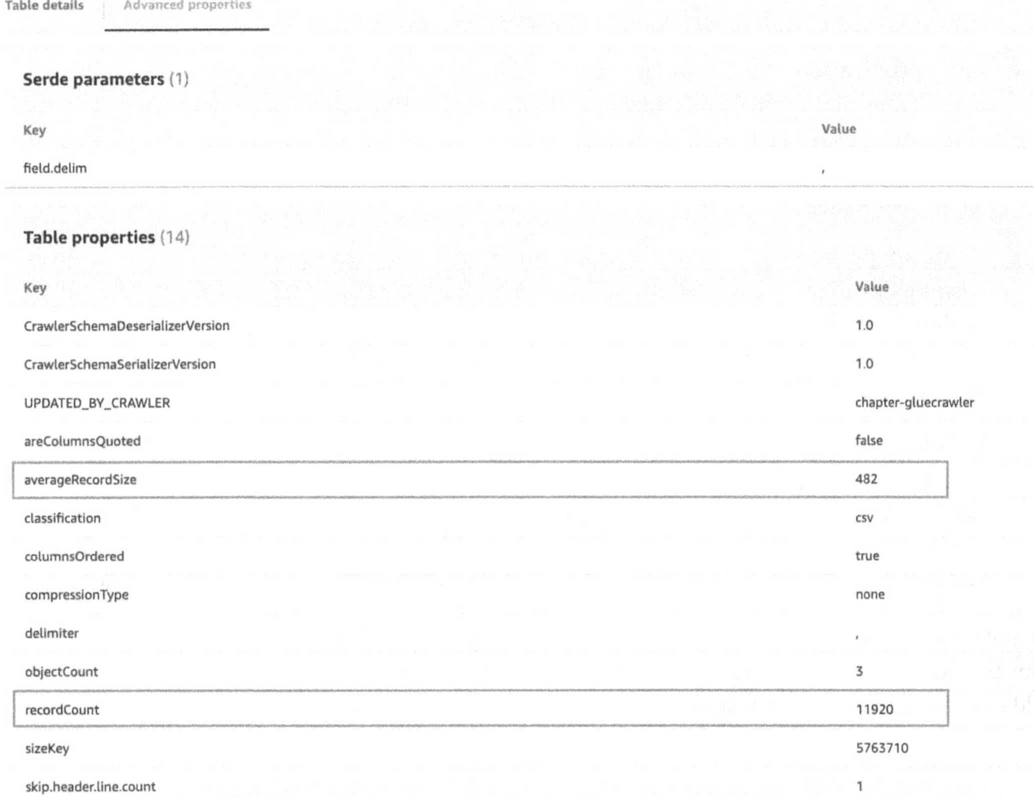
Table details | Advanced properties

Serde parameters (1)

Key	Value
field.delim	,

Table properties (14)

Key	Value
CrawlerSchemaDeserializerVersion	1.0
CrawlerSchemaSerializerVersion	1.0
UPDATED_BY_CRAWLER	chapter-gluecrawler
areColumnsQuoted	false
averageRecordSize	482
classification	csv
columnsOrdered	true
compressionType	none
delimiter	,
objectCount	3
recordCount	11920
sizeKey	5763710
skip.header.line.count	1

Figure 6.18 – AWS Glue Catalog – Advanced properties

Table stats can be viewed and updated through the AWS Glue console or the Glue API. They can also be automatically gathered by AWS Glue Crawler during the data discovery process.

Table stats in Glue Data Catalog provide important metadata about the tables stored in your data catalog. These stats include information such as the number of rows in a table, the size of the table, and the column statistics, such as minimum and maximum values, data distribution, and data type. These statistics play a crucial role in query optimization and performance tuning within AWS Glue.

These table statistics are utilized by AWS Glue and query engines such as Amazon Athena or Amazon Redshift Spectrum to make informed decisions about query execution plans. Here's how table stats are important and can be leveraged for query optimization and performance tuning:

- **Query planning**: The query optimizer uses table statistics to estimate the cardinality (number of rows) and data distribution of tables involved in a query. This estimation helps the optimizer choose the most efficient query execution plan. Accurate statistics enable the optimizer to make better decisions, resulting in faster and more efficient query processing.
- **Join optimization**: When joining multiple tables, the query optimizer utilizes table statistics to determine the optimal join strategy. By analyzing column statistics such as data distribution and value ranges, the optimizer can decide whether to perform a hash join, merge join, or other join algorithms. This information helps minimize data shuffling and improve overall join performance.
- **Predicate pushdown**: Table statistics are also used for predicate pushdown, which involves pushing down filtering operations to the data source before bringing the data into the query engine. By understanding the data distribution and value ranges of columns, the optimizer can determine if filtering at the data source would significantly reduce the data volume to be processed, leading to faster query execution.
- **Data skew detection**: Table statistics can help identify data skew, where the distribution of data across partitions or columns is uneven. Skew in data can negatively impact query performance, causing some tasks to take significantly longer than others. By analyzing table statistics, you can detect data skew and take corrective actions, such as redistributing data or using different partitioning strategies to achieve better load balancing and improve query performance.

To ensure accurate table statistics, it is important to regularly update them as data changes. AWS Glue provides functionality to automatically gather statistics for tables through the use of crawlers. Additionally, you can manually update the table statistics by using the `ANALYZE TABLE` command in query engines such as Amazon Athena:

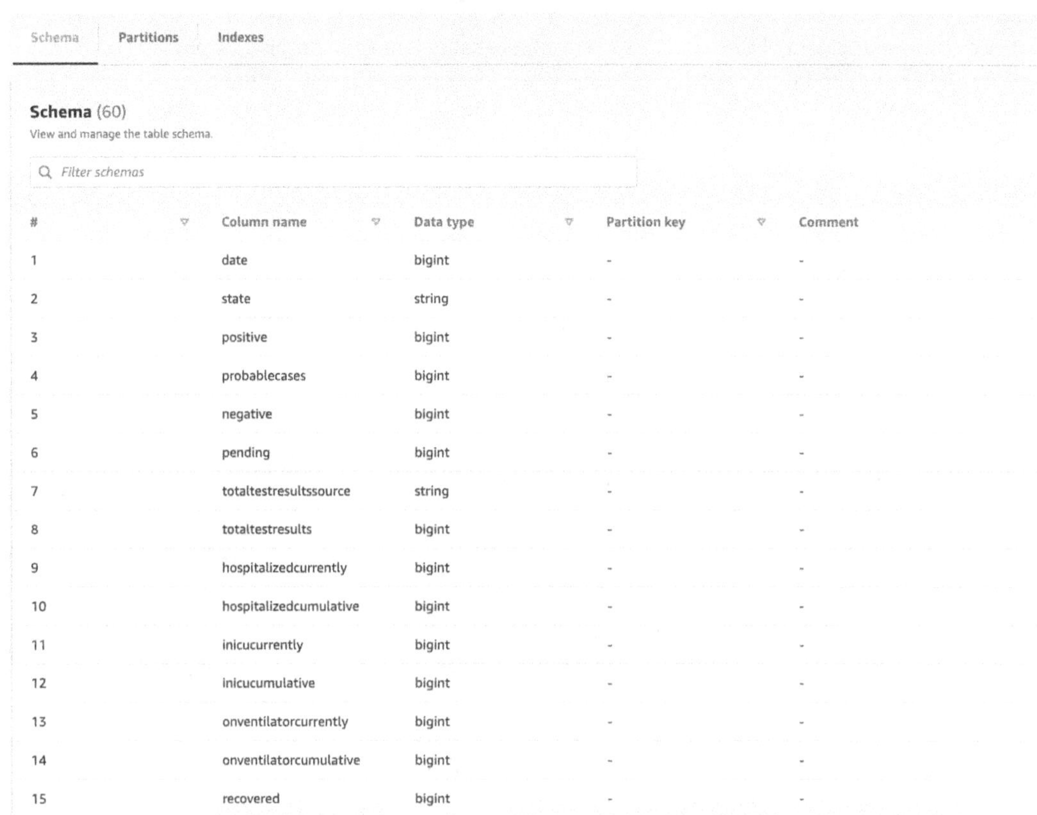

Schema | Partitions | Indexes

Schema (60)
View and manage the table schema.

Filter schemas

#	Column name	Data type	Partition key	Comment
1	date	bigint	-	-
2	state	string	-	-
3	positive	bigint	-	-
4	probablecases	bigint	-	-
5	negative	bigint	-	-
6	pending	bigint	-	-
7	totaltestresultssource	string	-	-
8	totaltestresults	bigint	-	-
9	hospitalizedcurrently	bigint	-	-
10	hospitalizedcumulative	bigint	-	-
11	inicucurrently	bigint	-	-
12	inicucumulative	bigint	-	-
13	onventilatorcurrently	bigint	-	-
14	onventilatorcumulative	bigint	-	-
15	recovered	bigint	-	-

Figure 6.19 – AWS Glue Catalog table schema definition

Having explored the table definition, we can now review the data using Amazon Athena.

Clicking on **Table data** will redirect us to the Athena console:

Tables (4)
View and manage all available tables.

Delete | Add tables using crawler | Add table

Filter tables

Name	Database	Location	Classification	Deprecated	View data
covid19_csv	chapter6_covid19	s3://covid19-lake/rearc-co\	csv	-	Table data
covid19_states_daily	chapter6_covid19	s3://covid19-lake/rearc-co\	json	-	Table data
covid19_us_daily	chapter6_covid19	s3://covid19-lake/rearc-co\	json	-	Table data
covid19_us_total_latest	chapter6_covid19	s3://covid19-lake/rearc-co\	json	-	Table data

Figure 6.20 – Tables list in AWS Glue Data Catalog

Here, we accessed the data of the `covid19_csv` table using Amazon Athena. By clicking on **Table data**, we were redirected to the Athena console, where we can see the data of the table. Other tables are also listed in Athena. In the upcoming chapter, we will explore Athena in more detail:

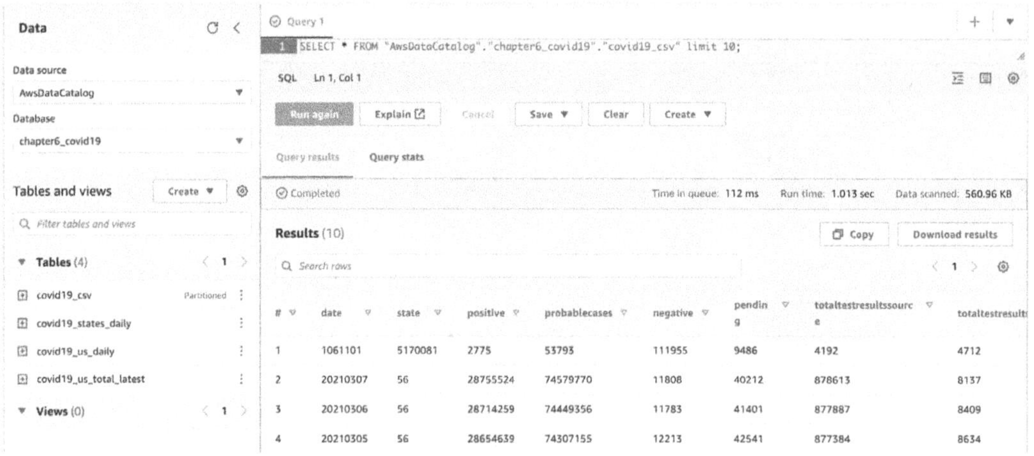

Figure 6.21 – Amazon Athena's query console

In this example, we demonstrated how to use AWS Glue Catalog to catalog the Covid-19 dataset and run SQL queries against it using Amazon Athena. In the next section, we will focus on how to perform data ingestion using AWS Glue ETL.

Data ingestion using AWS Glue ETL

In the previous section, we learned how to use various features of AWS Glue Crawler and AWS Glue Data Catalog to create a centralized data catalog for data discovery. In this section, we will explore the option of using AWS Glue ETL for data ingestion from various data sources, such as data lakes (Amazon S3), databases, streaming, and SaaS data stores. Additionally, we will learn about how to use job bookmarks to perform incremental data loads from Data Lake (S3) and JDBC.

Glue enables users to create ETL jobs using three different types of ETL frameworks – Spark ETL, Spark Streaming, and Python Shell. In the introduction section of Glue DataBrew, we learned how AWS Glue has evolved and that now, AWS Glue Studio is available to build ETL pipelines.

The AWS Glue user interface allows you to build your ETL pipeline with an interesting feature that converts your UI job into a script, which helps you scale when building similar pipelines or when you need some help to get started and then add customization.

In addition to supporting multiple Spark frameworks to process data, Glue provides advanced features during job creation, such as auto-scaling, job bookmarking, enabling continuous logging, the Spark UI, Flex instances, and passing Spark and job parameters.

In addition to the Spark framework, Glue ETL provides Glue-native advanced frameworks/APIs and formats for complex ETL, such as GlueContext, DynamicFrame, job bookmarking, Glue Parquet, Glue Interactive session, workflows, triggers, and more.

Let's explore these features one by one.

AWS GlueContext

The `GlueContext` class wraps Apache's `SparkContext` and can be initialized using the following code snippet:

```
sc = SparkContext()
glueContext = GlueContext(sc)
```

`GlueContext` allows you to communicate with the Spark framework and is the entry point for many Glue ETL features, such as DynamicFrame, job bookmarking, job parameters, and more.

DynamicFrame

Glue ETL's DynamicFrame is a vital feature that enables Spark developers to create more efficient Spark pipelines, and it is native to Glue. A Glue DynamicFrame is a distributed collection of self-describing `DynamicRecord` objects, but it does not require them to adhere to a fixed schema. Due to the self-describing nature of records in DynamicFrame, it does not require a schema to be created and can be used to read/transform data with inconsistent schemas.

You can create a Glue DynamicFrame using different APIs, depending on your use case. For example, the following code snippet creates a DynamicFrame object called `datasource0` for the `my_table` table in the `my_database` database:

```
datasource0 = glueContext.create_dynamic_frame.from_catalog(database_
name='my_database', table_name='my_table', transformation_
ctx='datasource0')
```

In this statement, we used the `GlueContext` object, which uses the Glue SDK, to connect to Glue Data Catalog and fetch the data source classifications and properties to create the object. Users can also pass additional options using the additional `_options` parameter, such as the `push_down_predicate` parameter.

Besides using the `from_catalog` method to create a DynamicFrame, you can create DynamicFrames using the following methods:

- `from_options`: This method allows users to create DynamicFrames by manually specifying the connection type, options, and format. This method provides users with the flexibility to customize options for a data store.
- `from_rdd`: This method allows users to create DynamicFrames using Spark RDDS.

To leverage the features available in DataFrame, you can convert a DynamicFrame into a DataFrame using the following syntax:

```
df = datasource0.toDF()
```

Similarly, you can convert a Spark DataFrame into a Glue DynamicFrame using the following syntax:

```
from awsglue.dynamicframe import DynamicFrame
dyf = DynamicFrame.fromDF(dataframe=df, glue_ctx=glueContext,
name="dyf")
```

Both DynamicFrame and DataFrame are high-level APIs that interact with Spark RDDs. However, the structure of a DynamicFrame is different from a DataFrame:

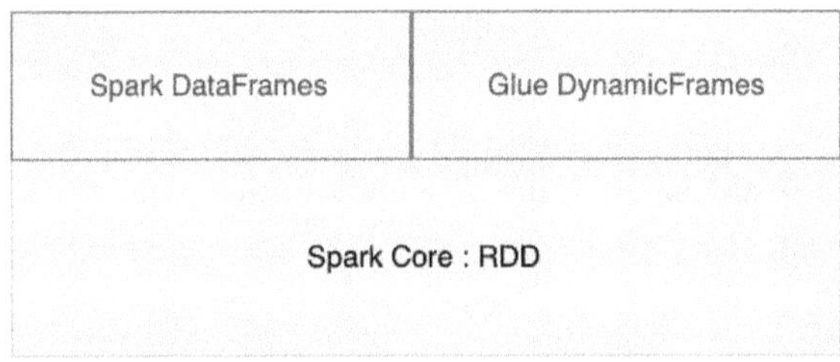

Figure 6.22 – AWS Glue ETL high-level architecture

It is important to note that converting a Glue DynamicFrame into a Spark DataFrame requires a full Map stage in Spark, which can be resource-intensive and add extra time to your job execution time. This is because converting a DynamicFrame into a DataFrame blocks Spark, using all the optimization done against DynamicFrame.

AWS Glue Job bookmarks

AWS Glue offers the unique capability of performing bookmarking, which distinguishes it from other Spark-based ETL solutions such as running Spark on Amazon **Elastic MapReduce** (**EMR**). Bookmarking enables incremental data loading by tracking the data that has already been processed and written. This is particularly useful when dealing with large datasets or extracting data from databases.

Job bookmarks are available for JDBC data sources, Amazon S3, and relational transforms. For Amazon S3, job bookmarks are available for the JSON, CSV, Apache Avro, XML, Parquet, and ORC file formats. When working with JDBC sources, users need to specify a column as the bookmark key; otherwise, AWS Glue will use the primary key as the bookmark key, provided that it is sequentially increasing or decreasing without gaps. If user-defined bookmark keys are used, they should be monotonically increasing or decreasing; gaps are permitted in this case.

For Amazon S3, AWS Glue uses the last modified time of the objects to determine which objects need to be reprocessed. There are various processing options available, such as resetting job bookmarks and rewinding. Resetting job bookmarks allows users to reprocess all the data using the same job, while rewinding enables them to go back to any previous job run. It is important to note that converting a Glue DynamicFrame into a Spark DataFrame requires a full Map stage in Spark, which can be resource-intensive and add extra time to job execution due to blocking Spark optimizations against DynamicFrames.

AWS Glue Triggers

AWS Glue Triggers enable you to schedule your Glue workflow, which includes Glue jobs and crawlers. You can create triggers that fire on-demand, scheduled, or based on events. Triggers can exist in several states, such as `CREATED`, `ACTIVATED`, and `DEACTIVATED`.

Three types of triggers are available:

- **Scheduled triggers**: These triggers are time-based and can be configured using cron expressions to define the schedule.
- **Conditional triggers**: These triggers execute based on the previous job or crawler states. For example, you can configure a trigger to execute Job 1 only when a crawler has completed.
- **On-demand triggers**: These triggers are activated manually, as the name suggests, and execute when you run them.

AWS Glue interactive sessions

AWS Glue provides an interactive environment for building, testing, and running your ETL jobs on AWS. This environment includes an open source Jupyter kernel that integrates with popular IDEs such as PyCharm, IntelliJ, and VS Code, allowing you to write and test code locally. To set up an interactive session, you can refer to the official Glue documentation at `https://docs.aws.amazon.com/glue/latest/dg/interactive-sessions.html`.

Now that we have a fair understanding of all the Glue components, let's learn about some ingestion patterns through examples:

- Ingesting data from Amazon S3 (Object Store)
- Ingesting data from SaaS applications
- Ingesting data from relational databases

AWS Glue Studio

Glue Studio is a powerful visual interface provided by AWS Glue for building and managing ETL workflows. It offers several features and benefits that enhance the data integration and transformation process. However, there are also some limitations and considerations to keep in mind. Let's provide an overview.

The features and benefits of Glue Studio are as follows:

- **Visual ETL development**: Glue Studio provides a user interface for visually designing ETL workflows. It simplifies the process of building data pipelines by allowing users to create, connect, and configure pre-built components called "transforms" without writing code.
- **Pre-built transform library**: Glue Studio offers a rich library of pre-built transforms, which are data processing operations such as filtering, aggregating, joining, and more. These transforms can be easily incorporated into the workflow, saving time and effort in developing complex data transformations.
- **Auto-generated Spark code**: Behind the scenes, Glue Studio automatically generates Apache Spark code based on the visual workflow. This enables users to leverage the power of Spark for distributed data processing while abstracting away the complexities of Spark programming.
- **Integration with Glue Data Catalog**: Glue Studio seamlessly integrates with Glue Data Catalog, allowing easy access to metadata, table definitions, and schemas. It simplifies the process of working with data stored in various AWS data sources such as Amazon S3, RDS, Redshift, and more.
- **Built-in data catalog and data lake**: Glue Studio leverages Glue Data Catalog as a central repository for managing and organizing metadata. It enables users to discover, catalog, and explore data assets within their data lake, promoting data governance and self-service data discovery.
- **Easy deployment and scheduling**: Glue Studio provides simple deployment options, allowing users to deploy their workflows as AWS Glue ETL jobs with just a few clicks. It also offers scheduling capabilities to automate the execution of workflows repeatedly.

One of the limitations and considerations of AWS Glue Studio is **limited customization**. While Glue Studio provides a visual interface for ETL development, it may have limitations when it comes to complex transformations or custom logic. In such cases, you may need to switch to traditional coding approaches using Glue ETL scripts or other AWS services.

Ingesting data from object stores

This example involves copying data from the COVID-19 data lake on Open Data on AWS (`https://registry.opendata.aws/aws-covid19-lake/`), which is stored in a public S3 bucket named `s3://covid19-lake/`. To achieve this, we will use the Amazon S3 Boto3 library, a Python package that's used to connect to data in different file stores such as SFTP, FTP, and others. In this case, a Glue Python shell ETL job will be utilized to read CSV data from Amazon S3, convert it into JSON, and then copy it to a target S3 bucket. The COVID-19 data lake on Amazon S3 contains various folders, and in this example, the `s3://covid19-lake/rearc-covid-19-testing-data/csv/us_daily/` folder will be used:

```
(base)                    ~ % aws s3 ls s3://covid19-lake/rearc-covid-19-testing-data/csv/us_daily/
2021-03-15 15:34:30      82926 us_daily.csv
```

Here is the code snippet:

```
import boto3,
import io,
import pandas as pd

client = boto3.client('s3')

##covid-19 data lake - https://registry.opendata.aws/aws-covid19-
lake/

src_bucket = 'covid19-lake' # SOURCE_S3_BUCKET_NAME
target_bucket = 'S3_TARGET_BUCKET_NAME'

src_object = client.get_object(
    Bucket=src_bucket,
    Key='rearc-covid-19-testing-data/csv/us_daily/us_daily.csv'
)

# Read CSV and Transform to JSON

df = pd.read_csv(src_object['Body'])

jsonBuffer = io.StringIO()

df.to_json(jsonBuffer, orient='records')

# Write JSON to target location

client.put_object(
    Bucket=target_bucket,
    Key='target_prefix/data.json',
    Body=jsonBuffer.getvalue()
)
```

The provided code snippet utilizes the `get_object()` method to retrieve data from Amazon S3, followed by data transformation from CSV to JSON format using the pandas library. Finally, the `put_object()` method is utilized to write the transformed data to the target.

Data ingestion from a database (JDBC data stores)

AWS Glue is commonly used to bring data from databases to a data lake. This is typically done using JDBC connections in a batch manner. To connect to a database, you can use an AWS Glue Connection, which stores the login credentials of the database, URI string, and **virtual private cloud**

(**VPC**) information. AWS Glue supports several types of connections, including JDBC, Amazon RDS, Amazon Redshift, Amazon DocumentDB, Kafka, and MongoDB. To create a JDBC connection, you can use the following format:

```
jdbc:protocol://host:port/db_name.
```

You can learn more about creating connections for various databases by reading the AWS Glue documentation (`https://docs.aws.amazon.com/glue/latest/dg/connection-properties.html#connection-properties-required`).

Here is an example of Microsoft SQL Server database connections:

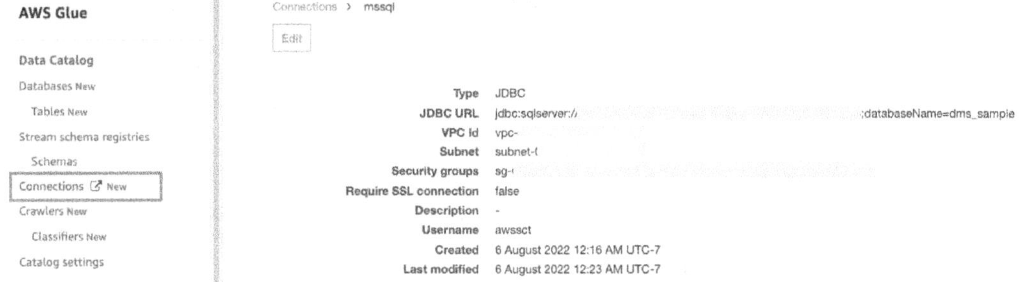

Figure 6.24 – AWS Glue JDBC connections

Here is the code snippet. Here, we are connecting the MSSQL database and moving data from the MSSQL database to Amazon S3 in Parquet file format:

```
MicrosoftSQLServer = directJDBCSource (
    glueContext,
    connectionName="mssql",
    connectionType="sqlserver",
    database="ec2-00-000-000-00.compute-1.amazonaws.com:1433;
    databaseName=dms_sample",
    table="dms_sample.sports",
    redshiftTmpDir="",
    transformation_ctx="MicrosoftSQLServer",
)

S3bucket_node3 = glueContext.write_dynamic_frame.from_options(
    frame=MicrosoftSQLServer,
    connection_type="s3",
    format="parquet",
    connection_options={"path": "s3://target_dir"},
    format_options={"compression": "uncompressed"},
    transformation_ctx="S3bucket_node3",
```

```
)
```

Data ingestion from SaaS data stores

So far, we have learned how you use AWS Glue to bring data from object stores such as Amazon S3 and relational databases such as Microsoft SQL Server. Now, we are going to learn how you use AWS Glue to ingest data from SaaS data stores.

To connect to SaaS data stores, you need to use an AWS Glue Marketplace connector; these were introduced in December 2020. At the time of writing, the Marketplace has a total of 66 connectors, which include AWS and third-party connectors such as SnowFlake, ServiceNow, Google BigQuery, ElasticSearch, Apace Iceberg, Delta Lake, and more:

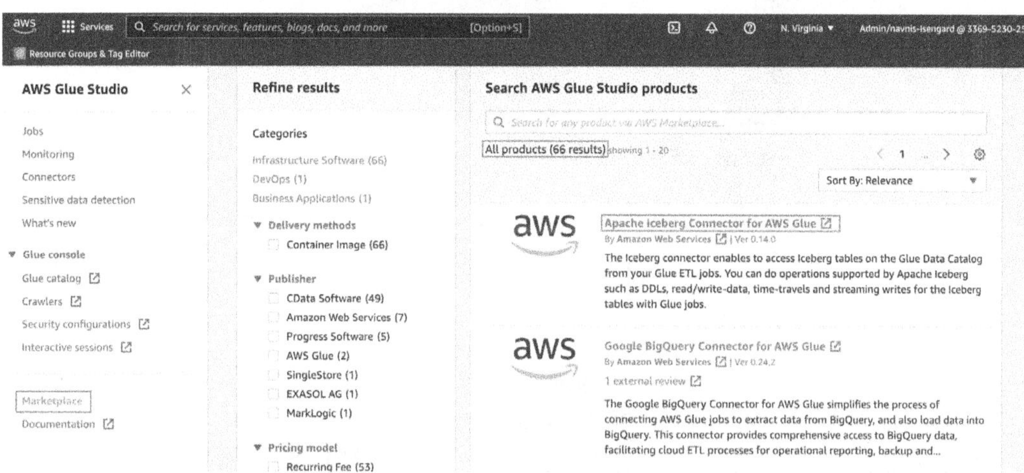

Figure 6.25 – AWS Glue Marketplace connectors

To connect ServiceNow and bring data to an Amazon S3 data lake, follow these steps:

1. Visit the AWS Marketplace (`https://us-east-1.console.aws.amazon.com/gluestudio/home?region=us-east-1#/marketplace`) and subscribe to the ServiceNow connector. Review the documentation, pricing, and user guide before proceeding.
2. Create a connection using the subscribed ServiceNow connector.
3. Build an ETL pipeline using AWS Glue Studio:

```
import sys
from awsglue.transforms import *
from awsglue.utils import getResolvedOptions
from pyspark.context import SparkContext
from awsglue.context import GlueContext
from awsglue.job import Job
```

```
args = getResolvedOptions(sys.argv, ["JOB_NAME"])
sc = SparkContext()
glueContext = GlueContext(sc)
spark = glueContext.spark_session
job = Job(glueContext)
job.init(args["JOB_NAME"], args)

# Script generated for node CData AWS Glue Connector for
ServiceNow
CDataAWSGlueConnectorforServiceNow_node1 = (
    glueContext.create_dynamic_frame.from_options(
        connection_type="marketplace.jdbc",
        connection_options={
            "tableName": "incident",
            "dbTable": "incident",
            "connectionName": "service-now-glue-connector",
        },
        transformation_ctx="CDataAWSGlueConnectorforServiceNow_
        node1",
    )
)
```

You can find a helpful blog post at `https://aws.amazon.com/blogs/big-data/extract-servicenow-data-using-aws-glue-studio-in-an-amazon-s3-data-lake-and-analyze-using-amazon-athena/`, which provides a detailed, step-by-step guide on how to build a pipeline that connects ServiceNow and brings data to an Amazon S3 data lake using AWS Glue Studio. This blog post includes instructions on subscribing to the ServiceNow connector in AWS Marketplace, creating a connection using the connector, and building an ETL pipeline using AWS Glue Studio. Additionally, it explains how to analyze the ServiceNow data using Amazon Athena once it has been ingested into the data lake.

Summary

In this chapter, we covered Apache Spark, its connection with AWS Glue, and the various features available in AWS Glue, including AWS Glue Data Catalog for data discovery, AWS Glue Crawler for metadata extraction, and AWS Glue Studio for building UI-based ETL pipelines. We also explored how to use the AWS Glue Marketplace to subscribe to different connectors so that we can extract data from SaaS applications.

In the next chapter, we will discuss another essential service that plays a significant role in the data wrangling and discovery process: Amazon Athena.

7

Working with Athena

In the previous chapters, you learned about the AWS Glue and Amazon S3 services and how they fit into the data wrangling pipeline. In this chapter, we will explore how Amazon Athena service can help in the data discovery, data structuring, data enriching, and data quality phases of the data wrangling pipeline. We will work with some practical examples and perform an analysis on the data to keep it more interesting.

This chapter covers the following topics:

- Understanding Amazon Athena
- Advanced data discovery and data structuring with Athena
- Enriching data from multiple sources using Athena
- Setting up a serverless data quality pipeline with Athena

Understanding Amazon Athena

Amazon Athena is an interactive, serverless analytical service that can help to explore data available in Amazon S3 without loading the data. Athena helps to analyze the data through SQL syntax or interactive Spark applications. It can help customers to analyze datasets stored in multiple data formats on Amazon S3 through familiar SQL. Since Athena is a serverless offering, users are charged based on the data scanned by the queries and there is no need to maintain separate servers to enable user queries. This has enabled business and analytics teams to quickly analyze, transform, and visualize data in the data lake for specific use cases without relying on the data engineering team to come up with complex ETL pipelines.

Amazon Athena was launched on *re:Invent 2016* and has gone through significant improvements over the course of time. It was launched as a serverless mechanism to query Amazon S3 data using managed Presto servers from the Athena catalog (different from the Glue catalog). Now, it supports querying data from the Glue catalog, Query federation, CTAS statements, Lake Formation integration, support for transactional data lake formats, Athena for Spark, and more.

Athena supports two modes for data analysis after the announcement of Athena for Apache Spark in *re:Invent 2022*, as follows:

- Users can query data using SQL syntax, which is similar to Presto/Trino but with limitations. This enables analysts without programming language expertise to analyze the data in the S3 data lake without support from anyone. The following blog contains best practices for Amazon Athena usage for optimizing cost and improving performance for SQL-based analysis: `https://aws.amazon.com/blogs/big-data/top-10-performance-tuning-tips-for-amazon-athena/`.
- Athena for Spark supported Apache Spark version 3.2 when it was launched. Refer to the Athena documentation for the support of recent Spark versions. For additional details about Athena for Spark, refer to the following blog: .

When to use SQL/Spark analysis options?

If you want to perform analytics on your data lake without loading it into another storage layer, use Athena SQL to catalog and query the data. You can also use CTAS statements to perform lightweight data transformations. If you want to execute Spark programs in an interactive and serverless manner for some of your analysis use cases, the Athena for Spark option can be used.

Advanced data discovery and data structuring with Athena

In this section, we will explore how Amazon Athena helps in performing advanced data discovery and data structuring phases of the data wrangling pipeline.

SQL-based data discovery with Athena

Amazon Athena provides SQL-based data exploration and supports advanced data types as well. The advantage here is that even people with no coding expertise can explore data with familiar SQL syntax on multiple formats of data and different storage types.

Before we query data using Amazon Athena, we need to create metadata for the table in the Glue catalog. Amazon Athena helps you to query data from different data sources, as follows:

- **AWS Glue catalog**—Access tables that are available in the AWS Glue catalog. We can create tables in the AWS Glue catalog in multiple ways, which we will explore later in this chapter.
- **Federated data sources**—Supports querying data from Apache Hive, AWS, and third-party databases and services. For an extensive list of supported data sources, refer to `https://docs.aws.amazon.com/athena/latest/ug/connectors-prebuilt.html`.

In addition to prebuilt connectors, you can also create custom connectors to query the data source of your choice. We will explore in detail federated data sources further in this chapter.

Let us understand more about the Glue catalog, which will be the central metadata store for most Athena queries. The Glue catalog is a persistent metadata store that lets users store, annotate, and share metadata. There will be a unique Glue catalog per region within each AWS account. You can use **Identity and Access Management** (**IAM**) policies to define and control access to users for the Glue catalog and tables. For fine-grained data access (record and column level), users will have to explore the AWS Lake Formation service.

If you look at the AWS Glue console, you can see different links under the **Data Catalog** section, as shown here:

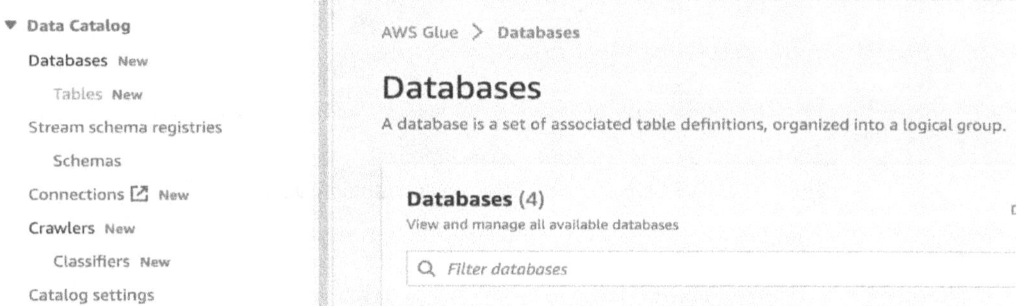

Figure 7.1: AWS Glue console – Data Catalog section

Let's look at these sections in a bit more detail:

- **Databases**: A database is a container for storing table metadata information from different data sources. Users can understand and relate this to the concept of schema/databases from the database world.
- **Tables**: Each table will have a schema definition of the source data. We want to emphasize that this is only a metadata definition of the actual data stored somewhere else, such as a S3 data lake. It also creates partitions in the table, when the files have the same schema, data format, and compression format.

  Tables can be created from three sources, as follows:

  - The crawler creates new tables when it's run. We can keep the schema updated with new partitions, additional columns, and so on by running the Glue crawler on a schedule.
  - Manually add the schema definition. You can go through this approach when you want to customize the name of the table/column, show only specific columns from the dataset, and so on.
  - Create a table from an existing schema from the schema registry for streaming data sources.

Glue catalog tables can have multiple versions. Each edit to the table metadata creates a new version of the table. You can compare the table versions on the AWS Glue console UI and verify the changes that are made between different versions of the table, as illustrated in the following screenshot. Also, we can revert back to a previous version by using the `delete-table-version` API:

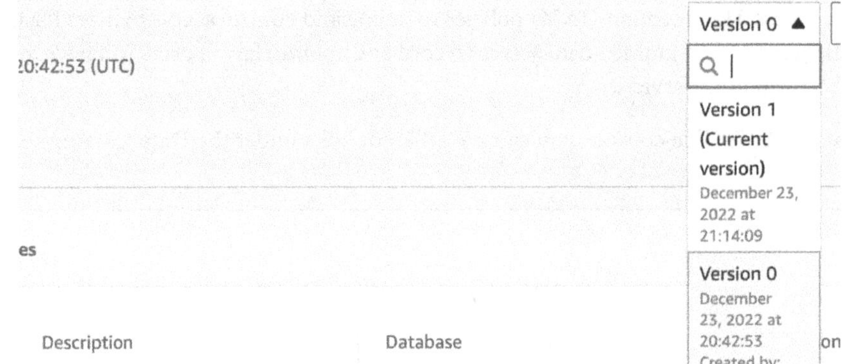

Figure 7.2: AWS Glue console – Table having multiple versions

- **Connections**: Store login credentials, URI, and VPC information to avoid providing this information every time a crawler/job is run. We can also create a network connection to access Amazon S3 or other services through VPC and not use the public internet.
- **Crawlers**: Glue crawlers discover data and catalog metadata (including semi-structured and log data) automatically for users. Crawlers use classifiers to infer and identify data types, both AWS glue created (CSV, JSON, and so on) and custom classifiers using grok patterns. Crawlers can detect schema changes and update the table definition automatically based on configurations provided by users.

In order to explore the features of Athena, we will use a sample dataset for Amazon reviews from `https://docs.opendata.aws/noaa-ghcn-pds/readme.html`. We have Parquet, CSV, and compressed CSV formats on which the data is available.

We will create a table in two formats, as mentioned earlier, through an AWS Glue crawler and a manual methodology.

Creating a table through an AWS Glue crawler and query in Athena

We'll get started as follows:

1. Navigate to the AWS Glue console, create a new crawler, and provide the S3 path for the `noaa` dataset, as shown in the crawler **Add data source** screen:

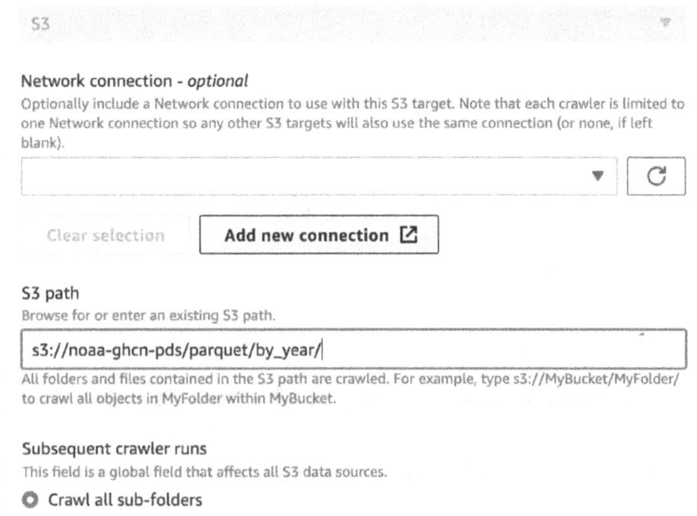

Figure 7.3: AWS Glue console – Configuring crawler

Provide an IAM role that has appropriate access (including S3 read access) and a database name to complete the crawler creation.

2. Once the crawler is created, click to run it, and wait for its completion. Once the crawler has finished, you can see a new table is added and partitions are added to the Glue catalog:

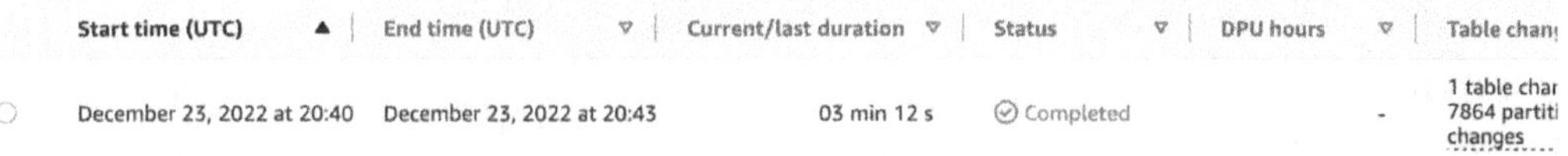

Figure 7.4: AWS Glue console – Result of a successful crawler run

3. Now, you can query the table in Athena and start analyzing the data. Run a `SELECT` query on the table, and you can also filter data using partitions that are available in the table:

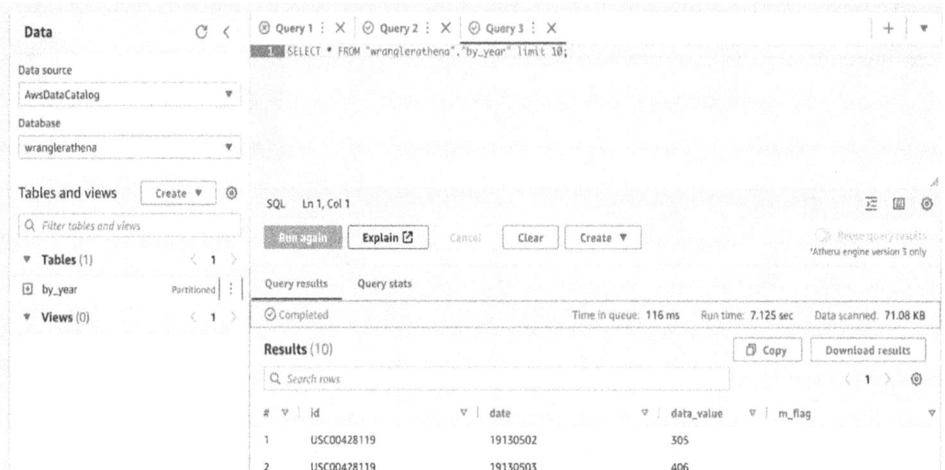

Figure 7.5: AWS Athena console – Querying the table created by the Glue crawler

Creating a table manually in Athena and querying the table

Here, we will create a table for the CSV format in a manual way. We will follow the approach as listed here:

1. Download a sample file and understand the table structure.

   Before creating a table manually, we need to understand the columns and data types in the source files so that we can create the table **data definition language** (**DDL**) statement appropriately. In this example, we will download the 2022 data alone using the command in the CLI (assuming the AWS CLI is installed in the machine already), as follows:

```
aws s3 cp s3://noaa-ghcn-pds/csv/by_year/2022.csv .
```

   As this is a CSV file, we can open it in an Excel application; there might be an error in some systems as this is a huge file with a size greater than 1 GB, but you could browse different columns and data types available in the data. You can see the file open in Excel here:

A1 fx ID

	A	B	C	D	E	F	G	H	I	J
1	ID	DATE	ELEMENT	DATA_VALUI	M_FLAG	Q_FLAG	S_FLAG	OBS_TIME		
2	AE00004119	20220101	TAVG	204	H		S			
3	AEM000411	20220101	TAVG	211	H		S			
4	AEM000412	20220101	TAVG	209	H		S			
5	AEM000412	20220101	TAVG	207	H		S			
6	AG00006039	20220101	TAVG	121	H		S			
7	AG00006059	20220101	TAVG	151	H		S			
8	AG00006061	20220101	TAVG	111	H		S			
9	AGE0014770	20220101	TMIN	73			S			
10	AGE0014770	20220101	PRCP	0			S			

Figure 7.6: Sample data file open in Excel to understand the column structure and data types

2. Now, we will create a DDL statement and execute that in Athena to create the table:

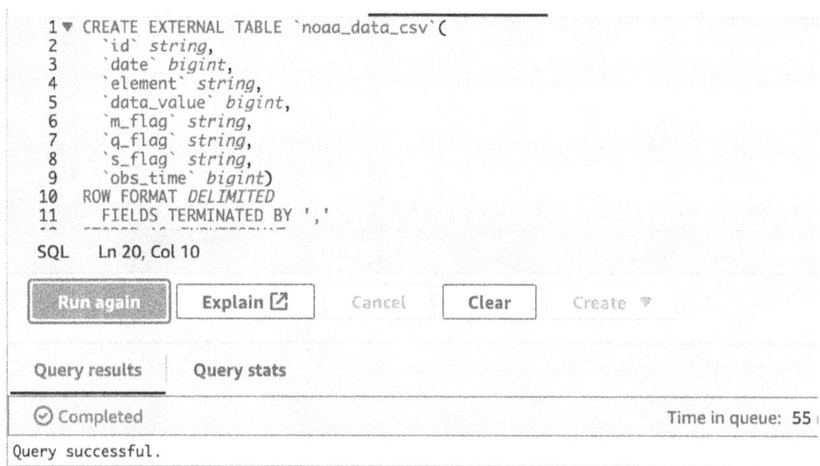

Figure 7.7: AWS Athena console – Creating a table manually using a DDL statement

> **Note**
>
> The DML statement used is shown next. The DML statement was taken from a different Glue crawler to save time and changed to meet our needs here.

```
CREATE EXTERNAL TABLE `noaa_data_csv`(
  `id` string,
  `date` bigint,
  `element` string,
  `data_value` bigint,
  `m_flag` string,
  `q_flag` string,
  `s_flag` string,
  `obs_time` bigint)
ROW FORMAT DELIMITED
  FIELDS TERMINATED BY ','
STORED AS INPUTFORMAT
  'org.apache.hadoop.mapred.TextInputFormat'
OUTPUTFORMAT
  'org.apache.hadoop.hive.ql.io.HiveIgnoreKeyTextOutputFormat'
LOCATION
  's3://noaa-ghcn-pds/csv/by_year/'
TBLPROPERTIES (
  'areColumnsQuoted'='false',
```

```
'classification'='csv',
'columnsOrdered'='true',
'compressionType'='none',
'delimiter'=',',
'skip.header.line.count'='1',
'typeOfData'='file')
```

3. Now, we can start querying the data from that table location using Amazon Athena, as follows:

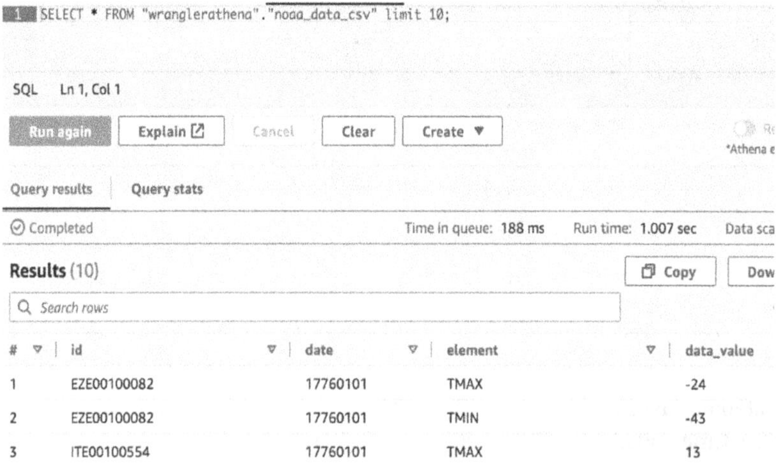

Figure 7.8: AWS Athena console – Querying the table that was created manually

Loading a fixed-width table using a regex parser

A better example is to load a table that is not supported by a Glue crawler. We will create a table for the inventory file (`http://noaa-ghcn-pds.s3.amazonaws.com/ghcnd-inventory.txt`). The file has the structure as pasted here from the documentation page of the data source:

The file structure is described in the table below.

Variable	Columns	Type
ID	1-11	CHARACTER
LATITUDE	13-20	REAL
LONGITUDE	22-30	REAL
ELEMENT	32-35	CHARACTER
FIRSTYEAR	37-40	INTEGER
LASTYEAR	42-45	INTEGER

- ID = the station identification code. Please see "ghcnd-stations.txt" for a complete list of stations and their metadata.
- LATITUDE = the latitude of the station (in decimal degrees).
- LONGITUDE = the longitude of the station (in decimal degrees).
- ELEMENT = the element type. See section III for a definition of elements.
- FIRSTYEAR = the first year of unflagged data for the given element.
- LASTYEAR = the last year of unflagged data for the given element.

Figure 7.9: File structure of the data

This means the first 11 characters are ID fields, the 12th character can be a space or anything, and the next 7 digits are latitude, as pasted in *Figure 7.9*. We can use a **regular expression** (**regex**) to parse the data and query it. We will perform the following steps to query and discover data from a fixed-width file:

1. Download and identify the structure of data within the file, like so:

    ```
    aws s3 cp s3://noaa-ghcn-pds/ghcnd-inventory.txt .
    ```

    Once the file has been downloaded to your local disk, you can open the file in any editor of your choice and analyze the data to understand the schema structure. We will understand the values that are available in each column, as seen here, to design a regex for parsing the file:

    ```
    AQC00914149 -14.2833 -170.6833 DAPR 1958 1963
    AQC00914149 -14.2833 -170.6833 MDPR 1958 1963
    AQC00914188 -14.2167 -168.5333 TMAX 1955 1957
    AQC00914188 -14.2167 -168.5333 TMIN 1955 1957
    ```

    Figure 7.10: Browsing the content of a NOAA inventory fixed-width file

> **Note**
>
> We can also use S3 Select to query data from files if the file doesn't have special characters or complex structures.

2. Design a regex to read data from the file.

    You can use any regex validator based on your organization's security needs to validate the regex before creating a Glue table. We will use `https://regex101.com/` for validating a regex in our use case.

    For those of you who are new to regexes, you can read more online materials and cheat sheets for regexes before getting started. We will copy some sample records that represent different data formats within our data file and start creating regexes one field at a time. The following screenshot shows the regex for capturing the first field to match a word of 11 characters along with a hyphen character that is present in some records (see *record 3* in the screenshot):

    ```
    / ^([\w-]{11})

    TEST STRING

    ACW00011604  17.1167  -61.7833 WT08 1949 1949
    ACW00011604  17.1167  -61.7833 WT16 1949 1949
    BR00B4-0340 -20.3300  -47.7700 PRCP 1943 1995
    AQC00914869 -14.3333 -170.7167 DAPR 1956 1966
    ```

    Figure 7.11: Creating a regex statement to load a fixed-width file

3. We will create a regex with a trial-and-error method until we are successful in matching the sample records from our input file, as shown here:

```
/ ^([\w-]{11})\s([\w\s.+-]){8}\s([\w\s.+-]){9}\s([\w]{4})\s(\d){4}\s(\d){4}
```

TEST STRING

```
ACW00011604  17.1167  -61.7833 WT08 1949 1949
ACW00011604  17.1167  -61.7833 WT16 1949 1949
BR00B4-0340 -20.3300  -47.7700 PRCP 1943 1995
AQC00914869 -14.3333 -170.7167 DAPR 1956 1966
```

Figure 7.12: Creating a regex statement to load a fixed-width file (continued)

A high-level explanation of the regex is provided in the following table:

Regex	Description
`([\w-]{11})\s`	Match the `id` column with the first 11 characters and then we will ignore the space with the `\s` character.
`([\w\s.+-]){8}\s`	Match the `latitude` column, which can have alphabets, numbers, and space (right-aligned _ and +/- signs). This is an 8-character field.
`([\w\s.+-]){9}\s`	Match the `longitude` column, which can have alphabets, numbers, and space (right-aligned _ and +/- signs). This is a 9-character field.
`([\w]{4})\s`	Match the `element` column with a 4-character word in the file.
`(\d){4}\s`	Match the 4-digit value for the starting year column.
`(\d){4}`	Match the 4-digit value for the ending year column.

Table 7.1: Table showing individual components of regex used for parsing data

4. Create a table using a regex in Athena.

   We will create a table using the `CREATE TABLE` statement in Athena, along with the regex that we designed in the last step. Please note we have to change all single backslashes to double backslashes before using them in the `CREATE TABLE` SQL statement (refer to the highlighted section from the following SQL statement):

```
CREATE EXTERNAL TABLE ghndinv
(
  `id` string,
  `latitude` string,
  `longitude` string,
  `element` string,
```

```
    `firstyear` int,
    `lastyear` int
)
ROW FORMAT SERDE 'org.apache.hadoop.hive.serde2.RegexSerDe'
WITH SERDEPROPERTIES (
    "input.regex" = "^([\\w\\s.+-]{11})\\s([\\w\\s.+-]{8})\\s([\\
w\\s.+-]{9})\\s([\\w]{4})\\s([\\d]{4})\\s([\\d]{4})")
LOCATION 's3://<<location your file/'
```

5. Query the data in Athena and validate it.

   Once the table is created, you can query the data and validate whether the data has been parsed correctly, as follows:

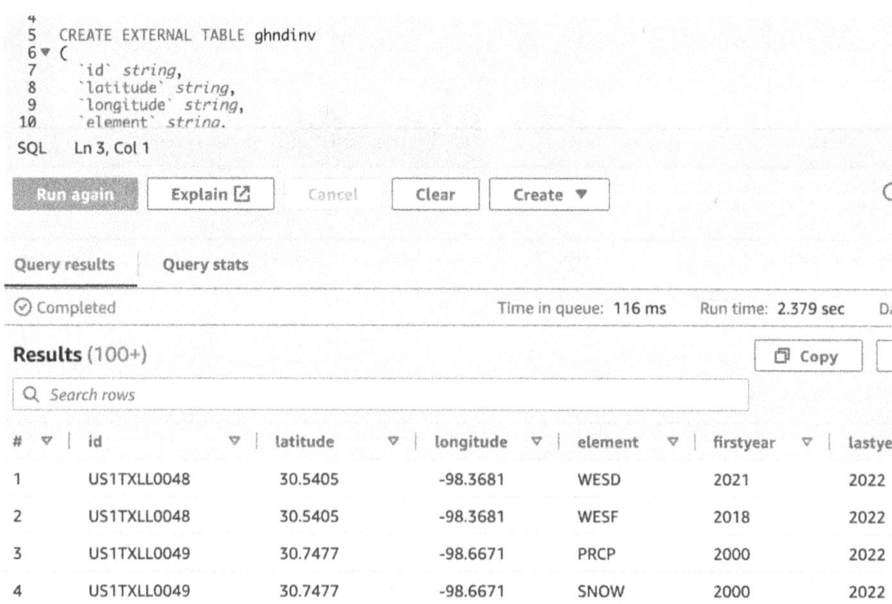

#	id	latitude	longitude	element	firstyear	lastye
1	US1TXLL0048	30.5405	-98.3681	WESD	2021	2022
2	US1TXLL0048	30.5405	-98.3681	WESF	2018	2022
3	US1TXLL0049	30.7477	-98.6671	PRCP	2000	2022
4	US1TXLL0049	30.7477	-98.6671	SNOW	2000	2022

Figure 7.13: AWS Athena console – Querying the inventory table created with a regex statement

Congrats! You have now created a table from a fixed-width file and used SQL statements to explore the data.

You have now understood different methodologies for creating tables to query in Amazon Athena, which is the first and important step before we proceed with analysis in Athena. You could also create tables in the Glue catalog in a programmatic manner or through ETL pipelines with services such as AWS Glue, and so on.

Using CTAS for data structuring

CTAS statements provide a powerful way to perform data structuring through SQL. You can convert data types, storage formats, and other smaller lightweight ETL as well with this command.

We will continue from our previous step where we created a table from the fixed-width file that was parsed using the `serde` regex. But if you expand the table definition and column types, you will find the `latitude` and `longitude` columns are of data type `string`. We can convert those two fields to a `float` data type and also store the output file in Parquet format, as follows:

```
create table ghndinv_parquet
with (
      format = 'Parquet',
      write_compression = 'GZIP',
      external_location = 's3://<<s3 bucket>>/ghndinv_parquet/')
as
select
    id, cast(latitude as real) as latitude,cast(longitude as real) as
longitude,element,firstyear,lastyear
from ghndinv
```

You can look at the S3 location and verify the Parquet files are created for the table and that it is not a fixed-width text file anymore, as follows:

20221224_233819_00007_wat2i_06c68780-b9e8-4a01-bfae-4fae9d1019ca
20221224_233819_00007_wat2i_179f1891-c2b8-42c8-a21f-2e3a56ae15fb
20221224_233819_00007_wat2i_223736c0-3bf7-469f-a026-fa862bae02b7
20221224_233819_00007_wat2i_3b745d06-b27b-4d40-a8a6-f2d2f374f6d6
20221224_233819_00007_wat2i_4622ef6b-49ba-4054-b649-66dafc90d76a

Figure 7.14: S3 location of the table that was created with the CTAS command

Also, the data types are changed to `float` for the `latitude` and `longitude` columns, as we can see here:

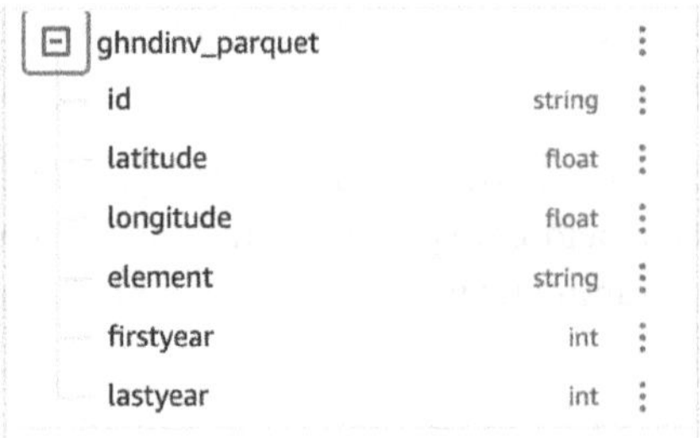

ghndinv_parquet	
id	string
latitude	float
longitude	float
element	string
firstyear	int
lastyear	int

Figure 7.15: Columns and data types of the table created with the CTAS command in Amazon Athena

We will also convert the CSV data into Parquet format, along with the partitioning schema that we require based on access patterns from data. We will partition the table based on country code to access the weather data for each country in a performant manner.

We have already loaded the CSV table manually, earlier in this chapter, into a `noaa_data_csv` table. We will use the data from the table and extract the `countrycode` value from the first two characters of the `id` column. We will also convert the date field into a `date` type for running efficient time-based filters in our queries:

```
create table noaa_data_parquet
with (
      format = 'Parquet',
      write_compression = 'GZIP',
      partitioned_by = ARRAY['countrycode'],
      external_location = 's3://<<bucketname>>/noaa_data_parquet/')
as
select
    id, element,data_value,m_flag,q_flag,s_flag,obs_time,cast(date_
parse(cast("date" as varchar(8)),'%Y%m%d') as date) as date_
field,substr(id,1,2) as countrycode
from noaa_data_csv
```

Please note that we have used a `partition` column in the preceding query, which we didn't use in the inventory table (`ghndinv`). We will get an error when this query is executed, as shown in the following screenshot:

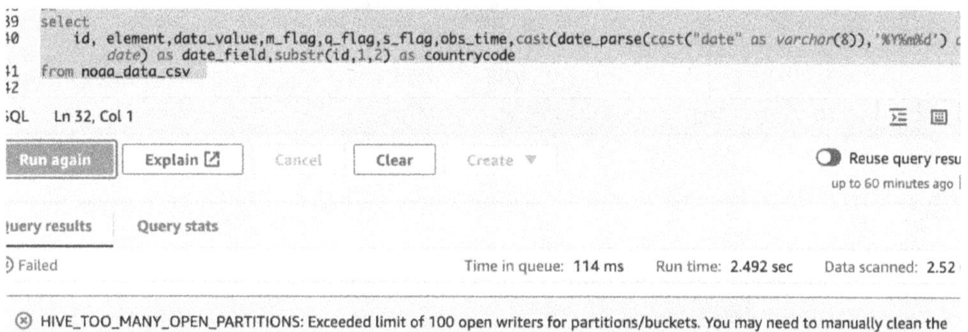

Figure 7.16: Athena error when creating a table with more than 100 values for the partition column

Athena supports inserting only 100 partitions at a time, and we have 218 unique country code values in our data, as shown in *Figure 7.17*:

```
Select substr(id,1,2) as countrycode
from noaa_data_csv
group by substr(id,1,2) order by substr(id,1,2)
```

217	WZ
218	ZA
219	ZI

Figure 7.17: Total number of unique values in the partition column

We will have to load the data in three batches with a maximum of 100 partition values each time. As we have sorted the `countrycode` values, we can structure the `INSERT` queries, as mentioned in the documentation at `https://docs.aws.amazon.com/athena/latest/ug/ctas-insert-into.html`.

We will insert data three times with `countrycode` filters based on the preceding query using CTAS and `INSERT INTO` statements. If the data only has <100 partition values, we can run this CTAS load query once without any additional steps. Proceed as follows:

1. Create a CTAS statement to load data with the first 100 partitions. You can see from the table in *Figure 7.18* that we have loaded data for countries before Jordan (`JO`) in alphabetical order:

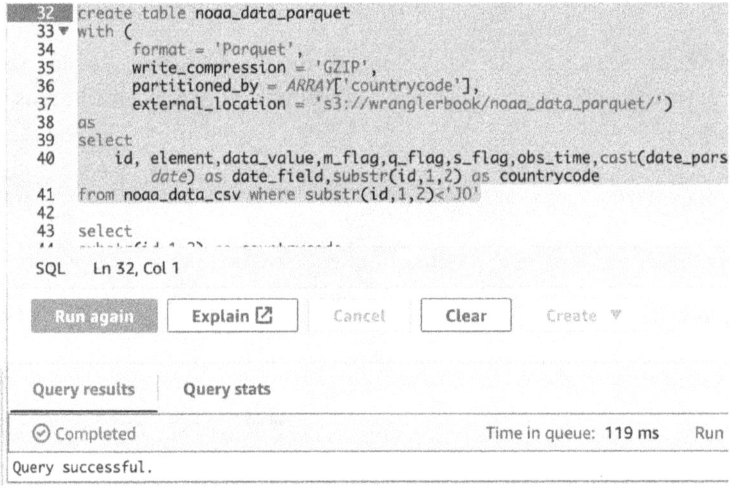

Figure 7.18: Running CTAS command restricting partition values to 100

2. N (Repeated multiple times as necessary): Insert statement to populate data into the target table, as follows:

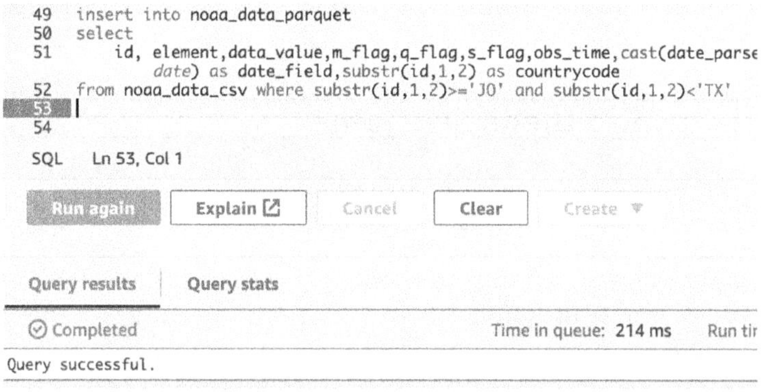

```
insert into noaa_data_parquet
select
    id, element,data_value,m_flag,q_flag,s_flag,obs_time,cast(date_parse
    date) as date_field,substr(id,1,2) as countrycode
from noaa_data_csv where substr(id,1,2)>='JO' and substr(id,1,2)<'TX'
```

Figure 7.19: Running CTAS command restricting partition values to 100 (continued)

Keep repeating the step until you have loaded all data from the source table. Once completed, you can verify whether all data has been loaded from the source table using count queries. You can also browse the S3 path to verify the data within country code partitions. You can see here that we have loaded data from all country codes (219 unique country code values):

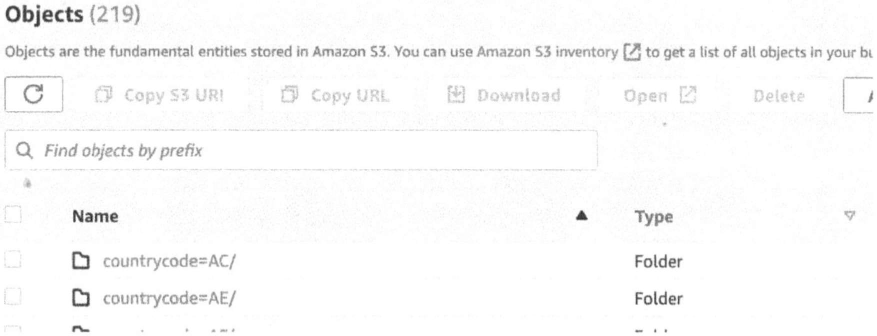

Figure 7.20: Verifying the CTAS table output in the S3 path

Now, you can explore the partitioned data efficiently based on the query access pattern. Alternatively, if you want to split your data into equal-sized buckets, you can use the bucketing command, as mentioned later in this chapter. You can also read about the difference between partitioning (which we did previously) and bucketing in the documentation at `https://aws.amazon.com/premiumsupport/knowledge-center/set-file-number-size-ctas-athena/`.

We have only made a small change to show the capability of Athena in restructuring data and also to perform ETL operations. You can play around with this more and create powerful data transformations as part of this exercise.

Enriching data from multiple sources using Athena

In this section, we will explore how to enrich data using Athena SQL and also using an Athena federation setup for enriching data from other supported data sources.

Enriching data using Athena SQL joins

In the previous section, we saw various ways through which we can explore data in Amazon Athena. Now, we will focus more on ways to enrich data with additional information through Athena queries.

In this phase, we can enrich raw data further by joining with other data sources. We will continue to use the same data source that we used in earlier sections. Let us assume a scenario where we want to identify the maximum recorded temperature of this century (after the year 2000) from a specific US state (Connecticut) for a specific year (2022). We will get the data for readings from the Parquet table (`noaa_data_parquet`) that was created using a CTAS statement in the previous section.

We can filter and get records from `Country code =US` based on our partition schema. But in order to get the records from the state of Connecticut, we need to join the `noaa_data_parquet` table with the stations data file (`http://noaa-ghcn-pds.s3.amazonaws.com/ghcnd-stations.txt`), which has the state information for all stations within the US and Canada.

We will follow the steps here to enrich our dataset with state data:

1. Load the state data file using the regex format. We will follow the same approach that we used for loading the inventory table in an earlier section. We will first design a regex for loading the table using a regex validator and sample records, as illustrated here:

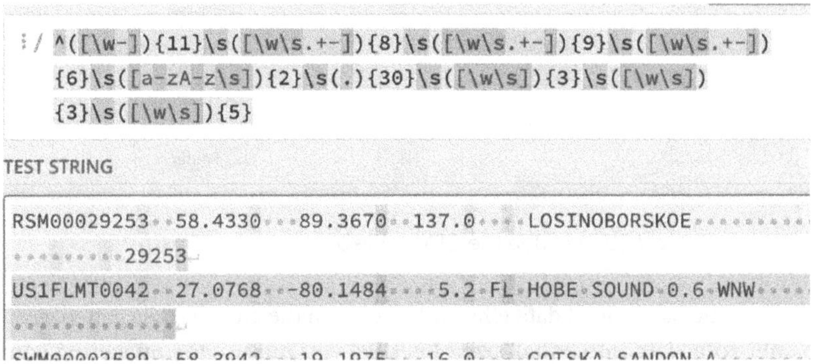

```
:/ ^([\w-]){11}\s([\w\s.+-]){8}\s([\w\s.+-]){9}\s([\w\s.+-])
   {6}\s([a-zA-z\s]){2}\s(.){30}\s([\w\s]){3}\s([\w\s])
   {3}\s([\w\s]){5}

TEST STRING

RSM00029253  58.4330   89.3670  137.0    LOSINOBORSKOE
          29253
US1FLMT0042  27.0768  -80.1484    5.2 FL HOBE SOUND 0.6 WNW
```

Figure 7.21: Designing a regex for loading a fixed-width file

2. Create a table and load the fixed-width file through Amazon Athena, as illustrated here. Verify whether the data is loaded successfully:

id	latitude	longitude	elevation	state	name
US1CTFR0002	41.4230	-73.5187	256.0	CT	DANBURY 2.8 WNW
US1CTFR0003	41.1486	-73.4591	71.6	CT	NEW CANAAN 1.9 ENE
US1CTFR0005	41.1028	-73.4893	60.0	CT	DARIEN 3.6 N

Figure 7.22: Amazon Athena querying the table loaded with a regex statement

3. We will join tables using the `id` column and then filter and aggregate on records only from state ='CT' and country code ='US' (partition column to speed up analysis) to identify the maximum temperature in the current century (21st century), as follows:

```
select max(data_value) from noaa_data_parquet t1 inner join
ghnd_stations t2 on t1.id=t2.id
where countrycode='US' and state='CT' and element='TMAX' and
date_field>cast('2000-01-01' as date)
```

We can see from the following screenshot that we have 54.4°C as the maximum temperature recorded within this century:

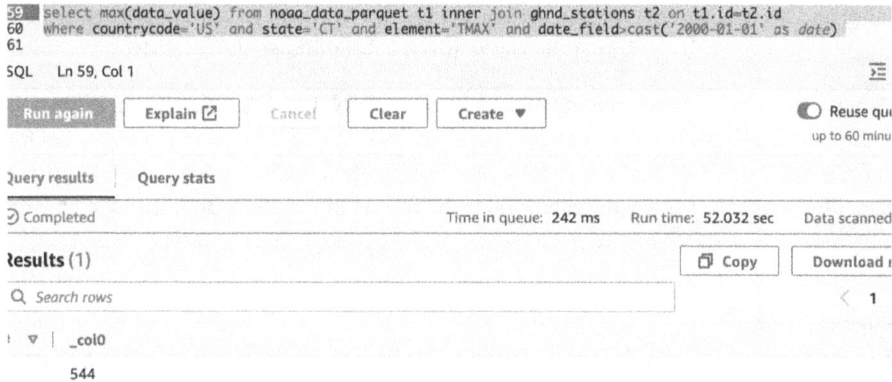

Figure 7.23: Amazon Athena query to identify the max temperature of the current century in CT state

4. Perform further analysis by identifying the places with the top three recorded temperatures in this century within Connecticut. We will use a partition and rank function to achieve this result by executing the following query:

```
select * from ( select t1.id,t1.data_value,t1.obs_time,t2.
state,t2.name,
ROW_NUMBER() OVER (PARTITION BY t1.countrycode,t2.state ORDER BY
data_value DESC) AS temp_rank
from noaa_data_parquet t1 inner join ghnd_stations t2 on
t1.id=t2.id
where countrycode='US' and state='CT' and element='TMAX' and
date_field>cast('2000-01-01' as date) ) TMP_TABLE
where temp_rank <=3
```

You can see the three places—Meriden, Danbury, and New Haven—with the highest recorded temperatures of this century. Also, as you can see from the analysis, the temperature has not been over 50° C since the year 2000:

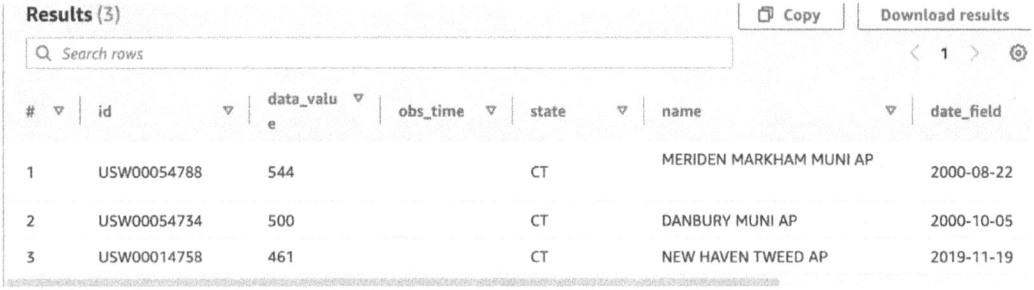

Results (3)

#	id	data_value	obs_time	state	name	date_field
1	USW00054788	544		CT	MERIDEN MARKHAM MUNI AP	2000-08-22
2	USW00054734	500		CT	DANBURY MUNI AP	2000-10-05
3	USW00014758	461		CT	NEW HAVEN TWEED AP	2019-11-19

Figure 7.24: Amazon Athena query to identify places where the top three highest temperatures were recorded in CT

The preceding exercise shows the power of doing this analysis using Amazon Athena, and it depends on the quality and accuracy of the data to get correct results. You will have to rely on data cleansing and data quality rules to create a cleaner dataset to provide accurate analysis results.

Amazon Athena supports all types of joins such as INNER JOIN, LEFT JOIN, RIGHT JOIN, OUTER JOIN, and CROSS JOIN based on your use-case requirements. In addition, there is a rich set of features that are available in Athena SQL that you can use to create highly complex analyses and transformations on your data. Please refer to the documentation for the full set of Athena SQL features at `https://docs.aws.amazon.com/athena/latest/ug/ddl-sql-reference.html`.

> **Challenge exercise**
>
> You can join the dataset from the sports betting use case that we will be using in *Chapter 10, Data Processing for Machine Learning with SageMaker Data Wrangler*. You can recreate the schedule for a sports team that we created in the data enrichment section of the chapter using Athena queries.

Setting up data federation for source databases

We will now explore more on joining datasets from different data sources. As the NOAA weather dataset is stored only in an Amazon S3 bucket, we will add some datasets to a **Relational Database Service** (**RDS**) MySQL database and show how we can query data without moving it to a central location. This helps business teams to run quick analyses using SQL without relying on data engineering teams to move data from one data source to another location. This would be extremely handy as business teams can run quick analyses without relying on other teams, but should only be used for ad hoc analysis where you need results within a quick time and to set up data pipelines for repeated data analysis for better performance.

Athena query federation works by creating Lambda functions with the necessary code to connect to the source database. The source code for supported sources can be found at this location: `https://github.com/awslabs/aws-athena-query-federation`. As this is open source code, you can develop this further and customize it for your needs and create the code for your own database with instructions provided on the repository. Once you deploy a serverless application in your AWS account, it creates a Lambda function that will be executed by Athena effectively in the backend for connecting to your database. Athena uses an effective mechanism to connect to the source database using multiple Lambda invocations, and Amazon Athena has a mechanism to circumvent Lambda 15-minute timeout and execute queries that run more than 15 minutes.

Prerequisite – creating a source table in RDS MySQL

Let us assume a scenario where we want to query weather data from Antarctica and understand what the lowest temperature during the current century was in a similar manner to before. We have country code values available in the `noaa_data_parquet` table, but we might not know the correct country code for Antarctica. We will emulate a scenario where the country lookup table data (with country code and country name) is available from a MySQL database. In order to create that scenario, we will load the data manually into a MySQL table. You can create an RDS MySQL instance as per the information available here: `https://aws.amazon.com/getting-started/hands-on/create-mysql-db/`.

You can use MySQL Workbench to connect to a public instance, and if you prefer to launch the RDS instance in a private subnet, then we will use an **Elastic Compute Cloud** (**EC2**) instance to connect to the RDS database. We will also create an EC2 instance in the same VPC as RDS MySQL, and we will use that machine to connect to the MySQL database. You can follow the steps for setting up an EC2 bastion host here: `https://aws.amazon.com/premiumsupport/knowledge-center/rds-connect-ec2-bastion-host/`.

In this section, we will log in to the EC2 instance and upload the countries file using the `scp` command. Before uploading the file, you can use any editor of your choice and replace the first occurrence of space with a comma, as shown next, and replace commas subsequently or enclose with double quotes. This will convert the data into a CSV file with two fields—country code and country name:

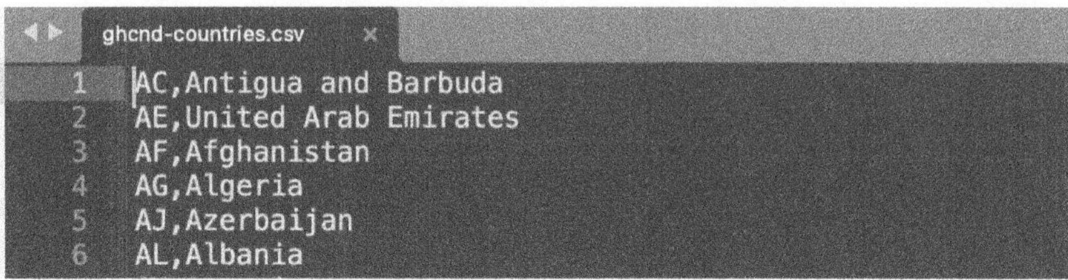

Figure 7.25: Browsing data in the country lookup file

After making the preceding change, save the file in CSV format and upload the file to the home directory of the EC2 instance using the `scp` command, as pasted here:

```
scp -i "yourpemfile.pem" <path/to/ghcnd-countries.csv> ec2-user@ec2-
XXX-XXX-XXX-XXX.region.compute.amazonaws.com:~/
```

We will log in to the EC2 instance using the `ssh` command (from the EC2 console connect screen) and then connect to the `mysql` instance using the following command:

```
mysql - h <<database endpoint string>>  -u <<db username>>  -P 3306 -p
```

We will create a new database, as shown in the following screenshot:

```
MySQL [(none)]> create database noaa;
Query OK, 1 row affected (0.01 sec)

MySQL [(none)]> show databases;
+--------------------+
| Database           |
+--------------------+
| dms_sample         |
| information_schema |
| mysql              |
| noaa               |
| performance_schema |
| sys                |
+--------------------+
6 rows in set (0.00 sec)

MySQL [(none)]> use noaa;
Database changed
```

Figure 7.26: Creating a database in RDS MySQL to load the country lookup file

We will create a table and load the data into the table, as shown next. At this point in time, we have completed the prerequisites for creating a source table in MySQL:

```
MySQL [(none)]> use noaa;
Database changed
MySQL [noaa]> CREATE TABLE noaa_country (
    ->      countrycode CHAR(2) NOT NULL,
    ->      countryname VARCHAR(255) NOT NULL,
    ->      PRIMARY KEY (countrycode)
    -> );
Query OK, 0 rows affected (0.02 sec)

MySQL [noaa]> LOAD DATA LOCAL INFILE '/home/ec2-user/ghcnd-count:
    -> INTO TABLE noaa_country
    -> FIELDS TERMINATED BY ','
    -> OPTIONALLY ENCLOSED BY '"'
    -> LINES TERMINATED BY '\n';
Query OK, 219 rows affected (0.02 sec)
Records: 219  Deleted: 0  Skipped: 0  Warnings: 0
```

Figure 7.27: Loading the country lookup file into RDS MySQL

Now, we will set up the query federation for this MySQL database in Amazon Athena. Navigate to the Amazon Athena console and create a data source. Alternatively, you can also go to the AWS Serverless Application repository and create an application to deploy the Lambda function and needed resources to support query federation, as shown here:

Figure 7.28: Searching for the application

In our use case, we will create the data source through the Athena console, as documented next.

Setting up data federation in your AWS account

Create a new data source from Amazon Athena, as shown here:

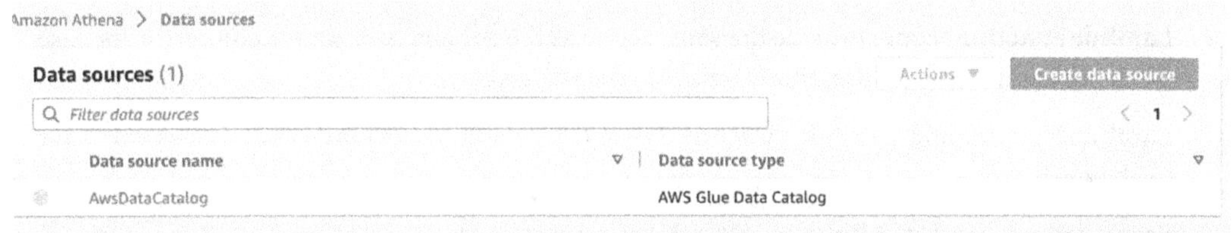

Figure 7.29: Amazon Athena data source screen

Here, we will choose `mysql` as the data source and click **Next**. You can choose your source database engine accordingly for different use cases:

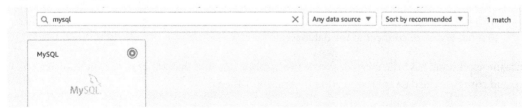

Figure 7.30: Amazon Athena data federation for MySQL data source

Enter a name for the application—`wranglerathena`, in our use case—and click on **Create Lambda function**, which will take you to the serverless application deployment screen. In order to understand more about the connector, you can read the license, README file, and template section to understand the resources that will get deployed. Under **Application settings**, you can enter the following values for our current use case:

- **Application name**: `AthenaMySQLConnector` (leave the default value).
- **SecretNamePrefix**: The name of the `SecretsManager` secret that has the username and password for the source database. For our testing, we will provide them in the connection string directly. But for production deployments, it is strongly recommended to use a secrets manager with password rotation for efficient security. So, enter a `dummysecret` value in this field.
- **Spillbucket**: Provide the name of the S3 bucket where the Lambda function can store data that is greater than its memory limits. This functionality effectively prevents Lambda memory errors for bigger query results.
- **DefaultConnectionString**: Provide the connection string in this format:

```
mysql://jdbc:mysql://<<database endpoint>>:3306/
noaa?user=<<username>>&password=<<password>>
##Replace << >> values in the above string with correct values
for your use case
```

- **DisableSpillEncryption**: `False` (unless you don't want to encrypt spill data in S3).
- **LambdaFunctionName**: Provide the same name as the Athena data source connector for ease of identification. In our case, this is `wranglerathena`.
- **LambdaMemory** and **LambdaTimeout**: Leave the default maximum values unless you want to change them.
- **PermissionsBoundaryARN**: Leave it empty for our use case.
- **SecurityGroupIds**: Provide the security group ID that you want to associate with the Lambda function. The security group needs to have rules to access the MySQL database.
- **SpillPrefix**: Leave this at the default value of `athena-spill`.
- **SubnetIds**: Provide the subnet ID where the Lambda function will be launched to get connected with RDS MySQL. Provide the subnet ID where the RDS MySQL instance is or a list of subnets that has access to connect to the database.

Once the application has been created, choose the Lambda function that was created from the previous step and complete the data source creation in Amazon Athena.

Validating the working of the federated data source

Method 1: Execute the query without the data source option in Athena by directly referring to the Lambda function by name, as shown here. If everything is set up correctly, you should be able to see the data from the source table, as shown next:

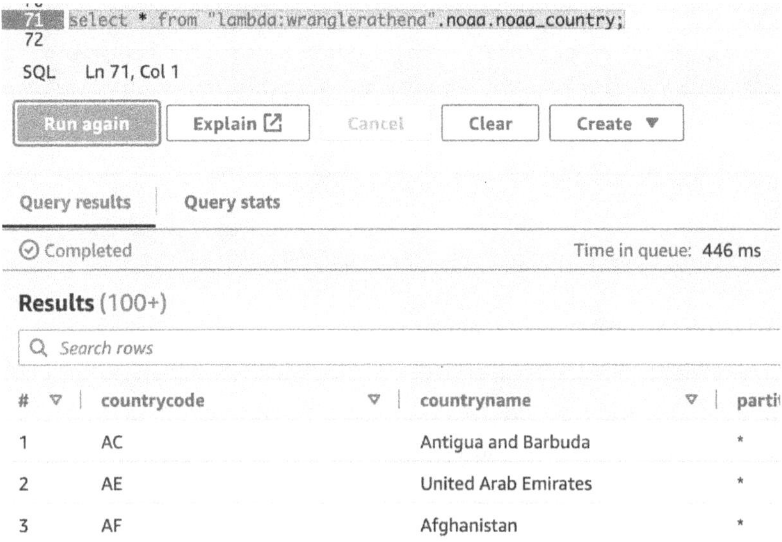

Figure 7.31: Amazon Athena querying country table from MySQL directly through the Lambda function

Method 2: Execute the query using the Amazon Athena data source that was created in the previous step. Before validating through this option, we need to make a change in the Lambda function that was created by the serverless application, as follows:

- Navigate to the Lambda console and choose the function name that was used in the configuration section—`wranglerathena`.
- Choose **Configuration** and then choose environment variables. Now, copy the environment variable from the `default` key name and create another key named `wranglermysql_connection_string`, as illustrated in the following screenshot. This key name should be of the format `athenadatasource_connection_string`:

Key	Value	
default	mysql://jdbc:mysql://awswrangler.ci2nx	Remove
disable_spill_encryption	false	Remove
spill_bucket	athenaresults-sankar	Remove
spill_prefix	athena-spill	Remove
wranglermysql_connection_string	mysql://jdbc:mysql://awswrangler.ci2nx	Remove

Add environment variable

Figure 7.32: Updating the configurations in the federation Lambda function

- Then, click **Save** to update the new environment variable change that we have made to the Lambda function.

Now, navigate to Amazon Athena console and choose `wranglermysql` as the data source, and you will be able to see the newly created table, as shown in the following screenshot:

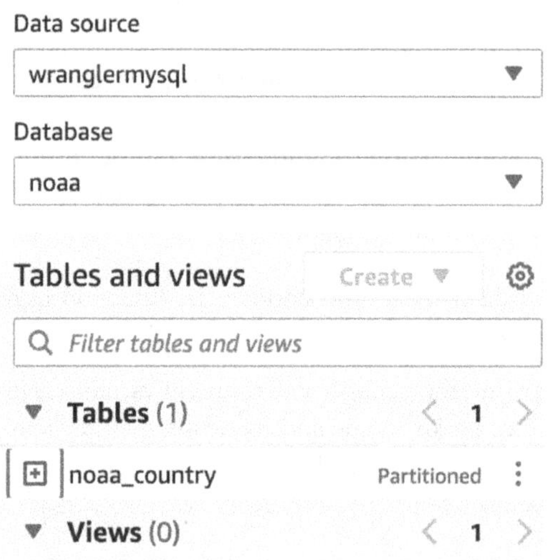

Figure 7.33: Accessing table list from the federated source in the Amazon Athena console

You can query the table using the `datasource.database.tablename` format and verify the working of the connector, like so:

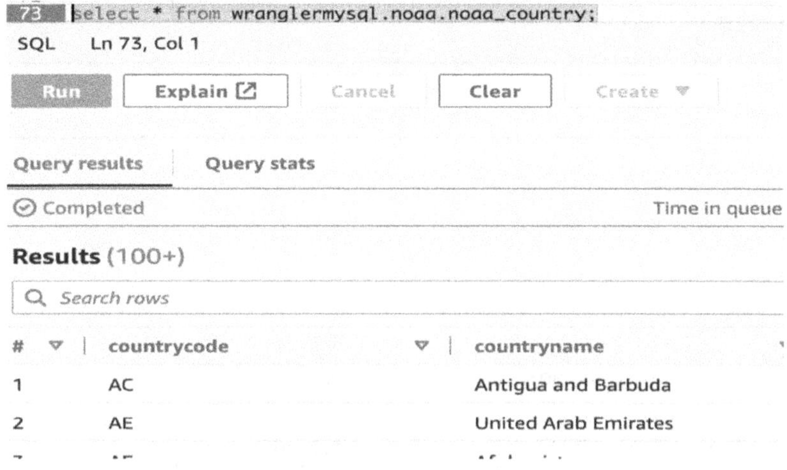

Figure 7.34: Querying the country table in RDS MySQL through the Athena console and registered data source

Now, we will explore how to use an Athena query to combine the country data in MySQL with the `noaa_paraquet` table, which is available in Amazon S3.

Enriching data with data federation

In order to demonstrate the benefits of Athena federation, let us consider a situation where your manager has asked you (as the data analyst in the company) to find the lowest temperature of this century from Antarctica and 10 other countries as soon as possible. You as a data analyst in the company know that you have to query the table `noaa_data_parquet` table, but you are not sure about the country code value for these countries. You also know there is a table in MySQL that has this information and don't want to wait for the data engineering team to move this table to Amazon S3 and create a data catalog on top of it to query in Amazon Athena.

Let us create a federated query that joins data from Amazon S3 and RDS MySQL and provides us with the output that was required for our use case. We will execute the following query to combine required datasets without data migration across data sources:

```
select min(data_value) as min_temp from AwsDataCatalog.wranglerathena.
noaa_data_parquet t1 inner join wranglermysql.noaa.noaa_country t2 on
t1.countrycode=t2.countrycode where trim(t2.countryname)='Antarctica'
and date_field>cast('1900-01-01' as date)  and element='TMIN'
```

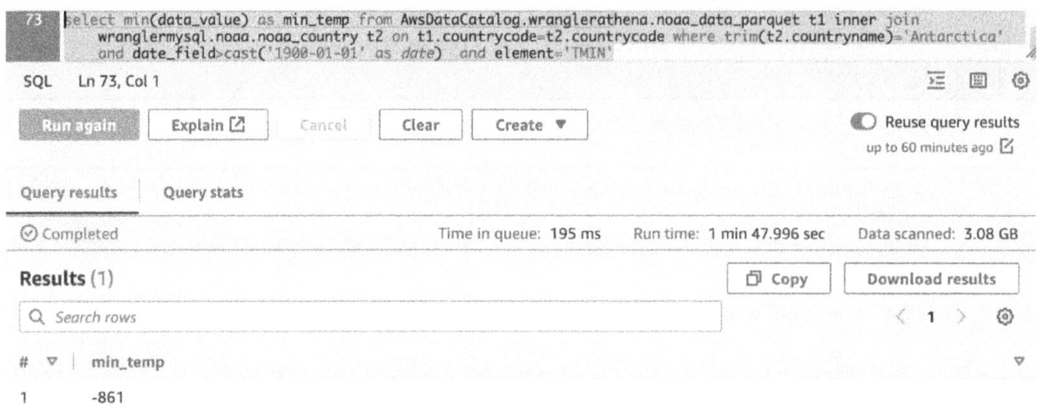

Figure 7.35: Amazon Athena query using a federated join to identify the minimum temperature in Antarctica

This demonstrates the capability of Athena to enrich your data from multiple sources without actually moving the data. This could come in handy a lot of times for various teams.

Now we have learned about various ways to enrich your data through Amazon Athena, we will explore in the next section how to set up a data quality pipeline using Athena queries.

Setting up a serverless data quality pipeline with Athena

Data quality validation is a very important step in data wrangling pipelines, ensuring the accuracy of data that will be used in analysis and visualization. We will explore in this section how to perform data quality validation through Amazon Athena.

Implementing data quality rules in Athena

Let us consider the rules that we want to validate in the NOAA weather dataset. What follows is only a high-level representation of some data quality rules and not a comprehensive ruleset for the weather dataset:

1. The state column should have two character values when the country code is `US`.
2. The date field shouldn't have any future-dated values that would be incorrect measurements.
3. Validate that the element column has only accepted the list of values as provided in the documentation.

We can have more rules that will ensure better data quality, but the preceding rules are sufficient for us to demonstrate the usage of data quality validation with Amazon Athena. We will first design the queries and then execute them in Athena to ensure syntactic and semantic correctness.

Data quality rule 1: For state code column validation, use the query given here:

```
--Identify incorrect state codes when Country is US
select * from ghnd_stations where substring(ID,1,2)='US'
and length(state)<>2
```

Execute the query in Athena and verify that we don't have any records that violate the data quality rule, as shown in the following screenshot. This ensures that the current data doesn't have any data errors and also validates our query is working correctly as expected:

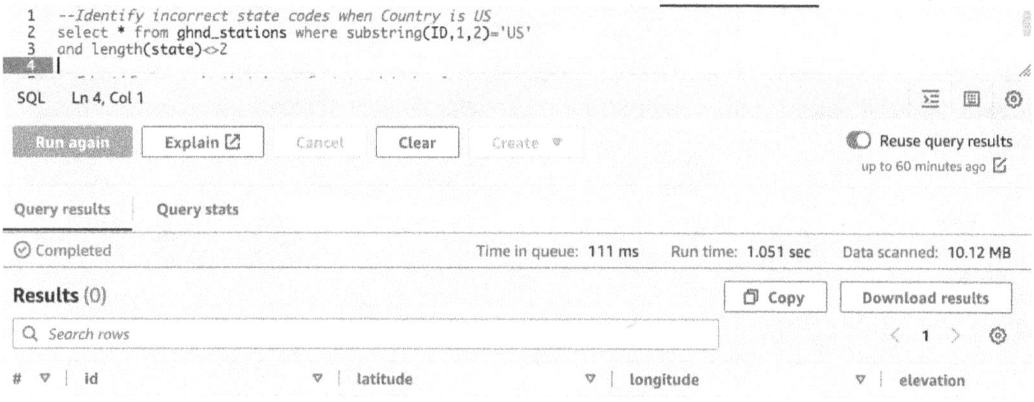

```
1  --Identify incorrect state codes when Country is US
2  select * from ghnd_stations where substring(ID,1,2)='US'
3  and length(state)<>2
4
```

SQL Ln 4, Col 1

Run again | Explain | Cancel | Clear | Create | Reuse query results up to 60 minutes ago

Query results | Query stats

Completed Time in queue: 111 ms Run time: 1.051 sec Data scanned: 10.12 MB

Results (0) Copy Download results

Search rows

#	id	latitude	longitude	elevation

Figure 7.36: Amazon Athena data quality to identify records with state code not equal to 2 characters

Data quality rule 2: In order to verify we don't have any weather observations from future dates, we will use the query given next. This ensures that we don't have incorrect observations from future dates:

```
--Identify records that have future dated values
select * from noaa_data_parquet where date_field > current_date
```

We can execute and validate the previous query in a similar way and ensure that we don't have any records with data quality issues.

Data quality rule 3: We will execute the query given next to validate whether the observations are made against valid dimensions only. This is done by validating against the `element` column. We got the `values` list by using the data from the NOAA dataset README file (`https://docs.opendata.aws/noaa-ghcn-pds/readme.html`). We copied the values to an Excel sheet, split them into two columns using the = delimiter, and then used them in the following query:

```
--Identify records with invalid values in element column
select element,s_flag,max(date_field) as latest_date,count(*) as cnt
```

```
from noaa_data_parquet
where countrycode='US' and element not in
('PRCP','SNOW','SNWD','TMAX','TMIN','ACMC','ACMH','ACSC','ACSH',
'AWDR','AWND','DAEV','DAPR','DASF','DATN','DATX','DAWM','DWPR','EVAP',
'FMTM','FRGB','FRGT','FRTH','GAHT','MDEV','MDPR','MDSF','MDTN','MDTX',
'MDWM','MNPN','MXPN','PGTM','PRCP','PSUN','SNOW','SNWD','TAVG','THIC',
'TMAX','TMIN','TOBS','TSUN','WDF1','WDF2','WDF5','WDFG','WDFI',
'WDFM','WDMV','WESD','WESF','WSF1','WSF2','WSF5','WSFG','WSFI','WSFM')
and element not like ('SN%') and element not like ('SX%')
and element not like ('WT%') and element not like ('WV%')
group by element,s_flag
```

When executing the queries, we found some element values that are not provided in the documentation but seem like valid values based on the availability of a huge number of records, as shown here:

Search rows

#	element	s_flag	latest_date	cnt
1	ADPT	W	2022-09-30	2213207
2	RHMX	W	2022-09-30	2224645
3	AWBT	W	2022-09-30	2213207
4	RHAV	W	2022-09-30	2224645
5	RHMN	W	2022-09-30	2223028
6	ASLP	W	2022-09-30	2208325
7	ASTP	W	2022-09-30	2208325

Figure 7.37: Amazon Athena data quality to identify element values that are not from the valid value list

Now, we have three data quality queries, out of which one has some records that we need to analyze more and understand. The next step is to set up the queries in a DynamoDB table so that they can be executed in Amazon Athena through AWS Step Functions in a serverless manner.

Amazon DynamoDB as a metadata store for data quality pipelines

We will use DynamoDB to store the queries so that they can be executed in an automated manner through the tool of your choice. Let us create a DynamoDB table to store the SQL scripts. Enter the table name, along with the partition key and sort key, and leave the rest of the settings at their default values, as follows:

Table name

This will be used to identify your table.

wranglerdq

Between 3 and 255 characters, containing only letters, numbers, underscores (_), hyphens (-), and periods (.).

Partition key

The partition key is part of the table's primary key. It is a hash value that is used to retrieve items from your table and allocate data across hosts for scalability and availability.

application String

1 to 255 characters and case sensitive.

Sort key - *optional*

You can use a sort key as the second part of a table's primary key. The sort key allows you to sort or search among all items sharing the same partition key.

queryid String

1 to 255 characters and case sensitive.

Figure 7.38: Amazon DynamoDB table creation process – for storing data quality queries

We used the application name as the partition key so that we can use the same DynamoDB table to store data quality queries for multiple applications. `queryid` can be a field that will help us to uniquely identify data quality queries within each application.

Once the table is successfully created, we will load the queries that we designed in the preceding step into the DynamoDB table that we created previously. Choose **Explore items** -> **Choose table name** -> **Create item** button. You should then see the following:

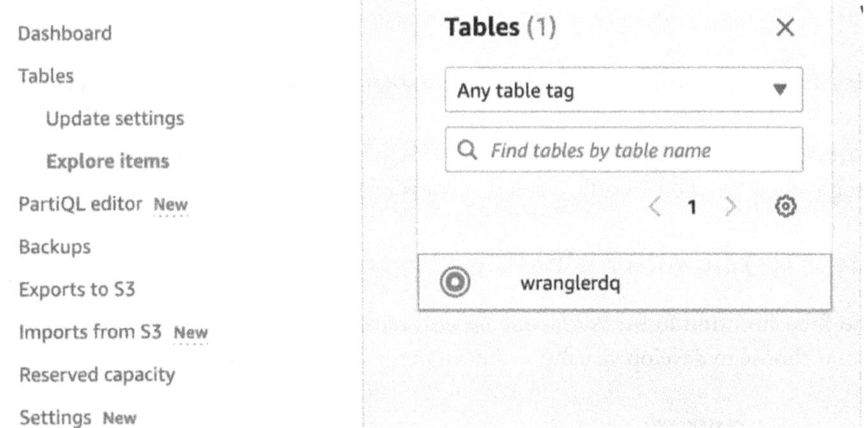

Figure 7.39: Amazon DynamoDB table – Adding items from the table storing data quality scripts

Enter the following values for each item and save them back in the table:

- `application`: Enter `noaa_weather`
- `queryid`: Enter `query<x>`
- `querystring`: Copy and paste the query string from the Athena console

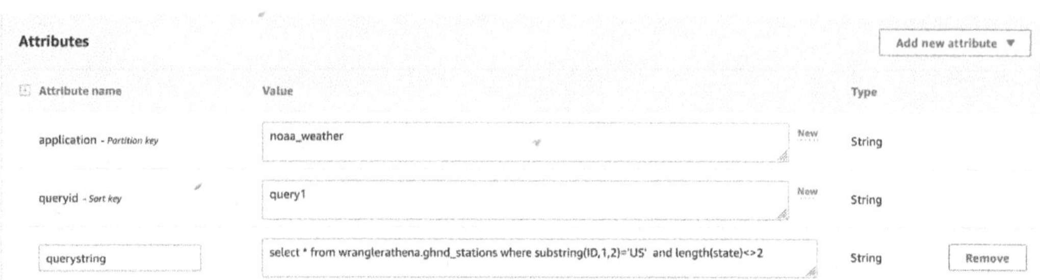

Figure 7.40: Amazon DynamoDB table – Adding an item to the table

Once all the values are stored in the table, you can verify whether they are loaded correctly by choosing a DynamoDB table name and then selecting **Explore table items**, which will take you to this screen:

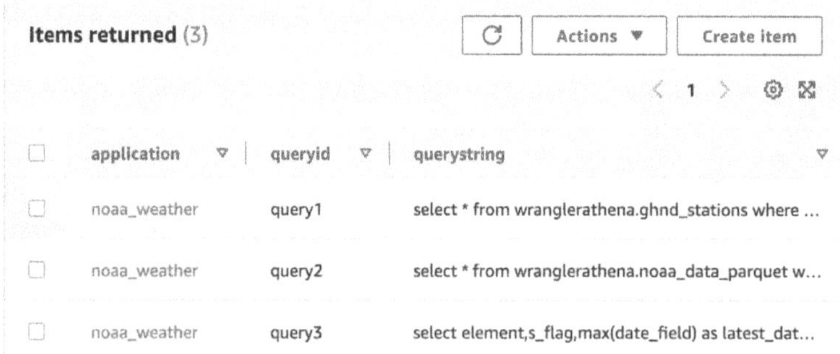

Figure 7.41: Amazon DynamoDB table – Viewing the data that was added to the metadata table

Now we have our queries ready in the DynamoDB table to be executed, we will see how we can execute them through a step function workflow in a serverless manner.

Serverless data quality pipeline

Navigate to **Step function** in the AWS console, and create a state machine. Choose the **Standard** workflow and choose to develop visually, as shown here:

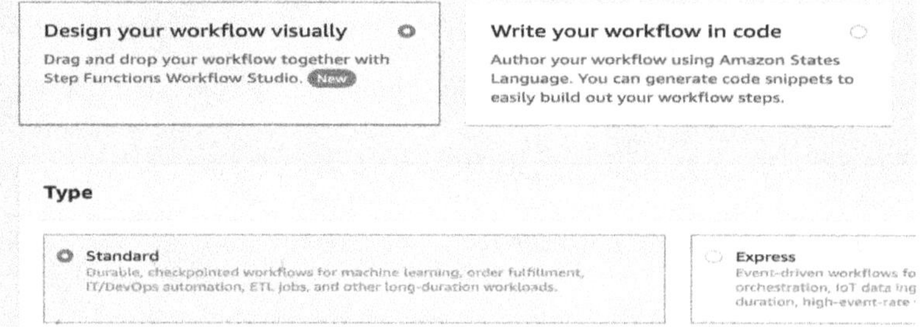

Figure 7.42: Step function console to create a new workflow

The following workflow should be designed in the state machine for our use case:

1. Run a query against Amazon DynamoDB and retrieve the data quality SQL script for our application.
2. Execute the data quality SQL scripts in Athena in a parallel manner.
3. Collect the results and consolidate them in a Lambda function.
4. Send the consolidated output from the Lambda function to a **Simple Notification Service** (**SNS**) endpoint. This will let a group of individuals be notified of the results of the step function to take appropriate action.
5. Execute and verify the working of the step function workflow.
6. Configure the step function to be executed on a periodic basis through Amazon EventBridge Scheduler.

Step 1: In the step function console for our state machine, search for `dynamoDB query` in the search box and drag the DynamoDB query icon to the visual palette.

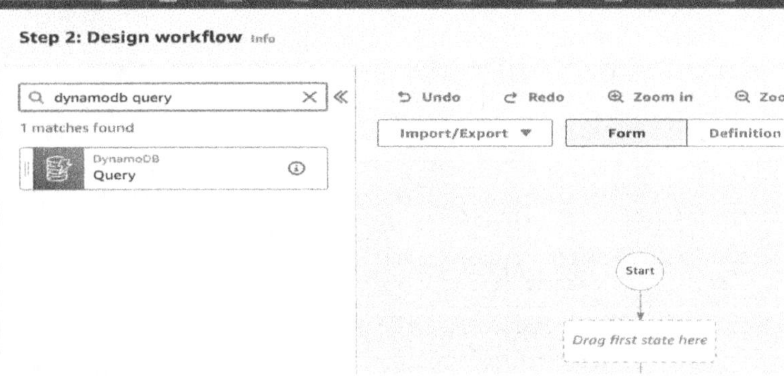

Figure 7.43: Step function workflow – Adding an API call to query the DynamoDB table

Now, update the parameters as given next:

```
{
  "TableName": "wranglerdq",
  "KeyConditionExpression": "application=:v1",
  "ExpressionAttributeValues": {
    ":v1": {
      "S": "noaa_weather"
    }
  }
}
```

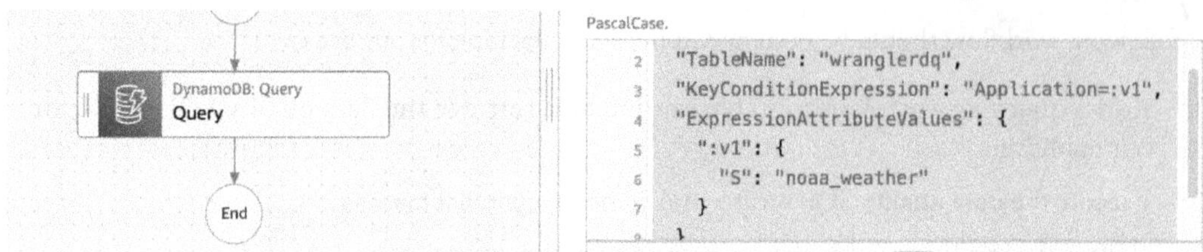

Figure 7.44: Step function workflow – Configuration options for querying the DynamoDB table API

This step will run a DynamoDB Query SDK against the `wranglerdq` table and filter results on the `Application = noaa_weather` attribute. You can see what will be the output of this API call by looking at the documentation for this API call at `https://docs.aws.amazon.com/amazondynamodb/latest/APIReference/API_Query.html#API_Query_ResponseSyntax`.

We can see it has an `Items` array field that will have the field name and field type. We need to extract only the SQL script and pass it to Athena for execution, as follows:

```
"Items": [
   {
      "string" : {
         "B": blob,
         "BOOL": boolean,
         "BS": [ blob ],
         "L": [
            "AttributeValue"
         ],
         "M": {
            "string" : "AttributeValue"
         },
         "N": "string",
         "NS": [ "string" ],
         "NULL": boolean,
         "S": "string",
```

Figure 7.45: Querying the DynamoDB table API – Snippet from response element structure

We will filter the output of this step using the `$.Items[*].querystring.S` JSON path. Under the **Output** section, choose **Filter output with OutputPath** and provide the JSON path as pasted here:

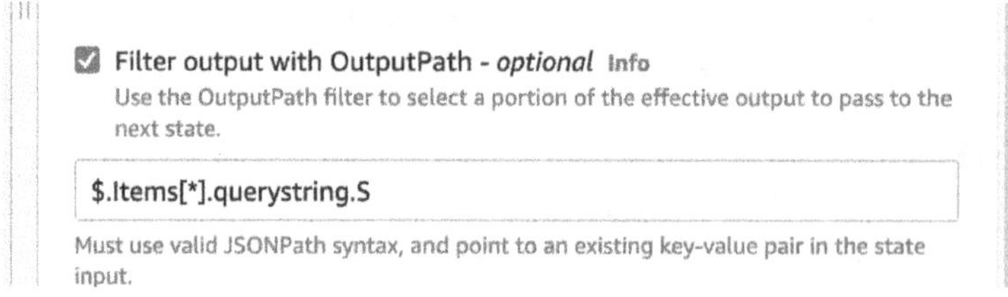

Figure 7.46: Querying the DynamoDB table API – Filtering the output to get only the query string DynamoDB query API response

Now, we will continue developing further steps for the serverless data quality workflow.

Step 2: We can use a map function to execute Athena queries in a parallel manner. This function will execute an action in parallel with different inputs from an array passed to it as an input. In our use case, we will pass the list of queries in an array to the map function, which will execute the `Athena-Startqueryexecution` API in parallel for each query from the input array.

Map functions will be available under the **Flow** tab, as shown in the following screenshot:

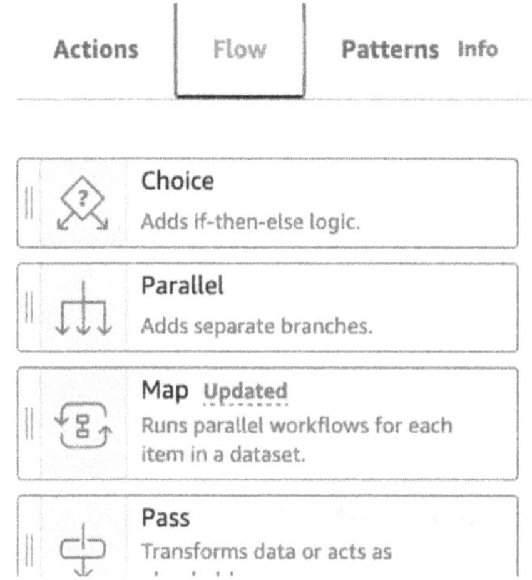

Figure 7.47: Adding a map function to execute Amazon Athena queries in parallel

We will provide the values to be updated for various parameters for the map function and you can update them in your workflow, as follows:

- **Processing Mode**: Choose `Inline`.
- **Provide a path to items array**: Enter `"$"`. As we have already filtered only the query string in the output of the previous step, we will get the data from the top-level JSON element (using `"$"`).
- **Maximum concurrency**: Enter `5`. You can enter a different value for your use case. We will see the performance of queries by executing in batches of five queries and then increase/decrease the parallel query execution count by using this parameter.

Search for `Athena start` and you should see the **Athena StartQueryExecution** API object in the results window. Drag that inside the map function, as shown here:

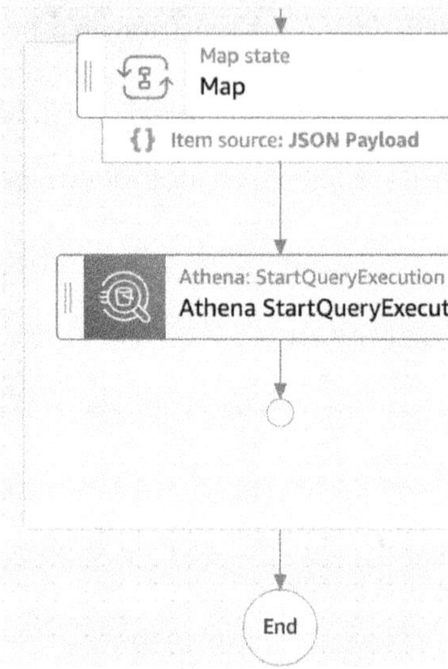

Figure 7.48: Step function workflow – Map function executing Athena queries in parallel

Enter the following parameters for the **Athena StartQueryExecution** API object:

API Parameters: Enter the following values. If you are using a different workgroup for specific features, update the input accordingly:

```
{
  "QueryString.$": "$",
  "WorkGroup": "primary",
  "ResultConfiguration": {
    "OutputLocation": "s3://<<path to store athena results>>/"
  }
}
```

Wait for task to complete: Check the checkbox. This is very important to do so that the workflow waits for the completion of the query. If you fail to check this checkbox, the subsequent steps will fail when they try to retrieve the results of an Athena query that has not finished yet.

Step 3: Consolidate the results from the previous step using a Lambda function.

Step 3a: We will add a "**pass step**" here to get the results from the map function and pass it to the Lambda function. Search for **"Pass" step** and drag it into our workflow after the map function. Click on **Pass step**, navigate to the **Input** tab, then choose the **Transform input with Parameters** checkbox and enter the following values:

```
{
  "Resultpath.$": "$[*].QueryExecution.ResultConfiguration.
  OutputLocation",
  "query.$": "$[*].QueryExecution.Query"
}
```

Step 3b: Create a Lambda function that will consolidate the results from the Athena query execution. Open the Lambda console in another tab and enter the function name as `Consolidateathenaresults` and runtime as `"Python3.9"`. Leave the rest of the arguments at their defaults and create the Lambda function.

Step 3c: Update the following code in the Lambda function. Click **Deploy** to save the Lambda code. The following code reads data from the S3 location and consolidates it to be sent through an email:

```
import json
import boto3
import csv
from urllib.parse import urlparse
s3 = boto3.resource('s3')

def Lambda_handler(event, context):
    # TODO implement
    i=0
    output=""
    for file in event["Resultpath"]:
        #Get a S3 URL from which we read the results of Athena
query.
        Parsed_path = urlparse(file, allow_fragments=False)

        #Read data from the S3 file and get results and split
each line
        s3_object = s3.Object(parsed_path.netloc,
        parsed_path.path.lstrip('/'))
        data = s3_object.get()['Body'].read().decode
        ('utf-8').splitlines()

        #Create a new section for each query output and print
the output from those queries
```

```
            output=output+"-------------------------------\n" +
    event["query"][i] +"\n "
            i=i+1
            lines = csv.reader(data)
            headers = next(lines)
            output=output + "Header -"+ ",".join(headers)+"\n"
            for line in lines:
                output=output+",".join(line)+"\n "
        return output
```

Step 3d: Update the IAM role attached to the Lambda function to have Amazon S3 permissions. We will attach an `AmazonS3FullAccess` managed policy with the IAM role. In a production setup, provide access only to the needed S3 location to further restrict access.

Step 3e: Search for `Lambda` in the step function console and pull that into our workflow after the pass step. Enter the function name parameter with the Lambda function that was created in *step 3b*, as illustrated here:

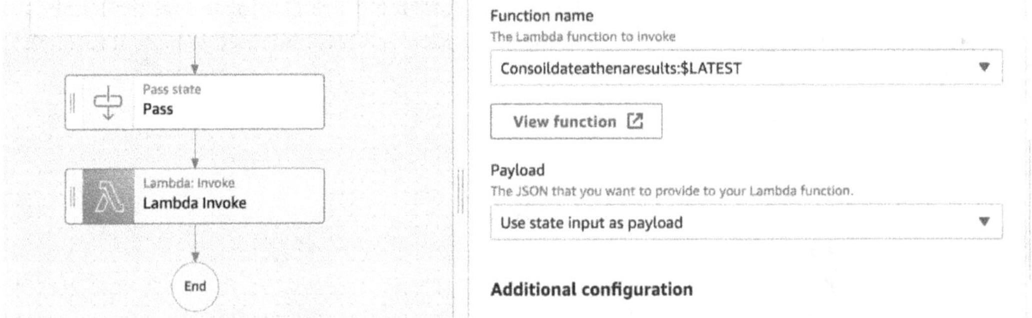

Figure 7.49: Step function workflow – Lambda function to consolidate the results from the Athena query execution

Step 3f: Filter the output path to fetch only the Lambda output to be sent in an email through an SNS topic. In the **Output** tab, choose **Filter output with OutputPath** and enter `$.Payload`.

Step 4: Send the consolidated results through email.

Step 4a: Navigate to the SNS console in a separate tab and create an SNS topic with a **Standard** topic type. Once the topic is created, click on the topic, and create a subscription from the topic. Select **Email** as the protocol and enter your email address (or a group) in the **Endpoint** field. Ensure that you click on the confirm subscription email.

Step 4b: Move back to the step function workflow and search for `SNS publish`. Drag the **SNS Publish API** icon to the workflow after the Lambda function.

We have now completed creating our workflow. Click on **Next** and verify that all the components and configurations are provided without any mistakes. This is how it should look:

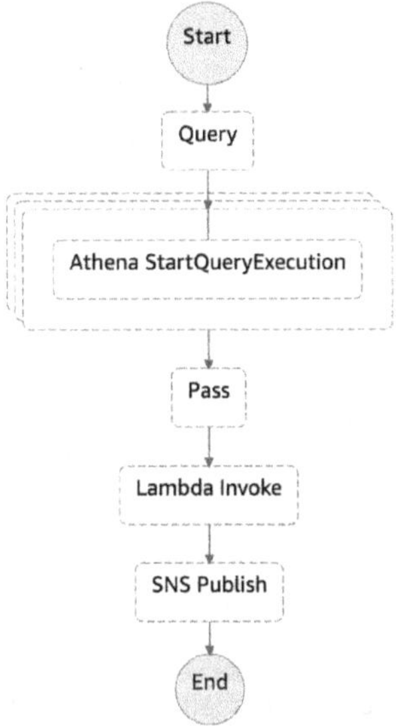

Figure 7.50: Step function workflow – Overall workflow for serverless data quality pipeline

Step 5: Enter a name for the step function workflow and leave the rest of the arguments at their defaults and create the state machine. We will verify if the IAM role attached to the state machine has all the required access. You can access the IAM role for the step machine by clicking on the state machine name and there will be a link to the IAM role under the **Details** section.

You might have noticed a warning while creating the step functions about DynamoDB permissions being not added to the IAM role attached to the state machine. We will add the `AmazonDynamoDBReadOnlyAccess` managed policy to the IAM role.

Now, execute the step function with default arguments and wait for its completion. If all the configurations and IAM permissions are provided correctly, you can see the state machine getting completed successfully, as follows:

Executions | Logging | Definition | Tags

Executions (2) View details Stop execution Start execution

Search for executions Filter by status 1

Name	Status	Started	End Time
e5513fec-fa06-411e-8b44-799dc4bc0e5d	Succeeded	Dec 26, 2022 07:05:39.205 PM	Dec 26, 2022 07:07:46.127 PM

Figure 7.51: Step function workflow – Successful execution of the data quality pipeline

You can also click on the current execution and explore the input and output values from each stage to understand the workings of the state machine:

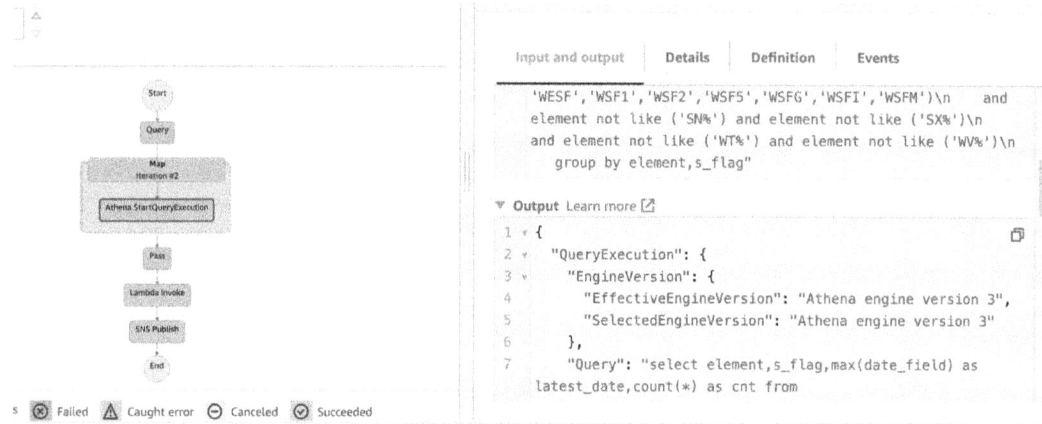

Figure 7.52: Step function workflow – Verifying the execution to understand its workings

You can then check your email to verify whether an email with consolidated results has been delivered to you. This is what it should look like:

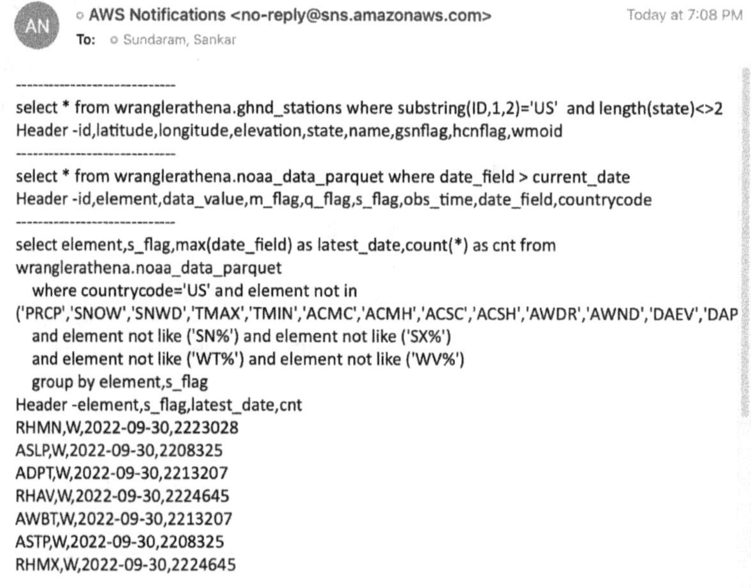

Figure 7.53: Snippet from the email received after the successful completion of the data quality workflow

We now have a working serverless data quality pipeline that is customizable. We can change the existing data quality queries, add more data quality queries, and add a new application with its own set of data quality queries. But the data quality pipeline will execute them without any changes.

Challenge exercise

Can you change the email output to have a summary table with rules executed and their pass/fail status along with sample records only from failed rules for further analysis?

Hint

Design data quality queries such that they output records that don't fit the rule. So, if there is no recorded output from the query, the data quality rule should be considered passed and vice versa. You can add this logic in the Lambda function. Collect the results of each query as you iterate through, and finally print the summary dashboard. Also, append sample records to output data in the email only when they are in failed status.

Automating the data quality pipeline

The serverless pipeline is currently executed in an ad hoc manner. We can make the pipeline execute on a custom schedule through EventBridge Scheduler.

Navigate to the EventBridge console and choose **Schedules**, as shown here:

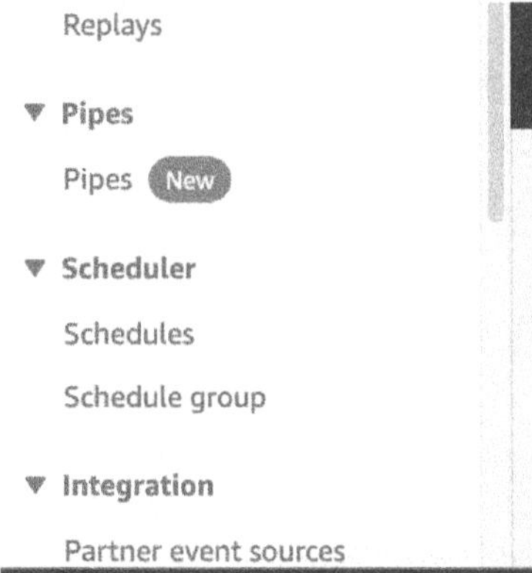

Figure 7.54: EventBridge Scheduler from the AWS console

Choose **Create schedules** and provide a name for the schedule. We will currently schedule the data quality pipeline to be executed every hour using a recurring schedule, but you can set up more complex schedules using a cron-based approach as well, as seen here:

Schedule pattern

Occurrence Info
You can define an one-time or recurrent schedule.

One-time schedule
Recurring schedule

Schedule type
Choose the schedule type that best meets your needs.

Cron-based schedule
A schedule set using a cron expression that runs at a specific time, such as 8:00 a.m. PST on the first Monday of every month.

Rate-based schedule
A schedule that runs at a regular rate, such as every 10 minutes.

Rate expression Info
Enter a value and the unit of time to run the schedule.

rate (1 hours)
Value Unit

Flexible time window
If you choose a flexible time window, Scheduler invokes your schedule within the time window you specify. For example, if you choose 15 minutes, your schedule runs within 15 minutes after the schedule start time.

Off

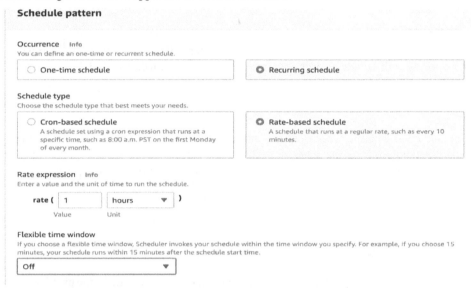

Figure 7.55: EventBridge Scheduler – Setting up a schedule to run every hour

Under **Target API**, choose the **AWS Lambda (Invoke)** option and select the step function that we created in the last section, as shown here:

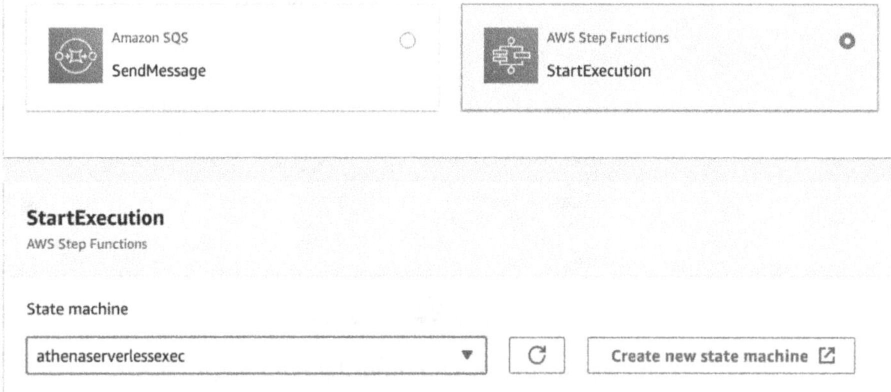

Figure 7.56: EventBridge Scheduler – Calling the step function as the target

Leave the rest of the arguments at their defaults and create the schedule. Congrats! We have now set up a serverless data quality pipeline that is executed on a schedule.

You can see from the following screenshot that the workflow has been running every hour and executing the data quality queries:

Executions (17) | View details | Stop execution | Start execution

Search for executions | Filter by status | 1

Name	Status	Started	End Time
5463ab1e-469c-4fc0-8693-bf0fb7c53ef7	Succeeded	Dec 27, 2022 11:33:50.027 AM	Dec 27, 2022 11:35:48.117 AM
5463ab10-369c-4fc0-8693-bf0fb7c53ef7	Succeeded	Dec 27, 2022 10:33:50.025 AM	Dec 27, 2022 10:35:53.609 AM
5463ab02-269c-4fc0-8693-bf0fb7c53ef7	Succeeded	Dec 27, 2022 09:33:50.022 AM	Dec 27, 2022 09:35:41.208 AM
5463aaf4-169c-4fc0-8693-bf0fb7c53ef7	Succeeded	Dec 27, 2022 08:33:50.030 AM	Dec 27, 2022 08:36:01.172 AM
5463aae6-069c-4fc0-8693-bf0fb7c53ef7	Succeeded	Dec 27, 2022 07:33:50.013 AM	Dec 27, 2022 07:36:02.410 AM
5463aad7-f69c-4fc0-8693-bf0fb7c53ef7	Succeeded	Dec 27, 2022 06:33:50.044 AM	Dec 27, 2022 06:35:43.237 AM
5463aac9-e69c-4fc0-8693-bf0fb7c53ef7	Succeeded	Dec 27, 2022 05:33:50.034 AM	Dec 27, 2022 05:35:57.894 AM
5463aabb-d69c-4fc0-8693-bf0fb7c53ef7	Succeeded	Dec 27, 2022 04:33:50.064 AM	Dec 27, 2022 04:36:00.090 AM

Figure 7.57: Step function workflow executed by EventBridge on an hourly basis

In the current scenario, we are executing the same queries on the data again and again. We can change the queries to run against only new data whenever they are populated using a timestamp column or a partition column that identifies new data. You can further customize the pipeline with more arguments and Athena prepared statements to suit your needs.

Summary

In this chapter, we explored the Amazon Athena service and how it helps in various phases of the data wrangling pipeline. Amazon Athena will provide functionalities that will help you to perform data discovery, data transformation, data structuring, and data quality in a better and performant manner with advanced functions in the SQL language.

In the next chapter, we will learn about Amazon QuickSight and how it helps in the data discovery and data visualization phases of the data wrangling pipeline.

8
Working with QuickSight

In the previous chapter, you learned about the Amazon Athena service and how it can be used for data discovery, data enrichment, and data quality pipelines effectively. In this chapter, we will explore how the Amazon QuickSight service can help with the data discovery and data visualization phases of the data-wrangling pipeline.

This chapter covers the following topics:

- Introducing Amazon QuickSight and its concepts
- Data discovery using QuickSight
- Data visualization using QuickSight

Introducing Amazon QuickSight and its concepts

Amazon QuickSight is a **Business Intelligence** (**BI**) service that helps you to generate interactive dashboards with visuals/charts from a wide variety of data sources, such as the cloud, on-premises, and third-party services. In addition, Amazon QuickSight provides advanced features such as embedded analytics and an AI-enabled search bar.

Why do we need a data visualization tool?

As mentioned previously, a picture is worth a thousand words. Users can understand patterns in data using visuals and charts more easily than tabular data. Also, when data insights are identified, they can be shared with business and executive teams through dashboards to convey the message more effectively.

How does QuickSight work?

QuickSight loads data from supported data sources and users can prepare data within QuickSight to suit their visualization requirements. The data is retrieved locally from the **Super-fast, Parallel, In-memory Calculation Engine** (**SPICE**) or through direct queries from data sources before rendering the visuals in QuickSight. The following screenshot shows the important components of QuickSight:

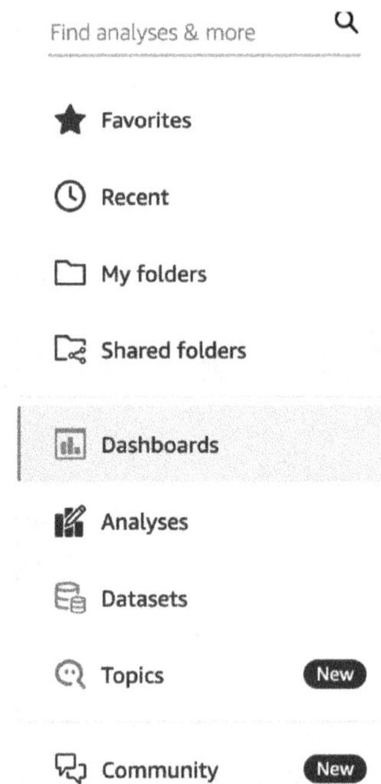

Figure 8.1: QuickSight menu dropdown

We will explore each of those components here:

- **Datasets**

  This section will help in setting up a connection to data sources and also in preparing the data for analysis. The data can be stored in SPICE or accessed in DirectQuery format. This is the first step to perform in any data visualization project within QuickSight (assuming the QuickSight initial setup and configurations are in place).

- **Analyses**

  Here, users will create different visuals and reports, which are published in dashboards. QuickSight users with author privileges will spend a lot of time in the **Analyses** section, creating visuals that can be shared with a wider set of users.

- **Dashboards**

  This section will have dashboards that are created in the **Analyses** section and can be shared with various team members. Users with read-only access can access this section and explore the visuals/reports from dashboards. Sharing dashboards on a schedule through email with different stakeholders can be configured here.

- **Topics**

  This is the section that enables business users to ask questions in English and get answers through machine learning techniques that understand relationships in your data. This avoids teams who would like to get quick answers from the data having to build reports and dashboards.

Now that we have learned about QuickSight at a high level, let us explore how we can perform data discovery using QuickSight from various data sources.

Data discovery with QuickSight

Amazon QuickSight supports loading data from various data sources, and we can then create visuals in the **Analyses** tab to understand the data. Data discovery can also be done using Jupyter notebooks with custom visualization libraries, but that might require programming expertise and complex setup before performing data discovery activities. In contrast, business users can perform data discovery in QuickSight with visuals in the **Analyses** tab.

QuickSight-supported data sources and setup

QuickSight supports a wide variety of data sources. The complete list can be found at `https://docs.aws.amazon.com/quicksight/latest/user/supported-data-sources.html`.

The sources could be classified into the following broad categories:

- **Relational data sources**: Covering cloud and on-premises data sources, including popular data engines such as MySQL, Postgres, SQL Server, Oracle, Snowflake, and Redshift. When connecting to on-premises data sources, you need to create a QuickSight VPC interface as well to import data through a secure connection.
- **File data sources**: Import files from S3 or a local network. Users can upload files from a local network for quick analysis or provide a symlink file with the locations of the S3 files that are needed for analysis.
- **Software-as-a-Service (SaaS) data sources**: Supports importing data from popular SaaS data sources such as Salesforce, Twitter, Jira, and ServiceNow. If your SaaS provider is not listed as supported in the QuickSight data source list, you can use the AWS AppFlow service to import data, or you can choose to import SaaS data into Amazon S3 programmatically through code running in ECS containers, AWS Glue, or Lambda functions.
- **Analytics data sources**: Supports importing data from analytics services so that the data from the analytics engine can be visualized. Supports importing data from Amazon Athena, Presto, Spark, Amazon OpenSearch, IoT Analytics, and so on.

Refer to the AWS documentation for some examples of how to set up connections for popular data sources: `https://docs.aws.amazon.com/quicksight/latest/user/connecting-to-data-examples.html`.

There are a couple of options for setting up data sources:

- **Creating datasets from new data sources**: We use this option when we set up a connection from a new data source that hasn't been used earlier in QuickSight. The following screenshot shows the list of connectors that can be used to create a connection for a new data source. Users can click on any of the sources and provide appropriate configuration options to create new datasets.

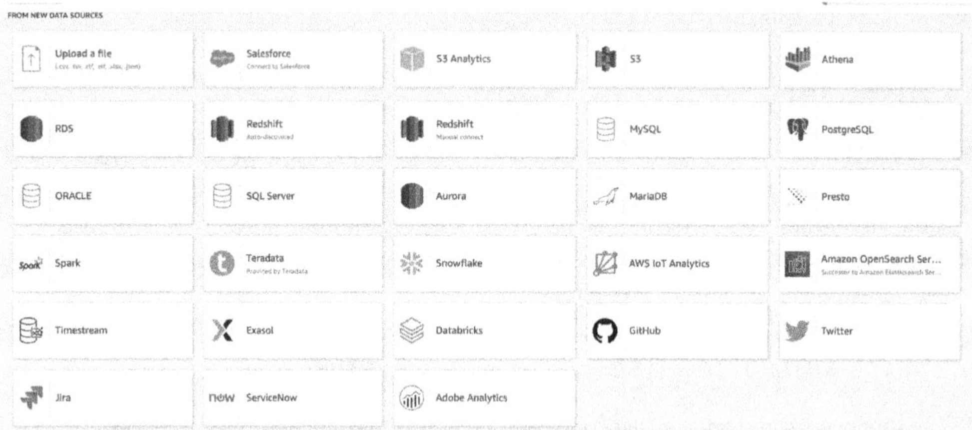

Figure 8.2: QuickSight – create datasets from new data sources

- **Creating datasets from existing data sources or datasets**: You can use existing connection information to create new datasets. This option is useful when you would like to use the same data source but perform different transformations before visualizing data. Consider an example of a Redshift warehouse connection that is used by the sales team. The sales team also removes certain attributes and transforms data differently for its BI needs. If the marketing team also wants to run reports from Redshift but doesn't need the changes made by the sales team, it can reuse the connection to create a new dataset for its visualizations.

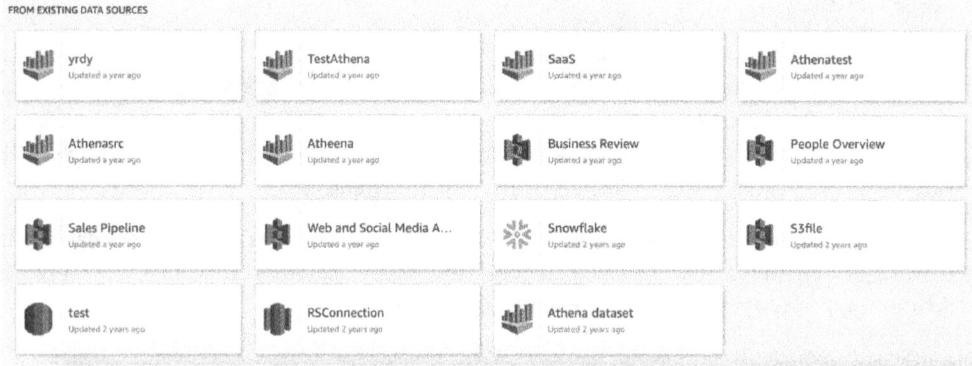

Figure 8.3: QuickSight – create datasets from existing data sources

Data discovery with QuickSight analysis

Now, we can look at data discovery with Amazon QuickSight by importing the sales pipeline data from sample datasets (refer to *Figure 8.3* for the sales pipeline dataset). You can import the data and create a new dataset for our analysis.

Once you have imported the data, it will show an empty canvas with the fields from our dataset shown on the left side. You can play around with it by creating visuals on the fields that you want to explore using QuickSight.

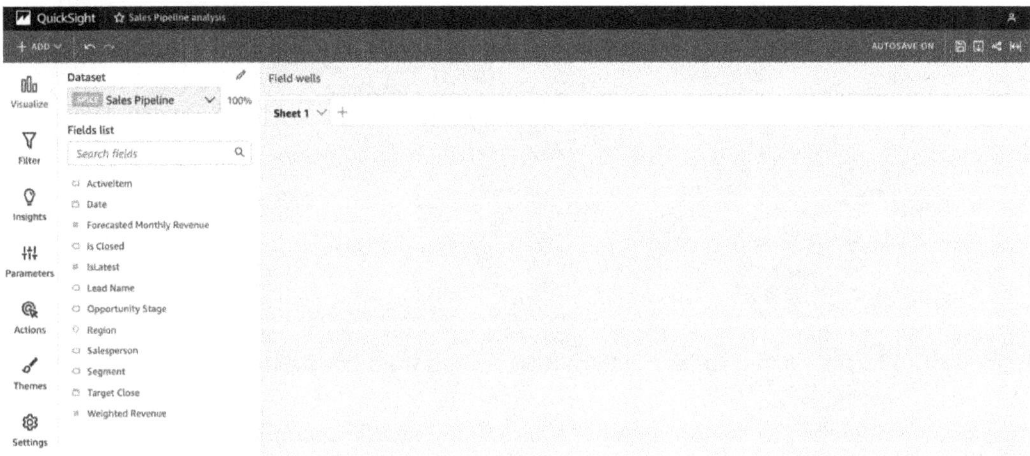

Figure 8.4: QuickSight – analysis screen in the QuickSight console

We will consider the following situation for performing a data discovery activity: a business user without coding expertise wants to explore and understand the sales dataset before making decisions on sales forecasting.

The advantage of using a visualization tool is that you can create quick visuals without any programming expertise. In order to visualize sales data over a time period, we will simply click on the **Date** column and QuickSight will automatically create a visual that is best suited to that type of data.

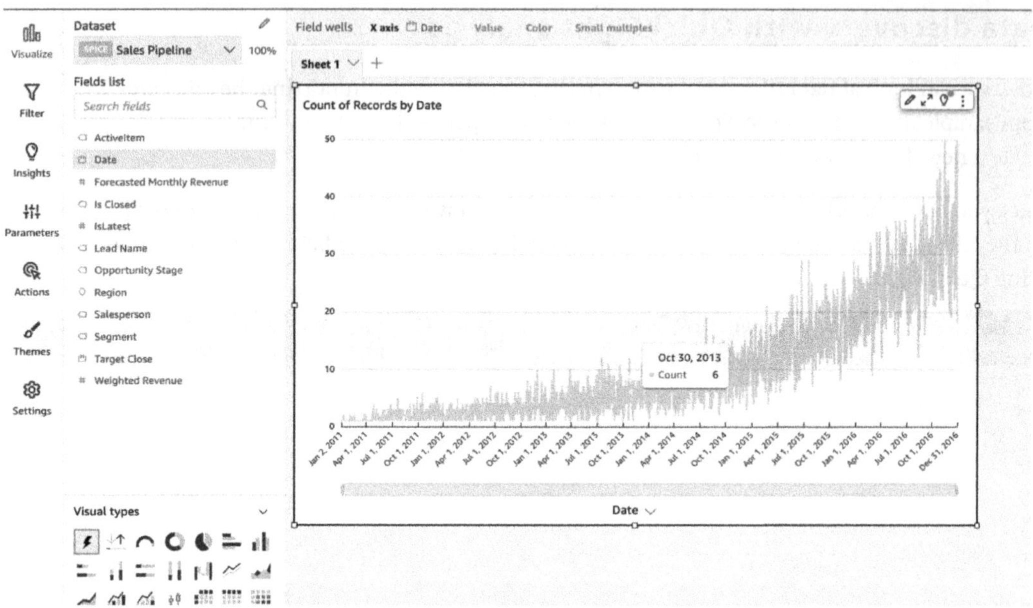

Figure 8.5: QuickSight – auto-graph that automatically chooses the best visualization for the Date field

As you can see from the preceding screenshot, QuickSight created an auto-graph for the date field with the count of sales records across dates. The chart shows an increasing trend in sales, and you can hover over the graph to see the count of records for a specific time period, as shown in the preceding screenshot.

But we still have data across a huge time period and we want to focus our analysis on sales records only for the year 2016, which is the latest year in this sample dataset. We will add a filter to visualize only data from 2016. Click on the **Filter** icon on the left side and it will show the **ADD FILTER** option, as shown here:

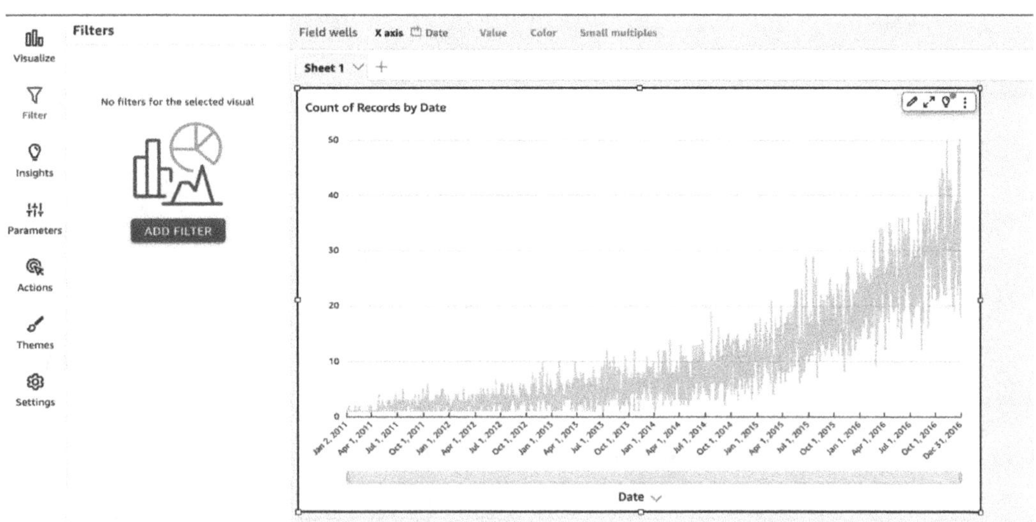

Figure 8.6: QuickSight – QuickSight Filter option to visualize only specific data

Click on **ADD FILTER** and choose the column/attribute from the dataset based on which the filter condition should be applied. Remember to choose the **Only this visual** option to avoid the date filter being applied to other visuals that we might create in this sheet. We will choose **After** for **Condition** and set the **Date** field to **2016/01/01**. We also have the option to choose a rolling window to keep looking at the latest data (visualize only the last 90 days of data). Once all options are chosen, click on **APPLY**. Now you can see the data is only shown for 2016, which makes the graph more readable:

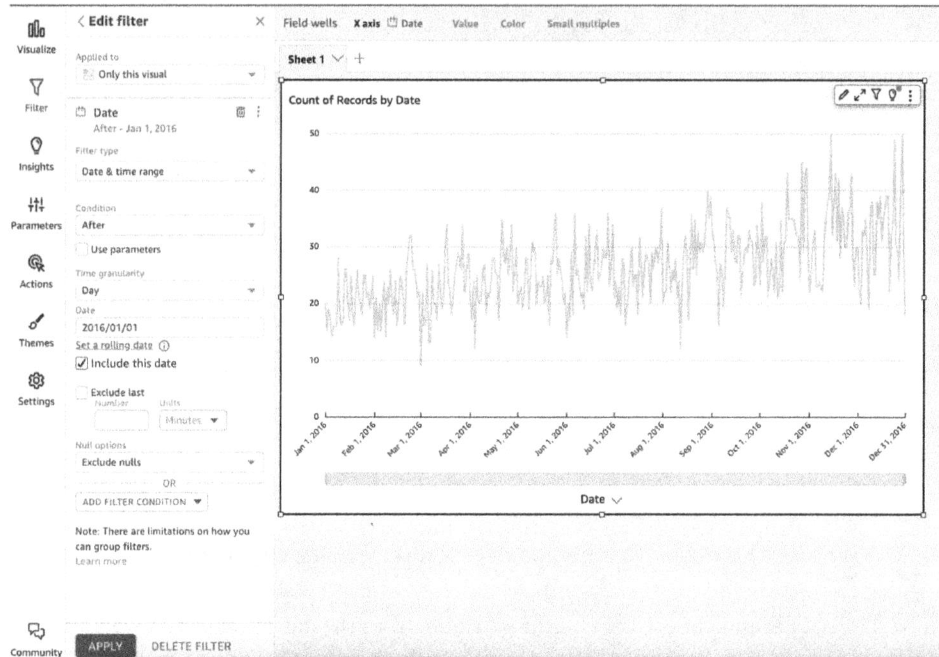

Figure 8.7: QuickSight – apply filter to visualize data in the QuickSight console

Still, the data is across 365 days and we want to see the aggregated numbers for each month so that we can understand the pattern of sales from the sales dataset. We can do this by clicking on the visual and looking at the **Field wells** section above the canvas. Refer to the following screenshot highlighting the **Date** field in **Field wells**.

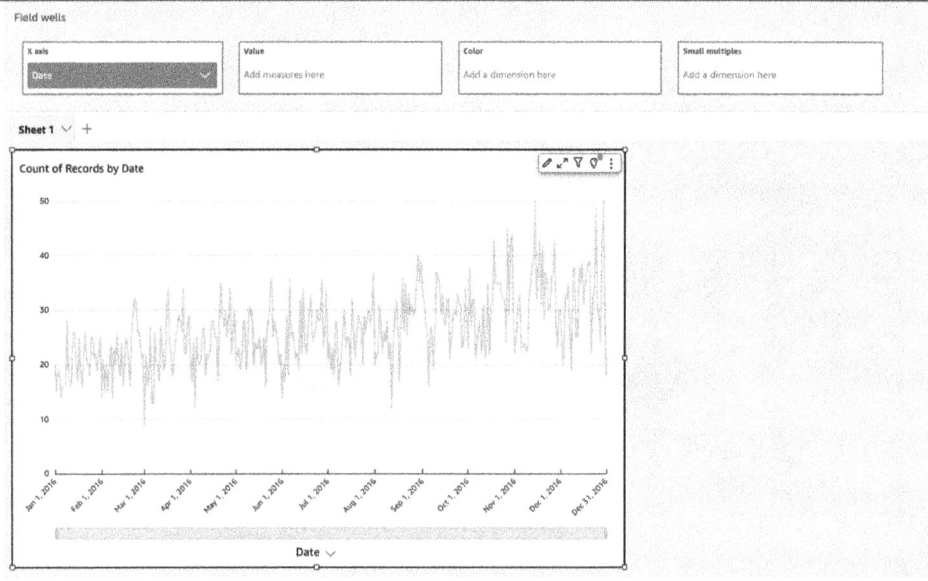

Figure 8.8: QuickSight – QuickSight Field wells demonstration

Now, we can click on the **Date** field under **Field wells** and aggregate the data on a monthly basis, as shown in the following screenshot:

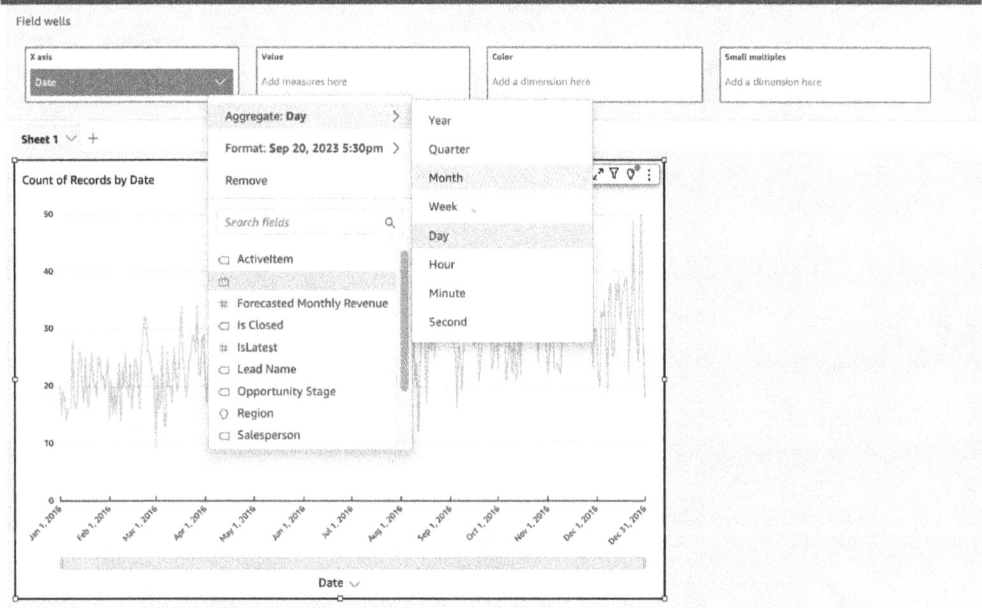

Figure 8.9: QuickSight – aggregate data in visuals through Field well

This will show the data aggregated at a monthly level, as shown here, which makes it much easier for us to visualize and understand the trend of sales in 2016:

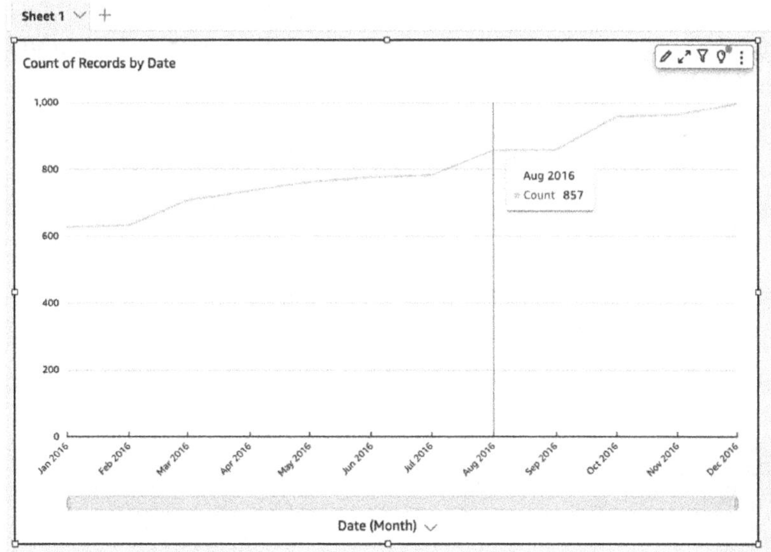

Figure 8.10: QuickSight – line chart – count of records aggregated on a monthly basis

This looks good, but we still do not have the data labels to clearly see the sales numbers and don't want to hover over the graph to get the sales numbers for a month. Click on **Format visual** in the top-right corner of the visual (refer to the following screenshot):

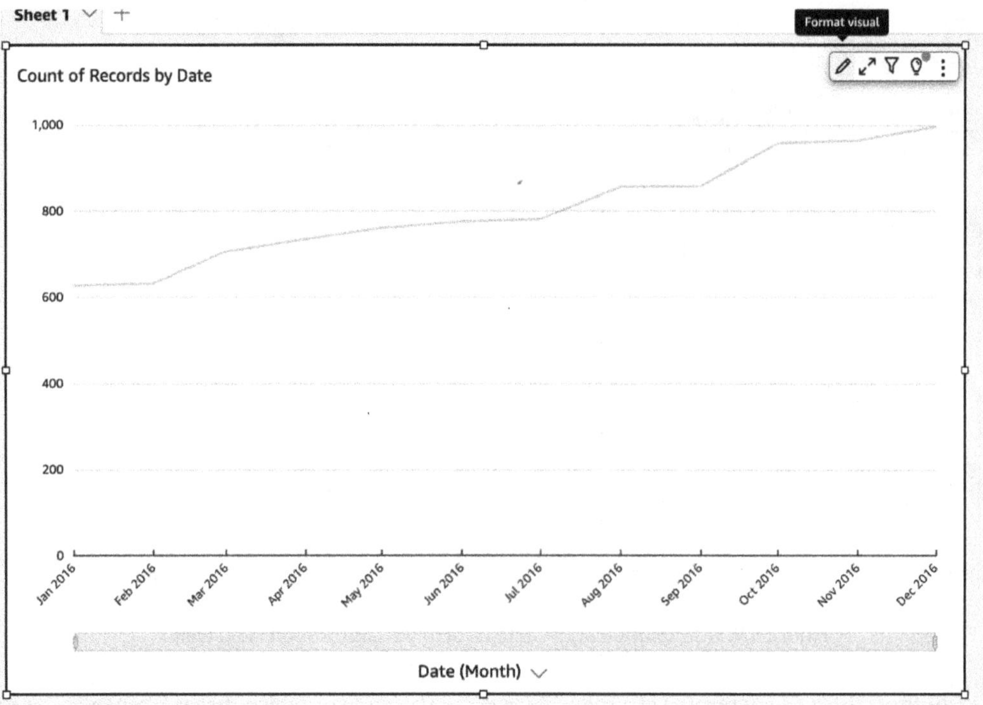

Figure 8.11: QuickSight – choose Format visual in the QuickSight console to customize the visual

You can now customize various aspects of this visual, including adding labels. We can add data labels by providing the following values under the **Data labels** section:

- Check the **Show data labels** checkbox
- Set **Font size** to **Large**
- Set **Font color** to **Black**

Now you can see the pattern of sales numbers over a period of time. We can see the increasing pattern in sales numbers in 2016.

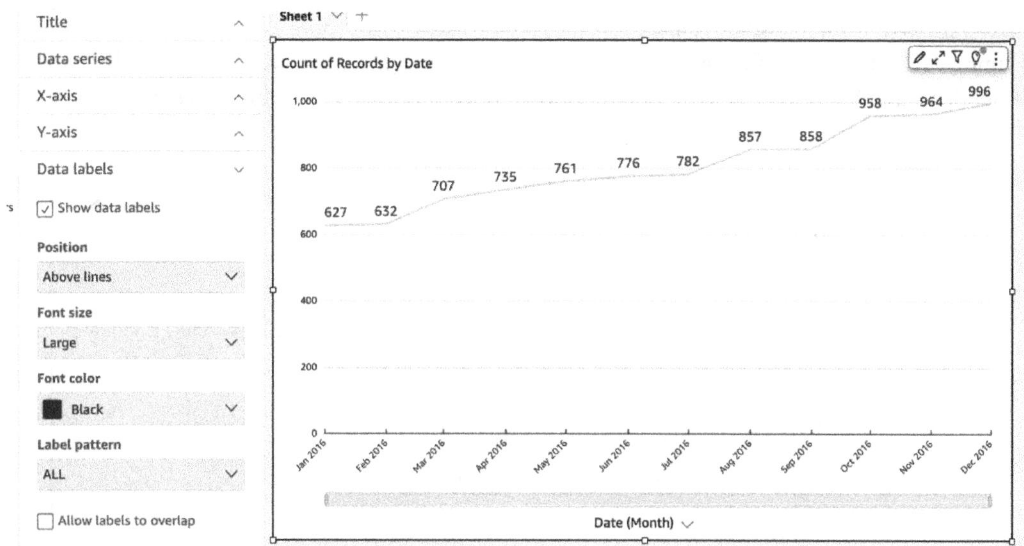

Figure 8.12: QuickSight – line chart with data labels

We can also add additional fields to this visual to analyze the sales numbers using a combination of different factors. We can add the **Segment** and **Region** fields to understand whether there is any particular attribute that has contributed to our sales increase significantly. This can simply be achieved by clicking on the **Segment** field under **Fields list**.

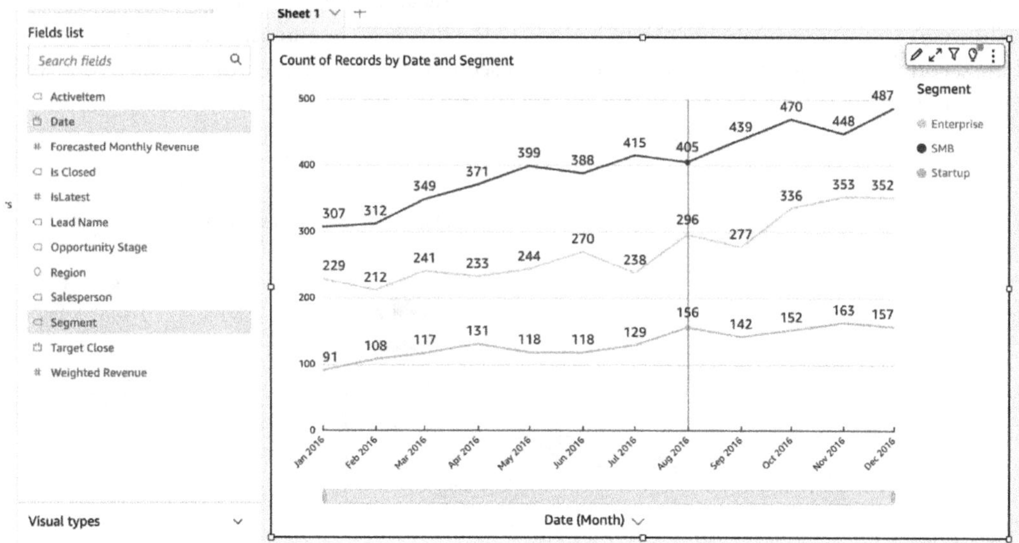

Figure 8.13: QuickSight – line chart with the Segment field added to the color segment in Field well

We still want to understand whether any particular region contributed more to our sales numbers. We will simply click the **Region** field as well under **Fields list** and QuickSight will automatically render sub-plots/sub-graphs within the main graph to provide region-level visualization, as shown here:

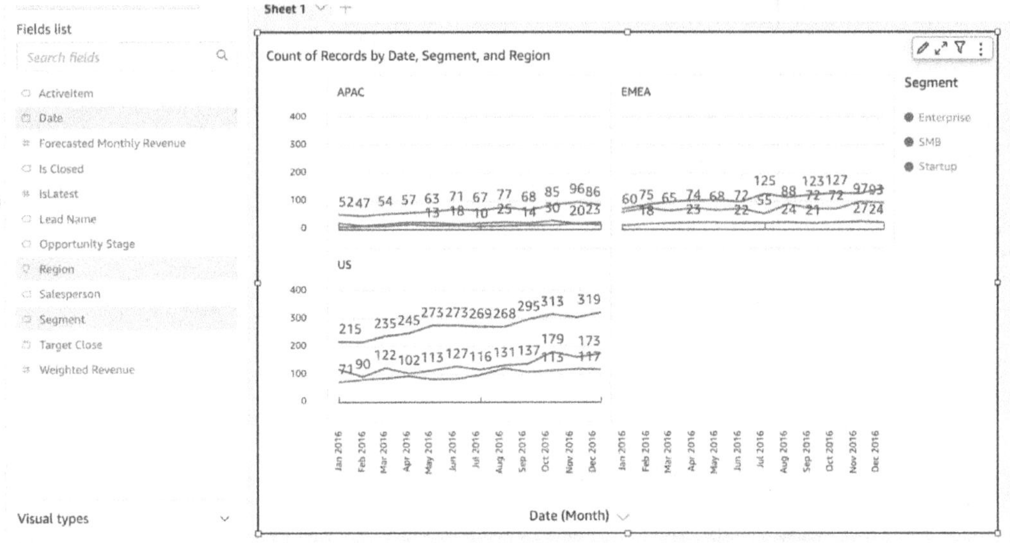

Figure 8.14: QuickSight – line chart with sub-plots/sub-graphs added

This all looks fine, but how does QuickSight keep creating these different visualizations? If you look at **Field wells**, you will see that QuickSight has added the first field, **Segment**, to the **Color** section and the second field, **Region**, to the **Small multiples** section and created the nice visualizations we saw previously:

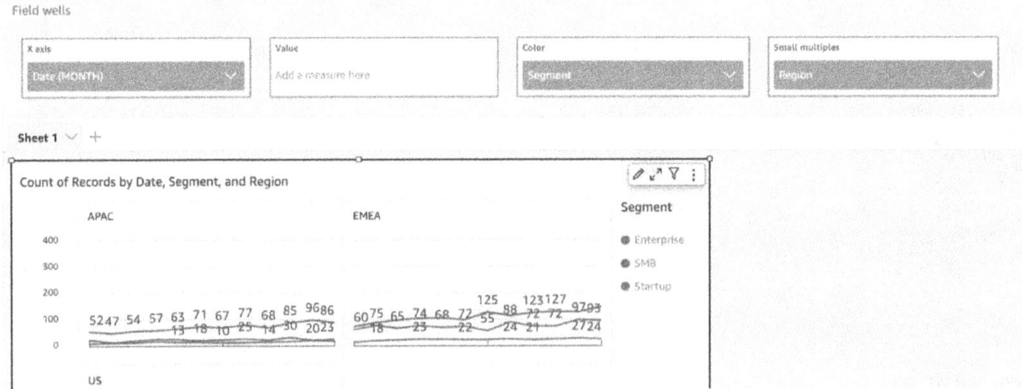

Figure 8.15: QuickSight – line chart with Color and Small multiples set, shown under Field wells

For curious minds, what will happen if we keep adding new fields by clicking on them? Let us go ahead and click the **Salesperson** field. You will now see that **Region** has been replaced in **Small multiples** with **Salesperson**. QuickSight uses mechanisms to understand the type of graph and keep adding attributes that are suitable for the current visualization option (here we have line charts).

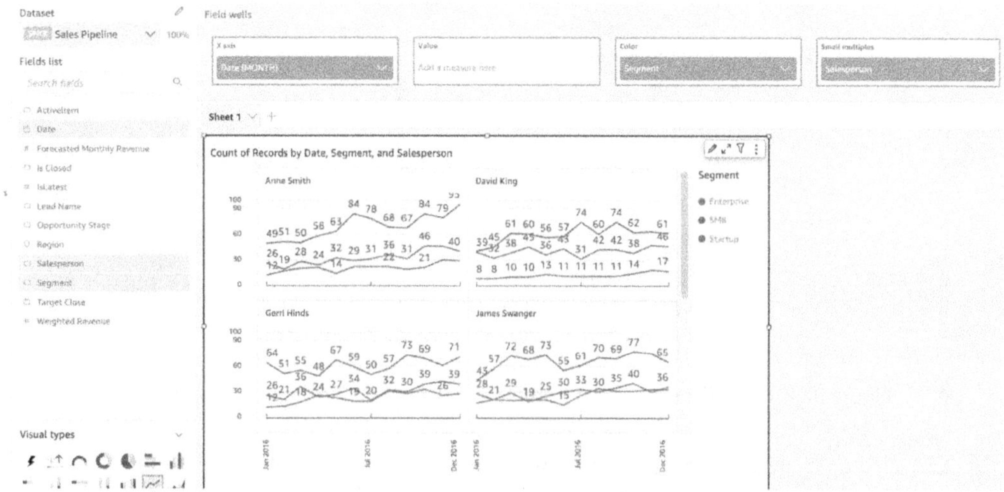

Figure 8.16: QuickSight – line chart working when adding new attributes to the visual in the QuickSight console

The same can be done for other fields as well, and QuickSight will render graphs based on the field type that is chosen. We will explore the **Salesperson** field further to understand the unique values within that field. Click outside the current line chart and choose **Salesperson** from the field list. You will see a bar chart is created with the salesperson names. QuickSight automatically determines the type of visualization that best fits the field chosen by the user. We can easily change the visualization in the **Visual types** section shown here:

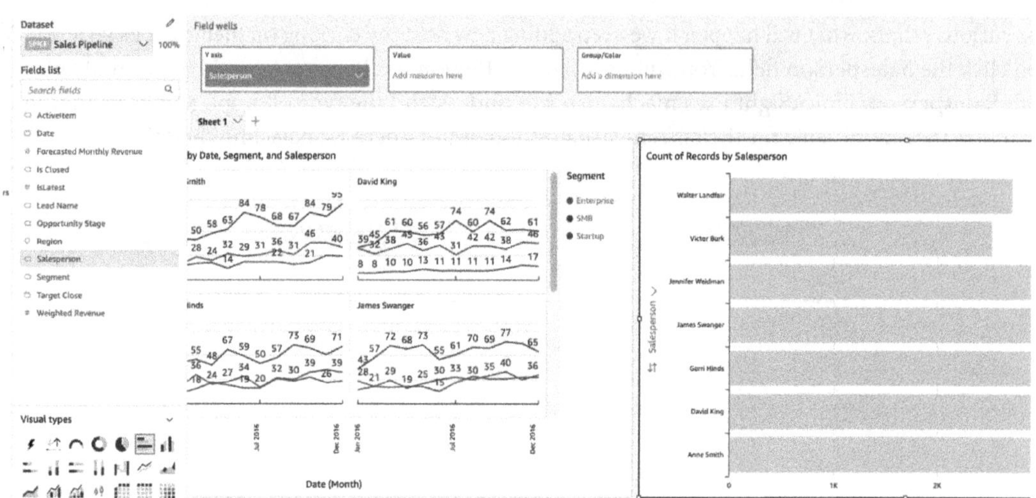

Figure 8.17: QuickSight – bar chart created for a field with distinct attributes

You can keep adding more visualizations and discover the data efficiently. But the key takeaway here is the ease with which users can explore data efficiently without any programming language expertise.

QuickSight Q and AI-based data analysis/discovery

Amazon QuickSight Q also provides advanced data analysis or data exploration through business language questions rather than SQL scripts or BI dashboards that need to be created by the IT team. QuickSight Q uses natural language processing models in the backend to answer the questions. This helps business and leadership teams to get answers from data without having any programming language expertise, and they also need not wait for the IT team to create dashboards for them.

You can ask QuickSight Q questions such as "Who are the best sales agents by sales?" and "Who were the top sales agents last year?" The words used can be different, but still, QuickSight Q can understand and provide meaningful results from the dataset.

Let us explore QuickSight Q with sample datasets provided by QuickSight. You can select topics and click on **Try Q** to explore Q using sample datasets. If you want to explore Q with your data and configure QuickSight Q, you can click on **Start free trial**. You can review the add-on pricing section to understand the cost details for using QuickSight Q. For the purpose of learning in this book, let us continue with the **TRY Q** option.

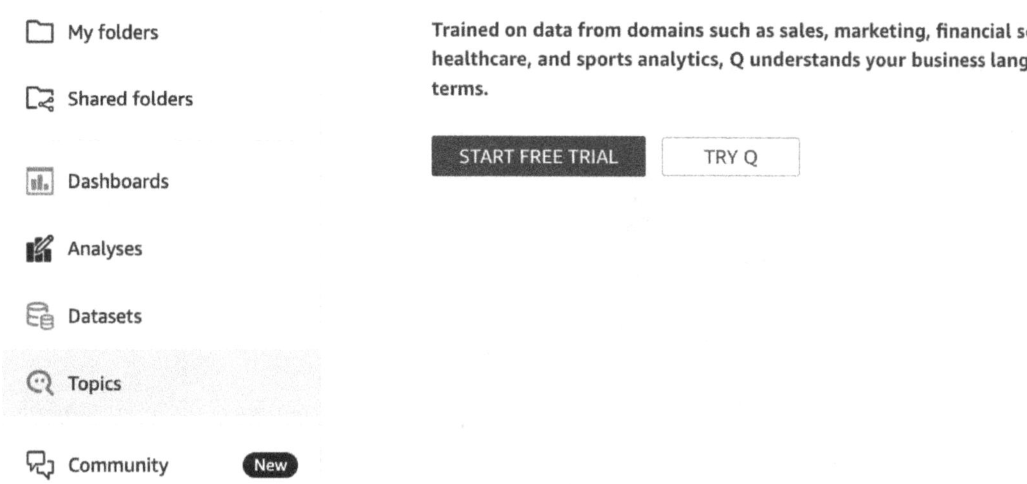

Figure 8.18: QuickSight – QuickSight Q enabled in console

From the sample datasets, choose **Product sales**. Now you will see the screen where you can ask questions through Q. It also provides suggested questions that can be asked about the sample dataset and a dashboard that already provides good visualizations of the data.

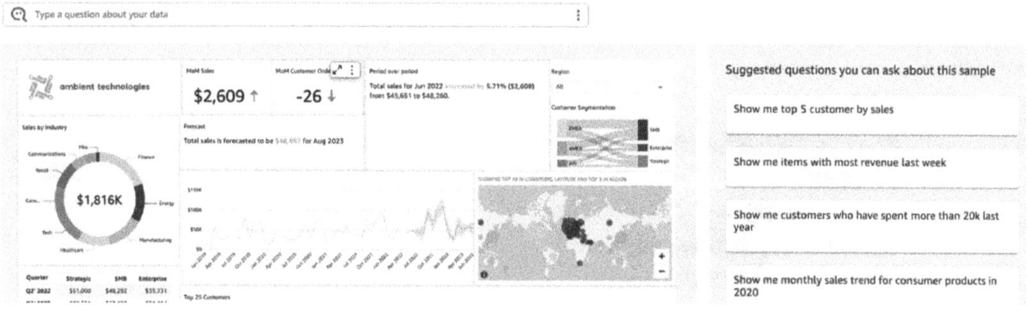

Figure 8.19: QuickSight – QuickSight Q home screen with search bar

We can start by using one of the sample questions that was suggested by Q. We can see the output with a horizontal bar chart showing the top five customers ordered by sales in dollars.

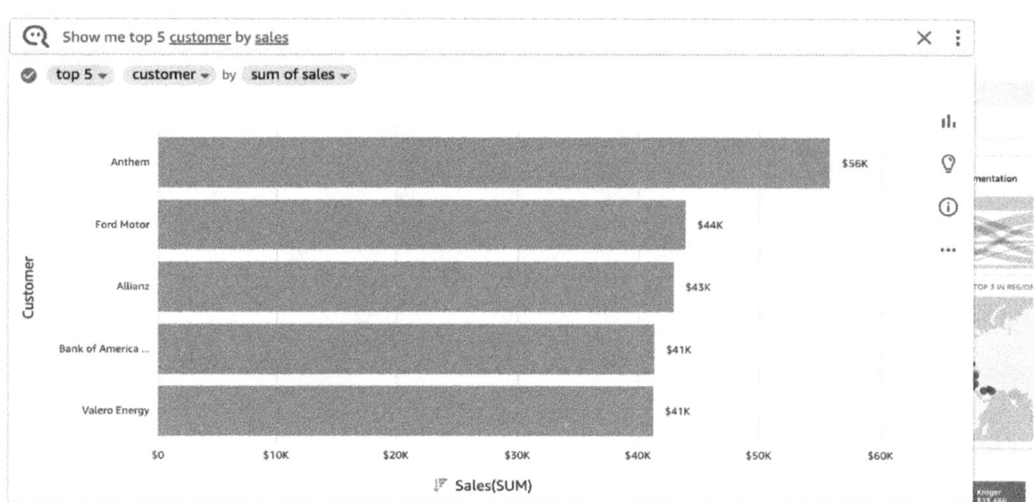

Figure 8.20: QuickSight – QuickSight Q showing results of a top suggested question

Let us explore this further by refining the question to get sales agents by region. We will see the results are now grouped by region.

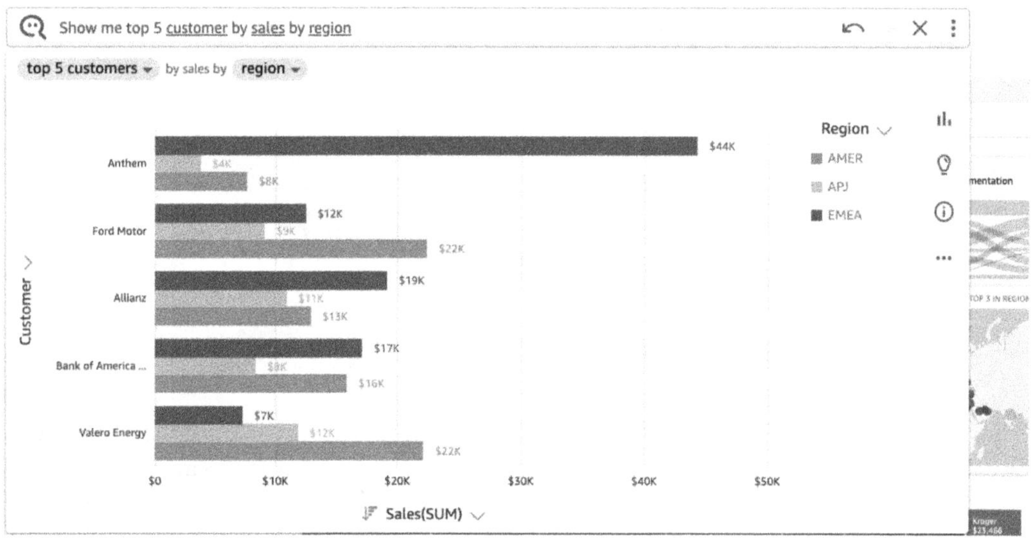

Figure 8.21: QuickSight Q – results for sales aggregated by region for top five customers

We can see the top customer has the highest revenue from the EMEA region. We would like to identify the top customers in the AMER region. Let us refine the question by asking for the top customers from a specific region.

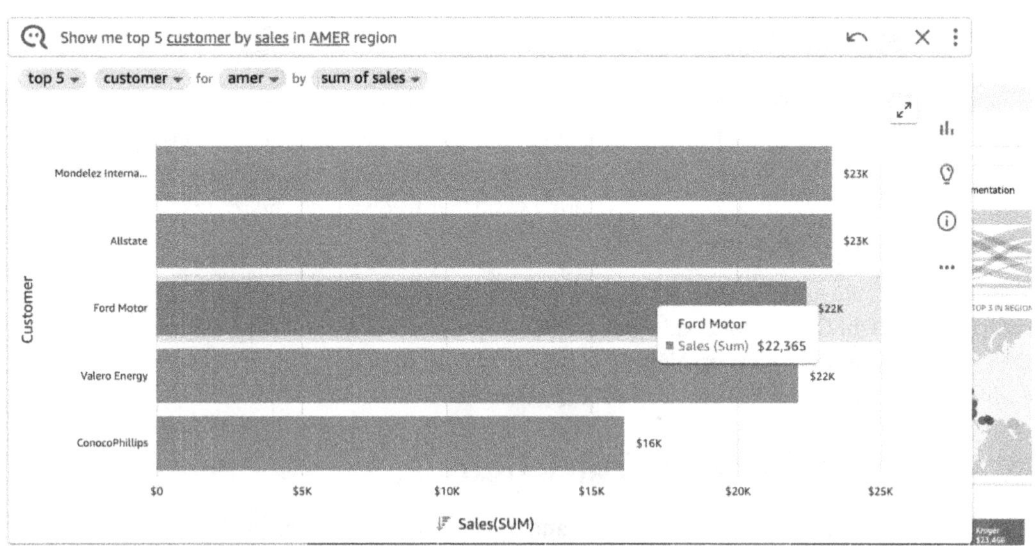

Figure 8.22: QuickSight Q – results for sales for top five customers only in the AMER region

Now, we would like to look at the top customers from the recent data. The business team wants to identify the top customers from the last two years of data to provide incentives/discounts to those top customers.

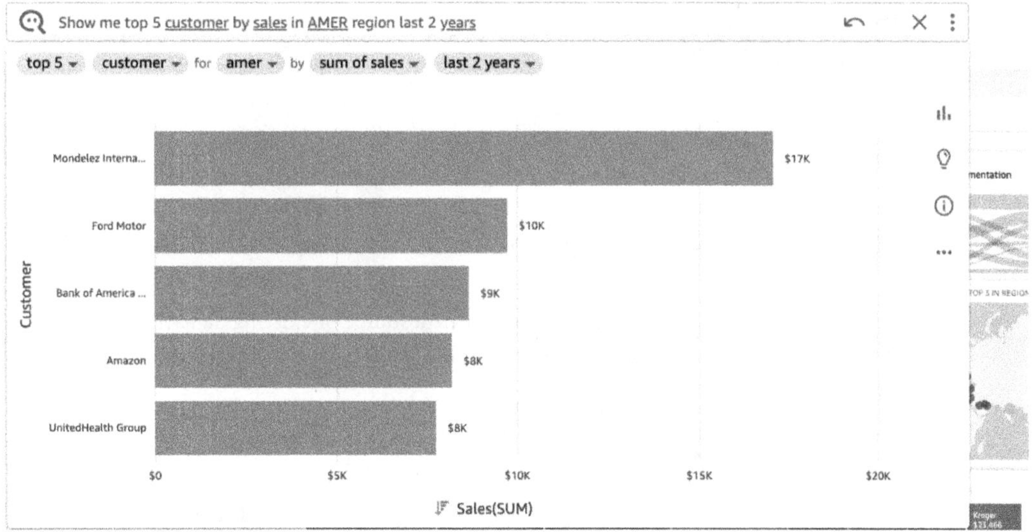

Figure 8.23: QuickSight Q – results for sales for top five customers only in the AMER region filtered for the last two years

Now, you can export the data or perform further analysis from these results. The important takeaway from this is the ease with which we can get the charts and visualizations using simple English language statements. The users don't need to know how to use any programming languages, SQL scripts, or BI tools but can still create visualizations to explore data using QuickSight Q. It can also take care of some spelling mistakes, acronyms, and synonyms and make auto-complete suggestions specific to each project's business needs. Users can also provide further feedback on the results, so QuickSight Q can learn and improve from user interactions.

We have explored the features of QuickSight Q only from a data discovery perspective using sample data. But QuickSight Q has a lot of advanced features that can be used to enable **Natural Language Querying** (**NLQ**) on your datasets. Now we have looked at ways of exploring data using QuickSight, we will look at data visualization options with QuickSight.

Data visualization with QuickSight

In this section, we will explore different visuals and options that are available within QuickSight. We will explore high-level concepts and different visuals and features within QuickSight in this section.

Visualization and charts with QuickSight

The following steps are performed when publishing a dashboard in QuickSight.

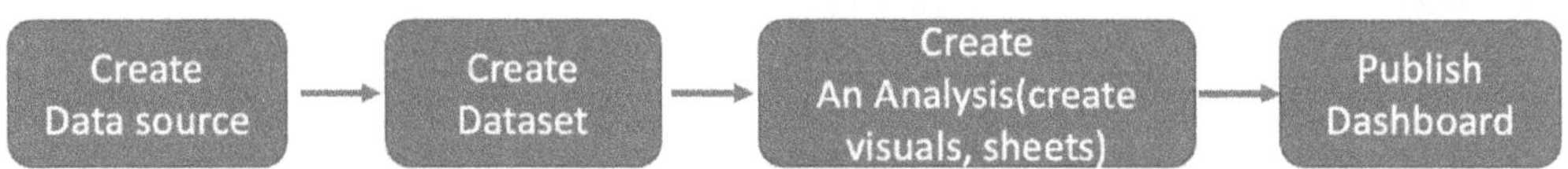

Figure 8.24: QuickSight – high-level dashboard publishing workflow

1. **Create data source**: This is the step where the connection to the data source is established. This can be a one-time activity and can be reused multiple times when new datasets are created from the data source.
2. **Create dataset**: A dataset can be created from a new data source or existing datasets for different analysis requirements. The datasets can be modified, parsed, or enriched based on specific analysis requirements.
3. **Create analysis (create visuals)**: Create visuals from a specific dataset. Here, the dashboard author will create interactive visuals that can be published to a dashboard for user consumption.
4. **Publish dashboard**: After creating a dashboard from the **Analyses** tab, the dashboard author can then publish the dashboard, which can then be consumed by users (readers or authors). The users can now subscribe to reports, export them as PDFs, or embed them into their applications as applicable.

The following are different types of visualization charts that can be used in QuickSight. We are not providing a complete list of visuals available in QuickSight, but will be highlighting some frequently used charts and scenarios in which you can use them:

- A **line chart** can help to visualize changes over time continuously. You can use a dual-axis line chart if one measure is smaller and one is very large, for example, comparing revenue (higher $ amount) and profit (smaller $ amount) over a period of time. Both line and bar charts can help to visualize changes in a dimension over a period of time.
- **Area charts** are similar to line charts but the area under the line is colored for better visualization. Area charts can be used when there are multiple measures and the area under them doesn't overlap. The following figure shows a line chart and an area chart:

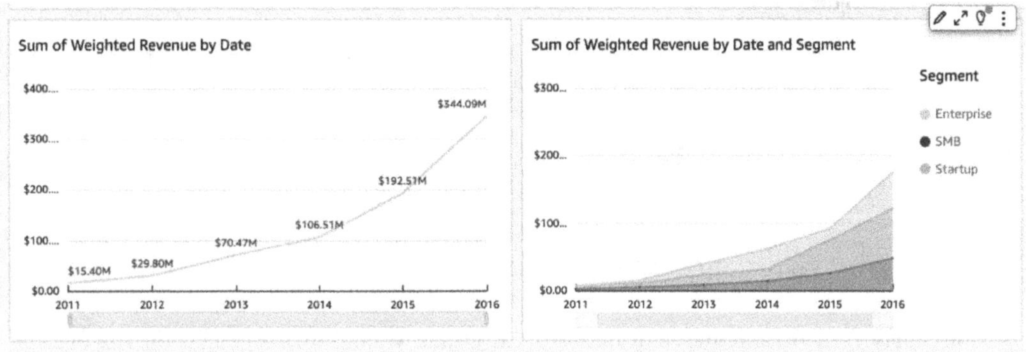

Figure 8.25: QuickSight – visualize changes over time using a line chart and area chart

- A **bar graph** can help to visualize and compare dimensions if there are discrete values in the dimension column:
  - **Single measure**: Add a dimension to the *x* (vertical) or *y* axis (horizontal) and the graph will show the count of each occurrence
  - **Multiple measures**: Each dimension is compared side by side for one or more measures, for example, compare cost and profit for each department
- A **stacked bar graph** can be used to visualize multiple dimensions grouped in a single stack over a single measure

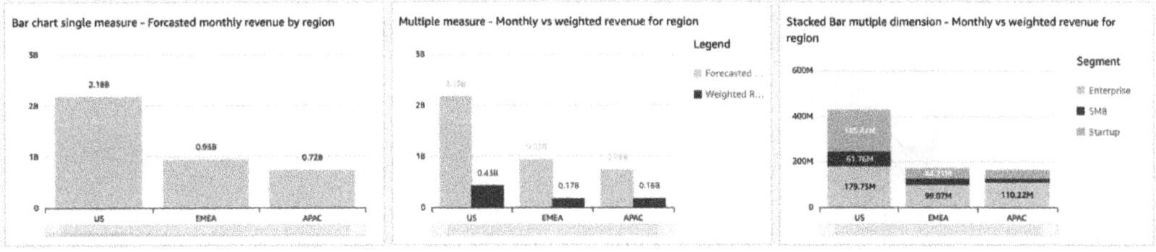

Figure 8.26: QuickSight – visualize and compare dimensions using a bar graph

- A **combo chart** can be used to show when there is a relationship between a bar and line graph. The following graph shows a visualization of the forecasted revenue on a line chart and the actual revenue on a bar chart.

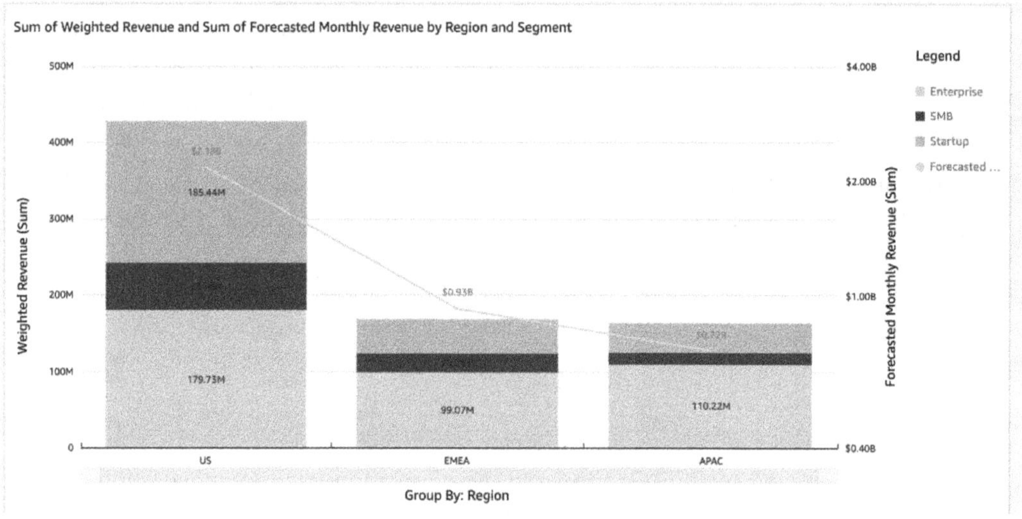

Figure 8.27: QuickSight – visualization using a combo chart

- **Pie charts** let us visualize the contribution of each value within a total segment. The size of each wedge/pie is representative of the percentage of that value within the whole segment. Any type of data that can be broken down into distinct categories can be used in this chart, but try to restrict the number of categories of data within the chart to less than five or it may be difficult to read and compare the slices in the pie chart.
- In a **donut chart**, in addition to the contribution of each value, the whole value is displayed in the center for easy reference. In the following figure, you can see the revenue contribution of each region in a pie chart and donut chart.

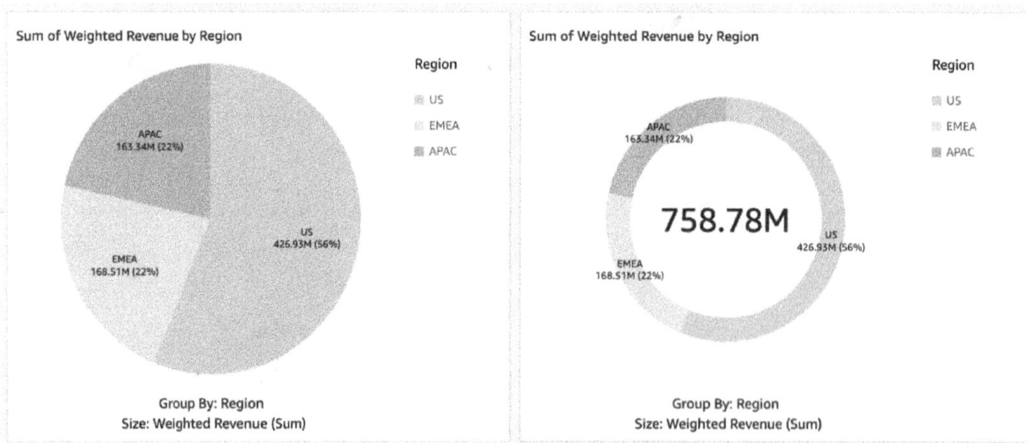

Figure 8.28: QuickSight – visualizion using a pie chart and donut chart

- A **gauge chart** helps us to understand the progress of a metric against an overall goal. In the following gauge chart, we can see the actual revenue compared to the forecasted revenue. It gives a clear indication that the current actual revenue is only 19.84% of the forecasted revenue. This chart can be used to track the progress of a metric against a goal on a periodic basis.
- A **KPI chart** shows key performance indicators by comparing them against a target value. We can also use this to compare the progress of a metric on a periodic basis, as shown here. The KPI chart displayed on the right side of *Figure 8.29* shows the weighted revenue grew by 8.82% between **Q3' 2016** and **Q4' 2016.**

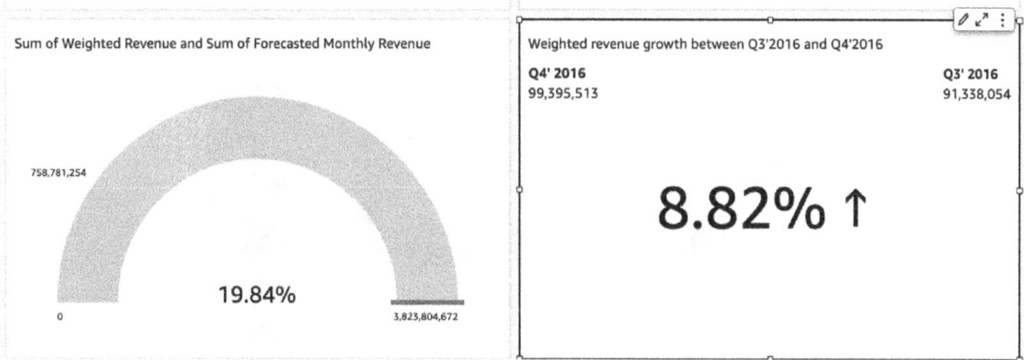

Figure 8.29: QuickSight – gauge chart and KPI chart

- A **heat map** will help to identify data outliers and data spread between two different dimension attributes. The data is displayed in tabular format and each box is color-coded based on the metric column chosen for the heat map. The higher the value for the metric, the darker the boxes are colored, and lower values are colored in a lighter color. In the following diagram, we can immediately see that EMEA enterprise customers should receive more focus as the revenue from this segment/region is lower compared to other regions (even though this is still the highest revenue segment within EMEA).

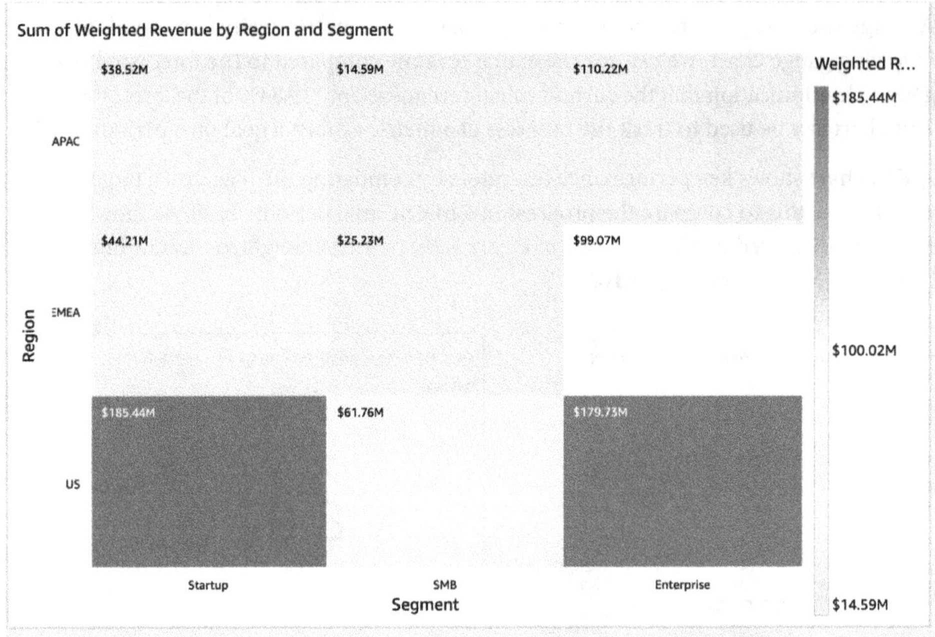

Figure 8.30: QuickSight – heat map

- A **box/whisker plot** helps in visualizing data distribution across an axis. In the following figure, you can see the distribution of revenue across different business segments. This helps us to see that the startup segment has revenue potential.

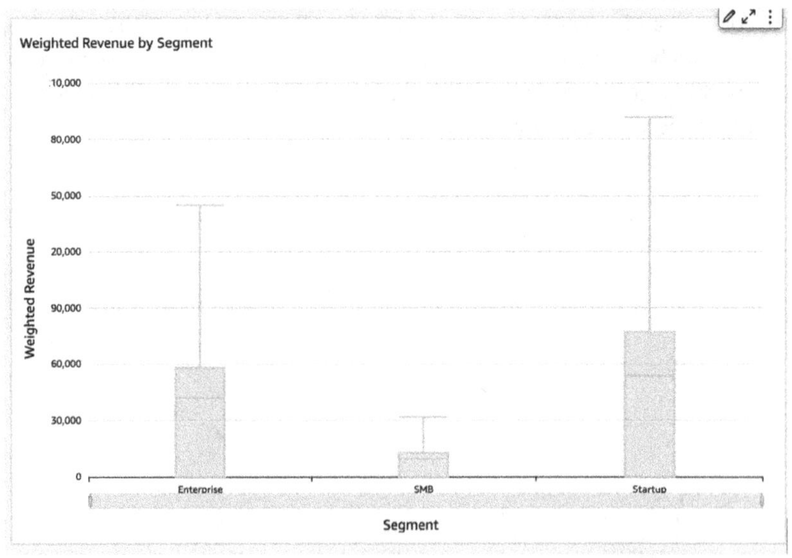

Figure 8.31: QuickSight – box plot/whisker plot

- A **sankey diagram** shows data flow from one dimension to another. The following diagram shows the revenue distribution between regions and business segments and the size of the connection path provides an idea of the volume of revenue generated in that region for that business segment.

Figure 8.32: QuickSight – sankey diagram

- **Map charts** let us visualize a metric on a map using a geo field (zip code, state, county, etc.). There are two types of map charts that can be created in QuickSight:
    - **Point maps** show the metrics as points with different sizes – bigger-sized points for higher values and smaller-sized points for lower values
    - **Filled maps** show the metrics in varying shades of colors – darker shades for higher values and lighter shades for lower values

  The following diagram shows a point map with weighted revenue from different hospitals. Each region is colored differently for easier analysis by business teams.

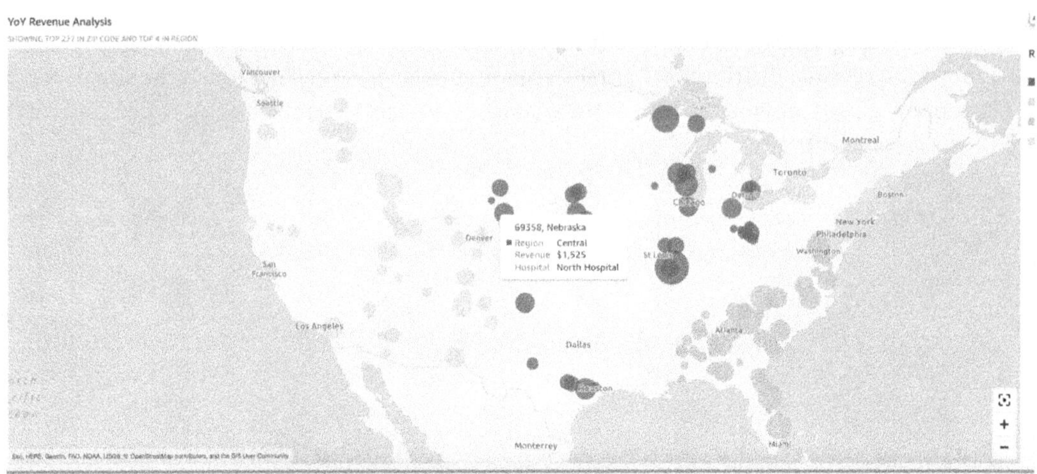

Figure 8.33: QuickSight – map chart – point maps

The following diagram shows a filled map with each state colored based on the revenue from the hospitals within the state.

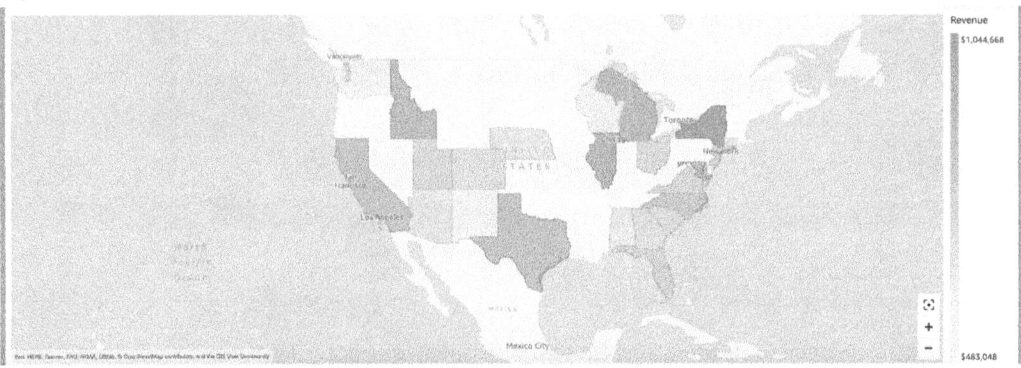

Figure 8.34: QuickSight – map chart – filled maps

In this section, you have learned about different charts. There are additional charts in Amazon QuickSight for visualizing your data for different use cases. Using the right charts in dashboards can help users narrate their story effectively to a wider audience. In the next section, we will learn about embedded analytics.

Embedded analytics

This section is very short and just aims to introduce you to the concept of embedding your dashboards. Organizations can embed dashboards into their applications or web portals so that users can explore QuickSight dashboards without logging in to the AWS console to access QuickSight. This makes life simpler for teams who can now publish advanced dashboards and visualizations on web portals and have enhanced user interaction. QuickSight supports embedding in three different flavors:

- The **QuickSight console**: Embed the entire QA console into a web portal so users can author and publish dashboards. This can be used by teams to embed the QuickSight authoring experience into their web portal with added functionalities for their employees.
- **Dashboards and visuals**: Embed dashboards that are developed in the QuickSight console and users will only view and interact with the dashboards. This can be used by teams who want to publish advanced dashboards to customers in their web applications.
- **QuickSight Q**: Embed a QuickSight Q search bar into web applications.

QuickSight supports one-click dashboard embedding. The steps are documented in this blog post: `https://docs.aws.amazon.com/quicksight/latest/user/1-click-embedding.html`.

In order to enable one-click public embedding, you need to change your QuickSight subscription to a session-based model.

Summary

In this chapter, we explored the Amazon QuickSight service and how it helps in various phases of the data-wrangling pipeline. We learned about various AWS services and how they fit into the data-wrangling pipeline and can perform certain data-wrangling activities in an efficient manner.

In the next chapter, we will learn about practical use cases for a data-wrangling pipeline.

Part 4: Advanced Data Manipulation and ML Data Optimization

In this section, we'll explore advanced data manipulation and machine learning data optimization using AWS Data Wrangler and AWS SageMaker Data Wrangler. *Chapter 9* showcases the powerful combination of AWS Data Wrangler and pandas, guiding you through advanced data transformations and analysis. *Chapter 10* delves into ML data optimization with AWS SageMaker Data Wrangler, helping you preprocess and prepare data for ML projects to maximize model performance and accuracy.

This part has the following chapters:

- *Chapter 9, Building an End-to-End Data-Wrangling Pipeline with AWS SDK for Pandas*
- *Chapter 10, Data Processing for Machine Learning with SageMaker Data Wrangler*

9

Building an End-to-End Data-Wrangling Pipeline with AWS SDK for Pandas

In the previous chapters, we learned about the data-wrangling process and how to utilize different services for data-wrangling activities within the AWS ecosystem:

- We explored AWS Glue DataBrew, which helps you in creating a data-wrangling pipeline through a GUI-based approach for every type of user.
- We also went through SageMaker Data Wrangler, which also helps users in creating a GUI-based data-wrangling pipeline, but it's more closely aligned with machine learning workloads with tighter integration with the SageMaker service.
- We also explored AWS SDK for Pandas, aka awswrangler, which is a hands-on coding approach to data wrangling that integrates the Pandas library with the AWS ecosystem. This will be used by users who are more hands-on with Python programming and are in love with the Pandas library and its capabilities.
- We also went through different AWS services such as Amazon S3, Amazon Athena, AWS Glue, and Amazon QuickSight and how those services help in different aspects of the data-wrangling pipeline.

In this chapter, we will explore an end-to-end data wrangling pipeline using the `pandas` library. We will use a fictional example and utilize various AWS services for performing data discovery, structuring, cleansing, enriching, validation, and publishing in a wrangling pipeline.

This chapter covers the following topics:

- A solution walkthrough for sportstickets.com
- Data discovery
- Data structuring

- Restructuring data using Pandas
- Data cleansing
- Data enrichment
- Data quality validation
- Data visualization

Let's get started!

A solution walkthrough for sportstickets.com

We will walk through a fictional example, sportstickets.com, which is a sports-ticketing franchise. This company manages different sporting events and sells tickets for sports events at a discounted rate. The business analysts from sportsticket.com want to set up an end-to-end data-wrangling pipeline for performing ticket sales analysis on the data.

We will explore the different phases of the data-wrangling pipeline and explain how the Pandas library will help in performing those operations in an effective and performant manner.

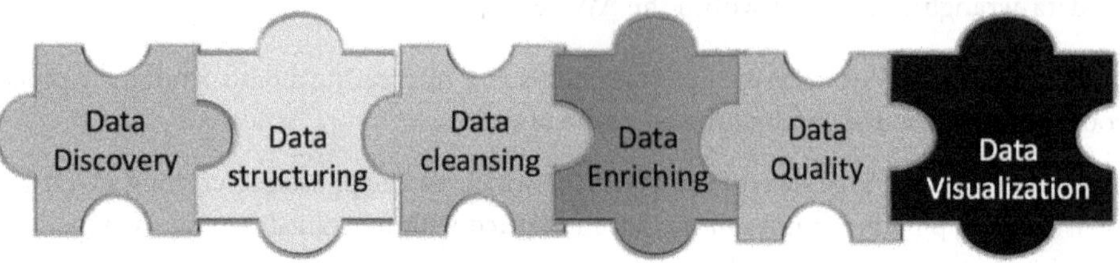

Figure 9.1: Different phases of the data-wrangling pipeline

Prerequisites for data ingestion

In order to perform data-wrangling activities for the preceding use case, we need to first ingest data into a data lake. In order to ingest data from on-premise databases into a cloud environment, we have the following options:

1. Extract data programmatically using SQL queries from services such as AWS Glue or containers deployed on **Elastic Kubernetes Service** (**EKS**)/**Elastic Container Service** (**ECS**).

   The advantages of this approach are these:

   - It can work with most databases as long as there is a package/library for connecting to the database
   - It doesn't need any additional setup other than login credentials with the needed permissions to extract data

- This approach reads data directly from tables and hence there is no additional workload from servers to create the database log files that are required for **capture data change** (CDC) streaming utilities

The limitations of this approach are the following:

- The data is extracted using SQL queries and requires an additional bookmarking column to incrementally extract data for subsequent runs. If there is a timestamp column that denotes when a record was last updated, we could use it to extract only new data.
- The additional burden of managing the state of the bookmarking column also rests with the user. So, the user has to store the metadata in a database like such as DynamoDB to get the value from the last successful data extraction.
- Deleted records can't be extracted with a bookmarking column and need additional setup, which is resource-intensive in databases.
- DDL changes are also not captured using this approach.
- As the extract process is done using SQL scripts, it competes with user queries for database resources and might impact the database performance.

2. Extract data from database change logs using tools such as AWS **Database Migration Service** (**AWS DMS**), Debezium, and so on.

   The advantages of this approach are as follows:

   - It can capture almost all of the data changes using database logs, including record deletes and DDL changes
   - Changes are captured in database logs and don't compete with user queries for database resources to extract data
   - Changes are captured incrementally and streamed immediately through the tool

   The limitations of this approach are the following:

   - Users will depend on the tool and its supported databases for this approach to work. Migrating from a database CDC streaming solution to another approach will require significant effort.
   - For scheduled data exports, continuous streaming wouldn't be a cost-effective approach. However, with AWS DMS, you can load only incremental data on a scheduled basis without running a DMS instance continuously, saving costs, as outlined in this blog post: `https://aws.amazon.com/blogs/database/build-an-incremental-data-load-solution-using-aws-dms-checkpoints-and-database-logs/`.
   - It needs additional permissions to read from database logs and the databases must be enabled to capture logs and retain them for a sufficient amount of time. If the logs are deleted before being captured by the database CDC tool, this will lead to a data loss scenario and users will have to recapture the entire data before proceeding ahead.

- The database will have a small overhead to capture full logs for every transaction as required by certain CDC tools.

When would you use them?

For most cases, starting with a CDC tool such as AWS DMS would be faster and simpler to set up. If you are starting fresh, use AWS DMS/Debezium based on your ecosystem. There are other CDC capture tools from different vendors as well, which you can explore further. If the CDC capture tools don't support your source database type or if you require a different configuration that the tool doesn't support (e.g., capturing changes from a replica database), you can use a programmatic approach to extracting data.

In our example, we will use programmatic extraction to showcase the abilities of AWS SDK for Pandas (awswrangler) in the data extraction process.

Loading sample data into a source database

We will use Amazon RDS MySQL as a source database, but this approach can be extended to on-premises databases as well.

We will create an RDS MySQL database using the steps mentioned at `https://aws.amazon.com/getting-started/hands-on/create-mysql-db/`. Please note the database is created with public access in the preceding approach. Restrict access to the Security group, which is attached to the database, to allow traffic only from the IP address of your client machine. For production deployments, the database should be deployed in a private subnet and accessed through more secure mechanisms with additional setup.

Here, we will use an Amazon EC2 instance to connect with the RDS MySQL database and load the sample database from the `aws-database-migration-samples` Git repository (`https://github.com/aws-samples/aws-database-migration-samples`). We will use the ticket database and load it into RDS MySQL with the following steps:

1. Log in to the EC2 instance and install MySQL client and `git`. Execute the following commands to install `git` and MySQL on EC2:

```
sudo yum update #as needed
sudo yum install git
git version
sudo yum install mysql
mysql --version
```

The following screenshot shows the successful installation of `git` and MySQL on the EC2 instance:

```
Dependency Installed:
  git-core.x86_64 0:2.37.1-1.amzn2.0.1                    git-core-doc.noarch 0:2.37.1-1.amzn2.0
  perl-Error.noarch 1:0.17020-2.amzn2                     perl-Git.noarch 0:2.37.1-1.amzn2.0.1
  perl-TermReadKey.x86_64 0:2.30-20.amzn2.0.2

Complete!
[ec2-user@ip-10-0-30-62 ~]$ git version
git version 2.37.1
[ec2-user@ip-10-0-30-62 ~]$ sudo yum install mysql
Loaded plugins: extras_suggestions, langpacks, priorities, update-motd
Resolving Dependencies
--> Running transaction check
```

Figure 9.2: MySQL installation on the EC2 instance

2. Connect to the `migration-samples` Git repository and clone the code. Execute the following commands on the EC2 instance:

```
git clone https://github.com/aws-samples/aws-database-migration-
samples.git
cd aws-database-migration-samples/mysql/sampledb/v1/
```

You can list the files under the cloned folder for MySQL to ensure the code is successfully copied.

```
[ec2-user@ip-10-0-30-62 ~]$ git clone https://github.com/aws-samples/aws-database-migration-sample
Cloning into 'aws-database-migration-samples'...
remote: Enumerating objects: 1015, done.
remote: Total 1015 (delta 0), reused 0 (delta 0), pack-reused 1015
Receiving objects: 100% (1015/1015), 2.58 MiB | 13.63 MiB/s, done.
Resolving deltas: 100% (449/449), done.
[ec2-user@ip-10-0-30-62 ~]$ ls
aws-database-migration-samples
[ec2-user@ip-10-0-30-62 ~]$ cd aws-database-migration-samples/mysql/sampledb/v1/
[ec2-user@ip-10-0-30-62 v1]$ ls
data  install-rds.sql  README.md  remove-sampledb.sql  schema  user
[ec2-user@ip-10-0-30-62 v1]$
```

Figure 9.3: Copying the sample data from GitHub to the EC2 instance

3. Connect to the MySQL database and ensure connectivity is working. Connect to the MySQL database using the following command and provide the password when prompted:

```
mysql -h <<database endpoint>> -u admin -P 3306 -p
```

You can get the database endpoint from the RDS console, as shown in the **Connectivity & Security** tab.

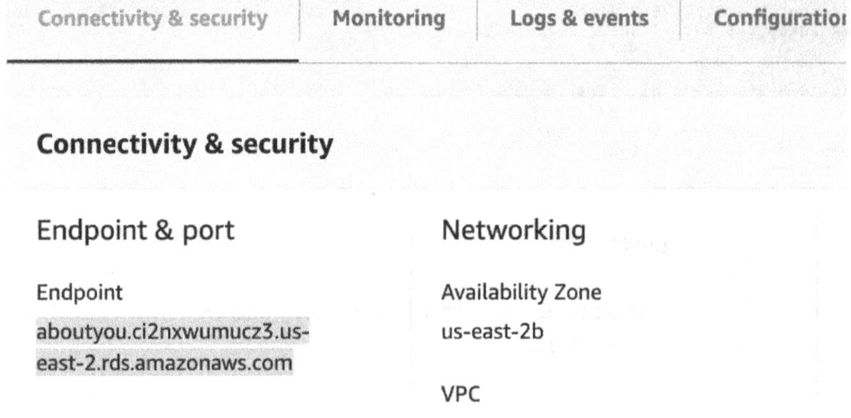

Figure 9.4: Database endpoint from the RDS UI console

4. Load the sample database into our source database. Execute the load script from the GitHub repository and it will load the ticket database into the MySQL instance. It will take some time to load the sample database. This step must be executed under the `aws-database-migration-samples/mysql/sampledb/v1/` folder, which we have navigated before connecting to MySQL. Execute the following command in MySQL:

   ```
   source install-rds.sql
   ```

   Once the load is complete, you can verify it by executing the following commands:

   ```
   show databases; --Display available databases, verify dms_sample
   is present in the list
   use dms_sample;
   show tables;
   ```

Data migration from source on-premises databases

As we mentioned earlier, we will use awswrangler to connect to source databases and extract data using a Glue Python shell job:

1. Create a Python shell job in the Glue console. Choose **Python Shell script editor** as shown in the following screenshot:

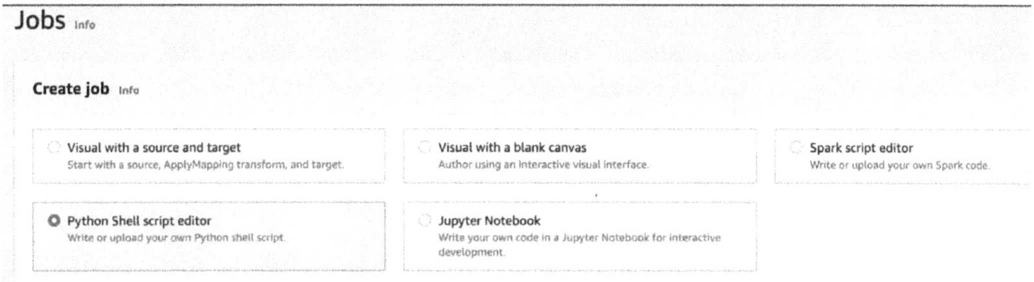

Jobs Info

Create job Info

- Visual with a source and target — Start with a source, ApplyMapping transform, and target.
- Visual with a blank canvas — Author using an interactive visual interface.
- Spark script editor — Write or upload your own Spark code.
- Python Shell script editor — Write or upload your own Python shell script.
- Jupyter Notebook — Write your own code in a Jupyter Notebook for interactive development.

Figure 9.5: Creating a Glue Python shell job

2. Enter the following code into the script editor and save the job:

```
import sys
import awswrangler as wr
import time
import csv
#Connect to MySQL using Glue connections
con=wr.mysql.connect("wranglerbook")
schema="dms_sample"
table_list=["mlb_data","name_data","nfl_data",
"nfl_stadium_data","person","player","seat","seat_type",
"sport_division","sport_league","sport_location","sport_team",
"sport_type","sporting_event","ticket_purchase_hist"]
for table in table_list:
    #Read data from MySQL tables into Pandas dataframe
    start_time = time.time()
    output_data=wr.mysql.read_sql_query
    ("SELECT * FROM "+schema+"."+ table +";", con=con)

    #Print one row for debugging
    #print(output_data.loc[1,:])
    #output_data['Name'] = output_data['Name'].apply
    (lambda x: '"' + str(x) + '"')

    if len(output_data.axes[0])>0:
        #Write Pandas dataframe into S3
        wr.s3.to_csv(
            df=output_data,
            path="s3://wranglerbook/awswrangler/"+table+"/",
            dataset=True,
            index=False,
            mode="overwrite",
            header=True,
```

```
                database="mysql_extract",
                table="mysql_"+table,
                compression="gzip")
            end_time=time.time()
            print(f"Completed the data extraction for table -
{table} .Loaded record count - {len(output_data.axes[0])} and
took {round(end_time-start_time,2)} seconds")
        else:
            print(f"Data load not performed for table {table} as it
is empty.")
print("Completed the data extraction process")
con.close()
```

3. We will now configure the job to have proper access to read the data from MySQL:

   I. Choose an IAM role that has access to reading RDS and also writing to S3, along with the other needed permissions for a Glue job.

   II. Change the Python version to **Python 3.9** under **Job details** as a Python 3.9 environment has AWS SDK pre-installed.

   III. Attach the Glue connection to the job so that the job is executed in an environment that has access to connect to MySQL. If you don't do this configuration under **Advanced settings** in the Glue job console, the job will fail to reach the MySQL instance on a private subnet.

4. Execute the job and verify the data is populated in the S3 bucket. Please note that the job will fail if the tables have empty columns since awswrangler expects some values to infer the data type. You can verify that the data was populated into the S3 bucket as shown here.

   Also, you could look at the AWS Glue job `output_logs` to understand the number of records that were populated. You could see that the `ticket_purchase_hist` table is skipped as it doesn't have any records from the source table as well.

```
Completed the data extraction for table - mlb_data .Loaded record count - 2230 and took 1.32 seconds
Completed the data extraction for table - name_data .Loaded record count - 5358 and took 1.15 seconds
Completed the data extraction for table - nfl_data .Loaded record count - 2928 and took 1.17 seconds
Completed the data extraction for table - nfl_stadium_data .Loaded record count - 32 and took 1.0 seconds
Completed the data extraction for table - person .Loaded record count - 7021016 and took 239.27 seconds
Completed the data extraction for table - player .Loaded record count - 5157 and took 2.63 seconds
Completed the data extraction for table - seat .Loaded record count - 3565082 and took 61.78 seconds
Completed the data extraction for table - seat_type .Loaded record count - 6 and took 1.62 seconds
Completed the data extraction for table - sport_division .Loaded record count - 14 and took 1.05 seconds
Completed the data extraction for table - sport_league .Loaded record count - 2 and took 1.62 seconds
Completed the data extraction for table - sport_location .Loaded record count - 62 and took 1.09 seconds
Completed the data extraction for table - sport_team .Loaded record count - 62 and took 1.1 seconds
Completed the data extraction for table - sport_type .Loaded record count - 2 and took 1.04 seconds
Completed the data extraction for table - sporting_event .Loaded record count - 1158 and took 1.18 seconds
Data load not performed for table ticket_purchase_hist as it is empty.
Completed the data extraction process
```

Figure 9.6: The Glue console output showing data extraction completion

You can see that the `person` table took almost 4 minutes to load 7 million records, and it took 1 minute to load the `seat` table. The rest of the table took almost a second. The total job took 5 minutes 31 seconds and we can understand the tables are loaded in sequential order. The job can be executed faster by executing it with multiple threads, but that will consume additional memory and lead to out-of-memory errors if the data volume is high.

> **Challenge**
>
> We have extracted the data from the MySQL database for a full load, but how do you extract data for subsequent loads that need to extract incremental data alone?

> **Hint**
>
> You must change the extraction script to query source tables to extract data only after a specific timestamp column. If such a column is not available currently in the source database, we have a couple of options:
>
> Option 1: Change the source database tables to add a timestamp column that can help you incrementally extract data. Please remember this approach still doesn't help you in getting deleted records and DDL changes.
>
> Option 2: Use AWS DMS or any other streaming solution to CDC from source databases.

Even though we have shown how to extract data programmatically using a Glue Python shell job using AWS SDK for Pandas, we recommend setting up data ingestion from databases using AWS DMS, which has multiple advantages and is more performant. The Glue job will fail with an out-of-memory exception if we are trying to load tables that are of a higher volume. You can try that by adding the `sports_event_ticket` table, which has a higher data volume. Also, for the rest of the chapter, we will explore all the tables from the MySQL database, and we have used AWS DMS to migrate data to the S3 raw layer for exploration purposes. You can follow this blog post to migrate data with DMS - `https://aws.amazon.com/blogs/database/replicate-data-from-amazon-aurora-to-amazon-s3-with-aws-database-migration-service/`.

Now we will explore the source data through various phases of data-wrangling activities, such as data discovery, data structuring, data cleansing, data enriching, data quality validation, and data visualization. Let us start with data discovery in the next section.

Data discovery

Data discovery is an important phase in the wrangling pipeline, as it helps users to understand the data and guides how the next steps should be done. For example, if the user looks at the data and determines certain columns have missing values, data cleansing should fix those values and any missing columns can be added by joining the data with other data sources or deriving them from raw data. Essentially, this step will give an idea of the completeness, usefulness, and relevance of the dataset to users.

There are multiple ways to perform data discovery including downloading small files on a local machine and using Excel files to explore the data. We will look at ways in which we can explore the raw data stored in a data lake. Some of the common steps that are performed during a data discovery phase are as follows:

- Identifying the source data structure/format and its associated properties
- Visualizing the data distribution on the dataset
- Validating the presence of useful data values across the dataset
- Exploring the dataset visually to understand the data patterns
- Slicing and dicing the dataset and exploring data for specific business needs

There may be additional data discovery activities for your specific project and you can still perform them using the options mentioned in the following sections.

Exploring data using S3 Select commands

The S3 Select (`https://docs.aws.amazon.com/AmazonS3/latest/userguide/selecting-content-from-objects.html`) feature helps to explore smaller datasets through the AWS console UI and code to look at sample records and run some exploration SQL queries. This is only expected to support files of a volume of less than 128 MB and can extract data up to 40 MB with limitations around row groups and record size. For analysis or discovery of datasets that are hampered by these limitations, it is recommended to use other forms of analysis.

> **Note**
>
> The 128-MB and 40-MB limits of file size/retrieved data apply to the console and **S3 Select** when used programmatically doesn't have this limitation. However, the row group and record size limitations still apply regardless of the access mechanism (via the console or programmatic).

We will explore the data that is available in the S3 raw bucket using S3 Select commands as shown in the following steps:

1. Navigate to the S3 path where the source file is available to explore. In our example, let us take one table and explore, which is `nfl_data`:

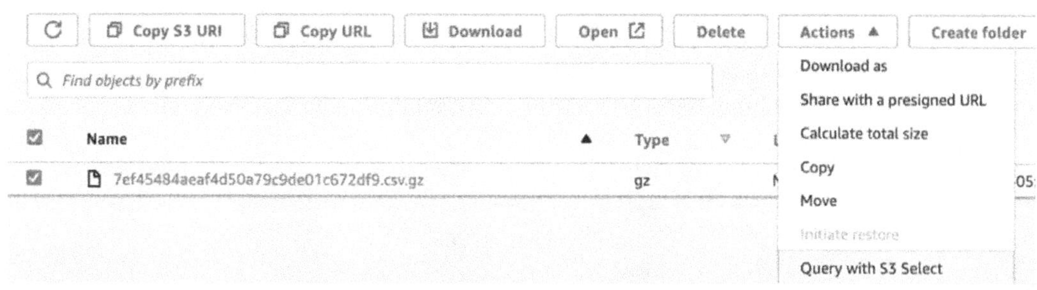

Figure 9.7: Querying the S3 file using S3 Select in the AWS console

2. In the AWS console, verify the input and output settings are correct. It will be auto-populated and inferred correctly for most use cases, but you can verify it for our use case as well. We stored our input data in the **GZIP** compressed **comma-separated values** (**CSV**) file format.

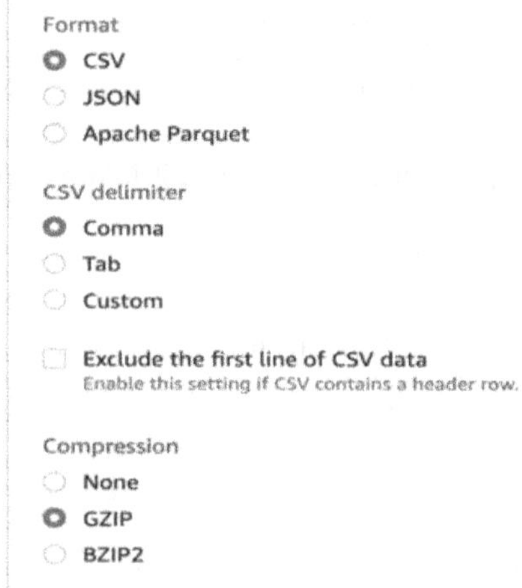

Figure 9.8: The AWS console S3 Select configurations

If you run a query with output format as CSV, you can see the header is populated correctly in the formatted view. However, there is an issue with the column and field alignment, and we will explore this further in the next steps. Look at the columns, starting with **name**:

position	player_number	name	status	stat1	stat1_val	stat2	stat2_val	stat3	stat3_val	stat4	stat4_val	team	
OT	66	Graf\	Kevin	ACT	G	--	GS	--					IND
FS	32	Green\	T.J.	ACT	TCKL	--	SCK	--	FF	--	INT	--	IND
FS	27	Guy\	Winston	ACT	TCKL	6	SCK	0	FF	0	INT	--	IND
OT	73	Haeg\	Joe	ACT	G	--	GS	--					IND

Figure 9.9: Exploring the CSV file data using S3 Select

3. If you want to look at the output in **JavaScript Object Notation** (**JSON**) format, check **Exclude the first line of CSV data** in the input settings and choose **JSON** under the output settings. Without this JSON setting, the output will not interpret the first line as a column header.

```
{
  "position": "OT",
  "player_number": "66",
  "name": "Graf\\",
  "status": " Kevin",
  "stat1": "ACT",
  "stat1_val": "G",
  "stat2": "--",
  "stat2_val": "GS",
  "stat3": "--",
  "stat3_val": "",
  "stat4": "",
  "stat4_val": "",
  "team": "",
  "": "IND"
```

Figure 9.10: Sample record explored as a JSON format output

Now, as you can see from the data, our CSV export file has columns with commas in them. The **Name** field is a combination of a first name and last name. You can refer to the original data either from the source (the MySQL CLI) or from the logs in the Glue job:

```
Position                    FS
player_number               32
Name                 Green, T.J.
status                     ACT
```

Figure 9.11: Sample record as seen from the Glue console output

Now we have discovered that our job writes the CSV output without wrapping the fields in a wrapper character, which is causing the field misalignment. However, we can't add the wrapper for these columns using awswrangler code, as the documentation on AWS SDK's GitHub site states that pandas keyword arguments will be ignored if we use Glue catalog syncing in the same code (which we are doing to query the final data in Athena).

4. If `table` and `database` arguments are passed, `pandas_kwargs` will be ignored due to restrictive `quoting`, `date_format`, `escapechar`, and `encoding` required by Athena/the Glue Catalog.

AWS SDK for Pandas will set `escapechar` to \\ to enable working with Athena. You can see from the following code snippet that pandas' extra keyword arguments are ignored and `escapechar` is set by default when we require Glue Catalog integration.

```
if database and table:
    quoting: Optional[int] = csv.QUOTE_NONE
    escapechar: Optional[str] = "\\"
    header: Union[bool, List[str]] = pandas_kwargs.get("header", False)
    date_format: Optional[str] = "%Y-%m-%d %H:%M:%S.%f"
    pd_kwargs: Dict[str, Any] = {}
```

Figure 9.12: AWS SDK for Pandas code snippet showing escapechar configuration

5. Let us re-execute the Glue job again to populate the data, manually wrapping the column with double quotes. Add the following code snippet to wrap the `Name` column with double quotes before writing it as a CSV file. Uncomment this line from the code snippet and run the job again:

```
output_data['Name'] = output_data['Name'].apply(lambda x: '"' +
str(x) + '"')
```

Now if we query the output file, we can see the data is aligned correctly with columns, but we will still have the escape character added in front of the comma separator:

position	player_number	name	status	stat1	stat1_val	stat2	stat2_val	stat3	stat3_val	stat4	stat4_val	team
OT	66	Graf\, Kevin	ACT	G	--	GS	--					IND
FS	32	Green\, T.J.	ACT	TCKL	--	SCK	--	FF	--	INT	--	IND
FS	27	Guy\, Winston	ACT	TCKL	6	SCK	0	FF	0	INT	--	IND
OT	73	Haeg\, Joe	ACT	G	--	GS	--					IND

Figure 9.13: Output file with columns containing an escape character wrapper in double quotes

Even if we fix a single file, there are more files with similar issues and the presence of an escape character will cause data filters on that column to not work correctly. So, based on our initial analysis, it would be appropriate to store the raw files in JSON format for further analysis.

6. Change the source code in the Glue console to store the data in a JSON file format. Clone the current Glue job and change the script to that shown here:

```
import sys
import awswrangler as wr
import time
import csv
#Connect to MySQL using Glue connections
con=wr.mysql.connect("wranglerbook")
schema="dms_sample"
#table_list=["mlb_data","name_data","nfl_data","nfl_
stadium_data","person","player","seat","seat_type","sport_
division","sport_league","sport_location","sport_team","sport_
type","sporting_event","ticket_purchase_hist"]
table_list=["nfl_data"]
```

```
for table in table_list:
    #Read data from MySQL tables into Pandas dataframe
    start_time = time.time()
    output_data=wr.mysql.read_sql_query("SELECT * FROM
"+schema+"."+ table +";", con=con)

    #Print one row for debugging
    #print(output_data.loc[1,:])
    if len(output_data.axes[0])>0:
        #Write Pandas dataframe into S3
        wr.s3.to_json(
            df=output_data,       path="s3://wranglerbook/
awswrangler/"+table+"/",
            dataset=True,
            orient='records',
            lines=True,
            mode="overwrite",
            database="mysql_extract",
            table="mysql1_"+table)
        end_time=time.time()
        print(f"Completed the data extraction for table -
{table} .Loaded record count - {len(output_data.axes[0])} and
took {round(end_time-start_time,2)} seconds")
    else:
        print(f"Data load not performed for table {table} as it
is empty.")
print("Completed the data extraction process")
con.close()
```

If you notice the difference, we have only changed the `to_csv` function into `to_json`. This illustrates the ease with which we can save files to S3.

Now you can see the data is correctly populated as JSON files and can verify this from S3 Select, as shown here.

```
{
  "position": "OT",
  "player_number": 66,
  "name": "Graf, Kevin",
  "status": "ACT",
  "stat1": "G",
  "stat1_val": "--",
  "stat2": "GS",
  "stat2_val": "--",
  "stat3": null,
  "stat3_val": null,
  "stat4": null,
  "stat4_val": null,
  "team": "IND"
}
{
```

Figure 9.14: Sample record from a JSON file format output

The `name` column is correctly populated now, but internally within the file, we will have an additional row name column because of a current Pandas limitation (`https://github.com/aws/aws-sdk-pandas/issues/1168`). Now we can explore the contents of the file to see whether there are any incorrectly populated fields, missing columns, and so on.

Raw data exploration with the Pandas library

The Pandas library provides a great set of tools for data discovery. We will perform these activities in SageMaker notebooks (Jupyter notebooks) for Python-based interactive data analysis. As a user, you can spin up a Jupyter notebook on your local instance using `pip` commands (`https://jupyter.org/install`), or use it from the SageMaker service. We have other services such as Glue and **Elastic MapReduce** (**EMR**) that support notebooks but they are mostly used for big data processing and wrangling. You can choose to use SageMaker or a local instance/EC2 installation if the data volume is small.

We will explore the ticket database data that was ingested into S3 buckets in the previous step. Open a SageMaker instance and start a Jupyter notebook for exploration. Follow the steps mentioned in the awswrangler introduction chapter and also install the `awswrangler` package first with the command:

```
!pip3 install awswrangler
```

Now load the data from the JSON file into a pandas DataFrame and explore the data using the `head` function. This will fetch sample records for you to browse through the record:

```
output_data=wr.s3.read_json("s3://wranglerbook/awswrangler/nfl_data/", lines=True)
output_data.head(2)
```

	position	player_number	name	status	stat1	stat1_val	stat2	stat2_val	stat3	stat3_val	stat4	stat4_val	team
0	OT	66.0	Graf, Kevin	ACT	G	--	GS	--	None	None	None	None	IND
1	FS	32.0	Green, T.J.	ACT	TCKL	--	SCK	--	FF	--	INT	--	IND

Figure 9.15: Exploring JSON data using a Jupyter notebook

Once data is loaded into pandas DataFrame, you can use pandas data exploration functionalities to analyze your data. Depending on the type of data and business usage, different types of explorations can be performed. We will explain some high-level data exploration activities here and identify the structure of the data including record count, column count, column types, memory usage, and so on using the info function. This gives you an idea of the data and its structure.

```
output_data.info()

<class 'pandas.core.frame.DataFrame'>
RangeIndex: 2928 entries, 0 to 2927
Data columns (total 13 columns):
 #   Column         Non-Null Count  Dtype
---  ------         --------------  -----
 0   Position       2928 non-null   string
 1   player_number  2916 non-null   Int64
 2   Name           2928 non-null   string
 3   status         2928 non-null   string
 4   stat1          2928 non-null   string
 5   stat1_val      2928 non-null   string
 6   stat2          2928 non-null   string
 7   stat2_val      2928 non-null   string
 8   stat3          2390 non-null   string
 9   stat3_val      2390 non-null   string
 10  stat4          2390 non-null   string
 11  stat4_val      2390 non-null   string
 12  team           2928 non-null   string
dtypes: Int64(1), string(12)
memory usage: 300.4 KB
```

Figure 9.16: Pandas DataFrame info function to explore all columns

If you are only interested in the number of records and the number of columns in the DataFrame, you could use the `shape` function. The usage of the function is `dataframe.shape`.

Suppose you want to focus on only certain columns for your analysis and the DataFrame has a lot of columns; you can select columns by name as shown here. Optionally, you can choose to get records from specific indexes using the `loc` function.

```
#Explore only first specific columns from specific records, if you iloc, need to p
output_data.loc[1:5,["player_number","Name"]]
```

	player_number	Name
1	32	Green, T.J.
2	27	Guy, Winston
3	73	Haeg, Joe
4	72	Harrison, Jonotthan
5	38	Hightower, Lee

Figure 9.17: Pandas DataFrame info function to explore all columns

If you want to focus on specific records that meet a selection condition, you can filter them as shown here. For the following screenshot, we will be filtering only records that have information about running backs (**RB**) from the Indianapolis (**IND**) team:

```
#Filter records for certain values
output_data[(output_data["team"]=="IND") & (output_data["Position"]=="RB")]
```

	Position	player_number	Name	status	stat1	stat1_val	stat2	stat2_val	stat3	stat3_val	stat4	stat4_val	team
38	RB	35	Price, Chase	ACT	CAR	--	YDS	--	AVG	--	TDS	--	IND
57	RB	28	Todman, Jordan	ACT	CAR	4	YDS	22	AVG	5.5	TDS	0	IND
59	RB	33	Turbin, Robert	ACT	CAR	50	YDS	199	AVG	4	TDS	1	IND
67	RB	40	Williams, Trey	ACT	CAR	2	YDS	12	AVG	6	TDS	0	IND
607	RB	34	Ferguson, Josh	ACT	CAR	--	YDS	--	AVG	--	TDS	--	IND
611	RB	23	Gore, Frank	ACT	CAR	260	YDS	967	AVG	3.7	TDS	6	IND

Figure 9.18: Filtering specific records from the Pandas DataFrame

Also, before proceeding with further analysis, you should identify the number of NULL/missing values in the DataFrame. The following code snippet shows you how to identify columns that are empty in the DataFrame. To demonstrate this example, we manually added an empty column in our Pandas DataFrame:

```
#Find empty columns from the dataset
empty_cols = [col for col in output_data.columns if output_data[col].isnull().all()]
empty_cols
```

```
[]
```

```
import numpy as np
output_data["new_column_null"]=np.nan
empty_cols = [col for col in output_data.columns if output_data[col].isnull().all()]
empty_cols
```

```
['new_column_null']
```

Figure 9.19: Identifying null columns in the DataFrame

If you want to identify the number of empty values in each column to understand the data completeness, use the following function:

```
output_data.isna().sum()
```

```
Position          0
player_number    12
Name              0
status            0
stat1             0
stat1_val         0
stat2             0
stat2_val         0
stat3           538
stat3_val       538
stat4           538
stat4_val       538
team              0
dtype: int64
```

Figure 9.20: Identifying the completeness of columns within the DataFrame

Optionally, you can visualize the data using `matplotlib` as shown here. This provides an idea of the columns with null values:

```
]: output_data.isna().sum().plot.bar()

]: <AxesSubplot:>
```

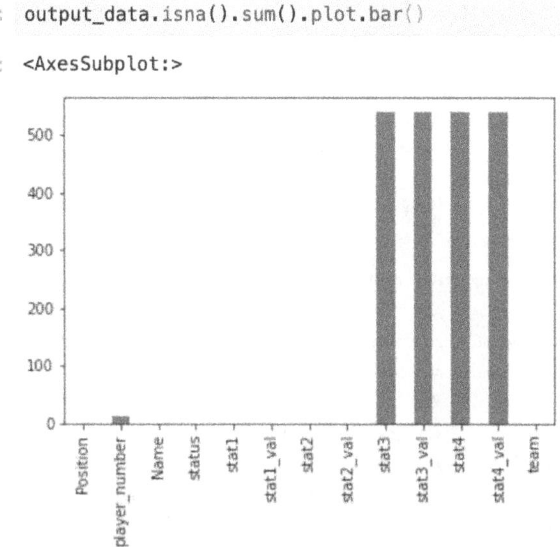

Figure 9.21: Visualizing the data completeness of the DataFrame

Then, we can explore the dataset in terms of the distribution of data values in certain columns, which will give you an idea of your dataset. The following function provides the count of values, the most frequently occurring value and least frequently occurring value, and also the overall count of distinct values (`4058` unique values):

```
]: output_data["last_name"].value_counts()

]: Williams    57
   Johnson     47
   Jones       40
   Smith       40
   Brown       27
               ..
   Forte        1
   Barney       1
   Bishop       1
   Bohanon      1
   Shead        1
   Name: last_name, Length: 4058, dtype: Int64
```

Figure 9.22: Distribution of data values in a specific column of the DataFrame

If you want to look at the players from the team with the highest number of sacks, you must explore the data further. The following snippet will help you browse the data:

```
output_data[["stat1_val", "stat2_val"]] = output_data[["stat1_val", "stat2_val"]].apply(pd.to_numeric,errors='coerce')
```

```
output_data[(output_data["stat2"]=="SCK")].groupby(["team"])["stat2_val"].sum().sort_values(ascending=False)[:3]
```

```
team
DEN    45.0
TB     44.5
MIN    44.5
Name: stat2_val, dtype: float64
```

```
output_data[(output_data["team"]=="DEN") & (output_data["stat2"]=="SCK") & (output_data["stat2_val"]>0)].\
dropna(subset=["stat2_val"]).\
sort_values(by="stat2_val",ascending=False)
```

	position	player_number	name	status	stat1	stat1_val	stat2	stat2_val	stat3	stat3_val	stat4	stat4_val	team
1399	OLB	58.0	Miller, Von	ACT	TCKL	35.0	SCK	11.0	FF	4	INT	--	DEN
1439	OLB	94.0	Ware, DeMarcus	ACT	TCKL	25.0	SCK	7.5	FF	1	INT	--	DEN
1359	OLB	48.0	Barrett, Shaquil	ACT	TCKL	50.0	SCK	5.5	FF	4	INT	--	DEN
1445	DE	95.0	Wolfe, Derek	ACT	TCKL	49.0	SCK	5.5	FF	0	INT	--	DEN
1416	LB	56.0	Ray, Shane	ACT	TCKL	20.0	SCK	4.0	FF	0	INT	--	DEN
1443	NT	92.0	Williams, Sylvester	ACT	TCKL	25.0	SCK	3.0	FF	0	INT	--	DEN
1365	DE	93.0	Crick, Jared	ACT	TCKL	48.0	SCK	2.0	FF	1	INT	--	DEN
1437	DE	96.0	Walker, Vance	ACT	TCKL	33.0	SCK	2.0	FF	0	INT	--	DEN
1438	SS	43.0	Ward, T.J.	ACT	TCKL	61.0	SCK	2.0	FF	2	INT	--	DEN
1396	ILB	54.0	Marshall, Brandon	ACT	TCKL	102.0	SCK	1.5	FF	2	INT	1	DEN
1406	OLB	52.0	Nelson, Corey	ACT	TCKL	16.0	SCK	1.0	FF	0	INT	--	DEN

Figure 9.23: Identifying players with the highest number of sacks in the team that has a greater number of sacks from all players

You could also visualize the data using the `matplotlib` library and export it as an image. The following code snippet provides an example of visualizing the teams with the most sacks:

```
#plotting values
import matplotlib.pyplot as plt
vis_data=output_data[(output_data["stat2"]=="SCK")].groupby(["team"])["stat2_val"].sum().sort_values(ascending=False)[:10]
vis_data1=vis_data.to_frame()
ax=vis_data1.plot.barh(color="red")
ax.bar_label(ax.containers[0]);
ax.get_legend().remove()
plt.title('Team with highest sacks')
plt.xlabel('Sacks')
plt.ylabel('Team');
```

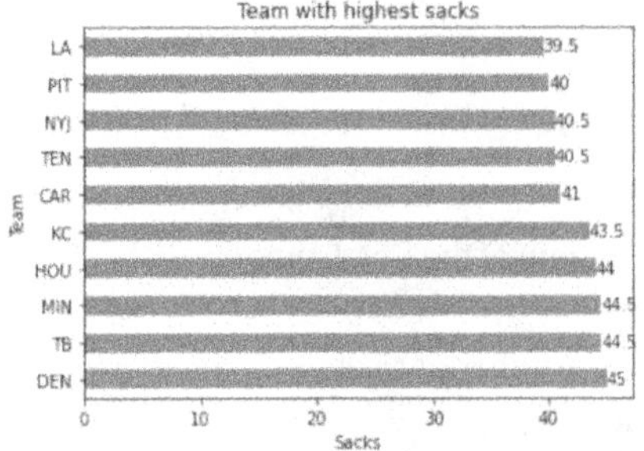

Figure 9.24: Visualizing the teams with the highest number of sacks

The preceding example is intended to show the power of Pandas DataFrames in performing deep-dive analysis on your data in whatever structure or format you want. You can continue to explore the data and visualize the results using `matplotlib` to visualize and understand more about your data.

Access through Amazon Athena and the Glue Catalog

To enable data discovery for users who are comfortable with SQL-based access, we can catalog the datasets in the AWS Glue Data Catalog and explore the datasets for more complicated analysis. Athena provides a SQL-based access mechanism to explore data without any file size limitation, supports SQL, and doesn't require Python programming to explore datasets.

Let us explore the `nfl_data` table for further analysis where we would like to run complex values from the `stat1_val` column:

```
select case when regexp_like(stat1_val, '^-?\d+$') then 'valid'
    else stat1_val end as column_spread,count(*)
from mysql1_nfl_data
group by case when regexp_like(stat1_val, '^-?\d+$') then 'valid'
    else stat1_val end
```

#	column_spread	_col1
1	--	1218
2	valid	1710

Figure 9.25: Amazon Athena query to identify valid stat values in the dataset

You could validate and see that the `stat1_val` column has close to 40% of values not populated with a valid stat value.

> **Note**
>
> The size of a single row or its columns cannot exceed 32 megabytes. This limit can be exceeded when, for example, a row in a CSV or JSON file contains a single column of 100 megabytes. Exceeding this limit can also produce the error message **Line too long in text file**. (`https://docs.aws.amazon.com/athena/latest/ug/other-notable-limitations.html`)

Now that we have looked at different data exploration techniques, let us discuss when to use the preceding data exploration approaches:

- If the file size is small and doesn't require you to explore data from multiple files, use S3 Select to explore the datasets. This will support you to quickly search datasets for incorrect values, missing columns, and so on.
- If the file size is huge and you would like a more in-depth analysis of the data (% of null values in a column, for example) and if the team is comfortable with Python programming, explore datasets using Pandas.
- If the file size is huge and the team is comfortable with SQL-based exploration activities, then use Athena along with the Glue Catalog. awswrangler helps in populating the Glue Catalog when writing files. For files from other data feeds, the Glue Crawler will help you infer the schema, which can be queried using Athena.

We have understood different techniques for data exploration and we can explore the next stage of the wrangling pipeline – data structuring.

Data structuring

Now we have to come to the part where we need to restructure the data into a usable format from its raw format. In our use case, we extracted data in JSON format and it is good for exploratory analysis that we used a raw data format. When we move further into the data-wrangling pipeline, different file formats and structures would be more efficient.

Different file formats and when to use them

There are different file formats that are commonly used in data pipelines:

- **Readable file formats**: CSV, JSON, and **Extensible Markup Language** (**XML**) are some file formats that are readable by human users:
  - CSV files are used mostly in the data extraction phase when the data needs to be shared with analysts for reading and performing further actions. The advantage is you don't need any programming language to read the files and can be opened in the most commonly available text editors. These file formats are widely popular earlier in the data analytics community along with Excel files. They are useful in performing quick pivots and other analysis/visualizations within the Excel application itself. However, they don't support the concept of data types or complex data formats (hierarchical data) and have limited scalability.
  - XML was created in the 1990s and quickly became a W3C standard for sharing hierarchical and complex data types. This was the first popular format to support hierarchical data formats and was widely used for data exchange between various systems. XML files are huge in storage size as they use open and close tags to represent data, unlike CSV file formats.
  - The JSON file format was mostly used by web applications for storing data and was passed on to downstream data pipelines for data analytics as well. JSON files became more popular than XML files as they are easier to read and understand than XML. They support more

complex data formats including hierarchical data, objects, and arrays. They also support schema evolution with key-value combinations, which helps us understand the data being stored. We can optionally skip certain fields if they are not applicable, unlike CSV files, which have a rigid schema that is advantageous to frontend applications. However, they consume more size and memory to process compared to CSV files.

The main reason to choose a readable file format would be for use cases where the users would want to download and use the file for different use cases (e.g., sharing a user list to follow up with a phone call from another team):

- You can choose the CSV file format if the data structure is relatively simple and doesn't have hierarchical fields as it is easily readable and lightweight. CSV files combined with Excel will provide good visualizations for lightweight data analysis.
- Choose the JSON file format if the data has more complex data types and you need to store different data formats. In the preceding example, we moved from the CSV to JSON file format as our data had commas in it and processing that data using the pandas library provided more challenges.

- **Binary file formats**: Parquet, Avro, and ORC are some common file formats that are not human-readable and are used in the data pipeline during the analysis phase. These file formats are stored in a machine-readable binary format and can be split and stored across multiple disks, thereby supporting parallel processing. These file formats are widely used in the big data processing landscape. They are self-described, meaning they store the schema and data together, so the processing systems can read the data easily.

  What is row versus column storage? Parquet and ORC file formats store data in a columnar format and Avro stores data in a record-level format. A columnar format stores data from the same column together for a chunk of records. This is helpful in analytical systems where the data is aggregated and visualized for specific columns. Storing data from columns nearby helps to read the data faster and skip reading other columns that are not used in the analytical query. For example, see the following:

Name	**stat1**	**stat2**
Test_user1	12	13
Test_user2	14	15
Test_user3	16	17

Table 9.1: Raw data (with a record chunk – 3 records)

Here is record-level storage:

Test_user1	12	13	Test_user2	14	15	Test_user3	16	17

Table 9.2: Record-level storage for the table

Here is columnar storage:

Test_user1	Test_user2	Test_user3	12	14	16	13	15	17

Table 9.3: Columnar-level storage for the table

The preceding tables are for illustration and understanding purposes alone and the real storage will have additional information stored with data chunks, along with compression.

When to choose a file format

Parquet files are most commonly used and you can start with them if you are unsure about the choice of data storage format but you know the data will be used for analytical use cases. You can choose to use the Avro file format in case of real-time streaming needs where schema evolution is of primary concern and the data will be used for exploratory purposes.

Restructuring data using Pandas

We will continue our example with the `seat` table within the `ticket` database. The structure of the table is as pasted here:

```
output_data.head(2)
```

	sport_location_id	seat_level	seat_section	seat_row	seat	seat_type
0	2	3	6	R	10	luxury
1	2	3	6	R	11	luxury

Figure 9.26: Exploring sample records in the seat table

We will consider a situation where we need to rename certain columns to better suit the data governance standards and also rearrange certain columns based on our needs:

```
#Rename and change order of columns
output_data.rename(columns={"sport_location_id":"sport_loc_id","seat":"seat_nbr"},inplace=True)
output_data=output_data.loc[:,["sport_loc_id","seat_type","seat_section","seat_level","seat_row","seat_nbr"]]
output_data.head(2)
```

	sport_loc_id	seat_type	seat_section	seat_level	seat_row	seat_nbr
0	2	luxury	6	3	R	10
1	2	luxury	6	3	R	11

Figure 9.27: Renaming and rearranging columns in the DataFrame

Pandas also provides powerful capabilities to convert the data shape from wide-format into long-format and vice versa using a pivot function. Consider an example where we want to convert the data from the raw format into an aggregated count of seats per category for each sporting location. This data will be used in a dashboard to visualize the type of seats available across different locations.

Pivot functions provide the capability to achieve similar aggregations. We will join the `sport_location` table data and `seat` table data, which is loaded already in `output_data` DataFrame, using a `merge` operation. We will explore joining DataFrames further in the data structuring section of this chapter. The pivot table will aggregate the number of seats based on their type and stadium name.

```
import awswrangler as wr
import pandas as pd
import numpy as np
con=wr.mysql.connect("wranglerbook")
sport_loc=wr.mysql.read_sql_query("SELECT * FROM dms_sample.sport_location", con=con)

pivot_data=pd.merge(output_data,sport_loc,left_on="sport_loc_id",right_on="id",how='inner')
final_data=pivot_data.pivot_table(values="seat_nbr", index="name", margins="True", columns="seat_type", aggfunc="count")
final_data
```

seat_type	luxury	obstructed	premium	standard	sub-standard	All
name						
AT&T Park	1000.0	NaN	13000.0	23915.0	4000.0	41915
AT&T Stadium	1000.0	1000.0	22999.0	42000.0	13001.0	80000
Angel Stadium	NaN	NaN	17001.0	26482.0	2000.0	45483
Arrowhead Stadium	3415.0	1000.0	16000.0	50001.0	6000.0	76416
Bank of America Stadium	8000.0	NaN	23001.0	33418.0	11000.0	75419
...	...	...	...	...	...	...
US Cellular Field	5000.0	1000.0	12614.0	18001.0	4000.0	40615

Figure 9.28: Pivot tables to aggregate and convert the dataset into the desired structure

In the preceding example, we could see that there are no **obstructed** seats in **AT&T Park** (remember this fictional data, though ☺). However, the seat counts are in a decimal type, which is misleading, as we can't have partial seats. Let us fix this by converting the data type of the column using the `format` function as follows:

```
]: final_data.head(5).style.format("{:.0f}")
```

seat_type	luxury	obstructed	premium	standard	sub-standard	All
name						
AT&T Park	1000	nan	13000	23915	4000	41915
AT&T Stadium	1000	1000	22999	42000	13001	80000
Angel Stadium	nan	nan	17001	26482	2000	45483
Arrowhead Stadium	3415	1000	16000	50001	6000	76416
Bank of America Stadium	8000	nan	23001	33418	11000	75419

Figure 9.29: Using data formatting and styling options in pandas

Now we have a different representation of data that was not available in the original raw data source. Similarly, you can convert data based on your project consumption needs using `pandas` operations such as `pivot`, `unpivot`, and so on.

Flattening nested data with Pandas

Pandas provides capabilities for structuring your data by removing unwanted columns, renaming columns, and also changing the index as needed. This helps in changing the data format to a more standard format that is suitable for each use case. In addition, there are functions that we can utilize in Pandas for flattening nested data within a single column to better analyze the data.

In order to demonstrate our work, let us consider a sample stadium data where the address and dining options from the stadium are available. We do not have the data in our sample dataset and hence will use a sample value to show how JSON data flattening works. We will use the `json_normalize` (`https://pandas.pydata.org/docs/reference/api/pandas.json_normalize.html`) function to flatten the nest JSON data into columns for analysis. Now we can use this data to query the columns much more efficiently. You can query how many stadiums are available in the state of California by filtering by the **Location.State** column.

```
stadium_address = {'Name':'Angel Stadium', 'Location':{'City':'Anaheim','Zipcode':'92806','State':'CA',
                                                       'Address':{'Street Name' :'E Gene Autry Way','Number':'2000'}},
                   'Dining':['The Sweet shop', 'Big A Burger']}
```

```
from pandas import json_normalize
flat1=json_normalize(stadium_address)
flat1
```

	Name	Dining	Location.City	Location.Zipcode	Location.State	Location.Address.Street Name	Location.Address.Number
0	Angel Stadium	[The Sweet shop, Big A Burger]	Anaheim	92806	CA	E Gene Autry Way	2000

Figure 9.30: Flattening hierarchical JSON data using the json_normalize function

However, we still have data in a list in the **Dining** column. If we wanted to have that column expanded, it would help us with our analysis further. For this, we need to create a function that will flatten both the dictionary and list data from a JSON string.

```
#Function referenced from https://towardsdatascience.com/flattening-json-objects-in-python-f5343c794b10
def flatten_json(y):
    out = {}
    def flatten(x, name=''):
        if type(x) is dict:
            for a in x:
                flatten(x[a], name + a + '_')
        elif type(x) is list:
            i = 0
            for a in x:
                flatten(a, name + str(i) + '_')
                i += 1
        else:
            out[name[:-1]] = x

    flatten(y)
    return out
```

Figure 9.31: Function to flatten both the list and dictionary columns with JSON data

Now, you can see the output has both dictionary and list data being flattened from the JSON string. We have used the `flatten_json` function that we created in the preceding step to achieve the desired output:

```
flat = flatten_json(stadium_address)
json_normalize(flat)
```

	Name	Location_City	Location_Zipcode	Location_State	Location_Address_Street Name	Location_Address_Number	Dining_0	Dining_1
0	Angel Stadium	Anaheim	92806	CA	E Gene Autry Way	2000	The Sweet shop	Big A Burger

Figure 9.32: Flattening JSON data with list and dictionary columns

Let's take a moment and understand how the function works so that you can develop it further. We will add comments to the function and demonstrate the working of the `flatten` function. The function will be called recursively to flatten the JSON string:

```
#For learning the working of the function.
def flatten(x, name='',out={}):
    print(x)
    a=""
    if type(x) is dict:
        for a in x:
            print("______________________________")
            print("Dictionary route " + a)
            flatten(x[a], name + a + '_')
    elif type(x) is list:
        i = 0
        for a in x:
            print("**********************")
            print("List route " + name + str(i) + '_')
            flatten(a, name + str(i) + '_')
            i += 1
    else:
        print("====> Found a value for target column --> "+ x)
        out[name[:-1]] = x
```

Figure 9.33: Understanding the working of the flatten function by adding comments

We have added the `print` statement immediately in the function to understand the input string that is being passed. We have added `print` statements to each of the sections, which perform the following functions:

- Flattening dictionary objects
- Flattening list objects
- Identifying an atomic value to be stored in the target column

How does the function work?

The function will iterate through the provided data and identify whether the current object is a dictionary or list:

- A dictionary object will have curly brackets and have a key-value pair structure, for example, `: {"name":"Angel stadium","state":"CA"}`. Dictionaries can have dictionary or list objects within them.
- List objects will have similar data items that are repeated multiple times. They are stored within a square bracket structure. They can be used to store multi-valued attributes. In the preceding example, we stored data about multiple restaurants within the **Angel** stadium in a list – for example, `: ["The sweet shop","Big A burger"]`.

Once it identifies the object, it will call the function recursively if it's a dictionary or list within another object.

The following screenshot provides an illustration of how the function parses the data before providing the final output. Follow through each step and you can better understand the workings of this function:

```
flatten(stadium_address)

{'Name': 'Angel Stadium', 'Location': {'City': 'Anaheim', 'Zipcode': '92806', 'State': 'CA', 'Address': {'Street Name': 'E
Gene Autry Way', 'Number': '2000'}}, 'Dining': ['The Sweet shop', 'Big A Burger']}
____________________
Dictionary route Name
Angel Stadium
====> Found a value for target column --> Angel Stadium
____________________
Dictionary route Location
{'City': 'Anaheim', 'Zipcode': '92806', 'State': 'CA', 'Address': {'Street Name': 'E Gene Autry Way', 'Number': '2000'}}
____________________
Dictionary route City
Anaheim
====> Found a value for target column --> Anaheim
____________________
Dictionary route Zipcode
92806
====> Found a value for target column --> 92806
____________________
Dictionary route State
CA
====> Found a value for target column --> CA
____________________
Dictionary route Address
{'Street Name': 'E Gene Autry Way', 'Number': '2000'}
____________________
Dictionary route Street Name
E Gene Autry Way
====> Found a value for target column --> E Gene Autry Way
```

```
____________________
Dictionary route Number
2000
====> Found a value for target column --> 2000
____________________
Dictionary route Dining
['The Sweet shop', 'Big A Burger']
**********************
List route Dining_0_
The Sweet shop
====> Found a value for target column --> The Sweet shop
**********************
List route Dining_1_
Big A Burger
====> Found a value for target column --> Big A Burger
```

Figure 9.34: Inner workings of the JSON flatten function

Now, we have successfully flattened the data into individual columns for better analysis. However, the list items are split into multiple columns in the same table, which could create wide column tables and sparse data, which is not good for querying the data. The better approach would be to split the data from the list into a separate table with foreign key relationships.

In order to achieve this, we will change our `flatten` function further. The following is a summary of changes made to the `flatten` function:

- Add logic to handle the primary key for the dataset so that the primary key can be stored in the child table to join them together.

- We will change the flattening logic for list objects to create a different DataFrame. The logic also will populate the primary key iterator column to identify different values from the original list object.
- Now we will have more than one dictionary item returned from our function, so we will change the output of the function to return a list of dictionaries/list objects.

```
#For learning the working of the function.
def flatten_v2(x, name='',df_name="df",pk="Name",pk_val="",out={},out_dfs={}):
    print("Input -->",x, "-", df_name,"-",name)
    a=""
    df1={}
    df_list=[]
    if pk_val=="":
        pk_val=x[pk]
    if type(x) is dict:
        for a in x:
            print("______________________")
            print("Dictionary route " + a)
            flatten(x[a], name + a + '_',"df",pk_val=pk_val)
    elif type(x) is list:
        i = 0
        for a in x:
            df1={}
            print("************************")
            print("List route " + name + str(i) + '_')
            df_name=name[:-1]
            df1[name[:-1]]=a
            df1[name[:-1]+"_pk"]=i
            df1[pk]=pk_val
            df_list.append(df1)
            print("Output in list-->",df_list)
            i += 1
        out_dfs[df_name]=df_list
        return out_dfs
    else:
        print("====> Found a value for target column --> "+ x)
        out[name[:-1]] = x
    out_dfs[df_name]=out
    print("Output-->",out)
    return out_dfs
```

Figure 9.35: Updated flatten function to split list objects into another DataFrame with a primary foreign key relationship

Explore the function and you can execute it on your own environment to understand the inner working better. Let us now bundle this into a working `flatten` function and verify the output:

```
def flatten_json_v2(y):
    out = {}
    out_dfs= {}
    def flatten(x, name='',df_name="df",pk="Name",pk_val=""):
        a=""
        df1={}
        df_list=[]
        if pk_val=="":
            pk_val=x[pk]
        if type(x) is dict:
            for a in x:
                flatten(x[a], name + a + '_',"df",pk_val=pk_val)
        elif type(x) is list:
            i = 0
            for a in x:
                df1={}
                df_name=name[:-1]
                df1[name[:-1]]=a
                df1[name[:-1]+"_pk"]=i
                df1[pk]=pk_val
                df_list.append(df1)
                i += 1
            out_dfs[df_name]=df_list
            return out_dfs
        else:
            out[name[:-1]] = x
            out_dfs[df_name]=out
    flatten(y)
    return out_dfs
```

Figure 9.36: Updated flattening code created as version 2 of the flatten function

Execute the function for our sample dataset here and we can now see that the function creates two DataFrames with one DataFrame having the contents from the list object along with the primary key value (the stadium name in the sample use case here) for joining purposes.

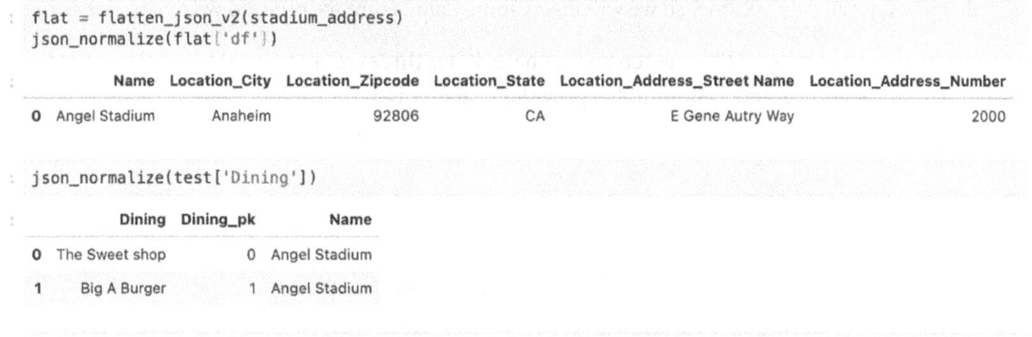

```
flat = flatten_json_v2(stadium_address)
json_normalize(flat['df'])
```

	Name	Location_City	Location_Zipcode	Location_State	Location_Address_Street Name	Location_Address_Number
0	Angel Stadium	Anaheim	92806	CA	E Gene Autry Way	2000

```
json_normalize(test['Dining'])
```

	Dining	Dining_pk	Name
0	The Sweet shop	0	Angel Stadium
1	Big A Burger	1	Angel Stadium

Figure 9.37: Verifying the workings of the updated flatten function

We have gone through this exercise to showcase that with pandas and Python, we can perform powerful data transformation to suit our needs. However, this logic can be further developed and fine-tuned.

Challenge

Can you also update the script to process nested lists? One example could be that a stadium has a list of food outlets and each food outlet has a list of menu items.

Hint

You can try to store the primary key separately for each table in the hierarchy and then add them to the child table along with the iterator column specific to that table.

In the next section, will learn more about using pandas' operations for performing data cleaning activities.

Data cleaning

Data cleaning is an important step in the process of data wrangling. A good amount of time is spent on identifying the right data source and cleaning the data. Pandas provides a lot of functionalities for cleaning your data.

The exact activities that are required during this phase are different for each type of dataset. Certain data sources will have data that requires only minimal cleaning and certain other data sources might require a lot of cleaning activities before the dataset can be used in your project. You could also use the output of data exploration activities to understand the level of cleaning activities to be performed on the data.

Data cleansing with Pandas

In order to demonstrate the data cleaning steps, we will use the `seat_type` table from our database. This table only has minimal data volume, so we will insert some data before we proceed with data cleansing.

The data in `seat_type` looks like the screenshot here. It has three columns for the seat type name, a description of that seat type, and a column that provides a relative ranking of the quality of that seat type:

```
con=wr.mysql.connect("wranglerbook")
cursor=con.cursor()
cursor.execute("show columns from seat_type")
cursor.fetchall()
```

```
(('name', 'varchar(15)', 'NO', 'PRI', None, ''),
 ('description', 'varchar(120)', 'YES', '', None, ''),
 ('relative_quality', 'tinyint', 'YES', '', None, ''))
```

```
cursor.execute("select * from seat_type ;")
cursor.fetchall()
```

```
(('luxury', 'Excellent seats - box seats, behind the plate, etc. etc.', 1),
 ('obstructed', 'Pretty crappy, partially obstructed seats', 5),
 ('premium', 'Really good seats - first level, mid field, etc. etc.', 2),
 ('standard', 'Standard seats - not super awesome but pretty good', 3),
 ('standing', "Really? That's not a seat at all now, is it?", 10),
 ('sub-standard', 'End zone, nose bleed, etc.', 4))
```

Figure 9.38: Exploring the current data available in the seat table

We will modify the data to emulate a dataset that will help us walk through the data-cleaning activities. Rather than deleting or updating the current data from the seat table, we will insert new records that are a mocked-up version of the current data.

The following screenshot shows the new mocked-up records with the same columns in the `seat_type` table. However, the `description` column has now additional details such as the level of the stadium in which the seat type is available and how many seats of that particular type are available, along with a description.

```
cursor.execute("insert into seat_type values('Luxury1','level5,1500 seats,Comfortable seats,Leather seats!!!',1);")
cursor.execute("insert into seat_type values('Obstructed1','level3,100 seats,Comfortable seats though,But wont have any v
cursor.execute("insert into seat_type values('Premium1','level4-5,500 seats,Comfortable but normal seats, good views for 
cursor.execute("insert into seat_type values('Standard1','level1,5500 seats,Comfortable seats,Leather seats!!!',3);")
cursor.execute("insert into seat_type values('standing1','Level1-5,Comfortable seats,Leather seats!!!',10);")
cursor.execute("insert into seat_type values('sub-standard1','level1,200 seats,Front row , risk of injury!!!',4);")
```

```
1
```

Figure 9.39: Mocked-up records for the seat table

For our current use case, we will extract only the data that we inserted into the table. We will filter records that have a seat type name column with values that begin with a letter (a-z) and end with a numeric value (0-9), which will only get the newly inserted records that have the number 1 appended at the end of the name column.

```
#Filter data that starts with characters and ends with a single number
cleanse_data=output_data[output_data["description"].str.contains("^[a-zA-z]*[0-9]+")]
cleanse_data
```

	name	description	relative_quality
1	Luxury1	level5,1500 seats,Comfortable seats,Leather se...	1
3	Obstructed1	level3,100 seats,Comfortable seats though,But ...	5
5	Premium1	level4-5,500 seats,Comfortable but normal seat...	2
7	Standard1	level1,5500 seats,Comfortable seats,Leather se...	3
9	standing1	Level1-5,Comfortable seats,Leather seats!!!	10
11	sub-standard1	level1,200 seats,Front row , risk of injury!!!	4

Figure 9.40: Extracting the mocked-up data records alone for data-cleansing activities

We will then split the data within the description column so that better analysis can be done on the data. We will use the `split` function on the comma delimiter and get the data into different columns as shown in the following screenshot:

```
#Extract data from column into different columns
pd.options.mode.chained_assignment = None
cleanse_data["Level_data"]=cleanse_data["description"].str.split(",",n=2).str[0]
cleanse_data["No_of_seats"]=cleanse_data["description"].str.split(",",n=2).str[1]
cleanse_data["Seat description"]=cleanse_data["description"].str.split(",",n=2).str[2]
```

Identify outliers Remove nulls with valid values

```
cleanse_data
```

	name	description	relative_quality	Level_data	No_of_seats	Seat description
1	Luxury1	level5,1500 seats,Comfortable seats,Leather se...	1	level5	1500 seats	Comfortable seats,Leather seats!!!
3	Obstructed1	level3,100 seats,Comfortable seats though,But ...	5	level3	100 seats	Comfortable seats though,But wont have any vis...
5	Premium1	level4-5,500 seats,Comfortable but normal seat...	2	level4-5	500 seats	Comfortable but normal seats, good views for t...
7	Standard1	level1,5500 seats,Comfortable seats,Leather se...	3	level1	5500 seats	Comfortable seats,Leather seats!!!
9	standing1	Level1-5,Comfortable seats,Leather seats!!!	10	Level1-5	Comfortable seats	Leather seats!!!
11	sub-standard1	level1,200 seats,Front row , risk of injury!!!	4	level1	200 seats	Front row , risk of injury!!!

Figure 9.41: Verifying the workings of the updated flatten function

Now we have data split into multiple columns but still have data that is not clean enough for final analysis. Let us fix the issue one column at a time for better understanding. The **Level_data** column provides information on which level of the stadium there are seats of that type available. However, some records have data such as Level1-5, indicating the seats are available in **level1**, **level2**, **level3**, **level4**, and **level5**. This is very clear to read to the human mind, but if you want to query the seat types available in **level3**, this data will not provide correct results. We want to expand the level data wherever applicable.

The following screenshot shows how we can achieve this using list comprehension in Python. We will split the string using hyphens (`-`) if available and then generate a sequence with numbers between the left-hand to right-hand number. For example, `Level1-4` will generate a sequence of numbers from 1 (left side) to 4 (right side), which will be appended with the string `Level` and joined together using commas. If the hyphen is not available, then the data will be populated as such:

```
#Iterate through data and fix issues
#Generate a string of level data from the list by parsing and appending data apprpriately
import re
cleanse_data['Level_data'] = [",".join(["level"+str(i) \
    for i in list(range(int(re.findall(r'\d+',x.split("-")[0])[0]),int(re.findall(r'\d+',x.split("-")[1])[0])+1))]) \
                                    if x.find("-")>-1 else x for x in cleanse_data['Level_data']]
cleanse_data
```

	name	description	relative_quality	Level_data	No_of_seats	Seat description
1	Luxury1	level5,1500 seats,Comfortable seats,Leather se...	1	level5	1500 seats	Comfortable seats,Leather seats!!!
3	Obstructed1	level3,100 seats,Comfortable seats though,But ...	5	level3	100 seats	Comfortable seats though,But wont have any vis...
5	Premium1	level4-5,500 seats,Comfortable but normal seat...	2	level4,level5	500 seats	Comfortable but normal seats, good views for t...
7	Standard1	level1,5500 seats,Comfortable seats,Leather se...	3	level1	5500 seats	Comfortable seats,Leather seats!!!
9	standing1	Level1-5,Comfortable seats,Leather seats!!!	10	level1,level2,level3,level4,level5	Comfortable seats	Leather seats!!!
11	sub-standard1	level1,200 seats,Front row , risk of injury!!!	4	level1	200 seats	Front row , risk of injury!!!

Figure 9.42: List comprehension to expand the level_data column

Now we can query which seat types are available in `level3` as shown next. Before the data was cleaned for the `Level_data` column, we would only get records for obstructed seats (which have a `level3` value in the `Level_data` column), and now we know that standing capacity is also available in Level 3:

```
cleanse_data[cleanse_data['Level_data'].str.contains('level3')]
```

	name	description	relative_quality	Level_data	No_of_seats	Seat description
3	Obstructed1	level3,100 seats,Comfortable seats though,But ...	5	level3	100 seats	Comfortable seats though,But wont have any vis...
9	standing1	Level1-5,Comfortable seats,Leather seats!!!	10	level1,level2,level3,level4,level5	Comfortable seats	Leather seats!!!

Figure 9.43: Querying the seat types that are available in Level 3 of the stadium

We can also capitalize the data within this column using the `capitalize` function as follows.

```
#Capitalize the first letter of the column
cleanse_data["Level_data"]=cleanse_data["Level_data"].str.capitalize()
cleanse_data
```

	name	description	relative_quality	Level_data	No_of_seats	Seat description
1	Luxury1	level5,1500 seats,Comfortable seats,Leather se...	1	Level5	1500	Comfortable seats,Leather seats!!!
3	Obstructed1	level3,100 seats,Comfortable seats though,But ...	5	Level3	100	Comfortable seats though,But wont have any vis...
5	Premium1	level4-5,500 seats,Comfortable but normal seat...	2	Level4,level5	500	Comfortable but normal seats, good views for t...
7	Standard1	level1,5500 seats,Comfortable seats,Leather se...	3	Level1	5500	Comfortable seats,Leather seats!!!
9	standing1	Level1-5,Comfortable seats,Leather seats!!!	10	Level1,level2,level3,level4,level5	None	Leather seats!!!
11	sub-standard1	level1,200 seats,Front row , risk of injury!!!	4	Level1	200	Front row , risk of injury!!!

Figure 9.44: capitalize function to change the first character of the column to caps

However, this doesn't capitalize the values that come after commas. If you want to capitalize every word, then use the `title` function to capitalize all words, as shown here:

```
#Capitalize the first letter of the column
cleanse_data["Level_data"]=cleanse_data["Level_data"].str.title()
cleanse_data
```

	name	description	relative_quality	Level_data	No_of_seats	Seat description
1	Luxury1	level5,1500 seats,Comfortable seats,Leather se...	1	Level5	1500	Comfortable seats,Leather seats!!!
3	Obstructed1	level3,100 seats,Comfortable seats though,But ...	5	Level3	100	Comfortable seats though,But wont have any vis...
5	Premium1	level4-5,500 seats,Comfortable but normal seat...	2	Level4,Level5	500	Comfortable but normal seats, good views for t...
7	Standard1	level1,5500 seats,Comfortable seats,Leather se...	3	Level1	5500	Comfortable seats,Leather seats!!!
9	standing1	Level1-5,Comfortable seats,Leather seats!!!	10	Level1,Level2,Level3,Level4,Level5	None	Leather seats!!!
11	sub-standard1	level1,200 seats,Front row , risk of injury!!!	4	Level1	200	Front row , risk of injury!!!

Figure 9.45: title function to capitalize the starting character of every word in a column

Next, let us assume we want to identify the number of seats available on a particular level. The **No_of_seats** column has both a number and a trailing value with seats. We can extract only the numeric part of the data and store it in the column. We will use the `extract` function with regular expressions to identify and extract only the numeric part of the data as shown in the following screenshot:

```
#Extract only numbers from the seat column
import numpy as np
cleanse_data["No_of_seats"]=cleanse_data["No_of_seats"].str.extract('(\d+)')
cleanse_data
```

	name	description	relative_quality	Level_data	No_of_seats	Seat description
1	Luxury1	level5,1500 seats,Comfortable seats,Leather se...	1	level5	1500	Comfortable seats,Leather seats!!!
3	Obstructed1	level3,100 seats,Comfortable seats though,But ...	5	level3	100	Comfortable seats though,But wont have any vis...
5	Premium1	level4-5,500 seats,Comfortable but normal seat...	2	level4,level5	500	Comfortable but normal seats, good views for t...
7	Standard1	level1,5500 seats,Comfortable seats,Leather se...	3	level1	5500	Comfortable seats,Leather seats!!!
9	standing1	Level1-5,Comfortable seats,Leather seats!!!	10	level1,level2,level3,level4,level5	NaN	Leather seats!!!
11	sub-standard1	level1,200 seats,Front row , risk of injury!!!	4	level1	200	Front row , risk of injury!!!

Figure 9.46: Extracting and storing numeric values from a column

Now the **No_of_seats** column only has numeric values and has **Not a Number** (**NaN**) value for the standing type. This is correct as standing is not really a seat type. However, we can replace the **NaN** value with **None** to better represent it as a NULL value to imply that the **No_of_seats** column is not applicable to this seat type.

```
#Replace Nan to None in the data
cleanse_data=cleanse_data.replace({np.nan: None})
cleanse_data
```

	name	description	relative_quality	Level_data	No_of_seats	Seat description
1	Luxury1	level5,1500 seats,Comfortable seats,Leather se...	1	level5	1500	Comfortable seats,Leather seats!!!
3	Obstructed1	level3,100 seats,Comfortable seats though,But ...	5	level3	100	Comfortable seats though,But wont have any vis...
5	Premium1	level4-5,500 seats,Comfortable but normal seat...	2	level4,level5	500	Comfortable but normal seats, good views for t...
7	Standard1	level1,5500 seats,Comfortable seats,Leather se...	3	level1	5500	Comfortable seats,Leather seats!!!
9	standing1	Level1-5,Comfortable seats,Leather seats!!!	10	level1,level2,level3,level4,level5	None	Leather seats!!!
11	sub-standard1	level1,200 seats,Front row , risk of injury!!!	4	level1	200	Front row , risk of injury!!!

Figure 9.47: Using the replace function to convert NaN into NULL values

We can the sum of seats on Level 5 as seen here. But before that, we have to convert the `No_of_seats` field into an integer type and replace null values with zeroes to sum them up:

```
cleanse_data['No_of_seats']=cleanse_data['No_of_seats'].fillna(0).astype('int')
cleanse_data[cleanse_data['Level_data'].str.contains('Level5')]['No_of_seats'].sum()
```

```
2000
```

Figure 9.48: Aggregate function to get the number of seats on a particular level in the stadium

In this section, we explored different functionalities to cleanse data for meaningful analysis. Users can further explore different Pandas functions for deduplication and other cleansing activities specific to their data sources. We will now explore the data enrichment phase of the wrangling pipeline.

Data enrichment

We have learned how to extract data from various sources, put them into a common or desired structure, and cleanse data issues. However, the data is still in silos from individual sources and it would be valuable to combine data from multiple sources to enrich the data with additional information.

Let us consider a use case where we will publish a schedule of football games for a specific team. Before we do that, we must understand our dataset in order to join relevant tables. We will first print the list of tables that is available in our source database.

```
con=wr.mysql.connect("wranglerbook")
cursor=con.cursor()
cursor.execute("show tables;")
cursor.fetchall()
```

```
(('mlb_data',),
 ('name_data',),
 ('nfl_data',),
 ('nfl_stadium_data',),
 ('person',),
 ('player',),
 ('seat',),
 ('seat_type',),
 ('sport_division',),
 ('sport_league',),
 ('sport_location',),
 ('sport_team',),
 ('sport_type',),
 ('sporting_event',),
 ('sporting_event_ticket',),
 ('ticket_purchase_hist',))
```

Figure 9.49: Printing all tables from the source database for a sporting ticket dataset

We have a list of tables, and the following diagram will illustrate the relationship across different tables in our dataset:

Table name	Description
mlb_data	Contains stats and details about players in the MLB.
name_data	Details about people/players' names such as last or first name.
nfl_data	Contains stats about players in the NFL.

nfl_stadium_data	Contains details about sports stadiums for NFL such as its surface, whether it is covered/open, etc.
person	Contains detail about people, linking to the ticket purchase history table.
player	Contains players' details and the sports team they belong to.
seat	Contains seat data with links to sports location.
seat_type	Contains details about seats in stadiums, different classifications, and their comfort ranking.
sport_division	Contains description about the sports league division the teams are playing for, e.g., NFL -> AFC South.
sport_league	Contains description about the sports league the teams are playing for, e.g., MLB, NFL, etc.
sport_location	Contains information about sporting locations/stadiums' addresses and seat capacities.
sport_team	Contains details about the teams, their short names, the leagues they belong to, and home stadiums.
sport_type	Contains description about different sport types – here we will have data about football and baseball alone.
sporting_event	Contains details on the teams playing along with location IDs for where they are playing, the dates when they are playing, etc.
sporting_event_ticket	Contains details about tickets purchased for each sporting event along with information on who purchased them, the price of the tickets, and also additional information on seating.
ticket_purchase_hist	Will have details about tickets' purchase history and any transfers made of the tickets.

Table 9.1: Table name and descriptions

We expect to see participating teams, the stadiums where matches are held, the city and state of the respective stadiums, the match dates, and the seating capacity of the stadiums in the final schedule that will be published. With the preceding information, we will prepare a schedule for a specific football team (the New York Giants, in this instance).

Pandas operations for data transformation

The first step is to fetch information from the sporting event table. Let us explore the data available in the sporting event table:

```
sporting_event
```

	id	sport_type_name	home_team_id	away_team_id	location_id	start_date_time	start_date	sold_out
0	1	baseball	33	34	20	2022-04-02 13:00:00	2022-04-02	0
1	2	baseball	33	35	20	2022-04-09 16:00:00	2022-04-09	0
2	3	baseball	33	36	20	2022-04-16 16:00:00	2022-04-16	0
3	4	baseball	33	37	20	2022-04-23 18:00:00	2022-04-23	0
4	5	baseball	33	38	20	2022-04-30 14:00:00	2022-04-30	0

Figure 9.50: Exploring the data available in the sporting_event table

Now we have the sporting event date and sport type, which we will filter for football teams. However, we still need to know the name of the teams that are participating in the match. Now we will join the `sporting_event` table with the `sport_team` table to fetch team name information. We will use pandas' `merge` (`https://pandas.pydata.org/docs/reference/api/pandas.DataFrame.merge.html`) command to make join DataFrames. We will use the `left_on` and `right_on` attributes to mention the key names that will be used in the join clause:

```
sporting_event_temp1=pd.merge(sporting_event,sport_team,left_on="home_team_id",right_on="id",how='left')
sporting_event_temp1
```

	id_x	sport_type_name_x	home_team_id	away_team_id	location_id	start_date_time	start_date	sold_out	id_y	name	abbreviated
0	1	baseball	33	34	20	2022-04-02 13:00:00	2022-04-02	0	33	San Diego Padres	
1	2	baseball	33	35	20	2022-04-09 16:00:00	2022-04-09	0	33	San Diego Padres	

Figure 9.51: Join tables using pandas' merge function

Now we understand the home team for the matches scheduled on April 2nd and April 9th is San Diego Padres from the MLB league. Watchful eyes will notice the `id` column is appended with `_x` for the `sporting_event` (left table) DataFrame and `_y` for the `sport_team` (right table) DataFrame. This is to avoid duplicate column names in the resulting dataset. Similar suffixes will be appended to other columns with similar names. We will have to make a note of this and use this name in the resulting DataFrame to access those columns.

This is great, but can you think of any problem with the preceding approach? What if you are joining with one more table that also has a column labeled `id`? This will cause the join condition to error. And it would be difficult to remember which table was used in `left` or `right` when the resulting dataset is exported for different consumption purposes. Luckily, Pandas also allows us to add custom suffixes to similar column names. We will use `_set` for the `sporting_event` table and `_se` for the `sporting_event_temp1` table as shown in the following screenshot:

```
sporting_event_temp1=pd.merge(sporting_event,sport_team,left_on="home_team_id",right_on="id",how='left',suffixes=('_se
sporting_event_temp1
```

	id_set	sport_type_name_set	home_team_id	away_team_id	location_id	start_date_time	start_date	sold_out	id_se	name	abbrev
0	1	baseball	33	34	20	2022-04-02 13:00:00	2022-04-02	0	33	San Diego Padres	
1	2	baseball	33	35	20	2022-04-09 16:00:00	2022-04-09	0	33	San Diego Padres	

Figure 9.52: Joining tables with custom suffixes

Now let us do the same join to get the away team information as well, as shown next. You can see that we made the join on different key columns, `home_team_id` and `away_team_id`, in the join statements:

```
sporting_event_temp1=pd.merge(sporting_event,sport_team,left_on="home_team_id",right_on="id",how='left',suffixes=('_set',
sporting_event_temp1=pd.merge(sporting_event_temp1,sport_team,left_on="away_team_id",right_on="id",how='left',suffixes=('_
sporting_event_temp1
```

ut	id_se	name_se2	...	sport_type_name_se	sport_league_short_name_se2	sport_division_short_name_se2	id	name_at	abbreviated_name_at
0	33	San Diego Padres	...	baseball	MLB	AL East	34	Tampa Bay Rays	TB
0	33	San Diego Padres	...	baseball	MLB	AL East	35	Atlanta Braves	ATL
		San Dieqo						New York	

Figure 9.53: Joining tables to get home and away team information

Now that we have the participating sports team information available, we still need the location information/stadium information for where the match is happening. We will fetch that information by joining the `sport_location` table so that it will have stadium information (name, city, and state) with seating capacity, as shown in the following screenshot:

```
sporting_event_temp1=pd.merge(sporting_event,sport_team,left_on="home_team_id",right_on="id",how='left',suffixes=('_set',
sporting_event_temp1=pd.merge(sporting_event_temp1,sport_team,left_on="away_team_id",right_on="id",how='left',suffixes=('_
sporting_event_temp1=pd.merge(sporting_event_temp1,sport_location,left_on="location_id",right_on="id",how='left',suffixes=
sporting_event_temp1
```

_at	sport_type_name	sport_league_short_name_at	sport_division_short_name_at	id_loc	name	city	seating_capacity	levels	sections
26	baseball	MLB	AL East	20	Petco Park	San Diego California	40162	2	40
27	baseball	MLB	AL East	20	Petco Park	San Diego California	40162	2	40

Figure 9.54: Joining with the sport_location table to get stadium/ location information for the sporting event

Now we have all the required fields, but we have a lot of additional fields that we need to filter out. We can utilize the `df.loc[: , list of columns]` function to achieve that by selecting only the required columns:

```
sporting_event_temp1=pd.merge(sporting_event,sport_team,left_on="home_team_id",right_on="id",how='left',\
                              suffixes=('_se1', '_ht'))
sporting_event_temp1=pd.merge(sporting_event_temp1,sport_team,left_on="away_team_id",right_on="id",how='left',\
                              suffixes=('_se2', '_at'))
sporting_event_temp1=pd.merge(sporting_event_temp1,sport_location,left_on="location_id",right_on="id",how='left',\
                              suffixes=('_se3', '_loc'))
sporting_event_schedule=sporting_event_temp1.loc[:,['id_se1','sport_type_name_se1','sport_league_short_name_se2',\
                              'start_date_time','name_se2','name_at','sport_division_short_name_se2',\
                                          'sport_division_short_name_at','name','city','seating_capacity']]
sporting_event_schedule
```

	id_se1	sport_type_name_se1	sport_league_short_name_se2	start_date_time	name_se2	name_at	sport_division_short_name_se2	sport_d
0	1	baseball	MLB	2022-04-02 13:00:00	San Diego Padres	Tampa Bay Rays	AL East	
1	2	baseball	MLB	2022-04-09 16:00:00	San Diego Padres	Atlanta Braves	AL East	
2	3	baseball	MLB	2022-04-16 16:00:00	San Diego Padres	New York Yankees	AL East	
3	4	baseball	MLB	2022-04-23	San Diego	Texas	AL East	

Figure 9.55: Selecting only the required columns from the pandas DataFrame

The preceding output still has column names that are lengthy and doesn't have meaningful business names. We can change the names to better represent the data as shown here using the `rename` function.

```
sporting_event_temp1=pd.merge(sporting_event,sport_team,left_on="home_team_id",right_on="id",how='left',\
                              suffixes=('_se1', '_ht'))
sporting_event_temp1=pd.merge(sporting_event_temp1,sport_team,left_on="away_team_id",right_on="id",how='left',\
                              suffixes=('_se2', '_at'))
sporting_event_temp1=pd.merge(sporting_event_temp1,sport_location,left_on="location_id",right_on="id",how='left',\
                              suffixes=('_se3', '_loc'))
sporting_event_schedule=sporting_event_temp1.loc[:,['id_se1','sport_type_name_se1','sport_league_short_name_se2',\
                              'start_date_time','name_se2','name_at','sport_division_short_name_se2',\
                                          'sport_division_short_name_at','name','city','seating_capacity']]
sporting_event_schedule.rename(columns={'id_se1': 'id', 'sport_type_name_se1': 'sport_name',\
                              'sport_league_short_name_se2': 'league_name','name_se2': 'home_team','name_at': \
                              'away_team','sport_division_short_name_se2': 'home_team_league',\
                                  'sport_division_short_name_at': 'away_team_league','name': 'stadium name'}, \
                              inplace=True)

sporting_event_schedule
```

ɔort_name	league_name	start_date_time	home_team	away_team	home_team_league	away_team_league	stadium name	city	seating_capacity
baseball	MLB	2022-04-02 13:00:00	San Diego Padres	Tampa Bay Rays	AL East	AL East	Petco Park	San Diego California	40162
baseball	MLB	2022-04-09 16:00:00	San Diego Padres	Atlanta Braves	AL East	AL East	Petco Park	San Diego California	40162
baseball	MLB	2022-04-16 16:00:00	San Diego Padres	New York Yankees	AL East	AL East	Petco Park	San Diego California	40162

Figure 9.56: rename function to change column names to align with the business use of the data

Now we have a working dataset that has the required data attributes, but we still need to filter it for football games and the games where New York Giants is a participant either as the home team or away team:

```
]: #Hand-out to individual team fans their schedule
sporting_event_schedule.loc[(sporting_event_schedule["home_team"]=="New York Giants") | \
                    |(sporting_event_schedule["away_team"]=="New York Giants")]
```

ort_name	league_name	start_date_time	home_team	away_team	home_team_league	away_team_league	stadium name	city	seating_capacity
football	NFL	2022-08-28 18:00:00	Dallas Cowboys	New York Giants	NFC East	NFC East	AT&T Stadium	Arlington, Texas	80000
football	NFL	2022-09-04 12:00:00	New York Giants	Philadelphia Eagles	NFC East	NFC East	MetLife Stadium	East Rutherford, New Jersey	82500
football	NFL	2022-09-11 14:00:00	New York Giants	Washington Redskins	NFC East	NFC East	MetLife Stadium	East Rutherford, New Jersey	82500
football	NFL	2022-09-18 14:00:00	New York Giants	Dallas Cowboys	NFC East	NFC East	MetLife Stadium	East Rutherford, New Jersey	82500

Figure 9.57: Filtering the DataFrame to extract data only for the New York Giants team

Now we have learned about creating new datasets by joining multiple data sources and transforming data. You can utilize pandas and Python functionalities to transform data in more powerful ways to suit your business needs. We will now move on to explore data quality validation using Pandas functionalities in the next section.

Data quality validation

Data quality validation is an important phase in data pipelines as it ensures the correctness of the data used in analyses. Without correct data, even if you use good analytical tools, the analytical insights will be incorrect. So, customers/developers need to focus more on the data quality phase to create accurate datasets for further analysis.

What is the difference between data quality and data cleansing? Some of us might be confused between data cleansing and data quality validation. In reality, there will be some overlap between the two phases, and some activities are used interchangeably:

- Data cleansing is the phase where we clean and deduplicate data and identify generic data issues, such as splitting data for more meaningful analysis, cleansing data errors, and so on. Without cleansing, the data might not be useful for analysis efforts. For example, in a student database and results table, the score column can have non-numeric values or missing values that need to be cleaned before using data for analysis.
- Data quality validation is the phase where we will configure rules and validate whether the data conform to these rules. The data would still look good even before data quality rules are applied and an outside person wouldn't be able to see any issues in the dataset. For example, in the results table, the score column can have only numeric values, but if the highest mark for a test is only 100, any value greater than that is not meaningful, which needs to be fixed before analysis.

With this understanding, let us continue working on the schedule that we created in the data enrichment step and validate it with data quality rules.

Data quality validation with Pandas

For those of you who are aware of NFL matches, a match is played every week during the season with a rest week somewhere in between. Let us first validate the schedule that was prepared for the New York Giants and validate whether the actual data conforms to those rules. Now, this is a data quality validation step, as the data doesn't have any issues on its own, but we expect the data to conform to our rules to match real-world situations. Please note this is fictitious data that was generated by a script to illustrate our use case.

We will first identify whether the New York Giants team has matches that are scheduled within the same time slot, which would make those matches impossible to play. We will use pandas' `groupby` functionality on the match start times and get the count of matches as shown here:

```
#We need to identify schedule issues where the same team is playing multiple games on the same day across different stadiu
#We can highlight the issues as the same team can't play games at the same time
sport_schedule_NYG.groupby(['start_date_time'])['start_date_time'].count()
```

```
start_date_time
2022-08-28 18:00:00    1
2022-09-04 12:00:00    1
2022-09-11 14:00:00    1
2022-09-18 14:00:00    1
2022-09-25 13:00:00    1
2022-09-25 15:00:00    1
2022-10-16 19:00:00    4
2022-11-13 14:00:00    4
2022-12-11 12:00:00    4
Name: start_date_time, dtype: int64
```

Figure 9.58: pandas' groupby function to identify duplicate matches that are scheduled

We have 4 matches scheduled at the same time during 3 weeks, which are impossible to play. But do we have issues in other weeks, such as September 25th, where there are two matches scheduled at different times? Even if we make a wild assumption that the same team can play two matches at different times within a day, let us understand that in the context of where the games are played. We will execute the `groupby` function on both the start times of the matches and the city where the matches will be played.

```
#Go one level further, to identify issues that have same team playing games on same day at different locations
sport_schedule_NYG.groupby(['start_date_time','city'])['start_date_time'].count()
```

```
start_date_time      city
2022-08-28 18:00:00  Arlington, Texas                1
2022-09-04 12:00:00  East Rutherford, New Jersey     1
2022-09-11 14:00:00  East Rutherford, New Jersey     1
2022-09-18 14:00:00  East Rutherford, New Jersey     1
2022-09-25 13:00:00  Philadelphia, Pennsylvania      1
2022-09-25 15:00:00  Landover, Maryland              1
2022-10-16 19:00:00  East Rutherford, New Jersey     4
2022-11-13 14:00:00  East Rutherford, New Jersey     4
2022-12-11 12:00:00  East Rutherford, New Jersey     4
```

Figure 9.59: pandas' groupby on location and time to identify further issues on matches within the same day

Now we understand that the team can't move between these cities on the same day to play multiple matches, so we have to modify the schedule for that week as well. The preceding verifications are intended to showcase the capabilities of pandas for data validation. Our business rule is to ensure each team gets only one match per week. Let us validate that business rule in our sample data. We will convert the start time into a date field, extract only the week part of it, and count the number of matches per week for the team.

The output is similar to our earlier validations. Now we will go ahead and correct the schedule for this team.

```
#Practically, a team can play a match per week and let us identify teams having more than one game per week
sport_schedule_NYG.loc[:,"week_nbr"]=sport_schedule_NYG['start_date_time'].dt.isocalendar().week
sport_schedule_NYG.groupby(['week_nbr'])['week_nbr'].count()
```

```
week_nbr
34    1
35    1
36    1
37    1
38    2
41    4
45    4
49    4
Name: week_nbr, dtype: int64
```

Figure 9.60: Validating whether there is only one match per week for NFL teams

We will use the `numpy` library and its `where` clause function to identify records using their start dates and also the opposing team when there is duplicate data for the start date. The following `update` statements are only for learning purposes in this book. We have updated the schedule manually to ensure there is only one match per week for the New York Giants team, but we haven't compared the schedule of other teams, and in reality, it would be a complex exercise to create a schedule reflecting this. So, we will only focus on the New York Giants and assume the schedule for other teams will not have any conflicts:

```
# The above gave an idea that the team is incorrectly scheduled on same week multiple times and some weeks are missing.
# We can then re-arrange our team schedule to better reflect the workload
import numpy as np
sport_schedule_NYG.loc[:,"start_date_time"] = np.where((sport_schedule_NYG["start_date_time"]=="2022-09-25 15:00:00")&\
                                    (sport_schedule_NYG["home_team"]=="Washington Redskins"), \
                                    sport_schedule_NYG["start_date_time"]+pd.DateOffset(7),sport_schedule_NYG["start_date_time"])

sport_schedule_NYG.loc[:,"start_date_time"] = np.where((sport_schedule_NYG["start_date_time"]=="2022-10-16 19:00:00")&\
                                    (sport_schedule_NYG["away_team"]=="Cincinnati Bengals"), \
                                    sport_schedule_NYG["start_date_time"]+pd.DateOffset(-7),sport_schedule_NYG["start_date_time"])
sport_schedule_NYG.loc[:,"start_date_time"] = np.where((sport_schedule_NYG["start_date_time"]=="2022-10-16 19:00:00")& \
                                    (sport_schedule_NYG["away_team"]=="Cleveland Browns"), \
                                    sport_schedule_NYG["start_date_time"]+pd.DateOffset(7),sport_schedule_NYG["start_date_time"])
sport_schedule_NYG.loc[:,"start_date_time"] = np.where((sport_schedule_NYG["start_date_time"]=="2022-10-16 19:00:00")&\
                                    (sport_schedule_NYG["away_team"]=="Pittsburgh Steelers"), \
                                    sport_schedule_NYG["start_date_time"]+pd.DateOffset(14),sport_schedule_NYG["start_date_time"])
sport_schedule_NYG.loc[:,"start_date_time"] = np.where((sport_schedule_NYG["start_date_time"]=="2022-11-13 14:00:00")&\
                                    (sport_schedule_NYG["away_team"]=="Denver Broncos"),\
                                    sport_schedule_NYG["start_date_time"]+pd.DateOffset(-7),sport_schedule_NYG["start_date_time"])
sport_schedule_NYG.loc[:,"start_date_time"] = np.where((sport_schedule_NYG["start_date_time"]=="2022-11-13 14:00:00")&\
                                    (sport_schedule_NYG["away_team"]=="Kansas City Chiefs"), \
                                    sport_schedule_NYG["start_date_time"]+pd.DateOffset(7),sport_schedule_NYG["start_date_time"])
sport_schedule_NYG.loc[:,"start_date_time"] = np.where((sport_schedule_NYG["start_date_time"]=="2022-11-13 14:00:00")&\
                                    (sport_schedule_NYG["away_team"]=="San Diego Chargers"), \
                                    sport_schedule_NYG["start_date_time"]+pd.DateOffset(14),sport_schedule_NYG["start_date_time"])
sport_schedule_NYG.loc[:,"start_date_time"] = np.where((sport_schedule_NYG["start_date_time"]=="2022-12-11 12:00:00")&\
                                    (sport_schedule_NYG["away_team"]=="Indianapolis Colts"), \
                                    sport_schedule_NYG["start_date_time"]+pd.DateOffset(-7),sport_schedule_NYG["start_date_time"])
sport_schedule_NYG.loc[:,"start_date_time"] = np.where((sport_schedule_NYG["start_date_time"]=="2022-12-11 12:00:00")&\
                                    (sport_schedule_NYG["away_team"]=="Jacksonville Jaguars"), \
                                    sport_schedule_NYG["start_date_time"]+pd.DateOffset(7),sport_schedule_NYG["start_date_time"])
sport_schedule_NYG.loc[:,"start_date_time"] = np.where((sport_schedule_NYG["start_date_time"]=="2022-12-11 12:00:00")&\
                                    (sport_schedule_NYG["away_team"]=="Tennessee Titans"), \
                                    sport_schedule_NYG["start_date_time"]+pd.DateOffset(14),sport_schedule_NYG["start_date_time"])
sport_schedule_NYG
```

Figure 9.61: Updating the schedule for the New York Giants team to have only one match per week

You could also verify the data has been successfully updated in the DataFrame to have only one match per week.

	id	sport_name	league_name	start_date_time	home_team	away_team	home_team_league	away_team_league	stadium name	city	s
930	931	football	NFL	2022-08-28 18:00:00	Dallas Cowboys	New York Giants	NFC East	NFC East	AT&T Stadium	Arlington, Texas	
933	934	football	NFL	2022-09-04 12:00:00	New York Giants	Philadelphia Eagles	NFC East	NFC East	MetLife Stadium	East Rutherford, New Jersey	
934	935	football	NFL	2022-09-11 14:00:00	New York Giants	Washington Redskins	NFC East	NFC East	MetLife Stadium	East Rutherford, New Jersey	
935	936	football	NFL	2022-09-18 14:00:00	New York Giants	Dallas Cowboys	NFC East	NFC East	MetLife Stadium	East Rutherford, New Jersey	
938	939	football	NFL	2022-09-25 13:00:00	Philadelphia Eagles	New York Giants	NFC East	NFC East	Lincoln Financial Field	Philadelphia, Pennsylvania	

Figure 9.62: Exploring the updated schedule for the New York Giants team

Alternatively, you could also run a query to verify that we have only one match scheduled for each week, as shown in the following screenshot. We will use the `groupby` function on the `week_nbr` column and we can see only a single match has been scheduled for each week. Now we have data that also conforms to our business rules so that it can be used for visualization and reporting purposes.

We can set up these data quality rules to execute and only show the records that do not conform with the rules and send an email to business team members to inspect the data in our data pipelines.

```
sport_schedule_NYG.loc[:,"week_nbr"]=sport_schedule_NYG['start_date_time'].dt.isocalendar().week
sport_schedule_NYG.groupby(['week_nbr'])['week_nbr'].count()
```

```
week_nbr
34    1
35    1
36    1
37    1
38    1
39    1
40    1
41    1
42    1
43    1
44    1
45    1
46    1
47    1
48    1
49    1
50    1
51    1
```

Figure 9.63: Verifying the updated schedule for the New York Giants team

We can also execute other validation rules as well. We can run a query against the `ticket_purchase_hist` table and see it's empty. In real production situations, this could be because the process that is supposed to populate ticket purchase data might be broken. However, in our current use case, the stored procedure that was supposed to insert the ticket purchase data was not executed during the initial setup. We will log in to the EC2 machine that was used earlier in the *Loading sample data into a source database* section. Once you have connected to the RDS MySQL database, select the `dms_sample` database with the `use` command and execute the stored procedure to insert 1,000 tickets, `call generateTicketActivity(1000,0);`:

```
MySQL [(none)]> use dms_sample;
Reading table information for completion of table and column names
You can turn off this feature to get a quicker startup with -A

Database changed
MySQL [dms_sample]> call generateTicketActivity(1000,0);
+--------------------------------------------------------------------------+
| CONCAT('Congratulations! You''ve just purchased ',p_quantity,' tickets.') |
+--------------------------------------------------------------------------+
| Congratulations! You've just purchased 6 tickets.                         |
+--------------------------------------------------------------------------+
1 row in set (0.22 sec)

+--------------------------------------------------------------------------+
| CONCAT('Congratulations! You''ve just purchased ',p_quantity,' tickets.') |
+--------------------------------------------------------------------------+
| Congratulations! You've just purchased 4 tickets.                         |
+--------------------------------------------------------------------------+
```

Figure 9.64: Stored procedure to generate ticket purchase activity

Now let us query the `ticket_purchase_hist` table and see records getting populated. This will ensure that we have all the data populated as expected across the data pipelines.

```
[99]: #After execcuting the insert tickets stored procedure. This SP is created but not called during initial run
      #We can insert 1000 tickets and validate the ticketing activity now. This ensures the data is complete
      ticket_purchase_hist=wr.mysql.read_sql_query("SELECT * FROM dms_sample.ticket_purchase_hist", con=con)
      ticket_purchase_hist
```

[99]:

	sporting_event_ticket_id	purchased_by_id	transaction_date_time	transferred_from_id	purchase_price
0	65536	410959	2022-12-07 03:23:29	None	43.13
1	65537	410959	2022-12-07 03:23:29	None	43.13
2	131071	4232646	2022-12-07 03:22:48	None	44.59
3	131072	4232646	2022-12-07 03:22:48	None	44.59
4	131090	4232646	2022-12-07 03:22:48	None	44.59
...	...	...	...	...	...

Figure 9.65: Exploring the data from the ticket purchase history table

We will query to see the tickets purchased for the match between the New York Giants and Philadelphia Eagles (`event_id - 934`). We will now see some records have `ticketholder_id` populated with values identifying the person who bought the ticket (which was populated from the stored procedure that we executed earlier):

```
sporting_event_ticket=wr.mysql.read_sql_query("SELECT * FROM dms_sample.sporting_event_ticket where sporting_event_id=934"
sporting_event_ticket.loc[sporting_event_ticket["ticketholder_id"].notnull()]
```

	id	sporting_event_id	sport_location_id	seat_level	seat_section	seat_row	seat	ticketholder_id	ticket_price
82496	63339564	934	32	2	10	A	1	2051116	29.44
82497	63339565	934	32	2	10	A	10	2051116	29.44
82498	63339582	934	32	2	10	A	8	2051116	29.44
82499	63339583	934	32	2	10	A	9	2051116	29.44

Figure 9.66: Verifying the ticketholder_id column is populated in the sporting_event_ticket table

Now we can perform analysis on which matches are being sold out and which matches are not selling tickets a lot.

We have validated data quality in our sample dataset using a couple of rules:

- Each NFL team needs to have one match scheduled per week for the entire season
- The ticket purchase history data should be populated to understand how many seats are still empty for each event

Data quality validation integration with a data pipeline

We can perform different validations on the dataset specific to each project's requirements. The data quality validation can be further improved with the following updates:

- Creating business rules that can be executed in SQL format and storing them in a metadata store (such as DynamoDB). For each run, execute the stored data quality rules and identify the records that do not conform. The load should only process new data using partitions or a custom bookmark functionality.
- `GreatExpectations` is a Python-based open- ource library for data validation, profiling, and documentation of the data. With this library, we can create assertions on what is expected out of the dataset. The library also supports several built-in expectations. Once the expectations are executed, you will get results in a formatted HTML document called Data Docs.

Now, we will explore data visualization, which is the last stage in the data-wrangling pipeline, in the next section.

Data visualization

Data visualization is the phase where you will create visuals and charts to better communicate the findings of your analysis to business users. A picture is worth a thousand words and an idea/message can be better communicated with charts/dashboards than tables/text data.

Visualization with Python libraries

In this section, we will explore creating dashboards using Python libraries such as `matplotlib` (`https://matplotlib.org/`) and Seaborn (`https://seaborn.pydata.org/index.html`). There are more Python libraries that can help in visualizing data, but we will not compare all those libraries here.

We will use the same sports dataset for this section as well. There are other datasets such as NY taxi trips datasets that we can use to cover different visualization aspects, but we will use the sports data for continuity purposes in this chapter. Let us consider a use case, where we want to visualize the following requirements:

- The number of tickets sold on a daily basis and their price range
- The price range for tickets sold per seat category to better understand how the ticket pricing band is structured

In order to get the number of tickets sold, we will use the data from the `ticket_purchase_hist` table. The data from the table will have the information as shown in the following screenshot:

```
]: ticket_purchase_hist
```

	sporting_event_ticket_id	purchased_by_id	transaction_date_time	transferred_from_id	purchase_price
0	1	3299597	2022-12-15 04:27:27	None	47.02
1	2	3299597	2022-12-15 04:27:27	None	47.02
2	22	3299597	2022-12-15 04:27:27	None	47.02
3	65536	410959	2022-12-07 03:23:29	None	43.13
4	65536	5909803	2022-12-15 04:27:30	None	43.13
...	...	...	...	...	...
5426	90143400	2496803	2022-12-15 04:22:07	None	34.82
5427	90143401	2453671	2022-12-15 04:24:00	None	34.82

Figure 9.67: Exploring the ticket_purcahase_hist table

The table has details on the ticket ID, transaction date, purchase price, and purchase person ID. We can use this table alone to visualize the number of tickets sold per day.

We will use a Matplotlib scatterplot to visualize the tickets sold on a daily basis. Please note this is only test data and we ran the stored procedure to populate ticket purchase history earlier in this chapter. In the sample data shown in the screenshot, the stored procedure was executed on two days to generate the ticket purchase data volume:

```
import matplotlib.pyplot as plt
plt.xticks(rotation=90)
plt.scatter(ticket_purchase_hist['transaction_date_time'].dt.date, ticket_purchase_hist['purchase_price'])
```

```
<matplotlib.collections.PathCollection at 0x7f9310af05b0>
```

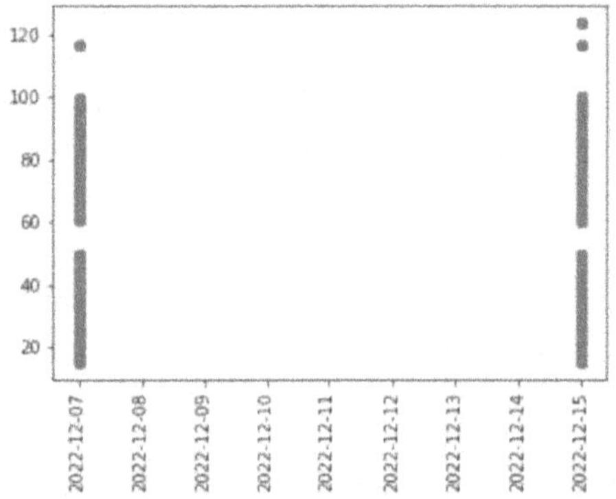

Figure 9.68: Matplotlib visualization of ticket purchase history data on a daily basis

We have used an `xticks` rotation argument to make the date values easy to read. We then create a scatterplot with transaction dates and purchase prices as shown here. We can see that there are more tickets sold in the lower price ranges (dots populated densely), but there are also some tickets sold at a high price range. Let us explore and find out how many tickets are sold above the price range of

$120. You could explore further by joining this dataset with other tables to understand the sporting event and also seat type to understand what these tickets correspond to.

```
ticket_purchase_hist[ticket_purchase_hist["purchase_price"]>120]
```

	sporting_event_ticket_id	purchased_by_id	transaction_date_time	transferred_from_id	purchase_price
4497	67075059	6294092	2022-12-15 04:24:15	None	123.81
4498	67075059	6928398	2022-12-15 04:25:53	None	123.81
4499	67075060	6294092	2022-12-15 04:24:15	None	123.81
4500	67075060	6928398	2022-12-15 04:25:53	None	123.81
4501	67075061	6928398	2022-12-15 04:25:53	None	123.81
4502	67075062	6928398	2022-12-15 04:25:53	None	123.81
4503	67075081	4360752	2022-12-15 04:25:27	None	123.81
4504	67075081	6294092	2022-12-15 04:24:15	None	123.81
4505	67075081	6928398	2022-12-15 04:25:53	None	123.81

Figure 9.69: Exploring the tickets that are sold at a high price

This is a starting point and Matplotlib still supports a lot of different visualization options. We will explore another Python visualization library called **Seaborn**, based on Matplotlib. Seaborn provides a high-level interface for drawing attractive and informative statistical graphics. We could use both Matplotlib and Seabor in the same visualization to create great graphs with little coding.

Before we start to use Seabor, we need to install the library in our environment. For SageMaker notebooks, we will use this command:

```
!pip install seaborn
```

We will create the same graph with Seaborn and now you can see the syntax is simple and intuitive and the graph is automatically populated with *x*- and *y*-axis names. For those of you with watchful eyes, we are still using Matplotlib along with Seaborn in the following visualization. We are using Matplotlib's `xticks` rotation argument to change the direction of the *x*-axis labels. This example shows how we can use both Matplotlib and Seaborn in the same visualization setting to create graphs as per our requirements.

```
import seaborn as sb
plt.xticks(rotation=90)
scatter_plot=sb.scatterplot(x='transaction_date_time' , y='purchase_price', data=ticket_purchase_hist)
```

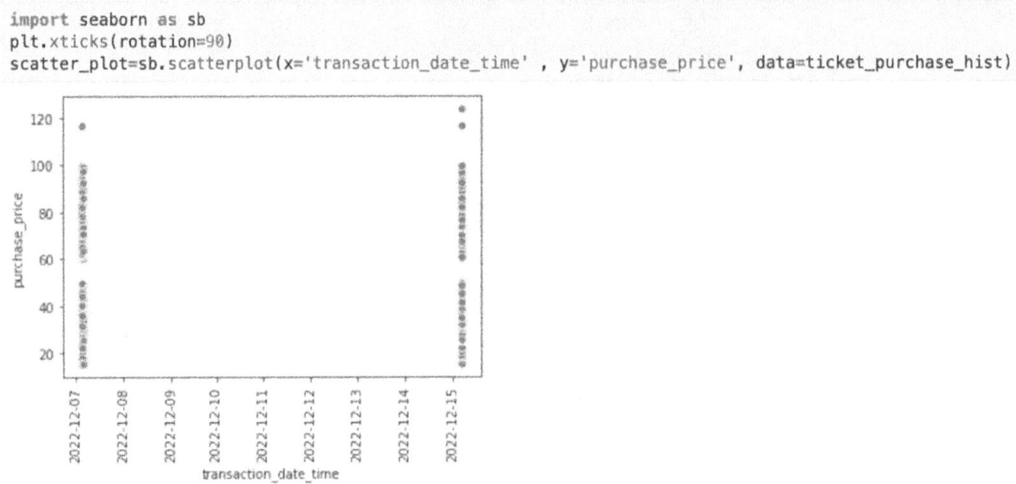

Figure 9.70: Ticket purchase history scatterplot drawn with the Seaborn package

To understand the impact of seat type on ticket pricing, we will join ticket purchase history with the `sporting_event_ticket` table and the `seat` table.

```
sporting_event_temp1=pd.merge(ticket_purchase_hist,sporting_event_ticket,left_on="sporting_event_ticket_id",right_on="id",
                    suffixes=('_tph', '_ht'))
sporting_event_temp1.head(5)
```

...

```
sporting_event_temp2=pd.merge(sporting_event_temp1,seat,left_on=["sport_location_id","seat_level","seat_section","seat_row
                    suffixes=('_tph', 'seat'))
sporting_event_temp2.head(5)
```

	sporting_event_ticket_id	purchased_by_id	transaction_date_time	transferred_from_id	purchase_price	id	sporting_event_id	sport_location_
0	1	3299597	2022-12-15 04:27:27	None	47.02	1	1	
1	2	3299597	2022-12-15 04:27:27	None	47.02	2	1	
2	22	3299597	2022-12-15 04:27:27	None	47.02	22	1	
3	65536	410959	2022-12-07 03:23:29	None	43.13	65536	2	
4	65536	5909803	2022-12-15 04:27:30	None	43.13	65536	2	

Figure 9.71: Joining the sporting event table with ticket purchase history to get seat details

With this new data, we will visualize the seat category in our earlier scatterplot as well. We will add `seat_type` as a `hue` parameter, which will color the data points based on seat type in our graph, as shown here:

```
import seaborn as sb
plt.xticks(rotation=90)
scatter_plot1=sb.scatterplot(x='transaction_date_time' , y='purchase_price',hue='seat_type', data=sporting_event_temp2, ma
```

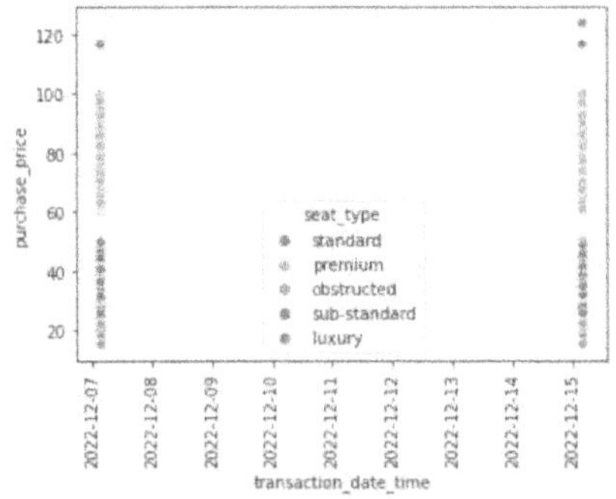

Figure 9.72: Ticket purchase history visualization along with seat type

This gives us the idea that luxury seats are costly and only sold infrequently, and premium seats and standard seats are sold a lot.

Let us explore this further by understanding the average ticket price for each seat type category. We will draw a bar plot for this use case. But before that, we need to understand the data type of the `purchase_price` column from the pandas DataFrame:

```
<class 'pandas.core.frame.DataFrame'>
Int64Index: 5431 entries, 0 to 5430
Data columns (total 15 columns):
 #   Column                     Non-Null Count  Dtype
---  ------                     --------------  -----
 0   sporting_event_ticket_id  5431 non-null   Int64
 1   purchased_by_id           5431 non-null   Int64
 2   transaction_date_time     5431 non-null   datetime64[ns]
 3   transferred_from_id       0 non-null      object
 4   purchase_price            5431 non-null   float64
 5   id                        5431 non-null   Int64
 6   sporting_event_id         5431 non-null   Int64
 7   sport_location_id         5431 non-null   Int64
 8   seat_level                5431 non-null   Int64
 9   seat_section              5431 non-null   string
 10  seat_row                  5431 non-null   string
 11  seat                      5431 non-null   string
 12  ticketholder_id           5431 non-null   Int64
 13  ticket_price              5431 non-null   object
 14  seat_type                 5431 non-null   string
dtypes: Int64(7), datetime64[ns](1), float64(1), object(2), string(4)
memory usage: 716.0+ KB
```

Figure 9.73: pandas DataFrame info function to understand the data type of columns

We could see the `purchase_price` column is of the `object` type, which will throw an error when aggregated on a bar plot. Let us convert it into a `float` object type and then create the bar plot. We will also add the `purchase_price` value on top of the bars to understand the price range of tickets better, as shown here:

```
]: sporting_event_temp2["purchase_price"]=sporting_event_temp2.purchase_price.astype(float)
   ax=sb.barplot(x='seat_type',y='purchase_price', data=sporting_event_temp2)
   for i in ax.containers:
       ax.bar_label(i,)
```

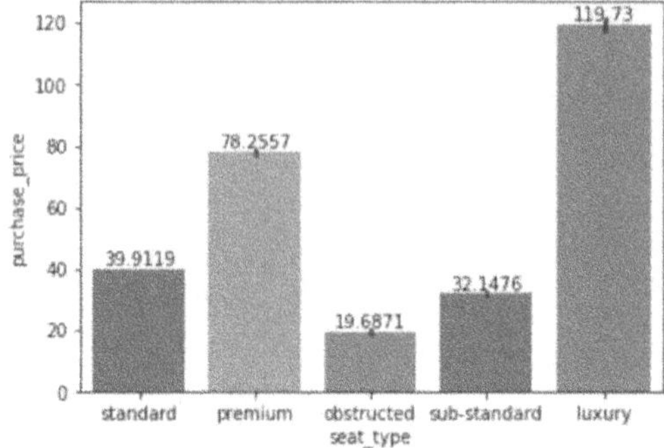

Figure 9.74: Bar plot showing the average purchase price for each ticket type

This graph is fine, but it would still be better if we could sort the graph in the order of `purchase_price` for us to visualize it better. So, we will sort the DataFrame by purchase price first and reset the pandas DataFrame index. We will also draw the graph in a more presentable manner with the `alpha` parameter to adjust the transparency of the bar plot.

```
]: sporting_event_temp2["purchase_price"]=sporting_event_temp2.purchase_price.astype(float)
   sporting_event_temp2 = sporting_event_temp2.sort_values(["purchase_price"]).reset_index(drop=True)
   ax=sb.barplot(x='seat_type',y='purchase_price', data=sporting_event_temp2, alpha=0.5)
   for i in ax.containers:
       ax.bar_label(i,)
```

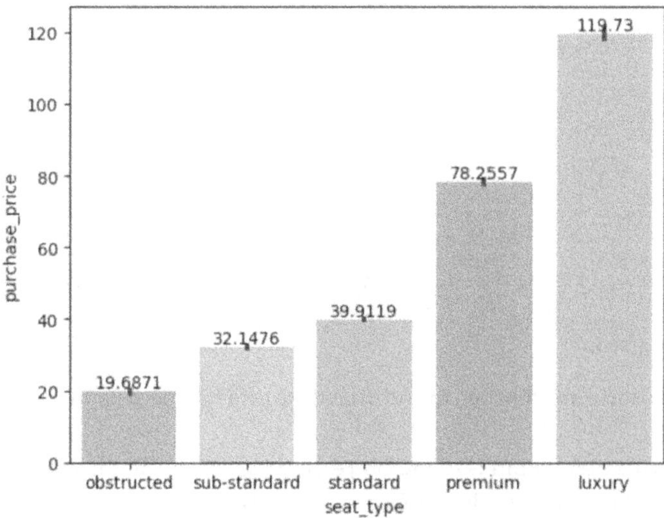

Figure 9.75: Sorted bar plot to understand the seat type and average price for that category of seats

Now we are able to visualize the impact of different seat types on the pricing band for tickets in a clearer manner. We can explore further how to maximize ticket sales with discounts on certain seat types based on the number of tickets that are sold for each seat type.

There are many more visualizations that are supported by these libraries and you can use the links provided earlier on these libraries to learn more about them. For most use cases, the preceding libraries should suffice for visualizing user data. Also, we recommend using Amazon QuickSight to visualize more complex use cases.

Summary

In this chapter, we learned how to perform pandas operations on datasets for data-wrangling purposes. We explored various stages of the data-wrangling life cycle, through discovery, structuring, cleansing, enriching, data quality validation, and visualization, and the usage of pandas operations to perform those activities seamlessly. Users can use AWS SDK for pandas, aka awswrangler integration, with pandas DataFrames to perform data-wrangling activities on AWS cloud services.

In the next chapter, we are going to learn about SageMaker Data Wrangler, which helps in performing data-wrangling activities as a part of ML pipelines.

10

Data Processing for Machine Learning with SageMaker Data Wrangler

In *Chapter 4*, we introduced you to SageMaker Data Wrangler, a purpose-built tool to process data for machine learning. We discussed why data processing for machine learning is such a critical component of the overall machine learning pipeline and some risks of working with unclean or raw data. We also covered the core capabilities of SageMaker Data Wrangler and how it is helpful to solve some key challenges involved in data processing for machine learning.

In this chapter, we will take things further by taking a practical step-by-step data flow to preprocess an example dataset for machine learning. We will start by taking an example dataset that comes preloaded with SageMaker Data Wrangler and then do some basic exploratory data analysis using Data Wrangler built-in analysis. We will also add a couple of custom checks for imbalance and bias in the dataset. Feature engineering is a key step in the machine learning cycle. It includes selecting and transforming raw data features into new features that better represent the underlying problem for the machine learning model. We will create a Data Wrangler flow and define data transformations on our sample dataset to do feature engineering. SageMaker Data Wrangler is a unified data processing tool enabling you to do a complete machine learning cycle, including training a machine learning model and deploying it for inference directly from within the tool. We will export our processed data and train and deploy a model from Data Wrangler.

This chapter covers the following sections:

- Logging in to SageMaker Studio
- Importing data
- Exploratory data analysis

- Adding transformations
- Exporting data
- Training a machine learning model

Technical requirements

If you wish to follow along, which I highly recommend, you will need an **Amazon Web Services** (**AWS**) account. If you do not have an existing account, you can create an AWS account under the Free Tier. The AWS Free Tier provides customers with the ability to explore and try out AWS services free of charge up to specified limits for each service. If your application use exceeds the Free Tier limits, you simply pay standard, pay-as-you-go service rates. In this chapter, we will get started by looking at how to access and get familiar with the SageMaker Data Wrangler user interface. As you follow along, you will use AWS Compute and also end up creating resources in your AWS account. This especially applies to the *Training a machine learning model* section of the chapter, which is both compute-intensive and creates an endpoint that you will have to delete. Please remember to clean up by deleting any unused resources. We will remind you again at the end of the chapter; for now, let's get started.

Step 1 – logging in to SageMaker Studio

In this section, we will cover the steps to log in and navigate inside the AWS console and SageMaker. If you are already familiar with using SageMaker, you can skip this section and move on directly to the next one.

After you have created your account and set up a SageMaker Studio domain and created a user, as covered in *Chapter 4*, you can log in to the AWS console and choose **SageMaker**. You can either navigate to SageMaker in the **All Services** section under **Machine Learning** or start typing `SageMaker` in the search box at the top of the AWS console.

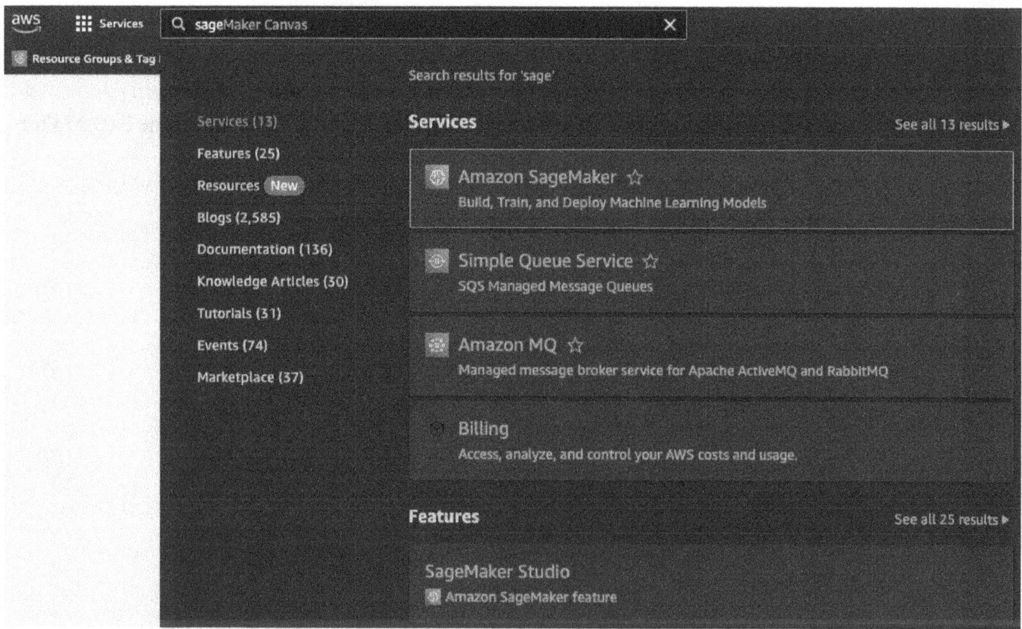

Figure 10.1: AWS console – SageMaker

Once you are on the SageMaker screen, you should see the domain you created in the prerequisite section in *Chapter 4*. Make sure that the status of the domain is **InService** before proceeding. If you do not see a domain at all, verify to make sure you are in the same region where you created your domain. Check and switch your region from the top-right section of the AWS console. Click on the domain name.

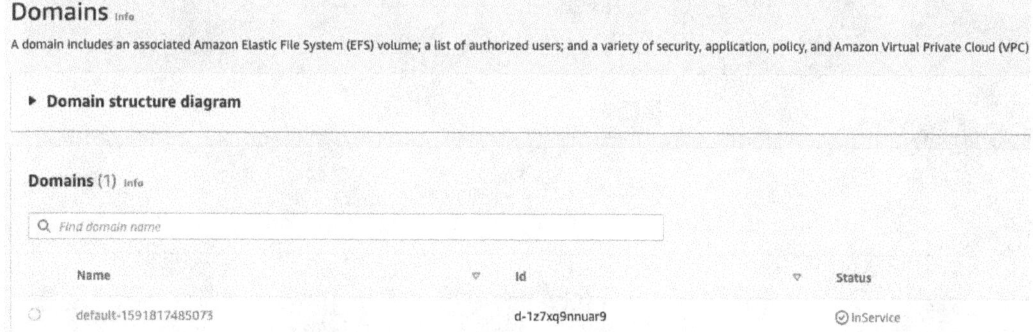

Figure 10.2: The SageMaker domain

This will take you to a list of registered users for the domain. If you followed the prerequisite steps in *Chapter 4*, you will see the user you created here. If you do not see a user, you can use the **Add user** button to create a new SageMaker Studio user. For details, refer to the prerequisite steps in *Chapter 4*. Use the drop-down option on the **Launch** button to select **Studio**. This will take you to the SageMaker Studio landing page.

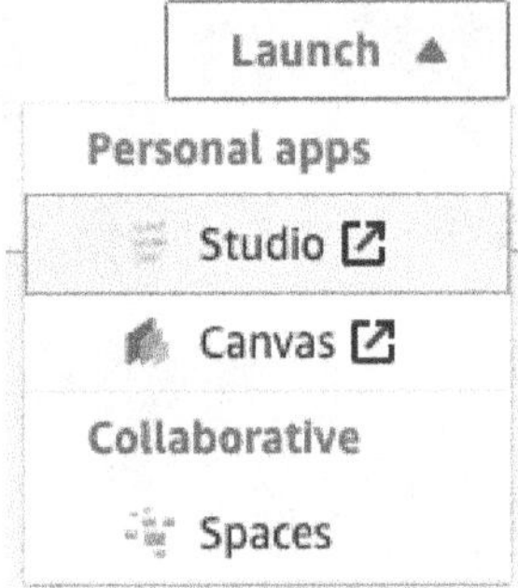

Figure 10.3: SageMaker Studio

If this is your first time logging into SageMaker Studio, it will take a few minutes to create and set up your user environment. On the SageMaker Studio landing page, click on **Import & prepare data visually**. This will take you to the Data Wrangler page and create a new flow.

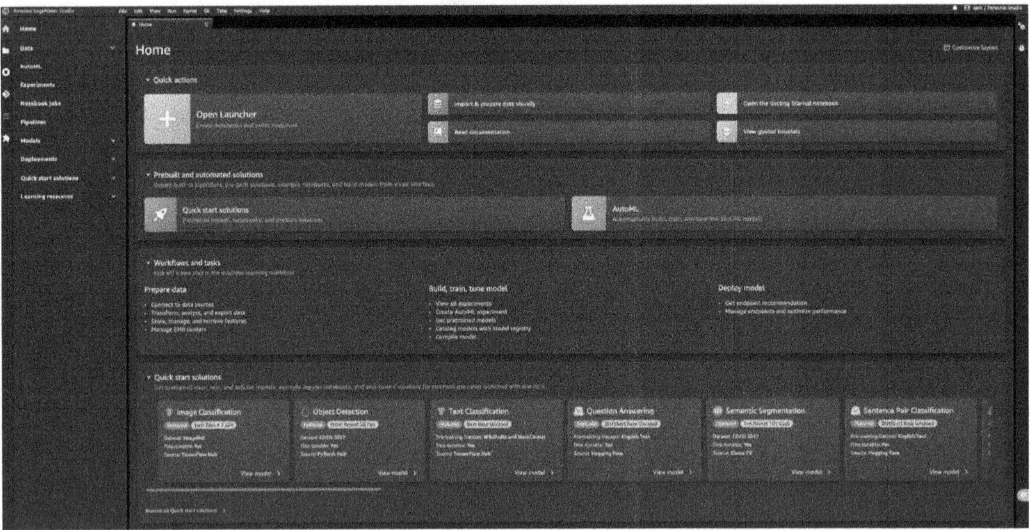

Figure 10.4: The SageMaker Studio landing page

Once you are signed in and have launched Data Wrangler, you will need to get your data into SageMaker. We will cover this in *step 2*.

Step 2 – importing data

Before we can start importing data into SageMaker Data Wrangler, we need to create a connection with our data source. SageMaker Data Wrangler provides out-of-the-box native connectors to Amazon S3, Amazon Athena, Amazon Redshift, Snowflake, Amazon EMR, and Databricks. Besides that, you can also set up new data sources with over 40 SaaS and web applications using Amazon AppFlow, a fully managed integration service that helps you securely transfer data between **software as a service** (**SaaS**) applications. The **Create connection** screen shows the connectors in Data Wrangler, along with additional data sources you can set up using Amazon AppFlow.

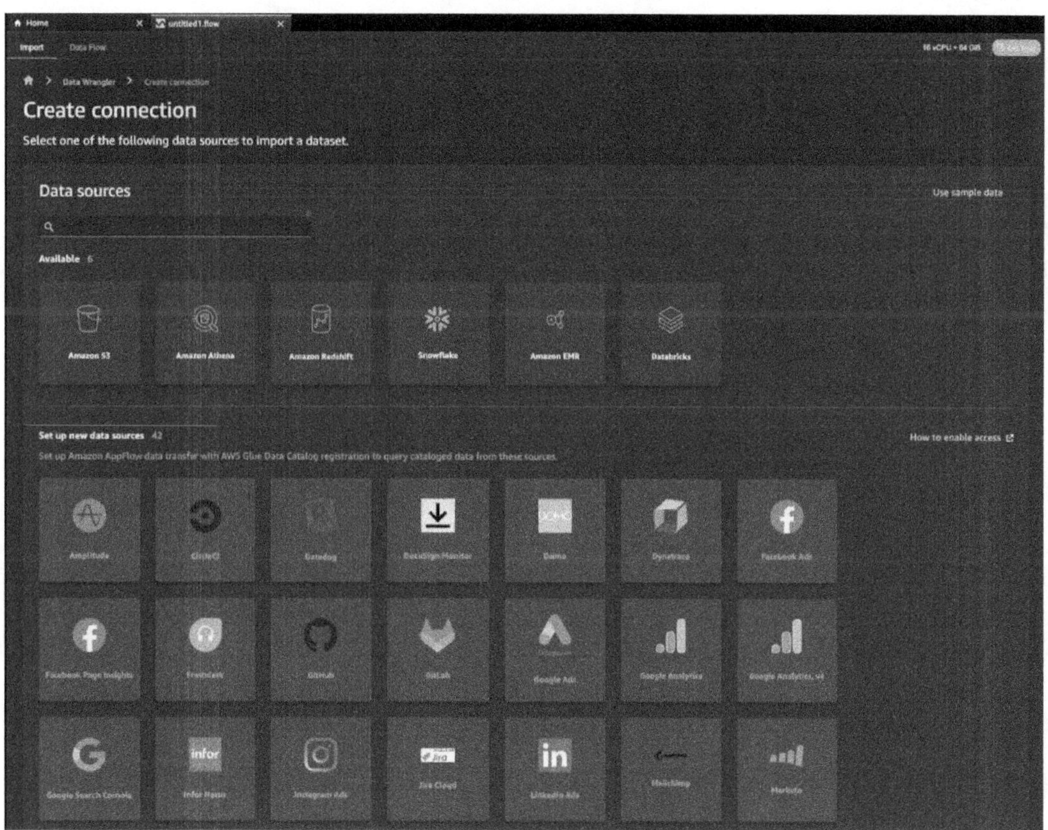

Figure 10.5: Data Wrangler data sources

In this chapter, we will use a publicly available example, the Titanic dataset. The Titanic dataset is considered the "Hello World" of machine learning datasets due to the number of commonly used data processing and machine learning techniques that are possible with this example dataset. We will use a slightly changed version of the Titanic dataset. You can learn more about the dataset here: `https://www.openml.org/search?type=data&sort=runs&id=40945&status=active`. The dataset is available via a public S3 bucket. To use this dataset with Data Wrangler, we can either upload it to an S3 bucket in our AWS account, or we can directly import the dataset directly into Data Wrangler via the **Use sample data** option at the top right of the **Data sources** section. In this chapter, we will use the latter option.

Figure 10.6: Data Wrangler sample data

After you click on **Use sample data**, a Data Wrangler connection is created in the S3 bucket hosting the dataset, and a sample subset of this dataset is loaded into Data Wrangler. This also creates the starting point for your data flow.

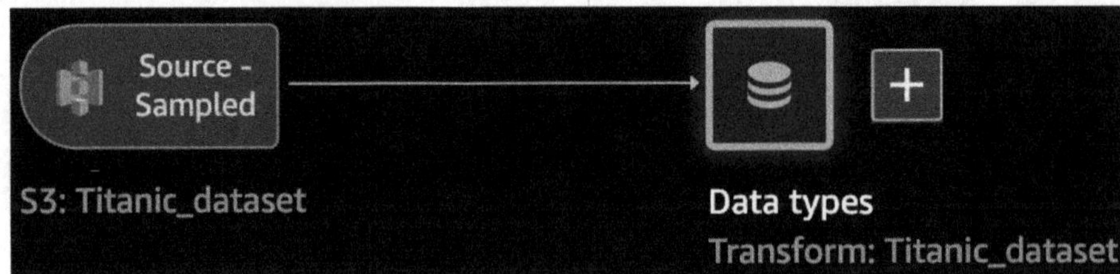

Figure 10.7: Data Wrangler data flow

You can examine the dataset sample by double-clicking on the source, which in our case is **S3**. This will display the first few rows of the dataset along with the headers or column names if they exist. Here, you can also check the data type for each of the features or columns that Data Wrangler has automatically determined.

Source - Sampled · S3: Titanic_dataset

Data Analysis Training NEW

Step 1. S3 Source

Export and train Export data

pclass (string)	survived (string)	name (string)	sex (string)	age (string)	sibsp (string)	parch (string)	ticket (string)	fare (string)	cabin (string)	embarked (string)
1	1	Allen, Miss. Elisabeth W...	female	29	0	0	24160	211.3375	B5	S
1	1	Allison, Master. Hudson...	male	0.9167	1	2	113781	151.55	C22 C26	S
1	0	Allison, Miss. Helen Lor...	female	2	1	2	113781	151.55	C22 C26	S
1	0	Allison, Mr. Hudson Jos...	male	30	1	2	113781	151.55	C22 C26	S
1	0	Allison, Mrs. Hudson J C...	female	25	1	2	113781	151.55	C22 C26	S
1	1	Anderson, Mr. Harry	male	48	0	0	19952	26.55	E12	S
1	1	Andrews, Miss. Kornelia...	female	63	1	0	13502	77.9583	D7	S
1	0	Andrews, Mr. Thomas Jr	male	39	0	0	112050	0	A36	S
1	1	Appleton, Mrs. Edward ...	female	53	2	0	11769	51.4792	C101	S
1	0	Artagaveytia, Mr. Ramon	male	71	0	0	PC 17609	49.5042	?	C
1	0	Astor, Col. John Jacob	male	47	1	0	PC 17757	227.525	C62 C64	C
1	1	Astor, Mrs. John Jacob (...	female	18	1	0	PC 17757	227.525	C62 C64	C
1	1	Aubart, Mme. Leontine ...	female	24	0	0	PC 17477	69.3	B35	C
1	1	Barber, Miss. Ellen 'Nellie'	female	26	0	0	19877	78.85	?	S
1	1	Barkworth, Mr. Algerno...	male	80	0	0	27042	30	A23	S
1	0	Baumann, Mr. John D	male	?	0	0	PC 17318	25.925	?	S
1	0	Baxter, Mr. Quigg Edmo...	male	24	0	1	PC 17558	247.5208	B58 B60	C
1	1	Baxter, Mrs. James (Hel...	female	50	0	1	PC 17558	247.5208	B58 B60	C
1	1	Bazzani, Miss. Albina	female	32	0	0	11813	76.2917	D15	C
1	0	Beattie, Mr. Thomson	male	36	0	0	13050	75.2417	C6	C

Figure 10.8: The dataset data types

You may have noticed that Data Wrangler automatically made certain assumptions about your dataset, such as the file formats, data types, sampling method, and quantity. You can change these by clicking on the **plus** and choosing the **Edit Dataset** option. Data Wrangler also automatically detected our dataset file format, its delimiter, and that the first row contained the header. You can change these settings. For example, you can change the file from **csv** to **Parquet** or change the delimiter from **COMMA** to **space**. Sometimes, your dataset may not have headers, so you can update the header settings here as well. By default, Data Wrangler will choose the **First K** method to sample the dataset. You can change this sampling method to **random** or **stratified**. You can also set the sample size here.

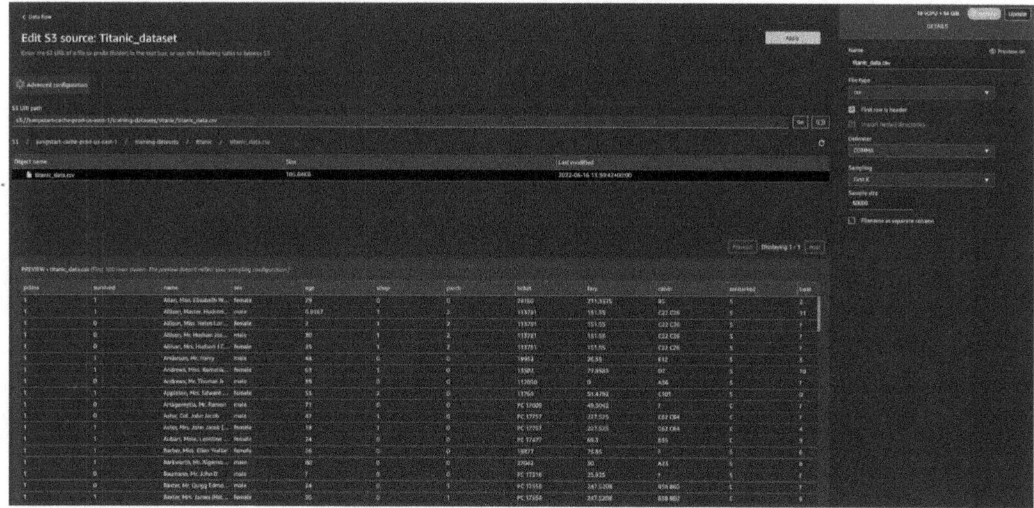

Figure 10.9: Editing the data types and source

A key tip to remember here is that, if you are planning to use Data Wrangler for your model training, you will need to re-import the data if you use sampling here. We will cover model training in the latter part of this chapter. In the next step, we will do some exploratory data analysis to understand our data better.

Exploratory data analysis

Before we do any data transformation or manipulations, we need to get a good understanding of our data. **Exploratory data analysis** (**EDA**) is a crucial step in data science because it allows us to understand the structure and characteristics of the data we're working with. EDA involves the use of various techniques and tools to summarize and visualize data in order to identify patterns, trends, and relationships. It is also important that we perform this step before we do any data transformations or modeling because EDA can help us understand which features are relevant and which are most important for the machine learning problem we are trying to solve. EDA can help you understand the distribution of data and identify any relationships that exist between the features in your dataset. When working with real-world data, you will inevitably encounter data quality issues such as missing data, imbalance in various classes, errors in data collection, and outliers. EDA helps to identify these data quality issues, which can have a detrimental impact on the quality of your machine learning models. Data Wrangler provides commonly used EDA tools via a built-in data analysis report, and you also can generate your own custom data analysis.

Built-in data insights

AWS Data Wrangler provides several commonly used data analysis tools out of the box. In this section, we will look at some of these. You can go to the **Data Analysis** section by clicking on the + button next to the data source icon and choosing **Get Data Insights**.

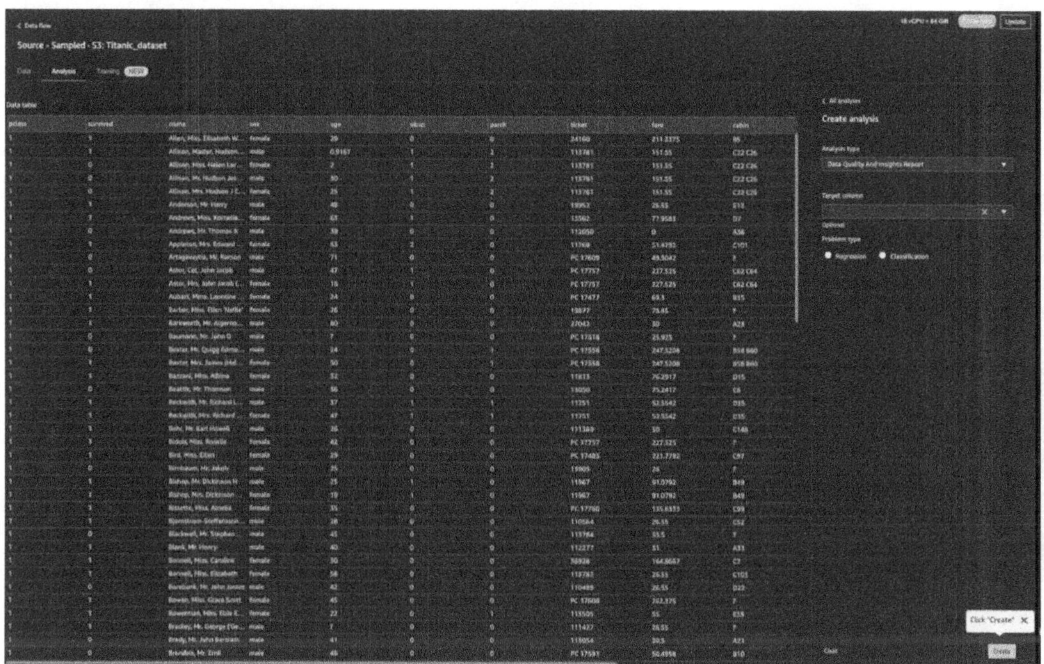

Figure 10.10: Data Wrangler data insights

Let's create a new analysis report:

1. Choose **Data Quality And Insights Report**.
2. Choose your target column or the column that your machine learning model will try to predict.
3. Here, we also choose the type of machine learning problem we will try to solve, whether it is a classification or a regression problem. In our case, we are trying to predict whether a passenger survived the *Titanic* tragedy. We will change the target column to **Survived**, set the problem type to **Classification**, and click on the **Create** button. Data Wrangler will take a couple of minutes to generate the report. This is, of course, dependent on your dataset and sample size.

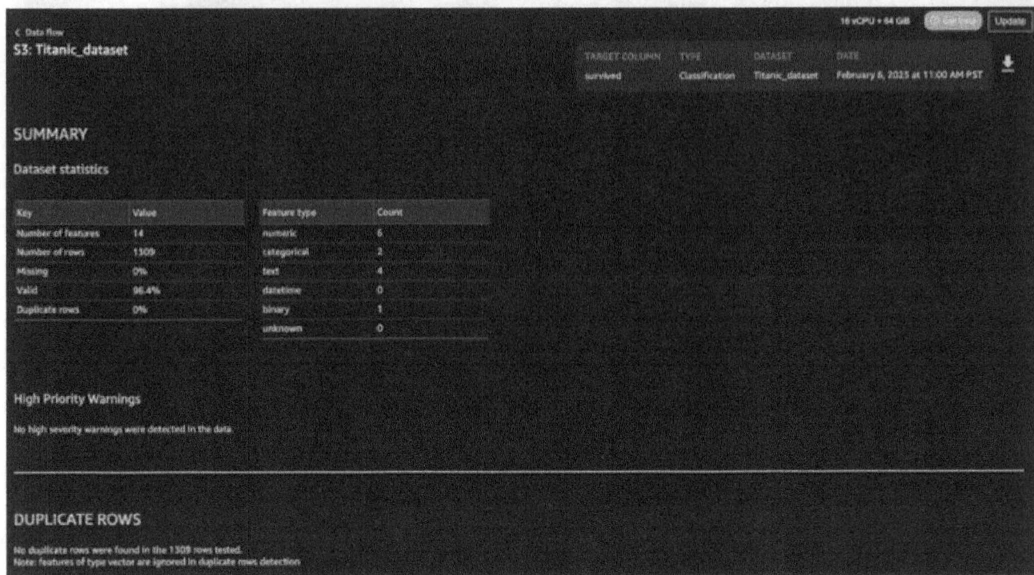

Figure 10.11: The data insights summary

Let's go over the different sections of the report, starting with the top summary. The summary includes key statistics of your dataset and the feature types. Here, we can see the total number of rows in your dataset, the number of missing rows, and the number of duplicate rows, if any. In the **SUMMARY** section, you can also review the number of features in your dataset and their count. If your dataset has critical errors that will significantly affect the quality of your machine learning models, they will display in the **High Priority Warnings** section of the report. An example of a high-priority warning is target leakage. Target leakage occurs when a feature is directly influenced by the target, resulting in high accuracy on the training set but poor performance on test data. To prevent target leakage, it's important to keep the target out of the training process, ensuring that we train the model only on independent features.

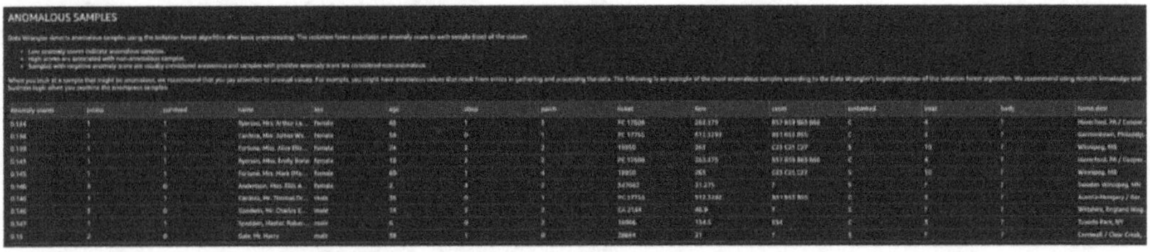

Figure 10.12: Data insights anomalies

The next section of the report shows any anomalies that may be present in our data. Data Wrangler detects anomalous samples using the **Isolation Forest** algorithm after basic preprocessing. The isolation forest algorithm detects anomalies based on how far a data point is from the rest of the data. The algorithm calculates an anomaly score for each record in the dataset. Negative scores are considered an anomaly and higher scores suggest the sample to be non-anomalous. While it is tempting to remove all samples that are classified as anomalies, sometimes, based on the machine learning problem and the dataset, it may be useful to leave the anomalies in the training dataset. In our example dataset, we can see certain records with low anomaly scores, but no negative values. We will leave these samples as part of the training data.

Figure 10.13: A data insights quick model

The target column section tells us about the distribution of the target variable and other relevant information, such as missing records. In our example dataset, we can see that the number of people who survived the *Titanic* tragedy is less than the number of people who did not make it. While there is a slight class imbalance in the dataset, it is not significant enough to be detrimental to our machine learning model. In cases where you find a significant class imbalance, such as a scenario where you have a certain class overrepresented or underrepresented, consider other data balancing techniques such as under-sampling the majority class or over-sampling the minority class.

The quick model section of the report is generated by automatically training an XGBoost model on a sample of your dataset. The quick model automatically holds 20% of the sample data and uses it for testing. The purpose of the quick model is to provide an estimate of the expected predicted quality of the model. Depending on the type of machine learning problem (i.e., classification or regression), the quick model generates various metrics to evaluate the model quality. In our example, since we have a classification problem, we can see metrics such as accuracy, F1 score, precision, recall, and AUC. For example, we can see an F1 score of .99 on the training dataset and a score of .96 on the validation dataset.

A higher F1 score means the model has better accuracy, with a better balance of precision and recall, indicating fewer false positives and false negatives, thus performing better at its classification task. As we are working with a regression problem, besides these key metrics, the quick model section also generates a confusion matrix that compares the actual class and predicted class for our sample dataset.

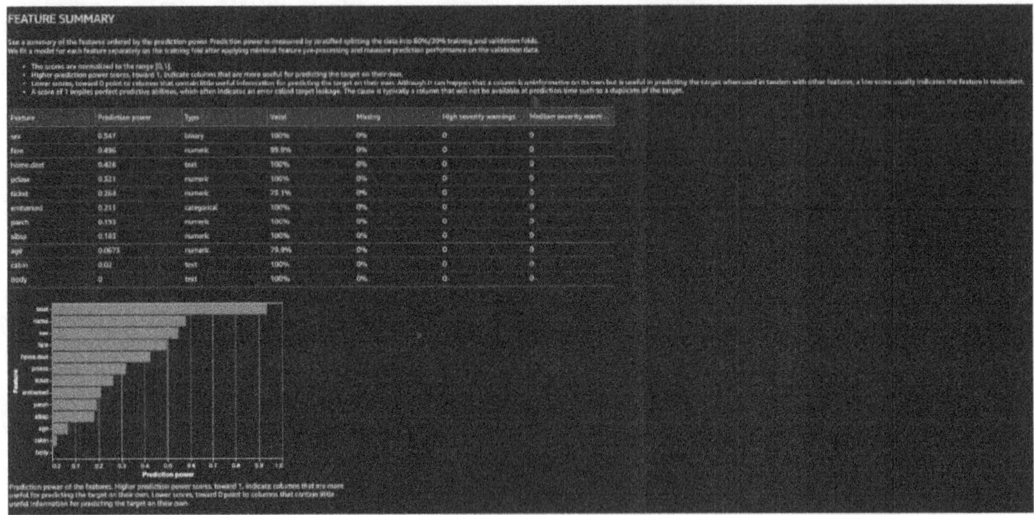

Figure 10.14: Data insights feature summary

The feature summary section of the report generates the feature importance or the prediction power of a feature. This helps make our machine learning models explainable. We normalize the values of feature importance on a scale of 0 to 1. Values closer to 1 show that the feature is highly important in the final prediction. A value equal to 1 can show target leakage. In contrast, lower scores, toward 0, point to columns that contain little useful information to predict the target. You might decide to feature-engineer these or drop them altogether.

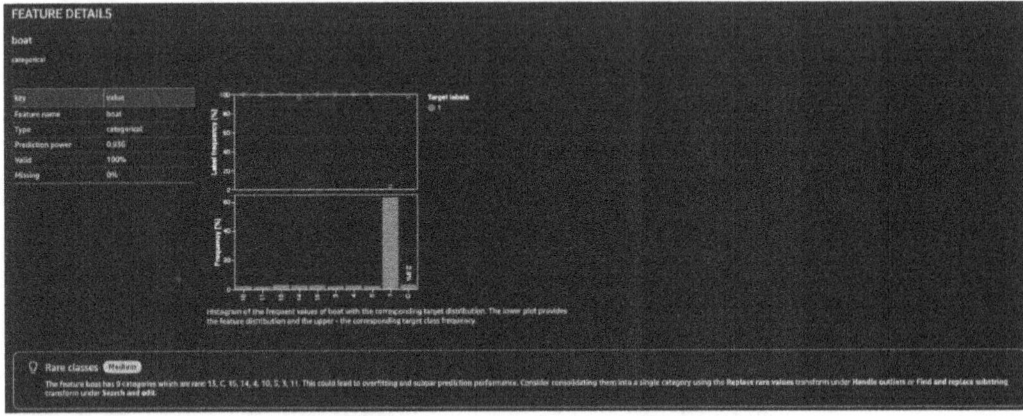

Figure 10.15: Data insights feature details

The **FEATURE DETAILS** section lists key information for each feature in our dataset. For example, it can highlight columns that may contain errors or unclean data. We can see a feature "boat," which is a categorical feature with nine categories. This is rare and could point to an error in data collection. During our data transformation stage, we might decide to drop or apply feature engineering to this column.

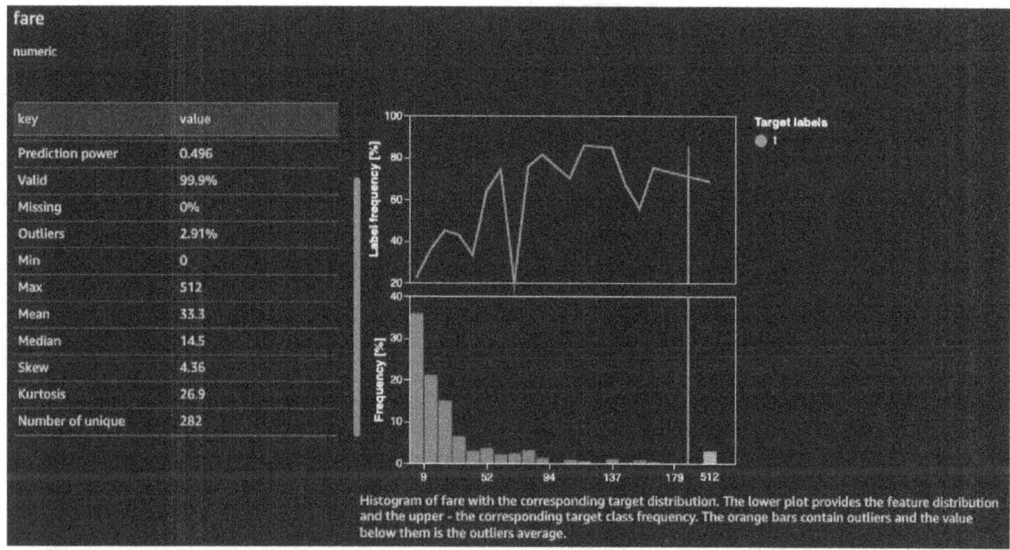

Figure 10.16: Data insights numeric features

Similarly, for numeric features, the **FEATURE DETAILS** section can list key descriptive statistics, such as the mean and median values besides the maximum, minimum, missing, and outlier values. You also get a frequency distribution for the values of these numeric features.

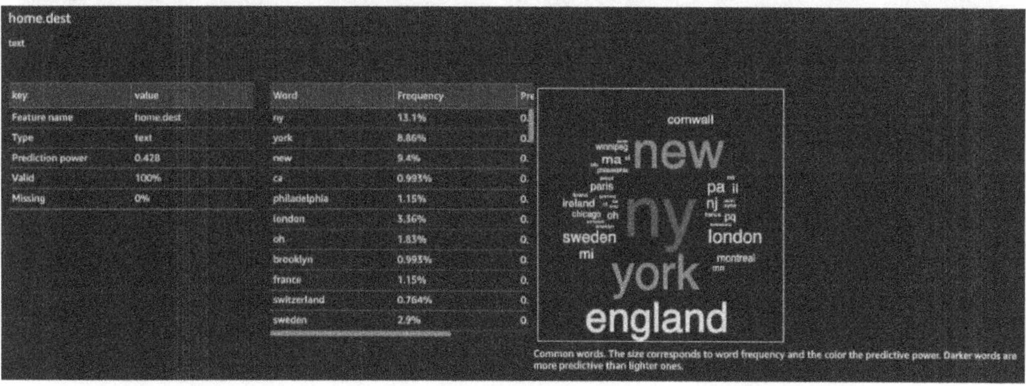

Figure 10.17: Data insights text-based features

Though we are dealing with structured tabular data, some columns contain pure text data, such as the destination or name feature. While it may seem obvious to drop these features, it might be possible to apply data transformation and extract useful information that can help make better predictions. When working with these features, the **FEATURE DETAILS** section of the report can tokenize the features that contain text and display useful information such as word frequency that can help us to make feature transformation decisions.

The **FEATURE DETAILS** section is an important place to determine what specific feature transformation steps we will add to our data wrangling process.

Step 3 – creating data analysis

As we covered in the preceding section, the built-in data analysis report that is available out of the box with Data Wrangler covers a lot of commonly used EDA in machine learning; however, you can also create additional analysis and custom analysis in Data Wrangler. In this section, we will cover some of these:

- **Target leakage** is a common issue in machine learning, where information from the target variable or outcome is used to create features or predictors, resulting in overly optimistic or biased models. Target leakage occurs when a feature that is created using information that is not available during the time of prediction or decision-making is used to train a predictive model. Target leakage analysis is crucial because it helps ensure that predictive models are built on valid and unbiased data. In Data Wrangler, you can generate a target leakage analysis by clicking on the + icon next to the datasets and choosing **Add Analysis**. In the **Analysis Type** dropdown, choose **Target Leakage**. Then, choose the problem type and an option from the **Target** dropdown.

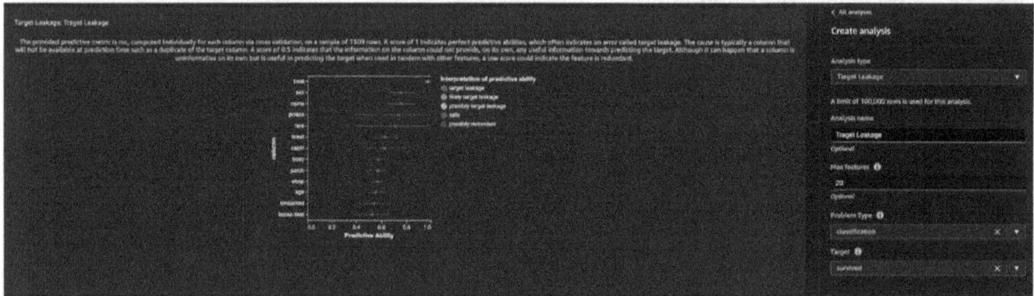

Figure 10.18: Target leakage

As you can see, in our dataset, the **boat** feature has a likely target leakage issue. The **boat** feature contains the lifeboat number if the passenger was on one. It is possible that this feature is not available for all the records of our dataset and was populated post-prediction. We will look at how to handle this in the data transformation and feature engineering step.

- **Scatter plot analysis**: Scatter plots represent the relationship between two or three variables. In our example dataset, we will use the scatter plot to visualize the relationship between **fare**, **age**, and the target variable, **survived**. You can add a new analysis in the same way as you added the previous analysis. In the **Analysis type** dropdown, choose **Scatter Plot**, and then choose **age** as the *X* axis and **fare** as the *Y* axis. To add the target as another variable, choose **survived** under the **Color by** dropdown.

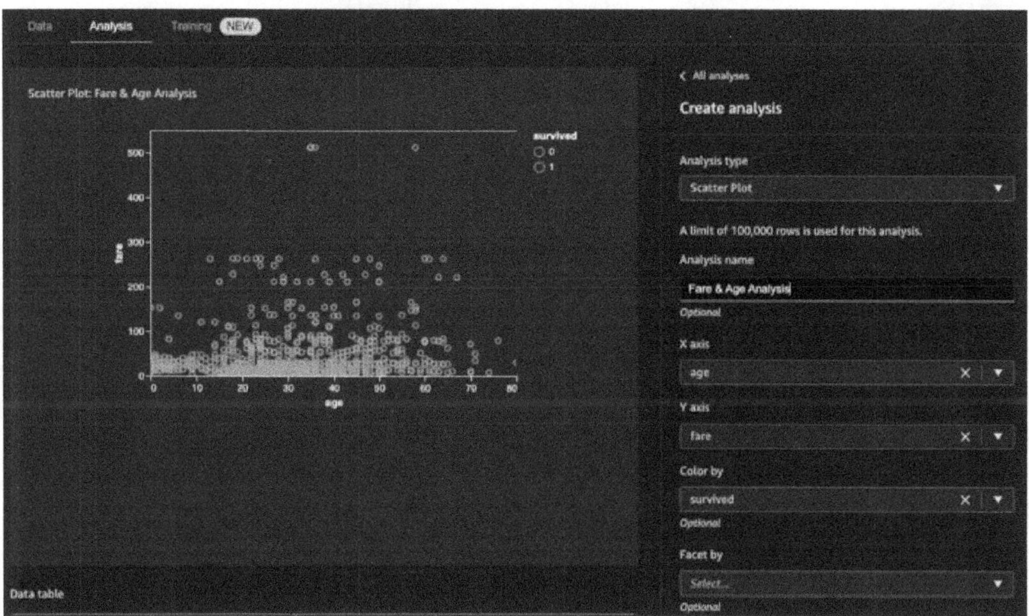

Figure 10.19: Scatter plot analysis

While there may not be a clear trend or relationship between age and fare, we can observe some patterns in the scatter plot that provide additional insights into the data. For example, we can find that passengers who paid higher fares had a higher survival rate. Alternatively, we can find that children had a higher survival rate compared to adults, showing a potential age-related factor in survival.

- **Custom visualizations**: Besides using the pre-defined analysis and visualizations, you can also create your own custom data visualizations in Data Wrangler using Altair. Altair is a Python data visualization library that allows users to easily create interactive visualizations with concise and intuitive code. It also integrates well with other Python data analysis libraries, such as pandas, NumPy, and SciPy, making it a popular choice for data scientists and analysts. Data Wrangler uses the `df` variable to store the dataframe, which is accessible by the user. You can add a custom visualization similar to the preceding by clicking on the + button of any step and choosing **Add analysis**. Set the analysis type as **Custom Visualization**. Here, we will create a custom visualization to show the age distribution and the average age of the passengers in our Titanic dataset. Use the following code snippet in the code section:

```
# Table is available as variable `df`
import altair as alt
df = df.iloc[:100]
df = df.assign(count=df.groupby('age').age.transform('count'))
df = df[["age", "count"]]
base = alt.Chart(df)
bar = base.mark_bar().encode(x=alt.X('age', bin=True),
y=alt.Y('count'))
rule = base.mark_rule(color='red').encode(x='mean(age):Q',
size=alt.value(5))
chart = bar+rule
```

You must also provide an output variable (chart) to store an Altair output chart. Once you click **Preview**, you should see a chart similar to the one in the following figure. This will create a histogram of the binned age of all the rows in our dataset on the *X* axis and the count on the *Y* axis. It will find the average and visually depict that in the histogram as a red line.

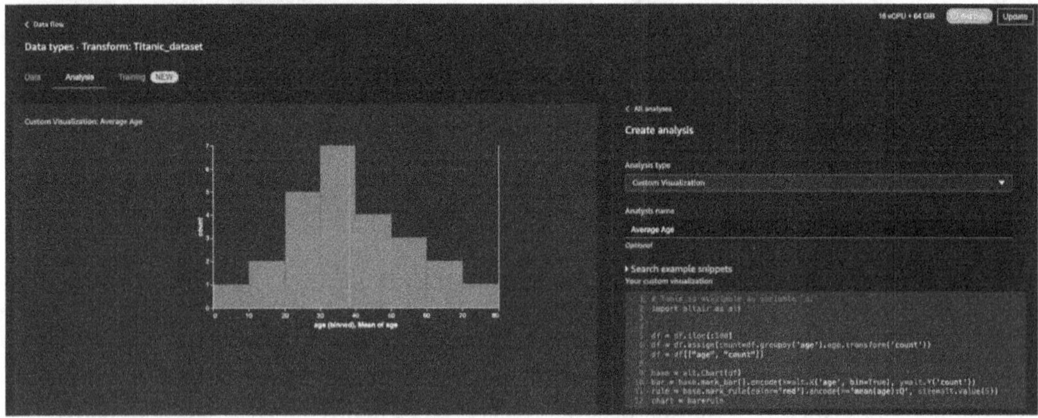

Figure 10.20: Custom visualization

- **Multicollinearity**: Understanding and addressing multicollinearity is important in data analysis to ensure that statistical models are accurate, reliable, and useful to make informed decisions. Multicollinearity is a high correlation between two or more independent variables in your dataset. It can make it difficult to isolate the effects of individual independent variables on the dependent variable. Last but not least, multicollinearity can also make models harder to interpret because when there are correlations between the independent variables, it is hard to understand the unique contribution of each independent variable. Data Wrangler provides out-of-the-box analysis options to detect multicollinearity in your data. There are a few different options to analyze multicollinearity. Let's see how to use some of these pre-built analyses on our Titanic dataset. The **variance inflation factor** (**VIF**) is a measure of collinearity among variables. We calculate it by solving a regression problem to predict one variable when given the rest. A VIF score is a positive number that is greater than or equal to 1, and a score of 1 means the variable is completely independent of the others. The larger the score, the more dependent it is. As a rule of thumb, we can drop or feature-engineer features with a VIF score of greater than 1. To create multicollinearity analysis with VIF, choose **Add Analysis** and then **Multicollinearity**.

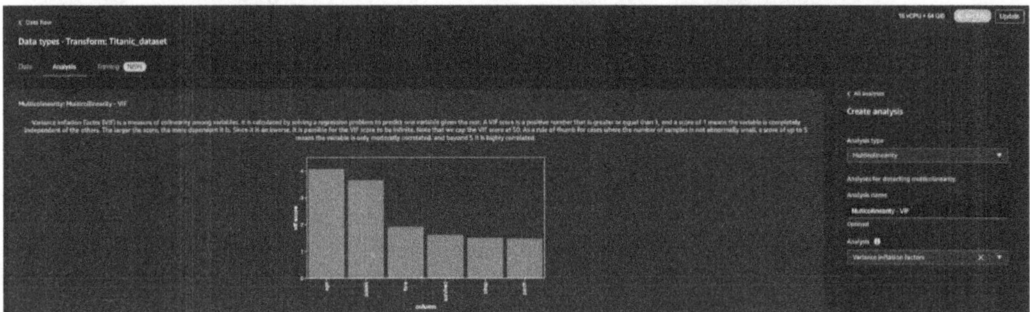

Figure 10.21: Multicollinearity using VIF

Once you click on the preview, you will see a histogram that has the feature names on the *X* axis and the VIF score on the *Y* axis. In our example, we can see that we do not have any features that have multicollinearity based on VIF.

- Besides VIF, there are a couple of other multicollinearity analyses that you can choose out of the box with Data Wrangler. Let's look at **Lasso feature selection analysis**. The Lasso method involves adding a penalty term to the regression model that shrinks the coefficients of the independent variables toward zero. This penalty term can help to identify which independent variables are most important to predict the dependent variable and can also help to address issues of multicollinearity. To use the Lasso feature selection method in Data Wrangler, choose the **Multicollinearity** analysis as discussed previously and then set **Analysis** as **Lasso feature selection**. You can optionally choose the L1 magnitude, which is the penalty term; the default value is **1**. Next, we set the problem type as **Classification** and the label column as **Survived**. This will create a baseline regression model, making all the independent variables in the dataset where the regularization parameter is set to be sufficiently large, causing some of the coefficients to be shrunk toward zero. This will create a histogram with the most important features – that is, features that have a non-zero coefficient.

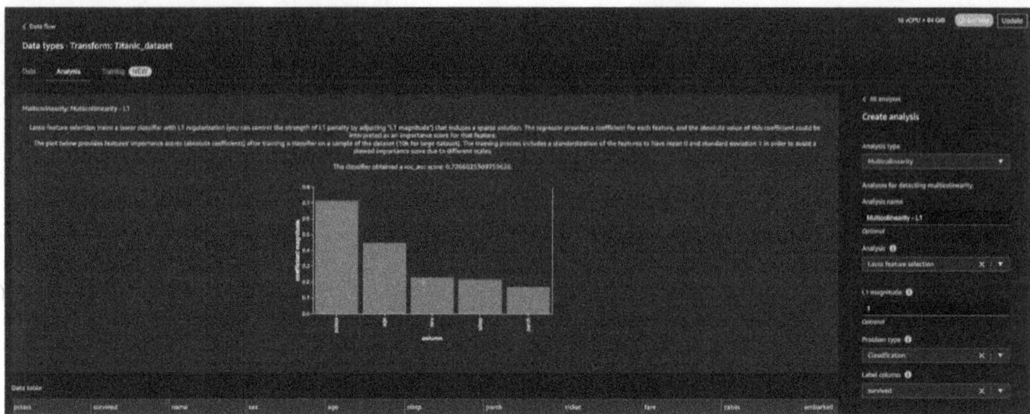

Figure 10.22: Multicollinearity using Lasso feature selection

Check the correlations between the selected independent variables to determine whether there are any issues of multicollinearity. By using the Lasso feature selection method in this way, you can identify and address multicollinearity in a regression model, which can help to improve its accuracy and reliability.

Besides the analysis that we covered here, Data Wrangler has the capability to analyze other specific types of datasets, such as time-series data. These let you do an additional analysis for anomaly detection and detecting seasonal trends. Now that you have a good understanding of your data and the underlying patterns, you can move on to the next step of modifying your data by adding transformations.

Step 4 – adding transformations

As part of your data analysis, you might have noticed elements of your dataset that you want to change or transform. The goal of data transformation is to make data more suitable for modeling, to improve the performance of machine learning algorithms, or to handle missing or corrupted values. Data transformations for machine learning can include things such as normalization, standardization, data encoding, and binning. Not all datasets are alike, and not all transformations apply to all datasets. The goal of data analysis is to identify specific transformations for your dataset. While we typically apply data transformation as an early step in the machine learning pipeline, before data is used to train a model, in real-world machine learning, we continually monitor our model performance and apply transformations as necessary. After you have imported and inspected your dataset in Data Wrangler, you can start adding transformations to your data flow. You may have noticed that some columns in our dataset do not have the correct data type associated with them. For example, the `age` feature in our dataset has a `String` type instead of `Numeric`. Before we apply transformations, we recommend reviewing and fixing the data types for all the features in our dataset.

You can review the data type that Data Wrangler automatically assigned to your features.

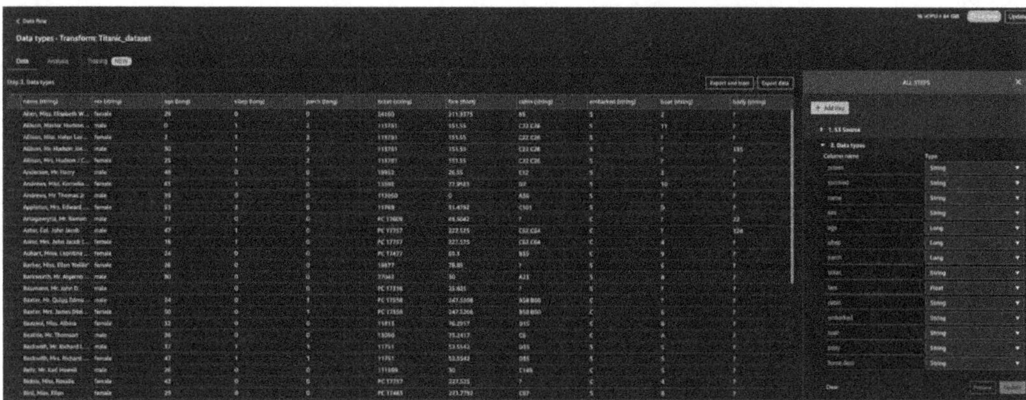

Figure 10.23: Data source data types

You can use the following steps to do this:

1. Go to the data flow screen and double-click on the **Data types** box. This will open a section that lists all your features, along with the automatically inferred data type for each of those features. The right side of the screen will also display a preview of your dataset in real time.
2. You can use the **Type** dropdown to change the datatype of a particular feature. Let's do some of these before moving ahead. Here, we will change the data type of **age**, the siblings (**sibsp**), and the parents (**parch**) to Long and the **age** feature to **Float**. In my case, Data Wrangler automatically classified all these features as **String**. If you try this in your account, you may have a slightly different result. Once you pick the data type you want for the features, you can preview it using the **Preview** button.
3. Once you are satisfied with the changes, you can click on the **Update** button to apply the changes.

Categorical encoding

After dropping the features in the preceding section, we still have two features in our example dataset that have text data representing categories, the **sex** and **boat** features. We will use categorical encoding to transform the **sex** feature. Categorical encoding is a common feature engineering technique that converts categorical data, which represents a set of discrete values, into numerical data that can be used for machine learning models. Categorical encoding is necessary because most machine learning algorithms work with numerical data, and categorical data cannot be directly used for many machine learning models. There are several common techniques for categorical encoding, such as "one-hot encoding," where each category value is converted into a new column and assigned 1 or 0 to the column. For example, the **sex** feature could be one-hot encoded to two new columns, `sex_male` and `sex_female`, with each column containing a 1 or 0 depending on the original value of the `sex` feature. Label encoding is another commonly used categorical encoding method that assigns a unique integer value to each category. For example, in our case, if we apply label encoding to the **sex** feature, we would end up with a value of 1 and 2 for `female` and `male` values, respectively. Since we are working with numbers, a higher value can be associated with the machine learning model that has a higher positive or negative correlation to our target, which we do not want for this feature. Besides one-hot encoding and label encoding, other categorical encoding methods include count encoding, which replaces each category with the number of times it appears in the dataset, and target encoding, which replaces each category with the mean of the target variable for that category. For now, let's apply one-hot encoding to the **sex** feature. We will start by adding a new transform step by clicking on the + sign next to the **Drop column** button in the data flow.

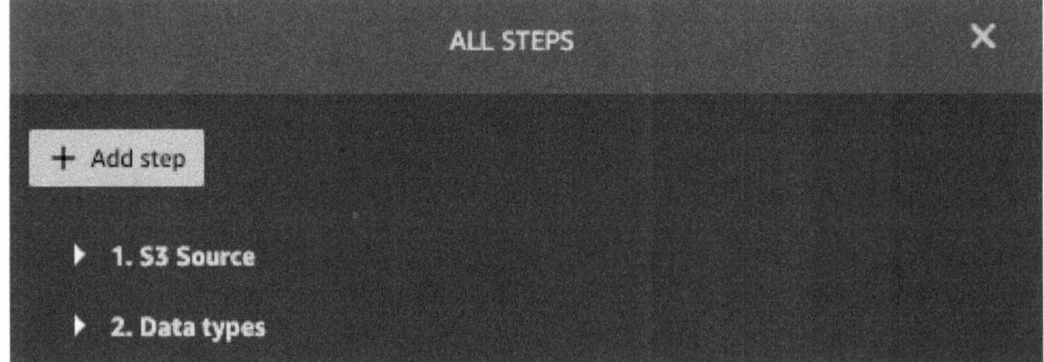

Figure 10.24: Data transform – Add step

Next, click the **Add step** button and choose the **ENCODE CATEGORICAL** section. Here, you can choose the type of encoding from the **Transform** dropdown. We will choose **One-hot encode**. We will specify the input column, which in our case is **sex**. Next, specify how you want to handle missing values in that column. You can either choose to keep them, skip them, or end the transform process with an error if it encounters missing values. You can preview the transformation, and once you are satisfied, you can click on the **Add** button to add the new transformation step to your flow.

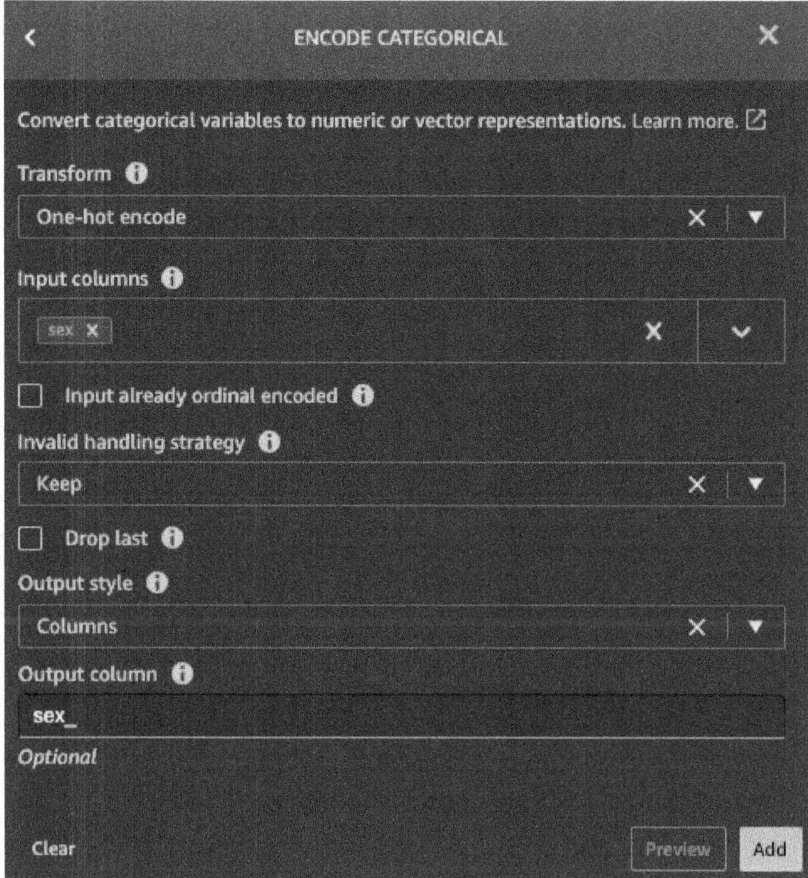

Figure 10.25: Data Transform – one-hot encoding

Check the data flow in the visualizer to make sure everything looks as expected. You should see an additional step now for one-hot encoding.

Custom transformation

Data Wrangler has several commonly used built-in transformations that are available out of the box, without the need to write code from scratch. We covered two of these in the previous sections – first, when we dropped redundant or irrelevant features from our dataset using the drop column transformation. The other built-in transformation we used was to apply one-hot encoding, using the categorical encoding transformation on the **sex** feature of the DataFrame. Besides these, there are other built-in transformations to work with text data and time-series data, handle missing and outlier data, and apply common data engineering tasks such as doing dimensionality reduction and working within balanced datasets. However, there might be scenarios where you would need to do transformations on your data outside of the built-in transformations. Data Wrangler provides you with the ability to do this via **Custom Transformations**, where you can provide your own custom code in PySpark, PySparSQL, and Python pandas and as Python user-defined functions. It is important to note the dataset size before choosing the specific type of custom transformation code that you want to use. For example, if you choose Python (pandas), your dataset should fit in the memory of a single instance. If you have a larger dataset, choose to provide PySpark code instead, which enables you to split your data across multiple instances and aggregate the results. In our example, the Titanic dataset has a **boat** feature that contains the lifeboat number of a passenger, if they could get on one. While the lifeboat number in itself does not hold significant information, a passenger having access to a lifeboat significantly increased their chances of survival. We will use a custom transformation to generate a new feature for our dataset that specifies whether a passenger had access to a lifeboat or not. The following custom Python code snippet does exactly that. It creates a new feature, **Lifeboat Exists**, and checks whether the **boat** feature has a value, and if it does, it adds a value of 1, and if it does not, it inserts 0. Finally, it drops the existing **boat** feature, as we no longer need it:

```
# Table is available as variable `df`
# Assign a target value to check, in our case '?' and use an escape as
this is a special character
target_value = '\?'
# Create a new column that will check if value exists for boat number
df['lifeboat_exists'] = (~df['boat'].str.contains(target_value,
na=False)).astype(int)
# Drop the existing "boat" column
df.drop('boat', axis=1, inplace=True)
```

Add a custom transformation in Data Wrangler using the following steps:

1. Go to the Data Wrangler flow to add a new transform step by clicking on the + sign next to the **Drop column** step in the data flow.
2. Next, click the **Add step** button and choose the **Custom Transformation** section. Here, we will give an optional name for your custom transformation step; we will call it `Lifeboat check`.
3. Then, we will choose the type; since we have a relatively small dataset, we will choose Python (pandas). You will get a warning message reminding you to check the dataset size and make sure you can fit it into the memory of a single machine.
4. You can then paste the code from the previous section. To make sure you do not have any errors, click on the **Preview** button and ensure everything looks alright. You should see a new column created, `lifeboat_exists`, and the previous `boat` column should no longer exist.
5. Once you are satisfied with the results, click on the **Add** button to add this transformation as an additional step in your data flow. You can also review your data flow in the visualizer as before.

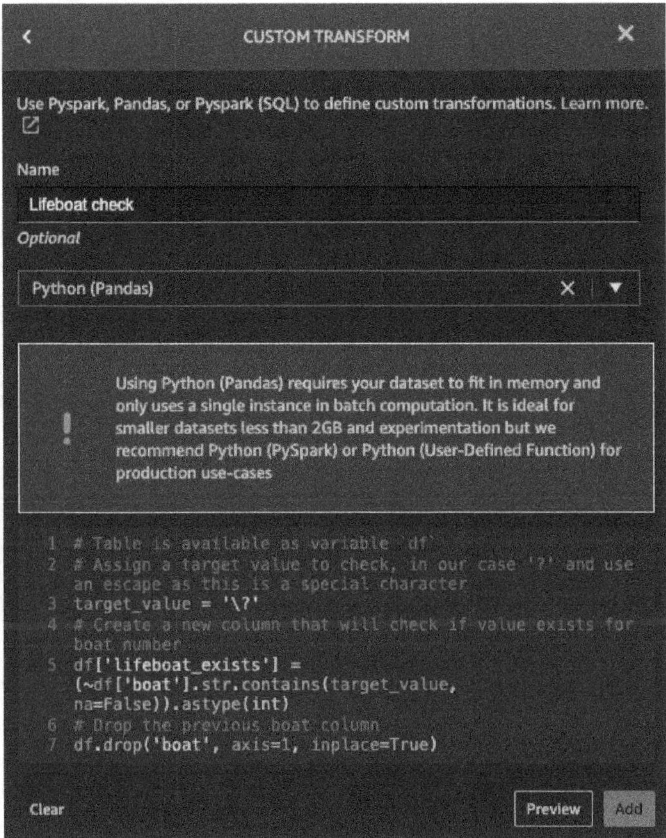

Figure 10.26: Custom Transform – Lifeboat check

The `cabin` feature of the dataset is another tricky feature. At the outset, the feature may not contain relevant information. However, as you further analyze the dataset, you may notice some correlation between the target. In other words, the survival chances of a passenger may be impacted by whether they were in a cabin and their cabin category. One challenge with the feature is that it has a high number of categories and a straightforward encoding might create too many columns, which in turn leads to a problem of dimensionality. To solve this, we use another commonly used data science technique called binning. Binning is a data preprocessing technique used to transform a continuous or categorical variable into a categorical variable with fewer categories, or `bins`. This can make it easier to analyze the data, identify patterns, and make predictions, particularly when dealing with large datasets or noisy data. Here, we will again use the **Custom Transformation** feature to implement binning in Python via the following code:

```
import pandas as pd
# define the number of bins you want to create
num_bins = 5
```

```
df['cabin_bin'] = pd.cut(pd.factorize(df['cabin'])[0], num_bins,
labels=False)
# Drop the existing "cabin" column
df.drop('cabin', axis=1, inplace=True)
```

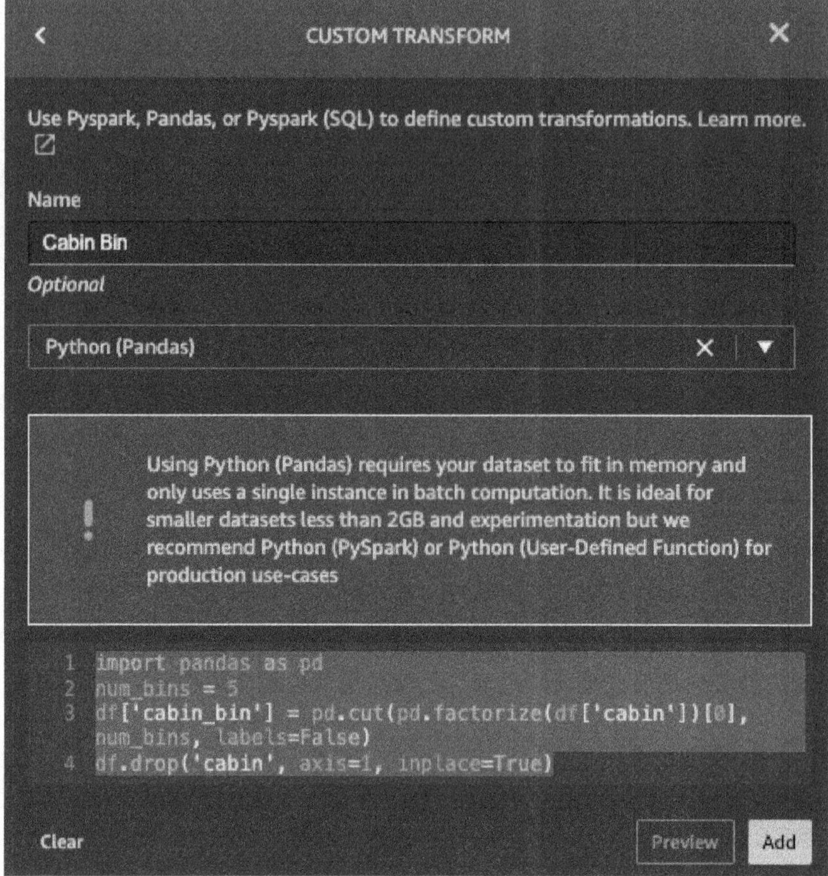

Figure 10.27: Custom Transform – Cabin Bin

You can add this transformation step by choosing a new custom transformation, similar to how we did for the lifeboat check.

Numeric scaling

Machine learning algorithms such as linear regression, logistic regression, neural networks, and so on that use gradient descent as an optimization technique require data to be scaled. There are two ways you can scale the features in your dataset. You can either apply normalization or you can choose standardization. The decision to use normalization or standardization depends on the normalization of the distribution of the features. We use standardization for features with a normal distribution. If the features have a skewed distribution, normalization may be more appropriate. Normalization scales the features to a range of 0 to 1, while standardization scales the features to have a mean of 0 and a standard deviation of 1. In our case, **fare** is highly skewed, and **age** is closer to the normal distribution. For the sake of simplicity, we will apply normalization to both these features. To apply scaling in Data Wrangler, go to the Data Wrangler flow to add a new transform step by clicking on the + sign next to the last step in your data flow. Here, it is the transformation step for creating bins. Next, click the **Add step** button and choose the **Process numeric** section. Here, choose **Min-max scaler** as the scaler. For Input columns, select **age** and **fare**. Specify the **Min** and **Max** values. We keep them as 0 and 1. Optionally, give the prefix for the new input columns as **scaled_**. Hit the **Preview** button to make sure that the data looks correct.

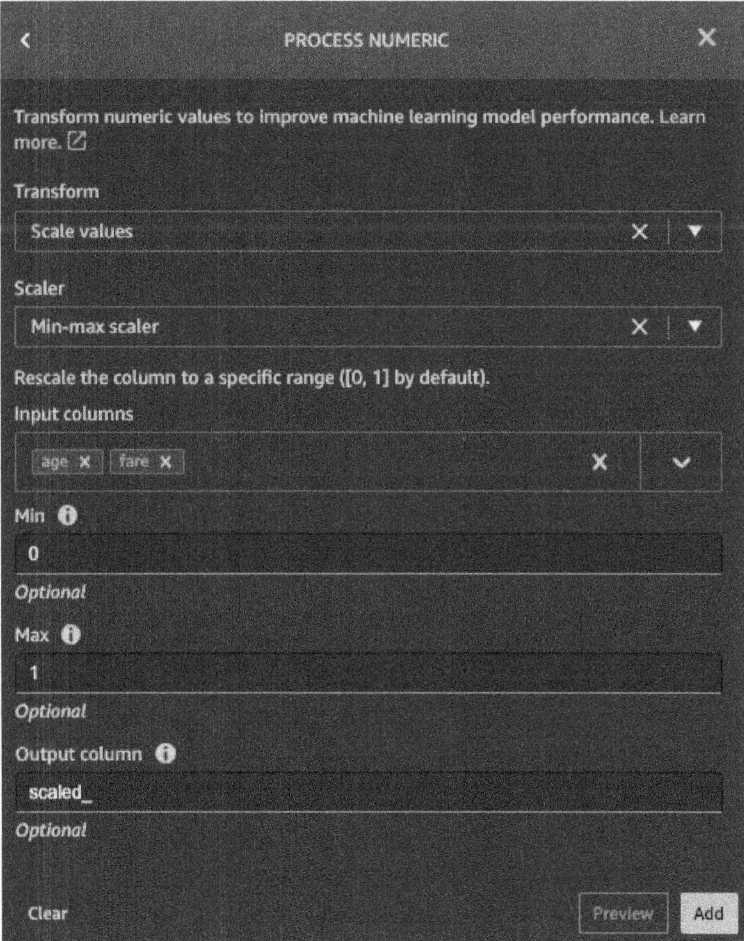

Figure 10.28: Scale values

Once you are satisfied with the results, click on the **Add** button to add this new transformation to your data flow. As usual, you can verify the flow in the Data Wrangler visualizer.

Dropping columns

Now that we have applied several transformations, there are likely columns and features in our dataset that are redundant or no longer needed. Let's review them now. Picking the right features and dropping irrelevant or redundant features are crucial steps in building a machine learning model because they can significantly affect the model's performance and the quality of the predictions it makes. While feature selection directly improves the accuracy of the model by preventing overfitting issues, it also helps to keep the model simple and easier to explain, as well as reduce the training time, leading to cost and performance efficiencies. In other words, adding too many features may cause a complex model that may overfit on the training data and be difficult to explain and train. But how do you choose which features to drop and which to keep? Choosing the columns or features from a dataset often depends on the specific machine learning problem and the analysis that you do. Let's look at some features in our example dataset that we could consider dropping, starting with the **name** feature. While we may deduce meaningful information about a passenger's name, such as the sex of the passenger perhaps, it is unlikely to have any direct impact on whether the passenger survived, and it would be difficult to derive any meaningful insights from this column. In addition, we already have the sex of the passenger as a distinct feature in the dataset, so it makes the information irrelevant. Similarly, the **ticket** number is unlikely to affect survival and may not provide any useful insights. We could try deriving other useful information from the **ticket** feature, such as the class of passenger, but that information is also already available in the dataset as a distinct feature. This also is not likely to influence the chances of survival. We will drop the **home destination** feature, which shows the final destination of the passenger, for similar reasons. The **body** feature represents the body number of the recovered body of the passenger. A value for that feature would show the person would not have survived the tragedy. The **boat** feature has the lifeboat number of the passenger, which would also show that the passenger survived. Both these features can be tricky. In our example, we will drop the **body** feature as it is a strong and independent predictor of our target. We will, however, keep the **boat** feature. Finally, since we have already encoded the **sex** feature and scaled the **age** and **fare** features, we also no longer need those. To drop a feature, click on the + sign next to the last step and choose **Add Transform**. Data Wrangler refers to each data transformation we define as a step. On the **All Steps** screen, click on **Add step** to create a new transformation. This will bring up the **Add Transform** screen. Here, we will get a comprehensive list of out-of-the-box transformations that Data Wrangler provides. Let's choose the **MANAGE COLUMNS** section and then choose **Drop column** from the **Transform** dropdown.

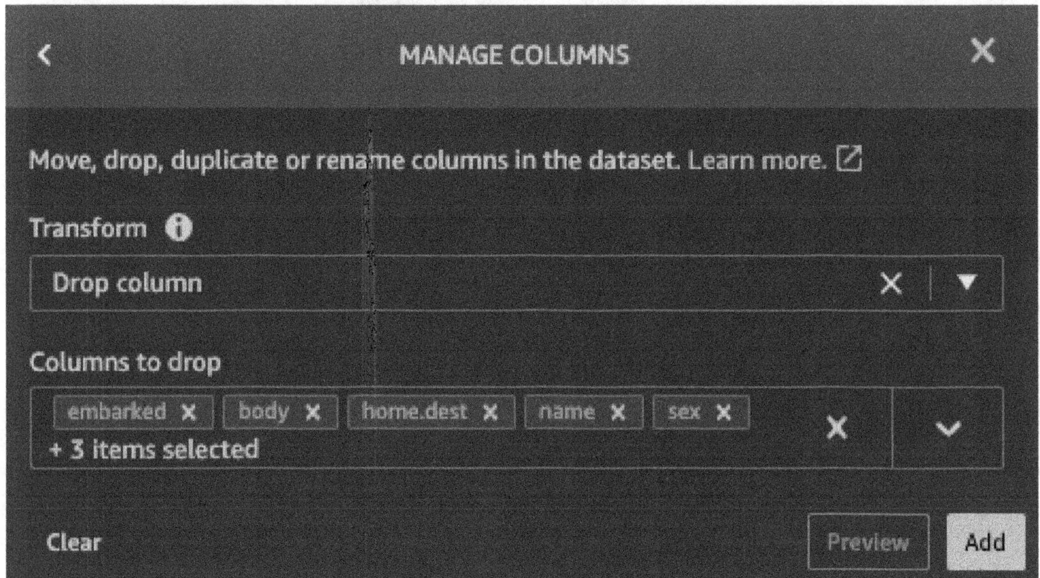

Figure 10.29: Drop column

The **Drop column** transformation allows you to select the columns you want to drop from your dataset. Once we have selected the features, we can preview the changes and click on the **Add** button to add the data transformation to our flow. You can also go back and check to see whether a new step added to your data flow in the data flow visualizer. Once we have defined all our transformations, we are ready to actually apply them and export our data. We will cover this in *step 5*.

Step 5 – exporting data

So far, we have performed several analyses on our dataset. We have also defined several feature engineering data transformations. However, it is important to remember that we have made no changes to the actual data itself yet. We have defined the data flow, which contains a series of analysis and transformation steps that can be executed before we build machine learning models. If you check the data flow, it will look something similar to the following:

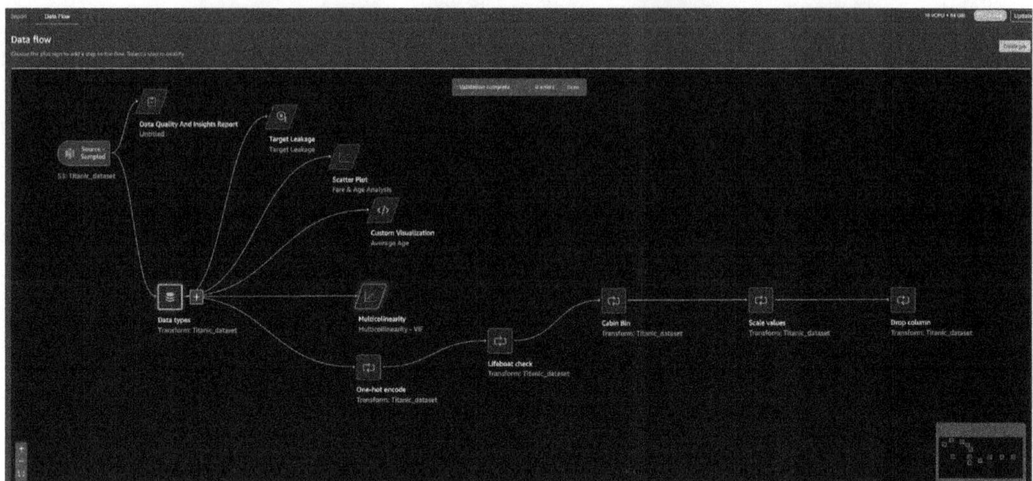

Figure 10.30: Completed data flow

Data Wrangler provides you with several options to export your data flow:

- **Exporting to S3**: Data Wrangler gives you the ability to export your data to a location within an Amazon S3 bucket. You can do this by clicking the = button next to a data transform step and choosing **Export To**, and then **Export to S3**. Data Wrangler will create a Jupyter notebook that contains the code to do all the transformations as defined in your data flow and export the data to an S3 bucket.

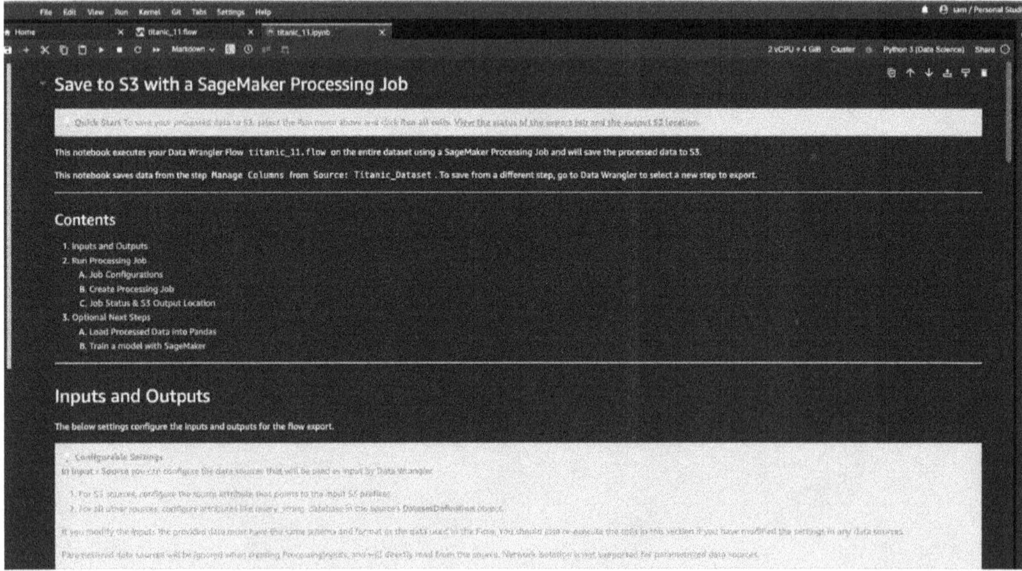

Figure 10.31: A Jupyter notebook for data export to S3

You can choose to update your sources and your destination locations directly in the Jupyter notebook before executing it. Data Wrangler uses a SageMaker Processing job to apply the transformations from your data flow, which are defined in the Jupyter notebook.

- **Export to SageMaker Pipelines**: SageMaker Pipelines is a fully managed service to build machine learning pipelines. When you choose this option, Data Wrangler creates a Jupyter notebook with code to create a SageMaker pipeline that executes your entire data flow. As with the Export to S3 option, you are able to update your input and destination sources directly from the generated Jupyter notebook.
- **Export to an inference pipeline**: Using Data Wrangler, you can directly export to a SageMaker inference pipeline that can be used with a SageMaker endpoint. When you choose this option, Data Wrangler creates a Jupyter notebook with code to apply all the transformations in your data flow and then train an autopilot model. It then creates an inference pipeline and deploys it to an endpoint. The inference pipeline uses the Data Wrangler flow to transform the data from your inference request into a format that the trained model can use.
- **Export as Python code**: This option creates a Python script file with code that contains all the transformations defined in your data flow. Depending on where and how you run this script file, you might need to provide additional permissions to access your AWS resources.
- **Export to Feature Store**: Finally, you can use Data Wrangler to export directly to SageMaker Feature Store. SageMaker Feature Store is a fully managed feature repository for storing and retrieving all your features and the metadata associated with those features. SageMaker Feature Store uses a feature group, which is a collection of features. Using Data Wrangler, you can either update an existing feature group or create a new one. When you choose this option, Data Wrangler will create a Jupyter notebook with the code to define and configure a feature group in SageMaker Feature Store. It will then run a SageMaker Processing job to apply the transformations defined in your data flow and update the feature group.

Once we have the data in the right format and the location that we want, we can move on to the next step of building and training a machine learning model.

Training a machine learning model

We have now used Data Wrangler to do data analysis and processing, which involved several steps, such as data cleaning, preprocessing, feature engineering, and exploratory data analysis. These steps are crucial before doing machine learning, as they ensure that data is in the correct format, we selected the relevant features, and we dealt with outliers and missing values using data transformation. Data Wrangler provides a unified experience, enabling you to prepare data and seamlessly train a machine learning model, all from within the tool.

SageMaker Autopilot is a tool that automates the key tasks of an **automatic machine learning (AutoML)** process. This includes exploring your data, selecting algorithms relevant to your problem type, and preparing the data to facilitate model training and tuning. With just a few clicks, you can automatically build, train, and tune ML models using Autopilot, XGBoost, or your own algorithm, directly from the Data Wrangler **user interface (UI)**. When you train and tune a model, Data Wrangler exports your data to an Amazon S3 location where Amazon SageMaker Autopilot can access it. Let's look at how we can get started with model training from within Data Wrangler:

- **Exporting the data**: Start by clicking on + next to the Data Wrangler step from where you want to start training.

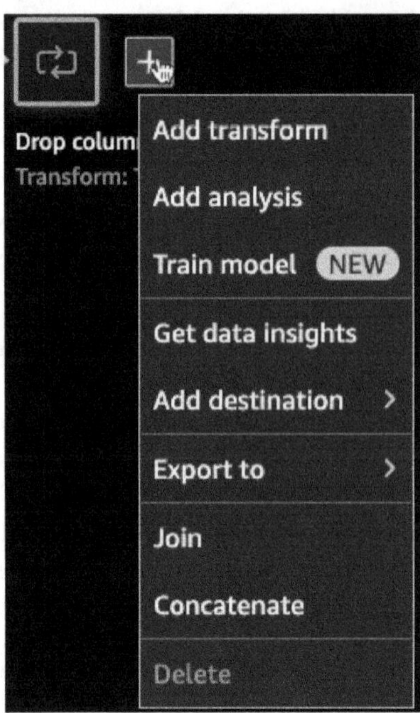

Figure 10.32: Data Wrangler – Train model

Then, choose **Train model**. This will bring up a data export screen where you can specify the S3 bucket where you want to export your transformed data. A SageMaker Processing job will apply all the data transformation up to the step from where you selected to train the model.

Next, you specify the file format of the exported data. By default, you have CSV selected, but you can also choose to export your data in parquet format. You can optionally specify an encryption key for your data.

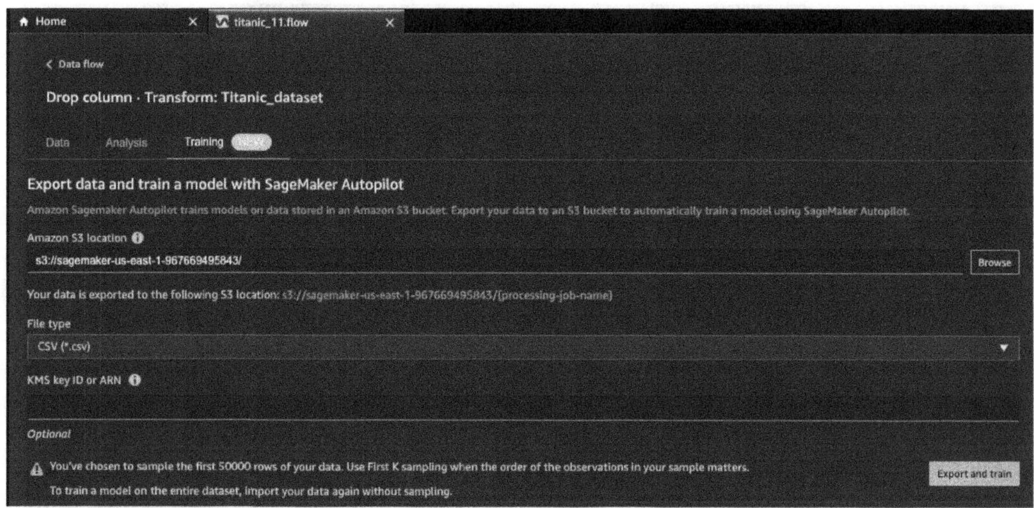

Figure 10.33: Train Model – data import

It is important to note that if you choose to import a sample of your records in Data Wrangler, you must re-import your data without sampling before starting model training to ensure the training process uses your entire dataset. When you are ready, click on **Export and train**. This will start the export process.

Figure 10.34: Train Model – starting the export process

- **Creating an experiment**: Next, we will create an Autopilot experiment. When you create an Autopilot experiment, Amazon SageMaker analyzes your data and creates a notebook with candidate model definitions. You start by giving a name for the experiment and the input location for your data in S3. If you have a manifest file, you can toggle the radio button here. SageMaker Autopilot automatically splits your training dataset and keeps 80% for training and the remaining 20% for validation; if you do not want to do that and use the entire dataset for training, you can disable it via the **Auto split data** toggle button. Finally, specify the output location for the Autopilot artifacts.

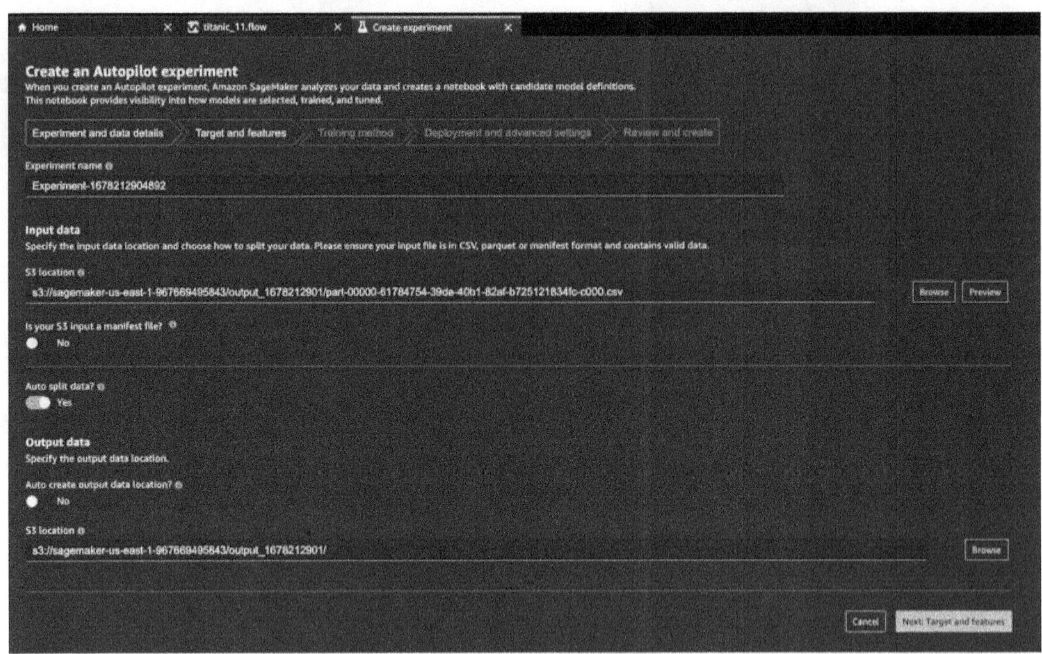

Figure 10.35: Train model – Create an Autopilot experiment

If everything looks as expected, click on the **Experiment and data details** button.

- **Specifying the target and features**: Here, you specify the target column that your model will predict. In our case, this is the **Survived** column. The following section allows you to pick the features that you want to use for training. By default, Data Wrangler will use all the features except the target for training. You can also specify the data type for your features here. Since we have already processed our data in Data Wrangler, we will use the defaults here.

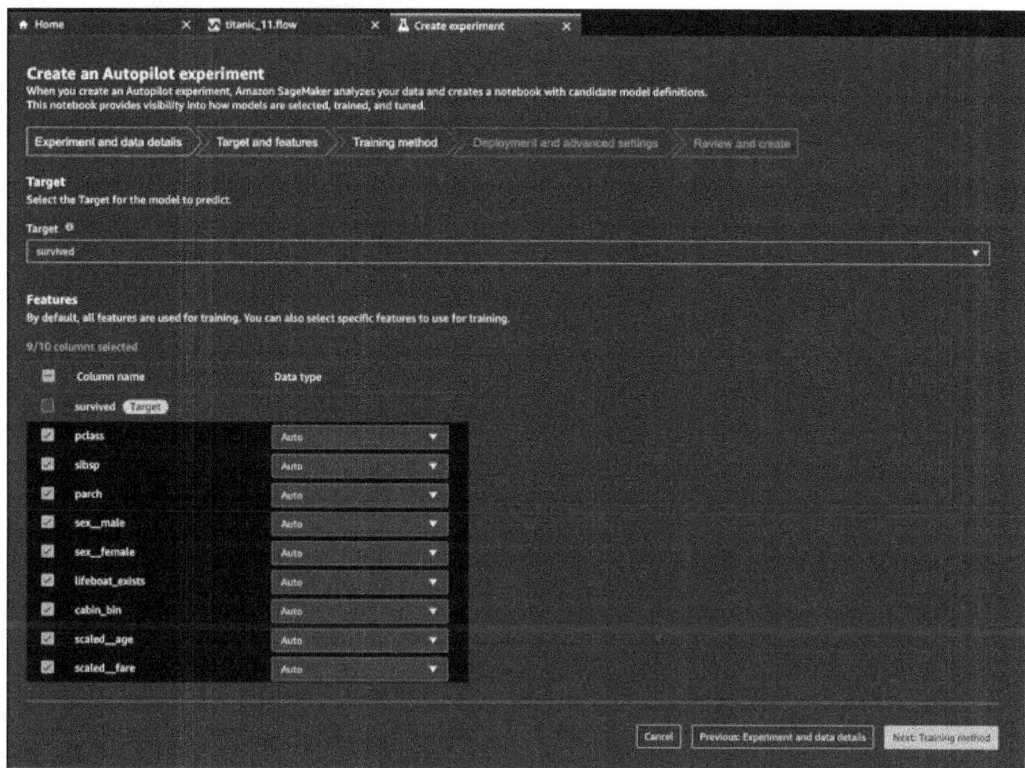

Figure 10.36: Train model – Target and Features

When you are ready, click on the **Next**: **Training method** button to proceed.

- **Pick a training method**: SageMaker Autopilot offers three different training methods. The default is **Auto**, where Autopilot will automatically decide the best method based on your training dataset size. Besides this, you can choose **Ensembling**, where Autopilot uses an AutoML algorithm that trains a multi-layer stack ensemble model to predict on regression and classification datasets, directly from your data. Finally, Autopilot provides a **Hyperparameter optimization** method, where Autopilot will find the best version of the model by tuning hyperparameters and running training jobs on our dataset.

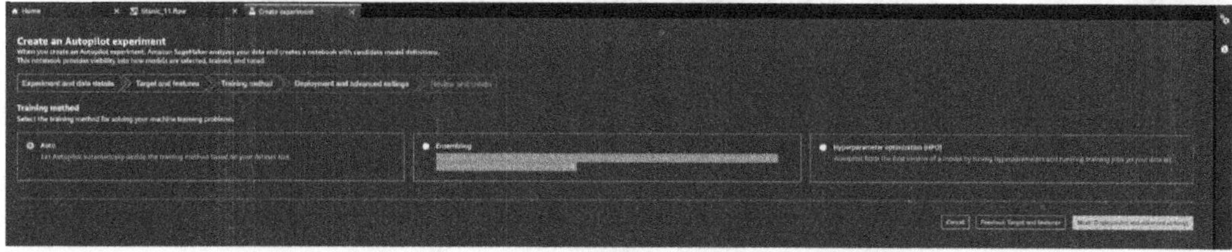

Figure 10.37: Train model – Training method

In our case, we will choose the default **Auto** method. Click on the **Next: Deployment and the advanced settings** button to move forward.

- **Specify deployment settings**: Here, we will specify the model deployment options. SageMaker Autopilot can automatically deploy a model to a real-time endpoint that we can use to run inference against. By default, SageMaker Autopilot will deploy the best version of the model along with the data transformations to the endpoint. You can, however, override this and choose to deploy with no data transformations or not deploy to the endpoint altogether. Next, specify a name for the endpoint. The advanced settings are optional. You can specify the type of the machine learning problem, which in our case is a binary classification – that is, we have only two outcomes that we are trying to predict, whether a passenger survived or not. You can also specify the metric used to evaluate the model; for **Binary classification**, an **F1** score is selected by default, which we will retain. There are several other advanced options that can be tweaked here. We will retain the defaults, but let's look at some of those.

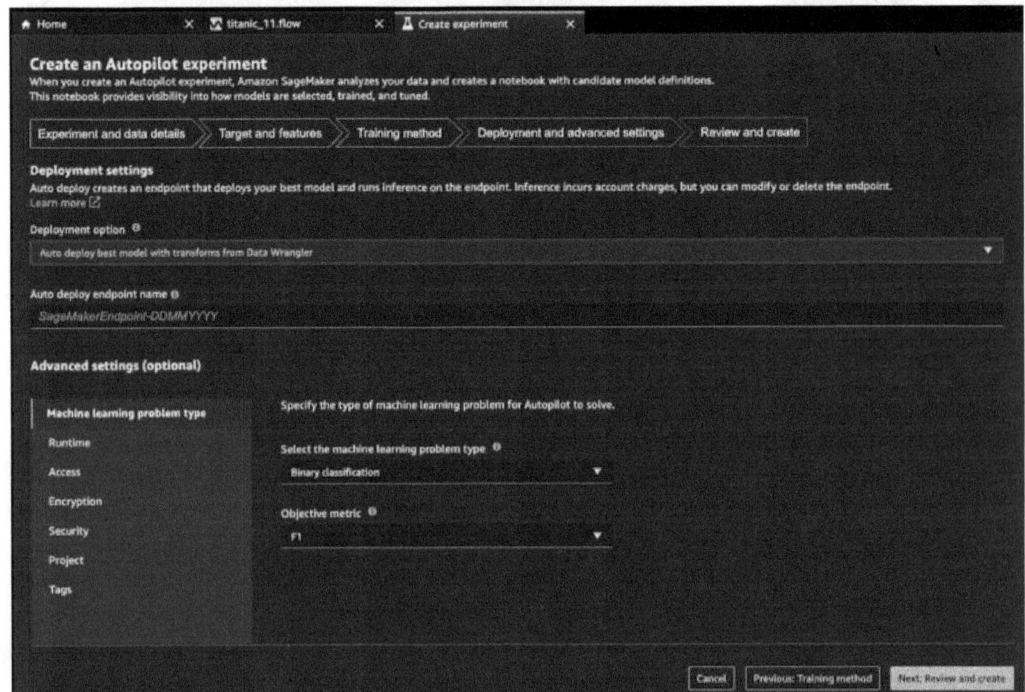

Figure 10.38: Train model – Deployment settings

By default, an Autopilot experiment will run several training jobs along with hyperparameter optimization jobs. If you want to restrict the duration of these jobs, you can do it in the runtime restriction section. You can also specify a specific IAM for SageMaker Autopilot to use to access your data, run the processing and training jobs, and deploy the endpoint. By default, the SageMaker role is selected. You can also choose to encrypt the S3 location and the storage volumes of the training instances by specifying the AWS key. In the security section, you can choose to run the Autopilot jobs in a private network by specifying a virtual private cloud. In the **Project** section, you can associate the experiment with a specific SageMaker project and specify additional tags in the **Tags** section. Next, click on the **Next**: **Review and create** button.

- **Review and create**: In the final section, review everything to make sure all the details look correct. When you are ready, click on the **Create experiment** button to start the SageMaker Autopilot experiment from Data Wrangler.

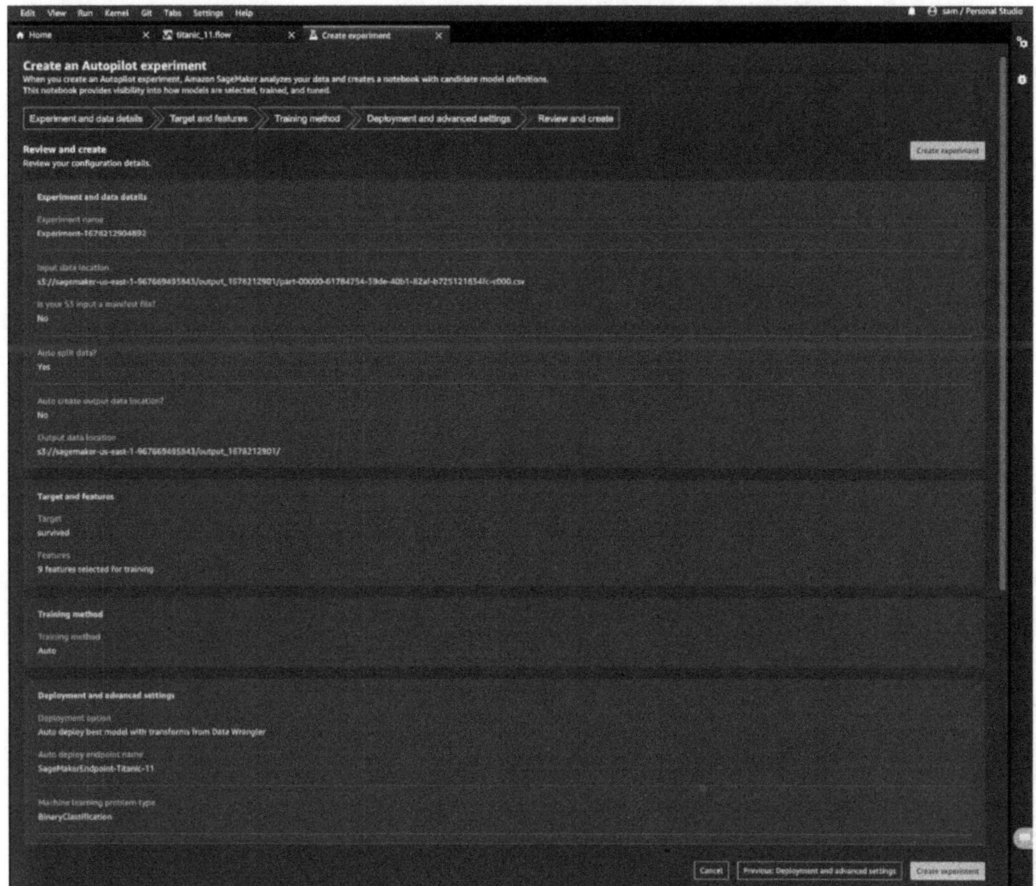

Figure 10.39: Train model – reviewing the experiment

You can view the training progress on the next screen, which starts from the data preprocessing stage. You can also find additional information on the job under the **Job profile** tab.

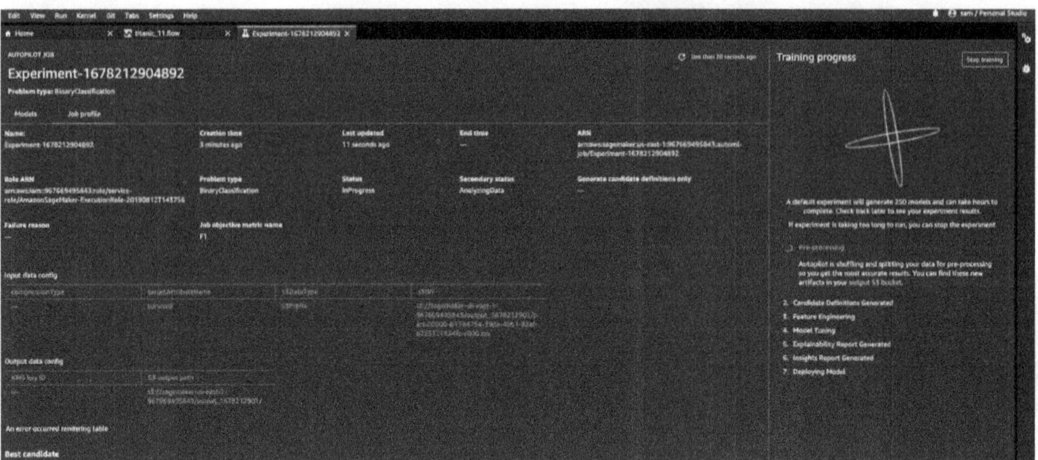

Figure 10.40: Train model – experiment progress

With our dataset and the default job settings, the process will take a couple of hours to complete. Once completed, SageMaker Autopilot will list all the experiments or job runs along with key evaluation metrics, status, and time. It will also show the best model that was used to create the deployment endpoint.

AUTOPILOT JOB

Experiment-1678212904892

Problem type: BinaryClassification

Best model endpoint: SageMakerEndpoint-Titanic-11

Best model	F1_binary (Objective)	F1	LogLoss	Recall	Precision	AUC	Accuracy	BalancedAccuracy	Algorithm
Experiment-16782129048927HjEHhOa-038-bf7f6f98	0.968	0.968	0.088	0.955	0.983	0.993	0.976	0.972	XGBoost

0 rows selected

Model name	Objective: F1_binary	Accuracy	AUC	F1	Status	Start time
Experiment-16782129048927HjEHh... Best model	0.968	0.976	0.993	0.968	Completed	55 minutes ago
Experiment-16782129048927HjEHhOa-059-51651...	0.968	0.976	0.992	0.968	Completed	47 minutes ago
Experiment-16782129048927HjEHhOa-099-aa510...	0.968	0.976	0.992	0.968	Completed	22 minutes ago
Experiment-16782129048927HjEHhOa-060-2a20f...	0.968	0.976	0.991	0.968	Completed	47 minutes ago
Experiment-16782129048927HjEHhOa-094-bcd43...	0.968	0.976	0.993	0.968	Completed	24 minutes ago
Experiment-16782129048927HjEHhOa-040-1ffd0...	0.968	0.976	0.986	0.968	Completed	55 minutes ago
Experiment-16782129048927HjEHhOa-024-92031...	0.968	0.976	0.992	0.968	Completed	59 minutes ago
Experiment-16782129048927HjEHhOa-068-18f19...	0.968	0.976	0.992	0.968	Completed	41 minutes ago
Experiment-16782129048927HjEHhOa-093-87aa4...	0.968	0.976	0.993	0.968	Completed	26 minutes ago
Experiment-16782129048927HjEHhOa-054-4bf83...	0.968	0.976	0.995	0.968	Completed	48 minutes ago
Experiment-16782129048927HjEHhOa-049-f56a5...	0.968	0.976	0.992	0.968	Completed	48 minutes ago
Experiment-16782129048927HjEHhOa-036-fa837...	0.968	0.976	0.992	0.968	Completed	56 minutes ago
Experiment-16782129048927HjEHhOa-066-e3c04...	0.968	0.976	0.992	0.968	Completed	42 minutes ago
Experiment-16782129048927HjEHhOa-043-671b5...	0.968	0.976	0.992	0.968	Completed	54 minutes ago

Figure 10.41: Train model – listing models

In this section, we trained a machine learning model on the data that we transformed using Data Wrangler and SageMaker Autopilot. We also ran a fine-tuning job and selected the best model. You can optionally choose to deploy the model.

Summary

SageMaker Data Wrangler is a purpose-built tool specifically for analyzing and processing data for machine learning. It is also one of the foundational platforms for machine learning on AWS. This has been a long chapter, and although we covered several key features of Data Wrangler, there are still a few features that we left out of this book. We started by looking at how to log in to SageMaker Studio and access Data Wrangler. For the sample dataset, we used the built-in Titanic dataset that is available via a public S3 bucket. We imported this dataset into Data Wrangler via the default sampling method. We then performed EDA, first by using the built-in insights report in Data Wrangler and then by adding additional analysis, including using our custom code. Next, we defined several data transformation steps for our Data Wrangler flow to do feature engineering. For this, we used several built-in data transformations in Data Wrangler. We also looked at applying a custom data transformation using Python (pandas). Once we defined our data transformations, we looked at various options to export the Data Wrangler flow to various destinations, including S3, SageMaker Feature Store, SageMaker Pipelines, and a standalone Python script. Last but not least, we looked at how easy it is to run a complete end-to-end machine learning cycle directly from within Data Wrangler that included all the data processing steps, pick the right algorithm, and run training experiments along with hyperparameter tuning jobs. As part of this exercise, we also deployed the best model from our experiments as a SageMaker real-time endpoint. As we wrap up this chapter, make sure you delete any used resources in your account that were created.

As we reach the concluding chapter of this book, we will focus on data security and monitoring. It is in this ultimate section that we will bring together all the different AWS services we have explored throughout the book, with a focus on security and monitoring.

Summary

Part 5: Ensuring Data Lake Security and Monitoring

In this final section, we delve into the critical aspects of implementing security and monitoring for your data lake. You will learn how to establish robust security measures, including access control, data protection, and encryption, to safeguard your valuable data. Additionally, you will explore monitoring options to ensure the effectiveness of your security framework, providing peace of mind and confidence in your data lake's integrity and protection.

This part has the following chapter:

- *Chapter 11, Data Lake Security and Monitoring*

11

Data Lake Security and Monitoring

In the previous chapters, we learned about the data wrangling process and how to utilize different services for data wrangling activities within the AWS ecosystem. By now, you should have enough knowledge on creating data pipelines using Glue DataBrew, SageMaker Data Wrangler, and AWS SDK for pandas. We also discussed the capabilities provided by AWS services such as AWS Glue, Athena, Amazon S3, and QuickSight, all of which support specific activities within your data wrangling pipeline more effectively. In this chapter, we will explore how to set up security and monitoring for the data wrangling pipeline for your workloads.

This chapter covers the following topics:

- Data lake security
- Monitoring and auditing

Data lake security

In this section, we will discuss bout various options and methodologies to enhance the security aspects of your data lake. We will talk about security across multiple layers; however, this should only be considered a starting point. You will have to work more and add additional security layers as applicable to your project.

Data lake access control

To secure a data lake, we can use a combination of user-based access policies and resource-based access policies. User policies are attached to users/roles and control the actions that a user/role can perform within an account. In addition to user-based control policies, we can attach access policies to resources such as Amazon S3, Amazon SQS, and more, to control access specifically for that resource. This provides another layer of security for protecting AWS resources. As a general best practice, the access policies should be kept least privilege to allow only required actions with specific conditions.

User-based access policies

AWS **Identity and Access Management** (**IAM**) helps with controlling access to AWS resources in a centralized manner for your AWS account. It helps with both authentication and authorization for your AWS account:

- Authentication verifies the identity of the resource/person using their credentials before they can access the AWS resources
- Authorization verifies whether a particular action is allowed for an authenticated user/resource

We will talk more about IAM authorization in this section to understand how it can secure access to a data lake.

Some of the best practices for IAM policies are explained in detail here. You should also follow the best practices outlined in the following AWS documentation: `https://docs.aws.amazon.com/IAM/latest/UserGuide/best-practices.html`. Let's take a look:

- You should apply permission guardrails for the entire account or multiple accounts within an organization using **service control policies** (**SCPs**). Guardrail policies are the maximum available permissions for the users on the accounts. Organizations can use these to prevent certain actions to ensure a strict security posture. One example could be to add an SCP policy to stop new roles/users being created by individual team members. The following link provides example SCP policies that you can use to get started: `https://docs.aws.amazon.com/organizations/latest/userguide/orgs_manage_policies_scps_examples_general.html#example-scp-restricts-iam-principals`.
- You can also provide **IAM permission boundaries** for a user or role to define the maximum boundary of permissions that can be added to that role. This will prevent additional permissions from being added apart from what was originally intended. Even if broader permissions are added to an IAM user/role through managed or in-line policies, a permission boundary will act as a preventive guardrail so that the user/role can still only have access defined within the permission boundary. One common use case would be to allow developers to create additional roles for performing their daily tasks but also to restrict those service roles from having broader permissions to avoid any security issues. Refer to the following blog post for additional details on using permission boundaries: `https://aws.amazon.com/blogs/security/when-and-where-to-use-iam-permissions-boundaries/`.

  You could attach permission boundaries to individual user roles either through your infrastructure provisioning code or the console for specific users:

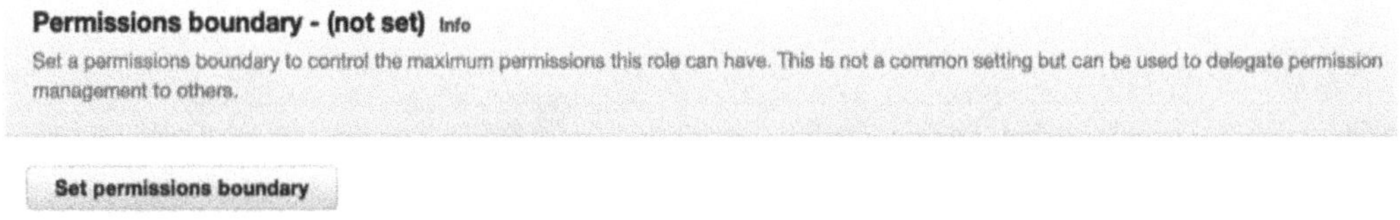

Permissions boundary - (not set) Info

Set a permissions boundary to control the maximum permissions this role can have. This is not a common setting but can be used to delegate permission management to others.

Set permissions boundary

Figure 11.1: Permissions boundary on the IAM console

To determine whether the user/role has permission to perform an action on a resource, IAM evaluates SCPs, identity-based policies, permission boundaries, session-based policies, and resource-based policies. An explicit deny statement takes precedence over allow statements. Read through the following documentation to understand more about policy evaluation logic: `https://docs.aws.amazon.com/IAM/latest/UserGuide/reference_policies_evaluation-logic.html`.

- You can leverage **least privilege permissions** and **IAM conditions** to further restrict your IAM policies for a better security posture. IAM provides managed policies for common use cases. However, those permissions might be more than what is required for some specific use cases. Also, customers used to create policies with wider permissions to avoid access errors during the development phase. For tighter security, create customer-managed policies that only provide access to specific resources and specific actions that are needed to get the work done. **IAM Access Analyzer** can be used to generate least-privilege policies based on access patterns.

  You can also use conditions on your IAM policies as an additional layer of security to provide access to resources when certain conditions are met. Consider, for example, that you want to provide access to users to assume a role but only if that request comes from a specific IP CIDR range (corporate network). Refer to the following document to learn how to use conditions effectively: `https://aws.amazon.com/premiumsupport/knowledge-center/iam-restrict-calls-ip-addresses/`.

Resource-based access policies

Users can attach access policies to S3 buckets, objects, and resources to secure access to S3 buckets. **Bucket policies** provide mechanisms to secure objects stored in Amazon S3 with specific access patterns. This provides mechanisms to control how/where/what objects are written/read from Amazon S3. With carefully designed bucket policies we can implement the following:

- Network origin control, which allows access only from a certain VPC, IP address range, browser, and so on. The best approach is to restrict access to the S3 bucket, except for the allowed IP CIDR/VPC settings:

```
{
    "Version": "2012-10-17",
    "Statement": [
        {
            "Sid": "Statement1",
            "Principal": "*",
            "Effect": "Deny",
            "Action": "*",
            "Resource": ["arn:aws:s3:::wranglerbook","arn:aws:s3:::wranglerbook/*"],
            "Condition": {
                "NotIpAddress": {
                    "aws:SourceIp": "172.0.0.0/24"
                }
            }
        }
    ]
}
```

Figure 11.2: S3 access policy statement restricting access only from a specific ID address prefix

- You can also control access by users at the folder level. Please note that Amazon S3 is an object data store that has a flat file storage hierarchy; the AWS console visualizes data with the same prefix as a folder for easier browsing purposes. So, only provide access to a certain prefix in the case of shared datasets. Consider, for example, that we have data from multiple clients stored under different folders. We can restrict access to specific user roles to a specific folder/prefix. Refer to the following documentation path for a bucket policy example for setting up folder-level access: `https://docs.aws.amazon.com/AmazonS3/latest/userguide/example-bucket-policies.html#example-bucket-policies-folders`.
- For situations where you need to provide access to objects in different folders for a group of users, use object tags to restrict access only to certain objects in the S3 bucket. Consider, for example, that we have three different data sources (e-commerce, agents, miscellaneous) that populate user data into the S3 bucket. Each source will upload two files daily, one that contains sensitive data (which shouldn't be accessed by users) and one that doesn't contain sensitive data (which can be accessed by all users). Each source will upload the files under a folder with their name. In this case, we can use object tags to provide access to files that don't contain sensitive data, as shown here:

```
{
    "Version": "2012-10-17",
    "Statement": [
        {"Principal":{"AWS":[
                "arn:aws:iam::<<accountid>>:role/role_name"]},
            "Effect":       "Allow",
            "Action":       ["s3:GetObject"],
            "Resource":     "arn:aws:s3:::wranglerbook/*",
            "Condition": {  "StringEquals": {"s3:ExistingObjectTag/dataclassification": "sensitive" } }
            }
        ]
}
```

Figure 11.3: S3 access policy statement restricting access based on tags attached to an S3 bucket

You can also ensure the objects are tagged correctly when the data is uploaded into the S3 bucket by making the tag mandatory for the `PutObject` action. Refer to the following AWS documentation for additional details on object-based tagging: `https://docs.aws.amazon.com/AmazonS3/latest/userguide/example-bucket-policies.html#example-bucket-policies-object-tags`.

Additional options to control data lake access

You can perform the following activities to secure data in your data lake:

- **S3 access points** help simplify access control for shared buckets that are accessed by many teams. They are named network endpoints that are attached to the S3 bucket with distinct permission policies. S3 endpoints help manage buckets with complex bucket policies that are difficult to maintain by segregating policies for each use case into a separate endpoint. Some common use cases are buckets that host large shared datasets, with each dataset having a different access policy, and testing new access policy changes on an S3 bucket without impacting the existing policies.
- **Object lambda access points** are useful if you want to use a lambda function in front of an access point. They help in cases such as redacting PII data using a Lambda object. Refer to the following blog post to learn how to implement the solution for this: `https://docs.aws.amazon.com/AmazonS3/latest/userguide/tutorial-s3-object-lambda-redact-pii.html`.
- **IAM Access Analyzer** can help validate policies for grammar and best practices, identify resources that are shared with external entities, and generate policies based on CloudTrail logs. It helps you apply policies that adhere to the least-privilege model and grant only the minimal permissions needed by users. This should be validated periodically to ensure the policies are updated based on recent user activity.

- **Amazon S3 logging options**: Amazon S3 provides a couple of logging options for capturing all user actions for auditing, compliance, and security purposes:

  - Amazon S3 server logs are used to capture logs in fine-grained detail (life cycle transition events, authentication failures, and so on). These logs have additional fields for object size, HTTP referrers, and more. There is no additional cost except for the storage cost of the logs.
  - AWS CloudTrail events (S3 API calls) capture object and bucket API operations through CloudTrail. The logs can be delivered to multiple locations and forwarded to Amazon CloudWatch for further analysis. There is an additional cost for CloudTrail event capture in addition to log storage costs, but it has better integration capabilities with other systems.

  Refer to the following documentation page to learn the difference between AWS CloudTrail and Amazon S3 server logs: `https://docs.aws.amazon.com/AmazonS3/latest/userguide/logging-with-S3.html`.

- **Amazon S3 Inventory** helps you export CSV/ORC/Parquet format files with a list of objects in an S3 bucket or prefix in a periodic manner. This report can be used to analyze the replication and encryption status of objects to ensure the data is secure. The inventory file can be queried with Amazon Athena to identify regulatory or compliance issues in the S3 bucket using SQL queries.

Monitoring, discovering, and identifying security issues

The following services can help you monitor, discover, and identify security issues in your data lake:

- **AWS Config** helps users continuously monitor AWS resources and audit configuration changes. Users can configure rules on AWS Config to monitor and tag resources that don't adhere to the configured rules. You can set up AWS Config to validate public read/write configuration for all buckets within your organization. Refer to the following blog post to learn how to use AWS Config to identify and update public settings for S3 buckets in your account: `https://aws.amazon.com/blogs/security/how-to-use-aws-config-to-monitor-for-and-respond-to-amazon-s3-buckets-allowing-public-access/`.
- **AWS Trusted Advisor** scans the AWS infrastructure on your accounts and provides recommendations that follow best practices. It can be used to identify any issues in your data lake configurations and fix them appropriately. This is available to AWS Enterprise support customers. Trusted Advisor provides optimized recommendations that help with the following:

  - **Cost optimization**: Identify unallocated, underutilized, and idle AWS resources to help users optimize costs.
  - **Performance**: Provides recommendations to improve performance by analyzing the throughput, latency, and compute usage of AWS resources.
  - **Security**: Identify and provide recommendations on exposed credentials, security group vulnerabilities, S3 bucket permissions that are more open, and more.

    - **Fault tolerance**: Identify and highlight EC2 autoscaling, health checks, data backups, and more.
    - **Service limits**: AWS has service limits for different services. They highlight when the user has hit 80% of the service limit so that they can be better prepared.

- **Amazon Macie** identifies sensitive data by using machine learning pattern matching in your S3 buckets. Macie also supports automated sensitive data discovery on S3 buckets. Refer to the following post for an automated, sensitive data discovery framework that can be used across multiple accounts using Amazon Macie: `https://aws.amazon.com/blogs/security/use-amazon-macie-for-automatic-continual-and-cost-effective-discovery-of-sensitive-data-in-s3/`.
- **AWS GuardDuty** is a threat detection service that continuously monitors your AWS account for suspicious activities. You can use GuardDuty to monitor S3 management events and data events so that you can identify security issues. A report will be generated so that the users can take action on them. Some common use cases are as follows:
    - Identify issues with files that are stored in an EBS storage volume
    - Identify issues with container deployments by analyzing EKS audit logs
    - Identify compromised credentials, suspicious logins and access patterns, and more

AWS Lake Formation integration

AWS Lake Formation offers fine-grained access control for data lakes, allowing you to grant permissions to individual principals on Data Catalog resources, Amazon S3 locations, and the underlying data. This enables precise control over data access and user actions.

There are two ways to perform fine-grained access control in Lake Formation:

- **IAM access control**: The recommended method involves granting IAM permissions to individual principals on Data Catalog resources, S3 locations, and the underlying data. This method provides maximum control over data access.
- **IAM and Lake Formation permissions**: This method combines IAM permissions with Lake Formation permissions. It is useful for enforcing additional security controls, such as row-level access control.

When configuring security rules effectively, consider the following factors:

- **Data security requirements**: Determine the level of security needed for your data, including protection against unauthorized access, modification, or deletion
- **Data access requirements**: Identify who needs access to the data and what actions they should be able to perform
- **Data governance requirements**: Take into account any data governance policies that need to be enforced

To configure security rules effectively, follow these tips:

- Start with the principle of least privilege and only grant permissions to those who require them to reduce the attack surface
- Use fine-grained permissions by granting access to specific resources such as tables or columns to gain more control over data access
- Implement **role-based access control** (**RBAC**) by assigning permissions to roles and then assigning those roles to users or groups for simplified security management
- Enable audit logging to track data access and actions taken by users to help troubleshoot security incidents

By considering these factors and following best practices for security rule configuration, you can effectively control access to your data lake, reduce security risks, and enforce data governance policies.

Data protection

Data must be protected with security and encryption where necessary. Encrypt data in S3 buckets and databases where applicable. Sensitive data can be tokenized to add another layer of security where necessary. Tokenized data cannot be reverse-engineered to the original data item unless you have access to the tokenization server. Refer to the following Protegrity/Athena blog on implementing a tokenization solution in AWS for more details: `https://aws.amazon.com/blogs/apn/data-tokenization-with-amazon-athena-and-protegrity/`.

To have robust security, we need to enable additional S3 data protection options to protect data against rogue or accidental deletions:

- **Enable object versioning**: Object versioning keeps multiple versions of the object in the bucket with every change. When an object is deleted, a delete marker is inserted and the object is not removed permanently from the bucket. This helps you roll back to a previous version of the object in case of issues.
- **Enable MFA delete to prevent accidental deletes**: This feature helps in preventing accidental file deletions by requiring two forms of authentication for deleting or changing the state of the object.
- **Block public access**: Enable this feature for data lake buckets to avoid everyone gaining access to the bucket. This adds another layer of security in addition to bucket policies and other access control mechanisms to secure data lake objects.
- **Object Lock**: Object Lock prevents objects from being deleted or overwritten for a certain period. This feature helps store objects for regulatory compliance (**Write Once Read Many** – **WORM**)
- **Enforce a TLS connection**: You can do this by using bucket policies and encrypting data storage.

Refer to the following Amazon S3 blog to learn more about the best practices for securing data: `https://aws.amazon.com/blogs/security/top-10-security-best-practices-for-securing-data-in-amazon-s3/`.

For Redshift/RDS databases, the best practice is to use IAM authentication to enhance security. Alternatively, you can use AWS Secrets Manager to securely store database usernames/passwords and automatically rotate secrets to increase your security posture. Redshift supports row-level and column-level filters natively to provide fine-grained access control. For other custom databases, you can utilize views to enforce security: `https://aws.amazon.com/blogs/big-data/achieve-fine-grained-data-security-with-row-level-access-control-in-amazon-redshift/`.

In terms of Redshift, refer to the following documentation for more information about security: `https://docs.aws.amazon.com/redshift/latest/dg/c_security-overview.html`.

Securing your data in AWS Glue

In the previous chapter, we learned how to use AWS Glue, which provides you with an easy and efficient way to prepare and transform data for analysis. In this section, we'll explore how AWS Glue can be used to secure data:

1. **Use encryption for data at rest**: One of the most crucial steps in securing data is to encrypt it. AWS Glue provides several encryption options for data at rest. You can use Amazon S3 server-side encryption to encrypt your data before storing it in S3. You can also use AWS **Key Management Service** (**KMS**) to manage your encryption keys securely. Additionally, you can use Glue's Data Catalog Encryption feature to encrypt metadata stored in the Data Catalog.
2. **Limit access to data**: To prevent unauthorized access to your data, you need to control access to your AWS Glue resources. AWS Glue provides several tools for limiting access to your data. You can use AWS IAM to create policies that define who can access AWS Glue resources. You can also use VPC endpoints to restrict access to your AWS Glue resources to your VPC. Furthermore, you can use AWS PrivateLink to securely access your AWS Glue resources over a private network.

   Let's look at an example. In this policy, the `Deny` effect is used to restrict access to the `glue:GetTable`, `glue:GetPartition`, and `glue:GetDatabase` actions. The `Resource` field is used to specify the resources that are affected by this policy, such as the catalog, databases, tables, and partitions. The `Condition` field is used to specify that the policy applies only to users or roles that are not specified in the `aws:PrincipalArn` field:

   ```
   {
       "Version": "2012-10-17",
       "Statement": [
           {
               "Effect": "Deny",
   ```

```
                "Action": [
                    "glue:GetTable",
                    "glue:GetPartition",
                    "glue:GetDatabase"
                ],
                "Resource": [
                    "arn:aws:glue:region:account-id:catalog",
                    "arn:aws:glue:region:account-id:database/
                    database-name",
                    "arn:aws:glue:region:account-id:table/database-
                    name/table-name",
                    "arn:aws:glue:region:account-id:table/database-
                    name/table-name/*",
                    "arn:aws:glue:region:account-id:partition/
                    database-name/table-name/*/*"
                ],
                "Condition": {
                    "StringNotEquals": {
                        "aws:PrincipalArn": [
                            "arn:aws:iam::account-id:user/username",
                            "arn:aws:iam::account-id:role/role-name"
                        ]
                    }
                }
            }
        ]
    }
```

By using IAM policies to restrict access to data in AWS Glue, you can ensure that only authorized users and roles can view, modify, or delete your data. You can find more examples in AWS Glue's official documentation: `https://docs.aws.amazon.com/glue/latest/dg/glue-policy-examples.html`.

3. **Monitor data access**: It's essential to monitor who is accessing your data and when they are accessing it. AWS Glue provides several monitoring and logging features to help you monitor access to your data. You can use AWS CloudTrail to log API calls and track who is accessing your AWS Glue resources. You can also use Amazon CloudWatch to monitor and alert you about specific events or thresholds. For example, you could create a rule that looks for `Glue.DataCatalog` events with the `eventName` field set to `GetTable`, `GetPartition`, or `GetDatabase`.
4. **Secure data in transit**: To secure data as it travels between different components of your architecture, you need to use secure protocols. AWS Glue provides several options for securing data in transit. You can use HTTPS to encrypt data as it travels between Glue jobs and S3. You can also use SSL/TLS to encrypt data as it travels between Glue jobs and other AWS services.

5. **Use IAM roles and policies**: AWS Glue uses IAM roles to control access to AWS Glue resources. You can create IAM roles that grant permissions to specific Glue resources. IAM policies define the permissions for each role. You can use IAM policies to control access to AWS Glue resources, including jobs, crawlers, and triggers.

With that, we have explored various options for ensuring data lake security. Even if a platform has the highest possible security standards, there should be a monitoring and auditing framework to ensure the security standards/rules are working as expected. We will continue to explore options for monitoring and auditing in the next section in detail.

Monitoring and auditing

In this section, we will look at different options for monitoring your data lake workloads. This will help you understand the performance and health of your data lake and other AWS services. We will also explore the auditing aspect of data lakes using Amazon CloudTrail.

Amazon CloudWatch

Amazon CloudWatch is a monitoring and observability service that provides users with visibility into the performance and health of their AWS resources and applications. It collects and stores metrics, logs, and events from a wide range of AWS resources, including EC2 instances, Lambda functions, RDS databases, and more. Users can then use this data to troubleshoot issues, optimize performance, and improve operational efficiency.

Overview of Amazon CloudWatch

- **Metrics**: Numeric data points that represent the performance or utilization of a resource over time, such as CPU utilization, network traffic, or database latency
- **Logs**: Text-based records of events and activities that occur within an application or system, such as server logs, application logs, and security logs
- **Events**: Notifications of significant changes or actions that occur within an AWS resource, such as a new EC2 instance being launched or a change to a security group

Key features of Amazon CloudWatch

- **Metrics and alarms**: CloudWatch collects and stores metrics from AWS resources and services and allows users to set alarms and triggers based on specific metrics. Users can receive notifications when a metric breaches a threshold and take automated actions in response, such as scaling resources up or down.
- **Logs and insights**: CloudWatch allows users to collect, monitor, and analyze logs from AWS resources and applications. Users can search and filter logs and use CloudWatch Logs Insights to gain insights into log data and identify issues.

- **Events and rules**: CloudWatch provides a centralized event management system that allows users to monitor and respond to changes and actions within their AWS resources and services. Users can create rules to trigger automated actions based on specific events, such as launching an EC2 instance or stopping an RDS database.
- **Dashboards and visualization**: CloudWatch provides a range of tools for visualizing and analyzing metrics and logs, including customizable dashboards, graphs, and charts. Users can create custom visualizations to monitor specific aspects of their AWS infrastructure and applications.
- **Integrations and APIs**: CloudWatch integrates with a wide range of AWS services and third-party tools, and provides APIs for programmatically accessing and managing CloudWatch data. Users can also use AWS CloudFormation templates to automate the creation and management of CloudWatch resources.

Benefits of Amazon CloudWatch

- **Real-time monitoring and visibility**: With Amazon CloudWatch, users can gain real-time visibility into the performance and health of their AWS infrastructure and applications, and respond quickly to issues and events
- **Automatic scaling and optimization**: Amazon CloudWatch allows users to set alarms and triggers based on specific metrics, as well as take automated actions in response, such as scaling up or down resources to optimize performance and cost
- **Improved operational efficiency**: Amazon CloudWatch provides a range of tools for monitoring and analyzing AWS infrastructure and applications, allowing users to identify and troubleshoot issues more quickly and efficiently
- **Reduced costs**: Amazon CloudWatch can help users reduce costs by optimizing resource usage and identifying and resolving issues before they cause outages or performance degradation

Monitoring an AWS Glue job using AWS Glue ETL job monitoring

To monitor the status and progress of your AWS Glue jobs using AWS Glue ETL job monitoring, follow these steps:

1. Go to AWS Glue and navigate to the **ETL Jobs** section. Click **Job run monitoring**.
2. Specify the date range for which you want to monitor the jobs. The system will provide a summary of all the jobs that have been executed within the specified date range, including **Total runs**, **Success**, **Failed**, **DPU hours**, and more:

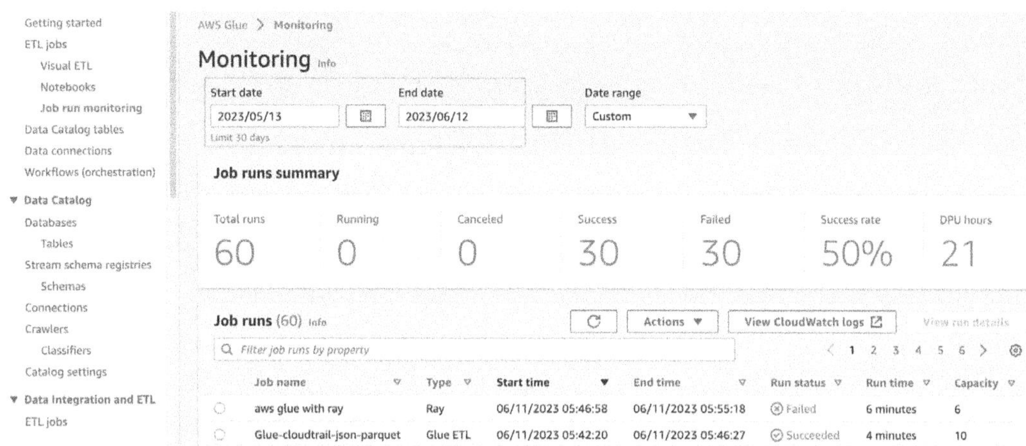

Figure 11.4: AWS Glue ETL monitoring

3. To monitor specific jobs, select the desired job and click **View run details**:

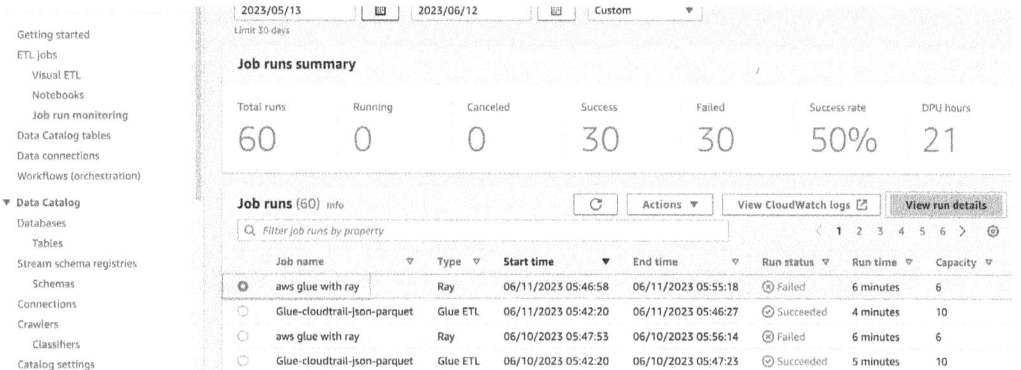

Figure 11.5: Monitoring an AWS Glue ETL job

4. The **Job Run** tab will show you the current status of the job, including the job's run ID, start time, and status.
5. If you wish to view detailed logs of a job, click on the hyperlinks under **CloudWatch logs**. This action will open a CloudWatch page that specifies the log's details:

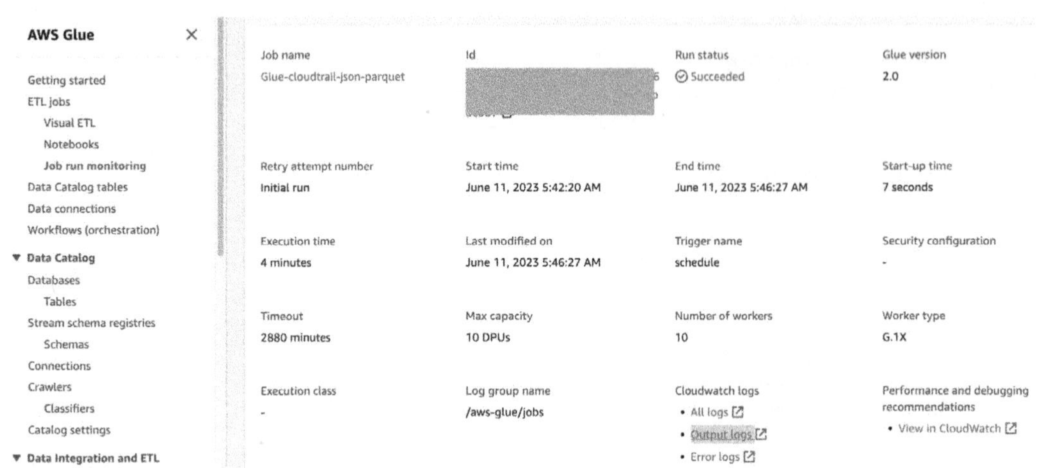

Figure 11.6: Opening AWS Glue ETL job logs in CloudWatch

6. The CloudWatch log will be listed, providing you with the necessary information:

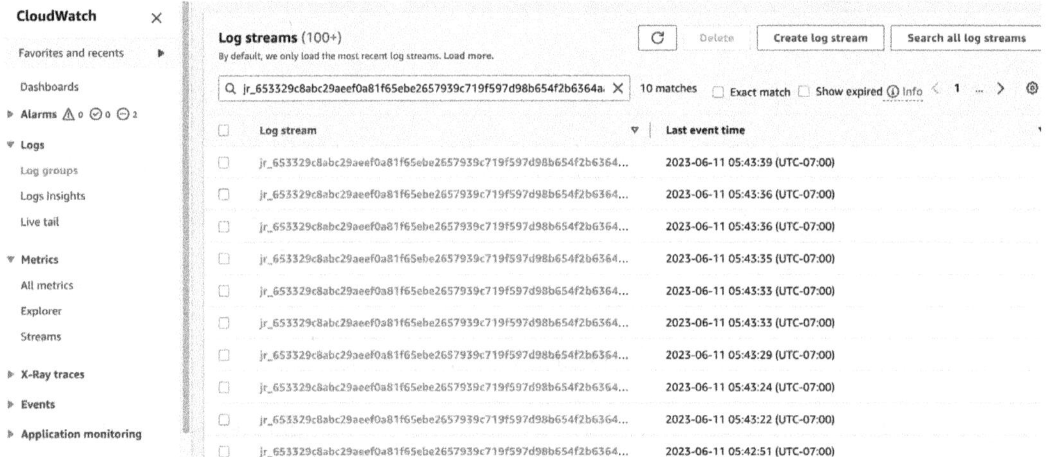

Figure 11.7: Monitoring an AWS Glue ETL job in CloudWatch

7. To obtain more details about the job, click on any of the available log streams.

By following these steps, you can effectively monitor your AWS Glue jobs using AWS Glue ETL job monitoring.

Amazon CloudTrail

CloudTrail is a service offered by **Amazon Web Services** (**AWS**) that enables you to log and monitor all API calls made within your AWS account. It provides a comprehensive audit trail that can be used for security analysis, compliance auditing, and troubleshooting.

Features of CloudTrail

- **API logging**: CloudTrail logs all API calls made to AWS services, including calls made through the AWS Management Console, SDKs, command-line tools, and other AWS services
- **Event history**: CloudTrail provides a detailed history of all API events, including the identity of the caller, the time of the event, and the parameters used in the API call
- **Log file integrity validation**: CloudTrail uses cryptographic hashing to ensure the integrity of log files, preventing tampering or unauthorized access
- **S3 integration**: CloudTrail can store its log files in an S3 bucket, which provides you with cost-effective, durable, and scalable storage for your log files
- **Real-time notifications**: CloudTrail can send real-time notifications to you when specific events occur, such as the creation or deletion of an EC2 instance

Benefits of CloudTrail

- **Improved security**: CloudTrail provides you with a complete audit trail of all API calls made within your AWS account, allowing you to identify and respond to security threats quickly
- **Compliance auditing**: CloudTrail helps you meet compliance requirements by providing a detailed history of all API events, which can be used for auditing and reporting
- **Troubleshooting**: CloudTrail enables you to troubleshoot issues by providing a detailed history of all API events, which can be used to identify the root cause of a problem
- **Cost-effective storage**: CloudTrail can store its log files in an S3 bucket, which provides you with cost-effective, durable, and scalable storage for your log files

How CloudTrail works

CloudTrail works by capturing and logging API calls made within an AWS account. When an API call is made, CloudTrail creates a JSON-formatted log file that contains information about the call, such as the identity of the caller, the time of the call, and the parameters used in the call. The log file is then stored in an S3 bucket.

You can configure CloudTrail to log API calls for specific AWS services or your entire AWS account. You can also configure CloudTrail to send real-time notifications when specific events occur, such as the creation or deletion of an EC2 instance.

To use CloudTrail, you must first enable it in your AWS account. You can then configure it to log API calls for specific services and send real-time notifications. Once enabled, CloudTrail will begin capturing and logging API calls made within the AWS account.

Summary

In this chapter, we discussed the options for securing, monitoring, and auditing your data pipeline within AWS. Earlier in this book, we explored various options for performing data wrangling activities within AWS. Let's summarize the data we discussed earlier in this book:

- First, we explored AWS Glue DataBrew, which helps you create a data wrangling pipeline through a GUI-based approach for every type of user. This is useful for teams who want to quickly set up a data wrangling pipeline without worrying about the coding and management aspects of the pipeline.
- We also covered SageMaker Data Wrangler, which helps users create a GUI-based data wrangling pipeline. However, it's more closely aligned toward machine learning workloads with tighter integration with SageMaker services. This is useful for teams who are planning to manage data wrangling for model training and inference in SageMaker.
- We also explored AWS SDK for pandas, also known as awswrangler, a hands-on coding approach for data wrangling that integrates the pandas library with the AWS ecosystem. This is used by users who are more hands-on with Python programming and are in love with the pandas library and its capabilities.
- We also covered different AWS services, such as Amazon S3, Amazon Athena, AWS Glue, and Amazon Quicksight, and how those services help with different aspects of the data wrangling pipeline. These capabilities should be used effectively to make your data wrangling pipeline more effective and performant.

We hope that the concepts you've learned about creating robust data pipelines in AWS have helped you. You can use what you've learned to start implementing data wrangling pipelines in your AWS accounts.

If you have any additional questions, please reach out to the authors of this book – we will be happy to help you. Happy learning!!

Index

Symbols

A

E

F

G

Packtpub.com

Subscribe to our online digital library for full access to over 7,000 books and videos, as well as industry leading tools to help you plan your personal development and advance your career. For more information, please visit our website.

Why subscribe?

- Spend less time learning and more time coding with practical eBooks and Videos from over 4,000 industry professionals
- Improve your learning with Skill Plans built especially for you
- Get a free eBook or video every month
- Fully searchable for easy access to vital information
- Copy and paste, print, and bookmark content

Did you know that Packt offers eBook versions of every book published, with PDF and ePub files available? You can upgrade to the eBook version at packtpub.com and as a print book customer, you are entitled to a discount on the eBook copy. Get in touch with us at customercare@packtpub.com for more details.

At www.packtpub.com, you can also read a collection of free technical articles, sign up for a range of free newsletters, and receive exclusive discounts and offers on Packt books and eBooks.

Other Books You May Enjoy

If you enjoyed this book, you may be interested in these other books by Packt:

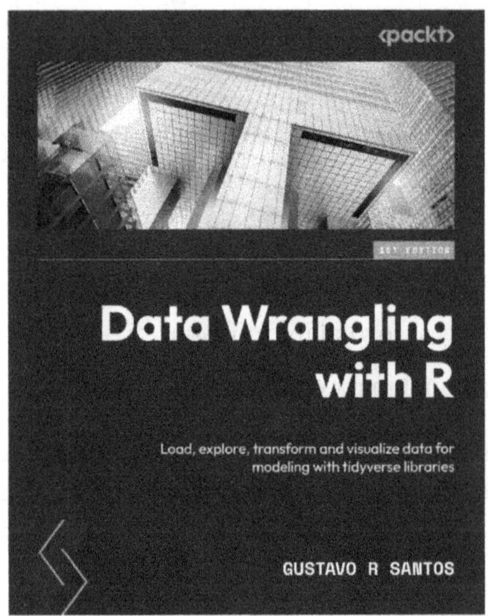

Data Wrangling with R

Gustavo R Santos

ISBN: 9781803235400

- Discover how to load datasets and explore data in R
- Work with different types of variables in datasets
- Create basic and advanced visualizations
- Find out how to build your first data model
- Create graphics using ggplot2 in a step-by-step way in Microsoft Power BI
- Get familiarized with building an application in R with Shiny

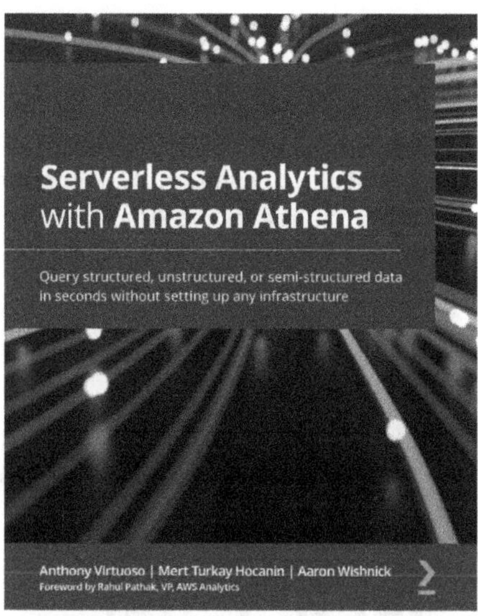

Serverless Analytics with Amazon Athena

Anthony Virtuoso, Mert Turkay Hocanin, Aaron Wishnick

ISBN: 9781800562349

- Secure and manage the cost of querying your data
- Use Athena ML and User Defined Functions (UDFs) to add advanced features to your reports
- Write your own Athena Connector to integrate with a custom data source
- Discover your datasets on S3 using AWS Glue Crawlers
- Integrate Amazon Athena into your applications
- Setup Identity and Access Management (IAM) policies to limit access to tables and databases in Glue Data Catalog
- Add an Amazon SageMaker Notebook to your Athena queries
- Get to grips with using Athena for ETL pipelines

Packt is searching for authors like you

If you're interested in becoming an author for Packt, please visit `authors.packtpub.com` and apply today. We have worked with thousands of developers and tech professionals, just like you, to help them share their insight with the global tech community. You can make a general application, apply for a specific hot topic that we are recruiting an author for, or submit your own idea.

Share Your Thoughts

Now you've finished *Data Wrangling on AWS*, we'd love to hear your thoughts! Scan the QR code below to go straight to the Amazon review page for this book and share your feedback or leave a review on the site that you purchased it from.

`https://packt.link/r/1-801-81090-7`

Your review is important to us and the tech community and will help us make sure we're delivering excellent quality content.

Download a free PDF copy of this book

Thanks for purchasing this book!

Do you like to read on the go but are unable to carry your print books everywhere? Is your eBook purchase not compatible with the device of your choice?

Don't worry, now with every Packt book you get a DRM-free PDF version of that book at no cost.

Read anywhere, any place, on any device. Search, copy, and paste code from your favorite technical books directly into your application.

The perks don't stop there, you can get exclusive access to discounts, newsletters, and great free content in your inbox daily

Follow these simple steps to get the benefits:

1. Scan the QR code or visit the link below

`https://packt.link/free-ebook/9781801810906`

1. Submit your proof of purchase
2. That's it! We'll send your free PDF and other benefits to your email directly

www.ingramcontent.com/pod-product-compliance
Lightning Source LLC
Chambersburg PA
CBHW081503050326
40690CB00015B/2901